8.50

The Slow Learner in Mathematics

YEARBOOKS
published by the
National Council of Teachers of Mathematics

First Yearbook: *A General Survey of Progress in the Last Twenty-five Years*
Second Yearbook: *Curriculum Problems in Teaching Mathematics*
Third Yearbook: *Selected Topics in the Teaching of Mathematics*
Fourth Yearbook: *Significant Changes and Trends in the Teaching of Mathematics throughout the World since 1910*
Fifth Yearbook: *The Teaching of Geometry*
Sixth Yearbook: *Mathematics in Modern Life*
Seventh Yearbook: *The Teaching of Algebra*
Eighth Yearbook: *The Teaching of Mathematics in the Secondary School*
Ninth Yearbook: *Relational and Functional Thinking in Mathematics*
Tenth Yearbook: *The Teaching of Arithmetic*
Eleventh Yearbook: *The Place of Mathematics in Modern Education*
Twelfth Yearbook: *Approximate Computation*
Thirteenth Yearbook: *The Nature of Proof*
Fourteenth Yearbook: *The Training of Mathematics Teachers*
Fifteenth Yearbook: *The Place of Mathematics in Secondary Education*
Sixteenth Yearbook: *Arithmetic in General Education*
Seventeenth Yearbook: *A Source Book of Mathematical Applications*
Eighteenth Yearbook: *Multi-Sensory Aids in the Teaching of Mathematics*
Nineteenth Yearbook: *Surveying Instruments: Their History and Classroom Use*
Twentieth Yearbook: *The Metric System of Weights and Measures*
Twenty-first Yearbook: *The Learning of Mathematics: Its Theory and Practice*
Twenty-second Yearbook: *Emerging Practices in Mathematics Education*
Twenty-third Yearbook: *Insights into Modern Mathematics*
Twenty-fourth Yearbook: *The Growth of Mathematical Ideas, Grades K–12*
Twenty-fifth Yearbook: *Instruction in Arithmetic*
Twenty-sixth Yearbook: *Evaluation in Mathematics*
Twenty-seventh Yearbook: *Enrichment Mathematics for the Grades*
Twenty-eighth Yearbook: *Enrichment Mathematics for High School*
Twenty-ninth Yearbook: *Topics in Mathematics for Elementary School Teachers*
Thirtieth Yearbook: *More Topics in Mathematics for Elementary School Teachers*
Thirty-first Yearbook: *Historical Topics for the Mathematics Classroom*
Thirty-second Yearbook: *A History of Mathematics Education in the United States and Canada*
Thirty-third Yearbook: *The Teaching of Secondary School Mathematics*
Thirty-fourth Yearbook: *Instructional Aids in Mathematics*
Thirty-fifth Yearbook: *The Slow Learner in Mathematics*

The Slow Learner in Mathematics

Thirty-fifth Yearbook

**National Council of
Teachers of Mathematics
1972**

Copyright © 1972 by
THE NATIONAL COUNCIL OF TEACHERS OF MATHEMATICS, INC.
1201 Sixteenth Street, NW, Washington, D.C. 20036
All rights reserved

Library of Congress Cataloging in Publication Data:
National Council of Teachers of Mathematics.
The slow learner in mathematics.

(*Its* Yearbook 35)
Includes bibliographies.
1. Mathematics—Study and teaching—Addresses, essays, lectures. 2. Slow learning children—Addresses, essays, lectures. I. Title. II. Series.
QA1.N3 35th [QA11]   512′.1′07   72-8350

Printed in the United States of America

Contents

Preface vii

Acknowledgments xii

1. Characteristics and Needs of the Slow Learner 1
   Richard W. Schulz, Cedar Rapids Community Schools, Cedar Rapids, Iowa

2. The Research Literature 26
   Len Pikaart, University of Georgia, Athens, Georgia
   James W. Wilson, University of Georgia, Athens, Georgia

3. Behavioral Objectives 52
   Henry H. Walbesser, University of Maryland, College Park, Maryland
   Heather L. Carter, University of Texas, Austin, Texas

4. A Favorable Learning Environment 104
   James R. Pearson, Dade County Public Schools, Miami, Florida

5. Adjustment of Instruction (Elementary School) 129
   Charlotte W. Junge, Wayne State University, Detroit, Michigan

6. Teaching Styles (Secondary School) 163
   Elizabeth A. Collins, Dade County Public Schools, Miami, Florida

7. Aids and Activities 182
   Evan M. Maletsky, Montclair State College, Upper Montclair, New Jersey

8. The Laboratory Approach 221
   Patricia S. Davidson, Boston State College, Boston, Massachusetts
   Marion I. Walter, Graduate School of Education, Harvard University, Cambridge, Massachusetts

9. Diagnostic-Prescriptive Teaching 282
   Vincent J. Glennon, The University of Connecticut, Storrs, Connecticut
   John W. Wilson, University of Maryland, College Park, Maryland

10. Classroom and School Administration 319
    Paul V. Rogler, Wilmington Public Schools, Wilmington, Delaware

11. Promising Programs and Practices 345

12. The Training of Teachers 402
    Dora Helen Skypek, Emory University, Atlanta, Georgia

Appendix A: Activities, Games, and Applications 444
    Thomas E. Rowan, Maryland State Department of Education, Baltimore, Maryland
    William G. McKenzie, Prince Georges County Public Schools, Upper Marlboro, Maryland

Appendix B: Sample Lessons 487

Index 521

Preface

In the revolution that has reshaped school mathematics over the past twenty years, the major efforts at first were in behalf of the capable student. Experienced teachers, however, have long been aware that mathematically capable students comprise only a part of the student population. A group often as large as the capable group, and in some schools larger, is made up of students who have considerable difficulty learning mathematics and whose achievement is noticeably below desired levels. Dedicated mathematics teachers have addressed themselves to the problems of these students for many years. By the sixth decade of the twentieth century, however, the need for greater mathematical competency on the part of all members of society was becoming increasingly clear. National, state, and local interest started to focus more than previously on the large number of students in our schools who have trouble learning generally; and among these, of course, are those who have trouble learning mathematics.

The Yearbook Planning Committee of the NCTM, at its April 1966 meeting, agreed to recommend to the Board of Directors a yearbook on the slow learner in mathematics, subject to the following limitations:

1. No attempt was to be made to identify such students beyond the general definition of "students who are not achieving at the desired level."
2. The yearbook was to deal with the subject matter objectives for slow learners and the methods for attaining these objectives at various levels.

The Board approved the recommendation, and a planning committee for the yearbook was formed. The planning committee had as its immediate work the development of a proposal for a conference on the slow learner in mathematics. It was hoped the conference would generate ideas that would culminate in the yearbook. The planning committee completed its work in April 1967, whereupon an editor and an editorial panel for the yearbook were appointed. Four of the original planning committee members remained on the editorial panel. Vincent Brant replaced Jack E. Forbes, who became chairman of the NCTM Yearbook Planning Committee at that time.

The conference approach to generating ideas for the yearbook did not prove feasible because of the cost of such an undertaking, and that approach was abandoned. During the early part of 1968 the editorial panel met twice. At those meetings we agreed on basic themes for the yearbook, selected tentative titles for the chapters, sketched chapter outlines, and selected prospective authors. In August 1968 a schedule and a budget for the yearbook were proposed to the Board of Directors. The Board approved the proposal later that year. By early 1969 the writing team for the yearbook was complete.

The editorial panel agreed with the first limitation set by the Yearbook Planning Committee and did not attempt to identify slow learners other than by noting that these are students who are not achieving at the desired level. We were well aware that there are a number of reasons why students do not achieve. We were also aware of the number of different labels—underachiever, low achiever, low-ability student, disadvantaged student, and so forth—applied to various groups of these students. We chose to use the term *slow learner* because the students we had in mind were those who learn mathematics slowly and who have a history of learning mathematics slowly. If speed of learning is a criterion of ability (there are those who say it should not be), then perhaps the basic group in mind is best described as those students of low ability, and in particular those of low mathematical ability.

Yet a variety of students, with various reasons why they learn mathematics slowly, are often placed in the same "slow learner" classes. The teacher is confronted with all these students. He is not always able to determine the cause of slow learning, although seeking the cause and working to eliminate it as best he can should be a major part of his efforts. The authors for the yearbook were particularly cautioned not to interpret "slow learner" in such a way as to leave out those whose apparently low ability is the result of cultural or educational deprivation.

The second stipulation of the Yearbook Planning Committee—that the yearbook deal with the subject matter objectives for slow learners and the methods for attaining these objectives at various levels—was subject to interpretation. We frankly admit that we chose to emphasize the latter. The main purpose of the book is to provide ideas for teaching the slow learner in mathematics. We felt that it should not be a book on curriculum; it should certainly not attempt to prescribe specific content in mathematics for all slow learners. Hence, the emphasis on objectives in the book is on how to make them clear to students and how to state them in terms of desired student behaviors; it is not on specific mathematical objectives to be attained.

Certainly, slow learners cannot be classified as being alike in all respects. However, teachers who have worked extensively with these students stress that, because of their history of failure and near failure, almost all of them have a low opinion of their worth, at least as mathematics students. They emphasize also that these students learn best when they are actively engaged in the learning activities. Contrary to the thinking of the panel, some learning materials and some teachers of slow learners seem to take the position that these children are able to function cognitively at relatively low levels only, as in the use of computational skills. With these three points in mind, the panel hoped to see the following strands running throughout the book; and we asked the authors to keep them foremost in mind: (1) enhancement of the self-image of the slow learner, (2) involvement of the learner in the learning activities, and (3) attention to the development of both skills and problem-solving ability. That the authors did keep these strands in mind will be apparent, we think, to anyone who reads the book.

The reader may find it helpful, as we have, to think of the yearbook as being divided into three parts. The first four chapters give background information the teacher will find useful. In order, these chapters treat the characteristics and needs of the slow learner, the research literature, the advantages of stating learning objectives in terms of student behaviors and some techniques for stating objectives in this way, and the creation of a favorable learning environment for the slow learner.

The second part, comprising chapters 5 through 9, is meant to provide more specific help for the classroom teacher. Adjusting instruction for the slow learner in the elementary school and finding teaching styles that are helpful to him in secondary school are the themes of chapters 5 and 6, respectively. Chapter 7 describes a number of simple, inexpensive multisensory aids and activities that can be used with slow learners; and chapter 8 is devoted to the laboratory approach to learning mathematics. Procedures for diagnosing mathematics difficulties and arriving at individual prescriptions to overcome these are developed in chapter 9.

The third part of the book, for want of a better name, might be called administrative considerations. Chapter 10 deals with classroom management and school administration. Chapters 11 and 12 deviate from this third theme somewhat but are related to it. Various programs for slow-learner groups are reported in chapter 11. The panel purposely chose programs representing a variety of philosophical and curricular approaches, wishing to leave open the question of what would constitute a complete and appropriate curriculum for slow learners and recognizing that a variety of approaches might be successful but with different kinds of slow-learner groups. Chapter 12 is devoted to descriptions of some programs for the in-service education of teachers—programs designed to help them do a better job in their work with these students.

The two appendixes should be of particular help to teachers. Appendix A presents a number of activities, games, and applications that have been found effective with slow learners; and Appendix B shows sample lessons that have been used successfully with slow-learner groups.

We would be remiss if we did not take this opportunity to thank those who have helped bring the yearbook to realization. In the early days of planning, help came from a number of people. Special thanks are due to Jack E. Forbes; L. Doyal Nelson, chairman of the Yearbook Planning Committee when the yearbook was proposed; and Donovan A. Johnson, president of the NCTM during the planning phase for the yearbook. Continued support for the project came from Julius H. Hlavaty and H. Vernon Price during their terms as president of the Council.

We are particularly grateful to the several authors of the yearbook. They kept close to schedule in submitting manuscript; made changes willingly when asked to do so; and, along with members of the editorial panel, reviewed chapters of the yearbook and made suggestions for changes. We are grateful also to the many persons who submitted excellent descriptions of their programs to be considered for chapter 11. We regret that, because of space limitations, only eight of these could be included. A list of those we did not have room to include is given at the beginning of chapter 11. We thank also the teachers who submitted the sample lessons for Appendix B. We shall not list here the names of the writers in any of these categories, since their names appear with their contributions in the yearbook.

Too numerous to mention by name are others who read all or parts of the yearbook in early or late draft stages and made helpful suggestions to the authors or the editorial panel members. Among these were a number of graduate students at Montclair State College and the University of Virginia.

Finally, special appreciation is due those at the Washington office of the Council. James D. Gates, executive secretary, has helped and advised us on a number of occasions. Charles R. Hucka, associate executive secretary, and his senior editorial associate, Julia A. Lacy, assisted by Charles Clements and Dorothy Hardy, receive our special praise for the careful work they did in editing and preparing the manuscript for the printer, and for the excellent job they did in seeing that the artwork, charts, diagrams, tables, and so on (there are a great many in the book) were skillfully and correctly done.

The Editorial Panel

Vincent Brant
   Baltimore County Public Schools

Shirley A. Hill
   University of Missouri at Kansas City

Mary V. Nesbit
   Formerly with the Dade County Public Schools

Max A. Sobel
   Montclair State College

William C. Lowry, *Editor*
University of Virginia

Acknowledgments

Grateful acknowledgment is made for permission to reprint extracts from the copyrighted sources named below. Individual articles are listed under the name of the journal or book in which each appears. (More complete bibliographical information appears in the reference lists at the ends of chapters.)

American Educational Research Journal. "Review of *Pygmalion in the Classroom*," by R. L. Thorndike.

The Art of Teaching, by Gilbert Arthur Highet. Reprinted by permission of Alfred A. Knopf.

The Changing Curriculum: Mathematics, by Robert B. Davis. Reprinted by permission of the Association for Supervision and Curriculum Development.

The Culturally Deprived Child, by Frank Riessman. Reprinted by permission of Harper & Row, Publishers.

"Development and Standardization of an Instrument for Assessing Video-Taped Data of Teacher Management in the Elementary Classroom," by David S. Steward and Margaret S. Steward.

The Disadvantaged: Challenge to Education, by Mario D. Fantini and Gerald Weinstein. Reprinted by permission of Harper & Row, Publishers.

Discovering Meanings in Elementary School Mathematics, by Foster E. Grossnickle, Leo J. Brueckner, and John Reckzeh. Reprinted by permission of Holt, Rinehart & Winston.

Educational Psychologist. "On Learning from Being Told," by John B. Carroll.

Education in Depressed Areas. "Ego Development among Segregated Negro Children," by David Ausubel and Pearl Ausubel. Reprinted by permission of Teachers College Press.

ACKNOWLEDGMENTS

Evaluation Comment. "Learning for Mastery," by Benjamin S. Bloom.

Fortune. "Technology Is Knocking at the Schoolhouse Door," by Charles E. Silberman.

Handbook on Formative and Summative Evaluation of Student Learning, edited by Benjamin S. Bloom, J. Thomas Hastings, and George F. Madaus. Reprinted by permission of McGraw-Hill Book Co.

How Children Fail, by John Holt. Reprinted by permission of Pitman Publishing Corp.

Ideas Educational. "Grouping in the Elementary Classroom," by Frances H. Redmond.

Journal of Negro Education. "The Overlooked Positives of Disadvantaged Groups," by Frank Riessman.

Learning and Individual Differences: A Symposium of the Learning Research and Development Center of the University of Pittsburgh. "How Can Instruction Be Adapted to Individual Differences?" by Lee J. Cronbach. Reprinted by permission of Charles E. Merrill Publishing Co.

Life Skills in School and Society. "The Changing Society and Its Schools," by Edward J. Meade, Jr. Reprinted by permission of the Association for Supervision and Curriculum Development.

"Mathematics for Basic Education." Reprinted by permission of the Baltimore County Public Schools.

"Mathematics for Spanish-speaking Pupils." Reprinted by permission of the Los Angeles City Unified School District.

Mathematics Teacher. "Positive and Negative Factors in Team Teaching," by Sister Mary Victor Korb.

National Elementary Principal. "Sex Ratios in Learning and Behavior Disorders," by Frances Bentzen. Reprinted by permission of the National Association of Elementary School Principals, NEA.

NEA Journal. "The Computer and the Student," by Kenneth E. Dawson and Morris Norfleet; and "The Prevention of Failure," by Walter B. Waetjen.

New England Journal of Medicine. "Pediatric Management of School Learning Problems of Underachievement," by A. Solnit and M. Stark.

The New Improved American, by Bernard Asbell. Reprinted by permission of McGraw-Hill Book Co.

Phi Delta Kappan. "Psychoneurobiochemeducation," by David Krech.

Psychological Issues. "Identity and the Life Cycle: Growth and Crises of the Healthy Personality," by Erik H. Erikson.

Saturday Review. "The Child: His Struggle for Identity," by Jerome Kagan; "Culture, Politics, and Pedagogy," by Jerome S. Bruner; and "Life Is Fun in a Smiling, Fair-Skinned World," by Otto Klineberg.

The Slow Learner Project: The Secondary School "Slow Learner" in Mathematics, by Sarah T. Herriot. Reprinted by permission of the School Mathematics Study Group.

Student Motivation and Classroom Management—a Behavioristic Approach. "CMC in a Disadvantaged Area," by David H. Moyer. Reprinted by permission of Behavior Technics.

Teachers College Record. "Taking Advantage of the Disadvantaged," by Mario D. Fantini and Gerald Weinstein.

Teaching Strategies for the Culturally Disadvantaged, by Hilda Taba and Deborah Elkins. Reprinted by permission of Rand McNally & Co.

"Teaching the Low Achiever—Success or Failure," by Terry Shoemaker.

Teaching the New Arithmetic, by Guy M. Wilson. Reprinted by permission of McGraw-Hill Book Co.

Today's Education. "Teaching the Slow Learner," by Regis F. Crowley.

1

Characteristics and Needs of the Slow Learner

RICHARD W. SCHULZ

LOW ACHIEVERS, *underachievers, educationally disadvantaged, culturally deprived, emotionally disturbed*—with an alacrity and confidence betraying only superficial understanding, some educators apply these euphemistic labels to children and adolescents. Whatever term is used, there is little evidence that human beings can be so categorized with any degree of precision.

Slow learners have been variously defined, in terms of IQ range, mathematical achievement, teacher grades, reading level, or various combinations of these. They do indeed demonstrate below-average intellectual capacity on the basis of at least one of these criteria and are likely to display mathematical atrophy, or arrested development. They thus have much in common. Nevertheless slow learners—by any definition—are not alike. Each has his own unique set of strengths and weaknesses, and each shares in the universal, though highly variable, attributes, concerns, and needs of other human beings.

It is commonly said that the child with a poor attitude or self-image is deficient in *affective* functioning and the child with weaknesses in intellectual skills is deficient in *cognitive* functioning. This is true; but it is also true—and it is a major thesis of this chapter—that slow learning can result from deficient affective functioning as well as from deficient cognitive functioning.

Solnit and Stark have warned that even a child with adequate intellectual endowment can be prevented from learning by a defective perceptual apparatus, reading and writing disabilities, an inner state of excitement or anxiety, overwhelming life experiences, inhibitions in curiosity and intellectual activity, and a home or school environment that interferes with the child's ability to concentrate and learn successfully (for example, a perfectionist parent or teacher whose demands arouse resentment and discouragement). They go on to say that "just as a successful school experience prepares the child for assuming responsibilities in later life, one fraught with anxiety and failure leads to the loss of self-esteem and to a self-defeating attitude" (36, p. 989).

Slow learners are likely candidates for such loss of self-esteem. In treating symptoms of slow learning, teachers must be wary of such generalized diagnoses as "They don't know their basic facts," or "They can't read," or "They must be grouped more accurately and with greater precision." Even a slow learner has already learned *something*. It is the job of the school to find out *how* he has learned, what learning disabilities he really has, and what channels of cognitive, affective, and physical activity are still intact. Ironically, schools may be the only treatment centers that blame the patient rather than the treatment when things go wrong. IQ groupings themselves often serve to mask instructional failures. By putting the blame on the child's innate capacity ("he is a slow learner"), schools have been able to escape the unsettling possibility that their own strategy or technology may be at fault.

This chapter examines the characteristics of slow learners. However, the reader is warned against assuming that all slow learners are alike or that the characteristics described below present an accurate profile of even a typical slow learner, much less a specific individual. The chapter concludes by reflecting on some important matters of fundamental need that are generally overlooked in the treatment of slow learners. Affective concerns of children and adolescents are stressed, with an underlying commitment to the position that the child's failure to learn may be partly the fault of the school or the teacher and not exclusively the fault of the child.

Characteristics of the Slow Learner

Cultural differences and deficient cognitive functioning are major influences on the behavior and achievement of slow learners. Before considering these factors in more detail, however, it should be stressed that differences are not necessarily defects. Concerned by the prevailing preoccupation with *negatives,* Eisenberg and Riessman have urged attention to the *positives,* maintaining that educational planning should capitalize on those differences that may actually represent strengths (10). In discussing the untapped verbal ability of disadvantaged individuals, Riessman points to these additional positive dimensions:

> . . . the cooperativeness and mutual aid that mark the extended family; the avoidance of the strain accompanying competitiveness and individualism; the equalitarianism, informality and humor; the freedom from self blame and parental over-protection; the children's enjoyment of each other's company and lessened sibling rivalry; the security found in the extended family and a traditional outlook; the enjoyment of music, games, sports, and cars; the ability to express anger; the freedom from being word bound; and, finally, the physical style involved in learning. [30, p. 230]

Fowler adds that even though an early tendency toward autonomy may be based on neglect, early independence can be handled adequately by involving the child in responsibility and thus can become a partial advantage (17, p. 7). One tragedy of contemporary education may be that so little has been done to identify and take advantage of these positives.

Poor self-image

A slow learner is likely to have a poor image of himself, both as a learner and as a person, to the extent that he has been unsuccessful in his school experiences. As new challenges lead him to question his own worth, he grows increasingly wary, and his endless frustrations lead to feelings of guilt and shame. He lacks confidence in his future. During adolescence a normal feeling of uselessness becomes still more onerous with the growing sense of powerlessness, particularly when the slow learner comes from a disadvantaged environment. Indeed, the slow learner is caught up in what Mager has called universal aversives—conditions and consequences people tend to avoid (27, pp. 50–57). These include fear and anxiety (for example, of threatened failure, exposing his ignorance at the chalkboard in front of his peers, or being sent to the principal); frustration (when information seems irrelevant or is presented too fast to assimilate); and humiliation and embarrassment (repeated failure, "special classes," and even the feeling of failure that is engineered into "the lower half of the grading curve").

Numerous studies appear to establish that a relationship does exist between self-concept and achievement or success (4; 8; 16). In commenting on the special problems of the black learner, Ausubel speaks equally well for the slow learner of any color whose self-image has been severely damaged:

> Before Negroes can assume their rightful place in a desegregated American culture important changes in the ego structure of Negro children must first take place. They must shed feelings of inferiority and self-derogation, acquire feelings of self-confidence and racial pride, develop realistic aspirations for occupations requiring greater education and training, and develop the personality traits for implementing these aspirations. [3, p. 130]

As the school attends to the mathematical deficiencies of the slow learner, whatever the matrix of causal factors and interrelationships may be, first priority should be given to reconstruction of his self-image.

Cognitive variables

Many slow learners are deficient in intellectual skills or cognitive functioning as measured by the predominantly verbal problems on intelligence tests. However, what seem to be cognitive defects may be simply differences in style that are incompatible with the standard list of school virtues or intellectual demands. Whichever the case, cognitive variables, like other human attributes, exist along a shadowy continuum rather than on either side of a have or have-not line.

Cognitive functioning: deficient. Intellectual deficiencies may, but do not necessarily, include some of the following characteristics of an impoverished language-symbolic system: a limited vocabulary; faulty grammar; inability to use abstract symbols; deficient formal speech patterns; restricted reading and listening comprehension; and a general paucity of information, concepts, and relational schemata (2; 13, pp. 47–55 and chap. 3; 17, pp. 5–6; 24, pp. 53–54). The slow learner is apt to possess these deficiencies. Moreover, he is apt to be less effective in classifying, ordering sequences of events, perceiving cause and effect relationships, generalizing, analyzing, solving abstract verbal problems, and maintaining an extended verbal thought sequence (37, pp. 5–9). Since the school is a heavily cognitive experience, the typical slow learner is achieving a year or more below grade level, particularly in academic subjects. If he has been held back in his normal school progress, he may also be a year or more older than his classmates. All in all, he exhibits a progressively deteriorating achievement pattern.

Learning style: physical, slow. In one sense, achievement is a testimony to an insidious sorting and rewarding process that prizes *head* orientation over *hand* orientation, or verbal skills and style over physical skills and style. In such a value system, the slow learner is often a loser, for in many cases his primary learning style is one of physicalization—confrontation with the immediate environment on a physical basis. While the importance of visual and action-based mathematical experiences has been hypothesized on a neurological basis for all children (15), tactile experiences with objects and events are indispensable to the learner who has no other effective input channel. To form concepts and work mathematical problems, he needs the physical input provided by such manipulative materials as fraction pieces, Dienes blocks, geoboards, puzzles, games, machine calculators, and in fact the entire mathematics laboratory.

But just as physicalization implies a physical *input*, it also hints at a physical *output* (17, p. 7). Mathematics teachers are familiar with the nuisance of the resulting "acting out" behavior: pencil tapping, rhythmic tapping of the feet, paper crumbling, muttering, waving fists, walking around the classroom, running in the halls, matching money, yelling, slamming books on a table, temper tantrums, name calling, fighting, and similar evidences that any teacher can cite. When an attempt is made to control physical output, the result can be sullen behavior, outright hostility, withdrawal, or daydreaming. None of these consequences is very pleasant, and any can make learning more difficult.

A learning style that is physical is also slow. Yet slowness should not be equated with stupidity. Riessman suggests that valid reasons exist for slow learning:

> A pupil may be slow because he is extremely careful, meticulous, or cautious. He may be slow because he refuses to generalize easily. He may be slow because he cannot understand a concept unless he does something physically. . . . A child may be slow because he learns in what I have called a "one track" way; that is, he persists in one line of thought and is not flexible or broad. He does not easily adopt other frames of reference, such as the teacher's, and consequently he may appear slow and dull. [30, p. 226]

Since speed of response is the dominant observable and *rewarded* behavior in most academic classrooms, many students may have been unfairly penalized for their slow styles. It has even been reported that, in one case study, science and mathematics teachers waited significantly *less* time for poor students to reply to questions. Students whom the teacher perceived as slow or less able had to answer more rapidly than those perceived as fast or bright (31, p. 13). If, in addition, slow learners find that speeding up their work increases not only the probability of error but the risk of some consequence that will further damage their self-images, it is not surprising that they continue to be *slow* learners.

Cultural differences

In general, cultural differences place the learner at a serious disadvantage—sometimes by impairing cognitive skills, sometimes by damaging affective functioning, sometimes by imposing between the learner and the school a cultural barrier or conflict with which neither the school nor the child is able to cope. For the slow learner who finds himself in a disadvantaged environment, life is not—to use Klineberg's words—"fun, filled almost exclusively with friendly, smiling parents, doting grandparents, generous and cooperative neighbors, and even warm-hearted strangers" (23). Rather, the disadvantaged legacy is one of poverty, often complicated by minority status, with a high potential for economic, emotional, and social disaster. Love of learning is certainly not a product of a slum home. The marginal family may be large, extremely overcrowded, noisy, disorganized, broken, highly mobile, presided over by someone other than a parent, marked by extremes of severe punishment and neglect, chronically insecure economically, and further weakened by poor diet and inadequate clothing. Because of the authority stance of the adult head of the family, culturally deprived children often have had little opportunity for intellectual interaction with adults. Furthermore, adults without an intellectual orientation may not be able to help with academic requirements, teach such "school virtues" as promptness and orderliness, or direct children toward long-range goals. (37, pp. 4–13.)

Thus, children who not only learn slowly but come from a disadvantaged culture may lack hope, tend to behave in a random manner, respond only to immediate or short-term goals, and neither expect to achieve nor fear not achieving (20). In contrast, most teachers come from a middle-class culture, which has given them a generally hopeful outlook, highly organized their behavior, made them conscious of long-range goals, and led them to *expect* achievement and success. Such cultural conflict can seriously impair the teacher's effectiveness in working with children from so discordant an environment.

A disadvantaged culture does not support the goals and patterns of school life. We need to remember, however, that individuals are not alike. Fowler repeats this caution when he says:

> There is a body of evidence now rapidly accumulating which reveals characteristic patterns associated with these conditions of life. . . . They are found in various combinations, although to some degree the presence of certain styles or traits tends to preclude the existence of others. It is important to underscore, however, that these must be considered ideal-type patterns which, while found more frequently in the poor and underprivileged, are not uniformly present throughout these subcultures. The range of variation, both in quantity and in quality of types of personality and cognitive styles, are as great here as in any other population. [17, p. 5]

Reality set

It has been said that many slow learners value education but dislike school. In a sense, they have a reality set. They are not satisfied by a phony world, and they raise serious questions about the relevance of their school experiences. As Fantini and Weinstein set forth the issue:

> The disadvantaged child has dared to call attention to the Emperor's clothes by asking, "What's really in education for me?" In a counterpoint of innocence and defiance, the ghetto student declares that the school is phony, that teachers don't talk like real people, that his reality and reality as painted by the language of the school are as night and day.
>
> In questioning whether the school has much intrinsic meaning, he has become the spokesman for the middle-class child as well. Middle-class students may drop out of college complaining of the irrelevancy of their classes, and middle-class America may betray its miseducation by its apathy toward social injustice. But even if they find the schools too distant from the reality of their lives they are little inclined to challenge the entire process because they have learned to play the game in order to make it to and through college. [14, p. 105]

Slow learners need to sense reality in the problems with which they are confronted, to sense at least occasionally that something important has happened in the school mathematics setting. While social pressures, adult views, and disciplined logic may affect curriculum choices, relevance must be based on the perception of the learner—in the way the slow learner views the school program as appropriate to his age, his social and ethnic background, and as an avenue to a useful adult role. School must be valid in *his* terms.

This is not to suggest that relevance must be based solely on vocational meaningfulness; for what is relevant to a slow learner is often related to his affective concerns, to his inner uneasiness. Fun, enjoyment, and discovery can also be relevant if they reach to the feelings of the learner. Unfortunately, as Bruner has noted, the problem is that learning is taken out of the context of immediate action just by dint of putting it into a school and "the result, at its worst, has led to the ritual, rote nonsense that has led a generation of critics to despair" (6, p. 71).

Need of immediate gratification

Slow learners often find it difficult to defer immediate gratifications in the interest of long-range goals. More often than not, their academic school experience is neither clearly nor convincingly related to long-range purposes. In lieu of responding to such future satisfactions as a good job or a college degree, slow learners tend to put their energy into immediately gratified desires: food, sports, cars, friends, sexual pleasures, and various other symbols of adult status. To a junior high school boy already one or two years retarded in school achievement, the distant outline of a high school diploma seems more illusory than real. Stated succinctly, in the light of available data, graduation is a bad bet.

Lack of school skills

Whatever the causes, slow learners are not likely to exhibit the skills required by typical school strategies and routines. One skill they often lack is that of *listening*—of paying attention. Poor listening may sometimes be the result of having been subjected to so much random noise that one has learned to tune out audio stimuli. As Asbell suggests:

> Psychologists are beginning to discern that the slum child's inattention may be a high skill, the result of intensive training. When the child lives with 11 people in three rooms . . . sharing their toilets, knowing when the man is drunk next door and [that] the baby is awake downstairs—a child must *learn* to be inattentive to survive. His ears become skilled in not hearing, his eyes at not seeing. [1, p. 89]

Children who have learned to be inattentive have acquired a characteristic of considerable concern to their classroom teachers.

Another skill that is typically deficient in slow learners is *persistence*. Many observers have noted the short attention span of slow learners. However, even slow learners persist well beyond expected limits when they are engaged in certain kinds of tasks that are either clearly relevant or unusually interesting.

> Slum children are not accustomed to attending to, or being an object of, the long, orderly, verbal sequences that teachers use in explaining

subject matter. . . . The much-noted short attention-span is thus only partly a habit built in disordered and discontinuous home life. It may also be a consequence of the meaninglessness of much of their school work and of an almost allergic reaction to an overabundance of commands, prohibitions, and directions which have flooded the ears of these students both at home and in school. [37, p. 9]

In problem solving, a *reflective response* is often lacking. Slow learners tend to be more impulsive than reflective. An impulsive response is frequently a request for personality support: the first person to respond at least wins some form of recognition. However, other factors may be at work. For one thing, a slow learner may have difficulty tolerating ambiguity and tend to close on an answer before collecting and evaluating all the available evidence. For another, with less understanding, he is more apt to guess.

Initiative is another school virtue in which slow learners are typically deficient. They need an unusual amount of prodding, and this is partly a result of their conditioning: they have been conditioned to expect their responses in the school setting to be self-defeating. They may be neither quick nor accurate, but they are clever enough not to expose themselves in a nonsupportive or threatening environment. Eventually, the teacher of slow learners must face the problem of how to initiate responsive behavior from the child.

Finally, a *sense of time, order, and sequence* is important for success in school. The slow learner is apt to have a deficient sense of time, a poor sense of order and sequence, and an inability to cope with sequential events. Since schools are organized around routines and time schedules, the slow learner easily becomes disorganized—a characteristic that shows up as lost pencils, forgotten notebooks, or unfinished homework, as well as in more serious manifestations. Disorganization leads, in turn, to a poor attitude toward school, a high incidence of withdrawal, regular absences, and a tendency to drop out.

Lack of social skills

In the absence of other sources of reward and reinforcement, many slow learners tend to measure success in terms of their personal relationships with peers. They seek strong peer identification and group support even as they may lack many of the social skills required for successful group work in the school setting. These social skills are even more likely to be wanting when the slow learner comes from a disadvantaged environment. He may unknowingly break the rules of conduct; for he may never have learned the school virtues of cleanliness, punctuality, orderliness, and responsiveness. He may chafe under the pressures of endless routines, commands, prohibitions, and directions. In another setting, however, he is a different person. When out of school and freed from its unacceptable constraints, he may exhibit aggressive, physical leadership.

Although a slow learner may seek group identification, a large group (class) may readily "turn him off." Particularly where intellectual performance is involved, exposing himself to his peers may be too threatening to his self-image. He is then likely to respond more skillfully in smaller, intimate groups, where the risks are smaller and where attention and reinforcement are more readily available. Thus at one time the slow learner may seek the support of a peer group, but at another time he may need to escape from group pressure, to seek temporary privacy—in a study cubicle, in a corner of the room, in the hall, or in the nonevaluative grasp of a headset as he responds to a carefully planned audio stimulus.

Deficient adult relationships

Kagan has suggested several broad classes of goals that motivate the child's learning of academic skills. Developmentally, the first goal is *recognition from significant others*. For the young child, this group includes parents and teachers. For the older child and adolescent, it includes peers and certain authority figures who have either the skills or the power that the adolescent values. A second goal is *identification with a model* who is seen as commanding desirable resources. The child will want to adopt behaviors and learn skills that he believes will make him more like the model. (22, p. 34.)

Unfortunately, significant others and appropriate adult models do not appear in the adult relationships of many slow learners, particularly those from disadvantaged backgrounds, where adult males are conspicuously unavailable to boys—not only because they find few male teachers in the elementary school but because the male parent is either missing or too busy to pay much attention to the family. Many such children seldom have an opportunity to sit down with an adult and hold a conversation of any personal consequence. Adults are creatures to avoid. ("They tell you to be quiet or to get out of the way, but they do not talk to you.") Yet the essence of a school experience is the *adult conversation* that these children have not learned. Often what passes for conversation is limited to such statements as, "Mathematics was one of my worst subjects, too," or, "That's not the way I learned it," or, "Why are they teaching you that?"

One of the most significant contingencies in a class of slow learners is that one of them will find in the teacher an adult model with whom he can identify, from whom he can catch a positive attitude toward mathematics, and with whom he can learn to engage in a mathematical dialogue. Bruner has suggested that "the courtesy of conversation may be the major ingredient in the courtesy of teaching" (6, p. 90).

Importance of sex differences

No listing of the attributes of a slow learner would be complete if it did not recognize the importance of differences associated with the sex of the learner. It makes a great difference whether the slow learner is a boy or a girl, especially when the school is searching for strategies and technologies relevant to the slow learner. Whether inherent traits or cultural imprints, sex-related differences have been observed in learning styles, role expectancies, sensitivities, aggressive tendencies, toleration of femininity or masculinity, and response to authority. How a child perceives his sex role can be a critical factor in his concept of relevancy, his self-image, his tendency to initiate behavior, and his willingness to complete a school assignment. (19, pp. 59–67; 26; 33.) The feminization of the elementary school may be more than coincidentally related to the fact that so many more boys than girls are "serious problem children" (5, pp. 13–17).

Kagan has developed the importance of the sex appropriateness of school tasks by relating this factor to modeling behavior, or his "identification motive."

> The peer group is not unimportant in the development of standards and motives surrounding intellectual mastery. The child selects models from among his classmates once he begins school. As with the lower-class family, the lower-class peer group is biased against school achievement in favor of those behaviors that the boys and girls themselves define as masculine or feminine. This situation has serious consequences for school performance. [21, p. 87]

Although arithmetic is one of the few school activities labeled as predominantly masculine by first-grade boys and girls, the influence of intellectual motivation has moderated by the fifth grade (22, pp. 36–37). Silberman has noted this important consequence of sex-linked behavior:

> The notion that intellectual activity is effete and effeminate takes hold among boys around the fifth grade. . . . (Curiously enough, the notion that intellectual activity is *un*feminine sets in among girls at about the same age.) [34, p. 203]

Thus the flight into femininity of preadolescent girls may spell additional trouble for the teacher of mathematics. This is but one example of the need for considering sex differences in planning mathematics curriculum. The implication in this case is that curriculum materials should include problems viewed by girls as feminine as well as problems viewed by boys as masculine.

There are, of course, other sex-linked characteristics of interest to the mathematics teacher. Girls are apt to exhibit the approved virtues of cleanliness, neatness, punctuality, and orderliness. They tend to function well in groups. They tend to be better with computation but less proficient in mathematical reasoning (18, pp. 49–50). Particularly at the onset of adolescence, they are preoccupied with personal appearance and social relations. They seek to marry and live happily ever after. They are more apt to respond to gentleness, soft voices, fairness, and democratic firmness. They are more apt to accept the teacher and the content on faith.

Boys, on the other hand, are preoccupied with things connected with their masculine status (33, p. 85). This is even more true of boys from disadvantaged homes where male-female roles tend to be more sharply drawn and where sex typing begins early (19, p. 64). Males, even adult males, from lower-class families gravitate towards male peers rather than their families. Males seek to dominate, and they fear femininity in any form. In most subcultures, however, boys are more apt to identify with activities that are mechanical, scientific, physically strenuous, adventurous, legal, political, sales-oriented, or technological.

A plea for more careful examination of sex differences as they relate to slow learners is made by Bentzen, who says that when a society only covertly recognizes the possibility of a relationship between a biologically determined differential between the sexes and the three- to ten-to-one male predominance in learning and behavior disorders, this itself may "precipitate stress and trauma, thereby frequently initiating the deviant behavioral response patterns that society has come to expect as 'normal' for boys" (5, pp. 13–14).

Managing Instruction to Meet the Needs of the Slow Learner

The teacher-manager as the strategic change agent

In building a mathematical program for the slow learner, the school has been notoriously unimaginative and unsuccessful. Its failure can be attributed to many factors. For one thing, learning theory has not provided an adequate base. For another, treatment has vacillated even as it has ranged from special worksheets to ability grouping, to preschool centers, to such technological resources as computers. Nevertheless, in the present composition of the real world, the teacher is the critical agent of change who can adapt the strategies and tactics of instruction to meet the needs of the slow learner. The living teacher, not an abstract program of instruction, is the manager of instruction, sensitive and responsive to the affective as well as the cognitive needs of the learner. He must diagnose with systematic care, plan for an extensive range of individual differences, and mediate effectively between the things of the classroom and the intellect on the one hand and the affections of the learner on the other. He brings to the task a bag of influencing techniques: proximity, signals, humor, constructive criticism, routines, reinforcements, and affections—to name but a few. In even the worst of circumstances he must try to be flexible, responsive, and nonthreatening. Let us now examine a few of the strategies of the teacher as an instructional manager who attempts to control, or at least influence, affective functioning, learning tasks, social interaction, and the schedule of reinforcements.

Just as there is no stereotype for the slow learner, so there is no universal prescription for his treatment. In the discussion that follows, the problem of individual differences is implicit in each dimension of the learning task and its management. Recognizing that it is impossible to assign a single teacher to every child, Sears has advocated the development of self-instruction devices that children can use at their own pace and has urged the designing of research studies to discover principles that apply to group-oriented teaching and learning as well as individual interactions between the teacher and the child (32, p. 6–7). The following paragraphs call attention to a few such principles—ones that are already known but commonly overlooked.

Affective control: A sense of trust

There is strong evidence that low achievement is as much a personality problem as an intellectual one. The student must feel good about himself (37, p. 265). When the slow learner comes to class with a seriously damaged self-image, he cannot do good work. Effective learning cannot take place until the teacher and the pupil trust and respect each other, until the pupil feels socially and emotionally secure in the classroom environment. Erikson has singled out basic trust as the first component of a healthy personality, defining it as follows:

> By "trust" I mean what is commonly implied in reasonable trustfulness as far as others are concerned and a simple sense of trustworthiness as far as oneself is concerned. . . . What we here call "trust" coincides with what Therese Benedek has called "confidence." If I prefer the word "trusts," it is because there is more naïveté and more mutuality in it. [12, pp. 56, 61]

To manage the environment in such a way as to build a sense of trust, the teacher must speak to the feelings of the learner. The slow learner must sense a special, warm, I-care-about-you relationship. He needs to *feel* the intimacy through hands-on reassurance or through carefully chosen words that manifest tolerance, understanding, and respect. He must find a clear frame of reference with consistent boundaries for classroom behavior. He must learn to respond and to engage in adult conversations with his teacher as well as his peers. The teacher, in turn, must learn when to talk and when to let students talk. This may not be easy, especially for teachers who have long defined teaching as telling and practiced it as such (37, p. 275).

Task control

Initiating responses. Anxious, withdrawn children seldom initiate a response, whereas confident, explorative children are seldom without something to do or say. It is not surprising, then, that slow learners, who are anxious because they are school-conditioned to expect failure, show avoidance and inhibitory reactions rather than desirable responses when presented with mathematical stimuli. Faced with this situation, the teacher-manager must find ways to overcome it.

One way to encourage initiatory responses is to make the classroom environment more attractive, appealing both to the mind and to the feelings. Physical arrangements can encourage the slow learner to ask a question, to inquire about a specific puzzle, or object, or display. Since questioning by the student is relatively nonthreatening to him (as long as the teacher refrains from making humiliating evaluations of the question itself), the teacher's ability to manage the environment to stimulate questions is an important technique for helping children begin to feel a part of a warm, human relationship. Questioning and curiosity should not be punished, and any reasonable questions should be encouraged, even when they are of a nonmathematical nature.

Physicalization. Sensorimotor involvement with real objects (and pictures of objects) is a crucial preliminary to effective verbalization and conceptualization by the slow learner. For him, learning must be more than passive reception. He needs to do things, sometimes even interacting with the environment in random exploration with his unique style and sensory mix. Such learning can be messy rather than elegant, uneven rather than predictable. Yet the understanding teacher will know that many children need to learn this way. Asbell makes a special plea for the culturally disadvantaged:

> No one ever tells slum children much about anything. Conversation is not a highly developed art in their families. Suddenly the child, accustomed to learning through his senses, is obliged to sit still all day before a talkative teacher—she can talk for hours without stopping. Moreover, she seems to think the most important thing in the world is to make out printed words on a page. [1, p. 91]

And Davis makes a final stinging observation:

> Large-scale observation of American classrooms reveals unquestionably that, in 1965, the usual (and nearly universal) mathematics class has children sitting in their seats, a teacher standing at the front of the room, no physical apparatus for the children to touch and play with, and a lesson involving merely talking, listening, reading, and writing. . . . This applies not only to the primary grades, but at least as broadly to K–12. . . . We need much more use of physical apparatus in the mathematics classroom, especially apparatus which the children manipulate themselves. [9, pp. 356–57]

Alternatives, novelty, and variety. Slow learners not only tolerate novelty and variety; they demand them.

Reasonable predictability is a prerequisite of classroom security, but novelty and reasonable *un*predictability are required to sustain *exploratory activity.* The point is forcefully made by Waetjen:

> Nothing erodes motivation more than constant exposure to the predictable and familiar situation. Of course, classrooms must be *somewhat* familiar to pupils, since this gives them guideposts for behavior and therefore facilitates motivation. But all classrooms should have some element of unpredictability which gently nudges pupils into an "off balance" position and which makes it necessary for them to obtain information in order to regain their balance. [38, p. 39]

Novelty and variety serve a further purpose by making *alternatives* available—the alternative approaches and procedures needed to accommodate the wide range of learning styles and affective concerns exhibited by slow learners. "More of the same" is seldom an effective solution to a learning problem that develops when a child fails to achieve a stated objective through a given set of stimuli. It is to be hoped that alternative stimuli, more lively and in tune with the learner's style and interests, will then be helpful. Available alternatives must range well beyond the unimpressive, unexciting, and overwhelmingly verbal format of the typical mathematics text—and beyond other resources that are commonly used. A workbook of problems all presented in a similar manner, all requiring the same form of response, and all leading to a single best answer does not stimulate persistent behavior or arouse curiosity. And the typical reading-lecture style of classroom activity is by no measure a close match with the physical-action style of the slow learner.

One important source of variety and novelty is the mathematical game. Children develop cognitive skills as they play games, making decisions and carrying out strategies. Aside from this fact, however, games have value because they are needed. The rationale for games, Riessman says, can be found in the learning styles and characteristics of slow learners:

> Their extra-verbal communication (motoric, visual) is usually called forth in games, most of which are not word-bound. Also, most games . . . are person-centered and generally are concerned with direct action and visible results. Games are usually sharply defined and structured, with clear-cut goals. The rules are definite and can be readily absorbed. The deprived child enjoys the challenge of the game and feels he can "do" it; this is in sharp contrast to many verbal tasks. [29, p. 71]

Teachers alert to the need for variety and novelty, however, must be equally alert to the danger that the mathematics presented to slow learners may degenerate into a series of completely unrelated topics, meaningless tricks, useless applications, or mere amusement and entertainment. Variety must be carefully managed and instruction organized to provide the feeling of security that slow learners seem to find when they look forward to a daily routine. Nevertheless, while a typical class period may include a "wake up" exercise, a review, a game, the discussion of a new idea, and written seat work or a "quiet time," within the context of each part of the lesson there is adequate opportunity for pleasant surprises, unpredictability, and variety.

One further point should be noted. When children are exposed to many alternatives, they are likely to find a preferred technique, strategy, or algorithm. As a result, students working side by side may be using different strategies and algorithms. Such flexibility allows for different learning styles and need not lead to mass confusion.

Psychological structure, sequencing, and pacing. That physicalization and variety are not sufficient in themselves is well argued by Kagan.

> [In preschool enrichment programs for lower-class children] there is a zealous attempt to bombard the lower-class child with pictures, crayons, books, speech, and typewriters, as if an intellectual deficit was akin to hunger and the proper therapy required filling of his cerebral gulleys with stuff.
>
> I would like to argue for a more paced strategy, a self-conscious attempt to intervene when the intrusion is likely to be maximally distinctive. [21, p. 82]

Fowler carries the thought further:

> Key principles are the concepts of structure and sequencing of materials, followed by the coordination and pacing of the learning according to each child's rate and level of mastery. . . . Selective organization and sequencing of the material is essential if the disadvantaged child is not to get lost in a walk in the woods. [17, pp. 13–14]

Instructional materials for the slow learner must be selectively organized and sequenced so that psychological organization (structure as the learner perceives it) is consonant with the logical organization (structure as the mathematician perceives it). Teachers of slow learners must attempt to step into the pupil's frame of reference and look matters over from there.

The following principles are presented as reasonable guides for the teacher who tries to manage instruction with both mathematical and psychological integrity:

1. The initial learning task must be geared to the learner's state of readiness, and the child must understand what he is supposed to do. Reduced persistence, excessive questions, and irrelevant behavior are frequently the result when the objectives and procedures are not clear.

2. Ongoing learning tasks must be consolidated and performance reasonably dependable before new, dependent tasks are introduced. Furthermore, newly developed concepts will have to be revisited frequently. Just as one plays a recording of a musical composition many times to appreciate its structure and meaning, mathematical ideas mature with each revisit. Unfortunately, in the interest of covering prescribed material, even slow learners are rushed to new concepts when they would better visit old ones. Superficial verbalizations can readily be memorized, but concepts develop in depth as they appear in a variety of instances and contrasting examples.

3. Successive learning tasks must be properly sequenced and paced. A child cannot be expected to persist in problem-solving activity if the ultimate solution of the problem lies beyond his ability or beyond his repertoire of skills and store of information. Nor is he likely to persist long if the successive stages are not relatively easy to attain, particularly during the early stages of instruction.

The third principle has implications that should be noted here. When long-range goals are absent, lessons and assignments in mathematics must provide unambiguous direction and well-defined, attainable endpoints. Children develop the confidence and persistence required for longer-range, goal-directed activity only as they frequently experience closure (that is, sense completion) in activities of much shorter duration. For the development of personality, it is probably more important to complete a short assignment than to leave a long assignment unfinished. Carefully designed worksheets, learning activity packets, and well-managed assignments are among the devices teachers can employ to ensure a reasonable amount of closure for slow learners in the daily classroom routine. Of course, the work span of a slow learner can be dramatically lengthened by such factors as perceived relevancy, fun, novelty, and social rewards.

Relevance. In arranging the learning task, adults often assume that what is meaningful to them is equally meaningful to the learner. The serious business of children's play may seem a waste of time to adults; yet the adult habit of accumulating knowledge merely to pass an examination may seem equally irrelevant to a child. For the slow learner, the critical test of relevance is not whether an activity is perceived as important by adult society or the mathematical community, but rather whether it is perceived as important and interesting to him. As long as a slow learner does not perceive relevance in intellectual activity, he is in the position of learning useless information. For example, a girl who views mathematical activity as predominantly masculine may well find mathematics irrelevant. Wasting time in useless activity is self-defeating for *anyone,* no less for the slow learner than for the bright scholar.

Before schools existed, relevancy was never a problem; for what was learned was learned in the context of an immediate application: farming, building a cabin, hunting, cooking. Today, the slow learner still seeks relevancy in the here and now. Long-range aspirations have little attraction and almost no holding power. Depending on his stage of development, the slow learner may find relevancy in a wide range of experiences: shopping; play stores; scales, graphs, and collected data of the natural and social sciences; student government; peer relations; family problems; cooking; newspaper ads; social situations; identification figures; blueprints; and office equipment—to offer a representative list. However, relevancy is not necessarily practicality. Children do like the excitement of finding out—of inquiring and discovering—as long as the adventure is not endless and aimless. With patience and considerable skill on the part of the teacher, even slow learners can want to learn for the sake of learning. It is toward this kind of relevancy that school experience should be directed.

Relevance can be magnified by permitting students to take part in the planning of learning activities. When a child is personally involved in selecting one option from a group of alternatives, he sees the task as relevant because he has committed *himself* to it. Something of his personal life will appear in the task itself, for he has examined his own interests and priorities and made his decision accordingly.

In any event, the teacher of slow learners must be continually ready with an answer to the question "What are we doing this for?"

Social control

For practical reasons, the school remains a group-centered experience for most children. Fortunately, group dynamics offers special help to the teacher who is attempting to manage the environment to accommodate the individual differences of slow learners. Since the motivation of a slow learner is particularly influenced by his strong peer orientation, improving the social system of the class or school has significant potential for favorably affecting the behavior of a slow learner (17, pp. 9, 15; 20, p. 14; 37, pp. 19, 267).

One of the most powerful applications of group dynamics is the use of peer helpers, student-to-student tutors. Classroom groups that are emotionally stable constitute a significant reservoir of peer helpers. Slow learners tend to be peer learners by style and by experience. Sometimes they find it difficult to work alone simply because of their need for attention and affection (37, p. 19). They are reassured that "at least two of us are in the same boat." They often ask to study together—sharing ideas, helping each other, sometimes just relaxing in occasional conversation as they do their assigned work. Furthermore, student-to-student interaction is readily managed to provide style matches and sex relevancy (for example, boys can be mutually supportive even when required to engage in work they perceive to be feminine).

Lippitt and Lohman point to assumptions they have made in designing projects to train student helpers: younger children model the behavior of their older tutors; older children communicate more effectively than adults at the younger child's level; the older child is less likely to be perceived as an authority figure; a slightly older child provides a more realistic level of aspiration than does an adult; and the older child profits from cross-age socialization as well as from developing a more realistic image of his own ability and present state of development (25).

In his more usual classroom routines, the teacher must manage a harmonious relationship with the group values of the learners. He must involve them in planning through discussion and guided activities and in decision making through affording an opportunity to choose for themselves among varied alternatives. He must be alert to any signs that a child lacks the skills required for effective group interaction, for there is constant danger that a slow learner may further damage his self-image if called upon to expose his disabilities before respected peers. On this account, the teacher must teach to strengths—to successes and to such positives as the student has in his bag of attributes.

A word of caution must be offered about the grouping of slow learners on the basis of deficient school achievement. There is some evidence that the homogeneous social groups that are a by-product of achievement groups may not be in the best interests of the slow learner (7, pp. 21–22) and that the "labeling of these groups with numbers or as 'bluebirds' and 'crows' undoubtedly affects the parents' and teachers' expectations for the students as well as the child's level of aspiration and his self-concept" (28, p. 44). The process of grouping may indeed be self-defeating, for when a student is labeled "slow" he may expect less of himself; and if he expects less, he may accomplish less. Much more needs to be learned about the effects of grouping and expectancy on the slow learner.

Reinforcement control

One of the most critical factors under the control of the teacher is the schedule of reinforcements. He must determine and provide for the optimal mix of rewards, successes, punishments, and failures as the student responds and learns. Skinner has suggested that tokens, sweets, privileges, and other contrived reinforcers are necessary, in some cases, to create a special (or prosthetic) environment to compensate for a defective sensitivity to normal contingencies of reinforcement (35, p. 708). In any event, contingency management and the scheduling of reinforcements underlies much of the work in performance contracting in which business and industry have been engaged.

While the slow learner must be relatively free from the threat of external evaluation and the anxious consequences of failure, he must also learn to tolerate a moderate amount of failure as he moves through a prescribed learning sequence. Unfortunately, the slow learner needs more powerful and individualized feedback mechanisms than are now generally available.

Some of the more crucial principles that should govern the control of reinforcements as they relate to the needs of the slow learner (or any learner, for that matter) are these:

1. *The risk of failure must be kept as low as possible.* No one chooses to invest much of himself in a task where he expects to fail. To threaten a slow learner with failure is meaningless and even counterproductive. An adolescent might rationalize that to study and fail is intolerable whereas to avoid study and fail is acceptable. A teacher must manage the structure and sequence of the learning tasks to minimize failure and manage the social environment so that failure is never a humiliating experience. An F must never stand for failure as a person, and under no circumstances should it speak with finality. Even the unsuccessful learner must continue to feel, "The teacher believes in me."

2. *Feedback must be informative and carefully scheduled.* This is much easier in basketball shooting than in long intellectual sequences. Children in their games have developed a helpful solution to continuous, nonthreatening feedback when they talk about "getting warmer" or "getting colder." Intuitively they seem to avoid the more final expressions "You're right" or "You're wrong." In any event, reinforcements that do not carry corrective or clarifying information must be used carefully if they are to be useful in guiding subsequent student behavior.

3. *Reinforcement should be positive and immediate.* Teachers of slow learners should be alert to every sign of success or even of good intent. Poor work should probably be overlooked more often than it generally is. Children are much better able to handle absence of praise for poor work than condemnation or constant carping. Appropriate rewards can include words (particularly affective-oriented words, such as "Well done" or "Much improved"), recreational activities (games or even free time), and tokens (especially when slow learners do not respond to normal reinforcing mechanisms and as long as the tokens

are deserved and reasonably accessible). If school grades are ever a suitable reward, they are certainly inappropriate for slow learners if they are restricted to the low end of the scale. What can a D convey to a slow learner who is trying, other than that his best is not good enough?

4. *Punishment should be avoided.* There is little if any evidence that punishment has value *except* to inhibit or stop dangerous or socially unacceptable behavior. Punishment carries a minimum of information. It is likely to cause enough anxiety to cripple a child's initiative and persistence in working at *any* mathematical activity. Punishment—whether physical or affective—is an aversive technique and a poor teaching device. Teachers of slow learners must be continually oriented to the positives and the successes. The effects of success cannot come unless the learner tries. And if reinforcements are not properly managed, the rich are likely to grow richer while the poor grow poorer as they travel along the increasingly complex continuum of mathematical skills and concepts.

Summary

Slow learners, no less than other human beings, are unique individuals. Each has his own set of strengths and weaknesses; each defies a stereotype. Yet in some respects they are alike; for it is common to find them deficient in affective functioning as well as in cognitive functioning. In fact, if slow learners in mathematics do share any common characteristic, it is probably that of a poor self-image with respect to mathematics. Accordingly, this chapter has maintained that work with slow learners must start with such affective concerns.

The other characteristics here discussed may or may not be attributes of a specific slow learner. These include various cognitive deficiencies and various learning styles in which action speaks louder than words; cultural differences that sometimes cause conflicts between the learner and the school; a reality set that continually asks, "What's in it for me?"; a tendency toward immediate gratification rather than long-range goals; a lack of certain components of school know-how (for example, listening skills, which may have been actually *unlearned* as a consequence of out-of-school experience); social needs and defective social skills; deficient adult relationships, which make adult modeling and conversation difficult; and various sex differences that may affect school behavior and achievement.

Instruction can be managed to meet the needs of students with these attributes. It is the teacher who, as manager of instruction, is the strategic change-agent in the classroom. As already noted, he can influence affective functioning, learning tasks, social instruction, and the schedule of reinforcements. His first responsibility is to establish and maintain a sense of trust. In controlling the learning task he should allow for sensorimotor involvement (physical manipulation and activity); novelty, variety, and alternate learning tasks; appropriate psychological structuring, sequencing, and pacing; and experience that is relevant on the learner's own terms. For social control through group dynamics, the teacher can take advantage of the slow learner's strong peer orientation by making use of student-to-student helpers. Finally, in his control of reinforcements, he would do well to create a success-oriented environment, of which informative feedback, immediate reinforcement, and a nonpunitive climate are essential components.

This chapter has made only limited and very general recommendations concerning the treatment of slow learners. More extensive suggestions follow in this yearbook. However, a final caution needs special mention here—one that bears careful attention. If slow learners are unique individuals, clearly each prescribed treatment must be based on a unique and well-defined set of strengths and weaknesses. The cure cannot be effective unless the *diagnosis* is accurate. The point is forcefully made by Taba and Elkins:

> A basic cause of defective teaching strategies, of ineffective selection of content and materials, of inadequate approaches, and of poor learning atmosphere is lack of systematic, all-encompassing, and continuing diagnosis. Just as a good physician administers treatment only after thorough diagnosis, a good teacher builds curriculum and instruction on analysis of data gathered by use of searching diagnostic procedures. [37, p. 23]

Better tools are needed both to pinpoint the learner's strengths and weaknesses and to monitor the progress of the learning program. Perhaps the computer is, as some have claimed, the only instrument capable of coordinating the complex network of diagnosis and instruction. Yet in the event that new strategies and technologies still fail to deliver a cure, it is to be hoped that the patients will no longer be blamed for what went wrong and that, instead, mathematics educators will search for even newer, more imaginative, and innovative strategies and technologies.

REFERENCES

1. Asbell, Bernard. *The New Improved American.* New York: McGraw-Hill Book Co., 1965.
2. Ausubel, David P. "How Reversible Are the Cognitive and Motivational Effects of Cultural Deprivation? Implications for Teaching the Culturally Deprived Child." *Urban Education* 1 (Summer 1964): 16–38.
3. Ausubel, David, and Pearl Ausubel. "Ego Development among Segregated Negro Children." In *Education in Depressed Areas,* edited by A. Harry Passow, pp. 109–41. New York: Teachers College, Columbia University, 1963.
4. Bachman, Alfred Morry. "The Relationship between a Seventh-Grade Pupil's Academic Self-Concept and Achievement in Mathematics." *Journal for Research in Mathematics Education* 1 (May 1970): 173–79.
5. Bentzen, Frances. "Sex Ratios in Learning and Behavior Disorders." *National Elementary Principal* 46 (November 1966): 13–17.
6. Bruner, Jerome S. "Culture, Politics, and Pedagogy." *Saturday Review,* 18 May 1968, pp. 69–72, 89–90.
7. Coleman, James. *Equality of Educational Opportunity.* U.S. Office of Education. Washington, D.C.: Government Printing Office, 1966.
8. Coopersmith, Stanley. "Studies in Self-Esteem." *Scientific American,* February 1966, pp. 96–106.
9. Davis, Robert B. "The Next Few Years." *Arithmetic Teacher* 13 (May 1966): 355–62.
10. Eisenberg, Leon. "Strengths of the Inner-City Child." *Baltimore Bulletin of Education* 41 (1963–64): 10–16.
11. Elliott, David L., and A. Harry Passow. "The Nature and Needs of the Educationally Disadvantaged." In *Developing Programs for the Educationally Disadvantaged,* edited by A. Harry Passow, pp. 3–19. New York: Teachers College, Columbia University, 1968.
12. Erikson, Erik H. "Identity and the Life Cycle: Growth and Crises of the Healthy Personality." *Psychological Issues* 1 (1959): 50–100.
13. Fantini, Mario D., and Gerald Weinstein. *The Disadvantaged: Challenge to Education.* New York: Harper & Row, 1968.
14. ———. "Taking Advantage of the Disadvantaged." *Teachers College Record,* [Columbia University] 69 (November 1967): 103–14.
15. Farnham-Diggory, Sylvia. "On Readiness and Remedy in Mathematics Instruction." *Arithmetic Teacher* 15 (November 1968): 614–22.
16. Fink, Martin. "Self-Concept as It Relates to Academic Underachievement." *California Journal of Educational Research* 13 (1962): 57–61.
17. Fowler, William. "Creative Science for Children from Disadvantaged Areas." Paper read at Council for Elementary Science International, 8 April 1966, Chicago, Ill. Duplicated.
18. Glennon, Vincent J., and Leroy G. Callahan. *Elementary School Mathematics: A Guide to Current Research.* 3d ed. Washington, D.C.: Association for Supervision and Curriculum Development, National Education Association, 1968.
19. Grambs, Jean D., and Walter B. Waetjen. "Being Equally Different: A New Right for Boys and Girls." *National Elementary Principal* 46 (November 1966): 59–67.

20. Henry, Jules. "Hope, Delusion, and Organization: Some Problems in the Motivation of Low Achievers." In *The Low Achiever in Mathematics*, edited by Lauren G. Woodby, pp. 7–16. U.S. Office of Education. Washington, D.C.: Government Printing Office, 1965.
21. Kagan, Jerome. "The Child: His Struggle for Identity." *Saturday Review*, 7 December 1968, pp. 80–82, 87–88.
22. ———. "Motivational and Attitudinal Factors in Receptivity to Learning." In *Learning about Learning*, edited by Jerome S. Bruner, pp. 34–39. U.S. Office of Education. Washington, D.C.: Government Printing Office, 1966.
23. Klineberg, Otto. "Life Is Fun in a Smiling, Fair-Skinned World." *Saturday Review*, 16 February 1963, p. 77.
24. Leiderman, Gloria. "Mental Development and Learning of Mathematics in Slow-learning Children." In *Report of the Conference on Mathematics Education for Below-Average Achievers*, pp. 45–66. Stanford, Calif.: School Mathematics Study Group, 1964.
25. Lippitt, Peggy, and J. E. Lohman. "Cross-Age Relationships—an Educational Resource." *Children* 12 (1965): 113–17.
26. Maccoby, Eleanor, ed. *Development of Sex Differences*. Palo Alto, Calif.: Stanford University Press, 1966.
27. Mager, Robert F. *Developing Attitude toward Learning*. Palo Alto, Calif.: Fearon Publishers, 1968.
28. Redmond, Frances H. "Grouping in the Elementary Classroom." *Ideas Educational* [Kent State University] 7 (Winter 1969): 41–45.
29. Riessman, Frank. *The Culturally Deprived Child*. New York: Harper & Row, 1962.
30. ———. "The Overlooked Positives of Disadvantaged Groups." *Journal of Negro Education* [Howard University] 33 (Summer 1964): 225–31.
31. Rowe, Mary Budd. "Science, Silence, and Sanctions." *Science and Children* 6 (March 1969): 11–13.
32. Sears, Robert. Introduction to *Learning about Learning*, edited by Jerome S. Bruner, pp. 3–8. U.S. Office of Education. Washington, D.C.: Government Printing Office, 1966.
33. Sexton, Patricia Cayo. *The Feminized Male*. New York: Random House, 1969.
34. Silberman, Charles E. "Technology Is Knocking at the Schoolhouse Door." *Fortune*, August 1966, pp. 120–25, 203.
35. Skinner, B. F. "Teaching Science in High School—What Is Wrong?" *Science*, 16 February 1968, pp. 704–10.
36. Solnit, A., and M. Stark. "Pediatric Management of School Learning Problems of Underachievement." *New England Journal of Medicine* 261 (1959): 988–93.
37. Taba, Hilda, and Deborah Elkins. *Teaching Strategies for the Culturally Disadvantaged*. Chicago: Rand McNally & Co., 1966.
38. Waetjen, Walter B. "The Prevention of Failure." *NEA Journal* 55 (April 1966): 37–40.

2

The Research Literature

LEN PIKAART
JAMES W. WILSON

ONE turns to the research literature for information. Ideally, the extant research would provide solid information for the identification of slow learners, for the understanding of their problems in learning mathematics, and for direct applications to the teaching of mathematics to slow learners. If enough research information were available, this chapter could be the source document for the rest of the yearbook. The chapter is not such a source document, for the research information about the learner in mathematics is insufficient.

Educational research is a young science. In less than half a century research design and statistical techniques have progressed from the relatively simple models described in classic works (e.g., 106, 55, and 54) to the highly sophisticated analyses available today. Educational research has progressed from that of the individual researcher attacking specific problems to systematic programs of research by teams of researchers. Educational researchers have begun to use models and theories for the identification of significant research problems. And mathematics education has just begun to emerge as a discipline with its own organized body of knowledge, empirical results, research activities, and practitioner's maxims. To some extent the problem of the slow learner in mathematics has had an easy "solution" in the past—the slow learners could be dropped from the mathematics classes. But modern society demands a greater mathematical literacy than the societies of past times, and modern educational philosophies of universal schooling up to the age of thirteen or fifteen demand the use of other alternatives for the slow learner in mathematics. The discipline of mathematics education must construct a body of information from well-chosen innovations, theorizing, and quality programs of research.

During this half-century of development, however, the impact of research on the teaching of mathematics has been relatively meager. Why? Why is there not a large body of research information on the teaching of mathematics to the slow learner? The answer has many facets; there are many influences. Researchers have been at the same time overwhelmed by a complex task and limited by inadequate theories, poor conceptualization of problems, and pedestrian research designs and statistical techniques.

Primarily, the many classes of variables associated with learning mathematics complicate the task of the researcher. For instance, he must consider previous learning experiences, environmental influences, personality characteristics, aptitudes, and the interaction of all these classes of variables. Moreover, the researcher must often conduct a study in a school setting, and this requires the cooperation of responsible administrators. Often, when the research is completed, the population to which the results apply is very limited. Reasonable compromises in the research procedure must be accepted. However, many times these compromises could have been avoided by the use of more sophisticated research designs if the researcher had been aware of them.

The results of learning research may be meager because researchers have not studied the appropriate variables. The burden of research is to discover or explain the unknown or unconfirmed. Research, as the primary method of science, must select, by means of an adequate theory, the appropriate variables to investigate. As ably stated by Thurstone: "It is the faith of all sciences that an unlimited number of phenomena can be comprehended in terms of a limited number of concepts or ideal constructs" (163, p. 51). It is one role of an adequate theory or model to specify the finite set of variables that may describe the phenomena—in this case, the problems of the slow learner in mathematics. Most research dealing with the slow learner in mathematics has been atheoretical, and it is no surprise that very little organized information has resulted from it.

Although it is true that one goal of research is to obtain knowledge and information, it is also true that productive research stimulates the construction of hypotheses and research questions. If productive research stimulates research, then any review of research will naturally lead to suggestions for additional research.

Therefore, in this chapter the authors will review extant research in the teaching of mathematics to slow learners, consider the limitations of this research, and suggest avenues of research that appear productive. The chapter's major sections consider the identification of slow learners, concomitant variables of slow learning, research on instructional programs, and studies that are predictive of future trends.

The Identification of Slow Learners

The history of research on slow learners approximately parallels the history of the development of the concept of intelligence as quantifiable. Indeed, it appears that the first modern interest in slow learners began when researchers learned that individuals differ in intelligence as measured by standardized tests and identified slow learners as those who have scores below the average on intelligence tests. One of the aims of this chapter is to convince the reader that such a definition is inadequate.

Intelligence

The concept of intelligence as a quantifiable and universal attribute emerged during the current century. The recent history of this concept is adequately described in most basic texts in educational psychology (e.g., see 116, pp. 245–70), so only the highlights will be mentioned here.

Unfortunately, the concept of intelligence has been misused as a theory to explain the failures of education.

In 1904 Spearman proposed a two-factor theory of intelligence. One factor was general intelligence, designated g; the other factor consisted of a large group of special abilities, designated s. The g factor was envisioned as relatively stable, but the several abilities of s were thought to depend on training and environment. Later E. L. Thorndike proposed a multifactor concept in which intelligence was thought to be the arithmetical sum of a series of varied and unrelated abilities. These abilities were classified as (1) abstract, (2) mechanical, and (3) social. About 1933 Thurstone proposed a concept of intelligence that embodied both the Spearman and the Thorndike notions. Thurstone's multiple-factor theory conceptualizes intelligence as composed of a great many abilities, but these abilities are clustered and it is the clusters of abilities that are seen as factors of intelligence. By means of the statistical technique of factor analysis, Thurstone was able to analyze the variance of a great many tests and to identify several specific factors. Thurstone's analysis is operational today and serves as a basis for the Primary Mental Abilities Tests (146).

Although Thurstone's concept of intelligence has been widely accepted, it has not been the concept most used in practice. Ever since the introduction of Binet's first test in 1905 and its Stanford Revision by Terman in 1916 (116, pp. 268–70), most teachers, counselors, and school administrators have relied on a single measure of intelligence—the intelligence quotient, or IQ.

Even if an IQ score is a valid measure of the construct intelligence—that is, even if it is a measure of aptitude to learn—there is good reason to believe that its use has been harmful to slow learners. The assumption that the IQ score is a sufficient measure of aptitude has led many people to exclude students from opportunities to study some subjects—thus further limiting their environments, with a likely consequence of retarding their mental ages (103, p. 45). To identify slow learners by specifying an IQ range—for example, between 75 and 90—may well be a confusion of cause and effect. Who is to know if slow learners typically have low IQ scores because they are underachievers (perhaps only because they learn slowly) or because they lack aptitude? Also, it is easy to find examples of students who have low IQ scores and high achievement in a school subject—and even easier to find students who have high IQ scores and low achievement in a school subject. The whole problem, as indicated elsewhere (103, p. 45), is that the exclusive use of IQ scores as a major classification variable for making decisions about the educational program for a student implies either (1) a belief that the IQ is genetically based and therefore inflexible or (2) a belief that a valid aptitude score can be obtained at one point of time—a score based on the student's learning (and environment) up to that time. Such beliefs are invalid. For the IQ, with all the body of research on its development and validation, is still an imperfect measure. Educators have often failed to recognize the limitations of IQ measures as they have adapted and used the measures in simplistic solutions to complex educational problems. These beliefs, and the educational uses that follow from them, do little more than excuse some failures of education; they contribute little to helping the underachiever to learn.

IQ score is not the only criterion that has been applied to identify slow learners. For example, in one significant study Herriot reports (76, p. 51):

> "Slow-learners" . . . were roughly defined to be the second lowest quartile. . . . In choosing students to benefit from the "slow-learner" study, some schools used previous standardized test scores, or teachers' recommendations, but, in general, the study classes chosen by principals, teachers, counselors, or coordinators were *existing classes of low-achievers.* The initial reasons for children being placed in these classes varied, e.g.:
>
> (a) below grade level in mathematics achievement
> (b) inadequate reading level
> (c) slow worker in mathematics
> (d) inaccurate computation
> (e) fearful of mathematics
> (f) antagonistic toward school
> (g) apathetic, indifferent toward learning
> (h) recent transfer to school
> (i) chronic absentee

Such operationally diverse classification criteria substantiate the absence of any single satisfactory method for identifying slow learners. This chapter will argue that slow learners can be best identified on the basis of their specific learning difficulties or, better, their specific learning abilities. Classification by any single general score has led researchers into unproductive investigations.

Implications of individual-difference studies

Research in psychology during the past seventy years has been very ably reviewed by Glaser to identify implications for the study of learning and individual differences (64). Much of the interest in the reviewed studies focused on the change in the spread of individual differences within a group after a period of learning.

As reported by Glaser (64, p. 2), Thorndike reasoned that an increase in the spread of differences following a learning period would imply that capacities for learning, or "innate aptitudes," were functioning rather than environmental factors; however, a decrease in the spread of differences could be caused either by differing native capacities or by differences in previous practice.

To further explain this notion, reference is made to figure 2.1. If the curve labeled t_1, with mean $\bar{x}_1$, represents a distribution of a sample before instruction, then a distribution such as the one labeled t_2, with

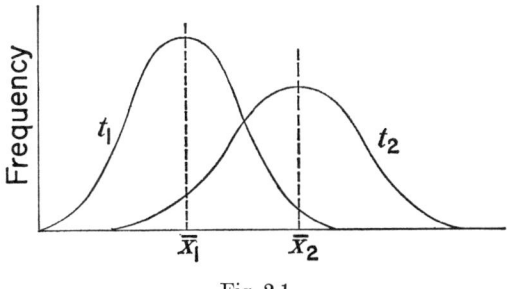

Fig. 2.1

mean $\bar{x}_2$, might occur after learning. In this case the spread of differences has increased, and one might guess that differences in capacities for learning handicapped low-ability students and helped high-ability students. Alternately, if the distribution t_2 were identical in shape to that of t_1, it might be inferred that everyone had simply increased his achievement by a fixed amount and thus capacities for learning had had no effect. Finally, if t_2 exhibited less spread than t_1 (was very steep), it would be difficult to hypothesize the cause. Perhaps the instruction or practice was so effective that everyone achieved similarly high achievement scores. In any case, a probable cause would not be indicated in this last situation.

Glaser marked two studies by Woodrow as classic (64, p. 3). In the first, Woodrow investigated the effect of practice on convergence or divergence of individual differences and concluded the change in the spread of the differences depended on the shape of the learning curve and the positions of individuals on it (174). Thus, relative individual differences may be a function of the way a task is performed. Later, Woodrow explored the relationship of measures of general ability, such as intelligence, and specific learning variables (173). In this study the general-ability measures were specified in terms of task accomplishments, while the specific learning abilities were defined as change measured by the difference between an initial score and the final score on given learning tasks. Woodrow concluded that a specific ability to learn is not the same as general intelligence and that the correlation is insignificant or close to zero, thus implying the futility of using general measures to identify slow learners.

This second study by Woodrow suffered from one impairment—the use of gain scores. Simply stated, the problem is that gain scores are dependent on the initial scores of individuals and subject to errors of measurement. More to be recommended is a technique that obtains a residual gain, which is the final score less the predicted final score. This predicted final score is determined by a regression function on the initial scores. (150.)

In spite of the criticism of the Woodrow research, the results have been corroborated by others (see 64, pp. 4–5). All these studies imply that there is great danger in using a general-ability measure as a predictor for student success on a specific learning task.

Concomitant Variables Associated with Slow Learning in Mathematics

Several studies have been conducted to determine variables associated with slow learning, and in general there are many variables.

Ross studied twenty fifth- and sixth-grade underachievers, defined as those students with an IQ of 100 or more on the California Test of Mental Maturity who were at least one year below grade level in achievement (141). He investigated arithmetic performance, general academic performance, intellectual abilities, physical characteristics, personal and social judgment factors, and home and family background. In general, he found specific deficiencies in basic arithmetical computation processes, in the solving of reasoning problems involving multiplication and division of whole numbers, and in all processes involving common fractions. Sixteen of the students (80 percent) were at least one year below their grade level in reading, and they were underachieving in other school subjects. Also, the children evidenced withdrawal and defeatist attitudes. Thirteen were identified as having emotional problems, and fifteen had shown immaturity or slowness of general physical development. Parents tended to be from a low socioeconomic class and to hold one or more teachers responsible for their child's inadequacies.

With regard to the socioeconomic level of the home environment, Dunkley found the achievement of disadvantaged kindergarten children to be significantly below that of children in the middle-class areas (41).

An investigation similar to Ross's was conducted by Sister Agnes Jerome (90), who studied twenty slow learners in grades 3 through 8. In the areas of achievement and social adjustment her results were similar to those of the Ross study. The subjects were in satisfactory physical condition, however, and Sister Jerome did find that thirteen subjects had Stanford-Binet IQ scores in a range from 74 to 90; the total group mean was 89.

Cawley and Goodman studied mentally handicapped children in special classes (28). They found many significant correlations between achievement in other content areas and achievement in arithmetic and between achievement and Primary Mental Abilities Test scores. The report is particularly interesting because profiles are provided that demonstrate the wide range for different factors of achievement within the age subgroups. For example, children in the age group from twelve to fourteen years old had mean-grade-equivalent scores that ranged from the second month of grade 2 in grammar to the tenth month of grade 3 in computation.

In a study of problem-solving ability, low IQ children, compared with those of average and high IQ, showed a greater incidence in nonpersistence, in offering an incorrect solution, and in using a random approach (100).

There is an excellent summary by Cronbach (36) of several studies conducted to investigate the affective domain in relation to cognitive learning (e.g., 51, 4, and 69). Cronbach identifies "constructively" motivated students as those who have a high level of achievement motivation and low anxiety, whereas "defensively" motivated students are those who have the opposite pattern. The research summary indicates that "constructive" students learn best when they are assigned moderately difficult tasks, immediate goals are not too explicit, and feedback is provided for judging themselves rather than for motivation. "Defensives," on the other hand, will function best when short-term goals are spelled out, there is a maximum of explanation and guidance, and feedback occurs at short intervals. Cronbach also points out that it is important to remember not only to capitalize on the existing aptitudes of students but also to attempt to improve these aptitudes. These generalizations have been corroborated by Leiderman (103, pp. 45–50) in an analysis of other studies (e.g., 108, 79, 91, and 101).

Glick, at the Olympic Center for Mental Health and Mental Retardation, University of Washington, is currently completing a paper on the relationships between attitude and achievement of 350 sixth graders. Although a positive relationship between these variables has been reported by Dodson (38, pp. 91–92), Glick is attempting to tease out the relative causal effect of achievement and attitude variables. He writes:

> Achievement is overwhelmingly the more frequent causal factor; however, more frequently than not, it occurs in an "incongruent" direction. That is, it operates to lower the attitude-achievement relationship. When

attitude is causal, which is in the minority of cases, the effects are, more frequently than not, congruent. That is, favorable attitudes enhance achievement and vice versa. Dissatisfaction for the learning task and the learning situation may be the price we pay for pushing kids toward high achievement.

This phenomenon may also explain the lack of correlation between attitudes toward school and achievement. Two variables are operating—one to increase the correlation and the other to decrease it—and perhaps they cancel each other.[1]

Research on Instructional Programs

Cronbach has suggested three major ways of adapting patterns of education to individual differences, as indicated in the third column of table 2.1, which is adapted from his summary (36, p. 24).

TABLE 2.1
PATTERNS OF EDUCATIONAL ADAPTATION TO INDIVIDUAL DIFFERENCES

Educational Goal	Instructional Treatment	Possible Modifications to Meet Individual Needs
Fixed	Fixed	1a) Alter durations of schooling by sequential selection 1b) Train to criterion on any skill or topic (alter duration)
Options	Fixed within an option	2a) Determine for each student his prospective adult role and provide a curriculum preparation for that role
Fixed within course or program	Alternatives	3a) Provide remedial adjuncts to fixed main-track instruction 3b) Teach different pupils by different methods 3c) Teach at an appropriate level on the learning curve

Fixed goals, fixed treatments

The first pattern is "adaptation within a predetermined program" in which both educational goals and instructional treatments are fixed. In order to meet individual differences the duration of schooling could be altered by a plan of sequential selection such as exists in many schools in England, Australia, and Sweden. However, the International

1. Oren Glick, 1969: personal communication.

Study of Achievement in Mathematics reported little support for selective retention (84, pp. 87–102). In the United States, academic programs or college-bound tracks, although part of comprehensive schools, may be thought of as examples of relatively fixed educational goals and fixed instructional treatments.

An alternative instructional pattern with fixed goals and fixed treatment is to train all students to a criterion, thus altering the time for instruction. Before the end of the nineteenth century, Sharpe has reported, it was found that students differ in the time needed to memorize a piece of information (148). Although the effect of Sharpe's report was to emphasize the existence of individual differences, it also pointed to a procedure for instructing slow learners. A recent study was reported by Begle at the First International Congress of Mathematical Education (8, p. 106). He found that fourth-grade slow learners learn mathematics as well as more able students when instructional time is increased for the slow learners. These results corroborated results found earlier by Herriot with seventh- and ninth-grade students (76, p. 44).

Goal options, fixed treatments

Another pattern identified by Cronbach is an "adaptation by matching educational goals to the individual." Thus the goals become options, and the instructional treatments may be fixed within a particular option. In order to meet individual differences, each student's prospective adult role might be determined and a curriculum provided that would prepare him for that role.

Margaret Cobb (34) indicated that there was a high risk of failure when any student entered first-year algebra, as it was usually taught in 1922, with a mental age of less than 15-6. Many general mathematics courses and shop mathematics courses were developed to provide less demanding goals for slower students. Both Castaneda and Hoffman have reported research supporting the pattern of matching educational goals to the individual (27; 82).

Fixed goals, treatment options

A third pattern identified by Cronbach is "adaptation by erasing individual differences"; goals are fixed within the course or program, but there are alternative instructional treatments. In order to accomplish the program objectives with individual differences, remedial adjuncts to the main track could become part of the program. For example, remedial work could be available and the student could be permitted to branch into the remedial adjunct, as in some forms of programmed instruction. Alternatively, hierarchies such as those recommended by Gagné could be established that would serve as bench marks in the learning process (61).

Several authors have reported research that supports the value of remedial programs (13; 23; 63). The results of studies of programmed instruction, regarded as a treatment alternative, are not conclusive (161; 78; 93). Nutting and Pikaart reported significant increases in computational speed and accuracy with disadvantaged pupils as a result of a special program of drill (123, pp. 1–39). Similar success has been reported in a computer-assisted instruction project of drill and practice in McComb, Mississippi (158, pp. 22–24).

A slight modification of the previous pattern is one in which the adaptation is made by altering instructional methods. This pattern appears to Cronbach to be one of the most promising. In a review of Cronbach's article, Carroll suggests that another modification might also be included (26). Because the school does not control the total history of the individual, Carroll suggests a procedure for locating the appropriate level on the learning curve for each individual and adapting instruction to him. It may be that this pattern, listed as 3c in the table above, would include patterns 3a and 3b in its scope.

Investigations of the effects of altering instructional methods have often involved a revision of content also. For example, Easterday reported the effectiveness of a special program that changed instructional methods and content (45). Callahan and Jacobson found success in the use of Cuisenaire rods (22), and Lerch and Kelly reported good results in units that employed mathematical structure and student exploration (104). Berger and Howitz studied the effectiveness of the NCTM series Experiences in Mathematical Discovery (EMD) and found the units were beneficial (12). The EMD series can be described as discovery lessons for ninth-grade students in the 30–50 percentile range. In two other studies of modified versions of the EMD series, Maynard and Strickland found no significant differences in achievement among three groups whether the method for each group was discovery, developmental, or expository (113, pp. 178–83; 155, pp. 169–73). Karnes found that the relative effects of various instructional programs can be very significant even as early as ages four, five, and six (94).

Individually Prescribed Instruction (IPI), or the Oakleaf Project, is a developmental project of the University of Pittsburgh Research and Development Center (159, pp. 78–79). A great many behavioral objectives have been specified for the elementary school mathematics program; and as each student achieves a given objective, a new learning sequence is assigned for other objectives. Although research reported at this writing is not comparative or summative, the formative research indicates that the instructional model is very effective (105). One of the most encouraging aspects of the IPI program is the premise accepted by its authors that the student cannot fail. If particular objectives are not achieved, the staff is committed to design a new learning sequence for the individual student. Thus, the focus is on instructional procedures for individual students, as opposed to general methods for whole classes.

Studies That Are Predictive of Future Trends

Almost all the reports of the implementation of mathematics programs have emphasized that slow learners need to succeed.

Rosenthal and Jacobson conducted two studies relating to this need (140). In one experiment twelve psychology students were each given five laboratory rats of the same strain. Six of the students were told that their rats had been bred for brightness in running a maze, while the other six students were told that their rats could be expected to be poor maze runners for genetic reasons. The students were assigned to teach their rats to run the maze. During the whole study the rats believed to be brighter in maze running performed better. At the end of the study the students were given a questionnaire, and the results indicated that those assigned the allegedly brighter rats rated their subjects brighter, more pleasant, and more likeable than the students who had the allegedly duller rats rated theirs.

In an analogous study by Rosenthal and Jacobson teachers were told that certain students in their classes could be expected to show unusual intellectual gains during the school year (140; 139). The names of these students had actually been chosen by means of a table of random numbers at the end of the previous school year, yet these randomly selected students demonstrated significant gains in intelligence as measured by the Flanagan Tests of General Ability (TOGA).

Although this study was not conducted with slow learners, it appears that it may have important significance and some important implications for teachers of slow learners. Teachers' expectations about students may be an extremely important variable.

It should be pointed out, however, that a review by R. L. Thorndike contains the following scathing comment about the Rosenthal and Jacobson study:

> The enterprise which represents the core of this document, and presumably the excuse for its publication, has received widespread advance publicity. In spite of anything I say, I am sure it will become a classic—widely referred to and rarely examined critically. Alas, it is so defective technically that one can only regret that it ever got beyond the eyes of the original investigators! Though the volume may be an effective addition to educational propagandizing, it does nothing to raise the standard of educational research. [162, p. 708]

Thorndike's review contains important questions about the reliability of the data reported in the study. It remains to be seen if additional research will support the original study.

A recurring theme in this chapter has been the notion that *classifying* slow learners as underachievers or low-aptitude students is not helpful and, in fact, may be harmful. A similar ill-advised use of classification may be the grading process common in this country. Bloom, Hastings, and Madaus have observed:

> As educators we have used the normal curve in grading students for so long that we have come to believe in it. Achievement measures are designed to detect differences among our learners—even if the differences are trivial in terms of the subject matter. We then distribute our grades in a normal fashion. In any group of students we expect to have some small percentage receive A grades. We are surprised when the figure differs greatly from about 10 percent. We are also prepared to fail an equal proportion of students. Quite frequently this failure is determined by the rank order of the students in the group rather than by their failure to grasp the essential ideas of the course. [15, pp. 44–45]

The thesis concerns the development of a "mastery" curriculum. This is analogous to pattern 3*b* in table 2.1: fixed goals within a program and alternative instructional treatments. The authors' hypothesis is this:

> Given sufficient time and appropriate types of help, 95 percent of students (the top 5 percent plus the next 90 percent) can learn a subject with a high degree of mastery. To say it another way, we are convinced that the grade of A as an index of mastery of a subject can, under appropriate conditions, be achieved by up to 95 percent of the students in a class. [15, p. 46]

They suggest some of the following techniques for individual teachers to find ways of modifying their instruction to fit the different needs of the students and therefore to work toward a mastery curriculum (15, pp. 48–49):

1. *Group study.* As students need opportunity for working in small groups (perhaps of two or three students), this kind of activity can be useful for discussing points of difficulty in the learning process. The small group should be noncompetitive in nature, with emphasis on cooperation.

2. *Tutorial help.* This is a costly procedure, to be used when other means of instruction are not available. Ideally, the tutor should be someone other than the teacher, in order to bring a fresh way of viewing the learning problem.

3. *Textbooks.* Since textbooks may vary in the clarity with which they explain a particular idea or process, one means for adapting instruction is to attempt to match alternative presentations with particular learning problems.

4. *Workbooks and programmed-instruction units.* These units may be especially helpful for some students who cannot grasp the ideas or procedures in the textbook form.

5. *Audiovisual methods and academic games.* Some students may learn a particular idea best through concrete illustrations and vivid and clear explanations.

At the heart of the mastery curriculum is the formative evaluation of classroom learning (15, pp. 43–57). This evaluation serves a diagnostic function and is used for making decisions about the next stage of instruction for each particular student. Learning outcomes are organized hierarchically and diagnostic tests prepared. Then for each stage in the hierarchy, if the student fails to reach mastery, an alternative instructional sequence is specified. Thus the instructional program is modified for each individual and structured so that he eventually achieves the desired terminal objective for the unit.

Bloom, Hastings, and Madaus reported several years' investigation of mastery learning procedures, where operating procedures such as formative evaluation, diagnosis, and prescription of alternative instruction were incorporated into existing classes. Results from algebra classes and test-theory classes were very encouraging. They reported significantly better class performance in a test-theory class as a result of incorporating mastery learning procedures. (15, pp. 53–56.) Wilson illustrated the use of mastery learning materials from Bloom's project in a first-year algebra course (170).

If the notion of a mastery curriculum is feasible, although its implementation is probably more costly than normal expenditures for education, it would appear that there is real hope of providing the education that slow learners have long needed. For, obviously, the procedure has direct implications for the slow learner.

Thus, in the mastery learning model, all students are helped to achieve a criterion mastery of the learning at hand. The focus is not on separating students into grade classifications of A, B, . . . , or F, but rather on helping students reach the mastery level. Such an instructional model avoids simply identifying those students who have not learned; instead, the instructional effort is to determine how each student can best learn. Research on the development, use, and validation of the mastery learning model for slow learners in mathematics is an obvious need.

A useful strategy for identifying problems for research in organizing instructional objectives, for identifying test items, or for analyzing results of an evaluation is to classify learning outcomes in terms of mathematics content and in terms of the level of behavior expected of students. Several classification schemata have been reported in the recent literature, most of them based on the Bloom *Taxonomy* (14). Schemata specific to mathematics have been reported by Wilson (170), Husén (84, pp. 93–94), Wood (171), Romberg and Wilson (138), and Begle and Wilson (9). Kilpatrick has questioned the predictive usefulness of such schemata precisely because so many different formulations have been reported (96). But validating the hierarchy of cognitive levels is not the major point in presenting these schemata here. Rather, their value lies in the heuristic direction they provide for organizing and specifying the problems of research, instruction, and evaluation. Organizational schemata for looking at the problems of studying the slow learner in mathematics are sorely needed.

The most comprehensive schema, or table of specifications, has been provided by Wilson (170). A simplification of that schema follows. The essential idea in the table of specifications is that objectives of mathematics instruction can be classified in two ways: (1) by categories of mathematical content and (2) by levels of behavior. The degree of specificity of the categories in either dimension is arbitrary and should be adjusted to the task under study. For example, a set of content categories might be number systems, algebra, and geometry. This could include most of the types of mathematics content slow learners might encounter in their school years. (In fact, a problem, perhaps an area of research, can be identified already in that slow learners in mathematics would tend to have limited contact with either algebra or geometry content.) A set of behavior levels might include computation, comprehension, application, analysis, interests and attitudes, and appreciation. See figure 2.2.

OBJECTIVES OF MATHEMATICS INSTRUCTION						
	BEHAVIORS					
CONTENT	Computation	Comprehension	Application	Analysis	Interest and Attitudes	Appreciation
Number Systems						
Algebra						
Geometry						

Fig. 2.2

Explicit definitions of the labels on each dimension need to be stated in order for the schema to become operational. One such set of definitions can be found in Wilson (170, pp. 653–63).

A cursory examination of the table of specifications suggests some possible areas of investigation of slow learners in mathematics. For instance, one would suspect that with slow learners there tends to be a heavy emphasis on the number systems-computation cell and little attention to other cells of the table. This might be the case because of the *assumption* that comprehension, application, or analysis behaviors (and even attitudes and appreciation) are dependent on a mastery of computation. The assumption is a dubious one, but in any event empirical questions for research can be generated. Can analysis-level behaviors be effectively taught to slow learners if they are deficient in computation-level performance? In what positive ways can a slow learner appreciate mathematics?

Summary

This chapter has examined the research on the slow learner in mathematics and found it lacking. Therefore, instead of summarizing research findings the task has been to look into the potential of research in this area.

Strong traditions were identified in this chapter with regard to the use of IQ scores as measures of aptitude. This was found to be inadequate. A more fruitful approach, bringing with it progress in the understanding of the problems of the slow learner in mathematics, is to consider specific learning aptitudes of slow learners and to adapt instruction to take account of these individual differences. It is in this direction that potentially fruitful programs of research on the slow learner in mathematics are identified.

REFERENCES

1. Amidon, Edmund, and Ned A. Flanders. "The Effects of Direct and Indirect Teacher Influence on Dependent-Prone Students Learning Geometry." *Journal of Educational Psychology* 52 (December 1961): 286–329.
2. Anderson, John E. "The Limitations of Infant and Preschool Tests in the Measurement of Intelligence." *Journal of Psychology* 8 (July 1939): 351–79.
3. Arthur, Lee E. "Diagnosis of Disabilities in Arithmetic Essentials." *Mathematics Teacher* 43 (May 1950): 197–202.
4. Atkinson, John W., and Walter R. Reitman. "Performance as a Function of Motive Strength and Expectancy of Goal Attainment." *Journal of Abnormal and Social Psychology* 53 (July–December 1956): 361–66.
5. Barber, Ralph W. "My Slow Students Are Personality Problems." *Clearing House* [Fairleigh Dickinson University] 29 (December 1954): 203–5.
6. Bassham, Harrell, Michael Murphy, and Katherine Murphy. "Attitude and Achievement in Arithmetic." *Arithmetic Teacher* 11 (February 1964): 66–72.
7. Beck, Hildegarde. "Adjusting the Course of Study in Ninth Grade Mathematics to the Ability of the Pupil." *Mathematics Teacher* 21 (January 1928): 24–30.
8. Begle, Edward G. "The Role of Research in the Improvement of Mathematics Education." In *Proceedings of the First International Congress on Mathematical Education, Lyon, August 24–30, 1969*. Dordrecht, Holland: D. Reidel Publishing Co., 1969.
9. Begle, Edward G., and James W. Wilson. "The Evaluation of Mathematics Programs." In *Mathematics Education*, Sixty-ninth Yearbook of the National Society for the Study of Education, pt. 1, edited by Edward G. Begle, pp. 367–404. Chicago: University of Chicago Press, 1970.
10. Beldin, Horace Otis. *A Study of Selected Arithmetic Verbal Problem-Solving Skills among High and Low Achieving Sixth Grade Children*. Ph.D. dissertation, Syracuse University, 1960. Ann Arbor, Mich.: University Microfilms (no. 60-2597).
11. Bereiter, C. "Some Persisting Dilemmas in the Measurement of Change." In *Problems in Measuring Change*, edited by Chester William Harris, pp. 3–20. Madison: University of Wisconsin Press, 1963.
12. Berger, Emil J., and Thomas A. Howitz. "Evaluation of *Experiences in Mathematical Discovery*." In *Research in Mathematics Education*, edited by Joseph M. Scandura, pp. 60–69. Washington, D.C.: National Council of Teachers of Mathematics, 1967.

13. Bernstein, Allen L. *A Study of Remedial Arithmetic Conducted with Ninth Grade Students*. Ed.D. dissertation, Wayne State University, 1955. Ann Arbor, Mich.: University Microfilms (no. 55-270).
14. Bloom, Benjamin S., ed. *Taxonomy of Educational Objectives: The Classification of Educational Goals*. Handbook 1, *Cognitive Domain*. New York: Longmans, Green & Co., 1956.
15. Bloom, Benjamin S.; J. Thomas Hastings; and George F. Madaus. *Handbook on Formative and Summative Evaluation of Student Learning*. New York: McGraw-Hill Book Co., 1971.
16. Borusch, Barbara Jane Neary. *Sibling Resemblance in Reading and Arithmetic Growth*. Ph.D. dissertation, University of Michigan, 1958. Ann Arbor, Mich.: University Microfilms (no. 58-7686).
17. Bowman, Herbert Lloyd. "Reported Preference and Performance in Problem Solving according to Intelligence Groups." *Journal of Educational Research* 25 (April/May 1932): 295-99.
18. Boyer, Lee E. "Provisions for the Slow Learner." *Mathematics Teacher* 52 (April 1959): 256-59.
19. Braunfeld, Peter, and Martin Wolfe. "Fractions for Low Achievers." *Arithmetic Teacher* 13 (December 1966): 647-55.
20. Brown, Andrew W., and Christine Lind. "School Achievement in Relation to Mental Age: A Comparative Study." *Journal of Educational Psychology* 22 (November 1931): 561-76.
21. Brunda, H. S. "Slow Learner in the Regular Classroom." *School and Community* 48 (October 1961): 28 ff.
22. Callahan, John J., and Ruth S. Jacobson. "An Experiment with Retarded Children and Cuisenaire Rods." *Arithmetic Teacher* 14 (January 1967): 10-13.
23. Callahan, Leroy. "Remedial Work with Underachieving Children." *Arithmetic Teacher* 9 (March 1962): 138-40.
24. Capobianco, Rudolph Joseph. *A Comparative Study of Endogenous and Exogenous Mentally Handicapped Boys on Arithmetic Achievement*. Ed.D. dissertation, University of Illinois, 1954. Ann Arbor, Mich.: University Microfilms (no. A54-1162).
25. Capps, Lelon. "A Comparison of Superior Achievers and Underachievers in Arithmetic." *Elementary School Journal* 63 (December 1962): 141-45.
26. Carroll, J. "A Model for School Learning." *Teachers College Record* [Columbia University] 64 (1963): 723-33.
27. Castaneda, Alberta M. "A Mathematics Program for Disadvantaged Mexican-American First-Grade Children." *Arithmetic Teacher* 15 (May 1968): 413-19.
28. Cawley, John F., and John O. Goodman. "Interrelationships among Mental Abilities, Reading, Language Arts, and Arithmetic with the Mentally Handicapped." *Arithmetic Teacher* 15 (November 1968): 631-36.
29. Chace, Harriett. "Slow Learners in the Elementary School." *Social Education* 21 (March 1957): 122-24.
30. Chambers, Margaret B. "My Plan for Developing Readiness in Subtraction." *Instructor* 62 (November 1952): 52.
31. Charlotte, Sister Mary. "Arithmetic Simplified." *Catholic School Journal* 59 (November 1959): 46-48.
32. Check, John Felix. *A Study of Retention of Arithmetic Learning with Chil-*

dren of Low, Average, and High Intelligence at 127 Months of Age. Ph.D. dissertation, University of Wisconsin, 1959. Ann Arbor, Mich.: University Microfilms (no. 59-3176).
33. Cieutat, Victor J., Fredric E. Stockwell, and Clyde E. Noble. "The Interaction of Ability and Amount of Practice with Stimulus and Response Meaningfulness (M, M') in Paired-Associate Learning." *Journal of Experimental Psychology* 56 (July–December 1958): 193–202.
34. Cobb, Margaret V. "The Limits Set to Educational Achievement by Limited Intelligence." *Journal of Educational Psychology* 13 (December 1922): 546–55.
35. Cook, Ruth. "Number Concepts for the Slow Learner." *Arithmetic Teacher* 1 (April 1954): 11–14.
36. Cronbach, Lee J. "How Can Instruction Be Adapted to Individual Differences?" In *Learning and Individual Differences: A Symposium of the Learning Research and Development Center of the University of Pittsburgh*, edited by Robert M. Gagné, pp. 23–39. Columbus, Ohio: Charles E. Merrill Books, 1967.
37. Davidson, Helen H., and Gerhard Lang. "Children's Perceptions of Their Teachers' Feelings toward Them Related to Self-Perception, School Achievement, and Behavior." *Journal of Experimental Education* 29 (December 1960): 107–18.
38. Dodson, Joseph Wesley. *Characteristics of Successful Insightful Problem Solvers*. Ed.D. dissertation, University of Georgia, 1970. Ann Arbor, Mich.: University Microfilms (no. 71-13,048).
39. Douglass, Harl R. "Remedial Work in Junior High School Mathematics." *Mathematics Teacher* 48 (May 1955): 344–46.
40. Duncanson, James P. "Learning and Measured Abilities." *Journal of Educational Psychology* 57 (August 1966): 220–29.
41. Dunkley, M. E. "Some Number Concepts of Disadvantaged Children." *Arithmetic Teacher* 12 (May 1965): 359–61.
42. Dunn, Lloyd M. "The Slow Learner: An Overview." *NEA Journal* 48 (October 1959): 19–28.
43. Dutton, Wilbur H. "Teaching Time Concepts to Culturally Disadvantaged Primary-Age Children." *Arithmetic Teacher* 14 (May 1967): 358–64.
44. Eagle, Edwin. "The Relationship of Certain Reading Abilities to Success in Mathematics." *Mathematics Teacher* 41 (April 1948): 175–79.
45. Easterday, Kenneth E. "An Experiment with Low Achievers in Arithmetic." *Mathematics Teacher* 57 (November 1964): 462–68.
46. ———. "A Technique for Low Achievers." *Mathematics Teacher* 58 (October 1965): 519–21.
47. Eisner, Harry. "The Challenge of the Slow Pupil." *Mathematics Teacher* 32 (January 1939): 9–15.
48. Elder, Florence. "Mathematics for the Below-Average Achiever in High School." *Mathematics Teacher* 60 (March 1967): 235–40.
49. Engel, Anna M. "The Challenge of the Slow Learning Child." *Educational Leadership* 11 (December 1953): 151–55.
50. Farnham-Diggory, Sylvia. "On Readiness and Remedy in Mathematics Instruction." *Arithmetic Teacher* 15 (November 1968): 614–22.
51. Feather, N. T. "The Relationship of Persistence at a Task to Expectation of Success and Achievement Related Motives." *Journal of Abnormal and Social Psychology* 63 (July–November 1961): 552–61.

52. Feldhusen, John F., and Herbert J. Klausmeier. "Anxiety, Intelligence, and Achievement in Children of Low, Average, and High Intelligence." *Child Development* 33 (June 1962): 403-9.
53. Ferguson, George A. "On Learning and Human Ability." *Canadian Journal of Psychology* 8 (June 1954): 95-112.
54. Fisher, Ronald Aylmer. *The Design of Experiments*. London: Oliver & Boyd, 1935.
55. ———. *Statistical Methods for Research Workers*. London: Oliver & Boyd, 1925.
56. Fitzgerald, William M. "On the Learning of Mathematics by Children." *Mathematics Teacher* 56 (November 1963): 517-21.
57. Fleishman, E. A. "The Description and Prediction of Perceptual-Motor-Skill Learning." In *Training Research and Education*, edited by Robert Glaser, pp. 137-75. New York: John Wiley & Sons, 1965.
58. Fremont, Herbert. "Some Thoughts on Teaching Mathematics to Disadvantaged Groups." *Arithmetic Teacher* 11 (May 1964): 319-22.
59. Fremont, Herbert, and Neal Ehrenberg. "The Hidden Potential of Low Achievers." *Mathematics Teacher* 59 (October 1966): 551-57.
60. Gagné, Robert M. "Ability Differences in the Learning of Concepts Governing Directed Numbers." In *Research Problems in Mathematics Education*, pp. 112-13. Cooperative Research Monographs, no. 3 (OE-12008). Washington, D.C.: Government Printing Office, 1960.
61. ———. "Some New Views of Learning and Instruction." *Phi Delta Kappan* 51 (May 1970): 468-72.
62. Gibney, Thomas C. "Multiplication for the Slow Learner." *Arithmetic Teacher* 9 (February 1962): 74-76.
63. Gilmary, Sister. "Transfer Effects of Reading Remediation to Arithmetic Computation When Intelligence Is Controlled and All Other School Factors Are Eliminated." *Arithmetic Teacher* 14 (January 1967): 17-20.
64. Glaser, Robert. "Some Implications of Previous Work on Learning and Individual Differences." In *Learning and Individual Differences: A Symposium of the Learning Research and Development Center of the University of Pittsburgh*, edited by Robert M. Gagné, pp. 1-18. Columbus, Ohio: Charles E. Merrill Books, 1967.
65. Glismann, Leonard W. *The Effects of Special Arts and Crafts Activities on Attitudes, Attendance, Citizenship, and Academic Achievement of Slow Learning Ninth Grade Pupils*. Ed.D. dissertation, Utah State University, 1967. Ann Arbor, Mich.: University Microfilms (no. 68-13,774).
66. Goldberg, Milton. "My Slow Learners' New I.Q.: Imagination Quotient." *Clearing House* [Fairleigh Dickinson University] 28 (February 1954): 337-40.
67. Greenholz, Sarah. "Successful Practices in Teaching Mathematics to Low Achievers in Senior High School." *Mathematics Teacher* 60 (April 1967): 329-35.
68. ———. "What's New in Teaching Slow Learners in Junior High School?" *Mathematics Teacher* 57 (December 1964): 522-28.
69. Grimes, Jesse W., and Wesley Allinsmith. "Compulsivity, Anxiety, and School Achievement." *Merrill-Palmer Quarterly* 7 (October 1961): 247-71.
70. Hagerman, Helen. "The Slow Learner." *Grade Teacher* 71 (May 1954): 26 ff.
71. Halloway, Robert L. "How We 'Repatriated' Our Slow Learners." *Clearing House* [Fairleigh Dickinson University] 27 (May 1953): 528-30.

72. Hammitt, Helen. "Evaluating and Reteaching Slow Learners." *Arithmetic Teacher* 14 (January 1967): 40–41.
73. Hawkins, G. E. "Adjusting the Program in Mathematics to the Needs of Pupils." *Mathematics Teacher* 39 (May 1946): 206–10.
74. Hayes, Keith J. "The Backward Curve: A Method for the Study of Learning." *Psychological Review* 60 (July 1953): 269–75.
75. Herkner, Melvin W. "How Shall We Provide for the Slow Learner in the Junior High School?" *Bulletin of the National Association of Secondary School Principals* 38 (April 1954): 95–100.
76. Herriot, Sarah T. *The Slow Learner Project: The Secondary School "Slow Learner" in Mathematics.* SMSG Reports, no. 5. Stanford, Calif.: School Mathematics Study Group, 1967.
77. Hess, R. D. "The Latent Resources of the Child's Mind." Paper read at the Regional Conference NASDTEC-AAAS Studies, Chicago, December 1961.
78. Higgins, Conwell, and Reuben R. Rusch. "Remedial Teaching of Multiplication and Division: Programmed Textbook versus Workbook—a Pilot Study." *Arithmetic Teacher* 12 (January 1965): 32–38.
79. *High-School Methods with Slow Learners.* National Education Association Research Bulletin 21 (October 1943).
80. Hirsch, J. "Individual Differences in Behavior and Their Genetics Basis." In *Roots of Behavior,* edited by Eugene L. Bliss, pp. 3–23. New York: Harper & Row, 1962.
81. Hoffman, Carl Bentley. *The Relationship of Immediate Recall, Delayed Recall, and Incidental Memory to Problem-Solving Ability.* Ph.D. dissertation, University of Pennsylvania, 1960. Ann Arbor, Mich.: University Microfilms (no. 60-3659).
82. Hoffman, Ruth Irene. "The Slow Learner—Changing His View of Math." *Bulletin of the National Association of Secondary School Principals* 52 (April 1968): 86–97.
83. Hull, Clark L. "The Place of Innate Individual and Species Differences in a Natural-Science Theory of Behavior." *Psychological Review* 52 (March 1945): 55–60.
84. Husén, Torsten. *International Study of Achievement in Mathematics.* 2 vols. New York: John Wiley & Sons, 1967.
85. Isaacs, Ann F. "A Gifted Underachiever in Arithmetic: A Case Study." *Arithmetic Teacher* 6 (November 1959): 257–61.
86. Jacobs, James N., Joan Bollenbacher, and Mildred Keiffer. "Teaching Seventh-Grade Mathematics by Television to Homogeneously Grouped Below-Average Pupils." *Mathematics Teacher* 54 (November 1961): 551–55.
87. Jenny, John H. "Motor Activities for the Slow Learner." *Instructor* 66 (January 1957): 63 ff.
88. Jensen, Arthur R. "Learning Ability in Retarded, Average, and Gifted Children." *Merrill-Palmer Quarterly* 9 (April 1963): 123–40.
89. ———. "Reinforcement Psychology and Individual Differences." *California Journal of Educational Research* 13 (September 1962): 174–78.
90. Jerome, Sister Agnes. "A Study of Twenty Slow Learners." *Journal of Educational Research* 53 (September 1959): 23–27.
91. Jewett, Arno, and J. Dan Hull. *Teaching Rapid and Slow Learners in High Schools.* U.S. Office of Education Bulletin 1954, no. 5. Washington, D.C.: Government Printing Office, 1954.

92. Johnson, George Orville. *Education for the Slow Learners.* Englewood Cliffs, N.J.: Prentice-Hall, 1963.
93. Jones, Thomas. "The Effect of Modified Programmed Lectures and Mathematical Games upon Achievement and Attitude of Ninth-Grade Low Achievers in Mathematics." *Mathematics Teacher* 61 (October 1968): 603-7.
94. Karnes, Merle B. "A Research Program to Determine the Effects of Various Preschool Intervention Programs in the Development of Disadvantaged Children and the Strategic Age for Such Intervention." Paper read at American Educational Research Association, Chicago, 1968. Mimeographed. Urbana: Institute for Research on Exceptional Children and Department of Special Education, University of Illinois.
95. Keiffer, Mildred C. "The Development of Teaching Materials for Low-achieving Pupils in Seventh- and Eighth-Grade Mathematics." *Arithmetic Teacher* 15 (November 1968): 599-604.
96. Kilpatrick, Jeremy. "Some Implications of the International Study of Achievement in Mathematics for Mathematics Educators." *Journal for Research in Mathematics Education* 2 (March 1971): 164-71.
97. Kincaid, Margaret. "A Study of Individual Differences in Learning." *Psychological Review* 32 (1925): 34-53.
98. Klausmeier, Herbert J., and John Check. "Retention and Transfer in Children of Low, Average, and High Intelligence." *Journal of Educational Research* 55 (April 1962): 319-22.
99. Klausmeier, Herbert J., and John F. Feldhusen. "Retention in Arithmetic among Children of Low, Average, and High Intelligence at 117 Months of Age." *Journal of Educational Psychology* 50 (April 1959): 88-92.
100. Klausmeier, Herbert J., and Leo J. Loughlin. "Behaviors during Problem Solving among Children of Low, Average, and High Intelligence." *Journal of Educational Psychology* 52 (June 1961): 148-52.
101. Krulik, Stephen. "The Use of Concepts in Mathematics New in Teaching the Slow Learner." Ph.D. dissertation, Teachers College, Columbia University, 1961.
102. Leary, Bernice E. "Using Books with Slow Learners." *Instructor* 65 (November 1955): 21-22.
103. Leiderman, Gloria F. "Mental Development and Learning of Mathematics in Slow-learning Children." In *Report of the Conference on Mathematics Education for Below-Average Achievers,* pp. 45-66. Stanford, Calif.: School Mathematics Study Group, 1964.
104. Lerch, Harold H., and Francis J. Kelly. "A Mathematics Program for Slow Learners at the Junior High Level." *Arithmetic Teacher* 13 (March 1966): 232-36.
105. Lipson, Joseph I. "Individualized Instruction in Elementary Mathematics." In *Research in Mathematics Education,* edited by Joseph M. Scandura, pp. 70-79. Washington, D.C.: National Council of Teachers of Mathematics, 1967.
106. McCall, W. A. *How to Experiment in Education.* New York: Macmillan Co., 1923.
107. Mackay, G. W. S., and P. E. Vernon. "The Measurement of Learning Ability." *British Journal of Educational Psychology* 33 (June 1963): 177-86.
108. Mallory, Virgil S. "Activity in Mathematics—the Slow-Moving Pupil." *Mathematics Teacher* 29 (January 1936): 23-26.

109. ———. "Mathematics for the Slow Moving Pupil." *Mathematics Teacher* 26 (November 1933): 391-98.
110. ———. *The Relative Difficulty of Certain Topics in Mathematics for Slow-moving Ninth Grade Pupils*. New York: Bureau of Publications, Teachers College, Columbia University, 1939.
111. Mandler, G., and S. B. Sarason. "A Study of Anxiety and Learning." *Journal of Abnormal and Social Psychology* 47 (1952): 166-73.
112. Manning, Winston H., and Philip H. DuBois. "Correlational Methods in Research on Human Learning." *Perceptual and Motor Skills* 15 (August 1962): 287-321.
113. Maynard, Freddy Joseph. *A Comparison of Three Methods of Teaching Selected Content in Eighth and Ninth Grade General Mathematics Courses*. Ed.D. dissertation, University of Georgia, 1969. Ann Arbor, Mich.: University Microfilms (no. 70-10,218). See also Strickland.
114. Melton, Arthur W. "Individual Differences and Theoretical Process Variables: General Comments on the Conference." In *Learning and Individual Differences: A Symposium of the Learning Research and Development Center of the University of Pittsburgh*, edited by Robert M. Gagné, pp. 238-52. Columbus, Ohio: Charles E. Merrill Books, 1967.
115. Merrell, Margaret. "The Relationship of Individual Growth to Average Growth." *Human Biology* 3 (February 1931): 37-70.
116. Merry, Frieda Kiefer, and Vickers Ralph Merry. *The First Two Decades of Life*. 2d ed. New York: Harper & Row, Harper Chapel Books, 1968.
117. Mintz, Natalie, and Herbert Fremont. "Some Practical Ideas for Teaching Mathematics to Disadvantaged Children." *Arithmetic Teacher* 12 (April 1965): 258-60.
118. Moyer, Haverly O. "Helping the Slow-Learner in Mathematics." *School Science and Mathematics* 55 (June 1955): 425-29.
119. Nachtman, William Robert. "An Instrument of Measurement to Appraise the Quantitative Abilities of the Educable Mentally Retarded Children." Ed.D. dissertation, Colorado State College, 1962. Ann Arbor, Mich.: University Microfilms (no. 63-1123).
120. Nelson, L. Doyal. "Textbook Difficulty and Mathematics Achievement in Junior High School." *Mathematics Teacher* 58 (December 1965): 724-29.
121. Newacheck, V. "Help the Slow Learner Adjust." *Educational Music Magazine* 33 (March 1954): 18 ff.
122. Noble, Clyde E., Janet L. Noble, and Wayne L. Alcock. "Prediction of Individual Differences in Human Trial-and-Error Learning." *Perceptual and Motor Skills* 8 (March 1958): 151-72.
123. Nutting, Sue Ellis, and Leonard Pikaart. *A Comparative Study of the Efficiency of the Flash-Math Drill Program with Second and Fourth Graders*. Practical Paper no. 7. Athens: University of Georgia Research and Development Center in Education Stimulation, 1969.
124. Orr, Kenneth N. "Helping the Slow Learner." *Social Education* 19 (March 1955): 107-8.
125. O'Rourke, Everett V., and Cyrus D. Mead. "Vocabulary Difficulties of Five Textbooks in Third-Grade Arithmetic." *Elementary School Journal* 41 (May 1941): 683-91.
126. Otto, Wayne. "Inhibitory Potential in Good and Poor Achievers." *Journal of Educational Psychology* 56 (August 1965): 200-207.
127. Painter, Helen K. "My Sales Talk to Slow Learners." *Instructor* 68 (November 1958): 22 ff.

128. Paschal, Billy J. "A Concerned Teacher Makes the Difference." *Arithmetic Teacher* 13 (March 1966): 203-5.
129. ———. "Geometry for the Disadvantaged." *Arithmetic Teacher* 14 (January 1967): 4-6.
130. ———. "Teaching the Culturally Disadvantaged Child." *Arithmetic Teacher* 13 (May 1966): 369-74.
131. Phillips, C. A. "Working with Slow Learners." *Catholic School Journal* 61 (September 1961): 65-66.
132. Pitts, Raymond J. "Relationship between Functional Competence in Mathematics and Reading Grade Levels, Mental Ability, and Age." *Journal of Educational Psychology* 43 (December 1952): 486-92.
133. Powell, Marvin, Henry A. O'Connor, and Kenneth M. Parsley, Jr. "Further Investigation of Sex Differences in Achievement of Under-, Average-, and Over-achieving Students within Five IQ Groups in Grades Four through Eight." *Journal of Educational Research* 57 (January 1964): 268-70.
134. Proctor, Amelia D. "A World of Hope—Helping Slow Learners Enjoy Mathematics." *Mathematics Teacher* 58 (February 1965): 118-22.
135. Reeve, William D. "The Problem of Varying Abilities among Students in Mathematics." *Mathematics Teacher* 49 (February 1956): 70-78.
136. Reynolds, Bradley, and Jack A. Adams. "Psychomotor Performance as a Function of Initial Level of Ability." *American Journal of Psychology* 67 (June 1954): 268-77.
137. Roberts, Gerhard H. "The Failure Strategies of Third-Grade Arithmetic Pupils." *Arithmetic Teacher* 15 (May 1968): 442-46.
138. Romberg, Thomas A., and James W. Wilson. "The Development of Mathematics Achievement Tests for the National Longitudinal Study of Mathematical Abilities." *Mathematics Teacher* 61 (May 1968): 489-95.
139. Rosenthal, Robert, and Lenore F. Jacobson. *Pygmalion in the Classroom.* New York: Holt, Rinehart & Winston, 1968.
140. ———. "Teacher Expectations for the Disadvantaged." *Scientific American* 218 (April 1968): 19-22.
141. Ross, Ramon. "A Description of Twenty Arithmetic Underachievers." *Arithmetic Teacher* 11 (April 1964): 235-41.
142. Rosskopf, Myron F., and Jerome D. Kaplan. "Educating Mathematics Specialists to Teach Children from Disadvantaged Areas." *Arithmetic Teacher* 15 (November 1968): 606-12.
143. Sawyer, Richard P. "Helping the Slow Learner in the Elementary School." *Elementary English* 36 (November 1959): 487-90.
144. Schacht, Elmer James. *A Study of the Mathematical Errors of Low Achievers in Elementary School Mathematics.* Ed.D. dissertation, Wayne State University, 1966. Ann Arbor, Mich.: University Microfilms (no. 67-10,488).
145. Schmitt, Clara. "Extreme Retardation in Arithmetic." *Elementary School Journal* 21 (March 1921): 529-47.
146. Science Research Associates. *SRA Primary Mental Abilities Test.* Chicago: Science Research Associates, 1954.
147. Sears, Pauline S., and Ernest R. Hilgard. "The Teacher's Role in the Motivation of the Learner." In *Theories of Learning and Instruction,* Sixty-third Yearbook of the National Society for the Study of Education, pt. 1, edited by Ernest R. Hilgard, pp. 182-209. Chicago: University of Chicago Press, 1964.

148. Sharpe, H. C. "Comparison of Slow Learner's Scores on Three Individual Intelligence Scales. *Journal of Clinical Psychology* 13 (October 1957): 372–74.
149. Shive, F. R. "Preparing the Slow Learner for a Place in Society." *Ohio Schools* 40 (February 1962): 18 ff.
150. Smith, H. Fairfield. "Interpretation of Adjusted Treatment Means and Regression in Analysis of Covariance." *Biometrics* 13 (September 1957): 282–308.
151. Smith, Sigmund A., and James H. Young. "Are Ye Able?" *New York State Education* 54 (January 1967): 44–45.
152. Stake, Robert E. "Learning Parameters, Aptitudes, and Achievement." *Psychometric Monographs* 9 (1961).
153. Stenzel, Jane G. "Math for the Low, Slow, and Fidgety." *Arithmetic Teacher* 15 (January 1968): 30–34.
154. Stolurow, Lawrence M. "Social Impact of Programmed Instruction: Aptitudes and Abilities Revisited." In *Educational Technology*, edited by John P. DeCecco, pp. 348–55. New York: Holt, Rinehart & Winston, 1964.
155. Strickland, James Fisher, Jr. *A Comparison of Three Methods of Teaching Selected Content in General Mathematics*. Ed.D. dissertation, University of Georgia, 1968. Ann Arbor, Mich.: University Microfilms (no. 69-9525). See also Maynard.
156. Sueltz, Ben A. "The Slow Learner." *Grade Teacher* 78 (April 1956): 41 ff.
157. Sugar, Anne. "Slow Learners Study the U.N." *Instructor* 66 (October 1956): 34 ff.
158. Suppes, Patrick, and Mona Morningstar. "Evaluation of Three Computer-assisted Instruction Programs: Technical Report No. 142." Psychology series of the Institute for Mathematical Studies in the Social Sciences. Mimeographed. Stanford University, Stanford, Calif., 1969.
159. Suydam, Marilyn N., and C. Alan Riedesel. "Developmental Projects." Interpretive Study of Research and Development in Elementary School Mathematics, vol. 3. ERIC Center, Ohio State University, and Center for Cooperative Research with Schools, Pennsylvania State University, 1969. Mimeographed.
160. Swenson, Esther J. "Rate of Progress in Learning Arithmetic." *Mathematics Teacher* 48 (February 1955):70–76.
161. Tanner, Glenda Lou. *A Comparison Study of the Efficacy of Programed Instruction with Seventh Grade Low Achievers in Arithmetic*. Ed.D. dissertation, University of Georgia, 1965. Ann Arbor, Mich.: University Microfilms (no. 66-2501).
162. Thorndike, R. L. "Review of *Pygmalion in the Classroom.*" *American Educational Research Journal* 5 (November 1968): 708–11.
163. Thurstone, Louis Leon. *Multiple Factor Analysis*. Chicago: University of Chicago Press, 1953.
164. Tryon, Robert C. "Individual Differences." In *Comparative Psychology*, edited by F. A. Moss. New York: Prentice-Hall, 1942.
165. Tucker, Ledyard R. "Determination of Parameters of a Functional Relation by Factor Analysis." *Psychometrika* 23 (March 1958): 19–23.
166. Vincent, Lois. "Peter Is a Slow Learner." *Arithmetic Teacher* 1 (December 1954): 24–26.
167. Wallach, M. A., and N. Kogan. *Modes of Thinking in Young Children*. New York: Holt, Rinehart & Winston, 1965.

168. White-Baskin, Jacquelin. "Making Arithmetic Live." *Instructor* 62 (June 1953) : 13.
169. Wilson, J. A. R. "Achievement, Intelligence, Age, and Promotion Characteristics of Students Scoring at or below the Tenth Percentile on the California Test of Personality." *Journal of Educational Research* 52 (April 1959) : 283–92.
170. Wilson, James W. "Evaluation of Learning in Secondary School Mathematics." In *Handbook on the Formative and Summative Evaluation of Student Learning,* edited by Benjamin S. Bloom, J. Thomas Hastings, and George F. Madaus, pp. 643–96. New York: McGraw-Hill Book Co., 1971.
171. Wood, R. "Objectives in the Teaching of Mathematics." *Educational Research* 10 (1968) : 83–98.
172. Woodby, Lauren G., ed. *The Low Achiever in Mathematics.* Report of a conference sponsored by the U.S. Office of Education and the National Council of Teachers of Mathematics. U.S. Office of Education Bulletin 1965, no. 31. Washington, D.C.: Government Printing Office, 1965.
173. Woodrow, Herbert A. "The Ability to Learn." *Psychological Review* 53 (May 1946) : 147–58.
174. ———. "The Effect of Practice on Groups of Different Initial Ability." *Journal of Educational Psychology* 29 (April 1938) : 268–78.

3

Behavioral Objectives

HENRY H. WALBESSER
HEATHER L. CARTER

Summary

You may find it peculiar to be confronted with the summary of a chapter at its beginning—but such unusual behavior is to be expected from behaviorists. Beginning at the end, as it were, may seem like playing a game. It is true that the authors are playing a game, as may be seen in the use to be made of cartoons. However, the purpose is entirely serious; and it is only fair to tell you at the start what the following narrative is intended to convey. The thesis being exposed here is elegant in its simplicity: *If a teacher describes his objectives for slow learners in terms of observable behavior, then he increases the likelihood of being successful in teaching them.*

Introduction

It is only fair also, and in line with the authors' faith in behavioral objectives, to tell you at the outset what the objectives for the reader are. A sensible notion, telling the reader what he should be able to do after reading something. Why is it not done more often? At any rate,

BEHAVIORAL OBJECTIVES

here are the authors' objectives for you. After reading this chapter and participating in its activities where indicated, you should have acquired the behaviors illustrated in figures 3.1–3.5.

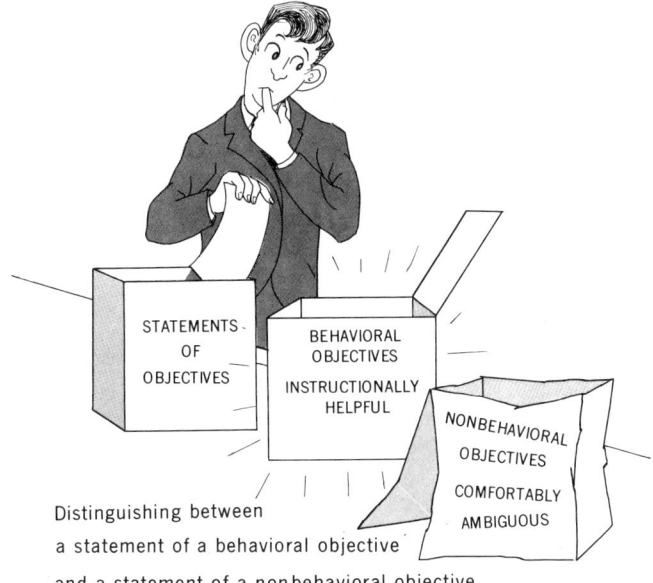

Distinguishing between a statement of a behavioral objective and a statement of a nonbehavioral objective.

Fig. 3.1

Describing the benefits of stating objectives in behavioral language for the slow learner and his teacher

Fig. 3.2

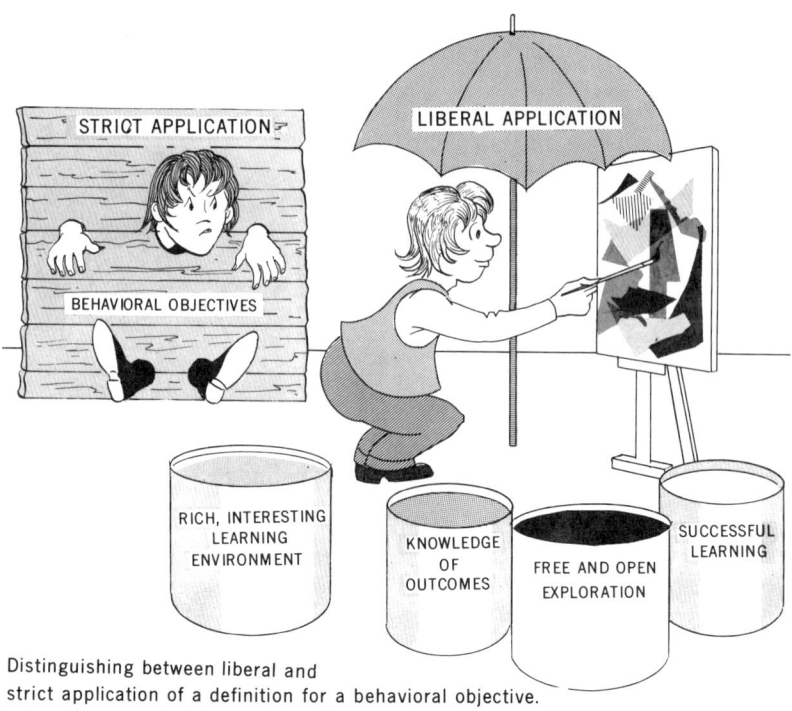

Distinguishing between liberal and strict application of a definition for a behavioral objective.

Fig. 3.3

Demonstrating the use of behavioral objectives in the design of instructional material for the slow learner

Fig. 3.4

BEHAVIORAL OBJECTIVES   55

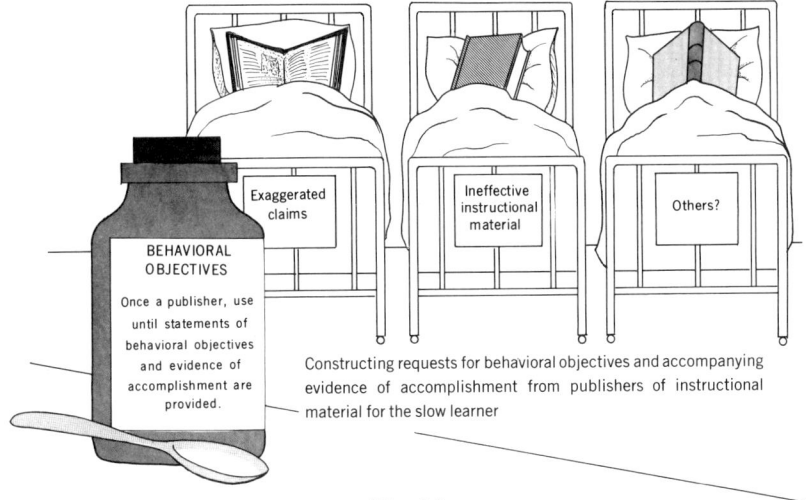

BEHAVIORAL OBJECTIVES — Once a publisher, use until statements of behavioral objectives and evidence of accomplishment are provided.

Exaggerated claims

Ineffective instructional material

Others?

Constructing requests for behavioral objectives and accompanying evidence of accomplishment from publishers of instructional material for the slow learner

Fig. 3.5

As you see, the commentary of this chapter is punctuated with visuals, which are employed to make important points. This maneuver is not frivolous; its purpose is to persuade you to read the entire chapter before making a judgment about the worth of behavioral objectives for the teacher of slow learners. However, should you abandon this chapter and need a reason for doing so, a few well-worn but still commonly used excuses are offered in the following illustrations.

The Too Confining Reason

I find writing behavioral objectives to accompany instructional materials too restricting for my discovery, inquiry, process, being aware of, interest, open-minded goals.

Fig. 3.6

The Really Important Reason

Behavioral objectives are all right
in their place, but the really important
purposes of mathematics instruction
cannot be described in that way.

Fig. 3.7

The Mind's Eye Reason

Sure I have objectives in mind
when I teach something, but it
isn't possible to write them down.

Fig. 3.8

Since behavorial objectives are not an altogether new idea, some readers may already possess the competencies identified as objectives for this chapter. For those readers, figure 3.9 and the invitation merely to skim this chapter are offered. Skimmers are also invited to try the assessment tasks at the end of the chapter.

The Most Competent Person

I need not read this chapter because
I already possess $\wedge$ each of
and practice
the behaviors described as objectives.

Fig. 3.9

An Unusual Committee

Once upon a time—and herein lies the truth to be found in fable—the community of Openminded decided to adopt a new instructional sequence for slow learners in mathematics. A selection committee was appointed, with representatives from classroom teachers, parents, students, mathematics supervisors, paraprofessionals, and building principals. The superintendent's charge to the committee was broad and ambiguous: "Select a mathematics curriculum most appropriate for the slow learners in our school system."

The committee asked publishers to send their representatives. An invitation was extended to each publisher of textbooks designed for the elementary or secondary grade level and intended for the slow learner. Each representative was to give a clear description of his program, including the materials available, with a brief review of the pedagogical approach. Most companies agreed to send representatives.

They came, they presented; the committee listened, asked for clarification, and recorded what was said.

After the final presentation, the committee met to decide on the texts to be adopted. They discussed the alternatives as each committee member perceived them. The discussions continued for several meetings with no resolution. Communication difficulties were obvious, so the committee decided to call in a consultant. Accordingly, a behavioral scientist was asked to provide advice on selection procedures.

The behavioral scientist came but did not offer the anticipated advice. No tried-and-true rules were given, no foolproof procedures outlined. What is more, no resolution of the selection problem was provided. Instead, the consultant raised hard-to-answer questions, such as, "What do you want slow-learning students to be able to do with respect to mathematics?" If someone lapsed into ambiguous language by replying "Know how to . . . ," he would tactfully reject the response by asking another question, "How do you know when the student knows?" This manner of probing offended some, embarrassed others, and frustrated most.

The consultant then focused on one topic, asking, "What do you want every slow-learning student to accomplish with respect to this topic?" At least half a dozen answers came from committee members, with twice as many "clarifying" remarks, which some decided were needed to interpret their responses. The variety of expectations for one competency was surprising and perplexing—surprising because of the many differences of opinion, which had never been so clearly voiced; perplexing because no one knew how to resolve the difficulty.

This procedure was repeated for two other topics, with similar results. By the end of the meeting the committee members began to realize that the consultant had made them focus their attention on the outcomes of instruction. More than that, he had led them to consider these outcomes in terms of observable student performance.

At the conclusion of the session, the behavioral scientist referred to a procedure employing carefully stated objectives. He suggested that this procedure be tried as a means of helping the committee members *to communicate with one another* as well as to select appropriate curriculum materials. The experience of the past hour was all the persuasion the committee needed to try this approach. They agreed that before any decisions could be made about the instructional sequence for mathematics, they would need to define the performance outcomes expected of their students.

But the committee members were not skilled at writing performance statements. Oh yes, some had heard of volumes like Gagné's conditions book (8), Bloom's *Taxonomy* (3), Mager's book (13), Cook and Walbesser's book on constructing objectives (5), and the work on affective taxonomy (12). Others recalled names of school systems or projects that had made use of behavioral objectives. Projects like the "Maryland Elementary Mathematics In-service Project" (MEMIP) and "Science—A Process Approach" were named; also, activities such as those carried out in the school systems of Anne Arundel County, Maryland; Baltimore County, Maryland; Bloomfield Hills, Michigan; Corpus Christi, Texas; Frederick, Maryland; Howard County, Maryland. However, no one was familiar enough with any of these procedures to be willing to assume the responsibility of teaching the others.

A decision was made to hold a series of instructional sessions which the behavioral scientist would lead. Objectives for this instruction were identified. At the end of the instructional sessions each committee member would be able to—

1. construct a behavioral objective;
2. identify instructional materials that should be used to help slow learners acquire a specified behavior;
3. construct evaluation tasks to measure the acquisitions of the performance;
4. demonstrate the use of behavioral objectives in making decisions about the design, construction, implementation, and assessment of instruction for slow learners.

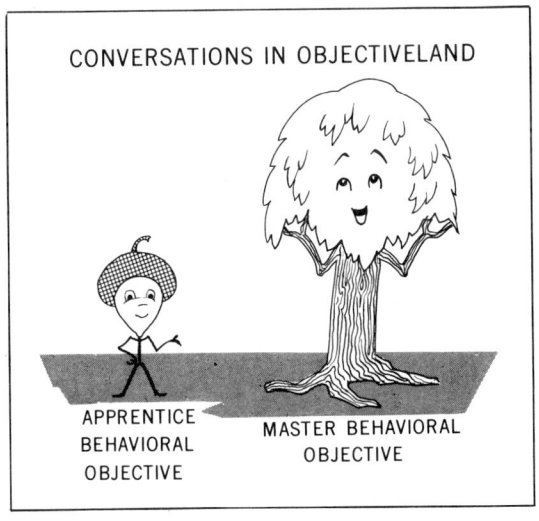

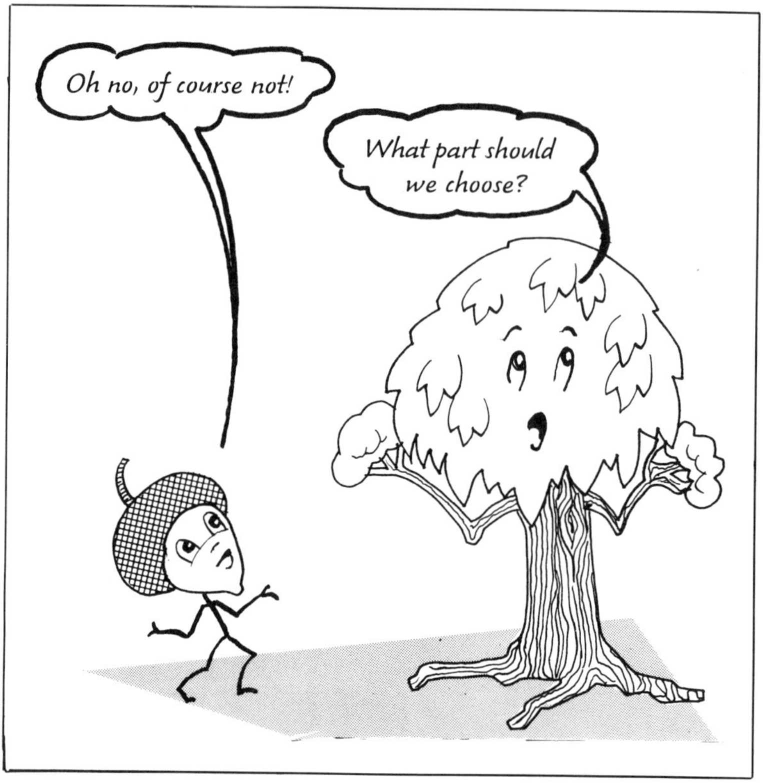

BEHAVIORAL OBJECTIVES

A log was kept of the instructional sessions when the consultant met with the committee. The following section is a description of that log.

The Committee's Log

Session 1: Characteristics of a behavioral objective

Each member of the committee was asked to write an objective for an exercise on fractions. Here is a selection of the written objectives:

A. Write a fractional numeral in the form of a decimal.
B. List four fractions in order from least to greatest. Name the fractions with decimal numerals.
C. Rename a fraction as a decimal numeral, given the name of the fraction in English words.
D. After instruction, each student will be able to distinguish the largest fraction, given a set of three fractions named by decimal numerals.

E. After instruction, each student will understand how to rename a fraction as a decimal numeral when he is presented with a fractional numeral.

The consultant identified some of the stated objectives (not all of which are listed) as descriptions of performance.

> Which of those listed (A, B, C, D, E) do you suppose he identified in this way? Write your response in the blank provided. _____. Go ahead, don't be bashful. Write a response—no one will grade you on it. Did you select any of the first three? No? Good for you! The consultant selected one statement, D.

The consultant then asked: "Why were statements A, B, C, and E not accepted as adequate descriptions of performance? Were these statements inaccurate as to content?"

"No" was the general response.

"Are these objectives unrealistic expectations?"

"We can't decide" or "No" were the responses.

"Were the wrong words used?"

About half of the group responded "Yes," while the other half said "No."

"What do you mean?" was asked of some who had responded "Yes."

Their pooled responses said that the words used in the four unacceptable statements did not make clear the desired student performance.

At this point the consultant asked, "With which objectives would there be the most agreement about how to determine whether an individual had achieved the objective?"

> Which do you think? Statements A, B, C, D, and/or E? _____. Go ahead, take a chance. Make a response.

The consultant then repeated the statement of the objective which he had said did describe an observable performance: "After instruction, each student will be able to distinguish the largest fraction, given a set of three fractions named by decimal numerals." Suggesting that the committee members reexamine the statements of the five objectives, he asked: "How is this one statement different from others? What characteristics does this statement include that the others do not?"

The group decided that the characteristics of a performance statement are determined by the types of information it provides. These types were identified as follows:

1. Who is to acquire the behavior

2. What behavior he is to acquire
3. When the behavior is to be acquired
4. Under what conditions, or given what situation, there is a high expectation that the behavior will be exhibited

The consultant then asked the committee to reexamine the five statements and decide which of the four characteristics each statement possessed.

While the committee is working that out, here is a task for you. Try naming each of these four characteristics for statement D above.

1. Who? _____
2. What? _____
3. When? _____
4. Given? _____

The acceptable responses are not going to be given, so you might as well respond now. When you have completed that task, try doing the same analysis for statement E above.

1. Who? _____
2. What? _____
3. When? _____
4. Given? _____

After the committee members had examined each of the five statements of objectives, the behavioral scientist led a discussion that considered each objective. "Did you find any of the four characteristics missing from the statement of the first objective?" he asked.

Responses that you can provide without any assistance were made by the group.

The discussion proceeded, each objective being considered. Everything went along without difficulty. That is, until the discussion of the fifth objective, there was no difficulty. The committee members could not reach agreement on this objective. Their discussion yielded this characterization:

1. Who? Each student.
2. What? Will understand how to rename fractions as decimal numerals.
3. When? At the end of instruction.
4. Given? A fractional numeral.

The consultant listened to their arguments but made no comments.

After the discussion had been going for about five minutes, he interrupted and drew this first session to a conclusion. He left the committee members with a task to be completed before the next session. The task was this: each member was asked to construct an assessment task (a test item) for objective D and an assessment task for objective E. The consultant said, "Each assessment task should be one that can be used with slow learners and should be such that passing or failing the task reveals whether the student has acquired the described behavior." He went on to say, "Your assessment tasks are not restricted. You need not use multiple-choice items. Your assessment tasks need not employ paper and pencil or otherwise be restricted to a format convenient to group administration. The principal restriction is that the task actually assess the behavior."

Session 2: Task fitting

At the end of session 1 each committee member was asked to write evaluation items for two objectives. Session 2 began with a presentation and discussion of the tasks constructed to assess objective D. Most of the tasks were similar, except for the particular fractions selected. One typical task was expressed this way: "Give the child a piece of paper on which three fractions have been written: 4.17, 1.47, and 4.71. Ask him to place an X under the name for the largest fraction."

Someone suggested that one variation on this task was to ask the student to "place an X under the name for the smallest fraction" rather than the largest fraction.

The consultant's response to this variant was "That is not an appropriate task."

> *Why did the consultant say that? Surely if an individual can pick out the largest fraction, he can also pick out the smallest fraction. Let's listen in and perhaps the consultant's reasoning will become clear.*

The person who suggested the variation observed, "Well, if I only test to see if the student can pick out the largest fraction, he will certainly get it right because that is what I taught him."

Someone then asked, "What do you want the student to be able to do? Do you want the student to identify the largest, the smallest, or both?"

Another person chimed in with, "He should be able to do both."

The consultant then remarked, "If this is so, shouldn't both be

BEHAVIORAL OBJECTIVES

stated in the description of the objective? Remember, the performance statement tells what you want the learner to be able to do—no more and no less."

The committee came to an agreement that tasks could be written for objective D and that, as the objective was then described, only the behavior of identifying the largest fraction should be assessed.

The group then proceeded to describe tasks designed to assess the behavior described by statement E. Here there was much less agreement. The consultant asked that several of the tasks be written on the overhead projector. Four of them are presented below:

1. Give the student a card on which $\frac{1}{6}$ is written and ask him to tell how the fraction can be changed to a decimal numeral.
2. Give the student a card on which are written $\frac{3}{4}$, $\frac{1}{5}$, and $\frac{1}{2}$. Ask him to write each of these fractions in decimal form.
3. Give the student a card on which $\frac{3}{4}$ is written and another on which 0.725, 0.75, and 0.57 are written. Ask him to select the decimal numeral that names the same fraction as $\frac{3}{4}$.
4. Give the student a card on which $\frac{1}{16}$ is written. Ask him to show you how to change this numeral to a decimal numeral.

The behavioral scientist then probed the committee, asking, "Are these tasks all equally difficult?"

The common response was "No."

He then asked, "Is there a similarity about these tasks?"

"No" and "Not as much as we should expect" were the two most common replies.

"Let us return now to statement D," the consultant said, "and examine its wording carefully: 'After instruction, each student will be able to distinguish the largest fraction, given a set of three fractions named by decimal numerals.' What one word in this statement of an objective helps you most in predicting the kind of performance most likely to be requested of the students during instruction and in an assessment task for this behavior?"

Several different responses were given, but the group finally decided that the word *distinguish* was the best clue to the assessment-task performance.

The consultant nodded and then asked, "What part of speech usually describes performance in English?"

Most agreed that it was the verb.

"Now consider statement E. What is the principal verb in that statement?"

Understand was the verb named.

The consultant observed, "The verb *understand* has a much broader collection of meanings than *distinguish* has. This may account for the variety in the assessment tasks you constructed. The greater the number of performance interpretations a word has, the less clear the meaning of the objective. The performance verb employed in the statement of an objective appears to be a central consideration."

It was apparent that some concern had to be directed toward a mechanism for classifying the meaning of performance verbs used in the statement of objectives.

The consultant ended this session with an assignment: "By the following session name three verbs which you feel describe different performances commonly called for in mathematics instruction."

You are invited to try your hand at this assignment before reading on.

Session 3: Verb limitations

At the beginning of the session the consultant asked for the performance verbs the committee members had named. Of the hundred or so verbs they named, here are the ones most frequently given:

write an answer	give a rule	write a name for
solve	subtract	add
make	know	compute
define	prove	substitute
identify	make an educated guess	estimate

Your collection probably included some of the same verbs and perhaps others not named in the list.

The most frequently used verbs were written on a transparency and displayed by using an overhead projector. The consultant asked, "What do you expect the student to do when the objective is indicated by the verb phrase *Write an answer?*"

After all the suggestions had been heard and considered, a similar question was asked about the verb *solve*.

This question-discussion format was repeated for each of the verbs in the list. For some verbs there were few responses; for others, many. Sometimes the student performances described were alike; sometimes there was little or no similarity.

The consultant observed, "We have already seen that some verbs are more likely to lead to misinterpretations, because a variety of meanings can be supplied. Maybe just stating that an objective should include a performance verb is not sufficient to assure specificity."

From the list of verbs they had already named, committee members were able to pick out several ambiguous verbs and verb phrases: *understand, develop an awareness of, gain facility with,* and *appreciate.* The consultant pursued this problem, saying: "One purpose of writing behavioral objectives was to assure clarity. How can the ambiguity difficulty be reduced?" He then suggested: "Here is a strategy that I find helpful. First attempt to identify each different type of performance you might observe. Don't pick out a specific instance in which the performance is exhibited, but name the class of performances itself. For example, suppose an objective dealt with the performance of writing a number sentence of some sort. Don't select *writing a number sentence* as the performance category, but, rather, the general performance *writing.*

"Each type of performance is named and that one name is used to identify all members of the performance class. For example, all performances that require the student to write something belong to the performance class *write*, whether he is to write a number sentence, write the name for, or write the name for a given number."

Some commonly occurring performances were seen to belong to the following nine performance classes, which can be used as operational guides in setting up instructional objectives:

1. *Identify.* The individual selects (by pointing to, touching, or picking up) the correct object when given a class name. For example, when presented with a set of small animals and asked, "Which animal is the frog?" the child is expected to respond by picking up or clearly pointing to or touching the frog. If the child is asked to "pick up the red triangle" when presented with a set of paper cutouts representing different shapes, he is expected to pick up the red triangle. This class of performances also includes identifying object properties (such as rough, smooth, straight, curved) and, in addition, identifying changes such as an increase or decrease in size.

2. *Distinguish.* Identifies objects or events when they are potentially confusable (square, rectangle), or when two contrasting identifications (such as right, left) are involved.

3. *Construct.* Generates a construction or drawing that

identifies a designated object or set of conditions. Example: A line segment is given, and the request is made, "Complete this figure so that it represents a triangle."

4. *Name.* Supplies the correct name (orally or in written form) for a class of objects or events. Example: "What is this three-dimensional object called?" Response: "A cone."

5. *Order.* Arranges two or more objects or events in proper order in accordance with a stated category. Example: "Arrange these moving objects in the order of their speeds."

6. *Describe.* Generates and names all the necessary categories of objects, object properties, or event properties that are relevant to the description of a designated object, event, or situation. Example: "Describe this object"—and the observer does not limit the categories by mentioning them, as in the question "Describe the color and shape of this object." The

child's description is considered sufficiently complete when there is a probability that any other individual is able to use the description to identify the object or event.

7. *State a rule.* Makes a verbal statement (not necessarily in technical terms) that conveys a rule or a principle, including the names of the proper classes of objects or events in their correct order. Example: "What is the test for determining whether this surface is flat?" The acceptable response requires mention of the application of a straightedge, in various directions, to determine touching all along the edge for each position.

8. *Apply a rule.* Uses a learned principle or rule to derive an answer to a question. The answer may be correct identification, the supplying of a name, or some other kind of response. The question is stated in such a way that the individual must employ a rational process to arrive at the answer.

9. *Demonstrate.* Performs the operations necessary to the application of a rule or principle. Example: "Show how you would tell whether this surface is flat." The answer

requires that the individual use a straightedge to determine whether its edge touches the surface at all points, and in various directions.

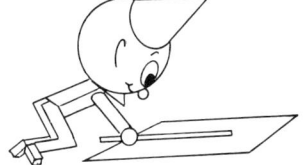

The consultant then suggested, "Let's try to use these nine performance classes. Suppose you work in groups of three trying to match each of the performance verbs we listed earlier with one of the nine performance classes." Each triple worked through the list.

You are invited to try this with the list he prepared or the list shown earlier in this chapter.

When everyone had finished, the consultant asked, "Suppose you wanted the student to tell someone how to do something. Which of the nine performance classes tells what you would expect him to do?"

Describe was the action verb chosen.

The committee tried several more of the verbs and found themselves largely in agreement. In fact, the group reported no difficulty in assigning most of their performance verbs to one or more of the nine categories. Difficulties came with the same verbs that had previously created indecision. One of these was the verb *know*. After some discussion, it was decided that the verb *know* was not a performance verb. The decision was made to practice with the nine performance classes in describing objectives, adding to the list as the need arose. It was acknowledged that the names for the nine performance classes were arbitrary, but they were seen to be helpful for communication among the committee members.

The consultant ended this session with an assignment. "For our next meeting, I want everyone to write one performance objective for an elementary school mathematics activity. The objective should deal with a performance expected to be acquired by all or nearly all slow learners. You may use only one of the nine action verbs in naming the performance in your statement of the objective. Each of the characteristics of a performance statement identified and named in the first session should be included in your description of an objective." Each committee member was asked to review these characteristics before preparing his statement.

You, too, are invited to review these characteristics before preparing your statement of an objective.

Session 4: Item writing

All members of the committee were successful with the assignment. Each person presented the statement of a performance objective and used one of the nine action verbs. Here is one of the statements: "At the end of the session the student should be able to construct a definition of *closed curve* when given a set of closed curves."

For this objective, the consultant presented the following five assessment tasks:

A. Look at this page of illustrations. Place a line segment below the illustration that shows a closed curve.

B. Here is a set of shapes. Each of these is called a closed curve. Make a definition for the term *closed curve*.

C. Here are a set of definitions and a set of shapes. Each of the shapes is called a closed curve. Place an X next to the definition that describes a closed curve.

D. Here is a definition of *closed curve*. Look at these illustrations. How would you use this definition to help you decide which of the shapes is a closed curve?

E. Make a definition for the term *closed curve*.

The consultant asked, "Which of these five tasks assesses the behavior named by the statement of the objective?" All five tasks were suggested by one person or another, but most selected two of them.

> *Can you guess which tasks were selected by most? Look at the action verb in the objective; that may assist you in making your choice. The tasks selected by most were _____ and _____.*

"What is the action verb in the performance statement we are discussing?"

Construct.

"What are some of the meanings of *construct*?"

To make something, or build something, or put something together, or assemble were the responses given.

"Which of the assessment tasks actually requires the student to do one of these things?"

Some discussion ensued because two tasks were suggested as appropriate by several individuals. B and E were the two candidates suggested. The support for the appropriateness of both was based on the observation that the same action was required in both instances.

"Is there agreement between the performance named in the objective

and that named by the assessment task for the objective?"
"Yes" was the answer for B, and "In a way" for E.
"Why?"
"Both ask for a definition to be constructed."
"Are there differences between tasks B and E?"
"Yes."
"What are they?"
"There is more information given in task B. In B, but not in E, the students are given a set of closed curves from which to devise a definition."
"What does the objective state as being given?"
"A set of closed curves" was the response from several committee members.
"So what's the problem? Which task fits the conditions specified by the objective?"

The committee finally agreed on task B as the only task that sampled the appropriate performance named by the action verb and satisfied the specification of what was to be given.

The consultant asked, "How will you decide whether a student's response is acceptable? Think about a response to assessment task B."

"Why, that's easy," someone said. "As long as he makes a definition of a closed curve, it's acceptable."

"Will you accept a definition if he says it, or must he write it?"

Some said yes, others no. The uncertainty of what constituted an acceptable response became clearer to everyone with this lack of agreement.

"How could the ambiguity surrounding an acceptable response be clarified?"

Several committee members contributed to the formulation of this general position: The statement of any assessment task should include a description of how to identify an acceptable response.

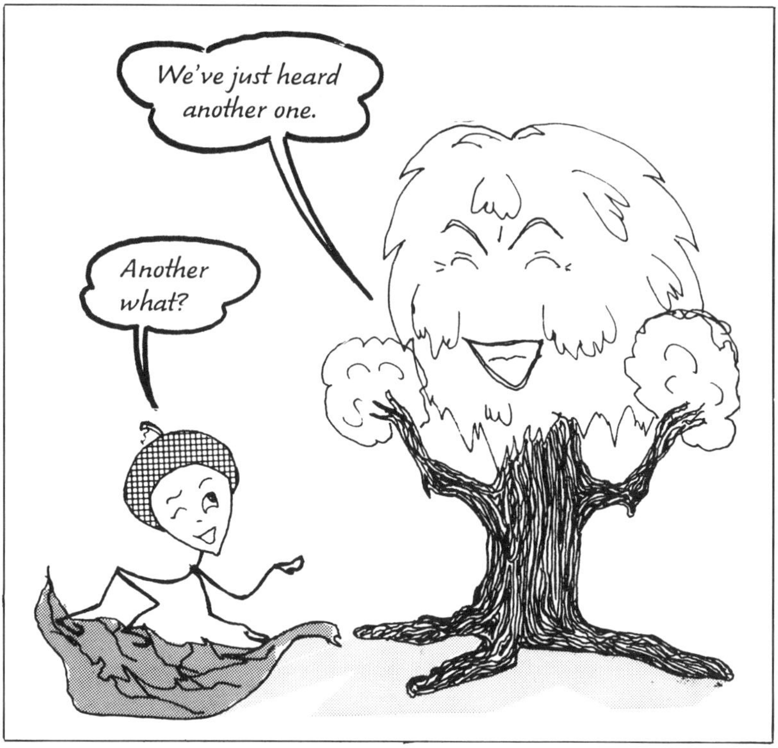

BEHAVIORAL OBJECTIVES 85

The consultant assigned a task to be completed before the next session: "Read two pages from one of the texts considered earlier by the curriculum committee. Identify the possible performance objectives for this instructional sequence. Name the action verbs for each objective you have identified. Keep a record of line and page numbers to show the section dealing with each performance." All agreed to use a table with these headings to report their findings:

ACTION VERB   LINE NUMBER(S)   PAGE NUMBER(S)

You are invited to attempt this task. Select two pages from an appropriate text and try completing a table like the one suggested. You might also want to try a page that deals with problems or exercises.

Session 5: Performance agreement between objective and student response

The consultant began this session by using an overhead projector to show four rectangles. A committee member was asked to place an X below the square region. He selected one of the figures, but not without some hesitation.

"What action verb describes the performance carried out by Mr. _____?"

Two responses were given; some said *identify*, and others *distinguish*. "What is the difference between *distinguish* and *identify*? We agreed on this earlier."

In reply, these distinctions were made: *Distinguish* implies a special collection of *identify* performances. *Distinguish* is used when some of the items are quite similar. The actions indicated by both verbs involve picking out, choosing, pointing to, or selecting; but one action is more difficult than the other.

"That's the right idea. *Distinguish* demands that the elements be very similar, whereas *identify* does not require this similarity. Remember that the choice of *identify* or *distinguish* depends on the items in the task and the characteristics of the learner who is expected to exhibit the performance."

Someone from the committee suggested that both responses could be acceptable for the performance with the square region.

"Why would you say that?" inquired the consultant.

"For some learners the performance would be difficult, while for others the figures would not be easily confused." The committee member continued, "If one could use a ruler, the task would be simple. But if he has to 'eyeball' it, the task is more difficult because two of the rectangular regions are close to being square regions."

"Good analysis," said the consultant, who went on to suggest, "Since we've looked at two of our nine action verbs, let's spend a few more minutes reviewing the performance meanings of the others."

For a start he asked, "What performance does this represent? Suppose I'm the student and the teacher has just said, 'Show me how you would find the quotient of 294 divided by 6.' The student wrote:

```
6 | 294
    190      30
    ---
    104
     60      10
    ---
     44
     24       4
    ---
     20
     19       3
    ---       ---
      1      47 r 1
```

The teacher considered it to be an acceptable performance."

Everyone "happened on" the errors made. Responses ranged from snickers to near belligerence about not putting down the correct answers. The consultant stuck to his rendering of the algorithm. He then repeated the task and the question, saying, "Remember the teacher's words—'Show me how you would find the quotient of 294 divided by 6.' For what performance did the teacher call?"

"*Demonstrate*" was the response from most.

The consultant continued, "Recall the definition of *demonstrate*. Did the student [pointing to himself] exhibit that desired performance?"

A verbal explosion followed. Calm returned. After the many comments were sorted out, it became clear that most responses belonged to one of two positions being advanced. One group held that the desired performance was exhibited; the other contended that the performance was not *completely* exhibited. The differences centered on the observation that the answer given was not the quotient.

The consultant refocused the discussion with this question, "Are there times when you grade on more than whether the student gives the correct answer?"

"Yes," came the reply.

"What else do you include?"

"Sometimes we are interested in the technique used or the strategy employed."

"So there are times when you are concerned with a technique or strategy."

"Yes."

"What did we name the class of performances concerned with exhibiting a tactic or strategy for procedure?"

"*Demonstrate*," came out hesitantly.

"Did the student demonstrate a procedure that would yield a quotient?"

"Yes" was the overall response, with some adding, "but he made an error."

"But did he demonstrate?"

"Yes."

"But what do we use if the teacher is concerned with the answer as well as the procedure?" was asked by several of the committee.

The consultant countered with the question, "How many different performances is that?"

"Two?" was suggested with a questioning voice.

"Which two?"

"Demonstrating and constructing."

"Good thought!"

"Is it acceptable to combine two performances in a description of an objective?"

"What does the committee think?"

It was agreed that when two performances were desired, both could be named in a statement of the dual objective. Someone cautioned that whenever this combining was done it would be necessary to remember that there were really two objectives. Listing the two performances in one statement is only a convenience.

Situations involving the action verbs *order, state a rule, apply a rule,* and *describe* were also "walked through" by the committee members.

The consultant then asked several committee members to record the verbs they had listed for the instructional material. In general, there was agreement about these. Where disagreements occurred, they involved the use of *distinguish* rather than *identify* or the use of *apply a rule* rather than *construct*. Each of these minor differences was resolved by the committee.

"Do you suppose this sort of performance description could be done for an entire chapter?"

"Yes," came back the response.

"For several chapters or an entire book?"

"Yes" was the opinion of all the committee members.

"Why might we want to write performance descriptions for textbooks? What possible purpose would be served?"

What purposes would performance descriptions of textbooks serve for the teaching of slow learners? Try naming at least two.

Discussion made it clear that with performance descriptions of the textbook's objectives, a teacher can more easily select those activities that will help achieve his instructional objectives. The possession of such information places the teacher in an excellent position to ask the publisher for evidence of the effectiveness of the publisher's product. For example, the teacher can ask for the percentage of learners who acquire each of the described performances if an instructor follows the recommended activities. If teachers insist on such information, then textbooks—their statement of objectives and the effectiveness of their activities—will certainly improve. This is especially true for slow-learner mathematics texts, where claims often far outreach reality. Quality-control standards are and have been lacking; this is one way of providing such standards.

For the teacher of the slow learner, information about time for acquisition would be especially valuable. Such questions as "How long does it take for 100 percent of the learners to acquire the behavior; for 90 percent of the learners; for 80 percent of the learners?" have special significance for this teacher, who needs to know whether slow learners, given time, can acquire the same mathematical behavior as other learners.

Interrupting the discussion, a committee member said: "That's all right; we see how behavioral objectives would help in the selection of material. But how about teaching? Do you see behavioral objectives directly helping instruction?"

"Good idea," the consultant replied. "Let's consider the question together. Is it important for the teacher to know when he has succeeded?"

"Yes" was the unanimous response.

"How will the teacher know when he has succeeded?"

"When the student learns what the teacher intends" was the first comment.

"No, that's not quite it," said another committee member. "The teacher will know he has succeeded when he can see the learner show the behavior the teacher is trying to help him acquire."

"In other words," someone interpreted, "if he shows the behavior, then the teacher has evidence of success." And another added," If he doesn't show the behavior, then the teacher has evidence of failure."

"Whose failure?" asked the consultant.

The consensus was, "If the behavior is not acquired, the instructional system is at fault."

The consultant then advanced this idea, "So if we write behavioral objectives to describe the purposes of instruction, all our troubles with slow learners learning mathematics will be over." And with a twinkle he added, "That's the way it is, isn't it?"

To this, the reply was negative. Becoming more clear about the performances instructors want students to exhibit won't solve all the problems of the slow learner in mathematics—all knew that.

"But it can't help but make a difference," added several. "If you know what you want to accomplish and how to recognize when you've succeeded or failed, it can't do anything but help."

In support of this conclusion, the consultant spoke of recent research.

"Investigations by Cook, Engel, Gray, Rowan, and Smith provide evidence of the benefits for the learner when instruction is planned around stated behavioral objectives," he said. "These five investigations [4; 7; 11; 16; 17] provide insight into the effects of behavioral objectives on acquisition, rate of forgetting, and generalizability. Each of these three learning dimensions is important for all learners but especially important for slow learners. For if teachers can help slow learners remember what they have learned longer and also generalize to new situations, one of the most persistent learning difficulties of the slow-learner population will have been resolved."

In this chapter it has been argued that behavioral objectives can benefit the schools in various ways: by helping them to select appropriate instructional activities and to organize curricula to take advantage of entry behaviors and the cumulative nature of learning; by making it easy for teachers and students to recognize success or failure; and, finally, by helping slow learners to retain longer, and to generalize, the behaviors they have acquired.

Now that you have read the log and participated with the committee in its activities, it is assumed that you have acquired the objectives of this chapter. To help you decide whether or not you have actually acquired these behaviors, you are invited to try each of the following assessment tasks. The behavorial objective being assessed by each task is named at the beginning of each item. The range of acceptable responses for each task is described at the end of the section. But try each task before looking at the acceptable response. Go ahead, give them a try; see how well you have learned or how poorly the writers have taught.

Assessment Tasks

For the five objectives illustrated in the introduction to this chapter (figs. 3.1–3.5), here are various assignment tasks:

1. *Objective in figure 3.1:* To distinguish between a statement of a behavioral objective and a statement of a nonbehavioral objective.

   Assessment task: Read each of the following statements and, by circling the *yes* or *no*, indicate whether it is or is not the statement of a behavioral objective.

   Yes No   a. After two weeks of instruction, every sixth grader can construct an explanation for a numerical puzzle, given a description of the puzzle and the instruction to explain how it works. Any explanation is acceptable that does account for the observed solution or solutions.

   Yes No   b. After one week of instruction, each seventh grader can order four or more rational numbers with different denominators from smallest to largest, given a set of names for rational numbers, paper, pencil, and the oral instruction to do the task. The order must be correct and completed in a single attempt.

   Yes No   c. After one week of instruction, the fifth grader can demonstrate an understanding of the properties of addition and subtraction. He should show he can add and subtract numbers whose numerals have several digits.

   Yes No   d. After two months of instruction, the secondary school geometry student can identify and name the errors in an argument, given a description of the argument and the instruction to analyze it for errors. The student must identify and name the errors in nine out of ten presentations.

Yes   No   e. After one semester of instruction, the ten-year-old will have strengthened his ability to solve problems involving mathematical sentences that require addition and subtraction of integers. Given a collection of situations involving mathematical sentences, the student will name the solution correctly for each sentence.

2. *Objective in figure 3.2:* To describe the benefits of stating objectives in behavioral language.

   Assessment task: Describe three benefits for the learner and three benefits for the teacher.

   a. For the learner:
   (1) _____
   (2) _____
   (3) _____

   b. For the teacher:
   (1) _____
   (2) _____
   (3) _____

3. *Objective in figure 3.3:* To distinguish between the liberal and the strict application of a definition of a behavioral objective.

   Background information:

   Sometimes the value of using behavioral objectives is diminished by overly strict applications of a particular definition of what the statement of a behavioral objective is. Such applications might lead some authors or teachers to omit important objectives simply because they cannot easily fit them into the description of an observable performance. This outcome would be sad indeed and should be viewed as a negative input in need of correction.

   Suppose you decide to use Walbesser's definition: The statement of a behavioral objective is a statement with six components telling (1) who the learner is, (2) what performance he is to exhibit, (3) what is given to him, (4) who or what initiates the learner's performance, (5) what the acceptable responses are, and (6) what the special restrictions are, if any.

   Assessment task: The following statements are interpretations of the application of the definition given above. For each statement, circle the appropriate word to indicate whether it is a strict or a liberal interpretation.

Strict	Liberal	a.	A behavioral objective must be so specific that only one acceptable response is possible.
Strict	Liberal	b.	A behavioral objective must be so specific that it applies to exactly one teaching environment.
Strict	Liberal	c.	Behavioral objectives should always be written before, not after, an instructional activity.
Strict	Liberal	d.	A behavioral objective must include some performance verb defined by the working team of writers.
Strict	Liberal	e.	A behavioral objective should not be so specific that it applies to only one stimulus setting.
Strict	Liberal	f.	A behavioral objective should not be so specific that it can be assessed by only one test item.

4. *Objective in figure 3.4:* To demonstrate the use of behavioral objectives in the design of instructional material for the slow learner.

   Assessment task: Obviously, any assessment of this long-range objective belongs to the future. The authors of this chapter invite you to share your demonstrations with them and the mathematics education community. Your productivity will be a measure of whether you have acquired this behavior.

5. *Objective in figure 3.5:* To construct requests for behavioral objectives and accompanying evidence of accomplishment from publishers of instructional material for the slow learner.

   Assessment task: On the supposition that you are about to select some instructional material for a mathematics course intended for slow learners, construct a letter to be sent to each publisher of materials you might purchase, requesting the behavioral objectives embedded in their materials and any evidence that slow learners have accomplished these objectives as a result of using these materials.

RANGE OF ACCEPTABLE RESPONSES

1. *Behavioral objective statements*
   a. Yes. b. Yes. c. No. d. Yes. e. No.
2. *Benefits of stating objectives in behavioral language*
   a. Examples of benefits for the learner:
      (1) The learner can name the competencies he is expected to acquire.
      (2) When he has acquired the competencies, the learner can identify what he is asked to identify.
      (3) The objectives act as cues to the learner to help him acquire skills in

a shorter time and retain acquired skills longer.

(4) The objectives act as guidelines to assist the learner in making generalizations.

b. Examples of benefits for the teacher:

(1) The teacher can identify what he has to teach.

(2) The teacher can objectively decide when the learner has acquired the skills.

(3) The teacher can construct instructional tasks related to the learner objectives.

3. *Strict and liberal interpretations*

a. Strict. b. Strict. c. Strict. d. Liberal. e. Liberal. f. Liberal.

4. _____

5. _____

Curriculum Materials Based on Behavioral Objectives

Some interesting curriculum materials employing behavorial objectives are being developed by school systems, projects, and individuals in the United States. Among these materials are some intended for the slow learner in mathematics. The following illustrations are taken from one set of such materials constructed by the Baltimore County Public School System of the state of Maryland (15). The content of the illustrations is intended to assist teachers and curriculum developers in the separation of behavorial objectives, their assessment tasks, and allied instructional activities.

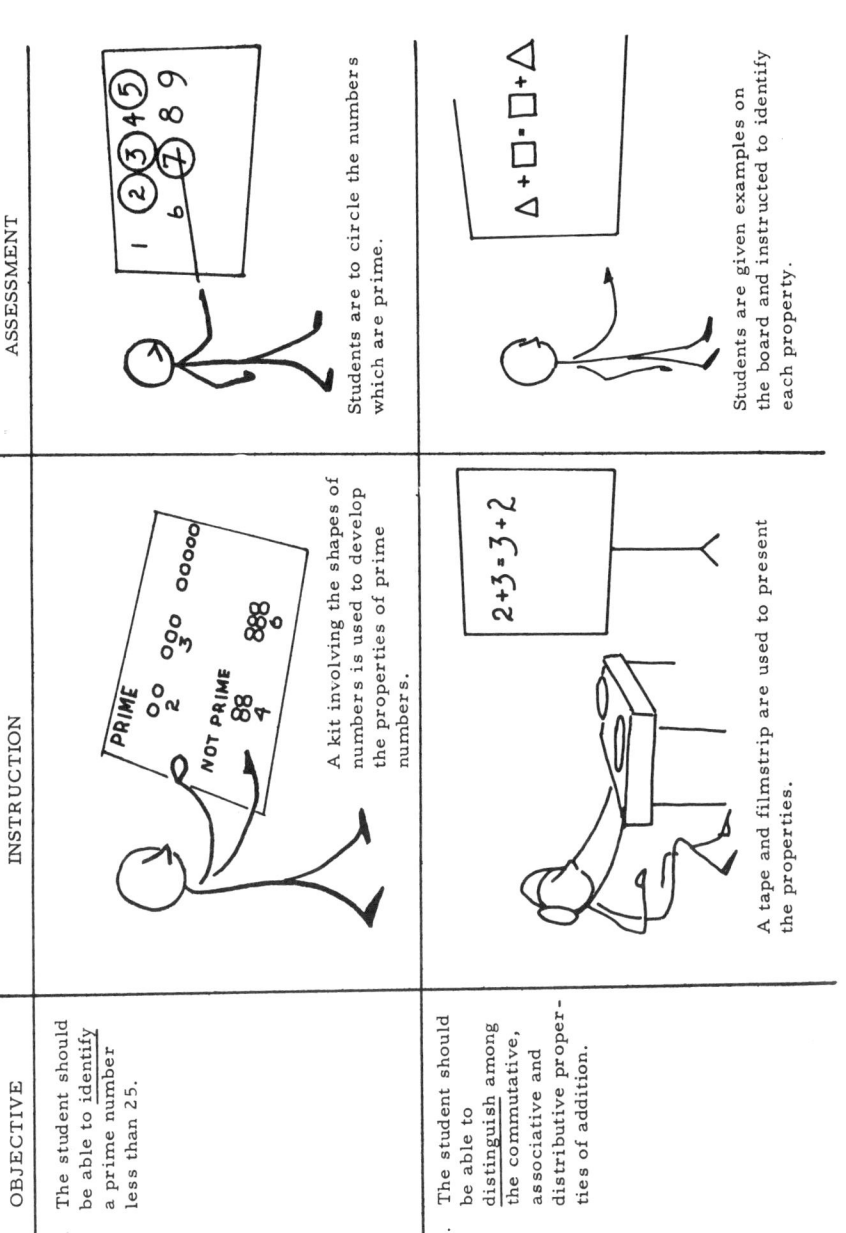

This material is taken from Mathematics for Basic Education, Grade 10 by the Baltimore County Schools, 1967

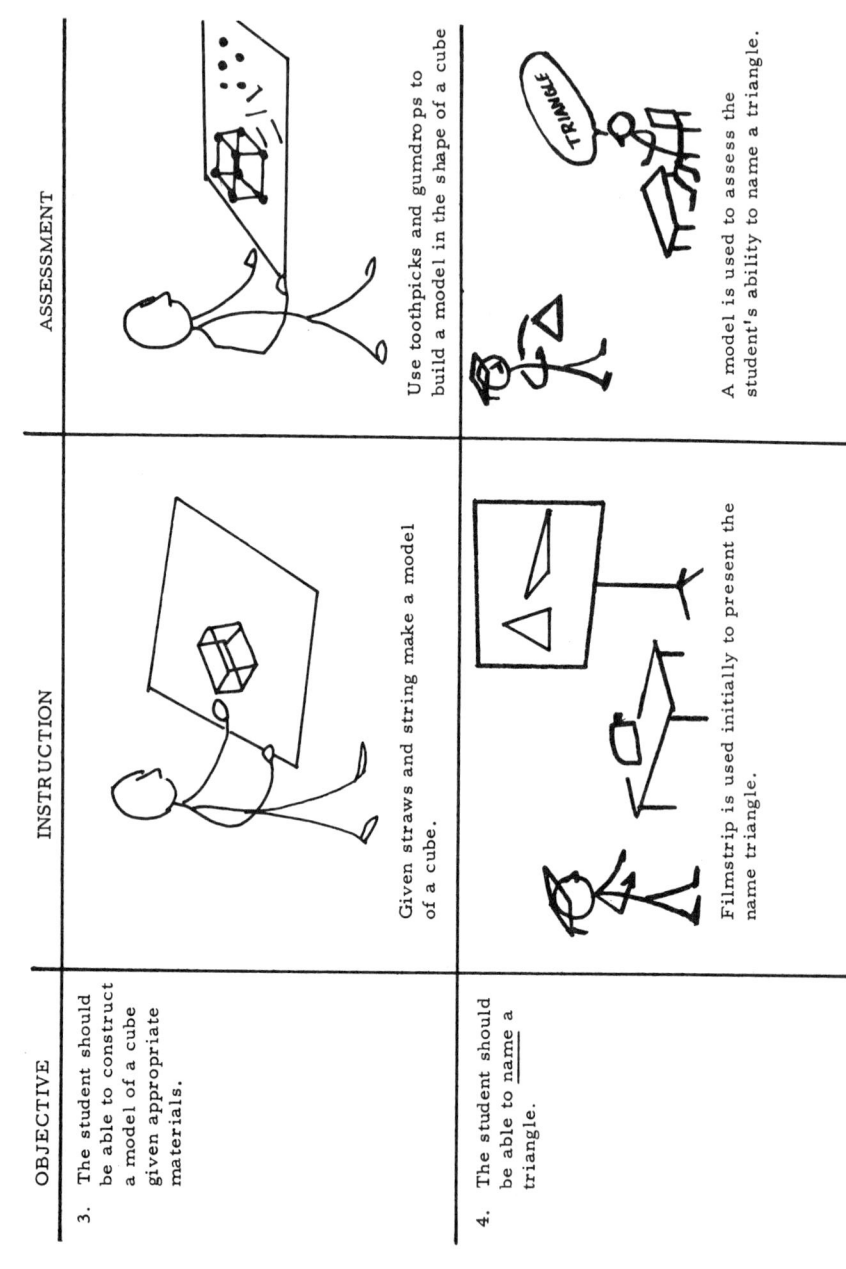

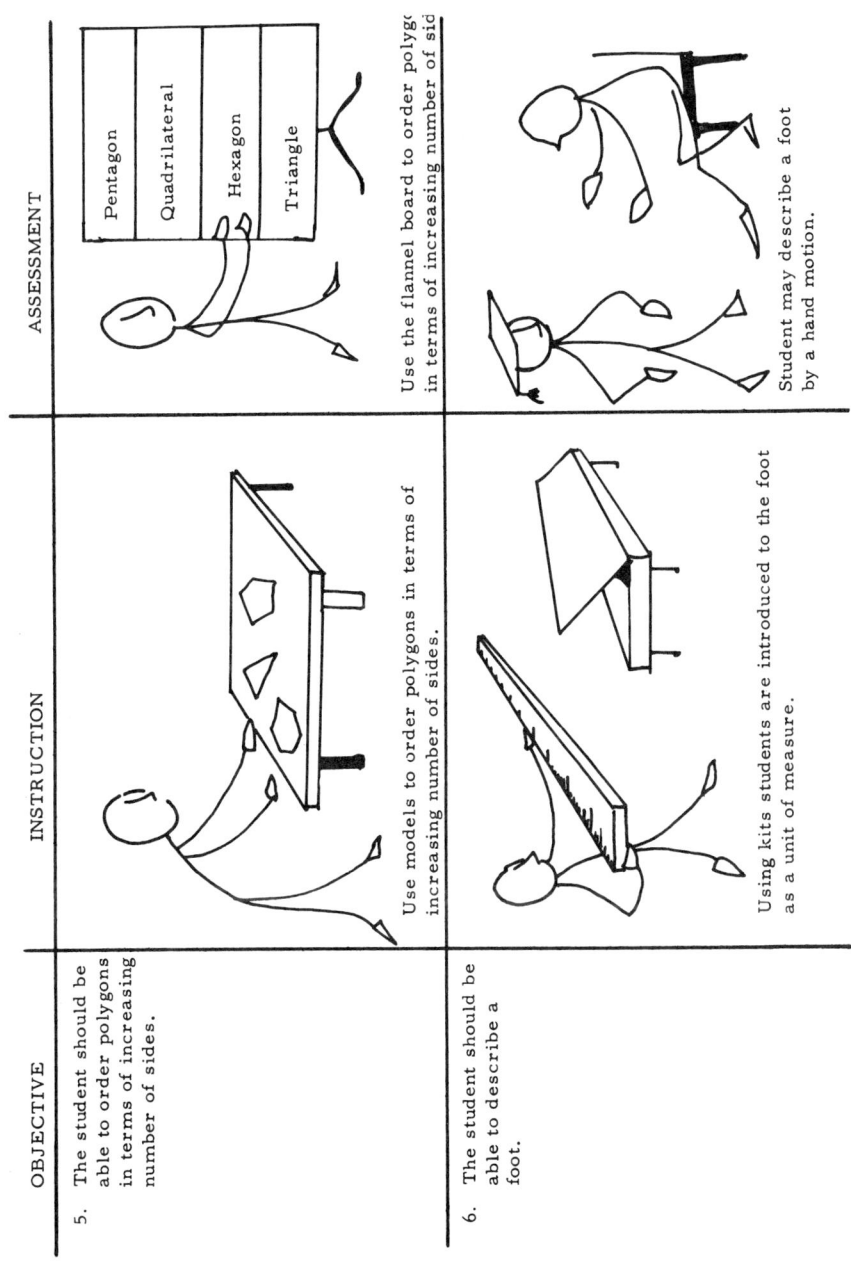

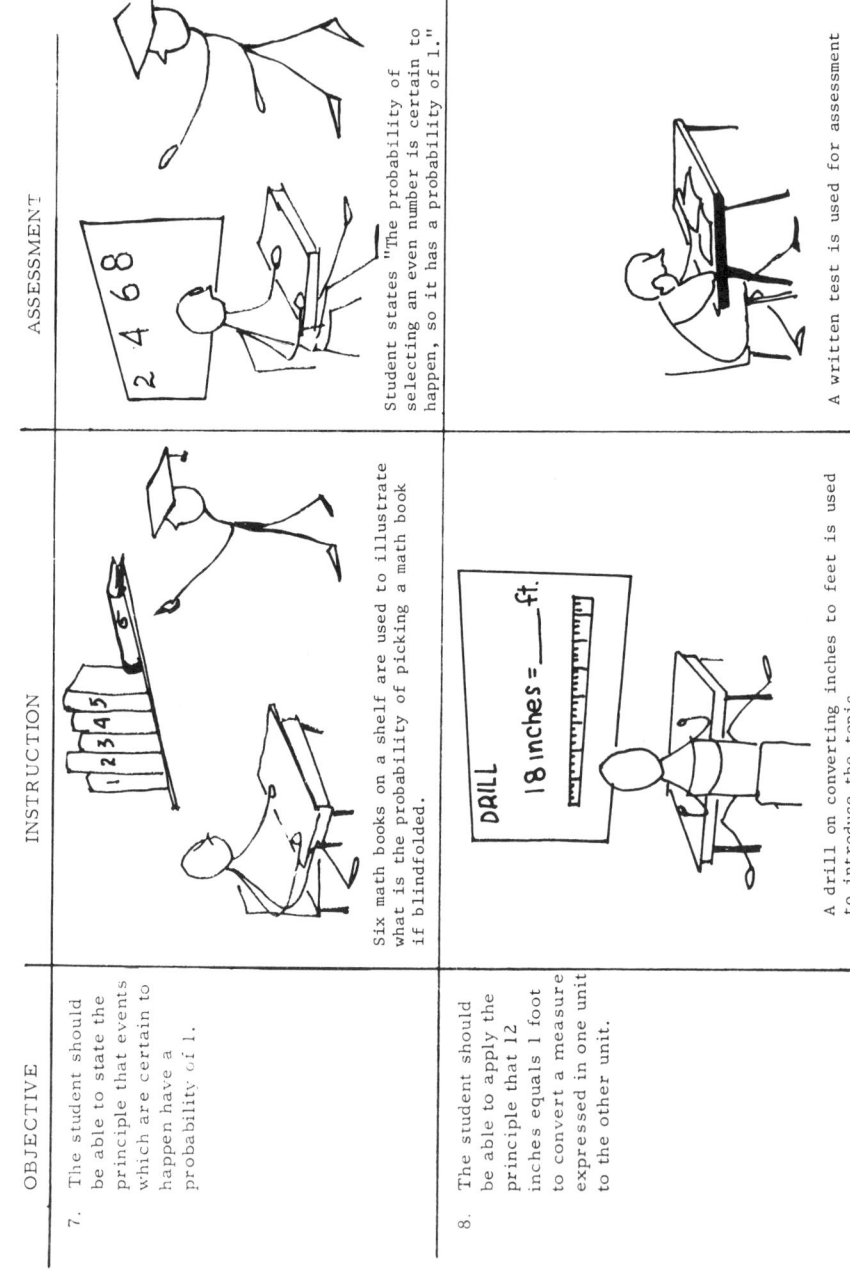

OBJECTIVE	INSTRUCTION	ASSESSMENT
9. The student should be able to demon- strate a procedure for constructing the product of two whole numbers.	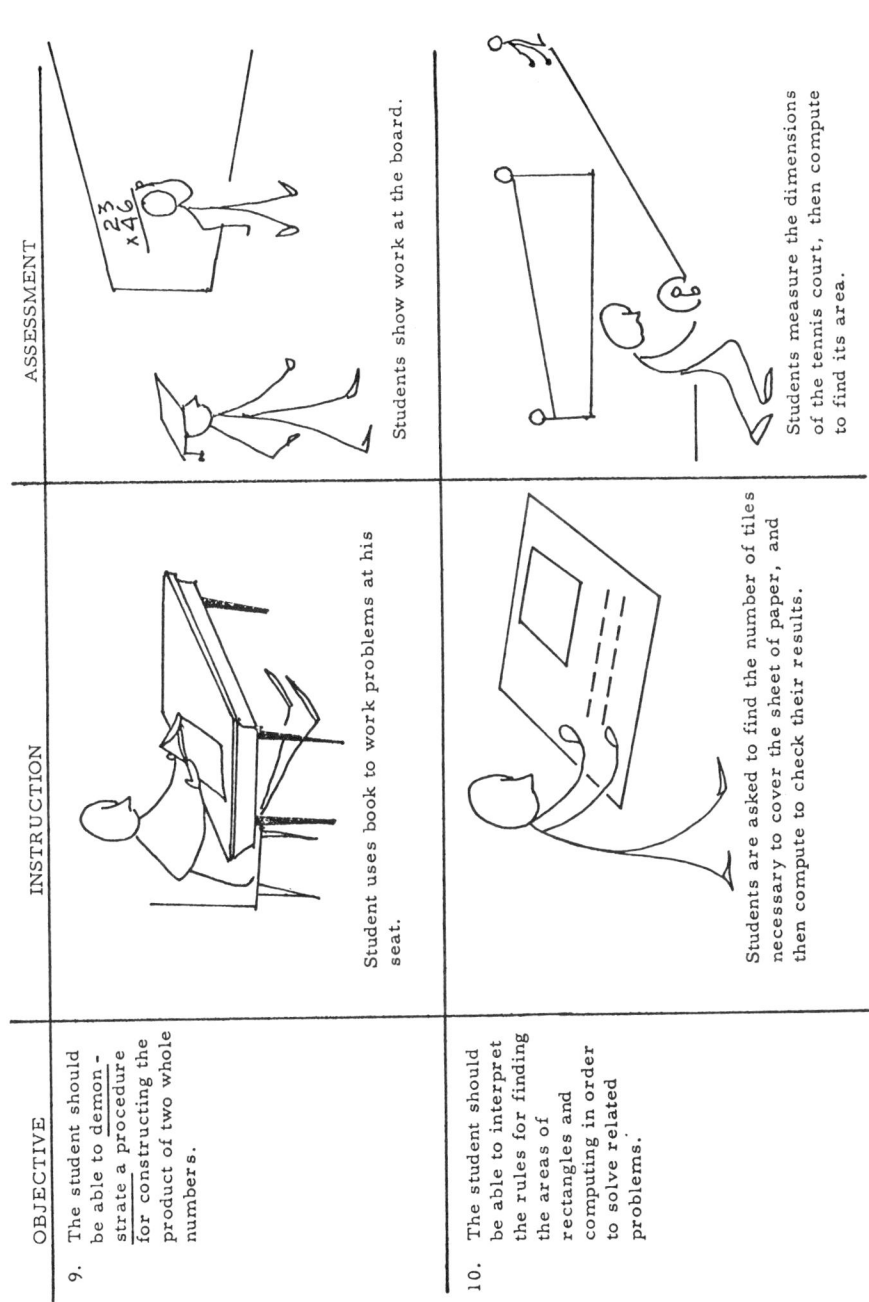 Student uses book to work problems at his seat.	Students show work at the board.
10. The student should be able to interpret the rules for finding the areas of rectangles and computing in order to solve related problems.	Students are asked to find the number of tiles necessary to cover the sheet of paper, and then compute to check their results.	Students measure the dimensions of the tennis court, then compute to find its area.

Points to Ponder

Behavioral objectives will not remake slow learners into average or fast learners.

Behavioral objectives for slow learners in mathematics will be like behavioral objectives for other learners in mathematics; behavioral descriptions are the same, but the expectation about how quickly each behavior is acquired will be different. Slow learners should not be shortchanged in content or expected capabilities. These are learners who are simply slower to acquire the desired behavior.

Behavioral objectives help the teacher determine when he and his selected instructional materials have failed.

Telling the learner the behavorial objective helps him to acquire the behavior.

The techniques of constructing behavioral objectives are easily acquired, but it is extremely difficult to maintain the discipline of putting them to use. It's too easy not to do it.

At first, try writing behavioral objectives for one or two lessons, not an entire course. See if stating the objectives in this manner helps your instruction and the children's learning. If it helps, continue to use it. You will find yourself becoming more and more proficient as you use these skills. If it does not seem to help, do not use it after the first attempts. But *try it* before judging its merits.

Prologue to Action

The literature on individual differences has an important message for effectively teaching the slow learner. There do exist individual differences with respect to rate of acquisition. Human beings learn at different rates, but the organization of schools and school subjects seldom acknowledge these differences. If school subjects, say mathematics, were a description of behaviors to be acquired rather than material to be covered in a given period, then the slow-learner problem would no longer be a problem. Children would be *expected* to learn at different rates.

This is a bold suggestion, which the authors recognize as such; but they submit it as a solution to a problem heretofore insoluble. Your participation in the implementation of the solution is invited.

REFERENCES

1. "Behavioral Objectives for the K-12 Curriculum." Duplicated. Bloomfield Hills, Mich.: Bloomfield Hills Public Schools, 1967.
2. "Behavioral Objectives for the Mathematics Curriculum." Corpus Christi, Tex.: Corpus Christi Public Schools, 1970.
3. Bloom, Benjamin S., ed. *Taxonomy of Educational Objectives.* Handbook 1: *Cognitive Domain.* New York: David McKay Co., 1956.
4. Cook, J. Marvin. "Learning and Retention by Informing Students of Behavioral Objectives and Their Place in the Hierarchical Learning Sequence." Ph.D. dissertation, University of Maryland, 1969.
5. Cook, J. Marvin, and Walbesser, Henry H. *Constructing Behavioral Objectives.* College Park, Md.: Maryland Book Exchange, 1972.
6. "A Curriculum Guide in Elementary Mathematics." 5 vols. Duplicated. Clarksville, Md.: Howard County Public Schools, 1969.
7. Engel, Roberta S. "An Experimental Study of the Effects of Stated Behavioral Objectives on Achievement in a Unit of Instruction on Negative and Rational Base Systems of Numeration." Master's thesis, University of Maryland, 1968.
8. Gagné, Robert M. *The Conditions of Learning.* New York: Holt, Rinehart & Winston, 1970.
9. "Games and Algorithms." Duplicated. College Park, Md.: Maryland Elementary Mathematics In-service Project and the Maryland State Department of Education, 1970.
10. "Geometry: A Multi-Media Approach." Duplicated. Annapolis, Md.: Anne Arundel County Board of Education, 1970.
11. Gray, William L. "The Effects of an Integrated Learning Sequence on the Acquisition and Retention of Mathematics and Science Behaviors in Grade Five." Ph.D. dissertation, University of Maryland, 1970.
12. Krathwohl, David R., Benjamin S. Bloom, and B. B. Masia, eds. *Taxonomy of Educational Objectives.* Handbook 2: *Affective Domain.* New York: David McKay Co., 1964.
13. Mager, Robert F. *Preparing Instructional Objectives.* Palo Alto, Calif.: Fearon Publishers, 1962.
14. "Mathematics Behavioral Objectives." Duplicated. Frederick, Md.: Frederick County Public Schools, 1967.
15. "Mathematics for Basic Education." Duplicated. Towson, Md.: Baltimore County Public Schools, 1967.
16. Rowan, Thomas E. "Affective and Cognitive Effects of Behavioral Objectives." Ph.D. dissertation, University of Maryland, 1971.
17. Smith, John M. "Relations among Behavioral Objectives: Time of Acquisition, and Retention." Ph.D. dissertation, University of Maryland, n.d.

4

A Favorable Learning Environment

JAMES R. PEARSON

IT IS said that the slow learner has a poor self-image; that he shows little curiosity, lacks verbal ability, is culturally deprived; that he has a short attention span, little initiative, and many other characteristics—including, of course, the fact that he learns slowly. A particular individual may exhibit all these attributes or only a few. Still another characteristic, however, is most common—one usually described as "a poor attitude." The very use of this term explains the total failure of the school to adapt to that multifaceted and complex phenomenon: the slow learner.

In too many instances, if judged by their actions, administrators and teachers alike have confused the relative positions of the slow learner and the school. Once again there is need to set the record straight: *the school operates for the learner, not the learner for the school.* This means that the total environment provided the child by the school must conform as nearly as possible to his uniqueness. It is also clear that slow learners present learning styles, intellectual de-

A FAVORABLE LEARNING ENVIRONMENT 105

velopment, social skills, self-concepts, and expectancy levels that challenge honestly attempted efforts to provide them with an environment conducive to learning.

Since the *total* school environment must adapt to the slow learner, the classroom facility itself must conform to his needs. Within the classroom are moods, motivations, and a general atmosphere, all having effects on the child. In this chapter these factors will be developed with specific illustrations. First the appropriate physical characteristics of the environment will be examined. Then the affective and cognitive aspects of the classroom situation will be discussed in terms of motivational methods, general atmosphere, and the psychological concerns of the slow learner.

Physical Characteristics of the Environment

A classroom that is gloomy and lacks variety or surprises in decor and arrangement hardly measures up as a favorable place to spend a school day. Architectural features are usually out of the teacher's control. Decisions have already been made about the lighting system and windows. Others have decided whether to have a classroom designed for about thirty pupils or a modern "open" classroom capable of housing two or three times that number. Occasionally this open classroom adjoins another in the so-called two-pack. Whatever the design, however, the teacher does have various means of controlling the physical environment.

The arrangement of the room's furnishings is one means of exercising control. For the slow learner, this arrangement should be open and flexible. Desks, chairs, and tables should be moved about as any activity dictates. Several tables, with three or four chairs at each, should be available for small-group work. The walls or corners should be reserved for the student who wishes to work on a project individually.

One part of the room should contain math games and other equipment, such as a tape recorder, a slide machine or filmstrip projector, and (if audio tapes are available) a listening center where several children can listen to tapes at the same time without disturbing others. Space should be designated for spare pencils and paper (both whole sheets and half sheets), for the slow student often loses or forgets material. A gaily decorated juice can or a block of wood drilled with holes will make a fine pencil holder. Manila folders stapled at the ends can hold paper.

A math table may have an activity file. This would contain task cards or worksheets for simple activities that could engage the student who "finishes first" and keep him from distracting others.

Activities with measurement are very popular with the slow learner. For this reason it is desirable to have on hand a great variety of measuring devices—yardstick, ruler, tape measure, scale, balance, egg timer, watch, clock, calendar, and so forth.

Many kinds of containers should be found in the room—milk cartons, boxes, cans, cups (paper or plastic), jars, and similar objects. The students are eager to bring these in because they cost nothing and they represent the real world, which too often goes unrepresented in the mathematics classroom. Use of these objects makes them believe that perhaps there is some mathematics outside the classroom.

Thousands of paper clips and tooth picks (for place value), some drinking straws, and a few jars of beans, peas, rice, or the like could be used for counting in puzzle situations. (The number of rice grains in a jar must be estimated quickly. Besides the large jar of rice, the student has two smaller jars, one larger than the other, and a paper bag. He may also use a balance or a scale. He places his estimate, his work, and his name on a slip of paper and puts it in a box. The beans and peas may be used in the same way.)

Through the use of directions on cards or worksheets, the teacher can develop self-directed student activities using—

road maps ("How far is it from A to B?" "Find the *shortest* route from X to Y");

TV schedules ("Which channel has the most time devoted to movies?" "Prove it." "How much time does channel 7 use for soap operas?" "For detective or police drama?");

food advertisements ("Using this ad, plan a picnic for 8 people and list the food and total cost." "What is the cost of 3 pounds of ground beef, $1\frac{1}{2}$ pounds of boiled ham, 3 dozen cans of Diet Cola, and 16 hamburger buns?" "Which is the better buy—the Del Monte can of peaches or the Libby can of peaches listed in this ad?" "Why?");

food recipes ("How many ounces of cream would you use to make this for 5 people?" "Here is a recipe for 6 people; use the attached advertisement and find the total cost for the ingredients needed").

All the material named above, and much more, should be used with the slow learner. This workaday material provides the sort of relevance he has been seeking but not finding in his school experiences. The physical environment described will provide the student with an informal setting that is comfortably familiar and at the same time not too familiar to evoke mild curiosity, enjoyment, and a few surprises.

The walls of the classroom are usually hung with bulletin boards and chalkboards. Bulletin boards provide the mathematics teacher with opportunities to display the usual posters and "well-done" papers. "Well-done" papers should not necessarily be limited to the so-called A papers. In fact, grading the slow learner at all except by growth is absurd. It may be desirable to display his pretest and posttest papers side by side when a great deal of growth has taken place. He should be allowed to choose, however, whether they will be displayed and how.

Still other purposes may be served by bulletin boards. Ones in well-traveled areas may be used to display difficult "facts," formulas, properly labeled geometric shapes, and tables. Such information can be placed on a board without fanfare or explanation. When there is something in the curriculum that can be divined by viewing it over a period of time (such as the patterns in a hundreds chart), it is a candidate for display on such a bulletin board.

When total class projects using charts and graphs are developed (such as graphing the sun's shadow at noon each day from the opening of school in September to the last day of school), a bulletin board may advertise the results. A trick that often gets the interest of the class is advertising on a bulletin board for help in solving a certain kind of problem. A student who has mastered that type of problem "answers the ad."

Finally, a word on the use of chalkboards in the classroom. *Keep them free* of murals, pictures, and displays of any kind so that students can use them as they choose. If this is done, the slow learner may elect to go to the board with another student who has a grasp of something with which he is experiencing difficulty. The slow learner makes greater use of the chalkboard when he can use it in this way. Then it poses no threat to him, as it would if he were sent to the board to work some problem before the whole class.

Methods of Motivation

Rewards such as candy, a trip to the zoo, "coins," and even trading stamps are forms of *extrinsic* motivation used today to encourage the student to work hard and learn. In some performance contracting, radios and other appliances are being offered for higher scores on achievement tests. Some of these extrinsic motivators, or rewards, actually do reinforce desired behavior in mathematics. However, the reinforcement that is most desired comes from some inner contentment for having achieved, which is a form of *intrinsic* motivation.

Intrinsic motivators

Expectation. Expecting a slow learner to do a job often motivates him to get the job done if he is mathematically ready for it. Knowing that someone expects him to be able to acquire a certain skill makes the student begin to doubt his own low evaluation of his ability. This approach must be used realistically, with the learner's progress kept in mind. Therefore, it is a good idea to begin with a task or skill below what he is ready for, so that he will be assured of fulfilling the teacher's expectations. For example, if a student is accomplished in multiplication but division is his present area of concentration, it might be well to give him partially completed division problems and let him practice multiplying "down." The teacher might write:

$$12 \overline{\smash{)}108}^{\,9} \quad \text{or} \quad 37 \overline{\smash{)}2{,}971}^{\,80}$$

Then the student would write:

$$12 \overline{\smash{)}\underline{108}}^{\,9} \quad \text{or} \quad 37 \overline{\smash{)}2{,}971}^{\,80}$$
$$\underline{108}\underline{2{,}960}$$
$$11$$

Merely providing workable problems, however, is not enough. In every action and word the teacher must exhibit his positive expectations of a student: (*a*) by waiting longer for an answer from the student during classroom work, (*b*) by using remarks like "I had an idea you'd get it" or "I knew it!" or "This is getting monotonous!" (after the student's second or third correct response in class or on a worksheet), (*c*) by including the slow student in groups with the more endowed students, taking care that his assignment and acceptance there will increase his own expectancy. For example, when a group is working on the weight of a number of objects for graphing, the slow learner could weigh, call out the weights to others, or record the weights called out by others. The level of his assignment would depend on the student. His activity doesn't have to be mathematically oriented. Knowing that his teacher does have *realistic* expectations of him motivates the slow learner (almost *any* learner) to want to accomplish the task.

A FAVORABLE LEARNING ENVIRONMENT

Hope. Many slow learners come from an environment that could hardly be expected to motivate them to succeed in school. They see older people from their culture not succeeding and so have little hope of improving their lot. In fact, hope is the most vital part of motivation. Few people can be motivated to act if they are convinced there is no hope of success; and when the acts desired by school result so *indirectly* in the economic success they desire, slow learners are completely indifferent.

To change this lack of hope, the teacher of the slow learner must provide frequent opportunities for him to exhibit success. It is obvious that these chances to do well must be carefully chosen so that they are within the capabilities of the learner. (This is discussed at length later.)

It is often suggested, and rightly so, that successful men from their own culture or geographic area or part of the city come in to talk individually to the students. This sort of "At least I did it" presentation is helpful. The person invited does not have to be a Jackie Robinson or a Lee Trevino. He can be a grocer, a used-car salesman, a mechanic, or any successful person who has established himself as a contributing member of the community.

The mere establishment of the fact that there is an "out"—a better world that can be obtained through school and socially accepted routes—is a big step toward increasing hope and thus promoting motivation.

Example. The biggest role the teacher of the slow learner plays in the classroom is that of example. If the teacher does not desire to learn, does not have a healthy respect for (in fact, uncontrolled enthusiasm for) his own learning, he may find it impossible to teach the slow learner. How can a student resist the honest, overt seeking and digging for an answer if the teacher is displaying this himself? To do this, the teacher must put himself in the position of puzzling out the solution to a vexing mathematical problem, or finding a new approach to it, and show that he is enjoying himself. During this activity he might even be thinking aloud so that the class can listen and be invited to join in.

Throughout his life the slow learner has said "I don't know"—or at least thought it—many times a day. What a fine, settling feeling to hear the teacher say "I don't know" once in a while. There is nothing more satisfying and identifying for the slow learner than to know that sometimes the teacher is in the same boat.

Success. Of course the slow learner must have goals he is able to reach. These goals, no matter how long-range, must be digested by the slow learner as many *short-term* goals. If there is a universal mistake made by the teacher of the slow learner, it is "too much too soon." When the goals are in sight and the student knows they are obtainable, there will be effort.

It is not enough, however, merely to have obtainable goals. Beyond this, the learner must receive some sort of satisfier along the way. As stated before, this can be a "Well done," a pat on the back, or even prizes or gold stars. He will be able to apply himself and exert the proper effort if the satisfaction is there. Bugelski (2) feels that concentration is not necessarily a special gift. If something has brought satisfaction previously, then applying oneself to it again is easy. He states that "a history of successes can be equated with such satisfactions." What satisfactions are worthwhile? Bugelski adds that even artificial motives such as money or honor rolls are reasonable as long as they are obtainable. "The learner may make his first efforts only for sordid reasons (such as money), but the satisfactions that come from success will eventually be adequate compensations" (2, p. 166).

Further, the teacher himself can be the satisfier through his efforts to assure that the student is *definitely going to be successful*, at least *initially*, in all material the student begins. The slow learner comes with a history of failures, which produced his lack of interest. The teacher sets about to change this history to one of successes through the careful organizing of the material. For example, to take a slow learner from 8×23 to 18×23 would be a mistake without the intermediate steps of 10×20 and 10×23 and more work with the distributive property of multiplication over addition. His chances of success with 10×20 and then 10×23 and finally 18×23 are more assured than if he were moved directly into the last problem. Success is probably the prime motivator, and all teachers of slow learners should provide for it.

Many teachers feel that progress charts on the bulletin board provide the learner with satisfaction. (The slow learner should be allowed the option of keeping his own chart and showing it as he feels it bears showing.) At any rate, a "picture" of the learner's progress is important. The teacher can provide additional motivation by establishing steps at various levels and recognizing each student when he masters a major step, showing his chart if he wants it shown and rewarding him with some privilege, such as extra time at the record player or tape machine to hear his favorite artists.

A FAVORABLE LEARNING ENVIRONMENT

Feedback. Information about the result of one's effort, or feedback, can be strongly motivating. But is it always? Telling a child he is wrong is certainly feedback, but does it help him to be right at some future time or even if he tries again immediately? Whenever possible, a wise teacher will use statements like "That's close," "Almost got it!" "How did you get that?" or "Check your decimal point." These allow the student to know he is on the right track.

When correcting papers, it is helpful to allow partial credit for the correct process or equation or number sentence—or even, in extreme cases, the neat alignment of digits. For example, partial credit has been allowed in the problems in figure 4.1, each of which is worth 5 points if entirely correct.

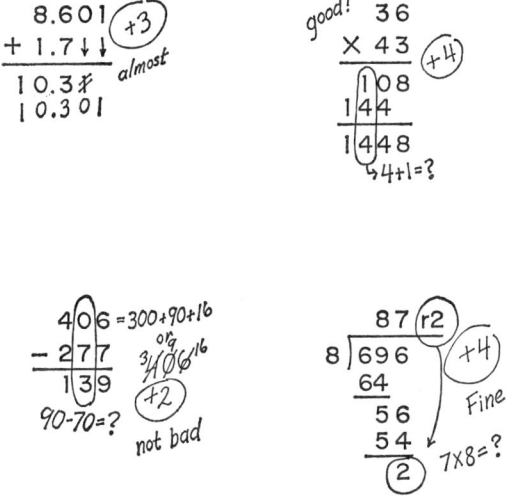

Fig. 4.1

The feedback, to be helpful to the slow learner, must be received as soon as possible. Papers kept longer than overnight have almost lost their value as teaching agents. In the classroom, it is ideal for the teacher to be literally at the student's elbow to make suggestions and answer questions about the work. Knowledge of results can be strongly motivating—but only if not delayed.

Extrinsic motivators

Because of the relatively worldly orientation of slow learners, it is not surprising that worldly goods and activities—*extrinsic* motivators

—are high on their list of satisfiers. On the surface, this may seem a negative virtue. Actually, it can be used to advantage; for the reasons why a slow learner begins to succeed in school are not really as important as the fact that now he is indeed succeeding. "Nothing succeeds like success" is not merely a bromide; it has been shown to be a fact.

Extrinsic motivators are strongly attractive to the student and may tempt him to fudge as he hurries toward success. When offering these rewards, therefore, the teacher must accept no shortcut; he must hold the line on what is or is not successful completion of a task.

Here are some extrinsic motivators that have proved successful and are now in use:

Time at the record player or tape machine to hear favorite artists

"Coins" that may be exchanged for time at the game table or the playground

Points that can accumulate to show that a student leads the class in his favorite game

Trading stamps (consult a local company) that may be collected in a book and redeemed for gifts

Sugarless gum and other types of sweets

Tickets for certain movies

Classroom Atmosphere

Mr. Smith, who was a specialist working with a group of inner-city first graders, opened his lesson with a counting game. He would knock on the door; a student would ask who was there; and Mr. Smith would give his number name by knocking, say, three times on a desk. The response would then be, "Come in, Mr. Three" (or Mr. Four, etc., depending on the number of times he knocked).

After playing this game successfully in one room, Mr. Smith entered another classroom. He knocked, only to be greeted with "Just a minute!" instead of "Who is it?" He explained the game again and received the desired response. Then when he knocked his "name" on the desk, a child responded with "Come in, Mr. Smith." The classroom teacher looked scornfully at the student who gave the response, and the child cringed in the silent room. But by this time Mr. Smith was unable to contain himself. Rushing to the child, he laughed, hugged the little first grader, and said, "By golly, I *am* Mr. Smith. I'd been playing this game so long I'd forgotten my name." The rest of the lesson was more successful than it had ever been, and that first grade was the leading "Knock-knock" class of the school.

The atmosphere in that room had been changed, at least while Mr. Smith was there; and it is hoped that, as the teacher saw the change, the tension was eased for good. Classroom atmosphere can stimulate the slow learner to better mathematics, or it can entirely prevent his learning. In fact, an undesirable atmosphere can lead to truancy and, at the legal age, dropout.

Routine and surprises

Because of the unorganized, random home life found in the environment of many slow learners, the promotion of "school attitudes" is quite difficult. Routine is necessary in order to have social control, but it is even more important to the slow learner. Routine provides him with a certain security reflected in "I know what comes next." This is the security that is provided by a schedule that is more or less followed.

A daily warm-up session of easy oral-mathematics problems may be used, typified by the "Number Trail" (the teacher says, "3 + 8 − 2 + 6," for example; then he calls on someone for an answer). To assure a quick appraisal of individuals in the class, "Show Me" cards may be used. The child represents his answers by inserting these numeral cards in pockets designed to hold and exhibit them for the teacher to see. Naturally any series of problems will have a limited range of difficulty—one governed by the needs of the class and changing whenever the needs change—but the teacher must be sure that each series is varied so that, within any range of difficulty, most levels are represented every day.

The warm-up session could be followed by assignments (to groups or individuals, depending on the goal) or by "open desk"—a period when some of the students work on puzzles or assignments and the others come, one at a time, to the teacher's desk for counseling, help, or just talk.

Although routine, or predictability, is required for a slow-learner classroom, novelty is a necessity. Novelty can be achieved by means of sudden humor, an unusual activity, a break in the schedule, or stopping to pursue a nonmathematical point through an encyclopedia. When should this be done? Probably when the teacher gets the feeling that "enough is enough" or when he receives signals that the group is restless.

Humor works best when it is well timed. A teacher of seventh-grade slow learners uses some very mild irony when a student is successful several times in a row during a verbal activity. Turning to another student, he says, "Minus five points for Joe—showing off!" The class roars with laughter, and Joe feels great. There is another teacher in an elementary school who occasionally writes a numeral backward so that he can be corrected by a gleeful class. Another elementary school teacher sang a silly song as he handed out papers: "Because the papers were so good, I feel like singing."

Occasionally, when some subject seems to have aroused the students' curiosity, stopping the class to explore the subject also adds needed variety. A third-grade teacher of slow learners was found on the floor on all fours with his students standing and kneeling around him. Before him was a sack of dried lima beans, and he was explaining how to plant them in small jars so that the root structure could be seen. Later, when the plants came up, and once a week thereafter, each child cut a strip of colored paper the length of his bean plant. These strips were pasted side by side on white newsprint to graph the growth of the plants.

Every once in a while a teacher might say to his group, "Well, no warm-up today. I'm going to show *Donald in Mathemagic Land.*" Or he might play some math-related game, such as Number Password (Is it greater than a hundred? Even? Odd? Greater than fifty? etc., until the number is guessed). Surprises such as these tend to maintain an atmosphere of informality and enjoyment of mathematics.

Variety of activities

The motor-centered learning style of the slow learner doesn't lend itself to an endless parade of the usual textbooks and worksheets. To suggest that a child be given more work in the same way and even in the same material that produced no results the first time is sheer folly. Coming from an environment that values the quick hand and strong, fast body, the slow learner is confused when placed in the school environment, which values the clear head and glib tongue. Although the thoughtful, verbal style is important, it is much better to capitalize on the motor skills and watch the other develop in time.

By employing a variety of activities that place things of a mundane nature *in the hands* of the child we can use the skills and curiosity the slow learner brings to school with him. To provide practice in addition, where proficiency was slowly slipping away through lack of use while the class was on other topics, the teacher of a fourth grade provided certain students with workbooks. At first some work was done. After a while boredom set in and no one was completing the sheets. The teacher brought some rocks to school and, providing a spring balance in grams, asked each child in the practice group to find the total weight of the rocks. The scale didn't reach far enough for all the rocks to be weighed at once, so addition was needed. Later some children brought their own rocks to school for weighing. In fact, one student left a rock at home only because, as he said, "I couldn't lift it"—much to the relief of the teacher.

Games such as Number Password, explained earlier, provide the child with variety in drill. A game that involves the child physically is even more successful with the slow learner. "Find Your Place" is popular with many students. Two or more teams are formed, with ten students on each team. Each member of a team is given a card on which is written one of the numerals 0 through 9. The teacher calls out "864." On each team the child with the 8, the child with the 6, and the child with the 4 must arrange themselves correctly so that the teacher can read 864. The first team to arrange itself correctly wins a point. This activity may be varied for more advanced groups by asking for the "shortest name" for 300 plus 180 plus 13. There are games to be played with Cuisenaire rods and with Dienes blocks, both of which may be purchased commercially. These offer excellent ways to vary approaches to mathematics teaching. In fact, the teacher of the slow learner should take advantage of any workshop in the use of manipulative and laboratory materials. (4.)

The activities of a class can be varied by moving out of the classroom into the out-of-doors. Laying out baseball diamonds, finding the area of the basketball court and the dimensions of the intersection nearest the school, timing the drinking fountain's use in a half-hour, counting passing cars at three different times in a day, and similar projects can add great variety at no loss to the mathematics program. Directions for many of these projects can be printed simply on cards and made available to a team or an individual. Many more may be found in the excellent book *Freedom to Learn*, by Biggs and MacLean (1).

Class activities can be varied also by the introduction of fractions earlier than usual—a practice that can reinforce the addition and subtraction of whole numbers if fractions with common denominators are used:

$$\frac{246}{3} - \frac{129}{3} = ? \quad \text{and} \quad \frac{646}{2} + \frac{295}{2} = ?$$

The learner is actually operating in the area where he needs strengthening but is using "harder numbers"—to quote a student friend. Obviously it helps the learner for him to be able to say, "We're working with fractions."

Finally, from the fact that there are many ways to add, subtract, multiply, and divide (not to mention many approaches to handling fractions) comes an obvious avenue to variety, namely, varying the algorithms presented to the children. A typical assignment might be not to do three subtraction problems but to find three ways to do one. Robert Davis, of the Madison Project, is quite proud of Kye's subtraction algorithm. When told by a teacher, "You can't take 8 from 4," Kye proceeded to show her that he could (3, p. X − 13):

$$\begin{array}{r} 64 \\ -28 \\ \hline -4 \\ 40 \\ \hline 36 \end{array}$$

Gelosian multiplication (fig. 4.2)—or lattice multiplication, as it is sometimes called—may be introduced as an alternate method. (It was good enough for Columbus!)

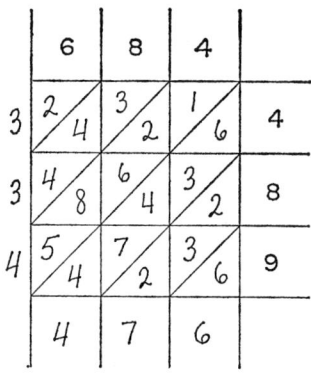

Fig. 4.2

A variety of materials increases the chances to provide the student with a "thinking model" for his mathematics. A child who at one point could perform subtraction only with paper clips can now use a standard algorithm. He had been presented with a variety of approaches and chose the one that best fitted his style and pace of learning. He still refers to the clips, but only occasionally.

Relaxed and informal

The slow learner adapts more readily in a classroom whose fluidity allows student movement and informal small-group work than in one where every movement is rigidly controlled. The student must be allowed a certain freedom of movement about the room and contact with other students, although not to the point of disruptiveness. (More will be said about this under "Behavior.") Generally, if the children are controlled by the mathematical activity they are engaged in, no further control will be needed.

More often than not, the slow learner benefits from work in groups of not more than three or four. There is a balance within these groups that allows interaction to be its own check. Several years ago it was unheard of to allow a student to ask another in class, "What did you get for the second one?" In small-group work, however, interaction is normal. The slow learner must be allowed this opportunity where mathematical activities and worksheets are concerned. The teacher must arrange his plans to allow *himself* time to aid each individual as he moves about the room. If schedules are in order, the teacher should schedule a part of the period for this interaction of students and their freedom of movement.

An important value of small groups has still to be mentioned. The slow learner fears exposure before a large group. For this reason he will gravitate toward a group where he doesn't feel threatened if he makes a "dumb mistake." The same purpose is served by certain programmed material and audiotapes used with earphones: they provide the slow learner with quiet feedback that doesn't threaten his prestige before the whole class.

Behavior

If the rules for the slow-learner classroom are few and to the point, and if they are consistently carried out, the chances are good that students will follow and uphold them. Children have a finely developed sense of fairness; the rules they make up for their own games demonstrate this. Indeed, by capitalizing on this, the teacher can allow the students themselves to develop the rules for desirable classroom behavior.

Much of the misbehavior in a mathematics classroom (or any classroom) stems from the nature of the material that is foisted on the student. For example, boys have a tendency to frown on learning in general as "girl's stuff" (especially at the ages of eleven through fourteen) and to reject it through antisocial behavior. In this case the teacher can make sure that the problems are of interest to boys as well as girls by adapting the ones presented in the lesson to a more masculine viewpoint. Girls need problems adapted to their interests also. Moreover, girls respond well to gentleness and an apparent interest in their activities. As often as possible the teacher should comment favorably on their clothes and general appearance. As always, the remarks should reflect genuine interest and not appear to be forced. By looking carefully, the teacher can find something complimentary to say every day.

Classes differ in the extent of their need for control and in the kinds of control they need. It is suggested, however, that the following general guidelines are applicable in some degree to every slow-learner classroom.

a) Noise. There is a learning noise; and there is a disruptive, nonlearning noise. Slow learners are not given to the so-called hum of activity. They seldom hum; they "carry on"—talk loudly, often yell, wave arms, and regularly contact one another. This is especially true among the boys. A teacher of the slow learner should expect an almost regular amount of noise, but this should be noise in which there are heard, at least occasionally, sounds of the task at hand.

An argument over how to proceed in an activity or who should handle what part of the activity is not nonlearning noise. It suggests that the part each should play in the mathematical activity at hand is *at that moment* more important than the activity. The fact that students are involved in the activity at all is the encouraging fact here. Their continuing involvement can be stimulated by arbitrating the dispute so that each has recognition for the part he is to play. Complimenting the children for their interest and expressing the opinion that their results will surely be great with all this enthusiasm will help significantly.

By contrast, merely playing with the materials or interrupting others intent on working is not *learning* noise. There is a tendency to take advantage of an informal classroom setting, and the slow learner seems more prone to do this than others. When the students in a group seem to be playing with the materials or worksheets, a teacher may ask if they are "getting used" to the equipment. At that point he may begin the activity *with* (not *for*) the students, taking great pains to see that there is initial success before he turns it over to the group. At this time, another remark about how well they seem to be doing is appropriate.

A FAVORABLE LEARNING ENVIRONMENT

A suggested rule, explained to the class beforehand, might be: NOISY NOISE, NO! LEARNING NOISE, YES!

b) *Moving about the room.* Here again is an action that should be encouraged but must be controlled. In a fluid classroom arrangement it is to be expected that movement about the room will create some problems, but these are increased with a classroom of slow learners. In fact, in a heterogeneous classroom, it is often the slower student who has the most difficulty adjusting to this relatively free movement about the room. If he is to feel free to work with others, ask questions of his peers, and move to resource centers when he needs this kinds of help, he must be given guidelines for such activity. If the child recognizes the importance of peer help and the rule governing this help is explained carefully, the child will not slip very often.

If a classroom is to be motor-centered, most activities will employ tangible materials. Therefore any jostling, pushing, or shoving may be unusually disruptive. At the same time, the action of going from area to area within the room is an important outlet for the slow learner. This, coupled with working on concrete materials and being allowed to share ideas and ask questions of others in a relatively free manner, provides a pathway to learning of inestimable worth to the slow learner. Since free movement will bring success in an enjoyable way, it is extremely important and the students soon realize this. The teacher should touch on all these points with the children, allowing them to come up with reasons for the following rule: Is THIS TRIP NECESSARY?

c) *Fighting.* Probably the most unsettling and potentially dangerous misbehavior in a classroom is fighting. Inner-city children especially bring to the school setting an aggressiveness learned on the streets. Boys have more of a tendency to fight than girls, but they do not have a monopoly in this area of misbehavior.

In a large city classroom in the heart of the ghetto, a sixth-grade teacher broke up a rather vicious fight between two young girls. As the rest of the class watched, he took each girl by the arm and led them to the hall. In minutes they were back. The girls were once again friends, and the teacher continued his class as though nothing had happened. In the hall he had said, as if talking to another person: "I can't get over this. Two pretty chicks, and they're scrappin'!" Although his tone was not gentle, his remarks were. Here was a teacher who looked at them as young ladies, pretty young ladies, and was completely taken aback that they would fight like boys. The expression on his face, an important part of any interaction with inner-city children, was one of concern that was close to tears. He had complimented them and scolded them in the same statement. They must have come back into the room feeling that this fellow couldn't possibly be wrong to expect better behavior from two "pretty chicks."

Fighting among boys has always been a problem, and approaches to handling this vary almost as much as the fighting itself.

A teacher of a seventh-grade class discussed the possibility that might makes right. He asked the students if they would accept pay for ten hours' work because the boss, who was bigger and stronger, was able to enforce this multiplication: Five eight-hour days equal a ten-hour week.

A boy remarked that "5 × 8 ain't 10" and that he'd "call a cop."

This was exactly where the teacher wanted to put things, in the hands of an arbitrator. Thereafter, whenever a fight seemed imminent, he would remind the participants of the big boss and it seemed to help. When the combatants tried to show how their situation was different from that of the big boss, the teacher continually found parallels, thus frustrating their "logic." Many times he averted possible fights by saying aloud before the group, "5 × 8 ain't 10." The class laughed, and the teacher "got on with it."

Still another method often used by men teachers is to have the boys "put on the gloves." They go to the gym and box under stringent amateur boxing rules. This has dubious value in that it seems to reinforce the idea that fighting may not be so bad after all. From the standpoint of working off their anger in a physical way, however, it may be justified.

A fourth-grade teacher, a woman, arranged for the boys to arm wrestle, with the class watching. The winner seldom won much because she invariably asked him to tell the class what he had shown by forcing down the other boy's arm. She asked questions like these: "Did it show that he didn't push you first, as you said?" "Did it show that he wasn't right when he said that you started it?" "Did it show that he started it?" Of course it became clear that victory only showed that the winner had the strongest arm and lasted the longest during the wrestle. This almost all the boys admitted. At last report the teacher still held arm-wrestling tournaments at the request of the class, but the fights had stopped, with only a few fiery arguments as reminders of what might have been.

A suggested rule for fighting:

FIGHTS SETTLE NOTHING! DON'T!

d) Copying others' work. The only time when copying is a serious mistake is when the child is being tested. Copying another's seatwork and take-home assignments often results when the slow learner is given work that is too advanced for him. If the copying amounts to getting another student to talk over the material and, in effect, explain it to him, then this is precisely what is to be desired for the slow learner. Often this is not the case and the student is simply taking the results of another's work and quietly putting them on his paper. When the student simply copies answers, two things invariably happen. First, the student doing the work begins to feel he's being used. The time it takes for this student to figure that out is in direct relation to the popularity, charm, and persuasiveness of the copier; but it *does* happen. It should be noted, however, that a class will "carry" a slow learner if they feel the fellow is being treated unfairly by the teacher or that demands made upon him are unrealistic. The second thing that happens is that the teacher discovers from the student's test results that he couldn't have understood the material he has been claiming for his own, since he performed so miserably on the test in the same material. After the student realizes that he must simply "go through" similar material again, he begins to see some value in trying to figure it out himself.

Copying is of course quite serious during a test. If the teacher handles tests for the slow learner effectively, he *does not test for a grade.* He tests to determine weaknesses and strengths. He is trying to find out what is wrong. When the students are convinced that they are being tested to find out what is wrong and that the score they make is of little importance to the teacher's opinion of them, any copying disappears. In short, when the testing does not pose a threat—and it shouldn't—the student performs appropriately. The slow learner responds to the analogy of the doctor taking a temperature to find out what is the matter. If the patient secretly places the thermometer in another's mouth, the doctor may well treat the poor fellow for an illness he doesn't have. Or worse, he may not treat him *at all* for the illness that is killing him. TAKE CREDIT ONLY FOR WHAT YOU HAVE DONE.

Briefly, these guidelines say to the teacher: Make rules that are reasonable, consistent, and agreed on by the group. Explain each rule and be firm in its imposition. If a rule can't be justified, discontinue it. Whenever possible, encourage the students to develop their own set of rules. Finally, be fair, considerate, and sensitive in the implementation of these rules.

Mathematical perspective

Presenting concrete models of a concept, operation, or algorithm gives the learner greater opportunity to develop his own "thinking model." Although he may internalize only a part of the concrete model into his personal "thinking model," it offers further chances to expand the way he will look at the process involved. An eighth-grade student subtracted integers by thinking of the vertical number line he saw in class, but he thought of it as "spring loaded" and moving past a fixed point located at the minuend. Removing (subtracting) positive integers caused the line to "spring up" past the fixed point, thus decreasing the minuend. Subtracting negative integers caused the line to "spring down" past the fixed point, thus increasing the minuend. Although the number line (an abstraction) helped him develop his "thinking model," the model itself was a semiconcrete adaptation of it. The model was how he looked at the operation—a particular perspective.

Planning mathematics lessons that will physically involve him (as in the "Find Your Place" game mentioned earlier) provides another perspective relevant to the slow learner. He finds it intolerable to sit behind his desk and "listen and think" throughout a mathematics period when his home environment places value on the physically involved aspects of life. He is seldom "talked to" outside school, but must adjust to a lecture as soon as he sits down in class. As a passive learner, this child will continue to fall behind. As one who is involved physically in what he is learning, he has a chance.

Placing the child with material he can manipulate will be capitalizing on that aspect of his background. The slow learner must have objects and situations he can relate to and is familiar with. The materials mentioned earlier reflect an environment he feels secure in and has learned to operate within. A teacher of migrant children put place-value concepts into proper perspective for his second graders. Since tomato picking is an important part of their lives, he related the ones, tens, and hundreds places to loose tomatoes, a quart basket (which held ten), and a crate (which held ten quart baskets). The children argued from experience that ten tomatoes would hardly fit into a quart basket unless they were cherry tomatoes, but they accepted this as well as the absurdity that ten quarts would fill a normal crate. (In fact, the children did manage to build, from cardboard and tape, a crate that held exactly ten quarts.)

The slow learner places a great deal of emphasis on what is important to him *now*. If the mathematical situations have here-and-now

A FAVORABLE LEARNING ENVIRONMENT 123

aspects, they will interest him. For example, situations involving the sports page will appeal to boys. Box scores with the totals eliminated may be used for practice in column addition and to answer such questions as: Which team had the most hits? Which team won? Or, if it's a doubleheader, How many hits did Mays have in both games? For girls, the food ads may be used to answer such questions as: How much would three pounds of hamburger cost? Given this recipe for a dish, how much would it cost to make it? Such activities bring a relevance to mathematics that is sorely needed by slow learners.

If all mathematics has come easily to the teacher of the slow learner, he may find it difficult, both psychologically and academically, to handle the situations that will arise in his classroom. Although it is not impossible, it would seem to be difficult for a teacher to empathize with the slow learner without recalling some of his own frustrating experiences with mathematics. Daniel Boone was said to be an excellent guide because he too had experienced difficulty finding his way around. However, when asked if he had ever been lost, Dan replied, "No, I was never lost, but once I was a mite bewildered for five days." The teacher of the slow learner should do his best to remember those times when he too was a "mite bewildered."

Arithmetic algorithms in the four fundamental operations really have their basis in counting. Counting and other approaches are tedious and time-consuming, so these quicker methods were developed. It is a fact, however, that these shortcuts are not always meaningful to the slow learner. (Many "meaningful" activities are not.) He is a special person who should not be made to conform to a set plan for working out a problem or to a so-called standard algorithm. For example, slow learners reject practice with the following:

$$432 = 300 + 120 + 12$$
$$-186 = -(100 + 80 + 6)$$

But after gaining some understanding of place value, they can acquire a mastery of

$$\overset{3}{\underset{}{4}}\overset{12}{\underset{}{3}}\overset{12}{\underset{}{2}}$$
$$\underline{-186}$$

Lattice multiplication (or Gelosian), already mentioned, is a workable algorithm for multiplication and is acceptable to the slow learner. The partial sums approach to addition and partial products for multiplication may also be used.

PARTIAL SUMS   PARTIAL PRODUCTS

```
   576              647
+  846            ×   9
   ---            -----
    12               63
   110              360
 1,300            5,400
 -----            -----
 1,422            5,823
```

Since long division presents a special problem to all students, especially slow learners, these children should be given instruction that will lead toward an algorithm they can master and put to use. Perhaps the short-division algorithm with a one-digit divisor will provide the workable process they need.

Finally, long-range goals fail to hold the attention of this child. In most cases, it is better for the child to complete short assignments than to leave long ones incomplete. In *Freedom to Learn* the authors tell about a boy who completed only seven problems out of twenty-seven on an addition test. When the principal asked why he had completed so few, the boy replied, "Sir, I did the first seven correctly; how many do I have to do to show her I can add?" (1, p. 7.)

Attention to the Needs of the Slow Learner

"We are all ignorant, but in different subjects," said wise old Benjamin Franklin. As if to prove the truth of the statement, a university professor was sent to school while in France with the armed forces—but he didn't know the subject was taught in French! He now claims an abiding empathy with the slow learner. And empathy is the basis for mutual respect.

Most children cannot respect a teacher who ridicules and scolds them, or their friends, before a group. The slow learner suffers even more because this teacher has now become a threat and an object of hatred by overtly reinforcing this student's own low opinion of himself as a contributing member of society. It is obvious that the teacher who broke up the fight between the two girls had the right idea when he led them from the room before talking. There are very few times when a scathing verbal attack upon a student can be justified, but to deliver it before his friends and classmates is unthinkable. Perhaps if the teacher alienated only the student receiving the tirade it would not be so disastrous, but he begins to lose the whole class with each stinging harangue he delivers.

A sixth-grade teacher of a low-average group had given the class an assignment in science that required a one-page essay on one of five topics. Clara handed her essay in to the teacher, who found that it was easily the finest job in the class. A few weeks later a test was administered and the same topics were given the class for the essay part of the test. Clara's was so well written and sounded so familiar that the teacher took the essay she had originally written and compared the two. They were almost identical. When the class assembled, the teacher accused Clara, holding the proof over his head before the class. Catching himself, he asked to see the now tearful girl outside the room. Clara pleaded that she did not cheat, that she had written and rewritten her original essay so many times for a "good grade" she knew it by heart. The skeptical teacher held the papers in his hand and asked the frightened Clara to repeat the essay. She did! Word for word! This teacher escorted Clara back into class. He apologized to the whole class and suggested they show better judgment than he did when they deal with people. The class loved him. Clara was a heroine again and immediately established a crush on the young teacher who accused, then vindicated, her. Although it may be human to lose one's temper, it is inhuman not to set the situation right by a very human apology. Teachers are human, and certainly each must show this aspect to the slow learner who comes to him with a long history of human error.

A sail with a skipper who doesn't seem to know the course is a very unnerving experience for both the skipper and the passengers. When a slow learner doesn't know where he is going, what he is supposed to do to get there, or how he knows when he is there, he is confronted with a similar unnerving situation. Insecurity develops; and when the work that is expected of him is not within his grasp, there is an almost complete indifference to the task. Security, then, lies in a confident feeling that one knows where to go, what's coming, and what it's like when he's there. For the slow learner, and all students for that matter, this entails beginning at a place that is comfortable for him, being able to see the next step, and knowing when he has completed this short trip. Many short objectives, each written in performance terms with an example of the behavior given, provide the child with specific references for judging his performance. This is a big step on the road to his feeling secure in an academic environment.

Respect and security are not obtained by clever worksheets and lessons alone. The feeling the teacher has for the students and they for him make or break a year with slow learners. Albert Schweitzer once said of respect, "Only those who have respect for the opinions of others can be of real use to them." Once again, the teacher who reacts to the child's opinions and academic efforts with respect and understanding will be able to reach and guide the child's further thoughts and efforts. Respect is seldom one-way. When it is established through fairness—as by Clara's teacher—and through patience, it becomes a mutual feeling.

A teacher of "low level" third-grade children seldom sat at his desk when he gave assignments. He was in constant movement about the room—sitting with the children, discussing the assignments and the problems, and *listening* to what the students had to say. He listened to mathematics and the nonsense that plays such a big part in the lives of eight-year-olds. He laughed at jokes that had whiskers and "bit" on riddles that came off the Ark. What is more important, he provided the adult half of the conversations with adults his pupils never had at home. He listened, reacted in an adult manner, and, by reacting, gave the children some much needed grown-up experience.

In one seventh grade the teacher makes his assignments from different places about the room. He invariably stands near a boy with his hand on the child's shoulder or neck, giving it a firm squeeze as he is talking. When he's finished he mutters something low to the boy in an aside and walks to his desk. The remarks he makes to the children are inconsequential and include things like "How's it goin'?" "Cool it, man!" and "Here we go again!" but the boys welcome them and hold these times as badges of honor. Should a boy fail to get a problem or worksheet correct, the teacher says something to him to let him know the world hasn't come to an end. "Don't sweat it!" or "Oh, I've done that same thing myself" are typical of the pacifying remarks he makes. If he is forced to do any scolding or harsh talking, he makes it a point never to let the scolded student leave the class without some sign that tells him all is forgiven. He's saying: "It's not *you*, son." He does this with what could be called "hands-on reassurance," mentioned in chapter 1. While walking by the student, he grabs his shoulder briefly and without so much as a glance at the boy walks on by. He stops by the girl's desk with a "How's it goin'? Cute dress!" Then he moves right along. He doesn't say he's sorry, or forget it, or something that amounts to a number of words for the child. He does it with a glance, a smile, a laugh, or a touch. He is *showing* real concern, real friendship, not *talking* about it.

The successful teacher of the slow learner teaches to the strengths of his students. The reasons for this are obvious. Teaching to strengths provides the slow learner with more opportunities for success. A student who seems gifted (yes, gifted) in art may find geometric constructions rewarding and, with the teacher's help, transfer this enthusiasm to other areas of mathematics. Another child, with a fine sense of humor, may well prosper with puzzles and cleverly worded problems. (One slow learner with a sense of humor made the following remarks: "If fractions was important, they'd legalize 'em" and "Ain't *not* doing homework a civil right?") Where chances for success are greater, that is the path to take.

The slow learner is in constant need of reassurance and some signs that his efforts will be rewarded and successful. This means reassurance from the teacher and signs of progress toward a goal that has been set and guided by both the teacher and the student. A fifth-grade teacher takes this so seriously that he uses checks on his class roll to be sure everyone has a reassuring remark each day. Whether this extreme is the answer is doubtful, but the successful teacher accomplishes the same thing in one way or another. Remember, the child's history of failure can change only by his stringing together little successes into big ones, which in turn assure him of progress; and many times a little success, to a slow learner, is that indefinable something the teacher shows that tells him he's doing fine.

Summary

Trading stamps, air conditioning, concrete materials, new texts, learning-activity packages, and every other individualized or nonindividualized approach imaginable mean nothing to the slow learner without a competent classroom manager—a sensitive teacher. This person, armed with a knowledge of his students and their backgrounds, can create in the classroom a compensating environment that is favorable to learning. He does this in various ways. He plans short steps that start with concepts the child already knows so that the child can experience initial success. He varies approaches and activities as well as the schedule to afford the learner the opportunity to find what fits his learning style. His hand is always out with offers of hope through obtainable goals. He encourages, listens, and sets an example. He provides a staff, both emotional and academic, for the slow learner to lean upon. Finally, he puts mathematics into a realistic setting that provides the relevance so lacking in the child's school environment.

Slow learners learn slowly, and to say they learn not at all is a contradiction. Provide a setting that gives them the chance they desire—the chance to learn!

REFERENCES

1. Biggs, Edith E., and James R. MacLean. *Freedom to Learn: An Active Learning Approach to Mathematics.* Don Mills, Ont.: Addison-Wesley (Canada), 1969.
2. Bugelski, Bergen Richard. *The Psychology of Learning Applied to Teaching.* New York: Bobbs-Merrill Co., 1964.
3. Davis, Robert B., et al. *Supplementary Modern Mathematics for Grades 1 through 9: Inservice Course No. 1 for Teachers* (Signed Numbers, Variables, Functions, and Cartesian Coordinates). Webster Groves, Mo.: Madison Project, 1966.
4. Fitzgerald, William M., et al. *Laboratory Manual for Elementary Mathematics.* Edited by John Wagner. Boston: Prindle, Weber & Schmidt, 1970.

5

Adjustment of Instruction (Elementary School)

CHARLOTTE W. JUNGE

One of the most important facts revealed by educational assessment in mathematics instruction is the wide range of achievement levels in any class in our schools. A recent study (see table 5.1) shows the

TABLE 5.1
VARIABILITY IN SCORES ON SECTIONS OF THE
CALIFORNIA ARITHMETIC ACHIEVEMENT TEST
OF 100 CHILDREN IN GRADE 6.1 WITH
IQs RANGING FROM 90 TO 100

	RAW SCORES			GRADE SCORES		
	Lowest	Highest	Mean	Lowest	Highest	Mean
I. Reasoning						
A. Meanings	2	13	8.6	2.7	8.0+	5.7
B. Signs and Symbols	5	14	11.8	3.4	7.4	6.2
C. Problems	1	12	7.0	2.6	8.0+	5.4
Totals on A, B, C	16	35	27.4	3.9	7.7	5.9
II. Fundamentals						
D. Addition	4	15	10.0	3.6	8.4	6.0
E. Subtraction	1	15	9.6	3.4	8.0+	5.9
F. Multiplication	3	15	7.5	4.5	8.0+	5.8
G. Division	3	15	8.7	4.4	7.9	6.1
Totals D, E, F, G	21	52	35.7	4.8	7.4	6.0

NOTE: Reprinted by permission of the publisher from *Discovering Meanings in Elementary School Mathematics*, 5th ed., by Foster E. Grossnickle, Leo J. Brueckner, and John Reckzeh (New York: Holt, Rinehart & Winston, 1968), table 18.2, p. 402. © 1947, 1953, 1959, 1963, and 1968 by Holt, Rinehart & Winston, Inc.

diverse scores made on a test given to sixth-grade students selected at random from the whole country (11, p. 402).

Note that on test C the grade scores range from 2.6 to 8.0+. On test E they range from 2.4 to 8.0+. The ranges are wider on tests of single skills than for the general abilities included in the totals.

Although this table represents but one set of data, its scores are typical of achievement scores in mathematics, and it portrays the difficulty of trying to teach the same mathematics lesson to all pupils. The able learner is not challenged to the full extent of his ability, and the slow learner meets steady frustration from tasks not paced to his level of achievement. It is not possible to maintain adequate levels of achievement for each child by giving standard prescriptions.

However, the most common practice among teachers of mathematics is to have all children work with the same instructional materials and to assign the same exercises to all. A survey of the intraclass grouping practices of 1,392 teachers in grades K-6 showed that only 33 percent of these teachers grouped pupils for arithmetic instruction. The majority did not believe grouping for mathematics instruction was as important as grouping for reading (2, p. 310.)

The fact that instruction in mathematics is still largely total-class instruction may be the result of failure to understand the proper use of new teaching materials, the concern for excellence and the maintenance of high standards, a lack of suitable instructional materials commensurate with the range of abilities within the class, or the fact that current curricula are described in terms of class or grade-level achievement.

The Nuffield Project (1), which is being developed in England, is a notable exception to this trend. The project directors seek to identify clearly defined developmental stages in a child's growth and to develop a curriculum around these stages. This project suggests a new approach to the organization of learning experiences in mathematics, one in which instruction is individualized and children do not necessarily move together as a group. Booklets from the Nuffield Project describe learning activities and tell exactly how children can work individually and in small groups in making mathematical discoveries and in recording their findings.

Diagnosing Pupil Performance

The slow learner, while resembling the average and the above average student in general physical development, chronological age, and interests common to his age group, may not learn intellectual things at the same rate as other children, owing either to lack of potentiality or to personal and emotional factors that interfere with the ability to achieve. Grossnickle writes that "the methods by which slow learners master the concepts and skills of mathematics are not unique or strikingly different from those used by children of greater learning ability. Slow learners, however, cannot learn skills as rapidly as children of higher ability." (11, p. 421.) Smith refers to research by W. M. Cruickshank indicating that retarded learners (1) are reasonably like other children in areas of computation, although they are more careless than average children and use more "primitive" habits, such as making marks and counting on their fingers, (2) have greater difficulty in identifying and understanding which process should be used in problem solving, (3) lack skill in separating irrelevant facts from the significant dimensions of a problem, and (4) have greater difficulty with the reading and language peculiar to arithmetic (26, p. 163).

One of the first responsibilities teachers have in adjusting instruction for the slow learner is to develop and use procedures for diagnosing learning difficulties and determining readiness for new learning. These procedures should focus not only on the types of errors made by each child but also on the processes used by the student in solving mathematical problems.

There are basically four ways to proceed in diagnosing pupil performance:

1. *Observe the child at work.* Note his patterns of study, his attitude toward his work, his interest or lack of interest in it. Observe his habits of work. Does he approach his assigned tasks with some plan, or does he seem to simply "try anything once"? Is he overly dependent on classmates for help? Conversely, are classmates "helping" by doing his work for him rather than helping him think through his problem? Observations can be facilitated by the use of checklists and attitude scales; but there is no substitute for the good teacher's careful, clinical observation in determining difficulties met by children in learning mathematics.

2. *Interview the pupil.* Have the pupil "think aloud" and tell the steps he has used in solving a problem. This is particularly helpful in locating errors in thinking, as well as in computation.

Develop short diagnostic exercises in which the child works without paper or pencil and responds orally to the teacher's questions.

This technique is particularly valuable in determining readiness for new learning. For example, the teacher can use the previous knowledge of the child in diagnosing his readiness to discover such relationships as

$$8 + 6 = 10 + 4$$

Ask the child to give "other names" for 6, such as

$$6 = 2 + 4$$

Ask what must be added to 8 to make 10:

$$8 + 2 = 10$$

Ask the child to study this exercise:

$$8 + 6 = 8 + (2 + 4)$$
$$(8 + 2) + 4 = \square$$

Encourage the child to take these steps mentally, using manipulative materials when they facilitate his thinking.

Provide opportunities for the children to estimate answers and to explain their thinking in arriving at the estimates. For example:

$$\begin{array}{r} 42 \\ -26 \\ \hline \end{array}$$

Slow child: More than 10; I count 26, 36, then [counting on fingers] 37, 38, 39, 40, 41, 42. It's 6 more than 10.
Slow child: About 20; if 42 was 46, it would be 20. So it's a little less than 20.
Slow child: About 20; I think 20 from 40.
Bright child: Think 20 from 42 is 22; take away 6.
Bright child: Think $(46 - 26) - 4$.

Tape recordings can be made of these interviews and the child's responses can be carefully studied to determine errors in thinking, faulty logic, and inaccuracies in computation. Portable video tape recorders are valuable tools in diagnosis. Videotaped interviews permit the teacher to observe student reaction while studying the mental processes used by the child. Recordings of class activities permit the teacher to assess the success of her work with children, and are helpful in planning follow-up lessons.

3. *Analyze written work.* Study the students' written assignments

(diagrams, examples, and problem solutions) to determine what kinds of errors are made and how often they are made, as well as to discover any errors being made by the entire class. Charts of the results of this analysis will be of assistance in arranging individual practice and small-group work.

Low achievement in mathematics is frequently accompanied by low achievement in reading comprehension and in language skill (8;25). In fact, low achievement in mathematics may be due to difficulty in reading and comprehending the precise vocabulary and abstract symbolism of modern programs. (See the discussion that follows under "Instruction in Reading Mathematics.") Mathematics shorthand (If $\triangle ABC \cong \triangle XYZ$, then $\overline{AB} \cong \overline{XY}$) can create serious problems for slow learners not yet ready for abstract symbolism. Diagnosis should include an analysis of the child's ability to read and comprehend directions, verbal problems, and mathematical symbolism.

4. *Use tests as clinical tools.* A well-coordinated testing program consisting of standardized achievement and diagnostic tests, teacher-made tests, and diagnostic assignments is a necessary part of a successful teaching program for slow learners. Available evidence (25) indicates that slow learners experience relatively less difficulty with computation than with those aspects of mathematics involving reasoning; however, assessment should be made of computation as well as reasoning and problem solving.

Standardized diagnostic and achievement test results provide a perspective of the class as a whole. An item analysis of errors and a determination of the nature of the errors on these tests are basic to planning appropriate learning experiences. Schacht (25) found, for example, that inability to read and comprehend diagrams is a common source of errors that low achievers make in problem solving, common fractions, and measurement. Failure to understand the decimal numeration system was also found to be a common difficulty in the four operations with whole numbers, common fractions, and decimal fractions.

Diagnostic assignments prepared by teachers and designed for easy scoring have special value in helping children appraise their progress and in reinforcing learning. The following are illustrations of kinds of items that might be used:

a) Here are some ways to name the number 12:

$$8 + 4 \quad 3 + 9 \quad 15 - 3 \quad 3 \times 4$$

Can you think of still other ways?

b) Write two facts shown by this number line.

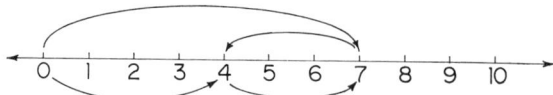

c) Write the missing numerals.

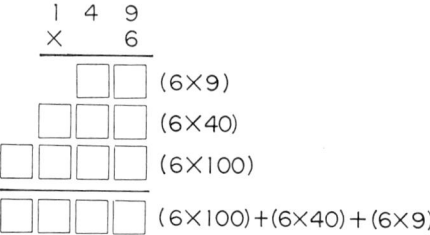

d) Here are sets of multiples for 2, 3, and 4:

$$A = \{2, 4, 6, 8, 10, 12, 14, 16, \ldots\}$$
$$B = \{3, 6, 9, 12, 15, 18, \ldots\}$$
$$C = \{4, 8, 12, 16, 20, \ldots\}$$

List four more multiples in each set. Name the multiples in set *A* that are in set *B*.
Which of these multiples are also in set *C*? What is the least common multiple of 2, 3, 4?

e) Finish this division example:

$$\begin{array}{r} 1 \\ 35\overline{\smash{)}6475} \\ \underline{35} \\ 29 \end{array}$$

f) Write an equation or inequality for these English sentences:
   (1) I am thinking of a number. Multiply it by 2, and the product is 56.
   (2) I am thinking of a number. Multiply it by 4, and the product is less than 32.
   (3) I am thinking of a number. Divide it by 3, and the quotient is 29.

Diagnostic assignments may be used as periodic tests, as inventories prior to introduction of more complex ideas, or as single items embedded in each lesson to assess understanding and guide review and reteaching.

Diagnosis of learning difficulties is not an easy affair; but it makes instruction easier in the end. Constant, careful diagnosis eases the work of the teacher and improves learning for children.

Educational Programs for Slow Learners

Basically, there are three ways of providing a setting in which children have an opportunity to realize their full potential. The first is through special forms of classroom organization, the second is through curriculum adjustments, and the third requires special instructional adjustments by the classroom teacher. The first two of these ways are discussed below as subtopics of this section. The third way, special instructional adjustment, the writer considers important enough to merit a separate section—"Strategies for Teaching Slow Learners"—which constitutes the latter part of this chapter.

Organizing the classroom for learning

Homogeneous grouping. Grouping on the basis of achievement and/or intelligence is one approach used frequently to provide for individual differences. This may result in one of these arrangements:

1. Special classes are organized for slow learners in mathematics. Here both content and methods of teaching are adjusted and class size is small, with work highly individualized.

2. Remedial classes enable slow learners to be removed from their regular class group for a specified number of periods a week. These remedial classes function best at late third-grade level, for a faulty foundation in fundamental understandings and skills blocks growth in the application of these understandings and skills to the more complex operations of the middle school years. The goal of remedial instruction at this point is to return the child to his regular classroom as soon as achievement warrants.

3. All mathematics classes are scheduled at the same hour and pupils are assigned to sections appropriate to their learning level. This arrangement provides each teacher with a small group of children having like abilities in mathematics and permits her to devote full class time to their needs. At the end of the class period the children return to their respective homerooms. Reading groups are frequently scheduled in a similar manner.

Mathematics laboratories. These are special classrooms equipped with individual study centers, or carrels, and a wide variety of manipulative and visual materials as well as printed materials at various levels of difficulty. Pupils are referred to the laboratory by the homeroom teacher for a few periods each week. Close cooperation between the laboratory teacher and the homeroom teacher is essential in maintaining a consistent pattern of instruction for each pupil.

Nongraded team teaching. This organization provides for small-group and individualized study as well as large-group instruction. One member of the teaching team should be a special teacher with preparation in mathematics as well as elementary education. This teacher guides instruction in mathematics and assists other members of the team in planning learning activities for small groups and individuals.

Computer-assisted instruction. A new development in classroom organization is the use of computers in diagnosing difficulties and prescribing appropriate instructional activities for individual pupils. Computer-assisted, individualized instruction is being tested in a variety of school situations and at various grade levels as a means of helping teachers with the arduous tasks of diagnosis, remediation, and drill. Notable among these experiments are those under the direction of Patrick Suppes at Stanford University.

Curriculum adjustments for slow learners

Lerch and Kelly state that the program of study for slow learners "should be a mathematics program in the true sense, and not primarily a remedial arithmetic program" (16, p. 232).

Remedial instruction has only immediate usefulness and temporary value. It is useful for minor problems but does not strike deep at the roots of any problem. The slow learner is in need of a program of study that will give insight into the operations and relationships of mathematics. The goals of instruction should be immediate, tangible, and practical. The curriculum should allow for flexibility and the application of mathematical processes in social and vocational situations. Specifically the curriculum should meet these conditions:

1. It should be well structured and systematic as well as paced to the individual's level of maturity. Pupils whose development is below average need a longer period of time than the average student to master new content. The timetable within a sequence of learning activities should enable pupils to proceed at a pace that will motivate and challenge but not frustrate.

2. It should establish a minimal program which includes new approaches to computation, new treatment of traditional topics (measurement, common fractions, graphs, and problem solving), and selected new topics (Paschal indicates that disadvantaged children appear to think in spatial terms and that instruction for these children might begin with a unit on geometry [20, p. 6].)

3. It should make wide use of visual and manipulative materials, progressing toward abstract representation but at a more deliberate pace than for average and above-average pupils.

4. It should give special help on the vocabulary of mathematics. Precise terminology should not be required until the teacher is sure understanding is developed.

5. It should include instruction on how to locate information, how to use the textbook, how to study, how to remember, and how to check computation.

6. It should relate mathematics to other curricular areas, particularly to science, social studies, and art.

Strategies for Teaching Slow Learners

Attitudes toward mathematics are of great importance among all students but are particularly important among those who experience difficulty in learning. Negative attitudes of fear, dislike, frustration, and outright rejection are often firmly fixed among these students. They do not respond to long-range educational goals. Their goals are immediate, practical, and self-centered. For this reason it is necessary to provide such a student with problems related to his experiences and to the real world in which he lives.

Familiar experiences

1. *The school lunchroom* can provide many opportunities for applying basic addition and subtraction understandings. A menu and price list, such as shown in table 5.2, can be placed on the chalkboard and toy money used for the transactions.

Every day give each child 25¢ to spend. In the beginning, have the children tell orally the selections they would make from the menu in addition to the regular lunch. The computation should be done by the individual child and checked by the class. After a few days ask the children to buy certain extras for a given amount and compute the change from a quarter. (Buy some fruit, milk, and cookies;

TABLE 5.2

Menu	Price
Regular lunch	20¢
Milk (one glass)	5¢
Bread (one slice)	1¢
Rolls (each)	2¢
Cookies (each)	2¢
Ice cream (one cup)	5¢
Orange	3¢
Apple	3¢

buy cookies and ice cream; buy a roll and milk, etc.) Finally "story problems" may be written by the children, placed in a card file, and used for additional practice in problem solving.

2. Readiness for multiplication and division can be built by *marching activities* similar to those used in the gymnasium. For example, select eight children and have them march single file, in pairs, and four abreast. Count the marchers by ones, twos, and fours. Using felt-board cutouts or magnetic disks, picture the groups as in figure 5.1. Children can observe that an increase in the size of the marching groups shortens the length of the marching line.

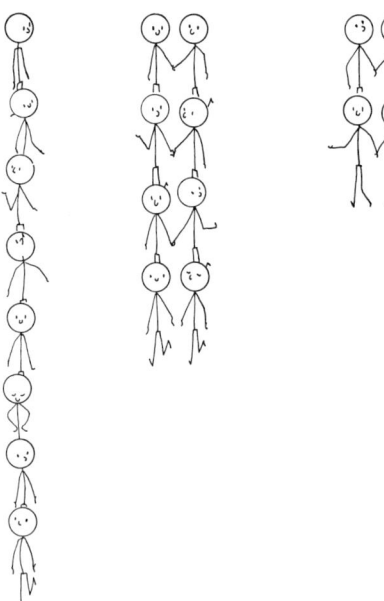

Fig. 5.1

ADJUSTMENT OF INSTRUCTION (ELEMENTARY SCHOOL) 139

Repeat this activity, using groups of six, ten, or twelve children. Each time illustrate the marching groups with objects or diagrams (arrays). Finally ask the children to use objects or diagrams to show all the ways a group of eighteen children can march so that the smaller groupings are the same in size (ones, twos, threes, sixes, nines).

Later these diagrams can be associated with appropriate multiplication and division facts, as in figure 5.2.

4 twos are 8 $4 \times 2 = 8$
2 fours are 8 $2 \times 4 = 8$
In 8 there are 4 sets of two.
In 8 there are 2 sets of four.
$8 \div 2 = 4$ and $8 \div 4 = 2$

Fig. 5.2

3. Current events can often provide the motivation for introducing new concepts or applying concepts already learned. One such activity in a sixth-grade classroom grew out of *the launch of Apollo 13*. At the time of launch the teacher carefully noted (from the TV screen) the initial launch data with respect to altitude, rate (feet per second), and distance down range from the launch site. These data were placed in two tables, one showing altitude and speed, the other showing altitude and distance down range in the first ten minutes of flight.

A large grid was placed on the chalkboard; and the children, with teacher assistance, made two graphs, using the information in the tables. The point at which Apollo 13 began its "pitch program" became readily apparent on the one graph. On the other, the children noted the vertical rise of Apollo 13 in early flight and the flattened trajectory as it moved at increasing velocity into earth orbit. Through this activity words and figures took on new meaning for these sixth-grade children. Incidentally, much computation was involved in changing feet per second to nautical miles per hour!

4. In another sixth-grade classroom, problems related to the spring *"paint up, clean up" activities* in the community were used to create interest in mathematics and to provide practice in problem solving. Many examples of the use of ratio were found in mixing liquid fertilizers, determining the amount of grass seed needed for a particular plot of ground, and mixing paint for prospective home repairs.

The girls in the class found and solved problems using jam and jelly recipes that called for a certain ratio of juice or pulp to sugar.

5. At holiday time a project related to *mailing parcel-post packages* provides opportunities for developing skill and understanding in measuring. Have packages of different shapes for children to measure. Apply the postal regulation that limits the weight to 70 pounds and requires that the package not exceed 100 inches in length and girth combined. (Girth is the distance around the widest part of the package.) Figure 5.3 gives one example.

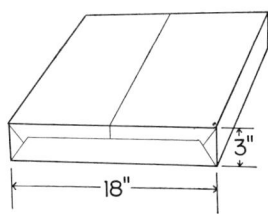

Length 18″
Girth 42″
       60″

Fig. 5.3

6. Geometry is implicit in many of the out-of-school activities of children. In one classroom a study of right triangles was introduced in the following way:

Teacher: "On your way to school this morning, how many cut across a vacant lot?"

Almost every pupil had crossed a lot somewhere en route. The others recalled crossing a vacant lot when going to a nearby store, or to church, or to a friend's house.

Teacher: "Why did you cut across the lot?"

Almost in a chorus they answered, "Because it's shorter that way!"

Teacher: "How do you know it's shorter? Could you prove it?"

The pupils couldn't prove it exactly, but they knew it must be shorter because everybody went that way whenever he could.

They were all anxious to know how to prove it arithmetically, so the teacher asked several children to go to the chalkboard and draw a diagram of themselves crossing a lot. They were directed to "be sure to name the intersecting streets."

When the drawings were finished, the pupils observed that all the figures had the same shape even though they were different in size—they all were triangles. Other pupils went to the board and measured the corner angles in these triangles. They discovered that all were ninety-degree angles, or right angles.

On the playground the children proved by actual measurement that by cutting across the lot they did save distance, and how much they saved. (The same type of demonstration can be done in a gymnasium.) Then back in the classroom, where the original triangles were still on the board, the children identified the base and altitude of each. (In an earlier study of triangles in general the children had become familiar with base and altitude.)

Teacher: "Now in the right triangle we give a name to the third line also. We call it the *hypotenuse.* See if you can tell me three facts that you know about the hypotenuse from what we have said and talked about so far. These facts refer to length and position."

All agreed that (1) it is the longest of all three lines; (2) it is a shorter line than the base and altitude added together; and (3) it is the side opposite the right angle.

7. Slow learners will develop basic understandings in geometry much more readily if frequent reference is made to the *use* of geometry in daily life.

a) A fourth-grade teacher skilled in the use of the camera took many colored photographs of buildings, bridges, streets, cars, airplanes, plants, and animals (fish, turtles, etc.) and had the children study them to find different shapes. The basic shapes—circle, square, rectangle, triangle, and pentagon—were identified again and again. Illustrations of point, ray, line segment, and line were also easily identified in the photographs.

b) Requiring young children to bring a toy or object from home to illustrate a geometric shape being studied adds meaning to their understanding of space and shape. Permit the child to describe the object he brings, naming the shape it represents.

c) In learning to understand the concept of volume, slow learners will profit from filling various familiar containers with water or sand and comparing the sizes of the containers by finding which hold the same amount or which of two containers will hold more. To help them find volume more precisely, it may be best to use cubes or rectangular prisms that hold an exact number of cubes of equal size (13, p. 427).

d) Often a child who has no difficulty in finding the perimeter or the area of a rectangle or a square will fail to see a relationship between what he has done and finding the amount of fencing needed for a yard or the amount of tile needed for a bathroom wall. "Matching activities" similar to the following may be used to build understanding of such relationships:

Match each item in column I with either item a or item b in colunm II.

I	II
What must I find when I—	I must find:
1. frame a picture?	a. perimeter
2. build a fence?	b. area
3. tile a bathroom wall?	
4. cover a floor with linoleum?	
5. measure glass for a window?	
6. put tape around a table cloth?	

Patterns and relationships

The slow-learning pupil has acquired some understanding and some skill. He needs the kind of instruction that enables him to collect in a unified way the things he has learned and helps him extend these learnings into new situations by careful emphasis on patterns and relationships. Here are several illustrations:

1. When pupils are involved in using two-place numerals in adding and subtracting, help them see relationships to previously learned concepts. For example,

$$4 + 3 = 7$$

so 4 tens and 3 tens are 7 tens, and

$$40 + 30 = 70$$

Illustrate with manipulative materials (bundles of tens and ones, dimes and pennies, tens blocks, Dienes multibase blocks, the abacus, etc.) and record the results with numerals. One teacher (10, p. 231) found that using a color code for place value helped the slow learner at this point. If money is used as a visual aid, the cents column in addition or subtraction is recorded with blue chalk or crayon, the dimes are recorded with red, and so on. This same color reference is used with the abacus; blue beads mark units, red beads mark tens, and so on. Once place value is understood, the color code is replaced and an addition grid or table is developed using multiples of ten, as in figure 5.4.

2. In developing number patterns with young children it is helpful to proceed as follows:

   a) Use large wooden beads (as in fig. 5.5) or kindergarten blocks

ADJUSTMENT OF INSTRUCTION (ELEMENTARY SCHOOL)

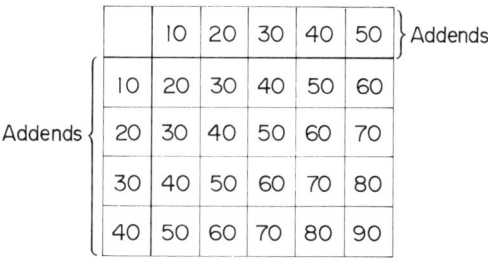

Fig. 5.4

arranged in a pattern dependent on color. Show the pattern once, repeat it in part, and have the children tell what should be added next.

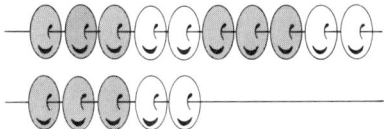

Fig. 5.5

b) Repeat the activity, this time varying the pattern in terms of shape (fig. 5.6).

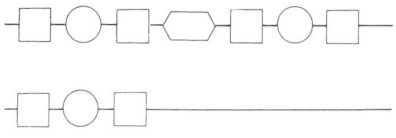

Fig. 5.6

c) Follow this with a pattern involving both shape and color (fig. 5.7).

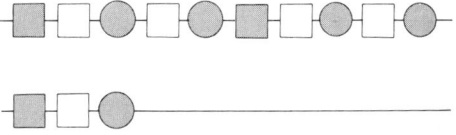

Fig. 5.7

d) Using rhythm sticks, tap out a pattern; ask the children to listen carefully and repeat the pattern by tapping on their desks. Permit the children to make up their own patterns to use with their classmates.

e) Ask the children to listen to a pattern tapped on a small drum and to record the pattern by using, first, markers, then tallies, and finally numerals. For example,

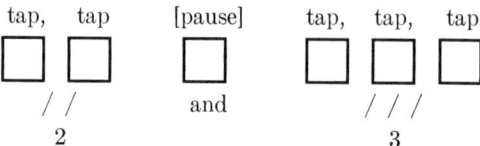

f) Build patterns using numerals. Begin with a number chart, erasing or removing numerals in a pattern. Inquire what numeral should be removed next.

1, —, 3, —, 5, —, 7, —, 9, 10, 11, etc.
2, —, 4, —, 6, —, 8, —, 10, 11, 12, etc.
10, —, 8, —, 6, 5, 4, 3, 2, 1

g) Start a number pattern on the chalkboard; ask the children to write the next three (or five) numerals in the pattern. These may be built to develop increasingly complex relationships.

2, 5, 8, 11, —, —, —
2, 4, 8, 16, —, —, —
3, 4, 6, 9, 13, —, —, —

3. When children are developing skill in basic multiplication facts, the following types of charts and diagrams can be used to build understanding of the commutative property, of the relationships between multiplication and division, and of patterns that exist in different multiplication tables.

a) Use arrays to visualize the commutative property. These may be pictured easily on graph paper. (See fig. 5.8.)

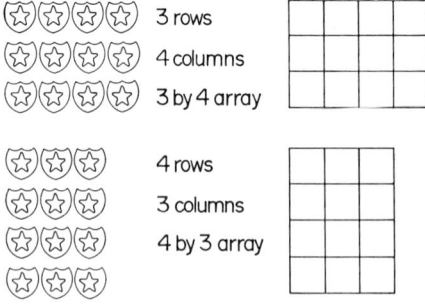

Fig. 5.8

b) Use number lines to visualize relationships and patterns.

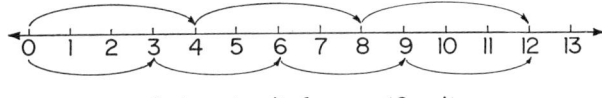

3 steps 4 units long = 12 units
4 steps 3 units long = 12 units

```
0    3    6    9    12   15   18   21   24   27   30
     1    2    3    4    5    6    7    8    9    10
```

This product line can be read "2 threes are 6; 3 threes are 9," and so forth, or "In 12 there are 4 threes; in 15 there are 5 threes."

c) Multiplication tables may be built first on an array pattern.

```
0 0 0 0 ← 4 ⎫
           ⎬ ← 8 ⎫
0 0 0 0    ⎭     ⎬ ← 12 ⎫
                 ⎭      ⎬ ← 16
0 0 0 0                 ⎪
                        ⎪
0 0 0 0                 ⎭
```

This array is read:

1 four = 4	1 × 4
2 fours = 8	2 × 4
3 fours = 12	3 × 4
4 fours = 16	4 × 4

d) The familiar multiplication table can be studied for patterns, too. In the table here shown, for example, notice that all products

4 × 1 = 4	4 × 6 = 24
4 × 2 = 8	4 × 7 = 28
4 × 3 = 12	4 × 8 = 32
4 × 4 = 16	4 × 9 = 36
4 × 5 = 20	4 × 10 = 40

are even numbers. Notice also that the ones digits form a repeating pattern of 4, 8, 2, 6, 0; 4, 8, 2, 6, 0. Comparing this table with that where 8 is a factor reveals similarities.

8 × 1 = 8	8 × 6 = 48
8 × 2 = 16	8 × 7 = 56
8 × 3 = 24	8 × 8 = 64
8 × 4 = 32	8 × 9 = 72
8 × 5 = 40	8 × 10 = 80

4. Practice should be more than a drill. Activities given for practice, which may be developed first as small-group or class activities and later used for individual study, should stress the seeing of patterns, the verbalizing of relationships, the search for clues that will help children use known learnings to solve new problems:

$$6 \times 30 = 180, \quad \text{so} \quad 12 \times 30 = \underline{}$$
$$7 \times 90 = 630, \quad \text{so} \quad 14 \times 90 = \underline{}$$
$$20 \times 5 = 100, \quad \text{so} \quad 20 \times 10 = \underline{}$$

$$32 \div 4 = 8, \quad \text{so} \quad 64 \div 4 = \underline{}$$
$$\text{and} \quad 64 \div 8 = \underline{}$$
$$80 \div 8 = 10, \quad \text{so} \quad 160 \div 8 = \underline{}$$
$$\text{and} \quad 160 \div 10 = \underline{}$$

5. At upper-grade levels, visual materials and diagrams prove useful in extending measurement to division of rational numbers. Here are two teaching strategies:

a) Start with a verbal problem: "Tom has 12 inches of paper tape. He wants to make as many ½-inch labels as he can for his rock collection. How many labels can he make?"

$$12" \div \tfrac{1}{2}" = \square$$

Provide each child with 12 inches of adding-machine tape and a ruler. Mark the tape in inches and half inches. Summarize:

In 1 inch there are 2 half inches.
In 2 inches there are 4 half inches.
In 3 inches there are 6 half inches.

So in 12 inches there are 2×12, or 24, half inches. Tom can make 24 labels.

b) Have the students use graph paper marked in 1-inch areas to solve this equation:

$$15\tfrac{1}{2}" \div 1\tfrac{1}{2}" = \square$$

Ask them to measure 15½ units on a grid like the one shown in reduced size in figure 5.9. Select 1½ inches as the unit of measure. Say, "Count to find the number of 1½ inches in the grid."

ADJUSTMENT OF INSTRUCTION (ELEMENTARY SCHOOL) 147

"There are 10 pieces (sized 1 ½ inches) and ½ inch over."

Fig. 5.9

Next have them count the half inches in 15 ½ inches. Say, "How many pieces 1 ½ inches in size can be measured on 31 half inches?" By folding the 1 ½-inch measure, help the children see that the ½ inch over is ⅓ of 1 ½. So

$$\frac{31}{2} \div \frac{3}{2} = 10\frac{1}{3}$$

Repeat this procedure many times, using other examples solved with graph paper and/or number lines to build understanding of measuring with like units as background for division with a fraction divisor.

Instructional activities that build step by step are important in teaching slow learners. A central idea or concept needs to be analyzed carefully and developed in such a way that the pupil is led from one level of learning to the next. Drill will be a necessary part of these activities, but it should be delayed until the pupil has some insight into the processes on which he must drill. *A slow learner is not helped by mere repetition. An enlarged view, carefully developed, is better for him than endless review and repetition.* The opening of a larger view is illustrated in the preceding paragraphs that describe a variety of visual and symbolic approaches to building understanding of the multiplication of whole numbers. It does a slow learner little good to be supplied with one explanation or one way of solving a problem. He needs to experience the understanding by development through as many sensory modalities as are useful (seeing, hearing, touching, writing) and with a variety of applications to his own experiences. The steps in learning need to be so carefully scaled that his progress toward mastery is like walking a ramp rather than climbing a stair!

Instruction in reading mathematics

Direct instruction in vocabulary, reading, and the use of verbal and symbolic cues in problem solving is basic to teaching slow learners in mathematics.

Learning the language of mathematics, like learning any language, develops as a result of interaction of the learner with his environment. Many slow learners are retarded in educational development because contact with their social and physical environment was limited in their preschool years. A deficiency in verbal development in these early years has an adverse effect on the pupil's later ability to abstract ideas, to use symbolic cues, and to solve verbal problems.

Reading in mathematics requires (1) careful attention to detail, (2) a questioning, critical, reflective frame of mind, and (3) a familiarity with mathematical language and symbolism as well as familiarity with the "usual," more general, vocabulary and symbolism. In the study of mathematics, children must read and interpret words that carry not only a usually understood meaning but also a special meaning. Words such as *set, power, point, product, root, rational, irrational,* require special interpretation, since many pupils already have nonmathematical referents for them.

Similarly, the precise symbolism and terminology in today's curricula must be carefully taught to make certain that children can not only "read," or recognize, them but also understand them. Examples are *congruent, rectangle, plane, region, array, set of points, rotation.* Even a cursory examination of a child's textbook impresses the reader with extensive use of mathematical shorthand. For example, such symbols as $\therefore, =, \neq, <, >, \leq, \geq, \pm, \cup, \cap, \sim, \overleftrightarrow{AB}$, $\overleftrightarrow{CD}$, and $\angle CDE$ are in common use in elementary textbooks, as is such punctuation as

$$A = \{1, 3, 5, 7, \cdots\},$$
$$B = \{1, 3, 5, 7\},$$
$$(4 + 6) + 3 = 4 + (6 + 3),$$

and

$$346_{eight} = [3 \times (8 \times 8) + (4 \times 8) + 6]$$

These words, signs, and symbols seldom appear in isolation: they are usually integral parts of grammatically correct mathematical sentences. Contemporary programs compound reading problems for children who have difficulty with handling abstract ideas and with reading per se. Consequently, systematic instruction in reading mathematics must be a part of any program of study for slow learners.

Lyda and Duncan (17) recommend that all teachers consider the feasibility of incorporating direct study of quantitative vocabulary as an important aspect of the class period in arithmetic. Their study with second-grade children showed that direct study of quantitative vocabulary contributed significantly to growth in problem solving.

In describing a Miami, Florida, project on teaching culturally disadvantaged children, Paschal advocates an audiolingual method. This, says Paschal, "is basically a method of sustained practice in the use of the language in the relationship of teacher-speaker, student-hearer, student-speaker situations" (21, p. 370). The teacher in this project always used the correct term in presenting the idea but did not insist that the child use the correct term at the initial learning level. Some activities used by this teacher follow:

1. The teacher displayed models of circles, triangles, rectangles, and squares and asked the children to identify them. If necessary, the teacher supplied the name of each shape and the children touched the models, ran their fingers around them, and found other objects in the room shaped like them.

2. The children placed their hands behind them, and the teacher placed an object in the hands of each, who told what shape he had by feeling the object carefully.

3. Different geometric shapes were placed around the room before the children arrived. When they had gathered, the teacher held up an object shaped like a triangle and had the children identify it. Then they were asked to look around the room and find other objects shaped like the triangle. This game continued with other geometric shapes.

As many sense modalities as possible should be used in helping slow learners form quantitative concepts. Cuisenaire rods, magnetic disks, felt pieces, and attribute blocks are excellent at this level. As objects are manipulated the pupil tells what he sees, what relationships he observes, and the teacher supplies more precise terminology where it is needed. The pace of instruction in building vocabulary and mathematical readiness will of necessity be slow. Stable understandings will not develop if instruction is rushed and symbolic representation introduced too soon.

At upper grade levels when children have gained some facility in reading, such activities as the following can be used in building vocabulary:

1. Words can be matched with definitions, objects, or pictures.
2. Geometric figures, parts of drawings, and steps in computation can be labeled.
3. The meaning of a phrase, a concept, or a word can be demonstrated by using concrete materials or diagrams. For example, the meaning of *average* can be demonstrated by the use of books, coins, or blocks. A mirror may be used to demonstrate symmetry, and congruence can be shown by placing one geometric shape upon another.
4. A picture dictionary of mathematical terms and meanings can be constructed, as a project for an individual pupil or for a small group.
5. Bulletin-board displays can be designed in which terms or definitions are connected by yarn to an appropriate diagram, picture, object, or example. This same approach can be developed on an electric board and used for individual practice.

When reading from a mathematics textbook slow learners should be given the same kind of direct vocabulary instruction as is commonly used in reading classes. New or difficult words or phrases should be identified and placed on the chalkboard or on charts for discussion and recognition. Guided silent and oral reading should precede individual solution of verbal problems. Problems should be read silently, discussed orally by the group, and solved individually by each child.

Children who have difficulty in reading and solving verbal problems need to develop a *way* of reading mathematics:

1. A first reading to get an overall picture
2. A more careful, slower reading for details
3. Scanning to locate specific data
4. Occasional reading between the lines to note implied data necessary for solution
5. Thinking about relationships in the problem before attempting solution

ADJUSTMENT OF INSTRUCTION (ELEMENTARY SCHOOL) 151

The mathematics textbook should be used, on occasion, in the reading class, and attention centered on reading for specific purposes rather than on solving problems. One skill at a time might be selected for this instruction. For example, the student might read—

1. to locate specific information;
2. to select appropriate data (to build an awareness of extraneous data);
3. to perceive relationships;
4. to interpret maps, scales, charts, graphs, diagrams, etc.;
5. to determine the question(s) asked;
6. to determine the operation(s) to use;
7. to get the main thought and express it in the student's own words.

Games, puzzles, and recreations

Games, puzzles, and recreations are appealing to almost all children. Paschal, in discussing a program for disadvantaged children, advocates the use of games in maintaining class attention and in giving practice in listening and speaking (21, p. 372). He indicates that the games used for these children should be sharply defined and structured, and the rules definite and easily understood. Furthermore, he recommends games that are person-centered and concerned with direct action and visible results.

Games may be used for practice, such as the various forms of bingo that are in common use for practicing on multiplication and division facts.

Another game that children find interesting is called "The Top." In the game as illustrated in figure 5.10, you begin with the number

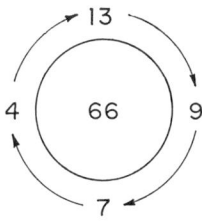

Fig. 5.10

13. You may choose whether to add, subtract, multiply, or divide the numbers. Follow the directions of the arrows. Calculate until

you reach 66. As the game starts, the children shout, "The top is spinning! In turn, each child carries out one operation. The first child may choose to subtract, saying,

$$"13 - 9 = 4"$$

The next child may elect to add, saying,

$$"4 + 7 = 11"$$

The third child may multiply,

$$"11 \times 4 = 44"$$

The next player may subtract,

$$"44 - 13 = 31"$$

The child who reaches 66 wins the game.

"Can You Match Me" is a game that two or more pupils can play on the chalkboard or with figures placed on a feltboard or even with small objects, which can be grouped and regrouped to show the operation called for. One player writes a mathematical expression which can be matched in several ways by other players. For example:

Given:

$$\frac{3 + 17}{4}$$

Matching equivalent expressions:

$$20 \div 4 \qquad \frac{23 - 3}{4} \qquad (2 \times 10) \div 4 \qquad 5 = (3 + 17) \div 4$$

"T Square" is a game that can be used to practice basic facts in any of the four operations. The first player calls out five numbers, which are written on the left side of the T square. He then calls something like "plus 6," "times 7," or "divide by 4," which the players write at the top of the "T" before immediately writing the correct answers on the right side of the "T." The first child to complete the T square with correct solutions wins the game.

+6	×7	÷4
9	4	28
7	6	36
8	8	16
6	5	24
5	3	32

ADJUSTMENT OF INSTRUCTION (ELEMENTARY SCHOOL) 153

A puzzle similar to a magic square is placed on the chalkboard (see fig. 5.11). The children copy it on graph paper and fill in the missing numerals. Similar puzzles can be made simply by changing the numeral in square A or by altering the directions.

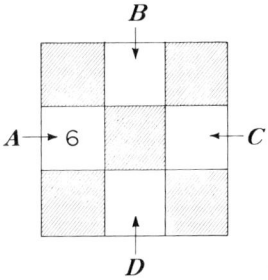

1. B is 6 times as large as A.
2. C is 4 less than B.
3. D is 8 more than A.

(If you work the puzzle correctly, the total of A, B, C, and D is 88.)

Fig. 5.11

Similar games can be found in teacher's guides to textbooks, the *Arithmetic Teacher,* and special books devoted to games and puzzles. A number of the references listed at the end of this chapter include descriptions of games.

Supplementary assignment sheets

Another successful way of adapting instruction to a range of learning abilities is to vary assignments in terms of depth and scope. Supplementary assignment sheets may be prepared in advance in such a way that they can be reused later. These assignments may be enclosed in clear plastic envelopes obtainable at most school and office supply stores, or they may be laminated. In either case the child marks directly on the plastic, using a marking pencil or pen suitable for transparencies. When corrected, the plastic may be wiped clear and reused by other children. Yet another procedure is to place the assignment sheets in file folders and have the child answer on separate sheets or answer strips. Keys for the exercises may be provided, and each child may check his own assignment, noting where he needs further study. For slow-learning children, the assignments should be limited to a few simple items with easily understood directions. Here are a few examples:

STRANGER IN THE FAMILY

In each column find the number sentence that does not belong in the family. Mark it out.

154 THE SLOW LEARNER IN MATHEMATICS

$$4 \times 6 = 24 \quad\quad 4 + 7 = 11$$
$$24 \div 4 = 6 \quad\quad 11 - 4 = 7$$
$$3 \times 8 = 24 \quad\quad 11 - 7 = 4$$
$$6 \times 4 = 24 \quad\quad 11 = 5 + 6$$
$$24 \div 6 = 4 \quad\quad 11 = 7 + 4$$

MAKING CHANGE

How many different ways can you make change for 11¢ which Bill and Joe can share?

Bill	Joe
10¢	1¢

USING THE HUNDRED CHART

Make a chart like the one shown in figure 5.12.
Draw a ring around multiples of 2.
Put a slash mark on the multiples of 3.
Draw a triangle around multiples of 5.

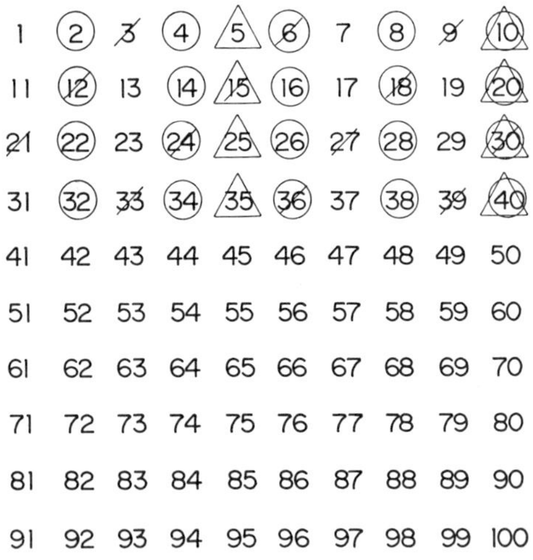

1	2	3	4	5	6	7	8	9	10
11	12	13	14	15	16	17	18	19	20
21	22	23	24	25	26	27	28	29	30
31	32	33	34	35	36	37	38	39	40
41	42	43	44	45	46	47	48	49	50
51	52	53	54	55	56	57	58	59	60
61	62	63	64	65	66	67	68	69	70
71	72	73	74	75	76	77	78	79	80
81	82	83	84	85	86	87	88	89	90
91	92	93	94	95	96	97	98	99	100

Fig. 5.12

WALLPAPER ARITHMETIC

[Provide each child with a set of directions and several sheets of graph paper.]

ADJUSTMENT OF INSTRUCTION (ELEMENTARY SCHOOL) 155

Here is a "3" pattern (fig. 5.13). What would a "2" pattern look like? What would a "9" pattern look like? Would a "5" pattern be attractive?

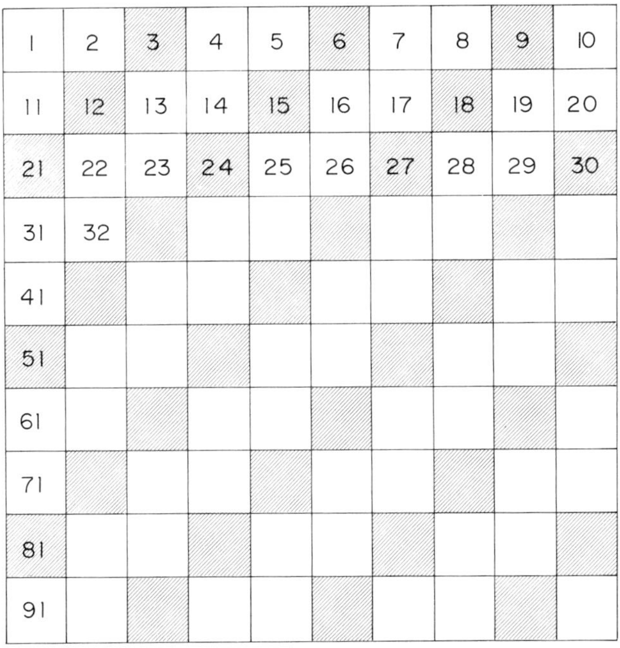

1	2	3	4	5	6	7	8	9	10
11	12	13	14	15	16	17	18	19	20
21	22	23	24	25	26	27	28	29	30
31	32								
41									
51									
61									
71									
81									
91									

Fig. 5.13

MATCHING VERBAL PROBLEMS WITH EQUATIONS

[Prepare sets of verbal problems and equations. Children read the problems and select the appropriate equation for each problem.]

Bill and Tom have 12 marbles.
Jane needs 2 more pennies to buy a 10¢ candy bar.
At 6¢ each, how many candy bars can Tom get for 30¢?
If one can of soup serves 3 children, how many cans are needed for 12 children?

$$2 + N = 10¢$$
$$6 \times N = 30¢$$
$$\triangle + \square = 12$$
$$N \times 3 = 12$$

PRACTICE IN PROBLEM SOLVING

Be careful. These problems have numbers that are not needed. Estimate each answer. Then find the exact answer. Check by comparing.

1. Bob had $1.50. He wanted to buy six 8-ounce packages of cookies at 29¢ a package. Did he have enough money?
2. Jim says that five 18-inch towel racks at $1.39 each should cost about $5 + $2, or $7. Is he right? What is the exact cost?
3. Jack bought five packs of notebook paper for 47¢. There were 50 sheets of paper in each pack. He estimated the cost of one pack to be $\frac{1}{5}$ of 50¢, or _____. Was his estimate a good one?
4. Find the cost of a game at 49¢, a 100-piece jigsaw puzzle at 28¢, and a pencil at 9¢.
5. Jane can get 27-inch-wide gingham for 49¢ a yard and 36-inch-wide gingham for 59¢ a yard. She needs $\frac{1}{2}$ yard of gingham. She has a quarter. Which kind of gingham should she buy?

PRACTICE FOR ESTIMATING QUOTIENTS

Which statements are true? Which are false?

$3 \times 6 < 19$ $3 \times 60 < 190$ $6 \times 90 < 520$
$30 \times 6 < 190$ $6 \times 6 < 52$ $6 \times 900 < 5,200$

Make these sentences true.

$22 = (\square \times 4) + 2$ $220 = (\square \times 40) + 20$
$43 = (\square \times 6) + 1$ $430 = (\square \times 60) + 10$

$19 = (\square \times 3) + \triangle$ $190 = (\square \times 6) + \triangle$
$52 = (\square \times 6) + \triangle$ $520 = (\square \times 60) + \triangle$

Find the quotients. What is the remainder in each example?

$3\overline{)19}$ $30\overline{)190}$ $60\overline{)190}$
$6\overline{)52}$ $60\overline{)520}$ $900\overline{)5,200}$
$7\overline{)26}$ $7\overline{)570}$ $70\overline{)640}$
$9\overline{)81}$ $90\overline{)635}$ $80\overline{)254}$

Written materials

A variety of written materials is necessary in any classroom where instruction is adjusted to the needs and abilities of the learner. Not only is a suitable textbook or textbook series necessary, but many different textbooks should be available in sets of six or eight. These textbooks may be individualized by removing the binding and mounting the separate practice units in file folders. Practice activities on problem solving, basic division facts, addition of fractions, and so forth, may be grouped according to learning difficulty and stapled into folders. The children work through the material in each folder, writing answers on separate answer sheets. Self-scoring devices may be included in the folder for ready use by the student. Old textbooks, or new textbooks other than the basic text, can be cannibalized and used in this way to provide needed extra practice.

Programmed textbooks and workbooks are available from many publishing houses. A variety of these should be available for individual use in each classroom. They should be purchased in small sets and handled in such a way that they, too, are reusable. Most publishers have such materials coordinated with their textbook series.

A wealth of good material is available from government agencies. For example, the U.S. Office of Education has "Space Oriented Mathematics for Early Grades," which is a set of workbook materials by Edwina Deans; a circular by Patricia Spross entitled *Elementary Arithmetic and Learning Aids;* and a bulletin, edited by Lauren Woodby, entitled *The Low Achiever in Mathematics.* Materials of the workbook type can be obtained also from the Treasury Department and the Forest Service of the Department of Agriculture. These are well done and are interesting to older students.

There are a growing number of supplementary books in mathematics written for elementary school children. Some of these are factual in character; others would be classed as fiction but are sound mathematically and carry high interest for elementary school children. Certainly a portion of the school's allotment for the library should be spent for such publications. Recent issues of the *Arithmetic Teacher* carry reviews as well as listings of these books as they become available.

Manipulative materials

Slow learners in mathematics should make frequent use of manipulative and visual materials. Many of these may be made by the teacher and the children; others can be collected and adapted to classroom use; still others may be purchased from school supply houses and textbook publishing houses.

Children's toys can be good mathematics materials in many instances! These should be used as teaching materials at all steps in learning—to aid discovery, to provide practice, to test understanding. They should be used by the children and by the teacher for demonstration. Various construction toys such as Tinkertoys, building blocks, link blocks, D-sticks, and parquetry tiles are useful in teaching geometry. Dominoes and various card games not only capture interest but provide practice in counting and computation. A trip through the toy department of any large department store will reveal, to the perceptive teacher, many toys and games that can serve the cause of mathematics! The writer discovered that the cardboard coin holders used by coin collectors can be used as arrays in multiplication and to develop concepts of percent. For the teacher who needs templates, they are excellent for tracing circles of various sizes!

It is impossible to list or describe the hundreds of visuals available for teachers. The *Arithmetic Teacher* often includes descriptions of teacher-made instructional devices. Books dealing with the teaching of elementary school mathematics are veritable gold mines of ideas for teachers seeking suggestions for making and using manipulative materials.

Slow-learning children need to resort constantly to objective materials, pictures, diagrams, and dramatization to help them "see" relationships. The written record and verbalization should accompany the visualization to make sure that the bridge is built between the operation and the algorithm.

Within-class grouping

Intraclass, or within-class, grouping of students is one of the more successful ways of adjusting instruction to the needs of the slow learner. This type of grouping should be flexible and temporary, with the size and the number of groups varying with the intent of the lesson.

For example, in a class working on division with a one-digit divisor, one group of children might be solving "248 ÷ 8" by using bundles of tens and ones. Their approach might be to expand 248 into 24 tens and 8 ones and to divide the 24 tens into 8 groups of equal size (or to separate the 24 tens into 8 groups of 3 tens each) and then to divide (or separate) the 8 ones. The written record could read:

$$24 \text{ tens} \div 8 = 3 \text{ tens} \quad \text{or} \quad 30$$
$$8 \text{ ones} \div 8 = 1 \text{ one} \quad \text{or} \quad \underline{1}$$
$$248 \div 8 = 30 + 1 \quad = \quad 31$$

A second group could be solving "248 ÷ 8" by subtracting, using the "ladder" algorism:

```
    8 |248
       80  | 10 × 8 = 80
      ---
      168
      160  | 20 × 8 = 160
      ---
        8
        8  | 1 × 8 = 8
      ---
       31
```

A more advanced group of children could be using a standard algorism, first estimating the answer.

```
      1
     30        Estimate: About 30, since 8 × 30 = 240.
  8 |248
    240
    ---
      8
      8
```

Working within this general framework of grouping according to levels of thinking, the teacher provides opportunities for the slow learner to make his discoveries under guidance, to share and discuss his findings with other children, to move slowly by well-graduated steps from objective materials to pictorial representation, and finally to move to the written record using numerals.

Grouping by maturity levels develops very naturally from a type of teaching that encourages discovery. In fact, the class sharing and discussion involved in group discovery may be one of the best ways to meet individual differences.

Grouping need not always be used for discovery lessons; it can be used effectively to arrange practice activities for small groups of children with similar needs.

1. Pupil teams can be formed for practice on basic facts and for remedial help on any of the operations with whole numbers and fractions. Usually one member of the team should be competent and able in the content being practiced. Assignment cards can be prepared in advance for each team and appropriate concrete aids set aside for use by those children who need to check their solutions with objective materials.

Occasionally a pupil team may be constituted of two children who both need help. Recently a sixth-grade teacher who was unable to motivate an underachiever to master basic multiplication facts assigned him the responsibility of helping a fourth-grade child who needed similar help. As the older boy assisted the younger one, he found it necessary to assume a teacher's role, to prepare his materials in advance each day, and when challenged by his young student, to learn the basic facts himself! At the end of one week the sixth-grade boy had mastered the facts he had not known, become interested in his participation, and developed more self-esteem.

2. A listening post equipped with a tape recorder and several sets of earphones makes it easy to administer special practice activities. Before class time the teacher reads practice activities or directions for individual work onto the audio tape. During class time, while the teacher works with part of the class, the children who need extra practice gather around the tape recorder, put on the headsets, and carry out the previously recorded activities.

Tapes may be developed with a pause, or "silent spot," to allow time for the pupil to produce the correct response. Sound effects such as those from rhythm-band instruments might be incorporated to help children perceive the meanings. (Beep, beep, beep, pause, beep, beep: $3 + 2 = 5$.) The children may reproduce the pattern with counters, with pictures, or with the appropriate algorithm.

Tapes may be indexed, stored, and used for group testing and practice in the same manner. However, many teachers prefer to create practice materials appropriate to the immediate needs of their students.

Help for teachers

Teachers need help themselves if they are to succeed in teaching slow learners. The strategies described above call for careful, time-consuming preparation. As a final strategy, therefore, administrators should provide clerical assistance for preparing materials and recording test data. They should also, perhaps, provide teacher aides and remedial tutorial help for disadvantaged children.

Summary

If mathematics instruction at the elementary school level is to be successful, then teachers must take cognizance of the variations in the groups taught and assign expectations to individual pupils instead of groups of pupils. Readiness for learning must be determined, learning difficulties diagnosed, and the classroom organization and environment made conducive to learning. Instructional materials commensurate with the needs of the children should be provided and teaching strategies employed that will help each pupil perform learning tasks in which he can be successful.

There is no single, easy solution in the education of the slow learner. His problem is complex. Teaching must take this into account.

REFERENCES

1. Biggs, Edith E. *Mathematics in the Primary School.* New York: British Information Service, 1965.
2. Brewer, Emery. "A Survey of Arithmetic Intraclass Grouping Practices." *Arithmetic Teacher* 13 (April 1966): 310–14.
3. Buffie, Edward G., Ronald C. Welch, and Donald D. Paige. "From Diagnosis to Treatment." In *Mathematics: Strategies of Teaching,* Modern Elementary Methods Series, pp. 182–214. Englewood Cliffs, N.J.: Prentice-Hall, 1968.
4. Chandler, Arnold M. "Mathematics and the Low Achiever." *Arithmetic Teacher* 17 (March 1970): 196–98.
5. Davidson, Patricia S. "An Annotated Bibliography of Suggested Manipulative Devices." *Arithmetic Teacher* 15 (October 1968): 509–12, 514–24.
6. Davies, Robert A. "Low Achiever Lesson in Primes." *Arithmetic Teacher* 16 (November 1969): 529–32.
7. Gibb, E. Glenadine. "Through the Years: Individualizing Instruction in Mathematics." *Arithmetic Teacher* 17 (May 1970): 396–402.
8. Gilmary, Sister. "Transfer Effects of Reading Remediation to Arithmetic Computation When Intelligence Is Controlled and All Other School Factors Are Eliminated." *Arithmetic Teacher* 14 (January 1967): 17–20.
9. Golden, Sarah R. "Fostering Enthusiasm through Child-created Games." *Arithmetic Teacher* 17 (February 1970): 111–15.
10. Green, Roberta. "A Color-coded Method of Teaching Basic Arithmetic Concepts and Procedures." *Arithmetic Teacher* 17 (March 1970): 231–33.
11. Grossnickle, Foster E.; Leo J. Brueckner; and John Reckzeh. *Discovering Meanings in Elementary School Mathematics.* 5th ed. New York: Holt, Rinehart & Winston, 1968.
12. Hammitt, Helen. "Evaluating and Reteaching Slow Learners." *Arithmetic Teacher* 14 (January 1967): 40–41.
13. Higgins, Jon L. "Sugar-Cube Mathematics." *Arithmetic Teacher* 16 (October 1969): 427–31.
14. Kaplan, Jerome D. "An Example of a Mathematics Instructional Program for Disadvantaged Children." *Arithmetic Teacher* 17 (April 1970): 332–34.
15. Keiffer, Mildred C. "The Development of Teaching Materials for Low-achieving Pupils in Seventh and Eighth Grade Mathematics." *Arithmetic Teacher* 15 (November 1968): 599–604.
16. Lerch, Harold H., and Francis J. Kelly. "A Mathematical Program for Slow Learners at Junior High Level." *Arithmetic Teacher* 13 (March 1966): 232–36.

17. Lyda, W. J., and Frances M. Duncan. "Quantitative Vocabulary and Problem Solving." *Arithmetic Teacher* 14 (April 1967): 289–91.
18. National Council of Teachers of Mathematics. *Instruction in Arithmetic,* Twenty-fifth Yearbook. Washington, D.C.: The Council, 1960.
19. National Society for the Study of Education. *Individualized Instruction,* Sixty-first Yearbook, pt. 1. Chicago: University of Chicago Press, 1962.
20. Paschal, Billy J. "Geometry for the Disadvantaged." *Arithmetic Teacher* 14 (January 1967): 4–6.
21. ———. "Teaching the Culturally Disadvantaged Child." *Arithmetic Teacher* 13 (May 1966): 369–74.
22. Reed, Mary Katherine Stevens. "Vocabulary Load of Certain State Adopted Mathematics Textbooks, Grades One through Three." Ed.D. dissertation, University of Southern California, n.d.
23. Richards, Pauline L. "Tinkertoy Geometry." *Arithmetic Teacher* 14 (October 1967): 468–69. Reprinted in *Readings in Geometry from the "Arithmetic Teacher,"* pp. 60–61. Washington, D.C.: National Council of Teachers of Mathematics, 1970.
24. Ridding, L. W. "Investigations of Personality Measures Associated with Over and Under Achievers." *British Journal of Educational Psychology* 37 (November 1967): 397–98.
25. Schacht, Elmer James. *A Study of the Mathematical Errors of Low Achievers in Elementary School Mathematics.* Ed.D. dissertation, Wayne State University, 1966. Ann Arbor, Mich.: University Microfilms (no. 67-10, 488).
26. Smith, Robert M. *Clinical Teaching: Methods of Instruction for the Retarded.* New York: McGraw-Hill Book Co., 1968.
27. Spitzer, Herbert F. *Enrichment of Arithmetic.* St. Louis: McGraw-Hill Book Co., Webster Division, 1964.
28. ———. "Providing for Individual Differences." In *Teaching Elementary School Mathematics,* pp. 314–30. Boston: Houghton Mifflin Co., 1967.
29. Stenzel, Jane G. "Math for the Low, Slow, and Fidgety." *Arithmetic Teacher* 15 (January 1968): 30–34.
30. Turner, Ethel M. *Teaching Aids for Elementary Mathematics.* New York: Holt, Rinehart & Winston, 1966.

6

Teaching Styles (Secondary School)

ELIZABETH A. COLLINS

SLOW LEARNERS have special needs calling for appropriate styles of teaching. Although such students may be defined in terms of a definite range of past scores on tests of academic achievement and potential, the teaching styles to which they respond defy bounding. Slow learners—or, more descriptively, students who have learned slowly—represent the total range of psychological constructs. It is likely, however, that any grouping of these young people will include many in need of emotional support or even emotional restructuring.

Teachers have special needs also when faced with slow learners in secondary schools; for all too often they have had less training in the subject matter than teachers assigned to advanced classes, yet they must teach content to students who have experienced failure with this same content for at least as many years as they have been enrolled at the secondary level. In this situation it is important that the teacher adopt teaching styles compatible with his personality, implement classroom management systems that are operable with a minimum amount of direction, and either locate or produce a variety of instructional materials that are easily available and cover a wide range of student interests and levels of difficulty.

This chapter presents—through "action shots," as it were—several different teaching styles that have proved successful. These snapshot views are then related and analyzed. Examples are provided of simple uses of various resources, and management systems for individualizing instruction are discussed.

Snapshots of Successful Teaching Styles

Teaching style A

A third-period, ninth-grade, phase 1 class had been under way for about fifteen minutes. The teacher was seated, busily engaged with two students. About ten students were at the chalkboard analyzing different sets of three problems in subtracting whole numbers. Some students were working alone and some in groups of two or more. A pair of students turned from the chalkboard and exclaimed to the teacher, "We did it! We did it! Did you bring the surprise?"

By this time several students had observed the presence of outsiders in the classroom, but the teacher had not. Responding to the successful students' joy and pride in accomplishment, he whirled and spoke in tones that matched their enthusiasm, "You did! I knew you could! Tell me, how did you solve the problems?"

Explanations spilled forth, a sentence from one student rolling into a sentence from the other.

The teacher continued, "Why were you having difficulties with the textbook problems?"

The students' answers included accurate but unsophisticated analysis of the faulty logic they had used, which they had now corrected. Their work on the chalkboard revealed different approaches being mastered, as illustrated by the following:

$$\begin{array}{l} 2{,}014 \\ -487 \\ \hline 3 \;+\;487\;=\;490 \\ 10 \;+\;490\;=\;500 \\ 500 \;+\;500\;=\;1{,}000 \\ 1{,}014 \;+\;1{,}000\;=\;2{,}014 \\ \hline 1{,}527 \end{array}$$

$$\begin{array}{r} 4{,}305 \;=\; 3\;|\;12\;|\;9\;|\;15 \\ -847 \;=\; \;|\;8\;|\;4\;|\;7 \\ \hline 3\;\;\;4\;\;\;5\;\;\;8 \end{array}$$

$$\begin{array}{l} 3{,}195 \\ -268 \\ \hline \overline{3{,}1}33 \;=\; (3{,}000\;-\;100) \\ \phantom{3{,}133 =}\;+\;(30\;-\;3) \\ \phantom{3{,}133}\;=\;2{,}900\;+\;27 \\ \phantom{3{,}133}\;=\;2{,}927 \end{array}$$

An uncertain quiet filled the room as both students and teacher became aware of the outsiders. Hesitating only momentarily, the teacher faced them and stated, "I promised yesterday to give a reward to those students who selected an appropriate method for solving the problems and achieved success with it in today's activities. These have, and the reward is theirs."

TEACHING STYLES (SECONDARY SCHOOL) 165

The reward was chocolate nuggets with permission to eat them in class. Almost immediately, the previous nonquiet state of purposeful study was resumed.

Teaching style B

A group of fifteen tenth-through-twelfth graders were enrolled in a course called Basic General Mathematics, taken for the sole purpose of fulfilling graduation requirements. The teacher opened the class by announcing that help was needed for measuring the 800 seniors for caps and gowns. Seeing this as an opportunity to escape from class for a few days, all fifteen students volunteered.

Seizing this opportunity to relate class instruction to immediate experiences, the teacher guided the group in organizing for the activity. Here are a few of the in-class activities that resulted:

1. Measurements were taken of each member of the class and also of the teacher.
2. Sample order sheets were completed.
3. Computations were made of the average height of the class and the average weight of the boys and the girls.
4. Graphs were made to show the distribution of the students' heights and weights.
5. Analyses were made of the weight-height distribution for boys and girls by using graphs and making comparisons with medical weight-height charts.
6. Three students decided to graph and analyze the collected weight-height data for the 800 members of the senior class.

Teaching style C

A tenth-grade class of boys convened on the school playground for a week of mathematics lessons in late April. The only practice exercises to be used were those that were available from this field experience. A teacher of physics was invited to discuss the aerodynamics of kite and rocket construction and flying.

At the beginning of the week kites and rockets, colorfully painted and interestingly labeled, were displayed. After several kites were put aloft, the teacher directed a discussion on measuring the altitude of each by using a measuring device made by the students. The device consisted of two yardsticks held together by a wing nut inserted in a hole bored into one end of each yardstick.

On the third day, the students measured the flight of single and multistaged rockets. Spotters had each made a simple device using a wooden demonstration protractor and a yardstick anchored at the center mark with a wing nut. The "textbooks" were technical papers distributed by a rocket company. After igniting several rockets for the sheer excitement of seeing them perform, the teacher and students together read the technical papers.

The role of teacher was continually changing, with students increasingly assuming the teaching role. The teacher's goal was to introduce trigonometric ratios informally through an involvement experience that was relevant. Soon the students arrived at the point of readiness; they were ready for this goal to be achieved, still using the technical papers as the textbook and validating processes through direct experiences.

In short order the students learned to read the tables. Arithmetic errors were minimal. Observational and listening skills were sharpened, as evidenced by an almost unanimous interest in determining the additional altitude attributable to the second stage of a two-stage rocket.

This field experience, initially planned for one week, evolved into a four-week unit in which many skills were retaught.

Teaching style D

It was a warm afternoon in mid-October when a group of slow-learning ninth-grade general mathematics students entered the classroom diagrammed in figure 6.1.

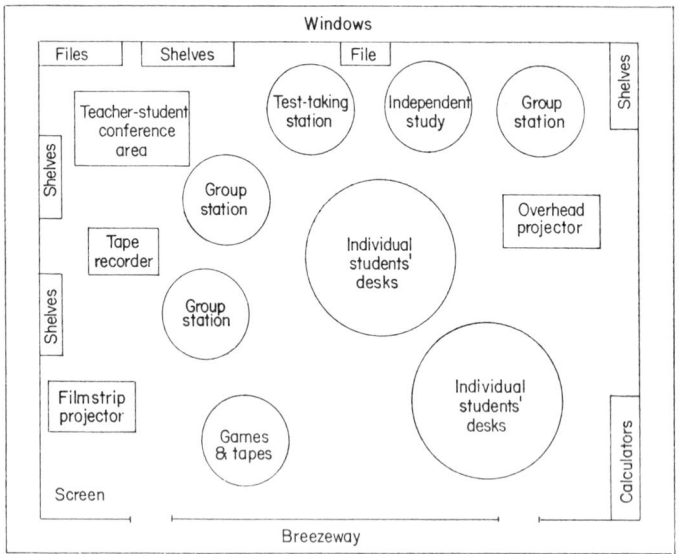

Fig. 6.1

TEACHING STYLES (SECONDARY SCHOOL)   167

Bulletin-board space was strategically used. Adorning one three-by-four-foot section, a clever cartoon showed the layout of the room and the location of materials—all depicted graphically by means of drawings, color, and bold type. Another section of the bulletin board was reserved for students' use.

On entering the room, students secured their individual folders and proceeded to different stations without receiving directions from the teacher. Each student's folder contained, in addition to actual work, two evaluation forms—one for the teacher to fill in and the other for self-evaluation by the student.

The teacher moved casually from one station to another discussing with an individual or with groups the activities for the day. Each of these discussions involved individual and joint assessment of accomplishments, needs, and alternatives that were available. Two students who had been working independently decided, after counseling with the teacher, to join forces with a small group working on the same problem. After each conference the teacher entered a few notes on the teacher evaluation form in the student's folder.

This classroom was a beehive of activity. After checking several exercises with the teacher's manual, two students became engaged in attempting to analyze the faulty logic that had led to their errors. Using this opportunity to present a short, purposeful lecture, the teacher moved briskly to the chalkboard, accompanied by the students. His short presentation was precisely sequenced, being at the same time designed to develop within each student confidence to challenge statements made by the teacher. He repeatedly asked, "Do you accept this?" and deliberately miscued to establish the idea that situations arise when acceptance is unwarranted even from an authority figure.

The varied activities in this classroom included use of a tape recorder. Three students were listening to a tape, which was part of a unit on sets, and were using the accompanying activity sheet (see fig. 6.2). The script for the tape included a simulated telephone call between two friends, Lisbeth and Kim. Lisbeth is inviting Kim to a party with the following conditions: All persons coming to the party will bring something. Seven are bringing cokes; ten are bringing hot dogs; four of those bringing hot dogs are also bringing cokes; and Kim is to bring only the coat hangers for roasting the hot dogs. The problem: How many persons are coming to the party? The tape explains the steps on the worksheet.

Shortly before the class period ended, the teacher gained the attention of the entire class to take stock of its progress and needs. Several

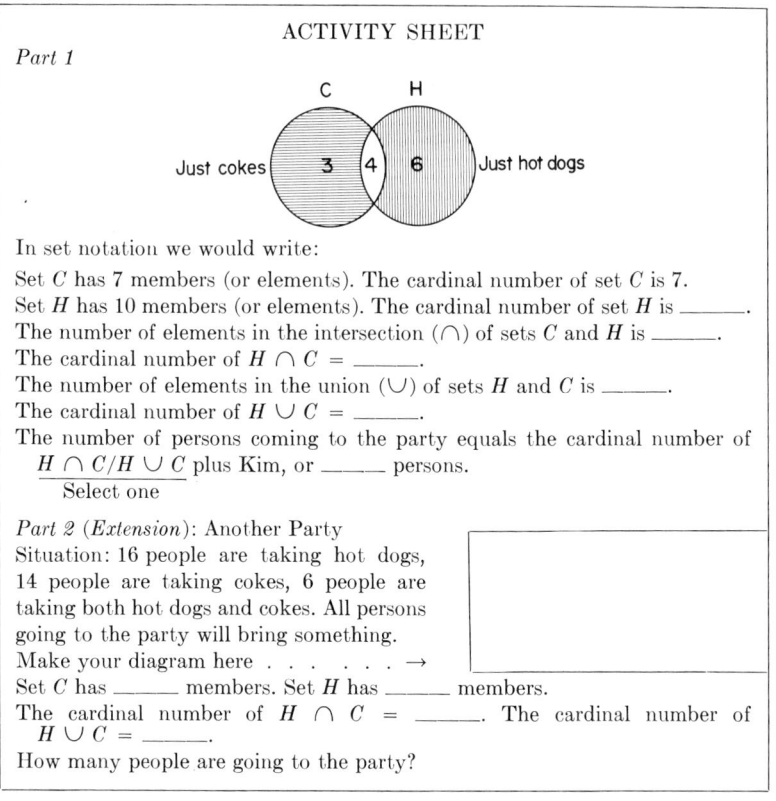

Fig. 6.2

mechanical problems that were interfering with individual pacing and comfort were identified. Objectives were established for the next day, designated student-choice day. On this day students had free access to the many involvement games and experiments found in the room, and they were free to select any other activity in which they had interest. The primary objective of student-choice day was to focus on enabling and fostering socialization and its development.

Composite Picture of Successful Teaching Styles

Each teacher described in the preceding discussion of teaching styles employed identifiable strategies for making learning relevant and purposeful. In teaching styles A and D, relevance and purpose were achieved by using the techniques of student success, immediate reward, and approval of student behavior by the adult model. In teaching styles

B and C, relevance and purpose were achieved through direct-involvement experiences. Slow learners respond favorably to immediate applications of reward systems and to instruction that follows experience in which they are directly involved, either in or out of school.

Significant features in teaching style A are (1) the open climate in which students are permitted to select different algorithmic methods and (2) the maintenance of students' trust by the teacher's following through on a promise. Slow learners tend to be very astute at interpreting human behavior; they respond generously to an adult who does not let them down, especially when that adult takes risks to keep their trust.

Teaching styles C and D give examples of a variety of short, specific learning experiences. The attention span of slow learners is likely to be short if they are not completely excited and involved. Since these young persons have difficulty delaying or postponing gratification, their learning experiences should be sequenced to allow for short-term concentration. Under favorable conditions, however, slow learners can and do exhibit the capacity for protracted attention. For example, in teaching style C the one-week activity evolved into a four-week unit when their interest was sparked by their direct experience in applying simple trigonometric ratios to rocketry. This interest was sustained long enough to give them a full review of decimals, ratios, and fractions. Consequently, they attained levels of computational skill that would have been thought impossible for them.

Identifiable strategies for individualizing instruction can be abstracted from each of the teaching styles that have been described. Styles A, B, and C all exhibit techniques for providing for the needs of individuals within the context of a group setting that is primarily teacher-paced. Differences in approach, however, are sharply delineated.

1. Style A accommodates individual differences by introducing and permitting different algorithmic methods. Presumably two assumptions are being made: (1) that individuality is incompatible with sameness and (2) that if a student has failed again and again with one approach, his conditioning and consequent positioning for failure must be reversed by getting him to try a new method.

2. Style B permits different student performance levels in that not all students completed an extra project, which implies that not all were expected to engage in this activity.

3. Style C provides an approach to individualization within an open and free environment that puts to the test the planning a teacher has done before actually beginning to teach. The quality of this advance planning is revealed by the degree to which the teacher is able to become a "learner," maintain control of the group, and use the stimulated interest for reteaching and extension.

4. Style D illustrates an approach to individualizing instruction that depends on student pacing and a partnership between students and teacher in decision making and assessment. This style—combining rich media environment, availability of alternative modes, and deliberate efforts to shape student behavior ("Do you accept this?") through actions of the teacher—demonstrates an effective approach applicable to the general population of slow learners. Furthermore, the classroom environment, by making it legitimate to move around, is suited to the motor inclinations of slow learners.

This style illustrates also an operational definition of individualized instruction, namely, that it consists of designing and conducting, in company with each student, programs of study that are tailor-made to fit his learning needs.

In the short glimpse we had of style D the teacher functioned as manager of the learning environment, consultant, diagnostician, and prescriber of learning alternatives.

Finally, elements in style D are helpful in counteracting the influences to which inner-city youth are exposed in their invidious, and often segregated, slum neighborhoods.

The ideal learning climate for slow learners is rich with varied media; it is structured, warm, facilitating, accepting of movement and purposeful noise; it is also nonthreatening, even though limits are clearly delineated and strictly adhered to.

The ideal teacher establishes trust, is supportive and sensitive to the emotional and learning needs of the students, employs teaching strategies that are compatible with his own style, provides students with options on which successful learning experiences can be built, and applies appropriate reward systems. Such a teacher sequences learnings along a similarity-dissimilarity continuum; that is, amenable aspects of new learning are related to and identified with earlier learnings, either formal or informal, thus facilitating transfer of learning from one setting to another.

Requisites for Viable Learning Environments

By the time slow learners enter secondary school, they have perceived themselves as persons who behave in ways that are out of accord with accepted norms for their age group. School grades have labeled them marginal. The nonverbal communications of teachers often scream rejection. Hence if the teacher and these learners are to achieve success, steps must be taken to at least neutralize such negative forces.

Understood objectives

Teaching and learning by objectives fosters teacher-learner partnerships that ensure mutually understood outcomes, direction of movement, and criteria for measuring success. Implied here is the need for clearly stated outcomes, or expected performances, expressed in language that enables the learner to know exactly where he is going. Successful implementation of this teaching-learning process depends on the quality of teacher performance during the preactive, or planning, phase of teaching. A model for guiding and sequencing activities during this phase is provided in figure 6.3.

For the teacher of slow learners, this model enables planning that—

1. recognizes that not all students need to achieve each objective for any given unit of study;
2. results in the creation of learning environments rich with stimuli that are useful for motivating student movement toward attainment of objectives especially selected for that student;
3. anticipates differing learning styles;
4. makes available appropriate instructional material using various media and modes;
5. judiciously uses media to disseminate information and thus frees the teacher to function increasingly as prescriber, diagnostician, and consultant during the interactive phase of teaching;
6. provides for systematic adjustment in plans based on feedback.

Teaching and learning by objectives gives the slow-learning student increased opportunities to achieve success because he is now responding to learning environments that consider his needs, styles, and characteristics. Stating objectives in language the student can understand suggests that these opportunities will be given to him. It is important that all adolescents understand where they are going. When a teacher shares this information with slow learners enrolled in secondary schools, he dramatically communicates respect for their social and

THE SLOW LEARNER IN MATHEMATICS

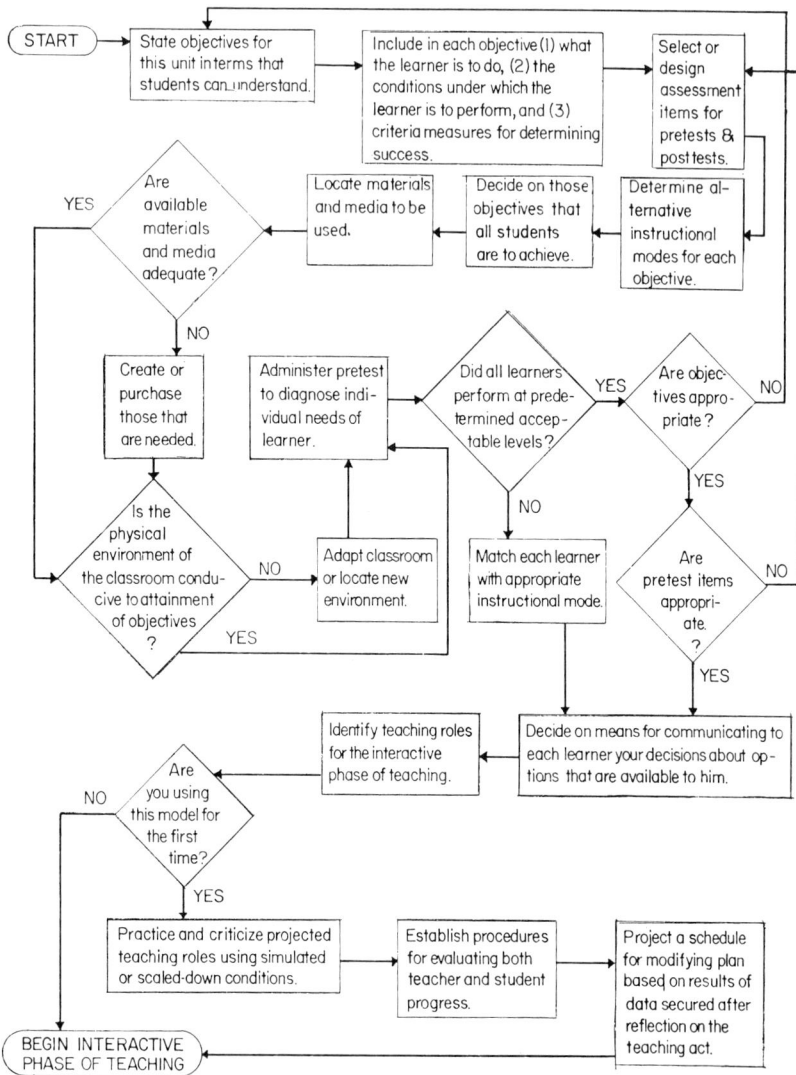

Fig. 6.3. A model for the preactive phase of teaching

physical maturity, thereby opening up many possibilities for joint decision making. Slow learners who share in decision making will also assume responsibility for their learning. Techniques for motivating students to exercise responsibility for their learning were provided in each teaching style presented in the preceding section.

TEACHING STYLES (SECONDARY SCHOOL) 173

Supports for independent learning

Low achievers often have difficulty following and understanding written directions. They encounter frustrations when required to sift out from written directions (*a*) what is expected of them, (*b*) the sequence of their activities, and (*c*) the sources of assistance. Directions should be given in a form that considers the low reading levels of these young people.

If a slow learner is expected to execute a learning activity independently, not only must the directions be clearly stated with a minimum of words but the ordering of his experiences must be indicated. Support should also be provided if he is to make generalizations. When independent learning activities are presented in charts, such as those illustrated in figure 6.4, most of these conditions can be met (3, pp. 123–27; 4, pp. 44–51).

CHARTS FOR INDEPENDENT STUDENT ACTIVITIES

EXAMPLE 1

Compare	First step		Second step	Therefore
			Use <, >, or =	
$\dfrac{2}{3}$ and $\dfrac{4}{5}$	2×5 3×5	4×3 5×3	$\dfrac{10}{15} < \dfrac{12}{15}$	$\dfrac{2}{3} < \dfrac{4}{5}$
$\dfrac{3}{8}$ and $\dfrac{2}{9}$	3×9 8×9	2×8	$\dfrac{27}{72} > \dfrac{16}{72}$	$\dfrac{3}{8}$ $\dfrac{2}{9}$
$\dfrac{5}{6}$ and $\dfrac{3}{5}$	——	——	——	—
$\dfrac{5}{10}$ and $\dfrac{45}{90}$				

EXAMPLE 2

Given	The divisor names	Multiply by one	New example	Same as
$.8 \overline{\smash{)}.16}$	tenths	$.8 \times 10 \;\;\overline{\smash{)}.16 \times 10}$	$8. \overline{\smash{)}1.6}$	$\underset{\frown}{.8} \;\; \overline{\smash{)}\underset{\frown}{.1.6}}^{.2}$
$.15 \overline{\smash{)}6}$	hundredths			
$8.3 \overline{\smash{)}2.49}$	tenths			
$.025 \overline{\smash{)}1}$	thousandths			

Fig. 6.4

The procedural flow chart is also useful when students are required to execute ordered sequences and make decisions at certain points along the way. Units on flowcharting are often motivational and are helpful for guiding slow learners in thinking through both mathematical and nonmathematical problems. Flow charts and calculators have been used together to add new dimensions to drill and practice with algorithmic methods.

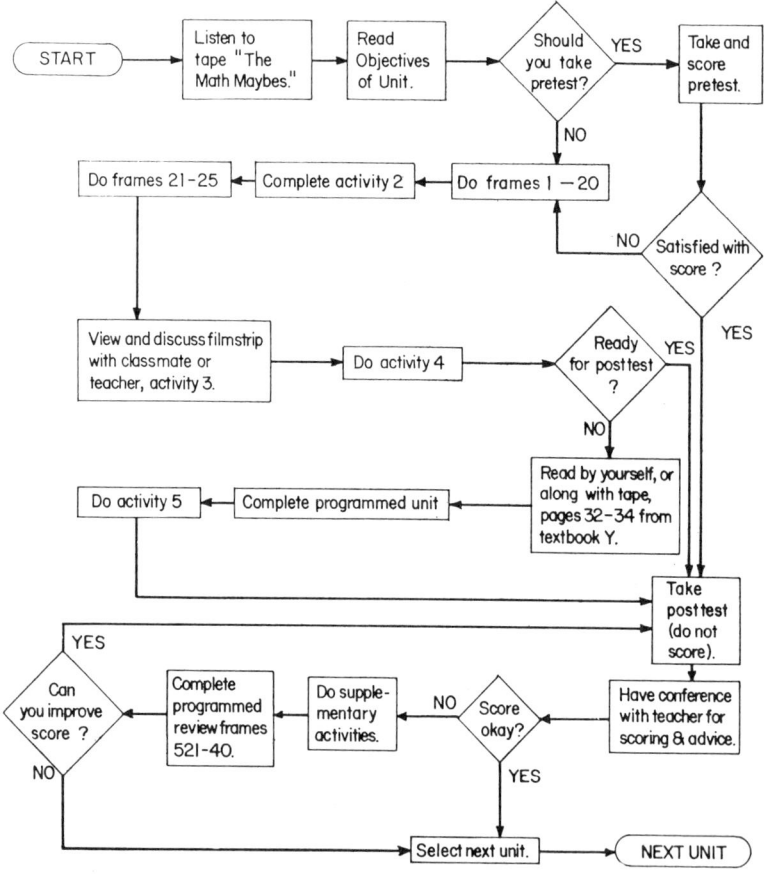

Fig. 6.5. Example of flow chart used by students: An introduction to probability

The procedural flow chart shown in figure 6.5 was developed for use in the individualized instructional program portrayed in teaching

style D. By flowcharting the sequence of learning experiences and the options that are provided, a systematic procedure is devised for—
1. involving students in evaluation and decision making;
2. promoting self-determination through self-pacing;
3. organizing and sequencing a variety of short, multimedia experiences.

It should be observed that the flow chart directs students to secure and use equipment and media. This provision capitalizes on the sensorimotor orientation of most slow learners. It also recognizes the need of adolescents to act without continuous adult supervision. If this need is to be met in the context here described, then sturdy, reliable equipment must be available and students must be taught to operate the equipment independently.

Organized instructional materials

The teacher of the slow learner should have ready access to a variety of attention-getters as well as varied media modes for student interaction. The Learning Activity Package is a device for organizing a variety of related activities.

A U.S. Office of Education grant to the Dade County (Miami) Florida School System made possible the organization and field testing of Learning Activity Packages with slow learners. Basically, each Learning Activity Package contains the following components:

LEARNING ACTIVITY PACKAGE

Student's Unit	*Teacher's Commentary*
1. Procedure flow chart (see fig. 6.5)	1. Introduction
2. Behavioral objectives stated in language students can understand	2. Prerequisites
	3. Sequence placements
3. Pretest (situational as well as paper-pencil)	4. Vocabulary
	5. Suggested required activities
4. Activities	6. Objectives correlated with pretest and activities
paper and pencil	
audio tapes	7. Comments on evaluation
films or filmstrips	8. Posttest (situational as well as paper-pencil)
laboratory experiments	
references to textbooks, magazines, etc.	9. Keys to tests and activities
games, puzzles, etc.	
drill and practice sheets	

For the most part, the student's Learning Activity Package refers to commercially produced activities available in the classroom; but some materials have been developed locally, such as:

1. Audio tapes using the teacher's voice or a student's voice
2. Short linear-programmed sequences
3. Visuals and sensorimotor situations using subject matter in which students have shown interest
4. Activities developed around data received from local businessmen

The following is an example of a locally produced audio tape:

TAPE COMMENTARY FOR ACTIVITY 2:
AN INTRODUCTION TO PROBABILITY

In order to do the activities that accompany this tape, you will need the mimeographed sheet entitled "Activity 2—Experiments and Spinner Labeled 'C.'"

Some examples of games of chance will be used to help you understand what probability means and how it may be used. The examples are not used with the idea that gambling is to be encouraged. Rather, the information in this unit should help you to understand why "most gamblers die broke."

The probability of an event is, roughly speaking, the fraction of the time we expect it to happen. For example, the circle on spinner C is ¾ blue and ¼ red. Therefore, on each spin you have a ¾ probability of the point's landing on blue and a ¼ probability of its landing on red. It would then seem that if you spin the dial 4 times, you should land on blue 3 times and red only 1 time. Don't bet on it, though! True, you might get lucky and have it happen just that way. However, it is far more likely that you would have to spin it many, many more times before the actual outcome would approximate the mathematical probability of landing on blue 3 out of 4 spins.

Ideally speaking, if you were to spin spinner C 8 times, how many times do you think you might land on blue? I'll wait while you think for a minute. [PAUSE.]

Did you say 6? You are right, because 3 out of 4 would be the same ratio as 6 out of 8.

Now, how about 12 spins of spinner C—how many times would you expect to land on blue? [PAUSE.]

Did you say 9? Remember, the probability is the number of favorable outcomes over the total possible outcomes: ¾ = ? Think about the proportion ¾ = $n/12$. To solve, you get $4n = 36$, or $n = 9$.

Let's actually try an experiment with spinner C—experiment 1 on the

TEACHING STYLES (SECONDARY SCHOOL) 177

mimeographed sheet that accompanies this tape. The objective of experiment 1 is to have you discover that in any one set of 8 spins you may or may not get 6 blues and 2 reds—indeed, you may even get all blue or all red, although all red is highly unlikely! However, the average of the number of times you land on blue after a number of sets of 8 spins will be very close to 6. The ideal probability is 3 out of 4 or 6 out of 8. But in actual practice it is not always possible to get the ideal probability.

Now follow the instructions on your mimeographed sheet after turning off the recorder. When you have completed experiment 1, turn the recorder back on.

How did your average number of blues work out? I hope it was fairly near 6.

Earlier on this tape I said that the probability of an event was the fraction of the time that you would expect it to happen. Look at spinner A—what fraction of the time would you expect to land on red? On blue? On yellow? Did you think $\frac{1}{3}$, $\frac{1}{3}$, and $\frac{1}{3}$? Right, this is the mathematical probability; but, again this only means that over the long run you would probably land on each close to $\frac{1}{3}$ of the time.

One false idea that many people have when thinking about chance is that if a particular side of a coin, or in this case a particular color, turns up several times in a row, chances are less that it will turn up again on the next flip or spin. This is not true—the coin and the spinner cannot think; they don't remember what has turned up previously. Think about it. If you flipped a coin 6 times and it turned up heads each time, you would probably be tempted to call tails for the seventh toss, thinking that the "law of averages should catch up." This is wrong—heads and tails each have an equally likely chance—that is, $\frac{1}{2}$—on the seventh flip. The same is true of our spinners. If, on spinner A, you spin an even number (2, 4, or 6) ten times in a row, the chance for ending up with an odd number on the eleventh spin is still the same—that is, $\frac{1}{2}$. Notice that $\frac{1}{2}$ the spaces on A are even and $\frac{1}{2}$ are odd. Use this spinner for the second experiment on your mimeographed sheet.

Rewind this tape and put it away before doing the experiment.

Since few Learning Activity Packages contain more than ten pages, students find them less threatening than standard textbooks. Learning Activity Packages provide for the organization of a series of learning experiences that are sequenced according to difficulty and varied as to instructional modes. They also facilitate independent student actions. It is imperative that such packages reflect the resources that are easily accessible to students, because slow learners tend not to be persistent in academic endeavors. Figure 6.6 shows relationships between the units of work for which Learning Activity Packages were designed for the project in Dade County. Provision is made for both vertical and horizontal progression.

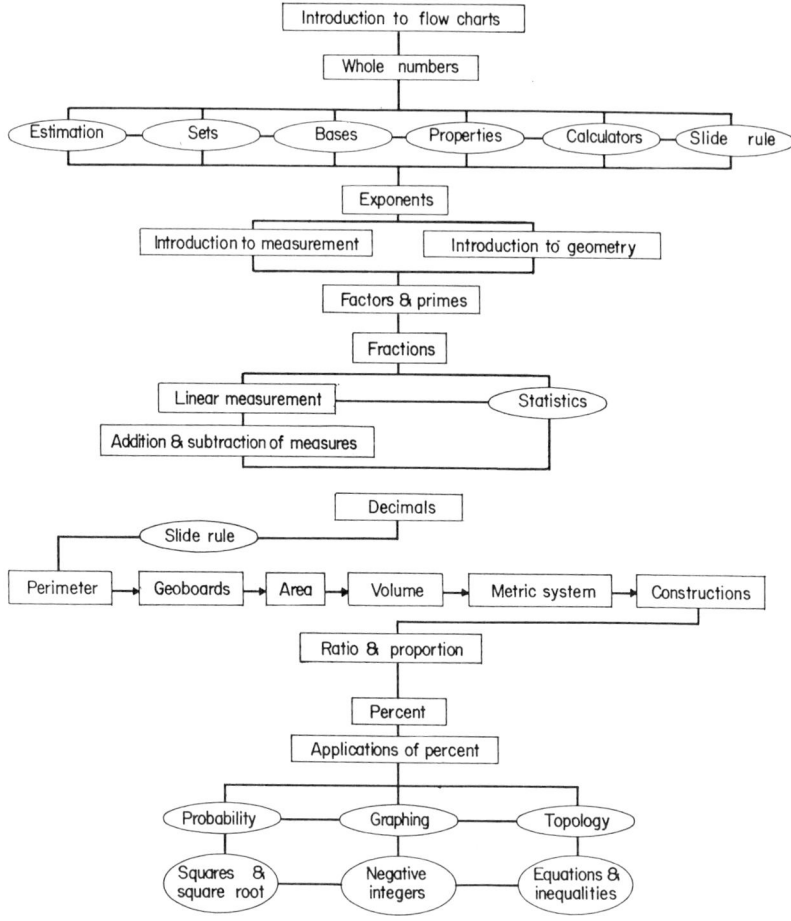

Fig. 6.6. Schema for low-ability students in general mathematics

The Baltimore County, Maryland, project for teaching slow learners developed a "banded approach" for organizing and varying instructional activities (1, pp. 58–60). The banded approach is a flexible way of organizing instructional activities in the class period. The class period is usually divided into three bands, with the first and third bands lasting from five to ten minutes each and the second band lasting about twenty-five minutes. The major portion of the lesson is presented during the second band. Each lesson provides for maintenance of computational skills. An outline of topics for a unit of banded lessons is presented in figure 6.7. Banded lessons permit sequential organization of instructional content and variety within the classroom period.

OUTLINE OF TOPICS FOR A SAMPLE UNIT OF BANDED LESSONS

Lesson	Band I	Band II	Band III
1	Drill—geometric figures	Parallel lines	4-digit numbers
2	Drill—patterns	Symbols for segment and ray, assessment of parallel lines	Puzzle—optical illusions
3	Math Builder[1]	Copying segments—straightedge	Tape—addition
4	Puzzle—multiplication and addition	Copying segments—straightedge and compass	Math Builder
5	Math Builder	Assessment—copying segments	Cross-number puzzle—place value
6	Drill patterns	Midpoint—paper folding	Construction of ruler
7	Math Builder	Symbols for angle, vertex	Puzzle—multiplication and addition
8	Puzzle—division	Assessment—midpoints	Cross-number puzzle—multiplication
9	Math Builder	Symbols for angle, vertex	Puzzle—renaming numbers
10	Tape—verbal problems	Copying angles—compass and straightedge	Tic-tac-toe games
11	Diagnostic test—addition of whole numbers	Copying angles	Continuation of tic-tac-toe games
12	Puzzle—calendars	Assessment—copying angles	Puzzle—hidden words

Source: Brant (1, p. 61).

[1] The Math Builder consists of a set of filmstrips and a projector. Each frame of the filmstrip elicits a recall response from the student. The projector can be set to flash the frames on a screen according to a predetermined time interval between the frames, thus permitting the responses needed for practice and drill.

Fig. 6.7

Contracts and Tasks Cards have also been used for organizing learning experiences and motivating slow learners to complete their tasks. When these tasks are related to out-of-school living, tenth, eleventh, and twelfth graders are especially amenable to them. These students often enjoy contracts and tasks that are not exclusively tied to the work world.

The Palm Beach County, Florida, Program for Underdeveloped Mathematics Pupils, a U.S. Office of Education project, resulted in the development of more than thirty-six units of work. Each unit is individually bound, thus providing many alternatives for anyone selecting instructional materials.

Removal of time constraints

The student who is the concern of this yearbook has a history of learning slowly. Even though measures of the learning potential of such students may be grossly inaccurate, their past rates of learning suggest that they will probably continue to learn at a less-than-average pace. If this is so, then secondary schools must provide the time these students need to acquire those mathematical concepts and skills that are projected for adult life. Therefore, mathematics programs that are based on continuous progress and are also available throughout the students' secondary school experience are needed. With these available, neither teacher nor student would be pressured to "cover" material. They would be motivated to create learning environments that permit vertical movement, without constraints of time.

Summary

There does not seem to exist a best teaching style to which slow learners respond. Instructional climates that slow learners and their teachers find helpful are filled with structures that develop identity and establish commitment.

Although slow learners may be dependent learners because their mathematical concept-and-skill development has been retarded, they can become self-propelling, independent learners. Conditions for encouraging independence and responsibility, however, are difficult to establish at the secondary school level. The primary task, then, of secondary school teachers of slow learners is to adopt the teaching style that has the greatest potential for counteracting the learned behavior that little is expected from these students. It is essential that the teaching style adopted be consistent with the personality of the teacher. Slow learners appear to have highly developed capabilities for detecting authenticity or lack of authenticity in behavior.

The attention spans of slow learners are functions of the type of activity they are engaged in, on the one hand, and the behavior of the adult model figure, on the other. Programs based on the premise that the attention span of slow learners is short provide learning episodes of ten-to-fifteen minutes' duration. Some slow learners, however, have sustained attention over several days when they are engaged in solving open-ended problems and when the skills needed for arriving at reasonable solutions are taught within the same context.

At the present time, few secondary schools provide slow learners with equality of educational opportunity. By definition, persons who are labeled "slow learners" learn slowly. If they are to be afforded equality of educational opportunity, it is the school's responsibility to provide the time they need to achieve the level of mathematical literacy demanded of fully functioning persons. It is unreasonable to assume that these learners can achieve this level of mathematical literacy when their experiences with formal instruction are often limited by the time requirement for earning one or two Carnegie units. It is expected that secondary schools will provide opportunities for continuous progress for the "college bound" and the accelerated learner. How can deliberate denial of opportunities to that segment of the school population who learn slowly be justified?

REFERENCES

1. Brant, Vincent. "Behavioral Objectives and the Slow Learner—an Action Approach." In *Report of a Conference: Programs in Mathematics for Low Achievers*, pp. 29–70. Charlottesville, Va.: Association of State Supervisors of Mathematics, 1970.
2. Collins, Elizabeth A. "Pedagogy and Accountability in Teaching Society's Rejects." In *Report of a Conference on Mathematics in the Inner City Schools*, pp. 55–74. Stanford, Calif.: School Mathematics Study Group, 1970.
3. Collins, Elizabeth A., J. Louis Nanney, and Agnes Y. Rickey. *Experiencing Mathematics, Book B*. Experiencing Mathematics, books A through E. New York: Random House, L. W. Singer Co., 1967.
4. ———. *Experiencing Mathematics, Book E*. Experiencing Mathematics, books A through E. New York: Random House, L. W. Singer Co., 1969.
5. Gagné, Robert M. *The Conditions of Learning*. 2d ed. New York: Holt, Rinehart & Winston, 1970.
6. Hunter, Madeline. *Teach More—Faster!* Theory into Practice Publications. El Segundo, Calif.: TIP Publications, 1969.
7. Kephart, Newell C. *The Slow Learner in the Classroom*. Columbus, Ohio: Charles E. Merrill Books, 1960.
8. Madsen, Charles H., and Clifford K. Madsen. *Teaching/Discipline: Behavioral Principles toward a Positive Approach*. Boston: Allyn & Bacon, 1970.

7

Aids and Activities

EVAN M. MALETSKY

A GREAT many multisensory aids can be used in the teaching of mathematics. Some can be bought through commercial manufacturers; others can be made by teacher or student. Some are elaborate and sophisticated, expensive, difficult to use, and hard to repair. Others are simple, obvious, and inexpensive. Some can be used to introduce and illustrate new topics, whereas others can help to clarify and reinforce old ones. Some are used seldom and only by the teacher. Others can be used regularly and by the student as well.

Whatever their size, cost, or purpose, multisensory aids in the classroom should help to make mathematical ideas, concepts, and examples more visual and meaningful. Remember that a slow learner is likely to be a physical, rather than an abstract, learner. If he is unable to use abstract symbols, he needs models and aids that can be made, touched, manipulated, and examined. It has already been mentioned that the slow learner, more than many others in his age group, prefers and needs tactile experiences. Hence he needs to be involved in the classroom activities. He frequently becomes motivated by doing things rather than by thinking concepts.

Often the poor self-image of the slow learner comes from his repeated failure and frustration in the classroom. For this reason the aids suggested in this chapter are simple to make and use. The activities are designed to be straightforward and brief to match his limited vocabulary and short attention span. The results are readily verified, and the student is frequently rewarded with a predictable degree of success.

Five basic areas are discussed in the chapter's major divisions: number patterns, arithmetic skills, geometric concepts, algebraic concepts, and the use of models. Thus the reader can see the role of each multisensory aid as it applies to some subject area. No attempt has been made to exhaust all possible uses of the aids; the intent is rather to give some specific, concrete examples of their effective use in the classroom.

Developing Number Patterns

Many slow learners lack simple number awareness and familiarity. Many have trouble recognizing number relationships because they have had all too few experiences with them. Many cannot see number patterns for the very reason that they are not presented in a physical, visual format. Unless these patterns and relationships can be associated with concrete representations, they mean little, if anything at all, to these children.

Slow learners need visual aids to give meaning to mental activities. It is very easy for the teacher to couch such experiences in real, physical, concrete situations. All it takes is a bit of concern and imagination and a few simple aids.

Some examples are given here to illustrate the point. Each involves doing something to produce a physical, countable result that is then related to a number pattern. When students are doing these things in class, be sure to have them guess each result first. Educated guessing is the first step toward discovery; so each activity begins with a very simple problem. In guessing the correct result, the student gains the needed self-respect that encourages him to guess again in a more difficult situation. Don't require generalization prematurely. The slow student is less effective in generalizing than most; he frequently needs more experiences to help him discover a number pattern or relationship.

Cutting paper

Fold and cut a sheet of paper as shown in figure 7.1. Find the number pattern.

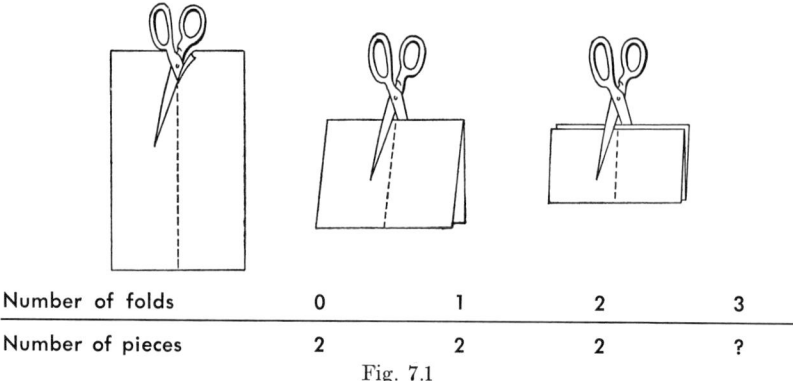

Number of folds	0	1	2	3
Number of pieces	2	2	2	?

Fig. 7.1

Now cut the paper the other way (fig. 7.2) and find the number pattern.

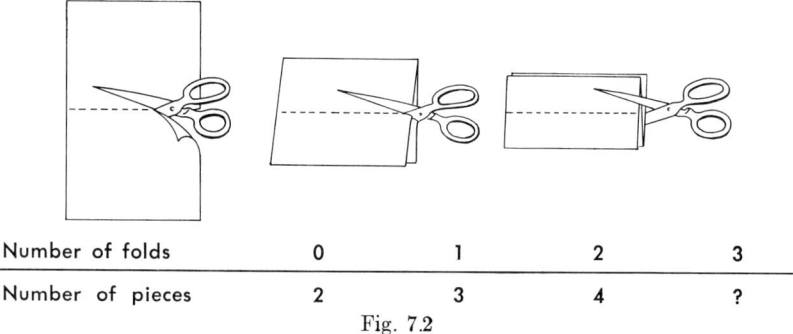

Number of folds	0	1	2	3
Number of pieces	2	3	4	?

Fig. 7.2

Cutting string

Repeatedly fold a piece of string around one blade of a pair of scissors and then cut as shown in figure 7.3. How many pieces are formed at each step?

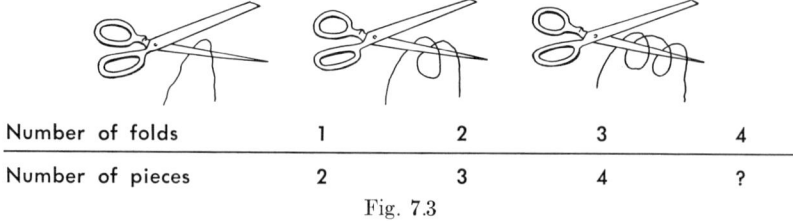

Number of folds	1	2	3	4
Number of pieces	2	3	4	?

Fig. 7.3

Fold a string once. Then fold it around the scissors and cut as shown in figure 7.4. How many pieces are formed at each step?

AIDS AND ACTIVITIES 185

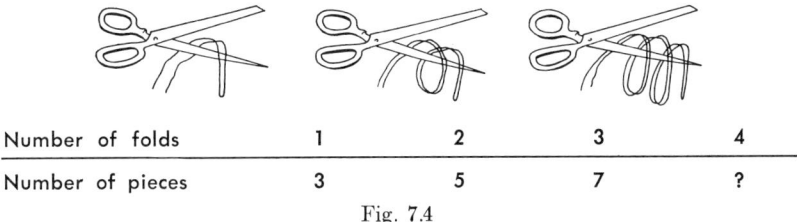

Number of folds	1	2	3	4
Number of pieces	3	5	7	?

Fig. 7.4

Folding a paper square

Make repeated folds across a square piece of paper as shown in figure 7.5. Find the greatest number of parts possible after each fold.

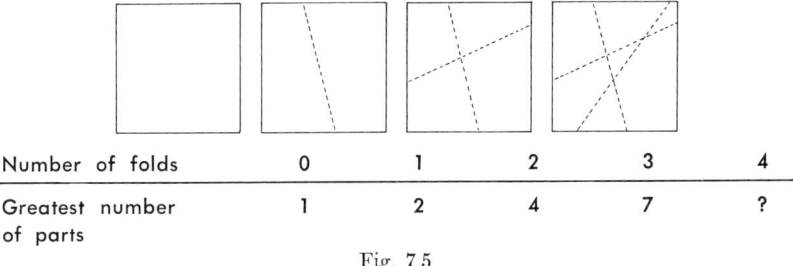

Number of folds	0	1	2	3	4
Greatest number of parts	1	2	4	7	?

Fig. 7.5

Folding a paper strip

Fold a strip of paper as shown in figure 7.6. How thick is it at each step?

 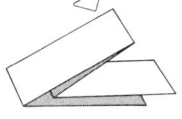 

Number of folds	1	2	3	4
Number of thicknesses	2	4	8	?

Fig. 7.6

Here is an interesting follow-up to this sequence: Have the class estimate the number of folds needed to get a stack as thick as the stack of pages in their textbook. This "thickness number" pattern gives powers of 2:

2^1	2^2	2^3	2^4	2^5	2^6	2^7	2^8	2^9	2^{10}
2	4	8	16	32	64	128	256	512	1,024

Most likely nine folds will do the trick. Bring in a large sheet from a newspaper and ask students to start folding it to see if they can make nine folds. They probably won't be able to, but they will have fun trying.

Folding a paper triangle

Cut out a piece of paper in the shape of a right isosceles triangle and fold it as shown in figure 7.7. Count the number of small triangles formed after each fold.

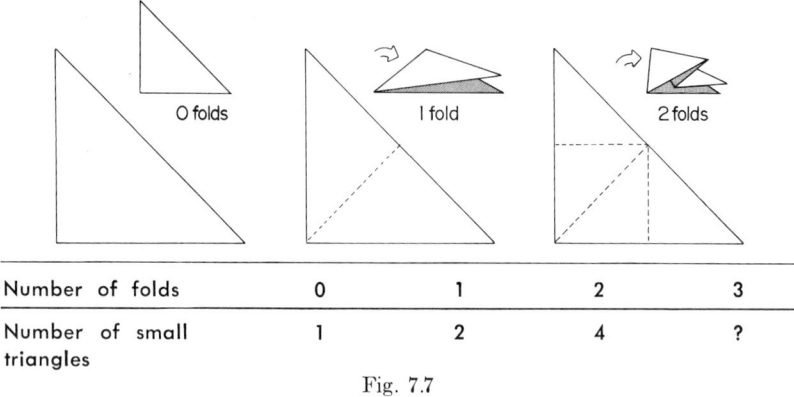

Number of folds	0	1	2	3
Number of small triangles	1	2	4	?

Fig. 7.7

This activity can be done by each student at his seat. It can also be demonstrated by the teacher with a large paper model or shown on the overhead projector by using a triangle cut from wax paper. Creases in the wax paper will show up clearly when projected.

Maintaining Arithmetic Skills

Invariably the slow learner in secondary school is weak in his arithmetic skills. More than likely this weakness stems, at least in part, from his failure to master the fundamental addition and multiplication facts while in elementary school. Hence it becomes increasingly important that attention be given to developing and maintaining arithmetic skills at the junior and senior high levels. The teacher needs to search for many imaginative and motivating aids and activities that either directly or indirectly lead to increased practice in arithmetic. Of all the problems confronting the mathematics teacher, this is probably the most difficult. There is no easy solution, no obvious method, and certainly no sure result.

There are some points to keep in mind, however. Try to teach the arithmetic skills in a format different from any used in the earlier grades. Be satisfied with gradual growth rather than expecting immediate, significant improvement. Strive for arithmetic competence rather than arithmetic mastery. Furthermore, concentrate on simple numerical examples rather than involved and complicated problems. Be realistic with the level of difficulty or the student will only get more discouraged with his inadequacies.

The slow learner needs novelty and variety to stimulate his interest and increase his attention span. The aids and activities described here can create visual, physical situations that are new to the student while at the same time helping to maintain and improve arithmetic skills.

Card games

Most students like games. They become motivated by competition, and they work under a self-imposed pressure often quite different from their normal level of interest and attention. The following card game can generate excitement and at the same time offer an opportunity to review arithmetic skills.

Number a set of cards from 1 through 9. Ask one student to pick five cards and another to pick a sixth card. Then see who can use the numbers on the five cards with addition, subtraction, multiplication, and/or division to get the number on the sixth card. Each number must be used exactly once. Numerous answers are possible for each set of cards. Some examples are given in figure 7. 8.

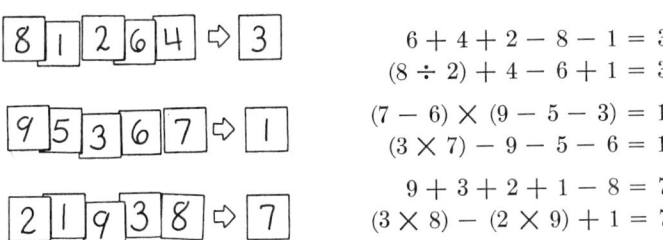

$6 + 4 + 2 - 8 - 1 = 3$
$(8 \div 2) + 4 - 6 + 1 = 3$

$(7 - 6) \times (9 - 5 - 3) = 1$
$(3 \times 7) - 9 - 5 - 6 = 1$

$9 + 3 + 2 + 1 - 8 = 7$
$(3 \times 8) - (2 \times 9) + 1 = 7$

Fig. 7.8

For slower classes, play a simpler game. Draw three cards and use them with the four fundamental operations to form other numbers. Some examples, with cards numbered 7, 8, and 3, are given in figure 7.9.

For a still simpler game, see how many numerals can be formed using some of the numbered cards as digits. There are fifteen possible

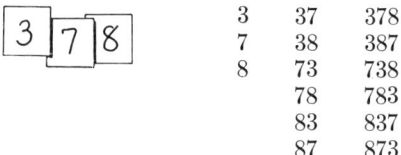

$8 + 7 + 3 = 18$
$8 + 7 - 3 = 12$
$7 + 3 - 8 = 2$
$7 \times 8 + 3 = 59$
$7 \times 8 - 3 = 53$
$8 \times 3 + 7 = 31$
$8 \times 3 - 7 = 17$
$8 \times 7 \times 3 = 168$

Fig. 7.9

solutions for three cards with different numbers. All the solutions for the digits 3, 7, and 8 are listed in figure 7.10.

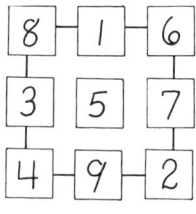

3	37	378
7	38	387
8	73	738
	78	783
	83	837
	87	873

Fig. 7.10

You can move around the class and let various students select the cards. You can cut out large squares and have the students arrange them at the board. Or you can prepare a set of small squares of acetate for use on an overhead projector, where the teacher or student can arrange them with ease.

Magic squares

For practice in adding, the same set of cards can be used to make magic squares. Tape the cards on the chalkboard arranged in a magic square. Have the students add the rows, columns, and diagonals to verify that the sum in each case is 15.

```
8  1  6
3  5  7
4  9  2
```

Fig. 7.11

By different rotations and reflections, eight arrangements in the magic squares can be formed from the nine cards. One is shown in figure 7.11. Three more are shown in figure 7.12. The remaining four arrangements have been started in figure 7.13. Begin these magic squares and have the students complete them at the board.

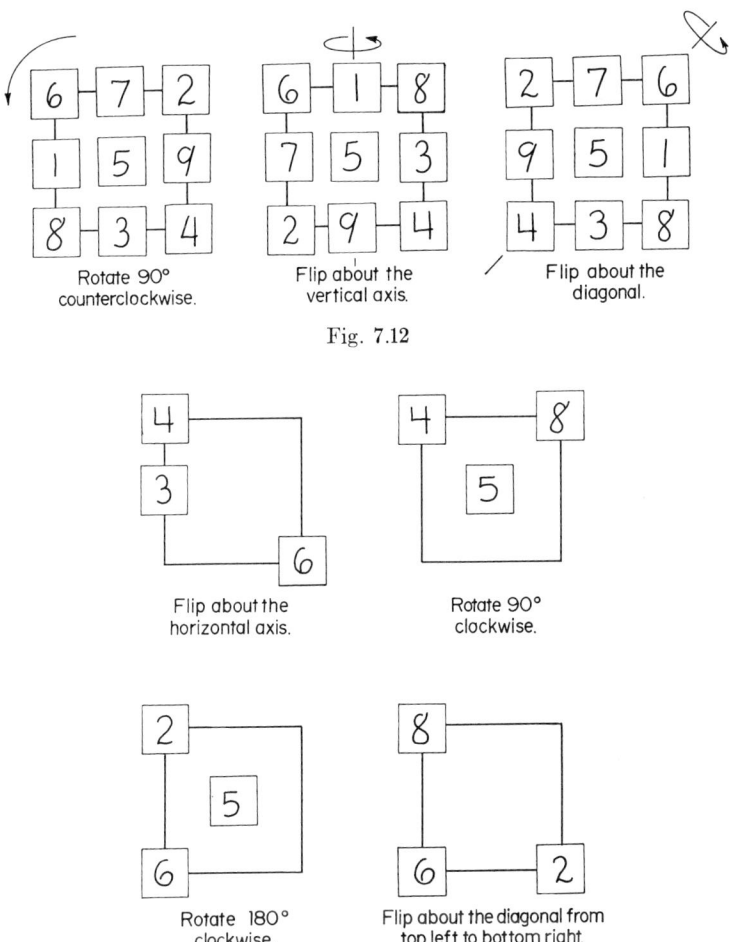

Fig. 7.12

Fig. 7.13

These eight arrangements can be shown effectively on an overhead projector by cutting out the magic square in its original position and then rotating it and flipping it over about the four axes indicated.

Many other activities can be developed from magic squares. Students might be asked, for example: "Can you add a given number to each entry or multiply each entry by a constant?" "Do you get a magic square when you subtract each entry from 10?"

Display cards

Here is a simple variation of a basic type of arithmetic problem. Have students order fractions and decimals by actually moving numbered cards that are taped on the blackboard or tacked on the bulletin board (fig. 7.14). The extra activity of having a student physically order the cards may add much to his understanding of the ordering property of numbers. Have one student put the greatest number on the right. Have another put the smallest on the left. Have a third order the rest in between.

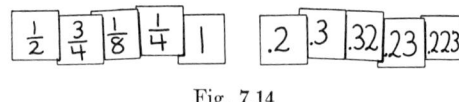

Fig. 7.14

Obviously, the same type of activity can be employed for more difficult problems, such as ordering the fractions and decimals shown in figure 7.15.

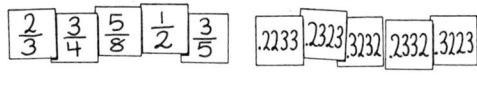

Fig. 7.15

This technique can be applied to many different situations, of course. Another is the equating of fractions and decimals (fig. 7.16). Have

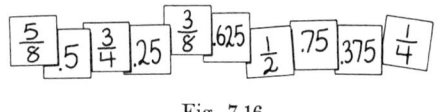

Fig. 7.16

students match each fraction with the correct decimal. Once the cards are matched, leave them on the board for easy reference. You may use them to introduce a large chart that shows many fraction-decimal equivalences. If such a chart is available, be sure to keep it displayed and refer to it frequently.

Flow charts

Many of the difficulties of teaching slow learners can be solved by finding new formats for the problems that have troubled these students in the past. A flow chart may be one such format. Suppose you want to review some arithmetic facts. First, cut out from a sheet of

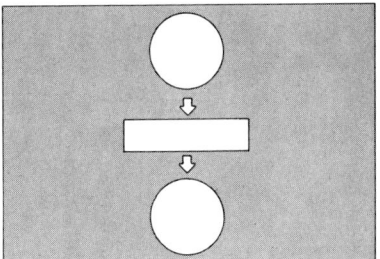

Fig. 7.17

paper several diagrams like the one shown in figure 7.17. When such diagrams are placed on the overhead projector, the light will shine only through the circles, rectangles, and arrows. Next, write some problems on clear sheets of acetate used as overlays. Put the input on the top, the operation in the center, and the output on the bottom, as shown in figure 7.18. Project the master diagram and an overlay on the screen. Of course, you may prefer to dispense with overlays by projecting the master diagram directly on the blackboard and writing in the values with chalk. The examples in figure 7.18 show some

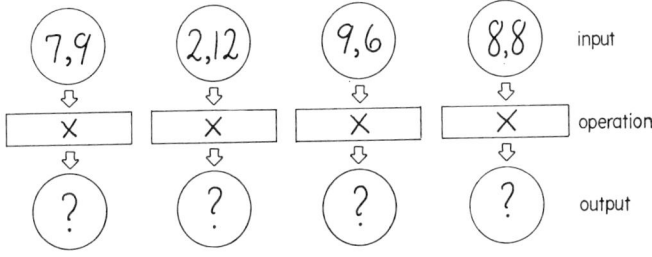

Fig. 7.18

typical problems used to review the multiplication facts, but you can vary the problems by asking for a possible operation, as in figure

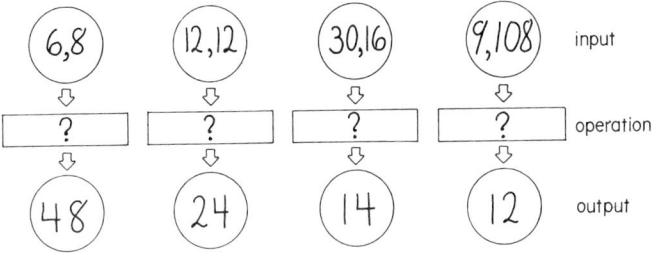

Fig. 7.19

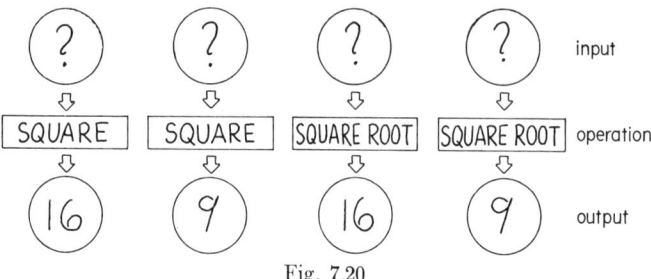

Fig. 7.20

7.19, or you can give the operation and output and have the students find the input, as in figure 7.20. Make problems like these fairly simple and move through them rapidly.

When you teach fractions or decimals or exponents, you will find the same diagram useful.

Another variation with flow charts can be used to give practice in arithmetic. Cut out a set of circular pieces of paper marked with various numbers and some rectangular pieces marked with different operations. Let one student come up to the board and make his own flow chart while the class tries to find what the output number is. The better students will enjoy putting several operation rules together in the same flow chart.

Percent scales and charts

The slow learner cannot be expected to master all the various types of percent problems. It is far better for him to get some basic feeling for a few commonly used percents and their meaning. Let the students make up tables of percent conversions, and encourage their use. Try to relate the percent concept to physical things and situations.

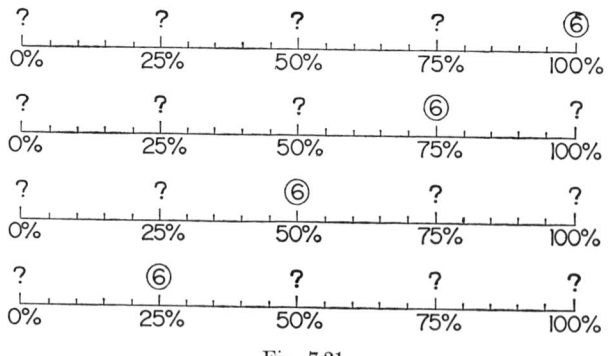

Fig. 7.21

AIDS AND ACTIVITIES

Mark a percent scale on a long strip of paper. Write a number above one of the percents. Then let a student write the corresponding numbers above other points on the scale. Point out the various problems that arise from placing the number in different positions on the scale (see fig. 7.21).

Another activity makes use of a percent chart like the one shown in figures 7.22-7.24. Rule the grid on a large piece of poster paper. Attach a string at the top and use it to locate the *base* along the bottom scale. Then read *percents* and corresponding *percentages* along the vertical and horizontal axes respectively. Once the student becomes familiar with the way the chart works, he should find it easy to solve the various forms of percent problems.

1. What is 40% of 50?

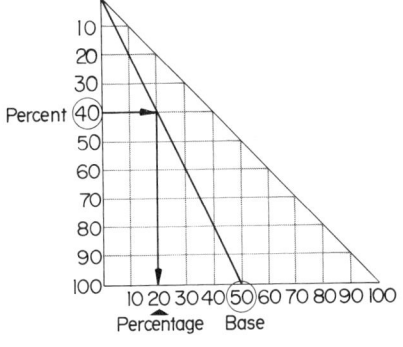

40% of 50 = ?
Rate = 40%
Base = 50
Percentage = ?
Locate the string for
a *base* of 50. Read
across at the *percent*,
40, to find the *percentage*,
20.
40% of 50 = 20

Fig. 7.22

2. What percent of 60 is 30?

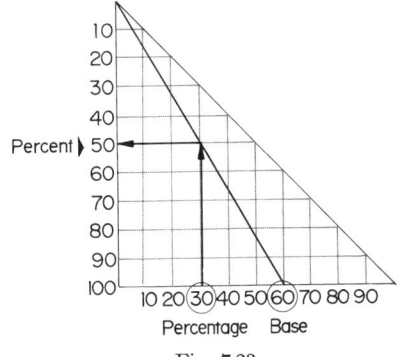

? of 60 = 30
Base = 60
Percentage = 30
Rate = ?
Locate the string for
a *base* of 60. Read up
from the *percentage*, 30,
to find the *percent*, 50.
50% of 60 = 30

Fig. 7.23

3. 60 is 75% of what number?

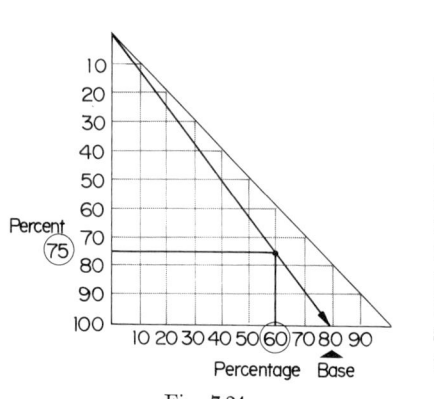

Fig. 7.24

75% of ? = 60
Rate = 75%
Percentage = 60
Base = ?
Read across from 75 on the *percent* scale and up from 60 on the *percentage* scale. Pass the string through this intersection point and find the *base* at the point where the string intersects the bottom scale.
75% of 80 = 60

Developing Geometric Concepts

Far too few mathematics teachers spend enough time on geometry with the slow and reluctant learner, and those that do frequently forget how important the use of aids can be in clarifying geometric ideas or concepts. There is an abundance of multisensory aids that can be used effectively in teaching geometry. Even pencil and paper can take on special meaning as aids in teaching geometry. Take time to illustrate important geometric concepts visually and in various ways. Help the slow learner to *see* the concepts he is asked to learn.

Congruence

The concept of congruency is all too often assumed to be simple, obvious, and self-evident. For most slow learners this is not the case—nor is it for many other students. A basic understanding of congruency comes best from visual and tactile experiences. Congruence must be seen, felt, and illustrated in many ways, and at the same time explained in simple, familiar terms.

Congruent figures have the same size and shape and can be made to coincide. Although this approach is decidedly intuitive, it is the only way the slow student can learn to see congruency. It is also the way the concept should be illustrated to the students through various aids and activities.

Cutting out congruent figures. Cut out some sets of congruent figures from heavy paper or cardboard—triangles, squares, circles, and figures of irregular shape.

Tape one triangle on the board. Hold a congruent one on top of it and show how they coincide. Then slide the second triangle to the side and show various positions in which it can be placed. Some positions give the obvious appearance of congruency whereas others do not (see fig. 7.25). Point out that the position of the triangle has

Fig. 7.25

nothing to do with whether or not it is congruent to another. Congruency is a property of the figures themselves and not of their relative positions. This is the big source of difficulty regarding congruency. When the figures are oriented favorably, students have no trouble recognizing congruency. But when they are not oriented favorably, students often say they are not congruent.

The idea that congruency is independent of orientation needs to be repeatedly illustrated in many different ways. It can be effectively shown with figures cut from colored acetate and moved about on an overhead projector. It can also be shown by tracing one figure and moving the tracing to a second figure. If the tracing can be made to coincide with the second figure, then the figures are congruent. These demonstrations may seem very crude, but they are particularly meaningful and visual to the slow-learning student.

Cutting and folding squares. Bring into class some square sheets of paper. Cut one square into two pieces so that the two halves are congruent. Then have your students come up and try to cut other squares in different ways but always so that the two pieces are congruent. Once a square is cut, hold one of its pieces on top of the other to see if they are congruent. Infinitely many different cuts are possible. Some cuts form pieces that are more obviously congruent than others (fig. 7.26).

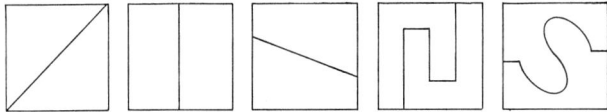

Fig. 7.26

For variation of this activity, pass a set of small square sheets of paper to each of the students. Ask them each to fold a square so that the crease divides the square into two congruent parts. Then have them make a variety of such folds, using their other squares, to see if they can find what property a fold must have for the parts to be congruent. Stacking four or five squares one on top of another and holding them up to the light may provide the clue. The fold forms a straight crease, and if it goes through the center of the square, the two parts are congruent. This can be vividly demonstrated by using an overhead projector with a series of creases folded into wax paper squares.

Better students may enjoy folding paper squares into more than two congruent pieces. The examples in figure 7.27 show folds forming four congruent parts.

Fig. 7.27

Drawing on grids and graph paper. Few aids are more useful in illustrating congruency than graph paper and a coordinate grid on a blackboard. Activities with these aids not only strengthen the student's understanding of congruency but also give him practice in translation, rotation, reflection, and orientation on a plane. The only skills required are two basic abilities: to count squares and to follow directions. Some slow learners, it is true, may not excel in these skills either; but they should be assured of at least some degree of success.

Start by drawing a vertical segment on the blackboard grid such that endpoints of the segment are points on the grid. Have a student

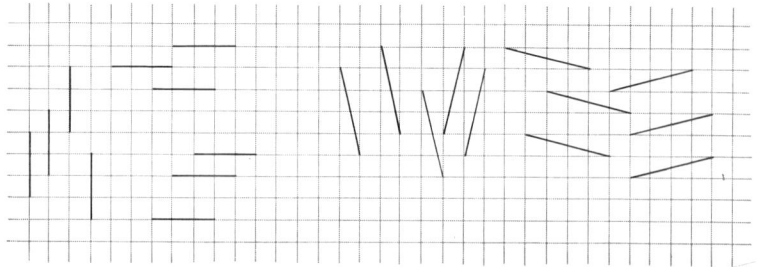

Fig. 7.28

draw several congruent segments in this position. Then let him draw some in another position. Now try the same with a diagonal segment. Let several students have the opportunity to draw congruent segments. See if they can find the four different positions possible. (See fig. 7.28.)

Next draw a rectangle on the blackboard grid. Have a student draw a congruent one in a different position. In general, for a rectangle only two positions are possible, vertical and horizontal.

Now draw a right triangle on the blackboard grid. Have several students come up and see how many congruent triangles they can draw in different relative positions. Your students should enjoy trying to find all eight, as shown in figure 7.29.

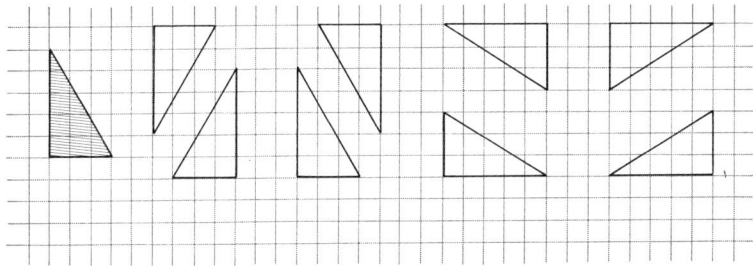

Fig. 7.29

A somewhat more difficult problem is to find all eight different relative positions of a general triangle whose vertices are points on the grid, as shown in figure 7.30.

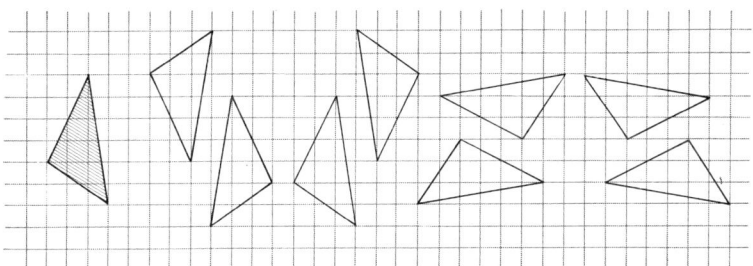

Fig. 7.30

One variation of this involves drawing the figures on an overhead projector rather than the blackboard. In either case, let a student come up and try to draw the congruent figures himself. Students become more actively involved this way, and they usually enjoy the opportunity to participate. The rest of the class will be eager to check for errors or duplications.

Needless to say, much can also be gained by having your students do several problems of this type on their own graph paper. In this case, be sure to draw the original figure on the board for them to copy.

Symmetry and reflections

Symmetry and reflections are very important geometric concepts, yet they seldom receive sufficient attention in the classroom. For the slow learner they are especially important because they are concrete, visual concepts. A few simple activities and aids appropriate for the topic and the student are given here. Be certain to relate each to the concept of congruency.

Cutting paper. However obvious and simple, the following illustrations of line and point symmetry are perhaps the most vivid. Fold a paper once and cut out a design across the fold. Then open it up to form an example of line symmetry. Point symmetry can be illustrated in much the same way but by folding the paper twice. (See fig. 7.31.)

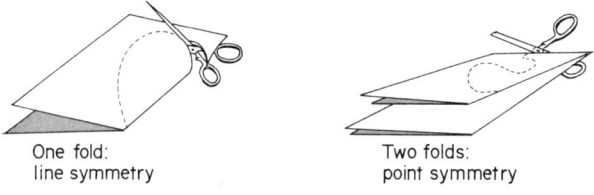

One fold: line symmetry   Two folds: point symmetry

Fig. 7.31

In this case, the figure formed has symmetry about two lines as well as about the point of intersection of these lines.

Folding squares. Cut out some squares of paper and punch two holes in each with a paper punch. Now, without revealing to the students the procedure, locate the line of symmetry between the holes in one of the squares by folding it so that the holes align. (Fig. 7.32.) Draw

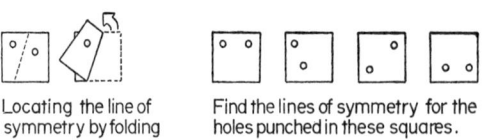

Locating the line of symmetry by folding   Find the lines of symmetry for the holes punched in these squares.

Fig. 7.32

the line clearly and show it to the students as you discuss with them the meaning of symmetry with respect to a line. Then ask some students to draw a line where they think the line of symmetry is for each pair of holes in the other squares. Finally, let them see how close they came by having them fold the squares so that the holes line up.

Writing reflections. Have a student go to the board and print his name. Have another draw a line nearby. Now have a third try to write the reflection of the name about the line. (See fig. 7.33.) Have a mirror

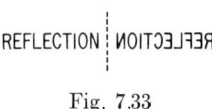

Fig. 7.33

handy to show the reflection if the student needs help.

A variation of this activity can be done at the students' seats. Distribute unruled paper and have each student print his name, draw the line, and try to write the reflection. Have each check his work by folding the paper on the line and holding it up to the light.

Drawing on grids and graph paper. Draw a line on a coordinate grid on the chalkboard. Then draw a triangle on one side of the line with vertices on points on the grid. Have a student, by counting squares, locate the reflection of the triangle on the other side of the line. The two triangles so found are symmetric about the line and, of course, congruent. (See fig. 7.34.) This activity is especially helpful

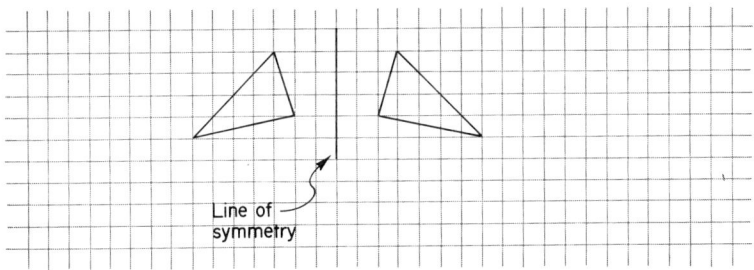

Fig. 7.34

to the slow learner. It improves his orientation on a plane yet requires no skill greater than that of counting.

Your better students can do a similar problem involving point symmetry (see fig. 7.35).

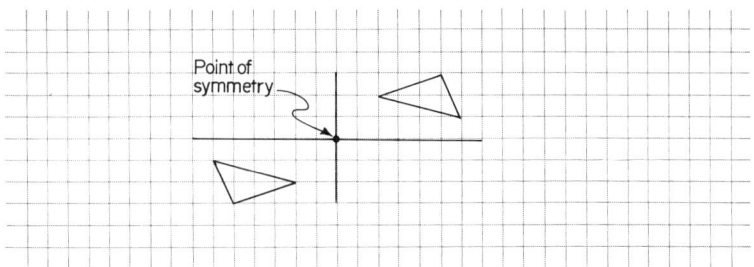

Fig. 7.35

Here again the activities can be varied by using an overhead projector or by having every student work at his seat with his own sheet of graph paper. In any case, draw the first triangle for him to copy.

Perpendiculars and parallels

Familiar examples of the geometric concepts *perpendicular* and *parallel* abound in the world, and many of them need to be brought to the attention of students. Slow learners especially need simple activities with such familiar examples in order to understand the concepts and establish them in their minds.

Folding paper. Construct some perpendiculars and parallels for the class by folding sheets of paper as shown in figures 7.36, 7.37, and 7.38. Then have each student fold paper at his desk in ways that show

Fig. 7.36. Folding a crease perpendicular to an edge of a paper

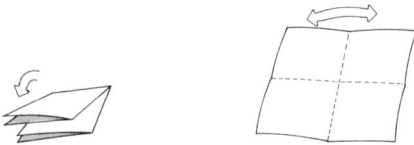

Fig. 7.37. Folding two perpendicular creases

Fig. 7.38. Folding two parallel creases

his understanding of what *perpendicular* and *parallel* mean.

Drawing on grids and graph paper. Parallels and perpendiculars are especially easy to illustrate on graph paper or on a coordinate grid on the board. Point out that the grid itself consists of many parallel and perpendicular segments and that many others can be drawn by simply counting squares. Draw a few of these at the board or use an overhead projector. Then have your students draw others on graph paper, taking the following procedure:

Choose a point and count as shown in figure 7.39. Then choose other

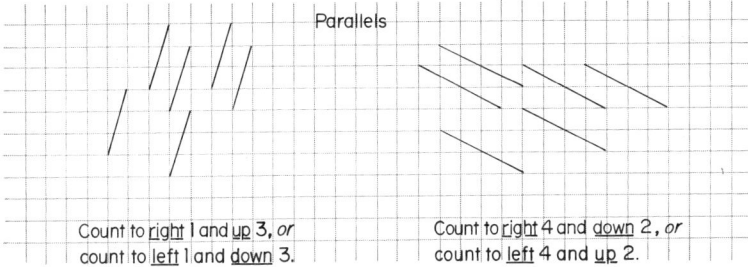

Fig. 7.39

points and repeat the process to draw parallel segments. Now segments perpendicular to these can easily be drawn. Start at either endpoint but reverse the number of units moved horizontally and vertically and also reverse one of the two directions (see fig. 7.40).

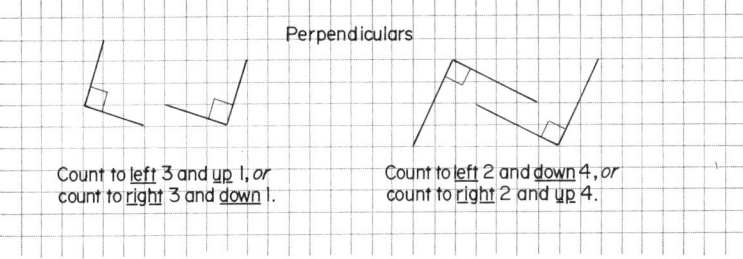

Fig. 7.40

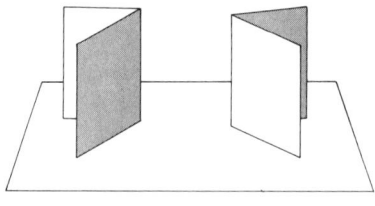

Fig. 7.41

Folding space models. It is easy to illustrate parallels and perpendiculars in space. Fold creases perpendicular to the edges of two sheets of paper and stand the folded sheets on a flat surface as shown in figure 7.41. Each crease represents a line perpendicular to a plane, since each is perpendicular to two lines in the plane. Together the creases represent two parallel lines in space, since both are perpendicular to the plane.

Other activities and aids to show perpendiculars and parallels in space are given later.

Length, area, and volume

All too many slow learners are unfamiliar with the basic units of length, area, and volume. One reason for this condition is that they need more time than they get in the classroom to study, use, and review these units of measure. Another reason is that they have not established good visual associations with these units. They haven't seen them represented enough, nor have they engaged in measuring activities that are sufficiently numerous and varied.

Ask a student to think of a hundred-yard length and almost invariably he has a mental picture of a football field; but ask him to think of a cubic-foot unit and he probably has no image at all. Even a square-foot unit is hard for him to visualize.

Begin by collecting some aids. Always have a *one-foot ruler* and a *yardstick* in the classroom. Keep cardboard models of a *one-inch square* and a *one-foot square* available. Make models of a *one-inch cube* and a *one-foot cube* (fig. 7.42) for the class. Use these aids frequently when working with measurement problems. Emphasize their visual comparison. It is probably just as important for a student to have a good visual idea of the relative sizes of a square inch and a square foot as it is for him to know that 144 square inches are equal in area to one square foot. It is common practice to teach students that 1,728 cubic inches are equal in volume to one cubic foot, but to

AIDS AND ACTIVITIES   203

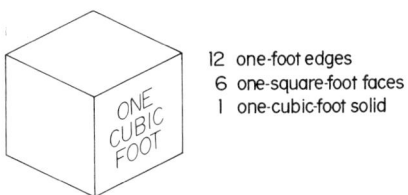

Fig. 7.42

most students this is only a number. By keeping models in class and referring to them often you can make the comparison much more vivid and much more meaningful.

A one-foot square has a square foot of area, but a half-foot square does not have a half square foot of area. Cardboard models resembling the sketches in figure 7.43 are very effective in illustrating this con-

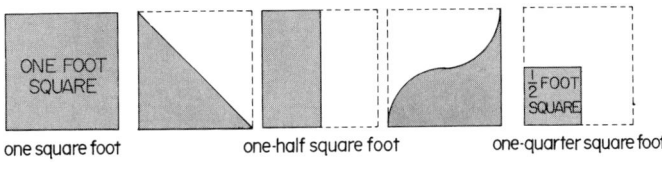

Fig. 7.43

cept. Make some models like these for the class. Or better, have some of the students make sets with the half-square-foot and quarter-square-foot areas appearing in different shapes or positions or locations.

A set of one-inch cubes can be a very valuable teaching aid. Arrange them in various ways, as in figure 7.44, and have the students

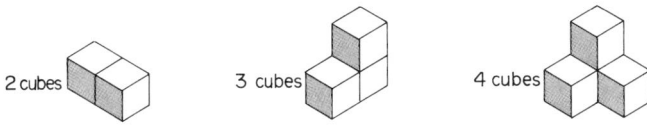

Fig. 7.44

find their volumes and areas. These problems offer good experience not only in using volume and area units but also in visualizing space figures.

Better students may enjoy finding which of the various solids that can be made from four cubes (fig. 7.45) has the least surface area.

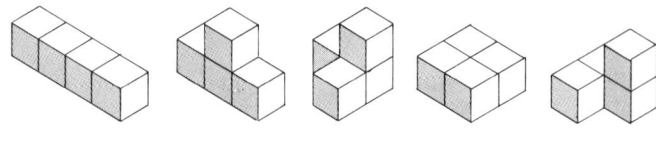

Fig. 7.45

Illustrating Algebraic Concepts

The basic concepts of algebra should be taught to all students. However, teaching them to the slow learner poses certain special problems. Invariably these students have done poorly in arithmetic; hence they lack the numerical foundation so vital to the algebra. Moreover, by its very nature, algebra is an abstract subject. It requires a high degree of mental dexterity, which the slow learner generally lacks. He understands best by doing, and he remembers best by seeing. In order to communicate the ideas of algebra to him, considerable attention must be given to the effective use of aids and activities in the classroom.

The slow student needs to study some of the basic concepts in algebra, but he needs to see them in many different ways. There are only a few skills in algebra he needs to master. There are many more he should experience.

Nomographs

Nomographs are simple to construct and easy to use. They are visual aids consisting of nothing more than number lines carefully spaced and calibrated. Prepare a large one for the bulletin board and another on a transparency for the overhead projector. Let the students make their own on graph paper.

The nomograph shown in figure 7.46 can be used for addition and subtraction of counting numbers. It consists of three equally spaced scales. The two outside scales are calibrated the same; the center scale has units half the size. To add two numbers, locate them on the outer scales and connect them with a line. The sum is read where this line crosses the center scale. Subtraction is done as the inverse of addition, with the difference found on the outer scale.

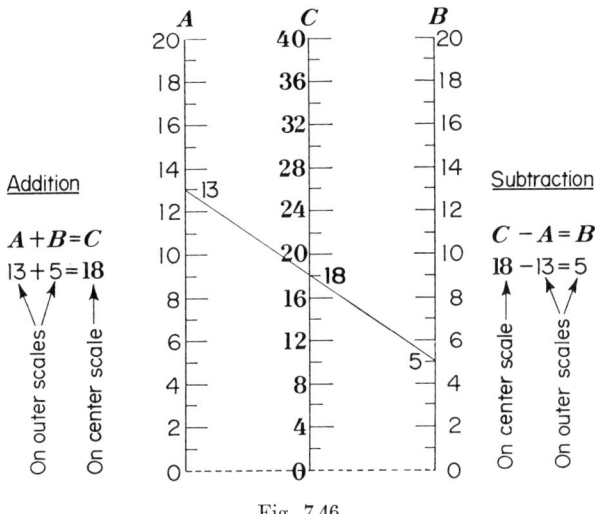

Fig. 7.46

The nomograph works this way because of a geometric property of trapezoids. The median of a trapezoid is equal in length to half the sum of the lengths of its bases. (See fig 7.47.) This median is located

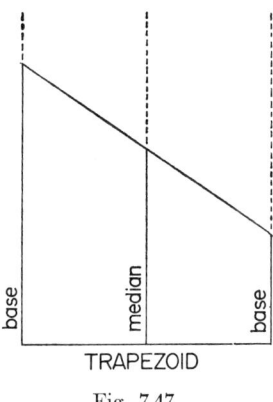

Fig. 7.47

along the center scale of the nomograph. By halving the unit length on this scale, the sums can be read directly.

A nomograph can be extremely useful in teaching addition and subtraction with integers. In teaching the addition and subtraction of integers, a demonstration nomograph like the one in figure 7.48

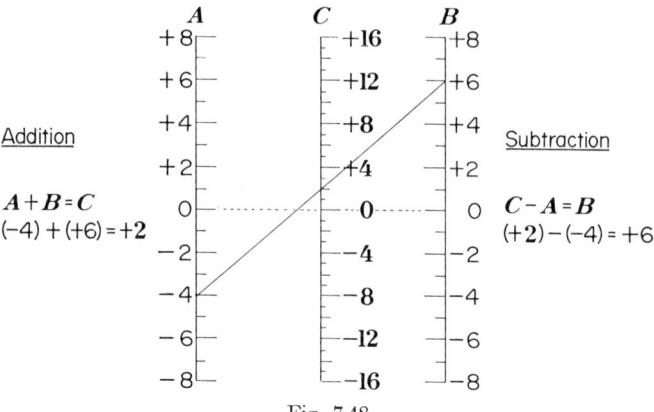
Fig. 7.48

serves several major purposes:

It gives the student a picture of the relative locations of the positive and negative integers.

It clearly illustrates the property that the sum of two positive integers is positive and two negative integers, negative.

It shows how the sum of a positive and a negative number can be positive or negative, depending on the magnitudes of the numbers.

It shows graphically why the sum of two opposite integers is zero.

It can be kept posted so that students can refer to it and use it any time they want.

There is much value in having students make their own nomographs as well. Have them draw the nomograph on graph paper. They get practice in measuring, marking off units, and numbering scales. Moreover, they have a chance to use what they make.

Paper folding

Try this simple demonstration of the relationship
$$(a + b)^2 = a^2 + 2ab + b^2$$
Take a paper square measuring $a + b$ units on each side. (See fig. 7.49.) Fold it twice to form two squares measuring a and b units

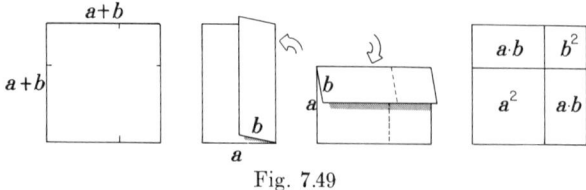
Fig. 7.49

respectively. Now find the areas of the two squares and the two rectangles formed.

Here is a simple demonstration of the relationship
$$a^2 - b^2 = (a - b)(a + b)$$
Take a square measuring a units on each side. (See fig. 7.50.) Fold

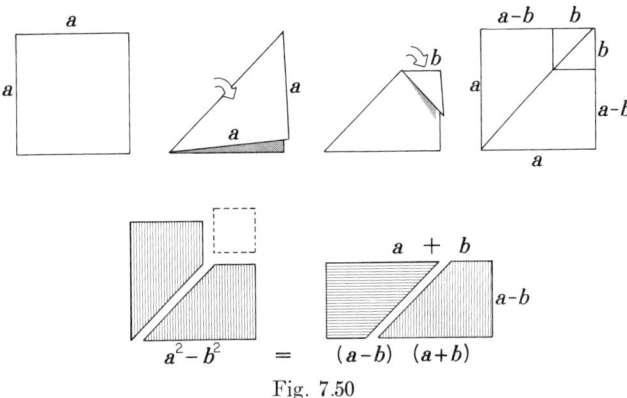

Fig. 7.50

it diagonally. Then fold back at a perpendicular distance b. Tear off this corner and tear down the remainder of the diagonal. The original piece measured a^2. The piece torn off measured b^2. The remainder measures $a^2 - b^2$. Rearrange the pieces into the rectangle shown. It measures $(a - b)(a + b)$.

Flow charts

Flow charts can be very valuable in teaching algebraic concepts to the slow learner. For example, such charts can illustrate the importance of clearly indicating the desired order of operations—the order typically shown by the presence or absence of parentheses. Cut out from construction paper the shapes shown in figure 7.51 and fill

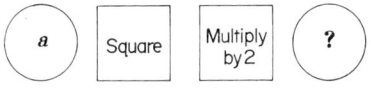

Fig. 7.51

them in. Now arrange them in two different ways on the board (fig. 7.52). Note how the flow charts help to emphasize the difference in these problems.

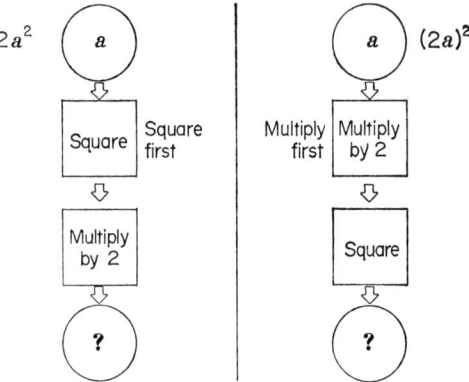

Fig. 7.52

Several different activities can be used for drill on this type of problem. Project the flow chart onto the blackboard, using an overhead projector. Write in the input and operations, and have the student write in the corresponding algebraic expression. Or give him the expression and have him write in the correct sequence of steps in the flow chart on the board. See figure 7.53 for examples. When the chart

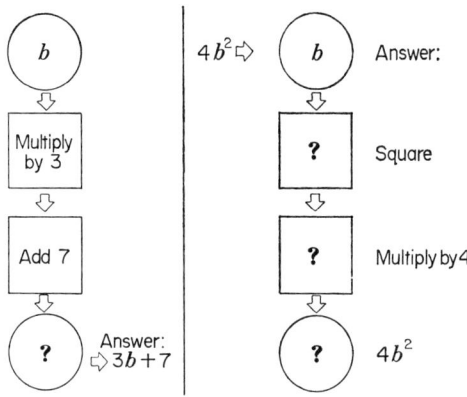

Fig. 7.53

is completed, simply erase the board and enter new data. The flow chart remains projected on the board.

A flow chart can outline the steps to follow in numerical substitution as well. (See fig. 7.54.)

AIDS AND ACTIVITIES

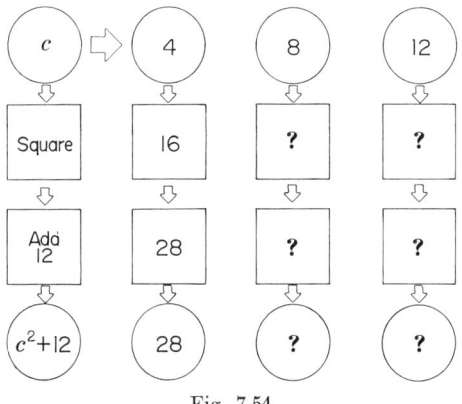

Fig. 7.54

Flow charts can also give meaning to the solving of equations. Notice how the steps are reversed to solve the equation in figure 7.55.

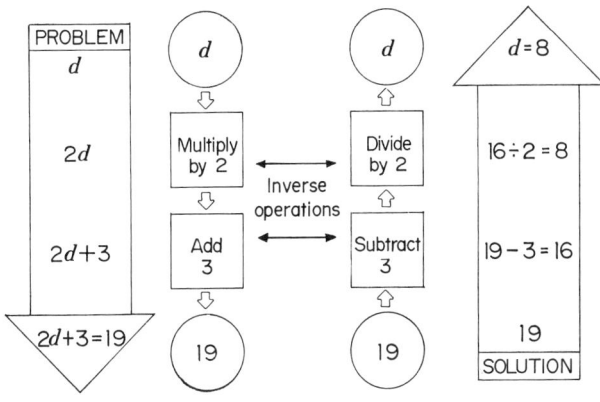

Fig. 7.55

Models for variation

Graphs show how variables are related, but frequently the students fail to see this relationship. The following example illustrates how a graph can be closely tied to a physical model.

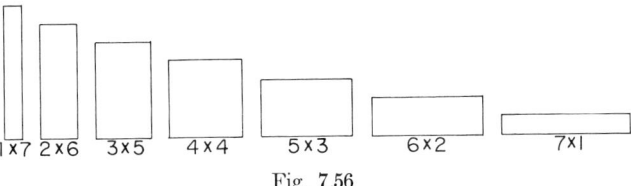

Fig. 7.56

Cut out a series of rectangles with perimeters of 16 inches and sides of integral lengths (fig. 7.56). Tape them to the blackboard in order of increasing length. Ask what happens to the width as the length increases, and discuss what might be the maximum possible length. Now stack the rectangles against the axes one at a time. Mark the upper righthand vertex of each. Then draw the graph through these points, as in figure 7.57. Have the students find the area of each

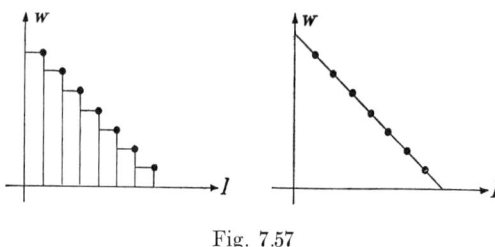

Fig. 7.57

rectangle. Point out that the square has the greatest area. Then see if a student can sketch how the area varies as the length increases.

Making Good Use of Models

The slow learner often learns by seeing things. One of the goals in teaching is to help him improve this skill in space perception. The clever, imaginative use of geometric models in the classroom can do a great deal toward achieving that goal.

By their very nature, geometric models can be seen, handled, and constructed. They are real to the student, even though teachers recognize them as representatives of abstract geometric figures that exist only in one's mind. Geometric concepts need to be expressed physically to the slow learner. New ideas need to evolve from established ones, and new ways of seeing things in space need to be supported with concrete illustrations. New, discovery problems need to be related to old, familiar ones.

All too frequently an insufficient amount of time is spent on geometry in the classroom. The reasons cited are many and varied. Some teachers argue that there is not enough time to master arithmetic skills, let alone geometric concepts. Some teachers feel that geometry is secondary in importance to arithmetic and algebra. Others find that they themselves have trouble visualizing things in space. Still others see only the synthetic structure and proof in geometry.

None of these reasons can be justified for the slow learner. Geometric relationships are part of the real world to him, and they can and should be seen and shown. Many aids and activities involving models can be used effectively in the classroom in teaching geometry. Here are some examples. They are concrete, not abstract. They are visual, not verbal. They are simple, not sophisticated. And they actively involve the student.

Making models

Making models is a valuable experience, especially for the slow learner. It gives him something to do with his hands and it gives him practice in copying patterns, in measuring, and in constructing. Many slow students are especially adept at these types of activities. For them, making models provides the much-needed feeling of accomplishment. For others, it gives good practice in organization, accuracy, and neatness.

The very slow class may do best by cutting out patterns supplied by the teacher, or by copying patterns, using the grid on graph paper.

In all classes, begin by cutting out a large paper model and showing how it can be folded. (See fig. 7.58.)

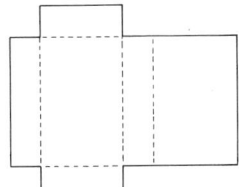
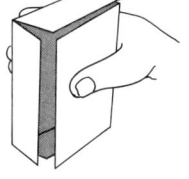

Fig. 7.58

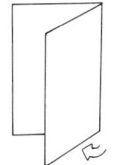
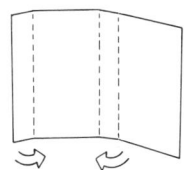
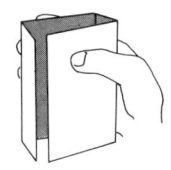

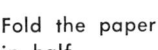

Fold the paper in half.

Fold each half the same distance from its left edge.

Fold to form the four lateral faces of the prism.

Fig. 7.59

For classes where the use of scissors and tape is inadvisable, a very simple representation of a right rectangular prism can be formed from a plain sheet of paper. (See fig. 7.59.)

Stacking models

Assign the construction of a particular rectangular prism to each student in class. A convenient set of dimensions is 1 × 2 × 4 inches. Then develop a lesson around solids that can be formed by stacking the prisms. Restrict the stacking to the joining of congruent faces only.

Three solids can be formed from two prisms, as shown in figure 7.60.

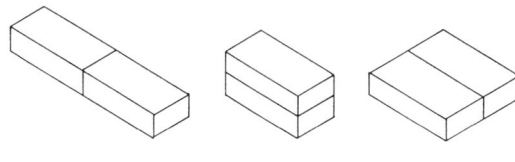

Fig. 7.60

Relate these solids to the volume and surface area of the original single prism, asking:
"Which solids have twice the volume?"
"Which have twice the surface area?"
"Which has the smallest surface area?"
"Which has the largest?"

For better classes, follow the same procedure with three prisms. Some of the possible figures are shown in figure 7.61. There are six altogether.

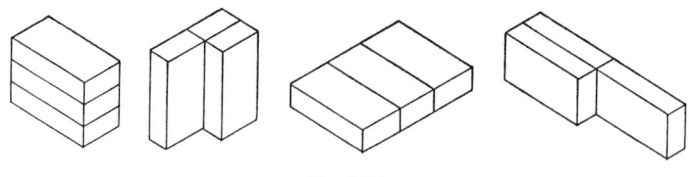

Fig. 7.61

Patterns for models

It is one thing to copy a pattern and make a model from it. It is another thing to make up one's own pattern. The slow learner can gain a great deal from making and studying patterns for models.

Cut six squares of paper all the same size. Fasten them on the blackboard with masking tape or a magnet, or on the bulletin board with

AIDS AND ACTIVITIES 213

thumbtacks. Then have a student come up and arrange them in a pattern for a cube. See how many different patterns can be found. Some are shown in figure 7.62. Don't count different positions of the same

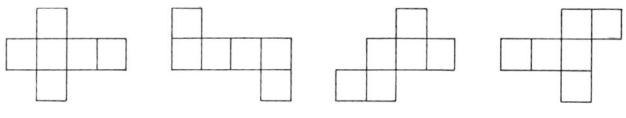

Fig. 7.62

pattern. Encourage students to recognize congruency and to see symmetries, reflections, and rotations.

Show some different positions of the same pattern (fig. 7.63). Let

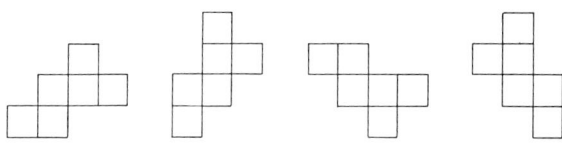

Fig. 7.63

students see how some positions can be reached by rotation, others by flipping the pattern over, and still others only by flipping the pattern and also rotating it.

Here are some variations on this same type of activity. Bring to class some figures formed from six squares joined side to side and see if the students can tell which can be folded to form a cube and which cannot. Once they guess, fold up the patterns to support or reject their answers. See if they can tell which of the patterns in figure 7.64 can be folded to form a cube.

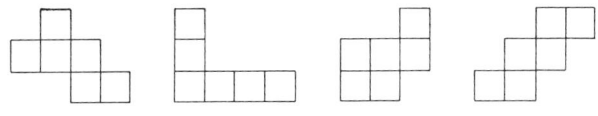

Fig. 7.64

Cut out a pattern that can be folded into a cube. Identify the top face and ask the students to locate the bottom one (fig. 7.65). In

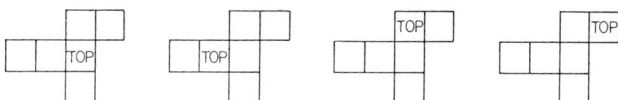

Fig. 7.65

each case follow up their answers by actually folding the pattern. If this one is too easy, use a harder pattern. If it is too hard, use a simpler one.

Still another related activity requires the identification of the incorrect face on the pattern for a rectangular prism (fig. 7.66). See if the students can identify each incorrect face.

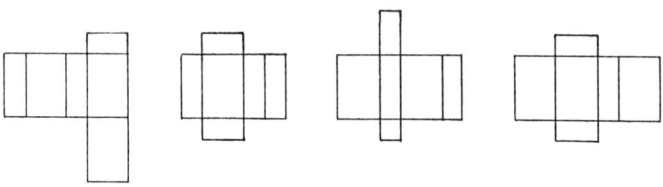

Fig. 7.66

Sketching solids

Many students, especially the slower ones, have trouble interpreting the two-dimensional sketches of three-dimensional solids. This trouble arises because few teachers explain the parts of a sketch carefully and because even fewer teachers give students much experience in sketching solids themselves.

Here are some aids and activities that give students valuable experience in sketching prisms. They should follow the construction of three-dimensional models and a discussion of these properties of prisms:

Opposite bases are congruent and parallel.
Lateral edges are congruent and parallel.

Take a rectangular and a triangular piece of paper. Have the class first view them head-on, then at an angle, as in figure 7.67. Discuss

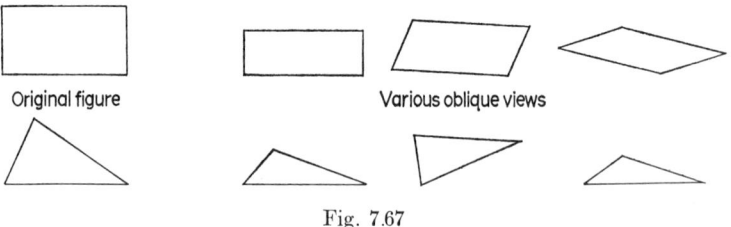

Fig. 7.67

which properties of the figures are seen to remain the same and which appear to change when viewed from different positions. Note that parallelism is preserved, as is the number of sides. Note also that dimension is not preserved.

Now begin the sketching activity this way. Cut out two large triangular pieces of paper of the same size and shape. Tape one to the board. Let it represent an oblique view of the upper base of a right triangular prism. Hold the other on top of it to show that they are congruent. Then move the second triangle to various positions below the first one. Seek out the position that appears best for the lower base. When this base is put in various positions, the students can see more clearly the reasons for positioning it directly beneath the upper base. Once the position is agreed on, tape the triangle there and complete the sketch of the right triangular prism. (See fig. 7.68.)

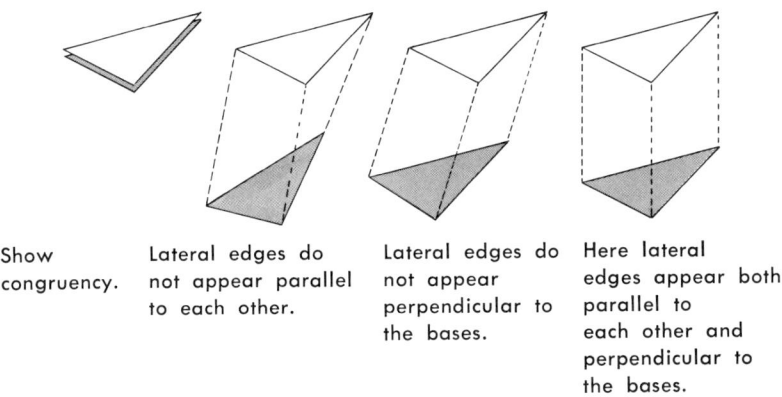

| Show congruency. | Lateral edges do not appear parallel to each other. | Lateral edges do not appear perpendicular to the bases. | Here lateral edges appear both parallel to each other and perpendicular to the bases. |

Fig. 7.68

This entire sequence could also be developed effectively by using an overhead projector.

Now illustrate these steps by using a coordinate grid drawn on the blackboard or projected from an overhead projector. (See figs. 7.69 and 7.70.)

Next, have the students copy these figures on their own graph paper. Suggest that they count the squares carefully in order to get the correct figure in each case.

Let the students sketch some other prisms on graph paper by themselves. Emphasize the importance of preserving the congruency and parallelism of the bases and of the lateral edges; these properties are what simplify the sketching technique. With a ruler and graph paper,

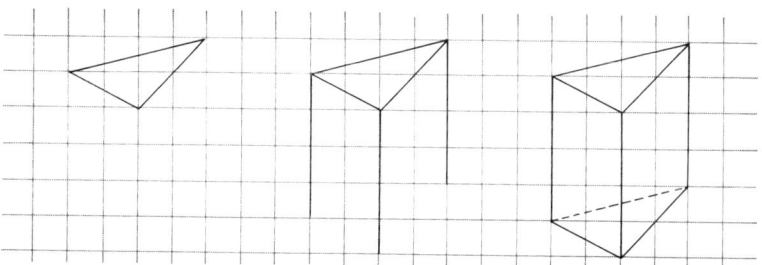

Step 1	Step 2	Step 3
Draw an oblique view of the upper base.	Draw the lateral edges congruent and parallel.	Draw the lower base. It must appear congruent to the upper base.

Fig. 7.69

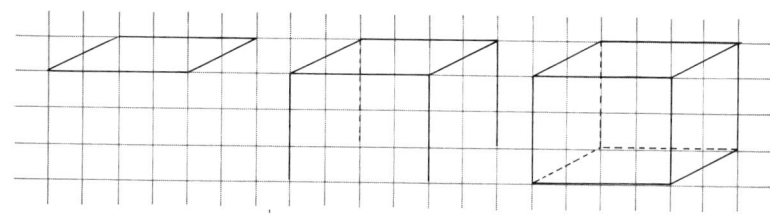

Fig. 7.70

even the slowest student will be able to sketch prisms with good results. Encourage the better students to follow the same steps but without graph paper.

Illustrating properties in space

Most teachers use the classroom itself to illustrate parallelism and perpendicularity of lines and planes in space. A cardboard model of a right rectangular prism can also serve as a valuable aid in illustrating these properties. Bring these supplies to class:

A large model of a right rectangular prism

Several large sheets of cardboard or a thin sheet of plywood

Several thin dowels, balsa strips, stiff wires, pointers, or even yardsticks

Use the dowels to represent lines and the cardboard, planes. Place the dowels along edges of the model to help locate lines, as in figure 7.71.

AIDS AND ACTIVITIES 217

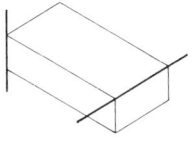 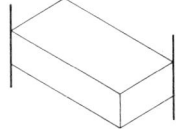 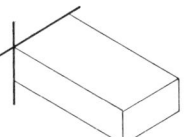

Skew lines — In all, 24 pairs of skew lines can be found.

Parallel lines — In all, 18 pairs of parallel lines can be found.

Perpendicular lines — In all, 24 pairs of perpendicular lines can be found.

Fig. 7.71

Place the cardboard against the model surfaces to illustrate planes, as in figure 7.72.

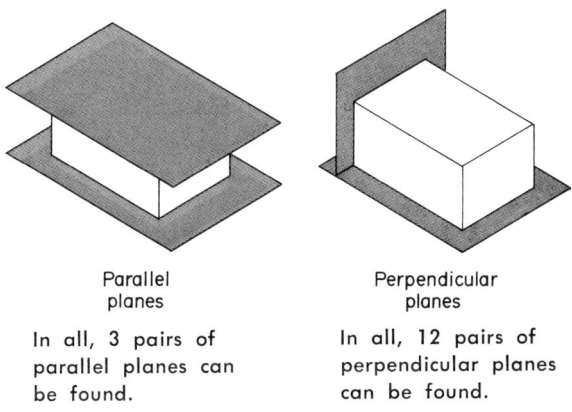

Parallel planes — In all, 3 pairs of parallel planes can be found.

Perpendicular planes — In all, 12 pairs of perpendicular planes can be found.

Fig. 7.72

This activity can be varied by using a sketch of a right rectangular prism drawn or projected on the blackboard. With colored chalk, mark one edge. Then have a student go to the board and mark the other edges that are parallel to it. Use the same procedure to show perpendicular and skew edges as well. If the sketch is projected on the blackboard from an overhead projector, the edges can be marked and readily erased without destroying the original sketch.

Summary

This chapter has set forth only a few of the aids and activities available to the mathematics teacher. These and many others are discussed in detail in the references listed below. Together they illustrate how simple, physical experiences can add to a student's understanding of a subject. The slow learner needs to see and do things to understand them; and he demands novel, meaningful experiences that will interest him and lengthen his short attention span.

As you teach, keep aware of the many uses of very simple things. *Folding paper* can illustrate the geometric concepts of parallelism, perpendicularity, congruency, and symmetry. It can produce many types of counting situations, and it can offer activities in which the whole class can become involved. *Graph paper* gives the students a chance to copy accurately and to follow the teacher's work in drawing geometric figures. It can help the student in drawing and studying parallel and perpendicular lines as well as congruent and symmetric figures through the simple skill of counting. The *overhead projector* allows for the advance preparation of materials and helps to focus attention through the use of color and the movement of figures. It is an aid that the student himself should be allowed to use. The *chalkboard* and *bulletin board* can serve to display key ideas, to hold numbered cards for ordering, and to serve as a screen for the overhead projector.

The only real limitation on the effective use of multisensory aids and activities in the classroom is the creativity and imagination of the teacher. As you teach the slow learner, use these resources to good advantage. They can make the difference between hearing without understanding, and seeing-and-doing *with* understanding.

REFERENCES

1. Adler, Irving. *Magic House of Numbers.* New York: John Day Co., 1957.
2. Association of Teachers of Mathematics [Great Britain]. *Notes on Mathematics in Primary Schools.* London: Cambridge University Press, 1967. Also available as paperback from the New York branch of Cambridge University Press and the Cuisenaire Company of America, Inc., 12 Church St., New Rochelle, N.Y. 10805.
3. Auclair, Jerome A., and Thomas P. Hillman. "A Topological Problem for the Ninth-Grade Mathematics Laboratory." *Mathematics Teacher* 61 (May 1968): 503-7.
4. Ball, W. W. R., and H. S. M. Coxeter. *Mathematical Recreations and Essays.* London: Macmillan Co., 1942.
5 Bruyn, D. L. *Geometrical Models.* Portland, Maine: Walch Publishing Co., 1963.
6. Collister, Larew M. "Punch-Card 'Adding Machine' Your Pupils Can Build." *Mathematics Teacher* 52 (October 1959): 471-73.

7. Cundy, H. M., and A. P. Rollett. *Mathematical Models*. New York: Oxford University Press, 1961.
8. Denholm, Richard. *Making and Using Graphs and Nomographs*. Teacher's ed. Pasadena, Calif.: Franklin Publications, 1968.
9. Elder, Florence. "Mathematics for the Below-Average Achiever in High School." *Mathematics Teacher* 60 (March 1967): 235-40.
10. Freitag, Herta T., and Arthur H. Freitag. "The Magic of a Square." *Mathematics Teacher* 63 (January 1970): 5-14.
11. Fukuda, Donald, Edwin Mookini, and James K. M. Siu. "A Straight Line Model for Multiplication." *Mathematics Teacher* 59 (April 1966): 342-47.
12. Gardner, Martin, ed. *Scientific American Book of Mathematical Puzzles and Diversions*. New York: Simon & Schuster, 1964.
13. ———. *Second Scientific American Book of Mathematical Puzzles and Diversions*. New York: Simon & Schuster, 1964.
14. Glenn, William H., and Donovan A. Johnson. *Number Patterns*. Manchester, Mo.: Webster Publishing Co., 1960.
15. Golomb, Solomon. *Polyominoes*. New York: Charles Scribner's Sons, 1965.
16. Horne, Sylvia. *Patterns and Puzzles in Mathematics*. Pasadena, Calif.: Franklin Publications, 1968.
17. Johnson, Donovan A. "How to Draw a Multiplication and Division Nomograph." *Mathematics Teacher* 49 (May 1956): 391-92.
18. ———. "How to Draw an Addition and Subtraction Nomograph." *Mathematics Teacher* 49 (April 1956): 281.
19. ———. *Paper Folding for the Mathematics Class*. Washington, D.C.: National Council of Teachers of Mathematics, 1957.
20. Johnson, Donovan A., and William H. Glenn. *Computing Devices*. Manchester, Mo.: Webster Publishing Co., 1960.
21. ———. *Fun with Mathematics*. Manchester, Mo.: Webster Publishing Co., 1960.
22. ———. *Topology, the Rubber-Sheet Geometry*. Manchester, Mo.: Webster Publishing Co., 1960.
23. Kraitchik, Maurice. *Mathematical Recreations*. New York: Dover Publications, 1953.
24. National Council of Teachers of Mathematics. *Enrichment Mathematics for the Grades*, Twenty-seventh Yearbook. Washington, D.C.: The Council, 1963.
25. ———. *Experiences in Mathematical Discovery*, 8 units. Washington, D.C.: The Council, 1966-67, 1970.
26. ———. *The Learning of Mathematics: Its Theory and Practice*, Twenty-first Yearbook. Washington, D.C.: The Council, 1953.
27. ———. *Multi-Sensory Aids in the Teaching of Mathematics*, Eighteenth Yearbook. Washington, D.C.: The Council, 1945.
28. Pearcy, J. F. F., and K. Lewis. *Experiments in Mathematics, Stage 1, Stage 2,* and *Stage 3*. Boston: Houghton Mifflin Co., 1966, 1967.
29. Ranucci, Ernest R. "A Tiny Treasury of Tessellations." *Mathematics Teacher* 61 (February 1968): 114-17.
30. Sobel, Max A. *Teaching General Mathematics*. Englewood Cliffs, N.J.: Prentice-Hall, 1967.

31. Spitznagel, Edward L., Jr. "An Experimental Approach in the Teaching of Probability." *Mathematics Teacher* 61 (October 1968): 565–68.
32. Steinhaus, Hugo. *Mathematical Snapshots.* New York: Oxford University Press, 1969.
33. Van Tassel, Lowell T. "Notes on a 'Spider' Nomograph." *Mathematics Teacher* 52 (November 1959): 557–59.
34. Walter, Marion I. *Boxes, Squares, and Other Things: A Teacher's Guide for a Unit in Informal Geometry.* Washington, D.C.: National Council of Teachers of Mathematics, 1970.
35. Wenninger, Magnus J. *Polyhedron Models for the Classroom.* Washington, D.C.: National Council of Teachers of Mathematics, 1966.
36. Willerding, Margaret. *From Fingers to Computers.* Pasadena, Calif.: Franklin Publications, 1968.

8

A Laboratory Approach

PATRICIA S. DAVIDSON
MARION I. WALTER

THE DOOR of the mathematics laboratory was already open, and as the visitor approached he heard an interesting hum of activity. On entering, he noticed groups of children sitting around tables, working busily with materials and talking quietly with each other. One group was using problem cards as they made shapes with rubber bands on their geoboards. Others were building three-dimensional models. At one table students were engaged in an exciting activity involving the trading of colored chips. At another the teacher was presenting a problem to some children working with balances.

A glance at the wide variety of "stuff" labeled and arranged on the shelves indicated to the visitor that if he had come at another time, he might have seen quite different activities.

Two students were reading booklets as they sat on a rug in the far corner of the room, and at this point the teacher moved on to talk with them. The visitor was pleased to see many written materials, including textbooks, among the resources in the lab.

Later, when visiting the classrooms, he saw many of the same manipulative objects and many activities similar to those he had seen in the lab. In some rooms students were both "doing" and writing. In others the teacher was at the front of the room presenting a lesson and the students were using only textbooks.

At the end of the day the visitor asked many questions about what he had seen. This chapter will deal with the visitor's questions as well as those usually asked about a laboratory approach and its implementation.

A Math-Lab Approach

What is a mathematics laboratory?

A mathematics laboratory should be thought of as an approach to learning mathematics rather than a particular place in a building. Such an approach encompasses exploring, investigating, hypothesizing, experimenting, and generalizing. It means that students are actively involved in "doing" mathematics at a concrete level. It provides abundant opportunities for them to manipulate objects, to think about what they have done, to discuss and write about their findings, and to build necessary skills. Problems are related to the children's own experiences and often emerge from the natural surroundings. The teacher acts as a catalyst and resource person, becoming an active investigator along with the students.

What are the purposes of a math-lab approach?

Several major considerations basic to this approach should be mentioned briefly before discussing specific materials and particular concepts.

INVOLVEMENT AT A CONCRETE LEVEL

Students need to go through concrete stages of learning before they can reach the higher levels of abstraction. If children are to achieve understanding, they cannot go straight to abstractions but first must handle things and be involved in "doing." It is vital that students be guided to carry out their own investigations and to think for themselves. In this way they can build firm foundations and achieve understanding through experience rather than rote learning.

NONVERBAL COMMUNICATION

The use of concrete materials offers opportunities for nonverbal communication. First of all, without any words it helps the student to comprehend a situation or a problem. Secondly, the student does not need to verbalize to demonstrate his understanding. Watching a student manipulate a physical apparatus can often give a teacher insight into how the student is thinking about the task—deeper insight than could be obtained by purely verbal means.

It should be made clear that the purpose here is not to avoid reading and verbalization. The purpose is to allow students to achieve and demonstrate mathematical understanding without letting reading and verbal disabilities stand in the way. As will be seen in a later section, problem cards and activities can be designed to help make transitions from concrete, nonverbal situations to more abstract levels involving mathematical terminology and symbols.

Positive Self-Image

One of the most important features of a laboratory approach is that each student can work at his own rate and can go as far as he can. Most of the time he is able to check his work by use of the materials and so has no need of an outside authority. Working in this way is nonthreatening, since the materials will tell him whether he is right or not. (For example, a balance shows if it is balanced.) Hence there is immediate feedback without any penalty. When a student tests his predictions against the materials, no harm is done if his first attempts are not correct, for he can always amend his predictions. Indeed, initial incorrect attempts sometimes serve to illuminate the problem and give deeper understanding of it.

Through laboratory experiences students will find that there are often many ways of approaching the same problem and that more than one answer may be right. Some tasks do not even involve so-called answers; it is the process of observing, hypothesizing, and checking that is important. Students enjoy talking about what they have done and how they have done it. In sharing their findings, they often come up with other problems to investigate and often gain deeper insights.

Working with materials is a confidence-building experience for many students not only because they are able to check themselves at every stage but also because they can feel success as they complete the action. This sense of doing and accomplishing gives them a feeling of control; they develop confidence that they do have enough power to be successful. Confidence and willingness to attack a problem are half the battle.

A Broader View of Mathematics

The use of manipulative materials enables students to obtain a broader view of mathematics than usual. For example, children can obtain firsthand experience with such topics as length, area, perimeter, volume, symmetry, and pattern by using various types of materials such as geoboards, Pattern Blocks, Mirror Cards, tangrams, various kinds of building blocks, and other devices. (A later section, entitled "What Are Some Useful Materials?" gives references to particular materials and information about how to obtain them.) Students can learn to classify and reason logically by using Attribute Materials and other objects. They can gather data to be graphed and examined for relationships that can be expressed by equations. Students can use dice, coins, or colored cubes to make predictions or do numerical computation by means of activities involving number patterns.

In a laboratory approach, the process of doing mathematics is as valuable as the content and the knowledge to be gained. Through experience with materials, students can see mathematics as patterns, order, and relationships. Instead of seeing mathematics as an isolated set of unrelated topics, students notice relationships between various concepts. When a student is involved in developing a concept from actual experience, it is likely to mean much more to him than when it is presented as a finished product.

When mathematics is treated from this broad viewpoint, every student is successful at something. That very student who has extreme difficulty with number facts may excel, for example, in fitting the tangram pieces together. The success a student achieves while doing one aspect of mathematics can help him feel confident enough to face those aspects that he finds more difficult.

Nothing is more damaging to a student than a steady diet of that same work which he cannot do well. Vitally needed are not only fresh approaches to help him with the things that cause difficulty but also opportunities for him to be involved in other aspects of mathematics that lead to excitement and success. A mathematics-laboratory approach offers both possibilities.

What are some of the activities?

When this question is asked, it often implies other questions, such as:

What materials are the children using?
What are the children doing with these materials?
To what mathematical concepts do the materials relate?

A LABORATORY APPROACH   225

Although these questions could produce almost endless answers, it will be helpful to discuss a few of these materials and their uses.

GEOBOARDS

What is a geoboard?

A geoboard (which was introduced by C. Gattegno) is a board with an array of nails on it. The most common is a 10-by-10-inch board with a 5-by-5 square array of nails spaced 2 inches apart. If a 1-inch border is left around the outside, the spacing is preserved when two boards are put side by side. Rubber bands are stretched around the nails to make various shapes. (See fig. 8.1.) Geoboards can be made of ⅜-inch or ½-inch plywood and ½-inch or ¾-inch escutcheon nails, or they may be obtained commercially (140).

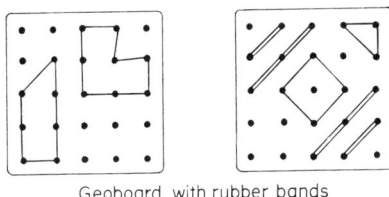

Geoboard with rubber bands

Fig. 8.1

Dot paper is useful with a geoboard. (This should be made by spacing the dots as far apart as the nails on the geoboard.) Grid paper is also useful for young children. (See fig. 8.2.) For older children, ½-inch or ¼-inch graph paper may be used.

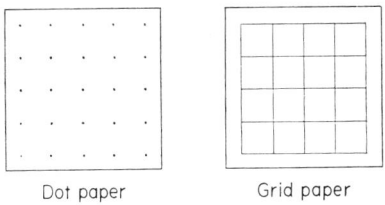

Dot paper   Grid paper

Fig. 8.2

A variety of other geoboards have appeared in recent years. Some have circular spacing; others "isometric" (or equilateral) spacing. (See fig. 8.3.)

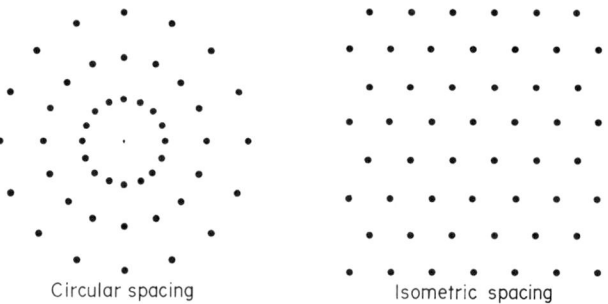

Circular spacing   Isometric spacing

Fig. 8.3

Who can use a geoboard?

Geoboards are used by schoolchildren of all ages and abilities. They are not specially designed for any one type or group of students. Children can work with geoboards by themselves, in pairs, in a small group, or even as a whole class. Every teacher, too, should have an opportunity to work with a geoboard.

How can a geoboard be used?

The boards can be used in many ways. For instance, students may use them—

for free exploration;

for solving problems posed by the teacher watching the student use the board;

for solving problems posed by the student himself;

for solving problems posed on a set of problem cards or in a textbook;

for solving problems posed by another student.

The children should have time to explore the geoboards freely. Some children, for example, may make a picture of a house, a boat, or a tree; others may make designs using various geometric shapes. (See fig. 8.4.)

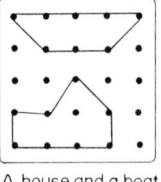
A house and a boat

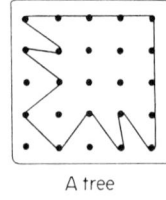
A tree

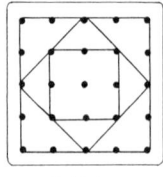
A design

Fig. 8.4

When the children are ready for some directed work, it is often possible to use a child's own picture for a question. It is one of the aims of mathematics teaching that the student should learn to pose his own problems. One way for him to learn to do this is to see the teacher pose problems related to his own work and then to be encouraged to add a question himself. The range of possible questions is broad. Below are a few examples of pictures that students have made, and beside each picture are questions that a teacher might have asked. Of course, the level of any question depends on the stage the student has reached.

STUDENT'S DESIGN　　　　POSSIBLE QUESTIONS

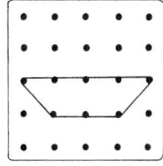

How many nails does the rubber band touch?
How many sides does the shape have?
Can you now make a five-sided shape?
Can you do it by moving the rubber band off only one nail?

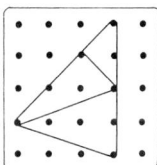

How many triangles can you see?
Draw them (using different colors) on a sheet of dot paper.
Which is the longest segment? (Use string.)
Calculate the length of each segment. (Use the Pythagorean theorem.)

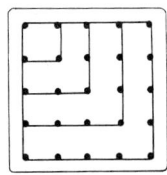

How many squares can you see?
How many nails does each square touch?
If the board were bigger, how many nails would the next square touch? And the next?
Do you see a pattern in the number of nails touched?

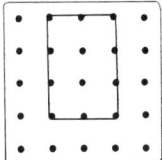 If your shape represents *one* unit, show 1/3 of the unit, then 1/2 of the unit.
Can you show these parts in more than one way?

Students should be encouraged to ask their own questions. It is important for them to learn that some questions are difficult or even impossible for anyone to answer.

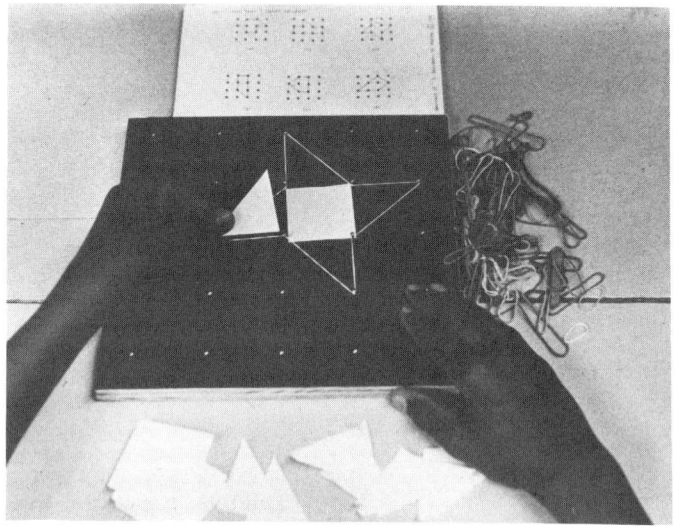

FINDING AREA ON A GEOBOARD

It is helpful to have some sets of problem cards that children can use independently with geoboards. As a sample, a small sequence of such cards has been developed to deal with a specific topic—that of area. The cards, which are shown below, are sequential: they illustrate one way of developing the topic in gradual stages.[1] No prior formal knowledge of the topic is assumed. The student should have had enough informal work dealing with area to understand the need for standard units for measuring area and the reason why square units are better than circles for this purpose (78). It is assumed that the children have had prior opportunities to explore geoboards.

1. The artwork on these cards was done by a student at a vocational high school.

GEOBOARDS

Introduction to Area

Patricia S. Davidson
Marion I. Walter

© 1969

MATERIAL

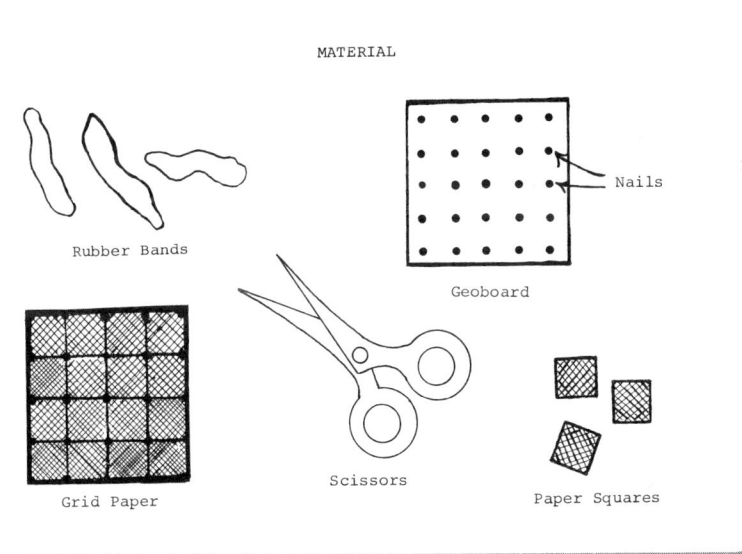

1

Cut some paper squares.

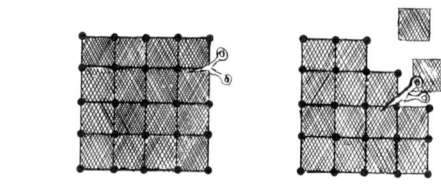

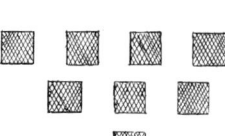

2

Make this square.

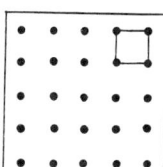

Check that your paper square covers it.

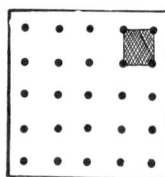

3

Make

How many paper squares do you need?

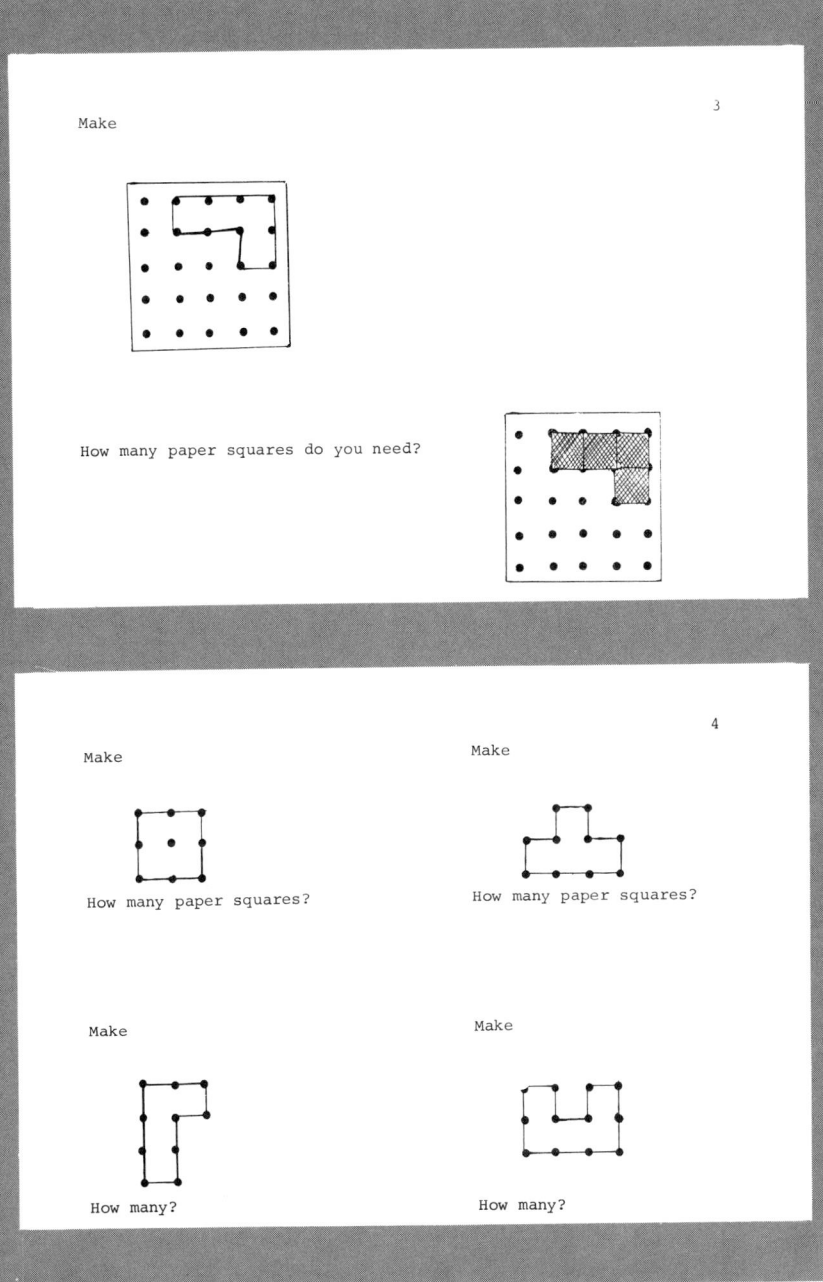

4

Make

How many paper squares?

Make

How many paper squares?

Make

How many?

Make

How many?

5

Make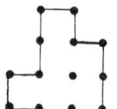

How many paper squares?

Make

How many?

Make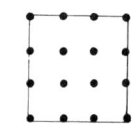

How many?

6

Which ones need 5 paper squares?

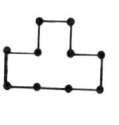

(a)

(b)

(c)

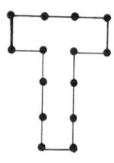

(d)

(e)

(f)

7

Make one that needs 6 paper squares to cover it.

Then ask a classmate how many he thinks are needed.

8

Make a pattern that needs 7 paper squares.

Make up other problems and exchange with a classmate.

9

Take a paper square.

Cut it into 2 triangles.

Check that the 2 triangles match.
Each is $\frac{1}{2}$ of the whole.

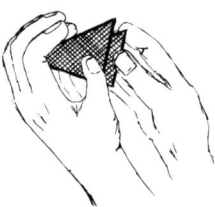

10

Make this square on the geoboard.

Check that the two triangles will cover it.

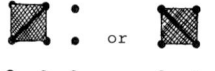

Make

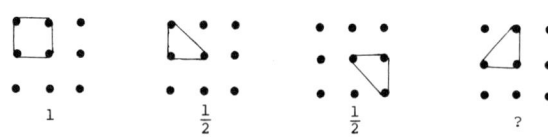

1     $\frac{1}{2}$ $\frac{1}{2}$?

11

Make

Check that ▨ ▨ ◣ will cover it.

You need   1 + 1 + $\frac{1}{2}$ = $2\frac{1}{2}$ squares to cover it.

Make

How many?

12

Make

Check that ▨ ▨ ◥◣ will cover it.

1 + 1 + $\frac{1}{2}$ + $\frac{1}{2}$ = 3

Make

Show that ▨ ◥◣ will cover it.

1 + $\frac{1}{2}$ + $\frac{1}{2}$ = 2

13

Make

Check that 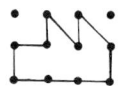 will cover it.

$1 + 1 + \frac{1}{2} + \frac{1}{2} = 3$

Make

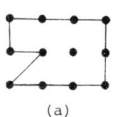

Check that 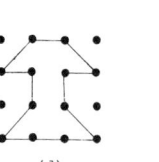 will cover it.

$1 + 1 + 1 + \frac{1}{2} + \frac{1}{2} = 4$

14

How many paper squares does each need?

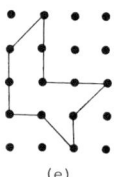
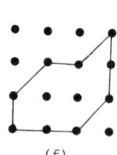

(a)   (b)   (c)

(d)   (e)   (f)

Cut the grid paper and use it to check.

15

Which ones need 3 paper squares?

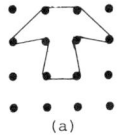
(a)

(b)

(c)

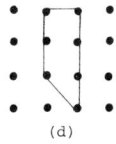
(d)

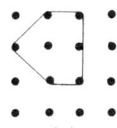
(e)

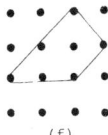
(f)

16

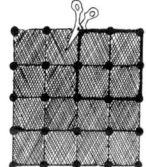   Cut out this square.

Make   Does the big paper square fit it?

How many small squares?

4 small paper squares

17

 Cut as shown. Check that your 2 paper shapes match.

Make  How many small paper squares do you need to cover it?

 Cut as shown. Check that  and match.

Make How many small paper squares do you need to cover it?

18

 Tom says, "I need 2 paper squares to cover it,

because  is $\frac{1}{2}$ of  and

$\frac{1}{2}$ of 4 is 2."

 Ann says, "I need 2 paper squares to cover it,

because I need   and

1 + $\frac{1}{2}$ + $\frac{1}{2}$ = 2."

What do you think?

19

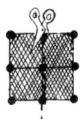 Cut as shown.   How many small squares?

Cut this rectangle 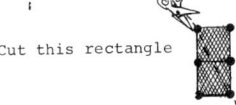 into 2 triangles.

Check that the triangles match.

Make and check that each of the paper triangles covers it.

20

Make How many small paper squares do you need to cover it?

Tom says, "I need 1 paper square, because

 is $\frac{1}{2}$ of  and $\frac{1}{2}$ of 2 is 1."

Ann says, I need 1 paper square because the missing bit is the same as the extra bit."

extra bit — missing bit

What do you think?

239

21

Make

Imagine an extra rubber band.

Now you can see it as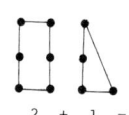

2 + 1 = 3

22

Make How many?

Make How many?

Make 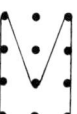 How many?

23

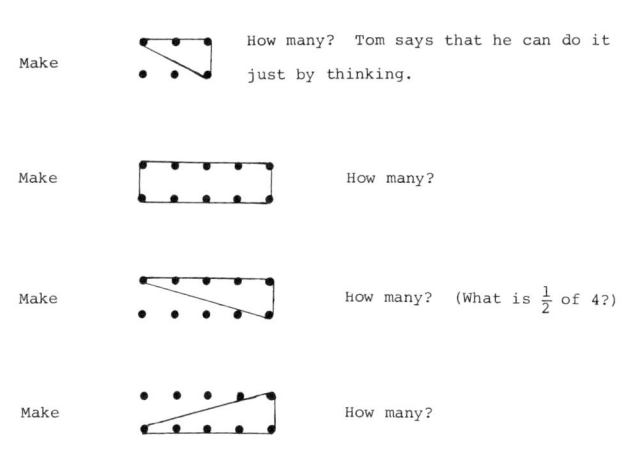

Make ⎰ How many? Tom says that he can do it just by thinking.

Make ⎰ How many?

Make ⎰ How many? (What is $\frac{1}{2}$ of 4?)

Make ⎰ How many?

24

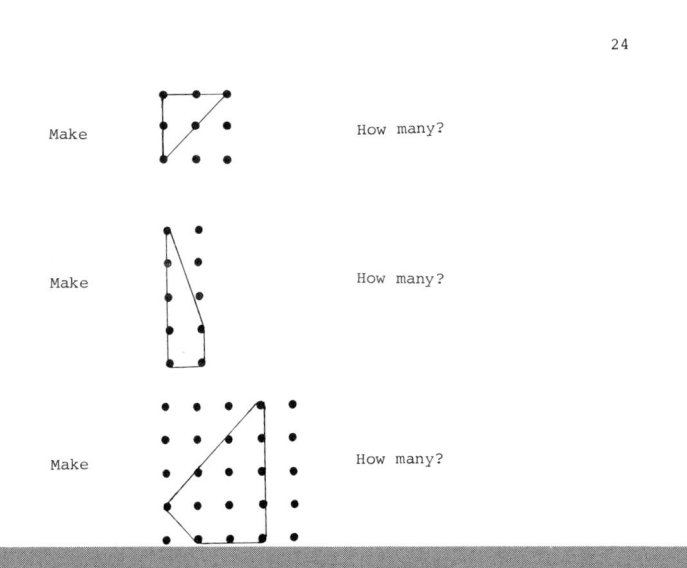

Make ⎰ How many?

Make ⎰ How many?

Make ⎰ How many?

25

 We have been using our small paper squares to measure shapes on a geoboard.

We will call 1 unit of area or 1 square unit.

  This represents $2\frac{1}{2}$ units of area or $2\frac{1}{2}$ square units.

How many square units does 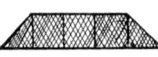 represent?

Make a shape which has an area of 4 square units.

26

Make Find its area.

Tom says that he used

$\frac{1}{2} + 1 + 1 + 1 = 3\frac{1}{2}$

The area is $3\frac{1}{2}$ square units.

Ann did it by putting an extra rubber band to make 4 square units. She then imagined taking away the extra bit.

 $4 - \frac{1}{2} = 3\frac{1}{2}$

She also got $3\frac{1}{2}$ square units of area.

27

Make  Find its area.

Tom did it as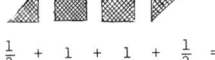

$\frac{1}{2} + 1 + 1 + \frac{1}{2} = 3$

The area is 3 square units.

Ann did it as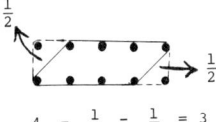

$4 - \frac{1}{2} - \frac{1}{2} = 3$

Both ways of doing it give the same answer.

28

Make 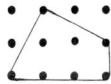 Find its area.

Tom's way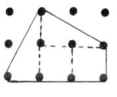

$1 + 1 + 1 + 1 = 4$

Ann's way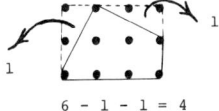

$6 - 1 - 1 = 4$

Both ways give the same answer.

29

Make Find its area.

Tom is thinking!

Ann's way works,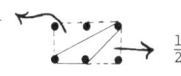

$2 - 1 - \frac{1}{2} = \frac{1}{2}$

The area is $\frac{1}{2}$ square unit.

30

Find the area.

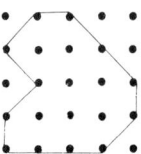 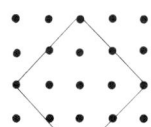

You may want to work on these.

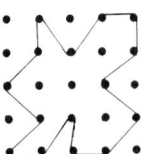 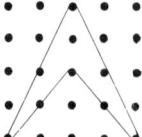

Now you make one, find the area, and then give it to a classmate.

A LABORATORY APPROACH   245

After working through these cards, students can find the area of shapes such as the following:

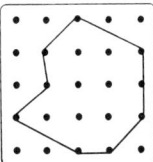

It is not difficult to continue the work so that children can find the area of any triangle, rectangle, parallelogram, or trapezoid on the geoboard. In fact, it is possible to find, without using any formula,

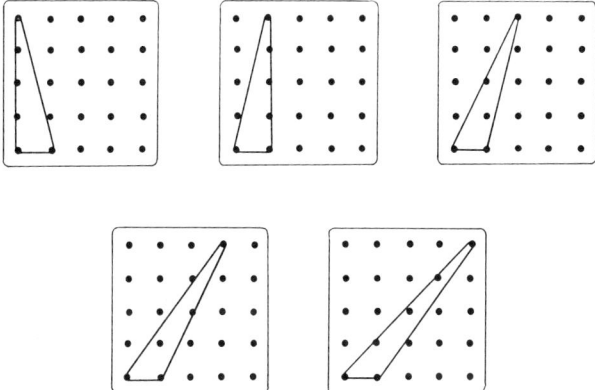

the area of any shape on the board if it is made with one rubber band that does not cross itself. Of course, it is more difficult to find the areas of some shapes than of others. This type of work should be carried out before children attempt to learn any formulas for the areas of triangles, trapezoids, and so forth.

What are some other topics for which a geoboard is useful?

It is not possible to make an exhaustive list. Many useful suggestions will be found in (2), (5), (9), (19), (21), (23), (24), (29), (56), (63), (69), (117), and (155). Just to indicate the richness of the material, a few topics with a few suggested questions are shown below.

Fractions. If

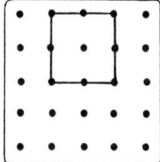

is one unit, show $\frac{1}{2}$, $\frac{1}{4}$, and $\frac{5}{4}$ of this unit.
If

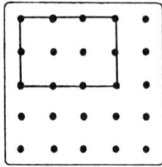

is one unit, show $\frac{1}{2}$, $\frac{2}{3}$, and $\frac{5}{3}$ of this unit. Using this same unit, show $\frac{1}{2} + \frac{1}{3}$.

Make a shape so that it is easy to show both $\frac{1}{3}$ and $\frac{1}{4}$ of it.

Counting problems. Make a shape. How many nails does the rubber band touch? How many line segments are there? How many nails are inside the shape, *not* touching the rubber band?

How many different-sized squares can you make on the geoboard? How many of each size can you make?

Congruence. Make a shape. Ask a friend to copy it on his geoboard. If you cannot decide whether the shapes really match, cut each out of dot paper and check.

Can you make these two shapes match?

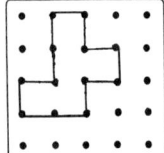 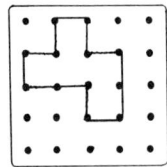

Is there another way that you can make this shape on your geoboard?

Shapes. Make and name various shapes.
Find various shapes within shapes.

Make a design out of squares. What other shapes can you now see?
On the board shown here, can you see a right triangle?

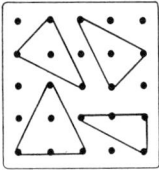

Can you make an equilateral triangle?
Can you make a five-sided shape? A six-sided shape? How far can you continue?

Symmetry. Make a design that looks the same after you have given the board a half-turn. Does it look the same after a quarter-turn?

Where on the geoboard shown could you place a mirror so that you could still see the whole design?

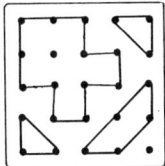

Can you make a picture that has one line of symmetry? Two lines of symmetry?

Patterns. What shapes do you see on the board below?
Do you see a pattern? Make the next one.
Ask a question about nails. About areas.

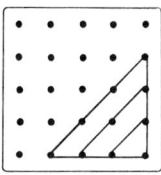

Scale and mapping. Make a simple design on a geoboard. Copy it on dot paper. Then copy it on smaller-scaled dot paper. In what ways is your design the same? Different?

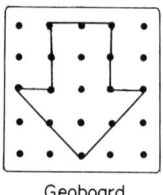 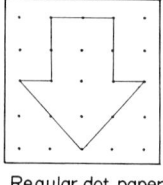 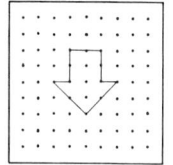

Geoboard   Regular dot paper   Smaller-scaled dot paper

Irrationals. Make a square of area 1 square unit (using the small square as a unit). Its side is of length 1 unit.

Make a square of area 4 square units.

Complete the following table:

Area of square	Length of side
1	1
4	2
9	?
16	?
25	?

Now make a square of area 2 square units. (Yes, it can be done.) How long is its side? Is it 1? 2? Between 1 and 2? Try 1.5. Between 1 and 1.5? 1.3? Between 1.3 and 1.5? How can you tell? Following this method, calculate the length of the side correct to two decimal places.

Make a square of area 8 square units.

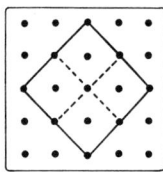

How long is its side?

Can you find a way of relating the $\sqrt{8}$ to the $\sqrt{2}$ in the diagram shown here?

Vocabulary. Geoboards encourage the use of words such as shape, square, triangle, rectangle, trapezoid, quadrilateral, segment, longer, shorter, inside, outside, more, fewer, straight, vertical, horizontal, oblique, slanted, length, unit, area, fits, matches, and symmetry.

What games can be played with the geoboard?

Since students will invent many new games, only a sample will be given here.

A LABORATORY APPROACH 249

The telephone game. One child makes a pattern with a rubber band on his board. Another has an empty board and a rubber band. They pretend that they are talking on the telephone and cannot see each other's board. The object of the game is for the second child to "copy" the pattern the first child made. This is a useful game to introduce coordinates, and it also provides good practice for coordinates.

Making shapes of area 3. Each child makes a shape having an area of 3 square units, transfers it to dot paper, and cuts it out. The cutouts are hung on the wall. Then each child tries to make another shape of area 3—one that is different from those already made. If there is an argument about whether a new shape is different, it can be settled by using the paper cutouts. The game is repeated several times. It can be played by children alone, in pairs, or in a larger group. In one class, students found over thirty different shapes with area 3 that can be made on a geoboard, but there are many more.

What are some of the advantages of using a geoboard?

A geoboard is very versatile because it can be used for a variety of topics and levels.

It gives concrete experience.

It enables children to check their own work.

It enables a teacher to observe children at work and to gain insight into their understandings as well as their misconceptions.

It can be made by parents, teachers, or students. Making geoboards has proved to be a worthwhile activity for students in some industrial-arts classes.

CHIPS

A topic that permeates much of the mathematics curriculum and turns out to be a stumbling block for many children is that of place value. Among the materials available to help students gain an understanding of this important topic are the abacus or counting frame, Cuisenaire rods (134), Dienes Multibase Arithmetic Blocks (136), Stern Structural Arithmetic Apparatus (149), chips (132), bottle caps, beads, and straws.

Because chips can be readily obtained, chip trading will be discussed. The basic idea of this section on chip trading stems from classes taught by L. Sealey and A. Gleason at the Cambridge Conference. For a fuller development of activities, games, and problems see (151).

What are the chips?

Chips are plastic disks available in various shapes and colors. Any variety of chips will serve the purpose—square ones and round ones are on the market—and they should be of five or six different colors and have a hole in the center so that they can be placed on an abacus board (59; 130) or on a simple board made with nails (see fig. 8.5).

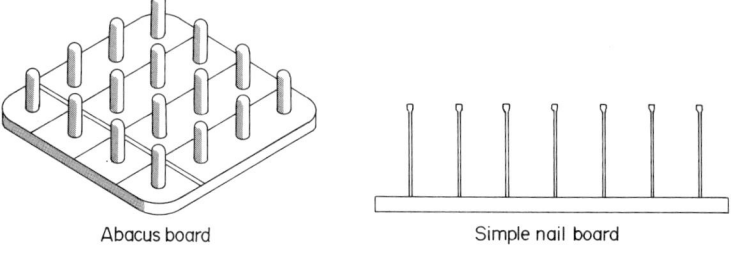

Abacus board   Simple nail board

Fig. 8.5

If plastic chips are not available, colored oak-tag squares can be used instead.

Dice will also be needed for some of the suggested activities.

Who can use the chips?

As the activities described in the next section will indicate, chips are suitable for use in all grades. Work with chips should not be considered as only remedial. One purpose of the chip-trading games is to prevent the usual difficulties with place value.

How can chips be used?

Chips can be used in many ways. For instance, students can use them—

for free exploration;

for games suggested by the children, by the teacher, or by instructions on a card;

for problems or calculations posed by the children, by the teacher, by the textbook, or by a problem card;

for work in which the whole class is divided into small groups;

for work in which only one or two groups are involved.

Some games that can be played with chips will be given here. Once the children learn these, they will want to make up other games and problems. A helpful way to introduce the games is for the teacher to

A LABORATORY APPROACH   251

play one game with a group and then have these students play it with others.

Basic trading game

The basic trading game, for three to five children, involves students in trading chips according to an established rate of exchange. Suppose that in the particular collection of chips being used the colors are yellow, blue, green, and red. The children can think of these chips as coins in some country and make up a rate of exchange such as the following:

$$3 \text{ yellows} = 1 \text{ blue}$$
$$3 \text{ blues} = 1 \text{ green}$$
$$3 \text{ greens} = 1 \text{ red}$$

Each student has a nail board or a paper till. One child in the group acts as a banker. He starts with a quantity of chips, as shown in figure 8.6, and the players with none. Each child in turn (except the

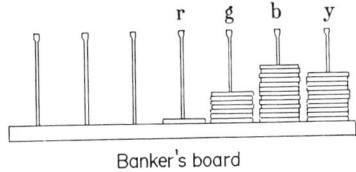

Banker's board

Fig. 8.6

banker) tosses a die, which tells him how many yellow chips the banker must give him. Whenever a player has three chips of one color, he must ask the banker to exchange them for one chip of the appropriate color. The banker can make the trade only after the player has told him the correct exchange. The player keeps his collection of chips arranged on his nail board or paper till. The first person who gets a red chip wins the game and becomes the banker for the next round.

Children enjoy this game, and even first graders are able to manage well with this small rate of exchange. The game is most effective when played at an early age, since its purpose is to help lay the foundations for an understanding of place value. However, it is also effective later as an initial activity in more advanced work.

There are many variations of this basic trading game. The children may wish to toss two dice and use the sum to determine the number of yellow chips each player receives. A different rate of exchange can also

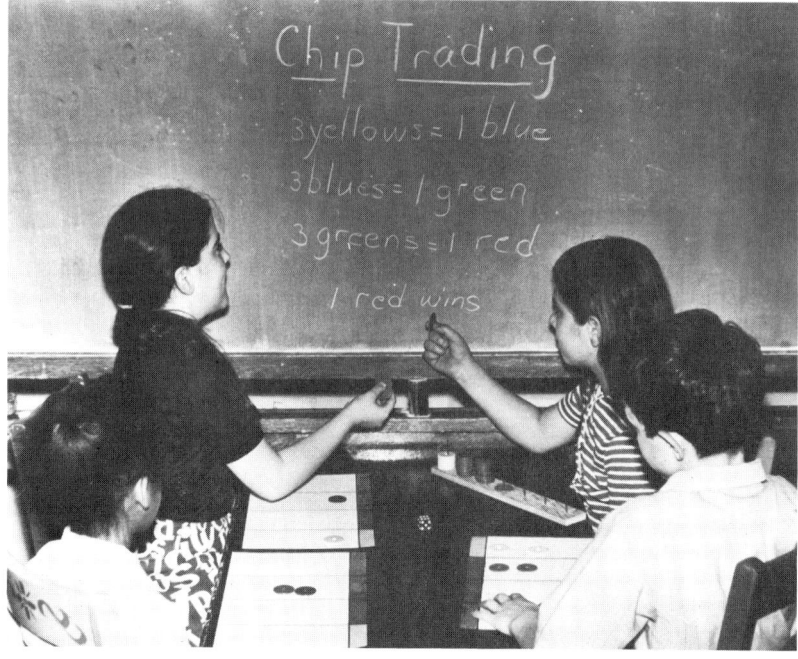

TRADING WITH CHIPS

be introduced; for example, the children might "fly to another country," where the rate of exchange is five to one:

5 yellows = 1 blue
5 blues = 1 green
5 greens = 1 red
5 reds = 1 black

Over a period of time, it is valuable for students to "fly to many countries" in order to gain experience with various rates of exchange.

When deciding on the rules for such games, one should keep in mind the value of the chips and the way they are obtained so that the number of turns necessary to win is small enough to keep the game exciting. For example, when the rate of exchange is three to one, the red chip is worth 27 yellows because

1 red = 3 greens = 3 × 3 blues = 3 × 3 × 3 yellows

The maximum number of yellows a player could obtain on each turn by tossing one die is six; hence a minimum number of five turns is necessary to obtain the red chip.

During a class period it is desirable for the children to play many

A LABORATORY APPROACH

short games, with different students being banker. The roles of banker and player require different thought processes, and both are valuable experiences.

A variation—ten to one

If the rate of exchange is ten to one, set the goal as a green chip, play with two dice, and use the sum of the numbers thrown. (Note that a red chip would require 1,000 yellows!) Older children could toss two dice and use the product instead of the sum. This variation not only gives children practice in multiplying but enables them to make physical and mental exchanges with larger quantities of chips. For example, if a 6 and a 4 are thrown, a player could ask the banker for 24 yellow chips; but with experience he will soon ask for 2 blues and 4 yellows.

Further variations include the use of three or four dice with sums or products being taken. One class suggested using two dice of one color and two of another color; the sums of the numbers on dice of the same color were then multiplied to indicate the number of yellow chips to be obtained. Another variation is to prepare index cards resembling those shown in figure 8.7.

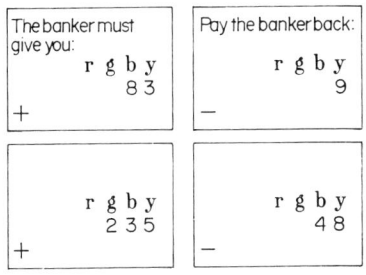

Fig. 8.7

Addition and subtraction

Experience with addition can be gained by combining two collections of chips. In the example given here the rate of exchange is ten to one. (A smaller rate is more manageable for young children.)

The children start by putting the two sets of chips on an abacus board or two nail boards. One set could consist of 5 greens, 2 blues, and 7 yellows; the other could have 4 greens, 8 blues, and 5 yellows. (See fig. 8.8.)

What is the sum of the two collections? Students tend to solve this problem in one of two ways. Some combine the two collections before

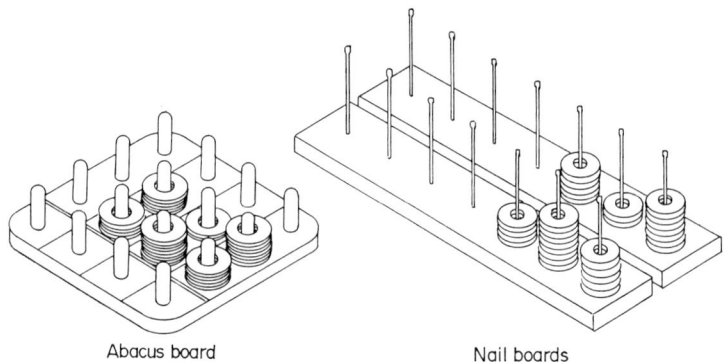

Abacus board   Nail boards

Fig. 8.8

they trade them:

   r   g   b   y
   9   10 12

Others combine and trade one color at a time. They work it out this way:

   r   g   b   y
   5   2   7
   4   8   5

Combine the 12 yellows (7 + 5); exchange 10 of them for 1 blue; and put the remaining 2 yellows on a nail board.

Combine all the blues (1 + 2 + 8 = 11); trade 10 of them for 1 green; and put the 1 remaining blue on the nail board.

Combine all the greens (1 + 5 + 4 = 10); trade them for 1 red; and put this red chip on the nail board, leaving the nail for the green chips empty. The result is

   r   g   b   y
   1   0   1   2

Children should be encouraged to talk about the combining and exchanging they are doing. They soon realize that exchanging 10 yellows for 1 blue is a concrete representation of the exchange of 10 units for 1 ten, and so on. After many such exchanges, "carrying" in addition will no longer be a mystery to them and they will be ready to record their activities. By using colored chalk or crayons that correspond to the colored chips, children can make a gradual transition from the physical exchanges to a written record of the numbers.

Exchanges with chips can be related to computation on paper as

A LABORATORY APPROACH

shown in the following example of subtraction:

```
  g   b   y
  3   2   9
 -1   5   6
```

The children take the 6 yellows from the 9 yellows, leaving 3 yellows. They now exchange 1 green for 10 blues and can rewrite and complete the problem as shown:

```
  g   b   y
  2  12   9
 -1   5   6
  1   7   3
```

The notation used here is that suggested by the Madison Project (12; 13; 82). The small numerals (like the "12" above) are called "Volkswagen numerals" because two can occupy one "parking place."

Multiplication and division

Chip trading helps children understand the operations of multiplication and division.

Here is a multiplication problem:

```
  r   g   b   y
  9   8   7   6
          ×   3
```

Again, students tend to proceed in either of two ways. Some children form three such sets, combine them, and then trade. Other children combine and trade one color at a time. For example, they get 18 yellows, trade 10 of them for 1 blue, and put 8 yellows on the nail board. Next they combine the blues [(3 × 7) + 1 = 22 blues], trade 20 blues for 2 greens, and keep 2 blues. Then they combine the greens [(3 × 8) + 2 = 26 greens], trade 20 greens for 2 reds, and keep 6 greens. And so they continue.

It is interesting for students to see the effect of forming and combining ten equal collections when the rate of exchange is ten to one.

Here is a division problem:

```
       g   b   y
    3│ 2   5   1
```

In order to solve the problem, children attempt to make three equal collections. Some students want to trade the whole collection for yellows, and it is worthwhile for them to see what happens when they try to do this. Others may realize right away that it is impossible to divide the 2 greens into three equal parts but that by trading the greens for 20 blues (giving a total of 25 blues) they can begin the division process. Eight blues can be placed in each of three piles, leaving 1 blue to trade for 10 yellows. The 11 yellows can be divided into three piles of 3 yellow chips each with 2 left over. Hence,

$$\begin{array}{r} \phantom{3\overline{)}}\ \text{g}\ \ \ \text{b}\ \ \ \text{y} \\ \phantom{3\overline{)}}\ \ \ \ 8\ \ \ 3 \\ 3\overline{)\ 2\ \ \ 5\ \ \ 1} \end{array}$$ 2 yellows left over

This type of concrete experience helps prepare children for written work. Even at the stage when they are working on problems from a textbook, the chips should be available for them to verify their work.

Further work

Eventually the children can use chips of just one color, which stresses the fact that place alone determines value.

Chip trading is useful also for formal work with other number bases. The four operations as outlined here could be done with any rate of exchange. Although the chip-trading activities can be done exclusively in base 10, it sometimes helps older children to see relationships in a system that is new to them.

Chips easily lend themselves to work with decimals. Children can keep the yellow chip as the unit and introduce tenths with chips of another color.

One can make up many questions related to chip trading. For example:

"Suppose I have some chips behind my back. They are worth 14 yellows (assume a rate of exchange of three to one). What possible collections of chips might I have? Which collection has the least number of chips?"

"Here is a collection of chips:

$$\begin{array}{cccc} \text{r} & \text{g} & \text{b} & \text{y} \\ 1 & 2 & 2 & 1 \end{array}$$

If the rate of exchange is three to one, how valuable is this collection in terms of yellows?"

What can be used instead of chips?

Among other materials that can be used for the work described here are painted bottle caps, colored beads, colored balls of clay,

A LABORATORY APPROACH 257

straws of different colors, tongue depressors tied in appropriate bundles, and tongue depressors with beans stuck on them (161). Further information can be obtained in (6), (41), (56), (59), (60), (79), (103), and (151).

CUBES

Cubes can be used for a wide range of activities and topics, including building, classifying, making one-to-one correspondences, graphing, counting, perimeter, area, volume, permutations, combinations, and probability.

What kinds of cubes are useful?

For the work described below, the cubes should all be the same in size, but a variety of colors is desirable. One hundred or more cubes are needed by one or two children.

Who can use cubes?

Although cubes are often associated with the work of young children, they can also be used for various challenging problems on a more advanced level.

How can cubes be used?

Cubes are probably best known for their use in free play and building. Young children will enjoy using cubes of various sizes, as well as blocks having other shapes.

Children can use cubes for problems dealing with one-to-one correspondence and counting. For example, class attendance can be obtained by asking each child present to drop a cube into a box and then having someone count the cubes. Cubes of two different colors can be used to obtain a separate count for boys and girls. Simple graphs can be made by using cubes. (47; 57.)

Patterns can be made with cubes (17; 93). For example:

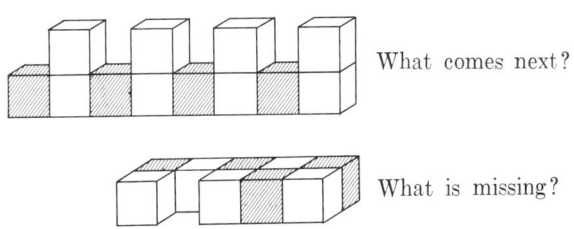

What comes next?

What is missing?

Cubes are useful for introducing the concepts of prime and com-

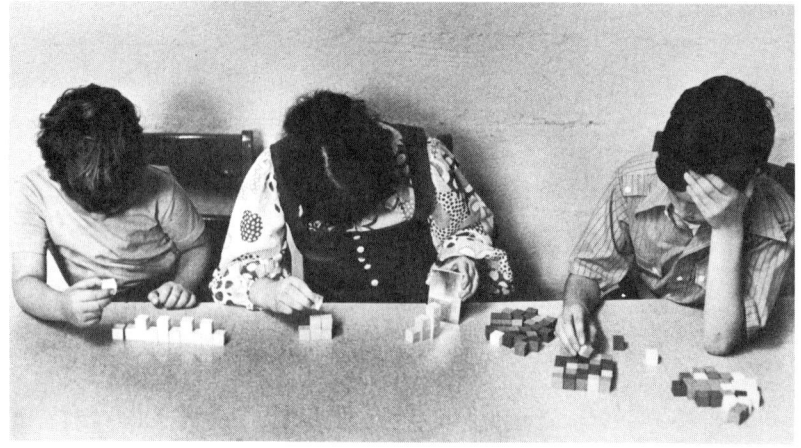

MAKING PATTERNS WITH CUBES

posite, even and odd, square numbers, and so forth. For instance, a child takes twelve cubes. Can he arrange them in one row? In two rows with none left over? In three rows with none left over? He may write:

I have 6 rows of 2 and none left over.
I have 4 rows of 3 and none left over.
I have 3 rows of 4 and none left over.
I have 2 rows of 5 and 2 left over.
I have 2 rows of 6 and none left over.
I have 1 row of 7 and 5 left over.
I have 1 row of

A LABORATORY APPROACH   259

Children can build cubes of larger and larger sizes and observe how they grow. They can build other shapes with cubes and count how many cubes are needed for each shape (52). Older children can explore

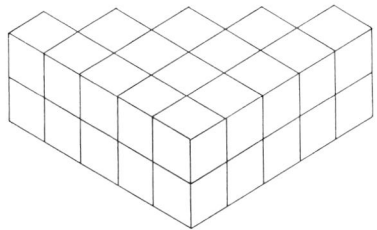

the perimeters, areas, and volumes of cubes and other shapes, such as the pieces in the Pattern Blocks (18; 145).

Simple mapping problems can be introduced by means of cubes. For example, "Make a pattern with blue and red cubes. Now make the pattern formed by replacing each blue cube with a green one and each red with a yellow. [17; 133.] Make another pattern and then build what you would see in a mirror. Check by using a mirror."

A variety of permutation and combination problems are suggested by cubes. Here the problems range from the very simple to the more difficult. For example, "How many different ways can you stack a red, a green, and a yellow cube?" is fairly simple; "In how many different ways can you color a cube if you have two colors?" is much more difficult and will raise some interesting questions. Problems of the type "How many different shapes can you make using four cubes? Five cubes? Six cubes?" are also of interest to students.

Properties of whole numbers can be demonstrated with cubes. Here are a few examples:

Make 7 rows of 6 cubes each. How many cubes are there in this array?

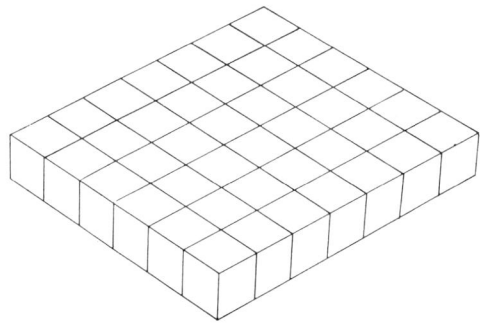

Make 6 rows of 7 cubes each. How many cubes are there in this array?

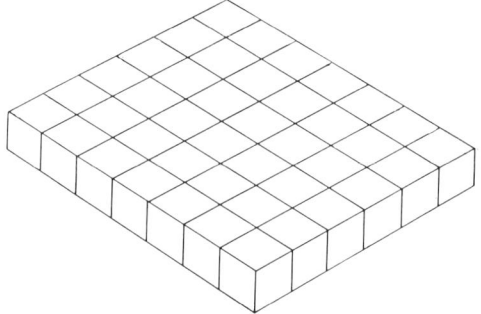

What do you notice?

Use cubes to show 5 × (3 × 4).

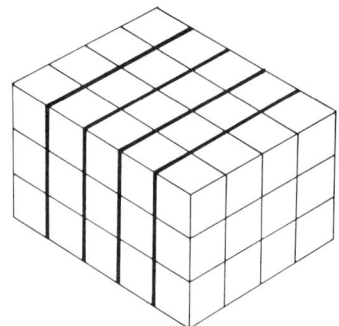

Use cubes to show (5 × 3) × 4.

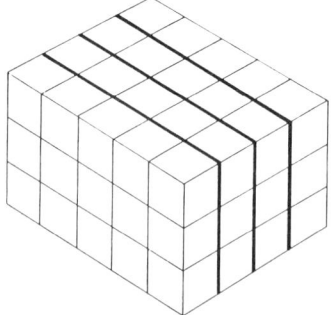

What do you notice?

A LABORATORY APPROACH   261

Make 6 rows of 3 cubes each and 6 rows of 4 cubes each.

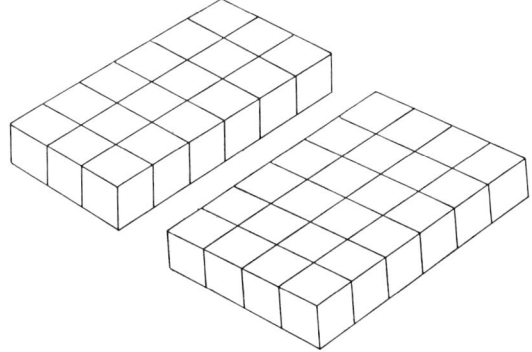

Make 6 rows of 7 cubes each.

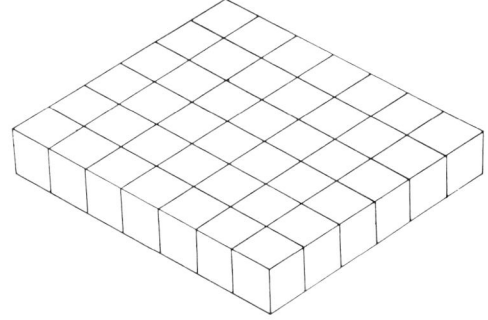

What do you notice?

Cubes can be used for work with fractions. For example:

Arrange 24 cubes. Show $\frac{1}{2}$ of them. Do this in several ways. Show $\frac{1}{4}$ of them. Arrange 24 cubes so that it is easy to show both $\frac{1}{3}$ of them and $\frac{1}{8}$ of them.
If

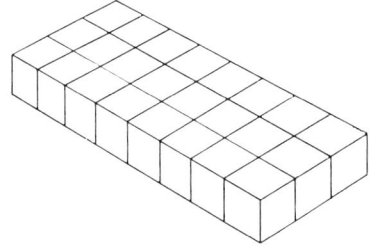

is considered a unit, then what part of the whole is one small cube?

Show $\frac{1}{3} + \frac{1}{8}$.

$\frac{1}{3}$ can be represented by 8 small cubes, or $\frac{8}{24}$;

$\frac{1}{8}$ can be represented by 3 small cubes, or $\frac{3}{24}$;

$\frac{1}{3} + \frac{1}{8}$ can be represented by 11 small cubes, or $\frac{11}{24}$.

What is the smallest number of cubes you would need to show both $\frac{1}{4}$ of them and $\frac{1}{5}$ of them?

Can anything be used besides cubes?

For several of the activities described above, sets of objects such as bottle caps can be used instead of cubes. For problems involving activities like coloring a cube, the children can construct their own models (30; 35; 68). For some of the work, materials such as Dienes Blocks or Cuisenaire rods can be used. For problems dealing with only a two-dimensional aspect of the cube, it is possible to substitute paper or wooden squares, ¼-inch or ½-inch graph paper, or geoboards.

Where can more ideas be found?

Many ideas can be derived from watching the children work and from working with cubes oneself. The following references will be useful not only for new ideas but also for expansions of the ideas presented here: (6), (20), (36), (57), (66), and (99).

What are some useful materials?

Although the few materials that have been discussed can be obtained commercially, much useful material can be homemade or rescued from the trash can.

Among the things that are ordinarily thrown away but that can be used in a variety of ways are:

Bottle caps
Cardboard
Containers of various shapes, sizes, and materials—e.g., coffee cans, matchboxes, metal containers, plastic jars, rectangular boxes, and small and large plastic bottles
Corks
Egg cartons (74)
Empty thread spools
Milk cartons (66; 115)
Plastic lids
Scraps of materials—e.g., acoustical tiles, fabric, linoleum tiles, paper, pegboard, plastic, and wood
Styrofoam packaging

A LABORATORY APPROACH

Other materials that are generally useful include:

Beads
Beans and other materials that can be used for estimating and counting
Clothespins
Coat hangers
Compasses
Construction paper
Crayons
Dice
Dominoes
Glue
Golf tees
Graph paper (various types)
Index cards
Magic markers
Masking tape
Mirrors (67)
Oak tag
Pebbles
Pipe cleaners
Plasticine
Playing cards
Protractors
Rubber bands
Rulers
Sand
Scissors
Scotch tape
Simple addition and subtraction slide rules (113)
Simple pendulums (77; 146)
Slide rules (95)
Stopwatches
Straws
String
Styrofoam
Tape measures
Tongue depressors
Toothpicks
Water
Wire
Yardsticks and metersticks

Of course, much "material" is in the environment itself—the children, the classroom, the school, the play area, the walls of bricks in the hall, the tiles in the cafeteria floor, and so on. The Nuffield Mathematics Project emphasizes the use of the child and his surroundings. It is impossible in a few paragraphs to convey the many ideas and fresh approaches presented in the various Nuffield booklets (40–51). The Nuffield Project has a short film also (126). Another rich source for the use of the environment is *Mathematics in Primary Schools: Curriculum Bulletin No. 1* (57).

The amount of commercially available material designed for learning mathematics is almost endless. A detailed, annotated bibliography of manipulative devices and a list of many distributors can be found in the October 1968 issue of the *Arithmetic Teacher* (85). For a more-up-to-date version, see (11). For many of the commercial materials, written guides are available in the form of cards or booklets. Some are written for the teacher and some for the children. Since budgets are generally quite limited, a list is given here of mathematical materials that teachers and students have found especially useful.

MANIPULATIVE DEVICES AND WRITTEN MATERIALS

Abacus (84; 92)
Attribute Materials (131; 135)
Balances (138; 147)
Building blocks (139; 141)
Calculators (137; 144; 148)
Chips and abacus boards (130; 132; 151)
Cuisenaire rods (10; 28; 64; 69; 134; 154)
Geoboards (2; 5; 9; 23; 24; 56; 69; 140; 155)
Mirror Cards (114; 116; 142)
Pattern Blocks (18; 145)
Tangrams (22; 55; 150)
3-D construction materials

Also available are small booklets for student use, (1), (3), (25), (26), (27), (33), (37), (39), (56), (67), (122); suggestions for individual projects and group activities for teacher and student use, (2), (4), (7), (12), (13), (14), (15), (21), (28), (31), (38), (53), (54), (57), (58), (61), (62), (65), (69), (70), (123), (143); sets of problem cards, (151), (152), (153), (154), (155), (156); and kits to give practice in computation, (157), (158).

In spite of its title, the book *Notes on Mathematics in Primary Schools* (2) provides a wealth of material at the junior high school level also. A number of references can help teachers relate science and mathematics, notably (8), (15), (16), (34), (77), (97), (100), (110), and (147).

Many useful articles have appeared in the *Arithmetic Teacher* (119)

A LABORATORY APPROACH

and the *Mathematics Teacher* (120), as well as in the British journals *Primary Mathematics* (124) and *Mathematics Teaching* (121). Among articles relating to a math-lab approach in general are (75), (76), (80), (81), (82), (86), (88), (91), (94), (96), (100), (105), (107), and (111). Among those that relate to specific materials or concepts are (63), (73), (83), (87), (89), (102), (108), (110), (112), and (118).

Some free materials of interest to teachers include (159), (160), and (161).

There are some delightful films for children; *Dance Squared* (125), *Notes on a Triangle* (129), and *Mathematics Peep Show* (127) have inspired many interesting activities at all levels.

For what mathematical concepts are the materials useful?

To illustrate some of the possible uses of manipulative devices, three particular materials—geoboards, chips, and cubes—have been discussed and related to various aspects of the curriculum. One can turn the problem around and ask what materials children can use to gain experience or practice in work that deals with a particular concept.

For example, in working with the concepts of area and volume, some materials that are likely to be needed are empty containers, water, sand, balances, Plasticine, rulers, cardboard, paper, pebbles, blocks of all types, geoboards, and tiles.

For work with geometry, some useful materials are building blocks, Pattern Blocks, Geo-Blocks, Geo-Sticks, cardboard, paper, graph paper, styrofoam, string, Mirror Cards, mirrors, and containers of all kinds.

USING TANGRAM CARDS, MIRROR CARDS, AND PATTERN BLOCKS

The following references are pertinent: (19), (43), (47), (50), (51), (57), (66), (72), (78), (94), (101), (104), (106), (109), (110), (115), (116), (117), (118).

For work with number skills, some useful materials are dice, pebbles, graph paper, chips, Cuisenaire rods, cubes, squared paper for number charts, number lines, dominoes. See (1), (2), (7), (16), (41), (42), (57), (69), (70), (74), (90), (98), and (154) for specific suggestions for the noncommercial material.

The best sources of all, however, are the teacher and the children who can invent games, problems, and strategies hand-tailored to their needs and interests.

Are there any mathematical games?

There are numerous games with a mathematical flavor that involve strategies based on patterns, chance, logical reasoning, perception, or problem-solving techniques. Here are a few:
Chess
Chinese Shuttle Puzzle
Dominoes
Dr. Nim
Hi-Q
Soma Cubes
Tic-tac-toe (ordinary, three-dimensional, and coordinate)
Think-a-Dot
Tower of Hanoi (Hindu Pyramid Puzzle)

Some of these games the children will play and leave at that; others they will want to analyze more carefully and perhaps relate to some mathematical concepts. These games can be played at home as well as at school. All can be explored on more than one level; for example, one may merely play tic-tac-toe, or one may analyze the game and get involved in such concepts as symmetry.

Many games relate directly to mathematical concepts. For instance, by playing coordinate tic-tac-toe (9), (12), (71), battleship (39), (56), (101), Point Set Game (12), and Go (32), children are prepared for the graphing of points. Kalah is a "count and capture" game whose rules can be adapted from the very simple for first graders to the more complex for adults. Many commercial games, as well as those the teachers and students can suggest, are good ways of reinforcing the basic computational skills with whole numbers and fractions. Rules can be changed for many of the games to make them more challenging for particular children. Once the spirit of improvising catches on, students will enjoy suggesting further activities.

A LABORATORY APPROACH   267

Games can serve many purposes. For some students, games may serve as enjoyment and motivation. Other students may come to realize that they *can* think several steps ahead or that they *can* concentrate for a long period of time. Through playing games together, students can learn to interact in a small group with other students. Careful choice of games, by giving engaging work to some of the children, allows the teacher to give close attention to another group of children. One should not underestimate the learning that can take place when children become really involved. The tossing of dice for learning number facts or generating computational problems is much more exciting and palatable than most worksheets are. The need for practice is always there, and games afford many good ways of getting it.

What about pencil and paper?

A math-lab approach does not necessarily mean the use of manipulative materials. Pencil and paper need not be thrown away! As described in this chapter, this approach enables children to be engaged in activities ranging from the very simple to the more advanced. Students certainly can, and often should, use paper and pencil along with the concrete experiences. Furthermore, they are free to abandon the manipulative materials when they are ready to do so: when a child can find the area of any polygonal region drawn on dot paper, he certainly will not be asked to redo the problem on a geoboard. Other work can be initiated by the use of pencil and paper: many examples of their use appear in the previous chapter.

The approach described in this chapter is not only for remedial work; in fact, much of the new work should at least be begun in this way. Each student can work at his own pace, using as much or as little concrete material as necessary.

In the scope of this chapter, it has been possible only to give samples of the types of things that can be done; no attempt has been made to exhaust the problem. This brief introduction to the flavor of a math-lab approach is to serve as an inducement to try it. The following section offers some practical suggestions for getting started.

Implementation

What are some ways of starting a math-lab approach?

Any teacher who is interested—even just one—can make a start. The effectiveness of the approach depends on how well the materials are used, not on how many different materials are used. A thoroughly implemented math-lab program does not happen immediately but takes time to evolve from whatever beginnings are possible.

A teacher who wishes to begin in his own classroom, whatever the level, should choose a few materials or ideas that he likes. The materials discussed in this chapter are among the most useful. If he is not able to purchase materials, he and the students can make things, or they can work on activities requiring noncommercial materials. If a budget is available, it is wise at first to buy in small quantities to avoid obtaining a large amount of material that turns out to be unnecessary or of little use. Sharing ideas with colleagues, visiting schools that use a math-lab approach, attending talks, and seeing displays at conventions are other valuable sources of help.

Although a whole class might work with a particular material such as geoboards, chips, or cubes, it is usually advisable for children to work in small groups. It is exciting for the students to swap materials and share experiences.

It may sound difficult to have the whole class divided into groups with each group working with a different material, but it really is not, provided the teacher introduces new materials to a small group at a time. One successful way to acquaint all the students with a new material is to introduce it to a small group first while the rest of the children work on their own with something familiar. When this small group knows what to do, the teacher can either work with another group or ask members of the first group to help introduce the material to others. Additional materials can be introduced gradually, and students may wish to use more than one material during a period. The teacher can circulate from group to group, taking part in the students' investigations and posing questions and problems as appropriate. Teachers must realize that they will not know all the answers. The math-lab approach requires that the teacher have a spirit of exploration—a spirit of wanting to make discoveries along with the children.

Bringing out few new materials at a time (or even just one) not only allows the teacher to work with each material himself before introducing it but also provides vitality and a spirit of anticipation. It is deadening to have materials around the room that either "can't be used yet" or are used only superficially. When a material is not in active use, it should not be part of the classroom environment; otherwise, it will not only lose some of its impact but no doubt some of its parts as well.

Proper storage is essential. The students must be taught to be responsible for the care of the materials; they must realize that in many cases the loss of one piece may make a whole device or game unusable.

Some teachers set up a "Math-Lab Corner" within the classroom. It might start with shelves and a table on which children can keep the devices being used at any particular time as well as those things that are always available to them (e.g., graph paper, rulers, balances, counters, rods, or whatever is appropriate to the level). Plastic washpans or boxes covered with contact paper are colorful and can serve as storage bins or tote trays for small materials. In addition, there might be a closet for storage of materials not in current use. Problem cards, project cards, and small booklets can be placed in the pockets of a simple rack made from cloth or paper and hung on the wall in this corner of the room. Students' projects can be displayed here also. Because supplementary textbooks, source books, and worksheets can provide additional ideas, room should be made for these too.

There are various ways of using the math-lab approach within a classroom. Some teachers try to incorporate more than one way into their plans. Here are several possibilities:

Small groups of children use the math-lab corner at various times during the day.

Children are involved in math-lab activities one day a week.

Some students work with manipulative materials while others are working with textbooks or other written materials. (The teacher might be with either group or share time between the two.)

Small groups of students work with different materials.

All students are working with the same material. (They need not be doing the same work nor be working at the same rate.)

The approach is used to relate mathematics to other areas of the curriculum, especially to art and to science.

Whenever one teacher adopts the math-lab approach, it almost always "spills over" to other classrooms. Often interest is aroused and momentum is gained through the informal sharing of ideas among both the teachers and the students. It is helpful for teachers to get together to work with the materials themselves. If there is no provision in the school system for workshops, each teacher can be responsible for getting to know one material well in order to help others. Communication resulting from the common experience of "doing" is most important; even with the best of teachers' guides, it is very easy to run out of energy and ideas. To be able to keep the materials open, alive, and challenging, teachers must work with these themselves, share ideas, and develop a repertoire of uses.

As a school becomes involved in a math-lab approach, it is helpful to pool resources. Since so many of the materials have uses in all the grades, it becomes essential to think of buying for the school rather than for each classroom. One teacher might help to provide an overview of what is needed in each classroom and what would be more economical to share, and then a loan service could be worked out.

What are some ways of using a math-lab room?

Some schools are fortunate to have space for a math-lab room. If this is the case, it can serve as a central resource for materials as well as a place where children work. Although it is not necessary, such a room has many advantages. Some schools even provide a teacher or an aide for the lab.

A math-lab room can be used in many different ways. Sometimes the children go to the math lab by classes with their teacher so that a particular unit can be introduced. Work with this unit might be continued in the lab, or appropriate materials might be taken back to the classroom.

Sometimes children in the same math group go to the lab for special work in some area. A student or small groups of students can work independently or on work suggested by the math-lab teacher, student teacher, or parent volunteer. The lab provides abundant opportunities for project work, for enrichment, for drill work, and for "catching up."

Nongraded sessions with a few children from several grades at once can prove very fruitful. Students of various ages can work at their own level with the same materials or with different materials. This type of situation provides an excellent opportunity for both the students and the teachers to see people as individuals. When children are given concrete situations, it becomes clear that the usual age and ability groupings can be very misleading.

As the program evolves, the children can help in the lab and in the classrooms as assistants. Children from any grade can act as helpers with topics in which they are well versed. A buddy system can be established for children with special needs. For example, older students might volunteer to work with first graders identified by their teachers as those who need either help or enrichment. The older children should have frequent opportunities to discuss their teaching and receive help from their teachers. High school students, also, can be helpful as assistants in an elementary, junior high, or senior high laboratory program.

How can the laboratory approach be coordinated with the rest of the curriculum?

Most of the math-lab materials are so rich and open-ended that they have implications from kindergarten through high school and beyond. There is need to coordinate their use with the rest of the curriculum. However, there is no need to set ceiling levels that restrict the use of a material in a particular grade. It is important that teachers be able to find out what prior experiences children have had in order to build on these experiences.

The math-lab approach can be applied to topics in the existing curriculum. Teachers can use textbooks, a scope-and-sequence chart, or curriculum guidelines as a basic outline from which topics are chosen. In this context, the lab activities provide a means for the students to gain understanding and to broaden their experiences. Ideally, there will be someone available to help coordinate the work, provide teacher training, and develop guidelines that integrate the math-lab approach into the curriculum. For a more detailed discussion and for many helpful suggestions, see the book *Freedom to Learn* (4) and the film *Math's Alive* (128).

Concluding Remarks

In the scope of one chapter, it is impossible to discuss all the reasons for a math-lab approach, all the ways of using the approach, all possible materials and topics, and all problems that arise. It is hoped that the samples of ideas presented here will encourage teachers to use the references and get started on what can be a most exciting and rewarding adventure.

REFERENCES

For the convenience of the reader, the reference materials pertinent to this chapter have been divided into the following categories:

Books (entries 1–70)
Journal Articles (entries 71–118)
Journals (entries 119–24)
Other Materials and Their Sources
    Films (entries 125–29)
    Manipulative Materials (entries 130–50)

Math-Lab Cards (entries 151–56)
Computation Kits (entries 157–58)
Free Materials (entries 159–60)
Unpublished Material (entry 161)

BOOKS

1. Allen, Charles E. *Adventures in Computing,* bks. 1 and 2. Boston: Ginn & Co., 1969.
2. Association of Teachers of Mathematics [Great Britain]. *Notes on Mathematics in Primary Schools.* London: Cambridge University Press, 1967. Also available as paperback from the New York branch of Cambridge University Press and the Cuisenaire Company of America, Inc., 12 Church St., New Rochelle, N.Y. 10805.
3. Bell, Stuart E. Mathematics in the Making series. 9 vols. London: Longmans, 1967. Available also from Houghton Mifflin Co., Boston.
4. Biggs, Edith E., and James R. MacLean. *Freedom to Learn: An Active Learning Approach to Mathematics.* Reading, Mass.: Addison-Wesley Co., 1969.
5. Bradford, John, and Harlan Bartram. *The Geosquare Teacher's Manual.* Ft. Collins, Colo.: Scott Scientific, Sigma Enterprises, 1967.
6. Bradford, John, and Marvin Karlin. *Sigma Chips: Teacher's Manual.* Ft. Collins, Colo.: Scott Scientific, Sigma Enterprises, 1970.
7. Braunfeld, Peter, et al. *Activities Handbook for Stretchers and Shrinkers.* UICSM Mathematics Program for Junior High School, Grade 7. New York: Harper & Row, 1970.
8. Cambridge Conference on the Correlation of Science and Mathematics in the Schools. *Goals for the Correlation of Elementary Science and Mathematics.* Published for Education Development Center. Boston: Houghton Mifflin Co., 1969.
9. Cohen, Donald. *Inquiry in Mathematics via the Geo-Board, Teacher's Guide.* New York, Walker Teaching Aids, 1967.
10. Davidson, Jessica. *Using the Cuisenaire Rods: A Photo/Text Guide for Teachers.* New Rochelle, N.Y.: Cuisenaire Co. of America, 1969.
11. Davidson, Patricia S., Grace K. Galton, and Arlene W. Fair. *Math Bibliography.* Newton, Mass.: Growth Activity Products, Box 637, Newton Lower Falls, Mass. 02162, 1971.
12. Davis, Robert B. *Discovery in Mathematics: A Text for Teachers.* The Madison Project. Reading, Mass.: Addison-Wesley Publishing Co., 1964.
13. ———. *Explorations in Mathematics: A Text for Teachers.* The Madison Project. Reading, Mass.: Addison-Wesley Publishing Co., 1966.
14. Denholm, Richard A. *Mathematics: Man's Key to Progress,* bks. A and B. Pasadena, Calif.: Franklin Publications, 1968.
15. Elementary Science Study. Working Papers series. *Mapping* and *Match and Measure* and *Musical Instrument Book.* Newton, Mass.: Education Development Center, 1968.
16. ———. *Peas and Particles.* Newton, Mass.: Education Development Center, 1966. Available from McGraw-Hill Book Co., Webster Division.
17. ———. *Teacher's Guide for Attribute Problems and Games.* Newton, Mass.: Education Development Center, 1968. Available from McGraw-Hill Book Co., Webster Division.

18. ———. *Teachers' Guide for Pattern Blocks.* Newton, Mass.: Education Development Center, 1968. Available from McGraw-Hill Book Co., Webster Division.
19. Elliott, H. A., James R. MacLean, and Janet M. Jorden. *Geometry in the Classroom: New Concepts and Methods.* Toronto, Ont.: Holt, Rinehart & Winston of Canada, 1968.
20. Fielker, David S. *Cubes.* Topics from Mathematics series. Cambridge: At the University Press, 1969. Also available from the New York branch of Cambridge University Press and the Cuisenaire Company of America, Inc., 12 Church St., New Rochelle, N.Y. 10805.
21. Fitzgerald, William M., et al. *Laboratory Manual for Elementary Mathematics.* Boston: Prindle, Weber & Schmidt, 1969.
22. Fletcher, David, and Joseph Ibbotson. *Geometry with a Tangram.* Glasgow: W & R Holmes, Ltd., 1965. Available from Selective Educational Equipment, Newton, Mass.
23. Foley, Jack L., et al. *Geo-Board.* Individualizing Mathematics: Skills and Patterns series. Reading, Mass.: Addison-Wesley Publishing Co., 1970.
24. ———. *Geo-Board 2.* Individualizing Mathematics: Patterns and Discovery series. Reading, Mass.: Addison-Wesley Publishing Co., 1970.
25. ———. Individualizing Mathematics: Discovery and Structure series. Reading, Mass.: Addison-Wesley Publishing Co., 1970.
26. ———. Individualizing Mathematics: Patterns and Discovery series. Reading, Mass.: Addison-Wesley Publishing Co., 1970.
27. ———. Individualizing Mathematics: Skills and Patterns series. Reading, Mass.: Addison-Wesley Publishing Co., 1970.
28. Hightower, Robert, and Lore Rasmussen. *First-Grade Diary.* New York: Learning Innovation Corp., Forest Hills, N.Y., n.d.
29. Jencks, Stanley M., and Donald M. Peck. *Building Mental Imagery in Mathematics.* New York: Holt, Rinehart & Winston, 1968.
30. Johnson, Donovan A. *Paper Folding for the Mathematics Class.* Washington, D.C.: National Council of Teachers of Mathematics, 1957.
31. Kennedy, Leonard M. *Models for Mathematics in the Elementary School.* Belmont, Calif.: Wadsworth Publishing Co., 1968.
32. Korschelt, O. *The Theory and Practice of Go.* Translated by Samuel P. King and George G. Leckie. Tokyo: Charles E. Tuttle Co., Rutland, Vt., 1965.
33. Marsh, L. G. *Let's Explore Mathematics,* bks. 1–4. New York: Arco Publishing Co., 1964, 1968.
34. Minnemast Project. *Minnemast Units 1–26.* Minneapolis: University of Minnesota, 1967–70.
35. Mold, Josephine. *Solid Models.* Topics from Mathematics series. Cambridge: At the University Press, 1967. Available also from the New York branch of Cambridge University Press and the Cuisenaire Company of America, Inc., 12 Church St., New Rochelle, N.Y. 10805.
36. ———. *Tessellations.* Topics from Mathematics series. Cambridge: At the University Press, 1969. Available also from the New York branch of Cambridge University Press and the Cuisenaire Company of America, Inc., 12 Church St., New Rochelle, N.Y. 10805.
37. Mollie Clarke Books. 18 vols. Exeter, Eng.: Wheaton, 1966. Available from Selective Educational Equipment, Newton, Mass.

38. National Council of Teachers of Mathematics. *Enrichment Mathematics for the Grades.* Twenty-seventh Yearbook. Washington, D. C.: The Council, 1963.
39. ———. *Experiences in Mathematical Discovery.* 8 units. Washington, D.C.: The Council, 1966–67, 1970.
40. Nuffield Foundation, Nuffield Mathematics Project. *Beginnings* 1/. New York: John Wiley & Sons, 1967.
41. ———. *Computation and Structure* (2). New York: John Wiley & Sons, 1967.
42. ———. *Computation and Structure* (3). New York: John Wiley & Sons, 1968.
43. ———. *Environmental Geometry.* New York: John Wiley & Sons, 1969.
44. ———. *Graphs Leading to Algebra.* New York: John Wiley & Sons, 1969.
45. ———. *I Do and I Understand.* New York: John Wiley & Sons, 1967.
46. ———. *Mathematics Begins* (1). New York: John Wiley & Sons, 1967.
47. ———. *Pictorial Representation* [1]. New York: John Wiley & Sons, 1967.
48. ———. *Probability and Statistics.* New York: John Wiley & Sons, 1969.
49. ———. *Problems—Green Set.* New York: John Wiley & Sons, 1969.
50. ———. *Shape and Size* 2/. New York: John Wiley & Sons, 1967.
51. ———. *Shape and Size* 3/. New York: John Wiley & Sons, 1968.
52. Page, David A. *Ways to Find How Many.* Watertown, Mass.: University of Illinois Arithmetic Project, Educational Services, 1965.
53. Pearcy, J. F. F., and K. Lewis. *Experiments in Mathematics, Stage 1, Stage 2,* and *Stage 3.* Boston: Houghton Mifflin Co., 1966, 1967.
54. Peck, Lyman C. *Secret Codes, Remainder Arithmetic, and Matrices.* Washington, D.C.: National Council of Teachers of Mathematics, 1961.
55. Read, Ronald C. *Tangrams: 330 Puzzles.* Toronto, Ont.: General Publishing Co., 1965. Reprint, Dover Publications.
56. School Mathematics Project. *School Mathematics Project,* bks. A–D. Cambridge: At the University Press, 1968–69. Available also from Cuisenaire Company of America, Inc., 12 Church St., New Rochelle, N.Y. 10805.
57. Schools Council. *Mathematics in Primary Schools: Curriculum Bulletin No. 1.* 2d ed. London: Her Majesty's Stationery Office, 1966. Available also from Selective Educational Equipment, Newton, Mass.
58. Seagrove, Bryan, and John Ward. *Mathematics with a Purpose: A Guide to Running a Math Workshop.* London: University of London Press, 1968.
59. Sealey, L. G. W. *The Creative Use of Mathematics in the Junior School.* Rev. ed. Oxford: B. H. Blackwell, 1965. Available also from New York Humanities Press.
60. Sealey, L. G. W., and Vivian Gibbon. *Communication and Learning in the Primary School.* Oxford: B. H. Blackwell, 1962.
61. Sobel, Max A. *Teaching General Mathematics.* Englewood Cliffs, N.J.: Prentice-Hall, 1967.
62. Spitzer, Herbert F. *Practical Classroom Procedures for Enriching Arithmetic.* St. Louis: Webster Publishing Co., 1956. Available from McGraw-Hill Book Co., Webster Division.
63. Tahta, D. G. *Pegboard Games.* Mathematics Teaching Pamphlet, no. 13. Nelson, England: Association of Teachers of Mathematics, Market St. Chambers, Nelson, Lancashire, England, 1967.

64. Trivett, John V. *Mathematical Awareness*, pt. 1 and pt. 2. New Rochelle, N.Y.: Cuisenaire Co. of America, 1962.
65. Turner, Ethel M. *Teaching Aids for Elementary Mathematics.* New York: Holt, Rinehart & Winston, 1966.
66. Walter, Marion. *Boxes, Squares, and Other Things: A Teacher's Guide for a Unit in Informal Geometry.* Washington, D.C.: National Council of Teachers of Mathematics, 1970.
67. ———. *Look at Annette* and *Make a Bigger Puddle, Make a Smaller Worm* (two children's books with mirrors). New York: M. Evans and Co., 1972. Available from J. B. Lippincott Co., Philadelphia.
68. Wenninger, Magnus J. *Polyhedron Models for the Classroom.* Washington, D.C.: National Council of Teachers of Mathematics, 1966.
69. Wirtz, Robert W., et al. *Math Workshop: Games and Enrichment Activities.* Chicago: Encyclopaedia Britannica Press, 1964.
70. Zimmerman, Joseph T. *L.A.M.P.—Low Achiever Mathematical Project.* Des Moines: Des Moines Public Schools, 1968.

JOURNAL ARTICLES

71. Ackerman, Judy. "Computers Teach Math." *Arithmetic Teacher* 15 (May 1968): 467–68.
72. Alspaugh, Carol Ann. "Kaleidoscopic Geometry." *Arithmetic Teacher* 17 (February 1970): 116–17. Reprinted in *Readings in Geometry from the "Arithmetic Teacher,"* pp. 30–31. Washington, D.C.: National Council of Teachers of Mathematics, 1970.
73. Auclair, Jerome A., and Thomas P. Hillman. "A Topological Problem for the Ninth-Grade Mathematics Laboratory." *Mathematics Teacher* 61 (May 1968): 503–7.
74. Baumgartner, Margery. "What Can You Do with an Egg Carton?" *Arithmetic Teacher* 15 (May 1968): 456–58.
75. Biggs, Edith E. "Mathematics Laboratories and Teachers' Centres—the Mathematics Revolution in Britain." *Arithmetic Teacher* 15 (May 1968): 400–408.
76. ———. "Trial and Experiment." *Arithmetic Teacher* 17 (January 1970): 26–32.
77. Blanc, Sam S. "Mathematics in Elementary Science." *Arithmetic Teacher* 14 (December 1967): 636–40, 670.
78. Bourne, H. N. "The Concept of Area." *Arithmetic Teacher* 15 (March 1968): 233–43.
79. Calvo, Robert C. "Placo—a Number-Place Game." *Arithmetic Teacher* 15 (May 1968): 465–66.
80. Clarkson, David M. "Mathematical Activity." *Arithmetic Teacher* 15 (October 1968): 493–98.
81. ———. "A Mathematics Laboratory for Prospective Teachers." *Arithmetic Teacher* 17 (January 1970): 75–78.
82. Cochran, Beryl S., Alan Barson, and Robert B. Davis. "Child-created Mathematics." *Arithmetic Teacher* 17 (March 1970): 211–15.
83. Crawforth, Denis. "What Is a Quadrilateral?" *Mathematics Teacher* 60 (November 1967): 778–81.
84. Cunningham, George C. "Making a Counting Abacus." *Arithmetic Teacher* 14 (February 1967): 132–35.

85. Davidson, Patricia S. "An Annotated Bibliography of Suggested Manipulative Devices." *Arithmetic Teacher* 15 (October 1968): 509–12, 514–24.
86. Davidson, Patricia S., and Arlene W. Fair. "A Mathematics Laboratory—from Dream to Reality." *Arithmetic Teacher* 17 (February 1970): 105–10.
87. Desmond, Florence. "Fractions in the Junior School." *Primary Mathematics* 7, no. 9, pp. 41–49.
88. Elder, Florence. "Mathematics for the Below-Average Achiever in High School." *Mathematics Teacher* 60 (March 1967): 235–40.
89. Girard, Ruth A. "Development of Critical Interpretation of Statistics and Graphs." *Arithmetic Teacher* 14 (April 1967): 272–77.
90. Golden, Sarah R. "Fostering Enthusiasm through Child-created Games." *Arithmetic Teacher* 17 (February 1970): 111–15.
91. Grossman, Rose. "Problem-solving Activities Observed in British Primary Schools." *Arithmetic Teacher* 16 (January 1969): 34–38.
92. Hamilton, E. W. "Manipulative Devices." *Arithmetic Teacher* 13 (October 1966): 461–67.
93. McKillip, William D. " 'Patterns'—a Mathematics Unit for Three- and Four-Year-Olds." *Arithmetic Teacher* 17 (January 1970): 15–18.
94. MacLean, J. R. "The Quest for an Improved Curriculum." *Arithmetic Teacher* 14 (February 1967): 136–40. Reprinted in *Readings from the "Arithmetic Teacher,"* pp. 13–17. Washington, D.C.: National Council of Teachers of Mathematics, 1970.
95. Martin, J. Gregory, Jr., "Discovering the Mathematics of a Slide Rule." *Arithmetic Teacher* 15 (January 1968): 23–25.
96. May, Lola J. "Learning Laboratories in Elementary Schools in Winnetka." *Arithmetic Teacher* 15 (October 1968): 501–3.
97. Mayor, John R. "Science and Mathematics: 1970s—a Decade of Change." *Arithmetic Teacher* 17 (April 1970): 293–97.
98. Nelson, Diane, and Marvin N. Nelson. "Pegboard Multiplication of a Fraction by a Fraction." *Arithmetic Teacher* 16 (February 1969): 142–44.
99. Olberg, Robert. "Visual Aid for Multiplication and Division of Fractions." *Arithmetic Teacher* 14 (January 1967): 44–46.
100. Olson, Lynn. "The Meaning of Meaningful." *Arithmetic Teacher* 16 (April 1969): 276–80.
101. Parker, Robert. "Graph Paper: A Versatile Visual Aid." *Arithmetic Teacher* 16 (February 1969): 144–48.
102. Pedersen, Jean J. "Dressing Up Mathematics." *Mathematics Teacher* 61 (February 1968): 118–22.
103. Phillips, J. A. "Starting Up—a Problem in Organization." *Teaching Arithmetic* 5 (Summer Term 6, 1967): 31–42. (This publication is now called *Primary Mathematics.*)
104. Ranucci, Ernest R. "A Tiny Treasury of Tessellations." *Mathematics Teacher* 61 (February 1968): 114–17.
105. Rosskopf, Myron F., and Jerome D. Kaplan. "Educating Mathematics Specialists to Teach Children from Disadvantaged Areas." *Arithmetic Teacher* 15 (November 1968): 606–12.
106. Sanders, Walter J., and J. Richard Dennis. "Congruence Geometry for Junior High School." *Mathematics Teacher* 61 (April 1968): 354–69.
107. Schaefer, Anne W., and Albert H. Mauthe. "Problem Solving with En-

thusiasm—the Mathematics Laboratory." *Arithmetic Teacher* 17 (January 1970): 7–14.
108. Schmid, John A. "Experiences with Approximation and Estimation." *Arithmetic Teacher* 14 (May 1967): 365–68.
109. Scott, Joseph. "With Sticks and Rubber Bands." *Arithmetic Teacher* 17 (February 1970): 147–50. Reprinted in *Readings in Geometry from the "Arithmetic Teacher,"* pp. 5–8. Washington, D.C.: National Council of Teachers of Mathematics, 1970.
110. Swart, William L. "A Laboratory Plan for Teaching Measurement in Grades 1–8." *Arithmetic Teacher* 14 (December 1967): 652–53.
111. Sweet, Raymond. "Organizing a Mathematics Laboratory." *Mathematics Teacher* 60 (February 1967): 117–20.
112. Thomashow, Beatrice E. "'Stock-Market' Unit." *Arithmetic Teacher* 15 (October 1968): 552–56.
113. Travers, Kenneth J. "Computation: Low Achievers' Stumbling Block or Stepping Stone?" *Arithmetic Teacher* 16 (November 1969): 523–28.
114. Walter, Marion. "An Example of Informal Geometry: Mirror Cards." *Arithmetic Teacher* 13 (October 1966): 448–52. Reprinted in *Readings in Geometry from the "Arithmetic Teacher,"* pp. 25–29. Washington, D.C.: National Council of Teachers of Mathematics, 1970.
115. ———. "A Second Example of Informal Geometry: Milk Cartons." *Arithmetic Teacher* 16 (May 1969): 368–70. Reprinted in *Readings in Geometry from the "Arithmetic Teacher,"* pp. 48–50. Washington, D.C.: National Council of Teachers of Mathematics, 1970.
116. ———. "Some Mathematical Ideas Involved in the Mirror Cards." *Arithmetic Teacher* 14 (February 1967): 115–25.
117. Wells, Peter. "Creating Mathematics with a Geoboard." *Arithmetic Teacher* 17 (April 1970): 347–49.
118. Woodby, Lauren G. "The Angle Mirror Outdoors." *Arithmetic Teacher* 17 (April 1970): 298–300.

JOURNALS

119. *Arithmetic Teacher*. Managing Editor, Jane M. Hill. National Council of Teachers of Mathematics, 1201 Sixteenth St., NW, Washington, D.C. 20036. Published monthly, October–May.
120. *Mathematics Teacher*. Managing Editor, Carol V. McCamman. National Council of Teachers of Mathematics, 1201 Sixteenth St., NW, Washington, D.C. 20036. Published monthly, October–May.
121. *Mathematics Teaching*. Editor, David Wheeler. Association of Teachers of Mathematics, Market Street Chambers, Nelson, Lancashire, England. Published quarterly.
122. *Mathex Pupil Bulletins*. Editor, W. W. Sawyer. Encyclopaedia Britannica Publications, 151 Bloor St., West, Toronto, Ont. Published monthly, September–June.
123. *Mathex Teacher's Bulletins*, nos. 1–20. Editors, W. W. Sawyer and L. D. Nelson. Encyclopaedia Britannica Publications, 151 Bloor St., West, Toronto, Ont.
124. *Primary Mathematics*. Pergamon Press, Maxwell House, Fairview Park, Elmsford, N.Y. 10523. Published three times a year.

OTHER MATERIALS AND THEIR SOURCES

Films

125. *Dance Squared.* Color, 4 min.
International Film Bureau
332 S. Michigan Ave.
Chicago, Ill. 60604
126. *I Do and I Understand.* 15 min.
Radim Films
220 W. 42d St.
New York, N.Y. 10036
127. *Mathematics Peep Show.* Color, 10 min.
For Rental:
University of Southern California, Film
Distribution Section
University Park
Los Angeles, Calif. 90007
For Purchase:
Charles Eames
901 Washington Blvd.
Venice, Calif. 90291
128. *Math's Alive.* 30 min.
Educational Foundation for Visual Aids,
National Audio-Visual Aids Library
Paxton Place
Gipsy Rd., London, S.E. 27, England
129. *Notes on a Triangle.* Color, 5 min.
International Film Bureau
332 S. Michigan Ave.
Chicago, Ill. 60604

Manipulative Materials

130. Abacus Board.
Scott Scientific, Inc.
P.O. Box 2121
Ft. Collins, Colo. 80521
Also:
Selective Educational Equipment (SEE)
3 Bridge St.
Newton, Mass. 02195
Also:
Math Media
P.O. Box 1107
Danbury, Conn. 06810
131. Attribute Games and Problems. Materials: A Blocks, People Pieces, Color Cubes, Stickers, and *Teacher's Guide for Attribute Games and Problems.*
McGraw-Hill Book Co., Webster Division
Manchester Rd.
Manchester, Mo. 63011
132. *Chips.*
Scott Scientific, Inc.
P.O. Box 2121
Ft. Collins, Colo. 80521

Also:
Selective Educational Equipment (SEE)
3 Bridge St.
Newton, Mass. 02195
Also:
Math Media
P.O. Box 1107
Danbury, Conn. 06810
133. Color Cubes.
McGraw-Hill Book Co., Webster Division
Manchester Rd.
Manchester, Mo. 63011
Also:
Selective Educational Equipment (SEE)
3 Bridge St.
Newton, Mass. 02195
134. Cuisenaire Rods.
Cuisenaire Co. of America
12 Church St.
New Rochelle, N.Y. 10805
135. Dienes Logical Blocks, Large Plastic Set, and *Learning Logic, Logical Games*, by Z. P. Dienes. New York: Herder & Herder.
Pitman Publishing Corp.
6 E. 43d St.
New York, N.Y. 10017
136. Dienes Multibase Arithmetic Blocks: M.A.B. New York: Herder & Herder.
Pitman Publishing Corp.
6 E. 43d St.
New York, N.Y. 10017
137. Divisumma GT 24 Calculator.
Olivetti Underwood Corp.
1 Park Ave.
New York, N.Y. 10016
138. First Balance and Invicta Math Balance.
Selective Educational Equipment (SEE)
3 Bridge St.
Newton, Mass. 02195
139. Geo Blocks, by Elementary Science Study: Materials for Geo Blocks, *Teacher's Guide for Geo Blocks,* and Problem Cards for Geo Blocks.
McGraw-Hill Book Co., Webster Division
Manchester Rd.
Manchester, Mo. 63011
140. Geosquare-Classroom Kit and *Teacher's Manual.*
Scott Scientific, Inc.
P.O. Box 2121
Ft. Collins, Colo. 80521
141. Lowenfeld Poleidoblocks, Set G with *Guide*.
Selective Educational Equipment (SEE)
3 Bridge St.
Newton, Mass. 02195
142. Mirror Cards, by Elementary Science Study. Materials for Mirror Cards and *Teacher's Guide for Mirror Cards.*

McGraw-Hill Book Co., Webster Division
Manchester Rd.
Manchester, Mo. 63011
143. Mobiles, by Elementary Science Study. Materials for Mobiles and *Teacher's Guide for Mobiles.*
McGraw-Hill Book Co., Webster Division
Manchester Rd.
Manchester, Mo. 63011.
144. Nippon Master Hand Operated Desk Calculator: Problem Cards, sets A and B, and Nippon Calculator Work Sheets.
Broughtons Calculators U.S.A.
31 E. 28th St.
New York, N.Y. 10016
145. Pattern Books, by Elementary Science Study.
McGraw-Hill Book Co., Webster Division
Manchester Rd.
Manchester, Mo. 63011
Also:
Selective Educational Equipment (SEE)
3 Bridge St.
Newton, Mass. 02195
146. Pendulums, by Elementary Science Study. *Teacher's Guide for Pendulums,* 1969.
McGraw-Hill Book Co., Webster Division
Manchester Rd.
Manchester, Mo. 63011
147. Primary Balancing, by Elementary Science Study. *The Balance Book: A Guide for Teachers,* 1969.
McGraw-Hill Book Co., Webster Division
Manchester Rd.
Manchester, Mo. 63011
148. SEE-Calculator.
Selective Educational Equipment (SEE)
3 Bridge St.
Newton, Mass. 02195
149. Stern Structural Arithmetic Apparatus.
Houghton Mifflin Co.
53 W. 43d St.
New York, N.Y. 10036
150. Tangrams, by Elementary Science Study: Tangram Cards, Tangram Pieces, and *Teacher's Guide for Tangrams.*
McGraw-Hill Book Co., Webster Division
Manchester Rd.
Manchester, Mo. 63011

Math-Lab Cards

151. *Chip Trading Activities,* Sets I–V. Patricia S. Davidson, Grace K. Galton, and Arlene W. Fair.
Scott Scientific, Inc., Sigma Division
P.O. Box 2121
Ft. Collins, Colo. 80521
152. *Macmillan Math Activity Cards, Levels A–E.* David M. Clarkson.
Macmillan Co., School Division

866 3d Ave.
New York, N.Y. 10022
153. Nuffield Foundation, Nuffield Mathematics Project. *Problems—Green Set.*
John Wiley & Sons
605 3d Ave.
New York, N.Y. 10016
154. Student Activity Cards for Cuisenaire Rods. Patricia S. Davidson, Arlene W. Fair, and Grace K. Galton.
Cuisenaire Co. of America, Inc.
12 Church St.
New Rochelle, N.Y. 10805
155. *Walker Geo-Cards.* Donald Cohen.
Walker Teaching Programs and Teaching Aids
720 5th Ave.
New York, N.Y. 10019
156. *The Workshop Approach to Mathematics.* R. A. J. Pethen. Mathematics Workshop Cards, Sets 1-4.
St. Martin's Press
175 5th Ave.
New York, N.Y. 10010

Computation Kits

157. Computational Skills Development Kit.
Science Research Associates, Inc.
259 E. Erie St.
Chicago, Ill. 60611
158. Individualized Mathematics: Drill and Practice Kits AA, BB, CC, and DD. Patrick Suppes and Max Jerman.
Random House, L. W. Singer Co.
Order Entry Dept.
Westminster, Md. 21157

Free Materials

159. *Elementary Science Study (ESS) Newsletter*
Education Development Center
55 Chapel St.
Newton, Mass. 02160
160. *Sets, Probability and Statistics: The Mathematics of Life Insurance*
Institute of Life Insurance, Health Insurance Institute, Educational Division
277 Park Ave.
New York, N.Y. 10017

Unpublished Material

161. Beryl S. Cochran. "Collection of Written Materials to Be Used with Primary Teachers in the Madison Project Teacher-Training Workshops in New Curriculum Mathematics." Duplicated.
Beryl S. Cochran
Box 1176
Weston, Conn. 06880

9

Diagnostic-Prescriptive Teaching

VINCENT J. GLENNON
JOHN W. WILSON

THIS chapter discusses four aspects of the problem of the nature and use of diagnostic and prescriptive teaching of mathematics to slow learners. First, the larger view of the problem is presented to enable the reader to see its furthest metes and bounds and be able thereby to view the narrow limits in which the writers are currently working. Second, and accepting the fact that their present efforts in diagnostic-prescriptive teaching are primarily oriented to cognitive learning, the writers present a taxonomy for the content of elementary school mathematics in the hope that it will enlarge the teacher's view to the fullest dimensions and potential of a symptomatic (observable behavior) approach to the problem. Third, some group (nomothetic) and some individualized (idiographic) procedures that are useful in diagnostic-prescriptive teaching are presented. And, fourth, lessons are presented from a case study in which the content taxonomy was used by the teacher to guide him in the selection of appropriate objectives and in the selection of relevant nomothetic and idiographic procedures. It is hoped that they will provide the interested reader with insights that will enable him to carry out similar diagnostic-prescriptive work with slow learners.

The Larger View

Prior chapters have presented discussions of several of the variables essential to a well-conceived theory of instruction for the slow learner (or any other child). These include knowing his characteristics and needs, using available research-derived knowledge about teaching him, using behavioral objectives, creating a favorable learning environment, adjusting instructional methods, using multisensory aids, and adopting the laboratory approach. If these and other variables essential to a theory of instruction were present in the initial teaching, and in appropriate amounts, the learning, retention, and transfer of learning would conceivably proceed at an optimum level for any given child. And, contrariwise, the fact that diagnosis and carefully prescribed teaching (a rifle approach rather than a shotgun approach) is presently needed by so many children and youth is prima facie evidence that one or more of the essential variables were missing or were present in inappropriate amounts during the initial teaching and subsequent consolidation phases of the instruction. To approximate an optimum level of learning and retention in this situation, teaching should have a large diagnostic-prescriptive element.

Some essential variables

From the above paragraph it can be seen that diagnostic-prescriptive teaching is a careful effort to reteach successfully what was not well taught or not well learned during the initial teaching. What, then, are the essential variables of a good diagnostic and prescriptive teaching program? At the outset let it be noted that such teaching can be viewed, on the one hand, as being as large as a theory of instruction itself or, on the other hand, as being fragmentary mechanical reteaching of each of many unrelated cognitive skills, such as renaming (carrying) in addition of the form $47 + 28 = n$ or "inverting the divisor and multiplying" in division of the form $3\frac{1}{2} \div \frac{2}{3} = n$. When diagnostic and prescriptive teaching of the higher cognitive abilities is viewed as mechanical reteaching of associations, it is most unlikely that any educationally significant amount of learning, retention, and transfer of learning will occur. In other words, if the slow learner has been the victim of a drill-oriented program of instruction for, say, six years and has not attained a level of scholastic performance consistent with his estimated capability, it is most unlikely that more of the same type of teaching will succeed in the seventh year.

The larger view of diagnostic-prescriptive teaching is here proposed and discussed as a set of constituent variables.

The curriculum variable. The first variable to be discussed within the larger theory of instruction is a worthwhile theory of curriculum. This asks the question What mathematical knowledge is of most worth for the slow learner? There are three possible theories, or subtheories, of curriculum to which one can turn to answer the question: a logical subtheory, a psychological subtheory, and a sociological subtheory. Each has its proponents and opponents, its advantages and limitations.

The logical theory of curriculum is about 2,500 years old. Its main tenet is that the curriculum is best organized for teaching and learning purposes when the subject matter (in this case mathematics) is organized and developed as a series of related ideas—regardless of its relevance as seen by the learner and regardless of its usefulness in the common business and social situations of adult life.

Presently its best-known advocate is the cognitive psychologist Jerome S. Bruner. As hypothesized by him: "Any subject can be taught to any child on any grade level in some intellectually honest form." This hypothesis and its implications for teaching neatly sidestep a more important prior question: *Ought* any subject be taught to any child?

Unfortunately, this and similar statements are used by some supporters to "justify" teaching a few "exciting" lessons in, say, algebra to third-grade children. Leaping to the untenable conclusion that slow learners can learn anything that other children can learn, they argue backward that because slow learners can learn algebra they ought to learn it. This theory in extremist form offers the teacher no reasonable guidelines for selecting the content of a diagnostic-prescriptive program for the slow learner.

A second point of view on what mathematics is of most worth is the clinical-psychological point of view. The essence of this view is that the only honest curriculum in mathematics is one that eventuates from the expressed needs of the child. A. S. Neill states the case for this theory of curriculum:

> Whether a school has or has not a special method for teaching long division is of no significance, for long division is of no importance except

to those who *want* to learn it. And the child who *wants* to learn long division *will* learn it no matter how it is taught. [17, p. 5]

Selecting the content for diagnostic and prescriptive teaching for the slow learner under this theory is essentially the responsibility of the child or youth. The teacher's role is that of a consultant to the child after he, the child, has identified and made known his interest in learning or relearning a particular topic. Presumably, his wanting to learn will compensate for any absence of the planning and motivating the teacher would provide under a more structured program. As with the logical theory, this theory offers the teacher little help in planning for the slow learner.

And, third, still others assert just as strongly that the only acceptable source of mathematical content is that body of knowledge which is widely used in business and in the common life situations of the adult population. For many years Guy M. Wilson has been the most articulate spokesman for this sociological point of view. He argues that for all children, not just slow learners, the amount of mathematics that should be "mastered" is very little. For the slow learner, whose adult mathematical needs may be less than those of the average person, the mastery program would be even less. After many years of investigating the mathematics used in common business and adult life situations, Wilson states the case for all children this way:

> The mastery [program] consists of simple addition—100 primary facts, 300 decade facts, carrying and other process difficulties; simple subtraction—100 primary facts, process difficulties; multiplication—100 primary facts, process difficulties; long division—no committed facts, general scheme and process steps; simple fractions in halves, fourths, and thirds, and, in special cases, in eighths and twelfths, general acquaintance with other simple fractions; decimals—reading knowledge only. . . . The essential drill phases of arithmetic for perfect mastery are as simple as that. The load is very small. [21, pp. 3, 4]

Two limitations to the sociological point of view, obviously, are the minimizing of structure and the failure to capitalize on the motivational power inherent in the expressed interests of children and youth.

Summary discussion of the curriculum variable. Above, then, are three very different subtheories on what mathematics is of most worth for all children (and therefore for the slow learner) and which must be drawn upon in various amounts in selecting that mathematics which should be diagnosed and prescribed for the slow learner. Each is an extremist point of view. It is the writers' opinion that no one of these in its extreme form should dictate the curriculum for the slow learner. Bruner and the structural, or logical, subtheory is no more correct than Wilson and his sociological subtheory, or Neill and his psychological subtheory. From the larger point of view, the question of what mathematics is of most worth for the slow learner (indeed, for any learner) is far too important and complex to be left to the mathematicians, or to the sociologists, or to the psychologists. Each of these has his own form of "the closed mind," each his own form of "Pied Piperism"—to use Lee J. Cronbach's apt figure of speech (10, p. 77).

Important checks are provided by the disciplines among the disciplines. Mathematics education is an interdiscipline. Mathematics educators cannot risk the danger inherent in any single subtheory. The harm to the slow learner would be too great.

Glennon (13, pp. 134–39) developed the model in figure 9.1 to picture the size of the ball park in which the curriculum game is played and the nature of a balanced theory of curriculum. The ring (x) in the "center" of the triangular region indicates the region of optimum balance for the average child. For any particular child the region of optimum balance and relevance may be shifted one way or another. For the slow learner with no significant emotional disabilities,

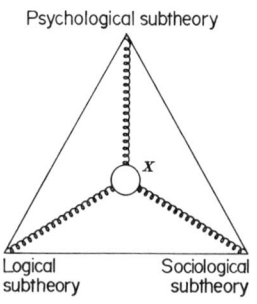

Fig. 9.1

the most appropriate curriculum will draw most heavily on the sociological subtheory and to a lesser but still significant extent on each of the other two subtheories. That is, the concept of a relevant curriculum will shift from region x to region y (fig. 9.2).

More specifically, not all number systems and not all numeration systems are of equal worth for the slow learner; and, indeed, not all

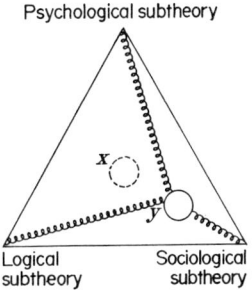

Fig. 9.2

topics within the real number system itself and in the decimal numeration system are of equal worth. Within the limited amount of time available for systematic instruction in, say, grade 5 (45 minutes per day for 180 days, or about 135 clock hours per year), a topic such as subtraction of whole numbers of the form $45 - 27 = n$ would be of greater relevance and social usefulness than division of fractional numbers of the form $1\frac{5}{7} \div 3\frac{1}{4} = n$ and hence would be more appropriately a part of the instructional program for the slow learner.

When one is diagnosing and prescribing the instructional program for the slow learner, the greater part of one's time and talents should be concentrated on diagnosing and prescribing within those topics of greatest relevance to the learner. The fact that, as the model shows, the other two subtheories are also connected to the ring in figure 9.2 means that the mathematical structure of the subject matter (the logical subtheory) and the expressed needs of the child are still important variables in curriculum decision making and must be used in appropriate amounts when diagnosing and prescribing for the slow learner.

The method variable. Any parent of school-age children is well aware of the fact that a given teacher will be liked by some of the children and disliked by others. These differing reactions are due to several causes. The cause of concern here is the teacher's perception of his role in the instructional process—a perception largely determining how he will teach. As with theories of curriculum, the theories of the teacher's method can be viewed as three very different subtheories: telling (didactic or expository), discovery, and psychotherapy. Glennon (13, pp. 139–41) illustrated their interrelationships with the model in figure 9.3.

In the discussion of curriculum theory above, it was noted that the

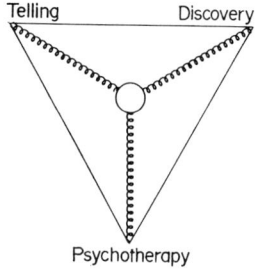

Fig. 9.3

selection of *what* mathematics is of most worth for the slow learner should be based primarily on the social usefulness of the topics. The answer to the companion question—What *method* is of most worth in the diagnosis and prescription for learning disabilities?—is a far more complex matter. The answer is intimately and intricately associated with such variables as the cognitive level of the topic being taught (i.e., understanding the commutative property, consolidation of a skill, ability to solve two-step verbal problems, etc.), the type of motivation being used, the personality traits of the teacher and the child as well as their mutual compatibility—to mention several relevant variables. Each of the three different methods is discussed briefly in its extreme form for purposes of comparison.

Certainly the most widely used method is that of "telling." In the typical elementary or secondary school classroom there is very little dialogue. Most of the talking is the teacher's and most of that is in the form of directions, commands, leading questions—all kindly, perhaps, but all authority-oriented statements. The teacher views this method as the one in which he is most experienced and hence most comfortable. Too, he views "telling" (perhaps because of the way he was taught) as the best way to get things done, to "cover the course." In recent years it has become fashionable by some other methods extremists to satirize and ridicule "telling" when done by the teacher. But, strangely enough, they applaud "telling" when done by one child in the classroom as he *tells* the other twenty-five children what he "discovered."

Although "telling" can be and perhaps is very often overused, the method has many excellent features for certain kinds of teaching situations, and it holds much promise for productive research in the future. Of this potential John B. Carroll says: "Despite its relative neglect [in being researched] in educational psychology, learning by being told has a glorious past. Its future may be even more glorious if we will take the trouble to examine it with the attention we have paid to other—less interesting—ways of learning." (9, p. 10.)

In the writers' opinion, the *au courant* extremism in method is the so-called discovery method. Much has been written about it; for example, see Shulman and Keislar, *Learning by Discovery: A Critical Appraisal*. When defined in a pure sense, discovery does not appear to exist in any real, recognizable, or usable form in education. In a pure sense, discovery would have to be defined as learning that takes place when (1) the purpose or goal resides wholly and singly within the learner, (2) the learning experiences are planned by him only, (3) the knowledge discovered is new to the learner, and (4) the knowledge discovered is new to that literate population. If any one of these criteria is not present, the method would be some variation of *guided* discovery. Within this definition, learning from reading a book could not be called discovery learning, since the book itself is a telling or didactic tool.

The guided-dicovery method appears to be used primarily to transmit subject matter. Its adherents also hold that it can be used as a method of bringing about such process outcomes as "learning to learn," "learning to inquire," and "learning to ask questions."

The third subtheory of method, and one the teacher should have available when working with the slow learner in diagnostic-prescriptive teaching situations, is psychotherapy. Unlike telling and guided discovery, which are primarily concerned with transmitting subject matter, psychotherapy is primarily concerned with the larger view of learning—the life skills of understanding of self, acceptance of others, and so on. Meade identifies five such "life skills": "powers of analysis, characterological flexibility, self-starting creativity in the use of off-job time, a built-in preference and facility for democratic interpersonal relations, and an ability to remain an individual in a mass society" (16, p. 38). *Dibs: In Search of Self*, by Virginia Axline, is an excellent case study in the use of play therapy—one form of psychotherapy—as she worked with a young boy struggling to learn about himself (2).

Although much has been researched and written (19) on the role of psychotherapy in teaching, the teacher's professional knowledge of and experience with the method is usually not complete enough to use it in the classroom or educational clinic. In one sense, however, almost all teachers are amateur psychotherapists to some children some of the time. That is, almost all teachers will identify with and empathize with a child who has evidenced some emotion-based problem in the classroom. The teacher behaves more like an artist or a humanist than like a scientist working with things or animals in laboratory situations. Gilbert Highet comments on this:

> I believe that teaching is an art, not a science. . . . Teaching is not like inducing a chemical reaction: it is much more like painting a picture or making a piece of music . . . or writing a friendly letter. You must throw your heart into it, you must realize that it cannot all be done by formulas, or you will spoil your work, and your pupils, and yourself. [14, pp. vii–viii]

Summary discussion of the method variable. As said above, selecting the most appropriate method or combination of methods for use in diagnostic and prescriptive teaching is a far more complex professional matter than selecting appropriate content. It may help the reader to see its complexity if a few questions are posed here about appropriateness of method in two teaching situations.

Mr. A is able to tolerate a rather high degree of ambiguity. He is teaching a slow learner who has a long history of inability to tolerate frustration. The topic is multiplication of whole numbers of the form 4×23. Should Mr. A *tell how* in the belief that this is the most efficient method even though previous teaching by telling has failed, and because he is most comfortable and secure with this method? Or, being able to tolerate ambiguity, should he *guide the discovery* of the algorithm in the belief that this is a more powerful method for building understanding of the distributive property—even though the child cannot tolerate the frustration that goes with the teacher's withholding of knowledge?

Now change the situation somewhat. Mrs. B is unable to tolerate frustration, is rigid in personality and in her didactic teaching methods. She is working with a slow learner who dislikes arithmetic and who is also quite hyperactive. When teaching the above computational skill, should she *tell*? Should she *guide discovery*? Or, using psychotherapeutic methods, should she *reflect the child's expressed feelings* of dislike for mathematics, hoping thereby to help the child see himself—an experience which, if successful over a period of time, should make it possible for him to attend better, to tolerate better, to learn better, and then to like better? Should this teacher change her prior, somewhat successful didactic methods to guided-discovery methods? To psychotherapeutic methods?

To summarize, many variables affect the diagnostic-prescriptive teaching of mathematics to slow learners in elementary and secondary schools. No longer can this teaching be viewed as simply reteaching (redrilling?) the computational skills of previous years. And no longer should reteaching use only a verbal-symbolic mode when the great significance attached to the necessary prior modes—the concrete-manipulative (enactive) mode and the representational, pictorial (ikonic) mode—is known.

Moreover, evidence is accumulating that the cultural background of children may determine to an educationally significant extent the ability of children to learn by these modes. Fort, Watts, and Lesser, in a summary of studies of the variability that exists among Chinese, Jewish, Negro, and Puerto Rican children in four mental abilities (verbal, numerical, reasoning, and spatial conceptualization), reported these findings (11, p. 387):

1. Chinese children performed spatial tasks better than any of the other tasks. They performed verbal tasks least well.
2. Jewish children evidenced their greatest proficiency in the verbal area and were next best in numerical concepts. Their spatial skills were poorest, and reasoning scores were only a bit higher than spatial.
3. Negro children showed their greatest skill to be in the verbal area. They performed least well in the numerical area.
4. Puerto Rican children evidenced the least difference in the four abilities. Their best area was space conceptualization; their worst, verbal concepts.

The space allotted to this chapter does not permit rendering the problem still more complex by discussing in detail other variables that significantly affect the success of diagnostic and prescriptive teaching. These variables, each of which has constituent subtheories, would include at least theories of motivation, theories of personality development, and theories of child and adolescent development. Although the preceding discussion, limited to theories of curriculum and of method, shows that diagnostic-prescriptive teaching is a complex task, it appears much more complex when these latter variables enter into the tutorial situation.

The patterns listed above and those for other ethnic groups should have implications for the mode of learning to be capitalized on in diagnostic and prescriptive teaching. Much has yet to be learned before these implications can be hypothesized, researched, and generalized. In the meantime, the teacher will have to work intuitively as he selects the mode of learning that will be most effective and efficient for a particular child.

A look into the future

All the preceding discussion has been concerned with diagnostic and prescriptive teaching from the point of view of teaching as a humanistic effort. While educational psychologists and curriculum workers are contributing the ideas above, a new breed of educator is working from what David Krech calls a psychoneurobiochemeducation point of view:

> There will be great changes made in the first and foremost and continuing business of society: the education and training of the young. The development of the mind of the child will come to rest in the knowledge and skills of the biochemist, the pharmacologist, and neurologist, and psychologist, and educator. And there will be a new expert abroad in the land—the psychoneurobiochemeducator. This multi-hybrid expert will have recourse—as I have suggested elsewhere—to protein memory consolidators, antimetabolite memory inhibitors, enzymatic learning stimulants, and many other potions and elixirs of the mind from our new psychoneurobiochemopharmacopia. [15, p. 374]

For the slow learner who cannot remember his addition facts, the prescription in the future may be chemical rather than practice and consolidation.

A Model for Cognitive Diagnosis and Prescription

The larger view of diagnostic and prescriptive teaching has been presented above and is admittedly complex because human learning is the result of many variables. The intent here is not that the larger view be used by all teachers today but that one should be aware of these many variables—particularly of what he teaches and how he teaches—as he works with the slow learner. Being thus aware, the teacher who is trying to diagnose the student's difficulties can look for causes other than the immediate, or cognitive, one.

However, from experience with diagnostic and prescriptive teaching over the past quarter century, the authors are aware that cognitive disability ranks high in the concern of the teachers and the parents and are aware also of the fact that a cognitive approach to affective disabilities can be a powerful one. A negative attitude toward mathematics can often be changed by approaching it from the cognitive rather than the affective route. Whatever the basic cause of the child's disability, one can often be successful in diagnostic-prescriptive work if he begins with the observable behavior symptoms of failure—say, the inability to rename (borrow) in subtraction of whole numbers.

The model for symptomatic diagnosis to be presented below is limited to a cognitive view and was constructed by Wilson (22) as a threefold guide for seeking answers to the following questions:
1. What specific mathematical learning products might be present/ absent, correct/incorrect, mature/immature?
2. What overt behaviors will indicate the presence, correctness, and maturity of each of these specific learning products?
3. What kind of psychological learning product does each of the specific mathematical learning products represent?

As a guide for question 1, Wilson has been developing a content taxonomy. For question 2, the authors are drawing on theories of tests and measurements, such as Bloom's *Taxonomy of Educational Objectives* (4). For question 3, the work of some learning theorists, currently the work of Robert Gagné (12), is being used. Each of these components of the model is treated briefly and separately below. Finally, a diagram is given of the cross-products model that these three components yield and an illustration of how this model guides the diagnosis for one of the main principles in the structure of mathematics.

A content taxonomy

Table 9.1 is an outline of a portion of the taxonomy of content objectives currently being used. This taxonomy reflects the view that mathematics is a system of related ideas composed of a vast variety of subsystems. Each subsystem dealt with in this portion of the content taxonomy has three essential aspects that identify it as a mathematical system: (*a*) a set of elements and symbols for these elements; (*b*) a set of operations on these elements; and (*c*) a set of properties and laws of the operations. Each of the subsystems for which elementary and secondary schools are responsible also has its socially useful aspects: (*d*) a set of computational procedures for processing the elements of the system; (*e*) a set of procedures for solving the sentences expressing the relationship within the system; and (*f*) a set of socially significant problem situations in which the elements and operations of that system are used.

As the reader can note in the outline (table 9.1), the first-order categories of the content taxonomy, designated by Roman numerals, are subsystems of the real number system: sets—the basis for real numbers—(III); whole numbers (IV); fractional numbers (V); integers (VI); and so on. Within each subsystem, second-, third-, and

TABLE 9.1
Content Taxonomy: Sets and Rational Numbers

III. Sets	IV. Whole numbers	V. Nonnegative rationals (fractional numbers)	VI. Integers	VII. Rationals

A. Concepts & notation
1. Concepts for
  a. Set
  b.
  c. Relation & properties
  d.
2. Notation for
	A. Number & notation
	1. Number concepts
	  a. Meaning of & models for
	  b. Special subsets of
	  c. Relations among
	  d. Uses of
	2. Notational systems for
	  a. Positional systems
	  b. Nonpositional systems
		A. Number & notation
		1. Number concepts
		  a.
		  b.
		  c.
		  d.
		2. Notational systems
		  a. Positional systems
		    1. Fraction
		    2. Decimal
			A. Number & notation
			1. Number concepts
			  a.
			  b.
			  c.
			  d.
			2. Notational systems
			  a.
				A. Number & notation
				1. Number concepts
				  a.
				  b.
				  c.
				  d.
				2. Notational systems
				  a.

B. Operations on: Meaning & symbols 1. Union 2. Complementation 3. Cartesian products 4. "Partition" 5. Intersection	B. Operations on: Meanings & symbols 1. Addition 2. Subtraction 3. Multiplication 4. Division 5.	B. Operations on: 1. Addition 2. Subtraction 3. Multiplication 4. Division 5.	B. Operations on: 1. Addition 2. Subtraction 3. Multiplication 4. Division 5.	B. Operations on 1. Addition 2. Subtraction 3. Multiplication 4. Division 5.

C. Properties under operations
1. Union
	C. Properties under operations
	1. Addition
	  a. Closure
	  b. Commutative
	  c. Associative
	  d. Indetity
	  e. Inverses ("compensation")
		C. Properties
		1. Addition
		  a. Closure
		  b. Commutative
		  c. Associative
		  d. Identity
		  e. Inverses (not compensation)
			C. Properties
			1. Addition
			  a.
			  b.
			  c.
			  d.
			  e.
				C. Properties
				1. Addition
				  a.
				  b.
				  c.
				  d.
				  e.

2. Complementation 2. Subtraction 2. Subtraction 2. Subtraction 2. Subtraction
   a. Closure a. a. a. a.
   f. f. f. f.
3. Cartesian 3. Multiplication 3. Multiplication 3. Multiplication 3. Multiplication
   a. Closure a. Closure a. a. a.
   f. Distributive f. Distributive f. f.
4. "Partition" 4. Division 4. Division 4. Division 4. Division
   a. a. a. a.
   f. f. f.

D. Algorithms: Principles for & skill with | D. Algorithms: Principles for & skill with | D. Algorithms | D. Algorithms
1. Addition | 1. Addition | 1. Addition | 1. Addition
   a. | a. | a. | a.
   z. | z. | z. | z.
2. Subtraction | 2. Subtraction | 2. Subtraction | 2. Subtraction
   a. | a. | a. | a.
   z. | z. | z. | z.
3. Multiplication | 3. Multiplication | 3. Multiplication | 3. Multiplication
   a. | a. | a. | a.
   z. | z. | z. | z.

TABLE 9.1 (Continued)

III. Sets	IV. Whole numbers	V. Nonnegative rationals (fractional numbers)	VI. Integers	VII. Rationals

	4. Division
	  a.
	  .
	  .
	  .
	  z.
	5.
		4. Division
		  a.
		  .
		  .
		  .
		  z.
		5.
			4. Division
			  a.
			  .
			  .
			  .
			  z.
			5.
				4. Division
				  a.
				  .
				  .
				  .
				  z.
				5.

	E. Sentence solving	E. Sentence solving	E. Sentence solving	E. Sentence solving

	F. Verbal problem solving
	  1. Addition
	    a.
	    b.
	    c.
	  2. Subtraction
	    a.
	    b.
	    c.
	    d.
	    e.
	    f.
	    g.
	  3. Multiplication
	    a.
	    b.
	    c.
	  4. Division
	    a.
	    b.
	    c.
	    d.
	  5.
		F. Verbal problem solving
		  1. Addition
		    a.
		    b.
		    c.
		  2. Subtraction
		    a.
		    b.
		    c.
		    d.
		    e.
		    f.
		    g.
		  3. Multiplication
		    a.
		    b.
		    c.
		  4. Division
		    a.
		    b.
		    c.
		    d.
		  5.
			F. Verbal problem solving
			  1. Addition
			    a.
			    b.
			    c.
			  2. Subtraction
			    a.
			    b.
			    c.
			    d.
			    e.
			    f.
			    g.
			  3. Multiplication
			    a.
			    b.
			    c.
			  4. Division
			    a.
			    b.
			    c.
			    d.
			  5.
				F. Verbal problem solving
				  1. Addition
				    a.
				    b.
				    c.
				  2. Subtraction
				    a.
				    b.
				    c.
				    d.
				    e.
				    f.
				    g.
				  3. Multiplication
				    a.
				    b.
				    c.
				  4. Division
				    a.
				    b.
				    c.
				    d.
				  5.

fourth-order categories are designated by capital letters, Arabic numerals, and lowercase letters, respectively. The first three second-order categories, A through C, define the learning products of the three aspects essential to a mathematical system—aspects identified above as (a), (b), and (c). The categories designated D through F contain the learning products involved in the various socially useful applications of that particular subsystem.

It is intended that the taxonomic plan suggest the content hierarchies within and across the number systems treated in elementary school mathematics.

First, the taxonomy suggests that, in general, a learner must acquire a knowledge of, and skill with, whole numbers (IV) before proceeding to the fractional numbers (V), since the meaning of, and the operations with, fractional numbers depend on the meanings, operations, and laws of the whole numbers.

Next, the second- and third-order categories of each subsystem are labeled in a parallel fashion (table 9.1). This suggests, for example, that the union of disjoint sets (III B-1) is a model for the addition of whole numbers (IV B-1), which in turn is the basis of the meaning of addition of fractional numbers (V B-1), and so on. Similarly, III B-2, complementation, is parallel to IV B-2, the operation of subtraction of whole numbers, and so forth.

Thirdly, within a subsystem, such as the whole number system (IV), the content taxonomy suggests that a child must, *in general*, acquire some level of meaning of the whole numbers and the notation for them (IV A-1-2) before he can acquire the meanings of the operations on whole numbers (IV B-1-4) and the laws governing those operations (IV C-1-4). In turn, at least some of the learning products contained in categories IV A through IV C must be acquired as prerequisites to the acquisition of the principles of, and skill with, the algorithms (IV D-1-4); principles for sentence solving (IV E-1-4); and principles for verbal problem solving (IV F-1-4).

Finally, for any specific learning product within a subcategory, there may be a hierarchy of levels of maturity or abstraction. For example, the meaning of addition of whole numbers (IV B-1) may have several levels of abstraction, ranging from concretely based meanings, such as "the union of disjoint sets is a model for addition," to such meanings as "addition is an operation used to find the sum of known addends," to "addition is an operation associating a pair of members with a third number," and so on.

Neither this content taxonomy nor those being developed for metric and nonmetric geometry are considered to be pure hierarchies. The expression "general hierarchy" must be emphasized. There are levels of completeness or abstractness for each of the learning products within each of the subcategories. This content taxonomy does *not* imply that learning products in any one subcategory must be at their highest level before a child begins to acquire those of the next subcategory. The arrangement of the subcategories, however, does imply that some level of acquisition must have been attained for the learning products in that category if effective learning is to proceed in the next subcategory.

To flesh out the content taxonomy outlined here, a large set of statements, essentially definitions, for each of the many learning products of the subcategories must be provided. The statements themselves are not learning products; they merely express the meanings of the products in adult terms. It is not suggested that the student should learn statements as statements. That would be the poorest of outcomes—empty verbalisms. Of course, at some point in the student's education the ability to use the statements meaningfully would be desirable. There is ample research that shows the retention and transfer power the learner acquires from being able to make verbalizations of his learnings. (See Brownell and Hendrickson [8] for a well-given distinction between verbalism and verbalization.) The fourth section of this chapter gives a session report of an actual case study conducted at the Arithmetic Clinic, Syracuse University. This report illustrates, among other things, how the statements in the content taxonomy are used as objectives in the planning of a session.

Behaviors that indicate the learning product

Each statement in the content taxonomy is essentially a definition of a mathematical concept or principle. Concepts and principles, as such, cannot be directly observed. Consequently, keyed to each of the various mathematically different specific learning products in the content taxonomy there must be a well-organized set of observable behaviors from which one can infer the presence or absence, correctness or incorrectness, and the level of maturity of that learning product possessed by the learner.

By far the most comprehensive plan for the classification of behaviors that indicate learning is the *Taxonomy of Educational Objectives: Handbook 1* (4). The chart below (fig. 9.4) lists the categories for the cognitive domain. In the complete *Handbook*, each category is described in detail and illustrated with behaviors for a variety of curricular areas. For each category, illustrative test items are also provided.

OUTLINE OF PART 2 OF
TAXONOMY OF EDUCATIONAL OBJECTIVES
HANDBOOK 1: COGNITIVE DOMAIN

Knowledge

1.00 Knowledge, recall of specifics
    1.10 Knowledge of specifics
    1.20 Knowledge of ways and means of dealing with
    1.30 Knowledge of the universals and abstractions in a field

Cognitive Abilities

2.00 Comprehension
    2.10 Translation
    2.20 Interpretation
    2.30 Extrapolation
3.00 Application
4.00 Analysis
    4.10 Analysis of elements
    4.20 Analysis of relationships
    4.30 Analysis of organizational principles

5.00 Synthesis
    5.10 Production of a unique communication
    5.20 Production of a plan, or proposed set of operations
    5.30 Derivation of a set of abstract relations
6.00 Evaluation
    6.10 Judgments in terms of internal evidence
    6.20 Judgments in terms of external criteria

Fig. 9.4

Bloom's taxonomy of the cognitive domain is not specific to any curricular area nor to any theory of learning. This is by intention. The authors of the *Taxonomy* leave to the specialist in each curricular area the analysis of his own field. The content taxonomy outlined in table 9.1 is intended to do this for elementary school and secondary school mathematics.

As an illustration of the cross product of the content taxonomy and *Handbook 1* of the *Taxonomy of Educational Objectives,* consider one of the content objectives under category IV A-2a: "The number named by a multi-digit numeral is the sum of the products of each digit's face value and place value."

To diagnose for this objective, one needs to have in mind a set of the observable behaviors a learner would display if he has acquired the above objective. There could be an infinite variety of specific behaviors that would be acceptable as indicators of the objective's presence. It is at this point that Bloom's *Taxonomy* is especially useful as a means of expressing these behaviors and classifying them by well-defined categories. The following are but a few of the statements expressing some of the behaviors that could indicate the above objective's presence in the learner in depth:

1. Be able to identify or reproduce 68 by using objects (rods, tongue depressors, etc.) and by using counting frames.
2. Be able to translate a two-digit numeral representing a whole number into an expression of so many tens and so many ones—for example, "68" means "six tens and eight ones."
3. Be able to translate a three-digit numeral into an expression of so many hundreds, so many tens, and so many ones.
4. Be able to translate any base-ten numeral representing a whole number into its expanded form—for example, "346" equals $(3 \times 100) + (4 \times 10) + (6 \times 1)$.

Such a list of behavioral indicators could, of course, be increased greatly. Each in turn could serve as a guide for the construction of a great variety of specific diagnostic test items or diagnostic interview questions that would elicit samples of the kinds of behaviors stated. It is evident also that all the above behavioral indicators call for the same general class of behaviors—translation. Hence, as behavioral statements, all would be in the same category of Bloom's *Taxonomy*, namely, "2.10 comprehension: translation." One of the great values of Bloom's *Taxonomy* is that it suggests higher-order behaviors that would indicate not only the presence of the given content objective but its level of maturity and transferability. Hence, to the same content objective cited above may be keyed higher-order behaviors such as the following:

5. Be able to analyze a set of numerals from nonspecified base systems to determine the face values and place values.
6. Be able to construct a set of single and multidigit numerals for the first twenty whole numbers by using unique symbols and any base.

These two behaviors would, of course, be classified under the *Taxonomy*'s "4.00 Analysis" and "5.00 Synthesis."

The lesson plans for Maria in the fourth part of this chapter illustrate both the specific content objectives and the expected behaviors that are keyed to each of the content objectives.

The joint use of both taxonomies—content and behavioral—by themselves is not sufficient for the diagnosis and treatment. Assume, for example, that there has been built a set of test items for interview procedures for all the behavioral indicators listed above for the content objective on the meaning of a multidigit numeral. Assume also that all the test items have been administered to a child and that all his behaviors indicate the absence of that content objective. To what does the diagnostician look next? The content taxonomy may indicate the category of learning products that must be diagnosed next, but it does not indicate by itself either the kinds of psychological learning products or which specific products must be diagnosed next. It is for this latter and most crucial task that the learning-theory component of the model is considered next.

The kinds of psychological learning products

Statements of the learning product in any one of the categories of the content taxonomy express a variety of *psychologically different* kinds of learning product as well as *mathematically different* categories of content. Hence the model should eventually be able to classify each of the mathematical learning products expressed in the content taxonomy according to its psychological type.

Expecting this of the model clearly implies allegiance to those learning psychologists who believe that there are not one or two but several kinds of human learning, each involving different laws of learning.

There are a number of unresolved taxonomic problems facing such learning theorists. An attempt at resolution offered by Gagné (12), however, seems to be a usable component, if only as a heuristic, in the construction of a model for symptomatic diagnosis in mathematics.

In his book *The Conditions of Learning*, Gagné partitions cognitive-learning products into eight different types. Each type differs from the others by reason of the different conditions of learning necessary for its acquisition. Gagné speaks of two classes of conditions: internal capabilities of the learner and external, or situational, conditions. The internal condition necessary for the acquisition of a given type of learning product is the presence in the learner of the lower types of learning products prerequisite to the desired type. The external conditions include all the stimuli, the sequence of the stimuli, and the reinforcing stimuli essential for the type of learning to be acquired. Both internal and external conditions are essential to the acquisition of any given type of learning and are different for each type of learning.

Gagné's eight types of learning are: type 1, signal learning; type 2, stimulus-response learning; type 3, chaining; type 4, verbal association or verbal chaining; type 5, multiple discrimination; type 6, concept learning; type 7, principle learning; and type 8, problem-solving learning.[1]

1. A more condensed categorization of types 2–7 can be found in Brownell and Hendrickson (8).

Perhaps the greatest potential of Gagné's theory is its application to the construction of what he terms "learning structures." The learning types 2–8 are supposedly related to one another in a truly hierarchical order. That is, problem solving (type 8) has as its prerequisite, principles (type 7), which has as its prerequisite, concepts (type 6), and so on. Within the types, especially principles (type 7), there are subhierarchies. That is, simple principles are prerequisite to higher-order principles. Theoretically, then, any given topic can be analyzed into the general types and the specific elements of each type of learning which are prerequisite to its acquisition.

The implication of Gagné's work for diagnosis and prescription hardly needs to be stated. Once a given mathematical learning product in any one of the content categories is diagnosed by means of the behavioral indicators as absent, immature, or incorrect, the classifying of the learning product as to its psychological type suggests which prerequisite types of learning must be diagnosed next. This could be termed "descending diagnosis," that is, higher to lower. "Ascending diagnosis" could also be used. For example, any desired learning product could be analyzed into its prerequisite types. One could then start with the diagnosis of lower types and proceed until the diagnosis found the highest type that was absent, immature, or incorrect. Prescriptive or remedial procedures would be directly suggested by the findings of either such diagnosis. For those children, then, whose underachievement is due primarily to not having been taught the prerequisite learning, this symptomatic diagnosis would also be etiologic. Unfortunately, far too few cases of underachievement are this simple.

The Gagné classifications and the precise stating of the content objectives, together with the keyed behavioral indicators, should all aid the diagnostician in identifying both the types of prerequisite learning products and the specific prerequisite mathematical learning products to be diagnosed next.

Consider again the content objectives used in the illustration above, "the number named by a multidigit numeral is the sum of the products of each digit's face value and place value." The statement expresses an objective that is clearly a chain of two or more concepts and therefore classified as Gagné's type 7—principles. Hence, if the behaviors keyed to this objective indicate that it is not present, the diagnostician is guided by Gagné's theory to diagnose for the lower-order principles and concepts of which this particular principle is a chain. Moreover, the precision of the content statement suggests which of the particular mathematical concepts and principles are involved in this principle. Hence the terms used in the statement—for example, "digit," "face value," "place value," "sum," and "product"—quite clearly indicate which specific mathematical concepts are chained to this particular principle. With a working knowledge of the content taxonomy, terms such as "sum," "product," and "place value" immediately suggest in which categories statements of these prerequisite concepts would be found.

For example, "sum" refers to a concept under the operation of addition. Since in this illustration the concern is with numerals for whole numbers, the pertinent category of the content taxonomy is IV B-1 (whole numbers, operations on, addition). The term "product" suggests IV B-3 (whole numbers, operations, multiplication); "place value," "digit," and "face value" suggest IV A-2-a. Provided the content taxonomy were comprehensive, statements expressing different levels of maturity for each of these prerequisite learnings would be found in these categories. Each statement would be classified as one of Gagné's types, thereby implying what *its* prerequisite types of learning are. Each would be precisely stated so that its terms would suggest in which categories and in which specific learning products statements of its prerequisites would be found. Each of these statements would also be keyed to a set of behavioral indicators classified according to Bloom's *Taxonomy*.

A diagram of the model

A diagram can now be constructed to help concretize the scope of the theoretical implications of the model produced by the Cartesian set of the content taxonomy and Gagné's and Bloom's taxonomies. For simplicity, the diagram will be restricted to just one number system in the content taxonomy—whole numbers (IV). The diagram will also be restricted to the major subcategories of IV (A–F) and to the major subcategories of Gagné and Bloom.

On one dimension one can represent the content taxonomy's categories for whole numbers (IV) as in figure 9.5.

On a second dimension one can represent the psychologically different kinds of learning Gagné recognizes. Connecting the segments gives the region of figure 9.6.

Thus far the region suggests that in each category of the content taxonomy there are theoretically a vast number of each of Gagné's eight types of learning products. Each could be specified. Each might need to be diagnosed.

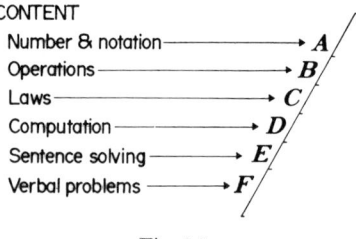

Fig. 9.5

Most probably some of Gagné's simpler types of learning (1, 2, and 3) would not be as significant in all categories of content. Gagné himself points out that there is little evidence to support the essentiality of type 1 (S-R) as basic to cognitive learning. However, the theoretical implications of the diagram thus far are clearly broad in scope.

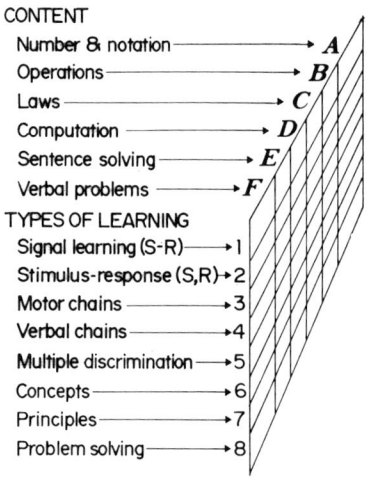

Fig. 9.6

A third dimension to the diagram can be used to represent the variety of behavioral indicators that Bloom's *Taxonomy* suggests might be used to infer the presence of the learning products. The result is figure 9.7.

The diagram helps concretize what the model for symptomatic diagnosis implies. In each category of the content taxonomy there could be a vast number of specific mathematical learnings of each psychologically different kind of learning. To each of these there could be keyed a variety of behaviors that would indicate its presence/absence, correctness/incorrectness, or maturity/immaturity.

It should be clear that the whole structure cannot be diagrammed into a simple cubical array when it is recalled that only one subsystem of content taxonomy is accounted for—and only the major subcategories of that. One can only muse on how to concretize a model that will need to account for all the other subsystems of dimensions of diagnosis: elementary school mathematics (e.g., geometry); other types of learning (affective); and the real problem—the etiology of the symptoms.

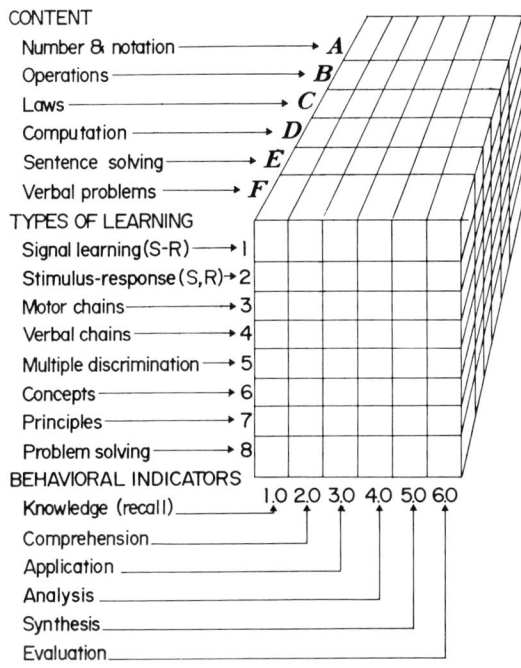

Fig. 9.7

Some Procedures for Diagnostic-Prescriptive Teaching

The commonly used procedures for diagnostic-prescriptive teaching can be divided, according to Windelband's distinction (23), into two groups—the nomothetic and the idiographic procedures. The former group consists of procedures that permit classifying and generalizing. The latter is concerned with the individual's unique and idiosyncratic responses and reactions to a given situation.

Specifically, it is one thing to study the scores made by a large group of children on a mathematics test in order to be able to state, say, that the mean number of correct responses on the addition facts for children in grades 1–6 increases in a given pattern. It is something else again to be able to say that Billy arrived at 16 as the sum of 7 and 9 by counting on his fingers, or by adding 9 and 9 and subtracting 2, or by any one of several other more mature or less mature ways of processing the numerals.

Psychologist Gordon Allport cites a well-known passage by William James which contrasts the nomothetic and idiographic procedures:

> The first thing the intellect does with an object is to class it along with something else. But any object that is infinitely important to us and awakens our devotion feels to us also as if it must be *sui generis* and unique. Probably a crab would be filled with a sense of personal outrage if it could hear us class it without ado or apology as a crustacean, and thus dispose of it. "I am no such thing," it would say; "I am myself; myself alone." [1, p. 53]

Each of the two classes of procedure is necessary; neither is sufficient. Of the two, the idiographic approach is the more relevant and the more neglected in diagnostic-prescriptive teaching.

Nomothetic procedures

The more commonly used nomothetic procedures include the standardized achievement tests, the teacher-made informal tests, the standardized diagnostic tests, the teacher-made diagnostic tests, the numerical section of certain mental-ability tests, and the tests that accompany the basic textbook series—both achievement and, in some instances, diagnostic.

The use of these nomothetic procedures rests on the assumption that the teaching-learning process can be separated from the evaluation process with no loss of information to the teacher, and with considerable gain. When used in a diagnostic-prescriptive situation, any or all of the above classes of instruments provide the teacher with data on a group of students, or an individual student, which he will use as a basis for prescribing future learning experiences and which will closely fit the student's cognitive-development pattern.

Bloom defends this assumption:

> The evaluation procedures used to appraise the outcomes of instruction (summative evaluation) help the teacher and student know when instruction has been effective.

Implicit in this way of defining the outcomes and preparing evaluation instruments is a distinction between the teaching-learning process and the evaluation process. At some point in time, the results of teaching and learning can be reflected in the evaluation of the students. But, these are *separate* processes. That is, teaching and learning are intended to prepare the student in an area of learning, while evaluation (summative) is intended to appraise the extent to which the student has developed in the desired ways. [3, p. 8]

Admitting that the kinds of nomothetically oriented procedures above have some overall diagnostic-prescriptive value (perhaps as much value as a patient's above-normal temperature would have for a physician), a more educationally significant approach sees the teaching-learning and diagnostic-evaluative aspects as inseparable.

Idiographic procedures

More than thirty years ago Brownell discussed the artificiality of the separation and the need for integrating instruction and evaluation —a statement as good today as when it was written. He noted that "some test technicians have not felt particularly handicapped by their ignorance of the purposes of arithmetic instruction. On the other hand, teachers, who supposedly know the nature and purposes of their subject matter, are regarded as unable to evaluate the learning they have directed" (6, p. 225).

He cites four unfortunate effects of the separating of teaching-learning from evaluation:

> One effect . . . has been to remove measurement further and further from the immediate learning situation. Tests to be used for diagnosis and the evaluation of achievement have been standardized, and in the process of standardization have lost touch with the features peculiar to the local classroom. . . .
> A second effect . . . has been to limit measurement to outcomes that can be most readily assessed. In arithmetic this has meant concern almost exclusively with "facts," with computational skills, and with "problem-solving" of the traditional sort. . . .
> A third ill effect . . . has been to limit unduly the techniques which are serviceable for evaluation. . . . There are other procedures which are now ignored. These other procedures . . . are easily managed by teachers and, what is more important, they uncover kinds of learning processes and products which at present elude paper-and-pencil [i.e., nomothetic] tests.
> The fourth harmful effect . . . has been to create confusion with respect to the purposes of evaluation. Learning may be evaluated for

a number of reasons. One may be the diagnosis of failure; another, the measurement of progress over short units or sections of content; yet another, the pre-testing of abilities before starting a new topic, as a means of "establishing a base line." [6, pp. 225–27]

Again, the important if limited values of the nomothetically oriented measurement instruments are recognized. But in this chapter the authors are concerned with procedures for diagnostic-prescriptive teaching, and they believe that for this purpose the idiographically oriented procedures are more effective.

For their contributions to the development and use of idiosyncratic procedures in mathematics development, two scholars are preeminent— in the United States, William A. Brownell; and in Switzerland, Jean Piaget. Each has spent a lifetime in the development and use of idiographic procedures in cognitive-development situations and with specific relevance to elementary school and preschool mathematics.

On the one hand, the procedures developed by Piaget for study of the development of such ideas as classifying, conserving, and the identity element for addition are more relevant to very young children and more applicable to the stages that precede the typical mathematical program for grades 1–9. On the other hand, the creative work of Brownell (who long ago recognized and cited the monumental contributions of both his teacher, Charles H. Judd, and Piaget) was developed and is still being further developed by him in more real, less clinical, school situations (7). Consequently, his procedures can be more easily understood and readily used by the classroom teacher, the mathematics education specialist, and the school psychologist.

The interview technique. Until such time as educators are able to learn from Krech's "psychoneurobiochemeducationists" just how learning takes place in the brain and is retained, they will be restricted to the study of learning as the outward, observable changes in behavior. The most powerful technique presently available to us is the interview. It can yield, as Weaver says, "big dividends" (20, pp. 40–47).

Brownell, in the study cited above, as well as in most of his prior classic studies, used the interview to gather data on the three systems of instruction being used in England and Scotland—the Cuisenaire, the Dienes, and the conventional programs. For effective use of the interview with children, he carefully selected the teachers and cautioned them—

1. to avoid cues and leading questions;

2. to refuse to stop questioning when only superficial answers—answers that could not reveal what was wanted—were given;
3. to adapt the pace of interviewing to the pace at which each child could respond comfortably;
4. to vary questions when responses were ambiguous, in order to draw children out;
5. to maintain a pleasant, friendly, warm atmosphere;
6. to stop interviews (they lasted about an hour on the average) as soon as any child showed rebelliousness or boredom or anxiety, bringing him back to complete the interview at another time if this was possible; otherwise, rejecting him as a subject;
7. to record exactly children's answers when the responses were especially interesting or resisted categorization.

The cautions are appropriate for all teachers who wish to make a serious effort to collect data from children as a sound basis for prescribing subsequent learning experiences.[2]

Modes of response. Over the years the authors have viewed the responses children can make to questions as being of three modes—the concrete mode, the pictorial mode, and the symbolic mode. More recently, the first two are sometimes referred to as the "enactive" and the "ikonic" modes. The first set of terms seems to describe more accurately the nature and purpose of each mode; the latter set seems unnecessarily "pedagese." "Enactive" erroneously implies that cognitive learning is the result of merely doing something with objects. No learning takes place through mere doing. How many times has a person dialed a telephone?—yet how rare it is to find a person who can draw a correct picture of the letters and numerals as they are positioned on the dial! Rather, one learns by *thinking about* what he is doing. And thinking can be done while a person is working with concrete things, or with pictures of things (e.g., the picture of a number line), or with symbols.

All three modes are essential to diagnosis, for it is a very real possibility that a child can respond correctly to $3\frac{1}{2} \div 1\frac{1}{4} = n$ on

---

[2]. In his *Classroom Questions: What Kinds?* (New York: Harper & Row, 1966), Norris M. Sanders used the *Taxonomy of Educational Objectives,* edited by B. S. Bloom, as a basic structure for the study of categories of classroom questions. Illustrative questions are presented in each of the seven Bloom categories: memory, translation, interpretation, application, analysis, synthesis, and evaluation.

the symbolic level, using the conventional algorithm, but be unable to do so on, say, the pictorial-representational level. Such overtly "correct" behavior would not represent true or complete understanding of the operation performed and the social significance of the work.

By way of a second illustration, a child could respond correctly to the sentence ½ = ?/4 by using the concrete mode to show that one-half of a disk can be represented by two-fourths of the same disk (fig. 9.8). Yet that same child, when questioned by the inter-

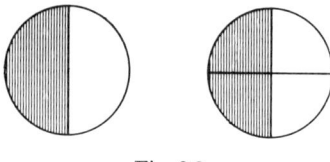

Fig. 9.8

viewer, might be unable at this stage of his development to use the symbolic mode and the identity element for multiplication:

$$\frac{1}{2} = \frac{1}{2} \times 1$$
$$= \frac{1}{2} \times \frac{2}{2}$$
$$= \frac{1 \times 2}{2 \times 2}$$
$$= \frac{2}{4}$$

One could say that this child has some partial and useful understanding of the equivalent values of 1/2 and 2/4 and hence is on the way to some more complete understanding. The prescription for him would be that at some appropriate time he, as a slow learner, might further develop his understanding by working on the pictorial (number line or ruler) level. But it might be some long time later, if at all, that the teacher would prescribe that this slow learner should progress to the symbolic level by using the identity element for multiplication in the algorithm above.

Diagnosing process. The above two situations point up the difference between *product* and *process* in diagnostic-prescriptive teaching—a difference that must be kept in mind by the person working with children and youth. By and large, diagnosis has, unfortunately, been limited to the product type of learnings, as Brownell has pointed out many times over many years (7).

The importance of process is presently being rediscovered, and with variations under such names as "learning to learn," "heuristic methods," "inquiry training," "process is the product," and others. The process by which a child arrives at the solution to a problem is at least as important as the product itself, if not more so. The recent renaissance of the "project method" of the 1910s, 1920s, and 1930s, which is current under the name of the "laboratory method" (the math lab), rests on the assumption that the development of learning strategies through solving unique problems is a more important outcome than the solutions themselves.

The audio tape and video tape in diagnosing process. As noted above, the use of the idiographic procedures in general and the interview in particular is not new in diagnostic-prescriptive teaching. However, the invention and widespread availability of the audio-tape and video-tape hardware now make it possible for the teacher to record and study more carefully children's responses. The former is useful when working and talking on the verbal-symbolic level. The latter adds a substantial diagnostic capability by making it possible to record and study behavior (levels of maturity) while working and talking on the concrete and pictorial-representational levels as well as the verbal-symbolic level. (See Appendix B, sample lesson 7, as an illustration.)

Levels of processing addition of whole numbers. It may help to clarify what is meant by "diagnosing process" if a common classroom situation is used. Assume that the child's ability to find the sum of a pair of numbers of the form 17 and 25 (i.e., when renaming of ones is required) is being diagnosed. Also, assume that these prerequisite abilities have been acquired:

1. The child can count rationally by ones to at least 42.
2. He can rename 17 as 1 ten and 7 ones; 25 as 2 tens and 5 ones; 12 as 1 ten and 2 ones. In general, he "understands" two-digit numerals and place values.
3. He can respond accurately to the addition facts—in this case, 7 + 5; 1 + 1; and 2 + 1.

One would begin to study the child's ability to find the sum on the concrete level (using objects), then move to the pictorial level, then to the symbolic level.

Table 9.2 illustrates some, but not all, of the ways a child could process the numerals 17 and 25 under the operation addition. This kind of diagnostic-prescriptive teaching permits the teacher to locate the level of thinking the child is using, and it suggests to the teacher the next level of ability that should be prescribed and achieved.

TABLE 9.2

CHILD'S MODES OF RESPONSE TO ADDITION PROBLEM: 17 + 25
(Maturity level increases from level 1 to level 4)

Maturity of response	Concrete level	Pictorial level	Symbolic level	
Level 1	Child counts 17 sticks. Counts 25 sticks. Puts them together. Begins at 1 and counts to 42.	On a number line, child counts from 1 to 17. Looks at 18 and says, "1." Counts by ones until he says, "25." Looks at sum, 42.	Using an algorithm, child says, "7 plus 5 is 12," Writes "12." Writes "3" in tens place. Adds.	17 +25 —— 12 3 —— 42
Level 2	Same as above, but begins counting at 18 or at 26.	Same as above, but begins with 26 and says, "1."	Says, "7 plus 5 is 12." Writes "1." Adds tens. Writes "4."	1 17 +25 —— 42
Level 3	Counts by twos or by fives.	Counts tens to 30. Renames 12 as 10 + 2. Associates 30 + 10. Says, "40, 42."	Says, "7 plus 5 is 12." Renames 12. Adds tens without need of helping figure. Processing is quick, accurate, and mature.	
Level 4	Groups by tens. Says, "10, 20, 30, 40, 42."			

The following section presents some lesson plans that set out in considerable detail, and from actual clinical situations, the procedure used to overcome identified disabilities.

Lesson Plans for Maria

IQ 80
SDAT Pretest 5.4
    Posttest 6.4

Case: Maria   Summary Report
Grade: 7   Clinician: Hoover

Maria is in the seventh grade. She has six brothers, four of them older. Her hobbies include cooking and sewing. She comes from a home on the lower socioeconomic level.

Maria is rather quiet. She seems willing to cooperate in the sessions but takes little responsibility for being at the sessions. If anything else comes up, she simply doesn't show up.

Maria has a pleasant sense of humor. She seems rather eager at times to learn new ideas, and at other times she seems frustrated by having to think through problems to gain new insights. She needs patient and friendly understanding.

Case: Maria
Grade: 7

Session: 3
Clinician: Hoover

I. Planned objectives
  A. To review:
   1. (IV A-2a)[3] Place values in the Hindu-Arabic system are special products of ten.
   2. (IV A-2a) Each place value in the Hindu-Arabic system is a power of ten.
   3. (IV A-2a) The exponent tells how many times the base is used as a factor.
   4. (IV A-2a) A multidigit numeral names a number that is the sum of the products of each digit's face value and place value.

  Expected behaviors:
   1. (2.10 translation)[4] Able to translate each place value as a product of ten.
   2. (2.10 translation) Able to translate each place value as a power of ten.
   3. (2.10 translation) Able to translate an exponential numeral to a product.
   4. (2.10 translation) Able to translate a base-ten numeral for a whole number to its expanded form. Able to translate a disarranged expanded base-ten numeral for a whole number to its standard form. Able to translate a base-ten numeral for a whole number to an exponential form.

  Procedure:
   1. I asked her to assign the place values and then to express products. She assigned the place values correctly and then expressed ten as 10×1, a hundred as 10×10, a thousand as 10×100. When asked if she could expand 10×100 further, she expressed it as $10 \times 10 \times 10$. We continued in like manner.
   2. I asked her to express the place values as powers. She did this correctly.
   3. I asked her the meaning of 10^4. At first she said "10×4"; but when I asked what 10×4 was, she replied, "40," and said that her previous answer was incorrect. She then gave $10 \times 10 \times 10 \times 10$. We did several others in like manner. (She had to be reminded that any number to the zero power is 1.)
   4. I gave her a decimal number and asked her to give it in expanded form, which she was able to do. Then I gave her a disarranged expanded base-ten numeral and asked for the standard numeral. She wrote the digits in the order in which they appeared. When I asked if the values were the same,

---

3. For the meaning of IV A-2a, see the content taxonomy in table 9.1 above. The IV refers to the set of whole numbers; the A refers to the subcategory "number and notation." The name 2a refers to "notational systems for positional systems."
4. The numeral 2.10 refers in the Bloom *Taxonomy* to the subcategory "translation" under the main category "comprehension."

she said, "I have mine mixed up." When I asked what she should do about that, she did the example correctly. Then I had her check her answer by multiplying and adding the expanded form. She had suggested this method of checking.

Inferences:

Maria is not quite sure about powers (exponents); so I will want to do some additional work in this area. She forgets to check what an expanded numeral says and thus makes mistakes. I'll give her one or two each time for a while to help her get in the habit of checking exactly what is expressed. She seems somewhat mixed up on the terms *product* and *factor*. I want to work on these next time.

II. Planned objectives:
   B. To review:
   1. (IV A-2a) A numeral based on grouping by tens is a base-ten numeral. Base-ten numerals are also called decimal numerals.
   2. (IV A-2a) The base of a notation system is a whole number, greater than one, multiples of which are used to yield place values.

Expected behaviors:
   1. (2.30 extrapolation) Can tell the base of our number system—also call it a decimal system. Can give the base of other number systems when shown the grouping process.
   2. (2.10 translation) Able to translate a three-digit base-five numeral for a whole number into an expression of so many twenty-fives, so many fives, and so many ones.

Procedure:
   1. I asked her the base of our number system; she was unsure. Then I asked her what number she had used when we had talked about place value in terms of products and powers, and she said, "Ten." I asked her how many symbols we had in our number system, and she said, "Ten." I asked her if she knew another name for our number system; she didn't. I asked her if she had ever heard it referred to as a decimal system; she had. We talked about *deci-* meaning ten. Then I gave her some examples of other number systems, showing the grouping process, and asked her to tell me the base of each one. She could do this.
   2. We developed an imaginary base-five numeration system using invented symbols. After carrying out our numeration to 35, I gave her a numeral and asked her for the next one, making hops to get quickly to 125. From time to time I had her tell me the value of the numeral and how she knew. At first she had trouble, but once she got the pattern going she was able to move along quickly. I then gave her a numeral in our imaginary numeration system and asked her to expand it in our base-ten system and find its standard name. She was able to do this quickly for three-digit numerals but had trouble with four-digit numerals.

Inferences:

Maria seems to understand the grouping process fairly well. She seemed to enjoy inventing our own numeration system. I will use this system in working on other aspects when it is applicable. She will need to review this a little later to make sure she knows it.

DIAGNOSTIC-PRESCRIPTIVE TEACHING

Case: Maria
Grade: 7
Session: 4
Clinician: Hoover

I. Planned objectives:
   A. To review:
      1. (IV A-2a) The exponent tells how many times the base is used as a factor.
      2. (IV A-2a) A multidigit numeral names a number that is the sum of the product of each digit's face value and place value.

   Expected behaviors:
      1. (2.10 translation) Able to translate an exponential numeral to a product.
      2. (2.10 translation) Able to translate a disarranged expanded base-ten numeral for a whole number to its standard form.

   Procedure:
      1. I gave her several exponential expressions, which she was able to translate as products. When I gave her 9^0, she answered, "Zero." We then went back to quickly making a place-value chart using both products of 10 and exponents of 10. From this she recognized that a number raised to the zero power was 1. She was able to respond correctly to subsequent examples.
      2. I gave her several disarranged expanded base-ten numerals, including some in exponential form, and asked her to give me their standard name. She did the first one by multiplying and then adding. I asked her if there was a quicker way for her to get the answer, and she said yes, she could look for the one with the highest place value and then work from there. She did the others quickly, making use of place-value knowledge.

   Inferences:
   Maria seems to comprehend the meaning of place value. She is beginning to be more careful in making sure she knows what the problem is. She seems to grasp exponentials, although she is a little unsure of the zero power.

II. Planned objectives:
   B. To diagnose:
      1. (IV C-1b) Addition is commutative.
      2. (IV C-1c) Addition is associative.
      3. (IV C-1d) The identity element for addition is zero.

   Expected behaviors:
      1. (2.20 interpretation) Illustrates the commutative property of addition on a number line. Uses the commutative property of addition to deduct a second addition expression from a given addition expression.
      2. (2.20 interpretation) Shows a set representation of the associative property of addition for a given group of addends. Uses the associative property of addition to deduct a second addition from a given addition expression.
      3. (2.20 interpretation) Uses the identity property to deduct a second addition from a given addition expression.

   Procedure:
      1. I gave her an addition expression and asked her to give me another that expressed the same idea; she responded by commuting the two addends. I asked her to show me on a number line that these two expressions named the same sum. She was unfamiliar with the number line but quickly saw how to use it when I showed her. Then she showed that her answer was

correct and also stated that this worked because addition was commutative.
2. I gave her an expression involving addition and asked her to express the same idea another way. She was able to give several different ways of associating the addends and stated that this worked because addition was associative. I asked her to show me it was true by using sets, which she did.
3. I gave her an addition example with a missing addend, which she supplied. I gave her several different examples using the identity property. She stated that if you add zero to any number, you get that number. For all the examples in this group, we did some using unknown variables, and she was able to use the properties to deduct the correct answers.

Inferences:

Maria seems to have a good grasp of the properties for addition. She is able to use the properties and also has labels for them.

III. Planned objectives:
  C. To diagnose:
  1. (IV B-1) The number obtained by addition is called a sum.
  2. (IV B-1) The numbers to be added are called addends.
  3. (IV B-1) Subtraction is the inverse of addition.
  4. (IV B-1) Parentheses indicate that an expression is to be regarded as a number.
  5. (IV B) In working examples, you usually carry out the operation within the parentheses first.

  Expected behaviors:
  1. (2.10) Can name the numeral that represents the sum.
  2. (2.10 translation) Can name the numerals that represent the addends.
  3. (2.10 translation) Expresses the number for the complement set as the number for the total set minus the number for the subset. Translates a given "addend plus addend equals sum" expression into the appropriate "sum minus one addend equals other addend" expression.
  4. (2.10 translation) Recognizes the number named in parentheses. Treats an expression in parentheses as a single number.
  5. (2.10 translation) Performs operation in parentheses first, before working with rest of problem.

  Procedure:
  1. I gave her several addition examples and asked her to name the sum and addends in each one. At first she had difficulty, but when I showed her that the numbers to be added were called addends, she was consistently able to respond correctly.
  2. I gave her a partitioned set. I asked her if she could give me an expression for the complement set in terms of the total and the subset. She gave me a subtraction expression. I gave her an "addend plus addend equals sum" expression and asked her to express it as a subtraction expression. She was able to respond correctly. I asked her in each of these expressions to name the sums and addends. A few times she got confused but was making good progress.
  3. I gave her a number of examples to work using parentheses. In some of them I provided for her to name the number expressed in parentheses.

She was able to do this and, in all the examples, worked the operation in parentheses before proceeding with the rest of the problem.

Inferences:

Maria had not learned the labels "sum" and "addend" and seemed to need these handles for adequately determining what was being asked of her. She seems to be quickly catching on to these.

REFERENCES

1. Allport, Gordon Willard. *The Use of Personal Documents in Psychological Science.* New York: Social Science Research Council, 1942.
2. Axline, Virginia M. *Dibs: In Search of Self.* New York: Ballantine Books, 1964.
3. Bloom, Benjamin S. "Learning for Mastery." *Evaluation Comment* 1 (May 1968).
4. Bloom, Benjamin S., ed. *Taxonomy of Educational Objectives, the Classification of Educational Goals: Handbook 1, Cognitive Domain.* New York: Longmans, Green & Co., 1956.
5. Brownell, William Arthur. *Arithmetical Abstractions: The Movement toward Conceptual Maturity under Differing Systems of Instruction.* University of California Publications in Education, vol. 17. Berkeley: University of California Press, 1967.
6. ———. "The Evaluation of Learning in Arithmetic." In *Arithmetic in General Education,* Sixteenth Yearbook of the National Council of Teachers of Mathematics, pp. 225–67. New York: Bureau of Publications, Teachers College, Columbia University, 1941.
7. ———. "The Progressive Nature of Learning in Mathematics." *Mathematics Teacher* 37 (April 1944): 147–57.
8. Brownell, William Arthur, and Gordon Hendrickson. "How Children Learn Information Concepts and Generalizations." In *Learning and Instruction,* Forty-ninth Yearbook of the National Society for the Study of Education, pt. 1, edited by Nelson B. Henry, pp. 92–128. Chicago: University of Chicago Press, 1950.
9. Carroll, John B. "On Learning from Being Told." *Educational Psychologist* 5 (March 1968): 1–10.
10. Cronbach, Lee Joseph. "The Logic of Experiments on Discovery." In *Learning by Discovery: A Critical Appraisal,* edited by Lee S. Shulman and Evan R. Keislar, pp. 77–92. Chicago: Rand McNally & Co., 1966.
11. Fort, Jane G., Jean C. Watts, and Gerald S. Lesser. "Cultural Background and Learning in Young Children." *Phi Delta Kappan* 50 (March 1969): 386–88.
12. Gagné, Robert M. *The Conditions of Learning.* 2d ed. New York: Holt, Rinehart & Winston, 1970.
13. Glennon, Vincent J. ". . . And Now Synthesis: A Theoretical Model for Mathematics Education." *Arithmetic Teacher* 12 (February 1965): 134–41.
14. Highet, Gilbert Arthur. *The Art of Teaching.* New York: Alfred A. Knopf, 1950; Random House, Vintage Trade Books.
15. Krech, David. "Psychoneurobiochemeducation." *Phi Delta Kappan* 50 (March 1969): 370–75.

16. Meade, Edward J., Jr. "The Changing Society and Its Schools." In *Life Skills in School and Society,* 1969 Yearbook of the Association for Supervision and Curriculum Development, pp. 35–51. Washington, D.C.: The Association, 1969.
17. Neill, Alexander Sutherland. *Summerhill: A Radical Approach to Child Rearing.* New York: Hart Publishing Co., 1960.
18. Shulman, Lee S., and Evan R. Keislar, eds. *Learning by Discovery: A Critical Appraisal.* Rand McNally Education Series. Chicago: Rand McNally & Co., 1966.
19. Stern, George G. "Measuring Noncognitive Variables in Research on Teaching." In *Handbook of Research on Teaching,* edited by Nathaniel Lees Gage, pp. 398–447. Chicago: Rand McNally & Co., 1963.
20. Weaver, J. Fred. "Big Dividends from Little Interviews." *Arithmetic Teacher* 2 (April 1955): 40–47.
21. Wilson, Guy Mitchell. *Teaching the New Arithmetic.* New York: McGraw-Hill Book Co., 1951.
22. Wilson, John W. "Diagnosis and Treatment in Mathematics." In *The Teaching-Learning Process in Educating Emotionally Disturbed Children,* edited by Peter Knobloch and John L. Johnson. Proceedings of the Third Annual Conference. Syracuse: Syracuse University Press, 1967.
23. Windelband, Wilhelm. *Geschichte und Naturwissenschaft.* Strassburg: Heitz & Mundel, 1904.

10

Classroom and School Administration

PAUL V. ROGLER

TEACHERS will find slow learners assigned to them in many different kinds and sizes of groups: some as a result of regrouping within their own classes, some as a result of regrouping within multigrading plans, some as a result of homogeneous grouping that tries to group whole class sections of slow learners together, and some as small remedial classes. This chapter reviews a number of principles and practices that have been found effective in managing slow-learner mathematics classes, in working with small groups within classes, and in evaluating student progress. Also included are points that administrators might consider in planning for slow-learner mathematics classes. Good general principles of class management hold, naturally, for working with slow-learner groups as well as with all other students; and many instructional techniques are allied to good classroom management. If the discussion here includes, in part, some techniques, it is in relation to their value to classroom management that they are included.

Classroom Management

Organization of the class

A first step is to know each student as well as possible. The teacher will find it helpful to consult guidance records and be aware of all important facets of each student's personality, his school development, and any special physical characteristics. Many teachers of slow learners keep a folder on each student in which are kept guidance data, diagnostic and achievement test data, parental reporting data, notes from other teachers, individual progress charts, and inventories of skills attained (for review by the student and his teacher—not to be made public).

The teacher may want to make a seating chart early, for it can help him to learn names quickly. This does not imply that seating must be static. Altering seating arrangements to permit varied interactions between students according to the activities being planned can be a resourceful way to manage productive learning situations. Seating changes help to assure that all students have equal opportunities, by the regrouping of social contacts, to develop friendships—as well as equal access to various preferred areas of the classroom. The chart should be kept up to date, of course, for use by substitute teachers.

Slow learners work best in an uncluttered environment where routines, established early in the year, are seldom varied. It is well known that when the slow learner understands what is expected of him, where materials may be found, and how they should be used, his performance is more likely to approach his potential. Such children perform best, therefore, in a somewhat structured environment. This does not mean that they require a classroom with a dictator in charge; it does mean that the children and the teacher, working together, establish rules and regulations for the smooth running of the classroom. In an elementary classroom these will include such details as the following:

Opening exercises: the time, the type, the person in charge
Recording attendance: how it should be done and who should do it
Recording lunch money: how it should be done and who should do it
Handling supplies: how it should be done and who should do it
 (One teacher gave each child strips of colored construction paper. When a child needed a compass, he wrote his name—his IOU—on red construction paper. The person in charge of

compasses picked up the red paper and gave the child a compass. At the end of the period, when the compass was retrieved, the red paper was returned to the owner. Orange paper was used for scissors, yellow paper for rulers, blue paper for pencils, pink paper for protractors, and so on. Each month the person and his assistant in charge of each material were changed.)

Higher-level classes can have a structure provided by a short written list of activities to which the student's attention is invited as he enters the classroom. The activities are planned so that doing them provides review and preparation for the principal work of the day. Students may participate in planning class routines; and, as a general rule, any learning activity should be organized so as to involve students in its planning and in participating physically in the activity. Many ways can be devised for using students to take care of physical needs in the room—distributing materials, cleaning chalkboards, planning bulletin-board materials, displaying projects, collecting papers, checking attendance, arranging desks, and so forth. These jobs should not be assigned as punishment. The class plan for handling equipment must be carefully explained (and reviewed as necessary) and should be consistently carried out. Many teachers have a plan for supplying pencils to those who forget. One teacher buys them in quantity and sells them at cost; another teacher keeps a box of stubs, which have been left behind in other classes, so that lax students may borrow a pencil for the day. Sometimes students can share instructional materials and benefit from sharing ideas about using the materials. In one class, on the day after students had prepared a number of sheets of folded paper to represent halves, fourths, and eighths, some students who had been absent or who had lost the materials were paired up with other students who did have the materials. Mutual discussion helped instill ideas of equivalent fractions. The class can sometimes be organized so that better students, from that class or other classes, can be assigned to help slow students work through a lesson or a project.

Classroom routine should include, each day, some way of allowing students to use large as well as small muscles. In elementary classes 24 children might get up and form 4 groups of 6 children, then 6 groups of 4 children. In higher-level groups, moving to one side of the room or the other for a short mathematics game or contest can accomplish this. In a classroom where the laboratory type of work is going on, noise connected with the work is likely to be a necessary concomitant and, as such, is allowable.

Since slow learners tend to learn best by doing and seeing, rather than by listening, activities of a manipulative nature are suggested. These students must be completely involved if they are to understand the various arithmetic processes. For this reason it is important that the classroom provide a place for motor activity as well as a place for the storage and use of many visual materials. Here is the way one teacher helps students who are doing an example such as

$$\begin{array}{r} 921 \\ -\ 187 \\ \hline \end{array}$$

to understand why regrouping is necessary:

> The teacher has a child take a desk at one corner of the room and label it "Banker." The teacher then gives him a supply of paper money in the form of $100, $10, and $1 bills. Another child at a desk nearby (but not too near) labels his desk "Clerk." A third child—the "purchaser"—is given nine $100 bills, two $10 bills, and one $1 bill. He deposits this with the clerk, who records it as a fourth child records it on the board and the others, remaining at their desks, record it on paper. The purchaser picks up a package that costs $187 (or several packages adding up to that amount if he is able to do the more complicated work) and takes it to the clerk, who tries to give him his balance. The clerk cannot give the proper change, so he takes a $10 bill to the banker and changes it for ten $1 bills. Later he takes a $100 bill and changes it for ten $10 bills. While this is happening, the child at the board and the children in their seats are also working on the problem. When one example is completed, other children become banker, clerk, and purchaser in turn.

Whatever the activity may be, it should be structured in advance, it should be carefully outlined to the students, and it should be consistently implemented.

If slow-learner groups are to work well, they must be helped in learning how to study—to organize materials and to follow directions and to check their work. Some elementary teachers use a shoe box for each student. The student decorates it and then uses it to hold ruler, compass, game counters, magic markers, and so forth. A good practice is to write assignments in concise, simple language on the chalkboard, using the same corner of the board every day. The teacher should be sure that each student understands what is expected of him, and he should give students sufficient time to complete assignments with success. It is often helpful to discuss what is to be done, including its purpose and a step-by-step interpretation of the work outlined on the chalkboard or on an assignment sheet.

There should be some activity every day that can be carried out with success by every student. Each should feel accepted no matter what limitations there may be on his appearance, or his clothing, or his ability to contribute to a discussion. The activity for the day might include a number of choices, so that each student can surely find one at which he can succeed. When a question in a developmental lesson is asked of students, a "guessing is allowed" situation should be instituted to encourage hesitant students who are reluctant to participate because they are often wrong. The teacher needs to support such students by an attitude that shows it is not bad to be wrong as long as you make a legitimate try. He also needs to be alert to ways of rewording student answers so that they still sound like the student's ideas yet point more directly to the correct development of the topic the teacher has in mind.

An occasional class party or class trip can help classroom rapport. It can also serve educational purposes. Planning a Christmas party involves practice in number work when costs are being considered, and it can involve informal geometry in the making of decorations. One class visited a hospital, where a nurse showed the many examples of measurement that she used. This led, naturally, to a follow-up discussion of metric measures.

The mathematics classroom

A mathematics classroom should look like a mathematics classroom. "Materials for classroom demonstration and materials for pupil manipulation were in display. . . . Bulletin boards were kept attractive, instructive, and interesting." (28, p. 120.) Student committees can be organized for this purpose. The teacher might build up a store of immediately available books and references. Storage space should be provided for student texts whenever these are to be kept in the classroom. A self-help corner might hold a variety of materials for manipulating, collecting, distributing, counting, classifying, arranging, and measuring. In another area within the room a number of mathematical games can be provided. An area set aside for small-group work can be helpful, especially if a teacher aide is available.

The principle that every mathematics classroom should be a mathematics laboratory is being accepted in many secondary schools. Others are providing mathematics laboratory rooms, staffed by aides, in which mathematics activities can be organized. Still others arrange a large room as a laboratory for reading and language study as well as mathematics so that the use of aides and audiovisual equipment can be efficiently handled. Commercial companies are now producing tables in a trapezoidal shape, thus permitting a variety of seating arrangements and orderings.

Silberman reports that many elementary classrooms today are organized to include a mathematics area, a science area, a reading area, and a social science area. Small groups work on assigned work or independent study in each area, and the teacher works with one small group at a time. All these plans are especially valuable for the instruction of slow learners in that they are activity-oriented and tend to aid the individualizing of instruction. (35, pp. 291-97.)

Planning for the substitute

In preparation for the day when he will not be present, the teacher should provide, in a place where the substitute will be sure to find it, such information and suggestions as the following:

Time children enter the school
Time children enter the room
Responsibility of the teacher before children enter the room
What children do between the time they enter the room and the time school starts
What is done about opening exercises
Time each class period starts and ends (a schedule of classes)
Time for recess, lunch, and other activities
Directions for fire drills and air-raid drills
Office signals if no public address system
Time of announcements
Directions for collection of money and what is to be done with receipts
Directions for taking attendance and reporting it
Location of necessary books and supplies
Routines that have been established for using supplies, using the pencil sharpener, leaving the room, etc.
Location of plan book
Grouping used and students in each group
Names of children who can be trusted to give accurate information about assignments, time for lunch, etc.
Names of children who may be troublesome and ways in which their cooperation may be obtained
Names of children who need special help
Names of children who will help with routines such as distributing rulers, pencils, compasses, etc.
A list of independent activities that children may perform when assigned work is finished

A plan worked out with one student to help a substitute teacher in naming the students in the class.

One plan might be to provide the teacher with a name-tag holder (the plastic pin-on type in which a card containing the child's name may be placed) for every child who attends class in his room. As the substitute presents the child with his name tag he has an opportunity to study the child and note where he sits. He also has the advantage of being able to call the child by name.

Homework

It is best to assign homework only when there is a specific purpose in mind, and after the activities that are described are well understood. The homework assignment should be written clearly on the chalkboard, or printed on a worksheet, or carefully outlined in some other way. If slow learners have problems about taking books home, the books may be kept in some orderly fashion in the classroom. Students fail to take books home for various reasons: perhaps they just forget; or their friends make fun of taking books home; or they play along the way home and mislay the books; or they have no place at home for their books. In some cases, then, students might be provided with paper sheets of homework problems or activities. The slow learner may well take home a sheet of paper when he wouldn't take home a book. A boy can put the paper in a folder, and a girl can put it in her pocketbook.

Homework should be checked and returned promptly. Its treatment will vary with its purpose. In all cases some form of reward is suitable. If it is drill work, the neatest or most accurate or most improved work might go on a bulletin board. If its purpose is developmental, refer to it and build on it for the lesson. Sometimes it may just be collected and then one or two of its problems given as a quick quiz. The teacher should not assume that a student knows the work just because he hands in his homework.

The contingency-managed classroom

A rather specialized plan for classroom organization is called the contingency-managed classroom. With this plan the teacher applies the principles of "operant conditioning." In brief terms, behavior patterns that are deemed acceptable are immediately reinforced; and behavior patterns that interfere are not reinforced and through nonreinforcement are extinguished. A contingency table lists acceptable activities, and children receive certain units of reinforcement contingent upon certain performances. For example, a credit system is set up based on listed academic or social tasks. A part of the contingency table used in a sixth-grade class might look like this (20, p. 118):

Academic Tasks	Number of Credits
1. One math assignment of 5 problems	5–10
2. One outside reading	25
3. Homework signed by parent	25
Social Tasks	
1. Neatness in class assignment	5
2. Courtesy to teacher	5
3. Books properly covered	10

The credits can then be used to buy the reinforcements that the student desires. Some are material rewards. Some are long-term rewards. Some examples of reinforcement items are shown below (20, p. 120):

1. "A" in mathematics		500 credits
17. Field trip to museum		75 credits
20. Go for drink of water		5 credits
21. Go to reinforcement area during activity period		10 credits

(The reinforcement area is a separate room where game activities are allowed during assigned times.)

A self-contained classroom can be divided into functional areas as diagramed in figure 10.1.

KEY TO DIAGRAM

1. *Credit Desk:* Assignments are given to students; credits for assignment completion are recorded by teacher's aide.
2. *Teacher's Desk:* Papers are corrected and student's progress is noted by the teacher.
3. *Materials Area:* Necessary student materials are kept in folders; reference materials and other instructions are kept in this area.
4. *Task Area:* Students work on individual assignments at their desks.
5. *Special Project:* Independent study area.
6. *Small Group Area.*
7. *Blackboard:* Psychedelic wall used for reinforcement.
8. *Blackboard:* The Mod Corner used for reinforcement.
9. *Time-out Area.*

This division helps to organize the instruction. Cards are kept on

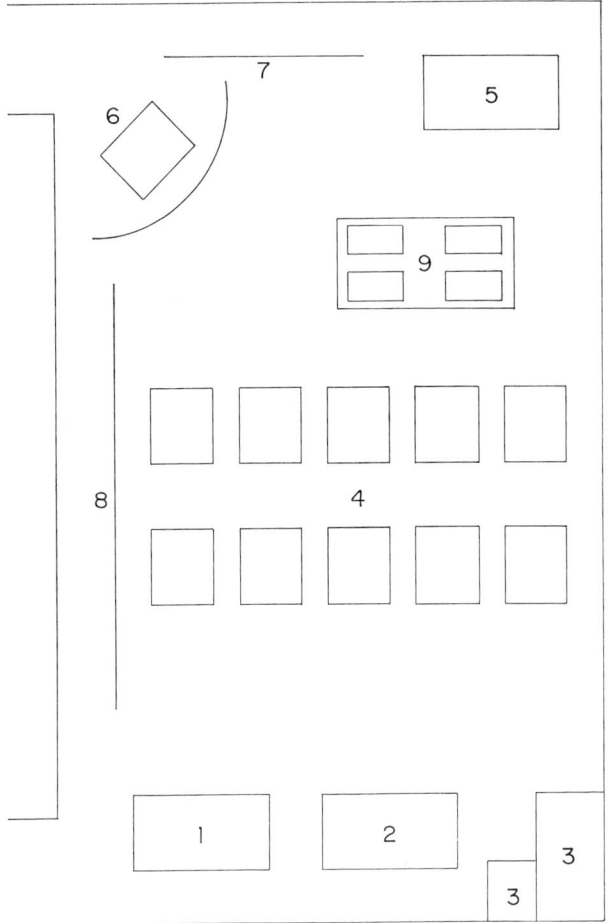

Fig. 10.1. Self-contained classroom. Reprinted, by permission, from David H. Moyer (20, p. 108).

each student to record credits. No credit is given for an assignment until errors are checked and corrected, but a way is always provided to get this done. To keep all these records, it is necessary to have a teacher aide.

Class control

A teacher's attitude toward his students is an important aspect of classroom management. He must be fair, firm, considerate, and consistent. An air of positive expectancy helps to produce positive student orientation to classwork. The teacher should meet every class with enthusiasm and a purpose. In applying rules of behavior, the teacher's point of view is important; a businesslike but pleasant approach can help to develop a relaxed atmosphere in which each student feels secure that he is not being too tightly controlled but, rather, is working in a setting of freedom with responsibility.

Class control may become a problem for the teacher in some situations. Basically the expectation is that good class control will result from the use of positive classroom management procedures and program planning along the lines suggested in this book. Where these practices are ineffective, possibly because of influences and situations outside the control of the individual teacher, some specific steps may be necessary to implement class control. As a starter, an all-school effort should be made to establish guidelines of accepted student behavior in school and society. General in-class rules should be added. These need to be worked out with the children so that they understand the reasons for the limitations on their actions and the possible variations that may apply according to the current activity of the class. Some of the most helpful procedures are those that work toward preventing disciplinary problems from arising and handle problems in a routine, impartial manner that indicates genuine interest in the students' social development. Teachers use some of the following principles as a guide:

1. Be sure that requests of students are understood by all.
2. Be aware of preserving the students' dignity and try to use experiences to help students learn self-discipline.
3. Show interest in all aspects of students' lives.
4. Group children in many different ways for various activities. If students are used to being grouped in various ways, regrouping at a particular time to separate certain children will be more readily accepted without exaggerating a disruptive incident.
5. Be aware of all that goes on in the classroom.
6. Follow through on requests made to students.
7. Deal with disruptive episodes quickly, positively, and in a manner that is consistent and impartial.
8. Be willing to listen to students tell what they felt happened in disrupting episodes.
9. Follow through on whatever corrective procedure has been worked out with the students.

Where there is a guidance counselor for his students, the teacher can get much help from him in understanding the student and in working out disciplinary problems as they are foreseen. When a child indicates upsetting tendencies, the teacher can make the guidance counselor aware of overt actions that indicate this. The counselor can help by checking all personnel who work with the student and by finding an opportunity to talk with the student to draw him out.

Mary Potter writes: "Don't act bothered. Believe that you can control them and you can." (26, p. 31.) If a student disobeys a rule, speak to him unobtrusively, without involving the whole class. One student should not be allowed to become a center of attention. It is better if instructions and direction of activity come from the teacher, not from students (this does not preclude having organized student-teacher planning). It is not a good practice to use ridicule and embarrassment of a pupil. Langworthy writes that this will "only widen the gulf between the student and the teacher, thus making objectives almost impossible to achieve. Even if these methods are used with only one student in the class, the remaining members of the class will identify themselves with him and the damage has been done to all and not only to one." (24, p. 74.) A firm, steady voice that assumes compliance and requests action in a kindly yet authoritative way is a helpful tool for the teacher in establishing a good classroom climate, thus fostering good discipline. Mary Potter also suggests: "If it is necessary to ask someone to do something, call on a pupil that you know will comply with your request first, choosing if possible a pupil with leadership. After this pupil does it, the others will follow his example." (26, p. 31.)

Every student is unique, and so is every series of offenses. The teacher needs to use judgment in being consistent, firm, and fair in all these procedures. The implication throughout that the teacher cares for the student and that these steps are part of the process of helping him to learn how to act in school and in society will help teacher-student relationships. In considering this problem it is recognized that having a class under control is not the ultimate goal of teaching. But this is a necessary step toward the goal of teaching accepted behavior.

With many students the great problem is getting them to participate in class discussions and activities. If careful planning is being done to assure that the teaching is relevant, purposeful, and as varied as needed for individuals and topics, then a series of steps might serve to lead the students into participating.

It is helpful for the teacher to be especially aware of the interests and abilities of students who tend to be introverted. He can call on them by name with questions they can probably answer. He can ask each of them, at one time or another, to explain some special interest or some method of doing a problem. Or he can involve them with students who are more outgoing but not domineering. Introverted students need support of this kind. They also need extra praise for any good attempts they make.

Evaluation

Objectives

Evaluation is an ongoing activity. An important aspect of evaluation is the stating of realistic objectives in behavioral terms. These will give proper direction to the teacher's planning and will allow for meaningful evaluation. Evaluation of a student's progress can be made with reference to these behavioral objectives and with consideration given to the student's mathematics aptitude. The evaluation indicates what growth has occurred and what levels of achievement have been reached. Setting reasonable goals for a student will allow him to attain success. Diagnostic testing will show where the student is and help to set, within reason, where he can be expected to go.

Students' daily work

Students like to have written work returned to them promptly after it is evaluated. Using a bulletin board to show off good homework or classwork promotes interest and indicates what papers seem to be closest to meeting stated objectives. The teacher may want to find ways of varying the criteria for bulletin-board presentations so that each student can see his work posted occasionally. To keep parents aware of progress, some papers might be sent home (mailed if necessary) for a parent to sign and return to school.

It is helpful if the teacher finds something positive to say about each day's work. For example, although John has every answer wrong, his work is neat and he shows increased understanding of the concept; what he needs is to learn his multiplication combinations. Rewards for slow learners are a form of evaluation. They are important and are most effective if given immediately—perhaps a personal remark, or being among the first to be dismissed, or receiving a badge. Some teachers have cookies or candies to distribute in small amounts as rewards.

One way to reward the student is to give immediate acknowledgment of successful work. Another is to post answers where the student can see them and check his work by them, thus gaining his own reward. Many variations of the old system of a "star" still work for many teachers. As described above, contingency management techniques can contain built-in evaluation plans. They establish points for various activities, and students are given many ways of gaining points, knowing that a certain number of points means that they will receive some reward or some "grade." Many slow learners come from homes where there is no known activity they can perform that will bring them a reward without fail (like being allowed to watch TV if homework is finished). There sometimes is just not that much interest in the children in the home. These students, especially, may respond favorably to a reward system that is very specific.

Once again, the teacher's folder on each student will include material on his evaluation. Frequent short quizzes help the student keep a high level of success on his record. A diagnostic checklist kept in the folder can be checked off and rechecked as a way of assuring that behavioral objectives are being attained and sustained.

Testing

Where within-the-class regrouping for mathematics instruction is done, diagnostic testing can be done weekly, or more often, so that children can be regrouped to receive the help they need. Students may check their own progress-record sheets and work on their own deficiencies. Initial tests can be oversimplified to provide some successes.

Before any new topic is introduced, it is helpful to give a brief pretest and to inform students that they are not being graded on the test (that it is merely help for the teacher).

Some teachers make a careful analysis of errors on student work. When students show all their work, including the intermediate steps, errors can be more easily identified. The student might be encouraged to try to find his own error; if he can't find it, the teacher can help him and give him a related example for practice.

In correcting papers it is good practice for the teacher to draw a circle around an error and indicate the correct procedure next to the student's work. If a number fact has been missed, the student can practice this fact. Students may be encouraged to make private sets of flash cards for the number facts they do not know. This identifying of individual difficulties helps with motivation. When the teacher recognizes the need to develop a concept or technique, he must teach it—not just tell it. The words "move the decimal point two places to the left" tell the student only what he must do; they do not help much in understanding.

Two important steps for the teacher, then, are (1) to analyze the error and (2) to teach the concept.

Teacher-made achievement tests should cover only small units of work. Reteaching and retesting at various levels on the mathematics sequence will help the teacher know where his students are. Many schools have a program that provides for standardized testing of some sort every year or two. These suffice for the long-term testing needs of slow learners.

Reporting to parents

In some schools methods of reporting to parents of slow learners are developed by teachers, principals, and parents as a joint effort. Many specific ways of working together are possible. Some ways are well suited to one situation but do not seem usable in another. The number of pupils for whom the teacher is responsible, the ease or difficulty with which parents can get to school (because of distance or work schedules), the extent to which ways of doing things (such as form or frequency of reports) are held inviolate—these and other factors in the situation itself influence ways of working together. Personality differences may also have an influence. People—parents as well as teachers—vary in the ways of working together that they find most satisfactory. At any rate, parents need to be aware of the reporting method being used, its philosophy, and its details. Johnson states: "The purpose of reporting is to inform parents clearly, concisely, and accurately how well their children are performing in school" (16, p. 283). Where reporting is realistic, realistic programs and expectations can be developed for students.

In the primary grades, two or three conferences, or anecdotal written reports, per year can probably best achieve the reporting goals. In grades 4 and above, as simple a report form as can be worked out is probably the best means of reporting. One part of the report should indicate the level of the student's performance in relation to that of children of his age. If A, B, C, and D categories are used on this part of the report, the slow learner will probably be graded only B with unusually good work, and A with outstandingly fine achievement. If groups are being delineated according to mathematics achievement, a B or an A grade would indicate that consideration should be given to moving the student into a group that is doing a higher level of work.

The report form should also show the student's progress as it relates to his ability. On this part of the form, the hard-working slow learner will be rewarded with an A, or a B, or whatever means is being used to show maximum effort.

Parents are not likely to read a long report that is hard to understand. They are often unfamiliar with the mode of marking and need help to interpret the report correctly. In spite of the need for brevity, however, many systems find that a place for comments is useful. This can provide a means for the teacher to add an encouraging note by indicating the most positive part of the student's class work. Crowley makes the following suggestion to the teacher:

> Adjust your own goals realistically. Don't expect to make waves—be satisfied with an occasional ripple. Success with the slow learner is best measured in terms of improvement in his attitude, and this cannot take place overnight.
>
> While fixing realistic goals for yourself, you can be of great help to the parents of the slow learner. In this competitive world, most parents want for their children the education that they themselves may not have had. The child we are discussing here is not likely to succeed in senior high school or more advanced education. You can often lead his parents to an understanding that this child has his own qualities to develop and that pressuring him to attain impossible goals is leading him to frustration and, perhaps, rebellion. You can help the parents of a slow learner to accept their child, and you can encourage them to encourage him to develop his own potential. [7, p. 49]

Grouping for Instruction

Setting up groups

If grouping is to work in the classroom, groups must be purposeful and each student should understand why he is in a particular group. Slow-learner mathematics groups that are set up within an elementary classroom should be made up on the basis of an analysis of needs.

Instruction in the skills should be based on the results of diagnostic tests, and a child should be allowed to transfer from one group to another to get the help he needs. Intraclass ability grouping can be worked out by starting the whole class together on a unit and then, after a short time, dividing the class into two groups—one composed of those who appear to learn more easily, the other of those who are having difficulties. Many initial developments can be worked out with a whole class group as various topics are considered, and then different levels of satisfactory operation can be established for different groups.

Operation of groups

Grouping should be flexible. One group might be composed of those needing drill on the multiplication combinations; another, of those learning to add unlike fractions; still another, of those learning subtractive division. At no time should a child be refused admittance to any group as long as he can receive the help he needs there. The names of those in each group should be posted after each diagnostic test, and the group should be designated, not as group 1 or group 2, but as James's group or the multiplication group, the division group or the fraction group.

Planning for the group work should be done with the children so they can know exactly when they should work with the teacher and what they should do while the teacher is working with another group. A teacher's board outline might look like the one shown in figure 10.2.

10:00–11:30

Multiplication Group	*Division Group*	*Fraction Group*
1. Do the examples on the board, using expanded notation.	1. Work with the teacher on multiplication of 6 × 8, 600 × 8, 50 × 9, 10 × 9, etc.	1. Do addition of fractions on p. 36, 1–10.
2. Work with the teacher. Use the football game for a drill on 6 × 4, 7 × 9, 7 × 7, 9 × 6, etc. Use these combinations to work on 890 ×7 948 ×6 764 ×6, etc.	2. Do the work assigned on the board, beginning with 9 × ? = 2,700 (or 9 × ? = nearly 3,000).	2. Continue working on p. 36. For extra credit, do p. 37, 1–10.
3. Continue working on multiplication examples.	3. Continue working on the examples on the board.	3. Work with the teacher on adding unlike fractions, using newspaper, fractional pies, etc.

Fig. 10.2

Secondary presentations for small groups of slow learners can allow for concrete, short-time, small-concept learnings. For example, a group of seven students might be set up because all within it are in need of reviewing one aspect of the division process. Where better students have progressed from long division to short division—that is,

from $\quad 7 \overline{\smash{\big)}458} \atop \underline{420}\ 60 \atop 38 \atop \underline{35}\ \underline{\ 5} \atop 3\ 65$ $\overset{65\ R\ 3}{}$ to $\quad 7 \overline{\smash{\big)}458} \atop \underline{42} \atop 38 \atop \underline{35} \atop 3$ $\overset{65\ R\ 3}{}$ to $\quad 7 \overline{\smash{\big)}458}$ $\overset{65\ R\ 3}{}$

—the slow learners may need to see again, in a different way from that first presented, the subtractive aspect of division. They might be allowed to stay with the level of work at which they can successfully perform, and to interrelate some manipulative method with the written algorism.

In speaking of individualized instruction, Wolfson writes: "For real learning to occur, the learner must see a purpose and meaning in the learning experience" (41, p. 33). To implement this, the teacher should meet with individuals and small groups for pupil-teacher planning and evaluation and for teacher assistance when it is needed. Also, students should be allowed to select from various alternative resources (human, material, and audiovisual). With regard to classroom procedures and organization, Wolfson prescribes "grouping for diversity (multi-age, nongraded) with opportunities for *temporary* subgroups to pursue special interests and competencies" (41, p. 33).

Team teaching

One organizational structure that allows great flexibility in the grouping of students is called team teaching. "Team teaching is an organizational procedure whereby a group of teachers pool their knowledge and talent to provide superior instruction for a larger number of students than one teacher could handle. They jointly share the responsibility for the planning, execution, and evaluation of the educational program for this group." (17, p. 50.) One advantage gained by this plan is that "team teaching utilizes teachers in different functions in accordance with their own special abilities, interests, and education and in keeping with the variety of the curriculum and the needs of individual students" (30, p. 39). Many types of team-teaching structure are used. "Although few plans are exactly alike, three patterns are emerging from activity across the country. These patterns might be termed the single-discipline team, the interdisciplinary team and the school-within-school team." (36, p. 16.) However the groups are formed, team teachers can organize the instruction so that slow learners in mathematics are grouped together for instruction at their proper level. Often one member of the team is designated team leader, responsible for organizing the planning. Together they plan ways to use the best abilities of each individual teacher. Sister Mary Korb observes that "team teaching is an educational innovation that offers a different perspective for the teaching personnel—namely, that the team members, not the administrator, make decisions concerning the program based upon their joint observations and evaluations" (17, p. 53). No matter what the structure of the teams, "the diagnostic, planning, and evaluative procedures employed in the teaching-learning process, when developed by a team of teachers, are generally superior to those developed by a single teacher" (3, p. 12).

Individualizing Instruction

Individually prescribed instruction

In addition to the use of grouping methods, a number of other innovative ways of individualizing instruction have been developed recently. Some schools are now using a system called "Individually Prescribed Instruction," developed in the Learning Research and Development Center at the University of Pittsburgh. IPI, as this system is called, "consists of planning and conducting with each student a program of studies that is tailored to his learning needs and to his characteristics as a learner" (31, p. 2). It is a nongraded program that is used with students at elementary school levels.

Materials consist of (1) pretests for each unit to aid in determining the program for the individual child and to identify individual strengths and weaknesses among students; (2) a written prescription made by the teacher on the basis of the pretests; (3) a series of individual instruction lessons in worksheet form at all levels in grades 1 through 6 (these worksheets are arranged in a sequential order called a continuum, and each student's prescription tells him what worksheets he will work on); (4) a series of curriculum-embedded tests to assess the mastery of each skill after it has been worked on; and (5) a series of posttests to determine when and where a student moves ahead in the continuum.

Teachers analyze progress and write the prescriptions. They also meet groups of students to discuss topics with them as the groups show that they have similar problems relating to some common skill or unit.

Teacher aides help keep records and score and check information.

Computer-assisted instruction

Another innovative approach to individualing instruction is called "Computer-assisted Instruction." In using it a student sits before a computer terminal. He identifies himself by typing his name or in some other established way. Then the computer presents him with information and questions, either by means of a display tube or on a printed output. The student responds by use of a light pen or by typing an answer. "The computer can assign each student to his level of ability based on previous performance and current progress. It automatically adjusts to the student's ability level and constantly leads him to more advanced problems as he progresses." (9, p. 47.)

Present CAI programs are expensive, noisy, slow, and undependable, but they still show much promise, especially when used with disadvantaged children. Experience in using a mathematics drill-and-practice program for elementary grades developed by Patrick Suppes at Stanford University indicates that "there is little significance between groups of high income, high I.Q. children on CAI and regular instruction (if teachers are comparable in ability) but startling results are obtained in favor of CAI in Negro and low-income groups regardless of teacher ability" (27, p. 2).

Mendelsohn reports that "an impartial evaluation of the New York City CAI program prepared by the City University of New York confirms that students using CAI learn more than students not using CAI" (19, p. 4) and that "CAI is extremely effective with disadvantaged children through the fourth grade" (19, p. 8). If costs can be brought down and more programs can be developed for slow learners, CAI shows much promise for the future.

Learning activities adaptable to individual instruction include using programmed materials; using IPI materials; using CAI materials; doing puzzles; individual flash-card review; problem solving; paper folding; geoboard exercises; research reading; preparing reports; and one-to-one teacher-to-student explanations, checking skills, and counseling.

Learning activities adaptable to small-group instruction include designing bulletin-board displays; playing games; measuring and comparing geometric objects; working with beads or blocks to show relationships; following tape-recorded instructions; chip trading; elementary surveying; and making and handling geometric models.

Learning activities adaptable to whole-class instruction include developmental learning presentations; class demonstrations by students; oral number games; guessing games; contests; simple paper folding or number-line work to show arithmetic relationships; "What's My Rule?" games; film and filmstrip presentation; testing; worksheet drills; flash-card drills; and class trips.

Administrative Responsibility

Grouping

An important administrative responsibility is to provide a productive pattern of grouping students for learning. There are many facets to the use of grouping. The administrator should be familiar with the many possibilities for the use of grouping and should plan for the grouping organization that best benefits the slow learner in his school. Goodlad indicates that "research into the merits of various patterns of interclass grouping is inconclusive, controversial, and misleading" (23, p. 71). And Miller says that "efforts to set up groups in terms of ability and/or achievement do little to reduce the over-all range of pupil variability with which teachers must deal. However, selective grouping and regrouping by achievement sometimes is useful, particularly at the secondary level." (22, p. 141.) Johnson and Rising recommend that ability grouping "be established wherever possible" as an aid in considering individual differences among students (15, p. 185).

G. O. Johnson also recommends some form of homogeneous grouping as an aid to organizing the teaching of slow learners. He says, "Only in this way can the purposes of education be achieved by the schools for the slow learners" (16, p. 118). He recommends that large developmental groups be organized on the basis of overall physical, social, emotional, intellectual, and academic growth; within this framework, grouping for instruction in specific subject areas should be on a homogeneous basis, with provision made for regrouping on the basis of successive testing.

These considerations point to the value of a nongraded or educational-need basis for school organization, possibly up through what has been traditionally labeled the eighth-grade level. This organizational plan allows for a block of time set aside for mathematics instruction, and for a special program for slow learners within this period. Teams of teachers can organize the instruction in the blocks of time so that by organizing and reorganizing large and small groups, individual students can work at a level that is success-oriented for them.

The program is benefited if administrators understand the time-

and-space needs of team teaching. They can plan for providing flexible spaces, a variety of instructional materials, teacher aides, team planning time, and adequate blocks of time for instruction. And they can help teachers learn how to organize for team teaching.

At the 9–12 grade levels, departmental scheduling and guidance can place the student in the mathematics class most suited to his ability. Many slow learners can learn algebra if they are placed in a two-year algebra sequence that covers the work traditionally taught as Algebra 1. If this class is scheduled back-to-back with a regular Algebra 1 class, students might be interchanged upon teachers' recommendations after the sixth or eighth week of the school year. After algebra these students can then go on to shop mathematics, business mathematics, consumer mathematics, or a geometry course. Many colleges today will accept students with this kind of program if they have done well in it.

For the non-college-bound student, a program that is related to job needs, student interests, and some algebra and geometry can be developed locally. Field trips can let students see people using mathematics. Local representatives of business and industry can supply forms and examples and are usually glad to talk to students about the mathematics they use. One teacher invited a car salesman to a mathematics class. He described a number of car buys to the students and then "sold" the cars. The next day he came back and showed how he had cheated students who "bought" his cars. His explanation aroused much interest in the importance of the mathematics involved in careful buying. Another teacher obtained a number of job-cost-estimate forms and a service-job-rate manual from a local car-service garage. Students described jobs that had been done on friends' cars, and then the costs were determined. In another case actual car-insurance-rate pages were reproduced. These not only helped students understand why their car-insurance costs were high but also showed how being a good student might benefit them in their insurance costs.

If such a program is developed as an ungraded one- or two-year course and if two or three sections meet at the same time, teachers can reorganize groups to provide remedial instruction for various learnings as the need becomes apparent. Students who have completed this course could benefit from a consumer mathematics course in the junior or senior year. In these classes, texts and workbooks should be available for use primarily as reference and practice materials, with local student interests and needs dictating the general program and the unit outline. Copeland states: "In the experience-centered, math laboratory approach to learning, books are also necessary. Their use, however, is as a resource material just as are the other materials in the math laboratory. They are not the only basis for learning mathematics as is the case in many classrooms." (6, p. 283.)

Administrators would do well to avoid making a slow-learner class a "dumping ground" for problem students. A slow-learner class is set up for a particular purpose, not related to solving problems of emotionally disturbed or troublesome students. Although slow learners tend to have a short interest span, they still need to have the equivalent of a full 45–60 minute daily period of time for mathematics. And they need to participate in all the school activities. Provision should always be made for a student to change to a more suitable class or group if he "wakes up" and improves to the point of being able to hold his own in classes that move along at a faster rate.

Use of teachers

Slow learners need a teacher who is highly qualified. Administrators can help by providing a pleasant schedule and a workable class size (less than twenty students where one class is assigned as a unit). In-service planning time provided for the development and continual updating of slow-learner programs is an important consideration. Teachers need time to contact representatives of local business and industry and to adapt their problems and business forms to the teaching in the classroom. They need time to exchange ideas with other teachers and to visit classes in mathematics and also, as Rosenbloom says, "in other subjects—shop, home economics, and commercial courses—and see to what extent they can draw mathematics problems out of the work students are doing in the subjects so as to make teaching more relevant" (29, p. 6). Meetings with parents can also be productive of understandings regarding needs and requirements of their children. Many administrators encourage teachers to attend professional conferences to hear about ideas that have worked; expense money is made available for this. Most NCTM meetings have a number of sections dealing with slow-learner problems.

Providing classroom teacher aides is an important way to help any teacher of slow learners. Although aides are now used mostly in elementary grades, they can be used in similar ways for slow-learner classes at any level. Aides should be carefully chosen "who will bring a whole new set of life experiences into the school and can become a real communication link between the school and the community" (1, p. 8). They should be people who can relate well to children and who like to work with children. Orientation sessions for both teachers and aides can be organized to establish procedures and to plan the program; and on-the-job sessions can be planned throughout the year for improving these practices.

The teacher who uses an aide effectively plans with the aide so both know exactly what the other is to do.

Some of the ways an aide may help are these:

Make sure all necessary supplies are on hand and ready for use.

Make and run off ditto materials.

Make mathematics games and play games with the children so the facts that have been taught will be reinforced.

Go over written directions to make sure children understand them.

Work with three or four children in some particular area.

When the teacher is working with one group, make sure the other children are doing correctly the work that has been assigned.

Make training aids, as planned with the teachers.

Operate audio and visual aid equipment.

Summary

Managing teaching so that slow learners can learn mathematics requires a resourceful teacher who can patiently discover and build upon whatever skills his students have. He plans to provide an uncluttered, structured environment where routines developed with the students are understood and consistently followed. He provides many success experiences, using a variety of activities that involve many muscles, as well as the brain. He seeks ways of working with various methods of grouping children so that he can find the one that works best for him, his students, his colleagues, and his school. The administrator who is aware of what students and teachers need in terms of space, equipment, and time will help to establish a smooth operation in the variety of teaching arrangements being used.

REFERENCES

1. Association for Childhood Education International. *Aids to Teachers and Children.* Bulletin no. 24-A. Washington, D.C.: The Association, 1968.
2. ———. *Reporting on the Growth of Children.* Bulletin no. 62. Washington, D.C.: The Association, 1953.

3. Blair, Medill, and Richard G. Woodward. *Team Teaching in Action.* Boston: Houghton Mifflin Co., 1964.
4. Brown, Kenneth E., and Theodore L. Abell. *Analysis of Research in the Teaching of Mathematics.* U.S. Office of Education Bulletin 1965, no. 8. Washington, D.C.: Government Printing Office.
5. Butler, Edward J. "The Art of Classroom Questioning—Have You Mastered It?" *Delaware School Journal,* November 1966.
6. Copeland, Richard W. *How Children Learn Mathematics: Teaching Implications of Piaget's Research.* New York: Macmillan Co., 1970.
7. Crowley, Regis F. "Teaching the Slow Learner." *Today's Education* 58 (January 1969): 48–49.
8. Cutts, Norma, and Nicholas Moseley. *Providing for Individual Differences in the Elementary School.* Englewood Cliffs, N.J.: Prentice-Hall, 1960.
9. Dawson, Kenneth E., and Morris Norfleet. "The Computer and the Student." *NEA Journal* 57 (February 1968): 47–48.
10. Glaser, Edward, and Irwin G. Sarason. *Reinforcing Productive Classroom Behavior.* Bethesda, Md.: ERIC Document Reproduction Service, 1970. (Available as ED 049469 from EDRS, 4827 Rugby Ave., Bethesda, Md. 20014.)
11. Greenholz, Sarah. "What's New in Teaching Slow Learners in Junior High School?" *Mathematics Teacher* 57 (December 1964): 522–28.
12. Hornburger, Jane M. *So You Have an Aide: A Guide for Teachers in the Use of Classroom Aides.* Wilmington, Del.: Wilmington Public Schools, 1968.
13. Holt, Irving. "The School Administrator and the 'Educationally Disadvantaged' Child." *Bulletin of the National Association of Secondary School Principals* 48 (March 1964): 85–98.
14. Jarvis, Oscar I. *A Statistical Analysis of the Relationship of Varying Time Allotments to Pupil Achievement in Reading, Arithmetic, and Language of the Elementary Grades in the Texas Gulf Area,* Ed.D. dissertation, University of Houston, 1962. Ann Arbor, Mich.: University Microfilms (no. 63-1092).
15. Johnson, Donovan A., and Gerald R. Rising. *Guidelines for Teaching Mathematics.* Belmont, Calif.: Wadsworth Publishing Co., 1967.
16. Johnson, George Orville. *Education for the Slow Learners.* Prentice-Hall Psychology Series, edited by Arthur T. Jersild. Englewood Cliffs, N.J.: Prentice-Hall, 1963.
17. Korb, Sister Mary Victor. "Positive and Negative Factors in Team Teaching." *Mathematics Teacher* 61 (January 1968): 50–53.
18. Mahan, T. W., Jr. "The Slow Learner: Fact or Excuse?" *School Review* 73 (Summer 1965): 77–88.
19. Mendelsohn, Melvin. *CAI in New York City—Application and Evaluation.* Mimeographed report. New York: Board of Education of the City of New York, 1969. (Available from Computer Assisted Instruction Project, 229 East 42d St., New York, N.Y. 10017.)
20. Moyer, David H. "CMC in a Disadvantaged Area." In *Student Motivation and Classroom Management—a Behavioristic Approach,* edited by John T. Neisworth, Stanley L. Deno, and Joseph R. Jenkins. Newark, Del.: Behavior Technics, 1969.

21. Muessing, R. H., ed. *Youth Education: Problems, Perspectives, Promises.* Yearbook of the Association for Supervision and Curriculum Development. Washington, D.C.: The Association, 1968.
22. National Education Association, Project on the Instructional Program of the Public Schools. *Education in a Changing Society.* Washington, D.C.: The Association, 1963.
23. ———. *Planning and Organizing for Teaching.* Washington, D.C.: The Association, 1963.
24. New Jersey Secondary School Teachers Association. *The Slow Learner in Secondary Schools.* Yearbook. Glassboro, N.J.: The Association, 1961.
25. Passow, A. Harry, ed. *Education in Depressed Areas.* New York: Bureau of Publications, Teachers College, Columbia University, 1963; Teachers College Press, 1968.
26. Potter, Mary, and Virgil Mallory. *Education in Mathematics for the Slow Learner.* Washington, D.C.: National Council of Teachers of Mathematics, 1958.
27. Prince, J. D. "A Practitioner's Report: Results of Two Years of Computer Assisted Instruction in Drill and Practice Mathematics." Mimeographed. U.S. Office of Education OEG-3-7-704721-5096 and McComb (Miss.) Public Schools, 1969.
28. Proctor, Amelia D. "A World of Hope—Helping Slow Learners Enjoy Mathematics." *Mathematics Teacher* 58 (February 1965): 118–22.
29. *Project Conference Report, CAMP.* Pella, Iowa: Concepts and Applications of Mathematics Project, 1966.
30. Research and Policy Committee of the Committee for Economic Development. *Innovation in Education: New Directions for the American School.* New York: Committee for Economic Development, 1968.
31. Research for Better Schools, Inc. *Individually Prescribed Instruction.* Philadelphia: Research for Better Schools, 1969.
32. Riessman, Frank. *The Culturally Deprived Child.* New York: Harper & Row, 1962.
33. Sassé, Katharine J. S. "Mathematics for the Noncollege-bound in Junior High School." *Mathematics Teacher* 58 (March 1965): 232–40.
34. Seyfert, Warren C., ed. *The Continuing Revolution in Mathematics. Bulletin of the National Association of Secondary School Principals,* April 1968. Reprint. Washington, D.C.: National Council of Teachers of Mathematics, 1968.
35. Silberman, Charles E. *Crisis in the Classroom.* New York: Random House, 1970.
36. Singer, Ora J. "What Team Teaching Really Is." In *Team Teaching—Bold New Venture,* edited by David W. Beggs III, pp. 13–28. Indianapolis, Ind.: Unified College Press, 1964.
37. Skinner, B. F. *Contingencies of Reinforcement.* New York: Appleton-Century-Crofts, 1969.
38. Sylvester, Robert. *Common Sense in Classroom Relations.* W. Nyack, N.Y.: Parker Publishing Co., 1967.
39. U.S. Office of Education. *National Conference on Education of the Disadvantaged.* Washington, D.C.: U.S. Department of Health, Education, and Welfare, 1966.

40. Weaver, J. Fred. "Differentiated Instruction and School-Class Organization for Mathematical Learning within the Elementary Grades." *Arithmetic Teacher* 13 (October 1966): 495–506.
41. Wolfson, Bernice J. "Individualizing Instruction." *NEA Journal* 55 (November 1966): 31–33.
42. Woodby, Lauren G., ed. *The Low Achiever in Mathematics.* Report of a conference sponsored by the U.S. Office of Education and the National Council of Teachers of Mathematics. U.S. Office of Education Bulletin 1965, no. 31. Washington, D.C.: Government Printing Office, 1965.
43. ———. *Preliminary Report of the Conference on the Low Achiever in Mathematics.* Washington, D.C.: National Council of Teachers of Mathematics, 1964.
44. Youne, William J. *Instructional Approaches to Slow Learning.* New York: Teachers College Press, 1967.

11

Promising Programs and Practices

IN THIS chapter various persons describe the programs with which they are, or have been, associated. These programs have been found to have promise, at least in working with certain groups of slow learners or, as in one case, in training teachers of slow learners. In selecting the programs to be included in this chapter, the editorial panel made an attempt to choose them so as to present a variety of philosophical and curricular approaches to working with various groups of slow learners.

William DeVenney describes two School Mathematics Study Group programs for low-achieving junior high school students.

Computer-assisted instruction is often used for all children, but it has been found in some instances to be especially effective with low-achieving students. Melvin Mendelsohn describes the computer-assisted instruction program in mathematics in the New York City Schools.

Special problems are associated with teaching children who come from homes where a language is used other than the language in which the instruction in the schools is given. Sidney Sharron and Gloria Cox report a program called MSP ("Mathematics for Spanish-speaking Pupils") developed by the Los Angeles City Unified School District.

The Baltimore County program called "Mathematics for Basic

Education (Grades 7–11)" is presented by Vincent Brant, who gives further details of a program referred to in chapters 3, 6, and 12 of this yearbook.

The mathematics laboratory of the Sir R. L. Borden Secondary School, a school specifically for underachievers in Scarborough, Ontario, is described by Mrs. Strobel.

Project SEED ("Special Elementary Education for the Disadvantaged") is a program designed to improve the academic achievement of disadvantaged elementary school children by teaching them abstract, conceptually oriented mathematics. This project is described by its director, William Johntz.

The attempts of a large city (Chicago) to meet the needs of inner-city children are recounted by Jessie Scott.

Finally, the University of Denver programs for teachers of low achievers are presented by Ruth Hoffman.

Limitations of space make it impossible to include all the descriptions of programs, practices, and facilities received by the editorial panel of the yearbook. Because the others received by the panel are certainly worthy of attention, they are listed below. The arrangement is geographical (alphabetical by state, then city) rather than by author or title of the paper. Many of the titles are self-explanatory. Interested readers are invited to write to any of the listed addresses for further information.

Oral Programming—Slow Learners
Kenneth Easterday
Department of Secondary Education
School of Education
Auburn University
Auburn, Alabama 36830

Mathematics Achievement Improvement Program in Birmingham, Alabama
Margaret M. Holland
Supervisor, Secondary Mathematics
Birmingham City Schools
405 Administration Building
Birmingham, Alabama 35202

Individual Advancement Laboratory Program in Mathematics
Marvin L. Johnson
Consultant, Mathematics
Long Beach Unified School District
Board of Education Building
701 Locust Avenue
Long Beach, California 90813

Outstanding Mathematics Laboratory Facilities in Los Angeles Schools
Arthur Freier
Mathematics Specialist
Instructional Planning Branch
Los Angeles Unified School District

P.O. Box 3307
Los Angeles, California 90054

A Sequential Approach to Individualization of the Mathematics Program
Los Angeles City Schools
Special Education Branch
Instructional Program
450 North Grand Avenue
Los Angeles, California 90012

TTT Mathematics Systems Laboratory
Viggo P. Hansen
Director, TTT Mathematics Component
San Fernando Valley State College
18111 Nordhoff Street
Northridge, California 91324

Project FOCUS—Mathematics
Harry Levitin
Supervisor of Mathematics
New Haven Public Schools
One State Street
New Haven, Connecticut 06510

Projects in Mathematics for the Underachiever and/or Slow Learner Involving Staff Members of the University of Connecticut
Robert A. Shaw
University of Connecticut
Storrs, Connecticut 06268

A Criterion for the Selection of Mathematics Curriculum for Low Achievers
Andria M. Troutman
Supervisor, Secondary Mathematics
Hillsborough County Public Schools
Instructional Services Center
707 East Columbus Drive
Tampa, Florida 33602

A Mathematics Resource Center, the Key to Improve Curriculum
Wallace S. Manning, Project Director
School District 91
150 North Water
Idaho Falls, Idaho 83401

Upward Bound, Southern Illinois University
Ronald G. Trimmer
Assistant Director, Upward Bound
Box 54-A
Southern Illinois University
Edwardsville, Illinois 62025

Readiness for Mathematics
Ruth Radcliffe
Coordinator of Mathematics
Fayette County Schools
Lexington, Kentucky 40503

Resource Center for Low Achievers in Mathematics, Grades 7–9
Lurnice Begnaud
Mathematics Consultant
Lafayette Parish School Board
P.O. Box 2158
Lafayette, Louisiana 70501

Using a Laboratory Setting for Slow Learners
Ingrid B. Weise and William J. Clark
Mathematics Supervisors
Montgomery County Public Schools
Educational Services Center
850 North Washington Street
Rockville, Maryland 20850

The Oakland County Mathematics Project
Albert P. Shulte, Project Director
Oakland Schools
2100 Pontiac Lake Road
Pontiac, Michigan 48054

Mathematics Experience Program
Dale R. Rapp, Project Director
Washington Junior High School
Lake Avenue and Third Street
Duluth, Minnesota 55806

Project SOSO (Save Our Slow Ones)
Daisy Howell, Director
Mathematics Department
Delta State College
Cleveland, Mississippi 38732

I.P.I., Grades 1-6 at Washington
School
John F. Almond
Washington School
Emory Avenue
Trenton, New Jersey 08611

Plus Program Mathematics
Donald W. Anderson, Administrator
Plus Program Mathematics
Buffalo Public Schools
Room 432, City Hall
Buffalo, New York 14202

The Development of Mathematics Materials in Cincinnati for Low-achieving Pupils in Grades 7 and 8
Mildred Keiffer
Cincinnati Public Schools
Education Center
230 East Ninth Street
Cincinnati, Ohio 45202

The Philadelphia Low Achiever Mathematics Project
Sol Weiss, Project Director
West Chester State College
West Chester, Pennsylvania 19380

MCLL 'Pops' into the Classroom
Lanetha C. Branch, Lead Teacher
Mathematics/Science Component
Memphis Community Learning Laboratory
370 South Orleans Street
Memphis, Tennessee 38126

On Building a Program of Instruction for the Low-achieving Mathematics Student
E. L. Likins
Consultant, Secondary Mathematics
El Paso Public Schools
100 West Rio Grande Avenue
El Paso, Texas 79999

Tailoring Teaching to Tantalize and Tease Tense Teenagers
Rebecca Ellsworth
Coordinator of Mathematics
Henrico County Schools
P.O. Box 40
Highland Springs, Virginia 23075

Milwaukee Project
Vincent F. O'Connor
Supervising Teacher
Milwaukee Public Schools
P.O. Drawer 10K
Milwaukee, Wisconsin 53201

SMSG Programs for Low-achieving Junior High School Students

WILLIAM S. DeVENNEY

In 1964, in order to obtain comments and suggestions from the mathematical community, the School Mathematics Study Group (SMSG) convened a conference to discuss all aspects of mathematics education for below-average achievers. As a result of this conference, one of the activities undertaken by SMSG was the preparation of experimental materials for junior high school students. One of the objectives was to design materials that would relieve the students from the burdens of computation whenever possible by providing them with mathematical tables.

The reason for this approach was the conjecture that many underachieving junior high school students had experienced failure in elementary school mathematics, had been forced to do extensive drill in computation, had continued to fail, and that this course of events had led to an expectation of continuing failure which, in turn, led to intense dislike and even fear of computation.

Main Study, 1966–68

As a first step, an exploratory experiment was conducted during the 1965/66 school year. The encouraging results of this experiment led to the decision to continue the exploratory experiment through 1966/67 and to try the materials and methods developed during the previous year with a greater number of classes during 1966/67 and 1967/68.

Ten schools in the area south of San Francisco agreed to contribute one experimental seventh-grade class each, and five others allowed a seventh-grade class, designated as a control class, to be tested at the beginning and the end of each school year.

The schools participating in this study were chosen on the basis of consistency in socioeconomic setting and, for the purpose of seventh-grade placement, consistency in testing procedures.

In most of these schools, the California Achievement Test, in both reading and arithmetic, is administered to all sixth-grade pupils in the spring of each year. The results of this testing are then used by the junior high school counselor for placement of students in the seventh grade. These reading and arithmetic tests served as the screening instrument from which students were selected to participate in the study.

The 261 students who initially participated in the study had a mean grade-placement score in "Total Arithmetic" that placed them 1.0 year below actual grade level in arithmetic achievement. They were chosen from the bottom 20 percent of those tested.

Initially, certain behavior and attitude patterns were observed which were characteristic of the students in the experimental classes. Generally:

1. There was a severe lack of organization in their approach to learning.
2. They appeared to be immature compared to other seventh-grade students.
3. Their attention and interest spans were exceptionally short.
4. Negative attitudes existed toward mathematics and, in some cases, toward school in general.
5. Students exhibited a defeatist attitude with regard to their ability to succeed in mathematics.

Most of the teachers of the experimental classes had been teaching six years, with a B.A. as their highest degree. They had acquired in this time more than thirty academic credits beyond the B.A. Most had taken no credits in college mathematics at the level of calculus or beyond, and none had an undergraduate major or minor in mathematics. They had, however, taken four to six credits in methods of teaching mathematics and had involved themselves in other types of preparation in mathematics.

Throughout the school year, seminars with the teachers of the experimental classes were conducted monthly. Discussions centered on methods of presentation of various subject-matter topics and on problems encountered by individual teachers.

During the summers of 1966 and 1967, material was prepared to be used by the pupils in the experimental classes. Each unit consisted of a number of daily worksheets. The lessons on these worksheets were constructed to be short and complete within themselves, with many examples for the pupil to follow. If, because of the nature of the topic, a lesson required a more lengthy explanation, the lesson was then partially programmed. With the attention span of these pupils being as short as it was, this approach put the pupil quickly to work, allowed ample time for supervised study, and required little or no homework.

The worksheets were handed out daily and contained ample space to do the required work. Worksheets were placed in individual binders which, in most cases, were kept in the classroom.

A battery of tests was administered in both the fall and the spring of the seventh-grade year and in the spring of the eighth-grade year to students in both the experimental and the control classes. Additional tests were administered to the students in the experimental classes in the fall of the eighth-grade year.

The Stanford Achievement Test, Intermediate II, in Arithmetic Computation and Arithmetic Applications, was used as the standardized pretest and posttest for grade 7. The Advanced Test for junior high school students was used as the posttest for grade 8.

In addition, SMSG-constructed tests which measure mathematical concepts different from those of computation and applications and tests constructed to measure attitudes toward mathematics were administered to students in both the experimental and the control classes.

Evaluation of the experiment

Analysis of the test data was conducted for each of the two years of this experiment. The following results, which stem from these analyses, are presented in an extremely abridged manner. For complete discussion of these analyses and their educational implications, the reader should refer to SMSG *Reports* 5, 6, and 7.

1. For the two different standardized achievement tests used in this experiment, one test (CAT) showed the mean grade placement of the students to be 1.0 year below grade level whereas the other test (SAT) showed them to be closer to 2.5 years below grade level in computation. Teachers felt that, initially, the latter figure came closer to indicating the actual mathematical skills of their students.

2. The analysis of the relationship of reading ability to mathematics achievement was undertaken by means of a stepwise regression procedure. The results indicated that when other variables are taken into account, reading accounted for a relatively small part of the total variance.

3. Approximately 13 percent of the students in the experimental

classes and 10 percent of the students in the control classes were absent from class about 11 percent of the time. The mean absence for both groups was in excess of twenty-one class periods. The within-group differences on gains in computation and application between the absentees and the nonabsentees were not meaningful.

4. Students in the experimental classes evidenced substantial losses over the summer in computation (approximately 0.7 year) while at the same time they showed substantial gains in applications (approximately 0.7 year).

5. Analysis of the data for both the first and the second year of the experiment indicated that the best predictor of achievement in computation is, in fact, the students' pretest scores on computation. The amount of variance accounted for by the pretest scores on computation, though, was substantially reduced as the experiment progressed from the first to the second year.

However, regression of posttest scores on the pretest measures show that in no case was computation a significant contributing variable in predicting achievement on any of the other posttest scales.

6. On the SAT Computation scale, at the end of grade 7, students in the control classes showed a mean gain of 1.7 years. Students in the experimental classes showed a mean gain of 1.2 years.

At the end of grade 8, the mean grade placement scores for both experimental and control classes were not meaningfully different from the scores recorded at the end of grade 7.

7. On the SAT Applications scale, at the end of grade 8 there was no meaningful difference between the mean scores for the experimental and the control classes, the mean gain being 1.7 and 1.8 years respectively.

8. Five SMSG scales were constructed to measure mathematical concepts different from those of computation and application. At the end of grade 7, students in the experimental classes showed greater gains than those in the control classes. These gains were significantly greater on three of the five scales.

9. Psychological scales were used to measure student attitudes toward mathematics. Students in both experimental and control classes entered junior high school with what could be considered negative attitudes. By the end of grade 8, scores on these same attitude scales indicated that pupils in the experimental classes had developed attitudes that could be considered highly positive toward mathematics.

However, pupils in the control classes evidenced no such reversal of attitudes. If anything, they now displayed attitudes that could be considered even more negative than those displayed on entering junior high school.

Conclusion

In the opinion of the author, the most important contribution of this experiment was its demonstration that very low achieving junior high school pupils *can* learn some significant mathematics and at the same time *want to learn more.*

"Secondary School Mathematics—Special Edition"

Another SMSG activity undertaken as a result of the 1964 conference culminated in the publication of a junior high school mathematics program, *Secondary School Mathematics—Special Edition,* designed for students whose mathematics achievement in elementary school is very low.

The mathematical content of this junior high school program is derived from the new SMSG *Secondary School Mathematics* program. However, the format of this special edition is a decided departure from that of the usual classroom textbook.

This change of format comes as a result of the experiment with junior high school very low achievers described at the beginning of this paper. The two aspects of the experiment that proved to be extremely successful from the point of view of both the student and the teacher were (1) the development of materials that would relieve the student from the burdens of computation whenever possible and (2) the use of daily worksheets rather than a textbook. These two features have been retained in this *Special Edition.*

A group of writers prepared experimental versions of nine chapters during the summer of 1969. During the 1969/70 school year, sixteen seventh-grade classes, taught by fourteen teachers in eleven different schools, tried out the experimental chapters. All students were low achievers in mathematics. Several classes consisted of black students predominately and two of Mexican-American students.

Throughout the trial period participating teachers attended biweekly seminars in which the materials and teaching problems were discussed. Problems that arose were carefully noted, and means of counteracting them have been incorporated in a short commentary for teachers. Teacher evaluations for each chapter were systematically collected, and these evaluations served as a basis for the revision of the nine chapters during the summer of 1970. In addition, nine more experimental chapters were prepared and tried out in the 1970/71 school year by the same teachers and students who used the seventh-grade material. These nine chapters were revised during the summer of 1971 and are now available.

Although this material is presented to the student in the form of worksheets, it is not, in the ordinary sense, a workbook. Topics in each chapter are developed lesson by lesson. Teacher-led class discussion exercises are carefully programmed to lead the student to successful experiences in the exercise sets. Every effort has been made to construct lessons that prevent failure. The quantity of reading has been reduced to a minimum and the reading level kept low. At the end of each chapter are (1) a cumulative "self-test," which enables the student, on his own, to determine how he is progressing; (2) a practice test, which, in essence, tells the student what he is expected to know; and (3) a chapter test, which is administered by the teacher.

This material comes to the teachers in bound volumes. Each chapter consists of a number of lessons of one or more pages. Each page is perforated for easy removal. These pages can then be reproduced in quantities sufficient for the class by means of spirit-master units. Although this reproduction process may appear to place an extra burden on the teacher, in practice the extra time required to reproduce the material is more than compensated for by the positive results, both mathematically and behaviorally, that appear in the classroom.

During the trial year 1969/70, students using the experimental versions of the first nine chapters were tested in the fall and spring by means of the SMSG Attitude scales. Also, a coverage test on the first nine chapters was administered at the end of the school year.

Results on the Attitude scales were similar to those observed in the original experiment. Although the intensity of attitude change differed across groups, gains that were significant indicated a change from a negative to a more positive attitude toward mathematics.

The purpose of the coverage test was to determine whether the students in the program had learned and retained what they had covered. At the time of testing, the fastest class had just started chapter 9 ("Congruence"), and several of the slowest classes were just finishing chapter 7 ("Probability").

Evaluation of the coverage test proved to be inconclusive for the topics contained in some of the chapters. This was due to the fact that most classes had not completed the last two chapters in the sequence and also that the coverage test proved to be too long for most of the students to finish in the time period allowed.

The students appear to have learned and understood the topics they were able to cover during the school year—in particular, the material contained in the chapters "Structuring Space," "Functions," "Number Theory," "The Integers," and "Rational Numbers." For those students who were able to complete the test through the items on probability, scores indicate that topics in this chapter were also learned and understood. The item construction and positioning of these items in the coverage test made it impossible to determine whether or not the students had a grasp of the topics in the chapter "Flow Charts."

These test results do show that low-achieving junior high school students can learn and understand topics that are just now being included in experimental junior high school mathematics programs for college-capable students.

Obviously, SMSG has merely scratched the surface of the problem of providing suitable mathematics programs for disadvantaged and low-achieving students. It is hoped, however, that these activities will point the way to more numerous and more powerful efforts in the future.

More information may be obtained by writing directly to SMSG. The address is Cedar Hall, Stanford University, Stanford, California 94305.

Computer-assisted Instruction in New York City

MELVIN MENDELSOHN

In March 1968 the New York City Board of Education implemented an innovative educational tool—computer-assisted instruction (CAI). CAI assists the teacher by providing daily individualized instruction to large numbers of students.

Computer-assisted instruction applies modern technology to the classroom. The computer, with its great speed and vast memory, uses the information given to it by a curriculum author to drill 192 students simultaneously. Each student is given lessons geared to his own learning ability. He is asked questions hard enough to make him work but not too hard for him to answer.

The RCA Instructional 70 System in New York City uses a Spectra 70/45 computer located at Forty-second Street and Second Avenue. The student terminals are modified teletypewriters linked to the computer by telephone lines.

Both students and teachers use the terminals to communicate with the CAI system. The computer sends messages or questions to the terminal by printing on the page printer. The student or teacher enters his response or questions through the keyboard. The response is transmitted for evaluation and processing as it types out on the page printer. The computer responds to each question or response in less than one second.

The 192 student terminals are installed in sixteen elementary schools in the Bronx, Brooklyn, and Manhattan. In fifteen schools nine to thirteen terminals are installed in a central classroom where students go for their daily lessons. In one school a student terminal is installed in each of thirteen classrooms. During the 1968/69 school year 4,000 second- through sixth-grade students took daily CAI arithmetic lessons.

New York City's CAI system was made possible by a three-year grant totaling $3.1 million from the U.S. Office of Education under Title III of the federal Elementary and Secondary Education Act.

Few educational innovations have been watched as closely (and as hopefully) as New York City's CAI system. Would CAI promote learning? Would CAI help educators solve some of the problems they face?

The student

A student begins taking daily CAI lessons the day after he is registered. The CAI arithmetic curriculum was developed by Patrick Suppes, director of the Institute for Mathematical Studies in the Social Sciences at Stanford University. It is organized as a series of concept blocks. A concept block is a set of material relating to a particular idea or concept. A brief description of the material in each concept block for grade 2 is given in table 11.1.

The CAI arithmetic curriculum provides material at five levels of difficulty within each concept block. A summary of the material in concept block 1 for grade 2 is given in table 11.2.

Seven days are devoted to every drill concept block, as shown in

TABLE 11.1

Concept Block Description, Grade 2

Block	Description
1	Addition; facts to 10; horizontal format
2	Subtraction; facts to 10; horizontal format
3	Addition and subtraction; facts to 10; vertical format
4	Addition; facts to 10; mixed horizontal and vertical formats with variables
5	Mixed addition and subtraction; facts to 10; mixed horizontal and vertical formats with variables
6	Counting by ones and twos (finding what comes before and after); inequalities
7	Addition; stressing sums to 11, 12, 13; horizontal and vertical formats
8	Subtraction; stressing differences for sums to 11, 12, 13; horizontal and vertical formats
9	Mixed addition and subtraction to 13; horizontal and vertical formats
10	Units to measure; counting; inequalities
11	Addition; stressing sums to 14, 15, 16; horizontal and vertical formats
12	Subtraction; stressing differences for sums to 14, 15, 16; horizontal and vertical formats
13	Mixed addition and subtraction; sums to 14, 15, 16; horizontal and vertical formats
14	Units of measure; counting to 200, inequalities; some word problems
15	Fractions; 1/2, 1/3, 1/4
16	Addition; stressing sums to 17, 18, 19; horizontal and vertical formats
17	Subtraction; stressing differences for sums to 17, 18, 19; horizontal and vertical formats
18	Mixed addition and subtraction to 19; horizontal and vertical formats
19	Units of measure; counting; inequalities; word problems
20	Multiplication, through 9×9
21	Commutative and associative laws for addition, subtraction, multiplication
22	Mixed drill: addition, subtraction, multiplication; vertical formats
23	Mixed drill: fractions, units of measure, inequalities, multiplication
24	Final review: multiple-choice, mostly word problems.

figure 11.1. The pretest, given on the first day of a concept drill, establishes the level of difficulty for the next day's drill. The student takes drill lessons on days 2–6, and his results on these drills (except for the sixth day, immediately preceding the posttest) determine his

TABLE 11.2

Grade 2, Concept Block 1

Level of Difficulty	Format
1: sums to 6	$a + b = $ _____
2: sums to 7	$a + b = $ _____
3: sums to 10	$a + b = $ _____
4: sums to 10	$a + b = $ _____, $a + $ _____ $= c$, _____ $+ b = c$
5: sums to 10	$a + b = c + $ _____, $a + b = $ _____ $+ d$

placement on the following day. If a student does well on a drill, scoring 85 percent or more, he is moved to the next higher level the next day. With a score of 60 to 84 percent, he stays at the same level. With a score below 60, he moves down a level. On the seventh day the student takes a posttest.

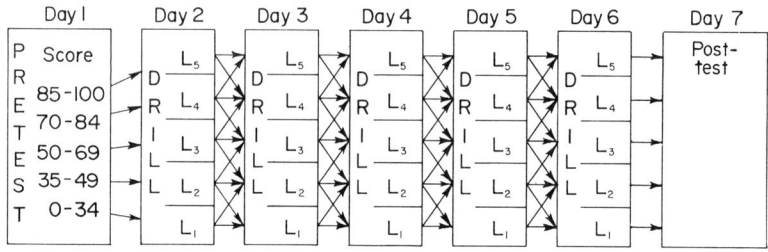

Fig. 11.1. Branching structure for drill lessons

After a student has completed four concept blocks, he is given review material in addition to drill material. Review lessons are selected from the concept block on which the student made his lowest posttest score. As figure 11.2 indicates, the student is given four review lessons (on days 2–5) and takes a review test on the sixth day. The review test score is substituted for the previous posttest score on that concept block.

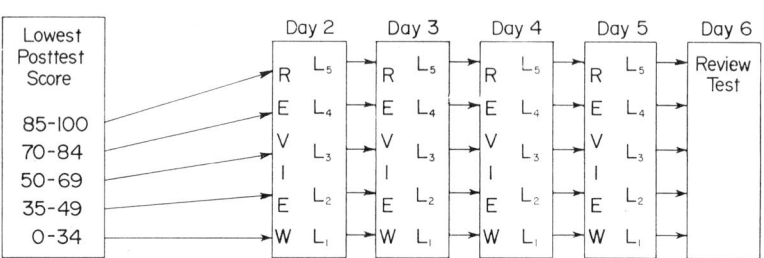

Fig. 11.2. Branching structure for review lessons

Each time a student takes a CAI lesson, he goes to a convenient terminal and taps out his assigned number and first name. The computer immediately confirms the student's identification by typing out his last name.

In the same split second the computer checks the student's previous performance and determines what material he is to study. It begins the day's lesson as soon as the student's name is completed. As the student answers the problems or questions, the computer identifies and helps him correct his errors and ends the lesson by telling him how well he did. Each lesson lasts approximately ten minutes. The flow chart in figure 11.3 depicts the problem-procedure program.

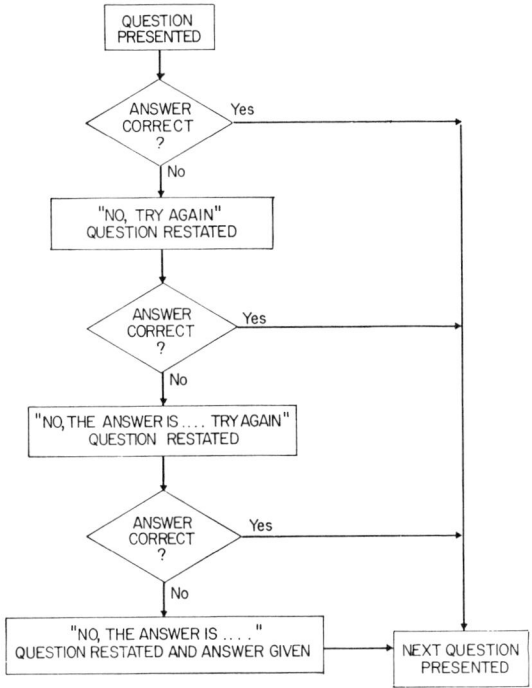

Fig. 11.3. Problem-procedure program

Evaluation, all students

An impartial evaluation of the New York City CAI program prepared by the City University of New York confirms that students using CAI learn more than students not using CAI. Consistently, in nearly all groups, the CAI students made greater gains in arithmetic achievement than the non-CAI students with whom they were compared. This study ("Evaluation of the 1968–69 New York Computer-Assisted Instruction Project in Elementary Arithmetic") was prepared by the Division of Teacher Education at the City University of New York. The dual purpose of the evaluation was to determine the effect of the CAI drill and practice program on pupil achievement and to describe the opinions and attitudes of pupils, teachers, and administrators.

Students in sixteen experimental schools and four control schools were pretested in January 1969. Their progress was charted for the next five months. A posttest was administered during the last two weeks in June. The pretest was taken by 4,573 students (4,077 CAI and 496 non-CAI). The posttest was taken by 3,282 students (2,940 CAI and 342 non-CAI).

The City University of New York (CUNY) selected the Metropolitan Achievement Test (MAT) for the evaluation study because it is used by the New York City Board of Education in evaluating pupil achievement. Form C of the MAT was administered in January 1969 for the pretest, and the same form was administered in June 1969 for the posttest.

The principal statistical method used in the study was the comparison of groups in terms of the means and standard deviations of test scores. The significance of differences was tested by analysis of variance. Differences were considered significant if they were less than the ".01 level of significance."

Data based on all students who took the pretest and the posttest were analyzed separately by grade. The mean raw score gains were higher in all grades for the CAI groups. The difference in gain scores is significant for all students in grades 2, 3, 4, and 5, as indicated in table 11.3.

TABLE 11.3

COMPARISON OF MAT ARITHMETIC COMPUTATION
RAW-SCORE GAINS EARNED BY ALL STUDENTS

GRADE	CAI Gains			Non-CAI Gains			p
	N	Mean	SD	N	Mean	SD	
2	340	6.78	5.16	79	3.50	4.51	$<.01$
3	726	12.68	5.92	98	9.31	5.34	$<.01$
4	790	8.34	5.85	93	6.10	6.75	$<.01$
5	717	8.13	6.08	49	2.89	8.09	$<.01$
6	367	5.54	6.83	23	2.69	7.44	n.s.

Raw score gains were analyzed by grade-equivalent levels. (A child theoretically starts in grade 1 at level 1.0. After one month in school he should gain one "point" and be at level 1.1; after two months, at level 1.2; and so on.) CAI students made significant gains in grades 2, 3, 4, and 5. Figure 11.4 illustrates the grade-equivalent score gains.

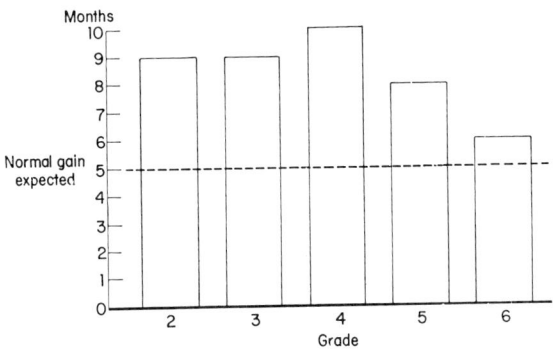

Fig. 11.4. MAT Arithmetic Computation grade-equivalent score gains earned by CAI students, grouped according to grade

Socioeconomic status

In large urban schools the student's socioeconomic status is an important variable in evaluating student progress. CUNY evaluators determined that CAI is extremely effective with disadvantaged children through the fourth grade. The statistics are illustrated in figure 11.5 (where the numbers of students in each class is shown in parentheses). The fact that fifth- and sixth-grade children did not show major gains may be attributable to the "cumulative-deficit phenomenon." Learning deficits are cumulative, since learning builds on learning. That is, all learning beyond the first few weeks or months of life depends on previous learning. When prerequisite habits or skills have not been learned, the capacity for new learning is impaired. Data from the CUNY evaluation seem to corroborate the theory that it is easier to overcome the cumulative-deficit phenomenon in the earlier years of school.

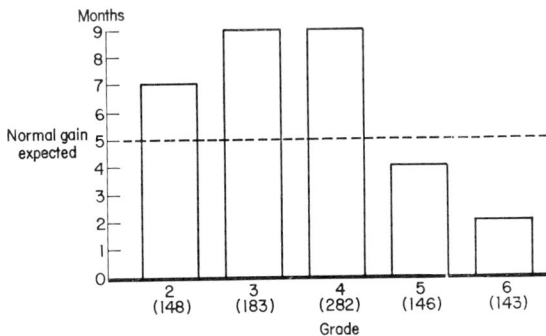

Fig. 11.5. MAT Arithmetic Computation grade-equivalent score gains earned by CAI students in schools located in predominately low socioeconomic areas

Matched pairs

Students in the non-CAI group were matched with students in the CAI group, and their score gains were compared (see table 11.4 and fig. 11.6). Scores from the computation pretest were listed by

TABLE 11.4

COMPARISON OF MAT ARITHMETIC COMPUTATION
RAW-SCORE GAINS EARNED BY MATCHED STUDENTS

| | | Pretest | | Gains | | | | |
| | | CAI & Non-CAI | | CAI | | Non-CAI | | |
Grade	N	Mean	SD	Mean	SD	Mean	SD	p
2	76	18.0	5.7	7.3	4.2	3.7	4.5	<.01
3	96	19.8	6.1	13.0	5.4	9.3	5.4	<.01
4	91	31.5	8.1	7.3	5.5	5.8	5.6	n.s.
5	47	20.7	9.4	10.7	6.8	3.2	8.1	<.01
6	23	35.3	7.6	4.2	5.2	2.7	7.4	n.s.

grade. For each non-CAI computation pretest raw score, a match was found in the CAI group. If an exact match was not found, a score within one point of the score to be matched was selected. If more than one CAI student earned a score that could be matched with a non-CAI student's score, a match was selected at random. A

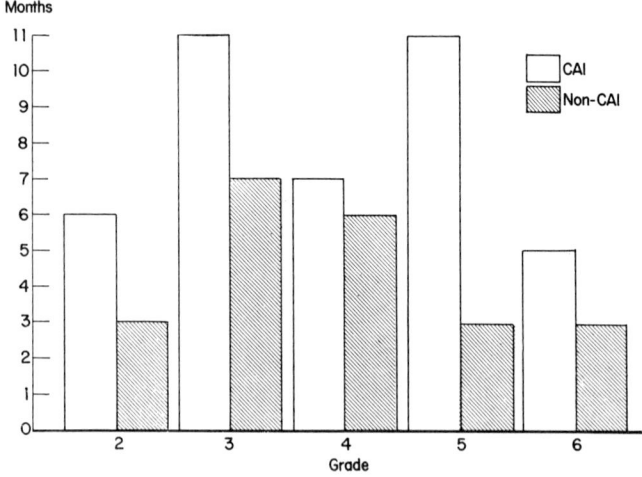

Fig. 11.6. Comparison of MAT Arithmetic Computation grade-equivalent score gains earned by matched students

total of 333 matched pairs were identified; the CAI students scored higher gains than the non-CAI students. As table 11.4 indicates, the most significant differences were found in grades 2, 3, and 5. The raw-score gains earned by matched students are analyzed by grade-equivalence levels in figure 11.6.

Problem-solving concepts

Statistics in the CUNY evaluation indicate that the CAI student has higher computational skills than the non-CAI student. There is a high correlation between computation scores and problem-solving concept scores on the MAT. The correlation between computation scores and problem-solving concept scores ranges from .72 in grade 2 to .88 in grade 6. This means that CAI assists the student in mastering the ideas (problem-solving concepts) involved in computation (see fig. 11.7). For example, he understands > and <. He knows what "1" means in 135 and that $\frac{4}{3} > \frac{3}{4}$.

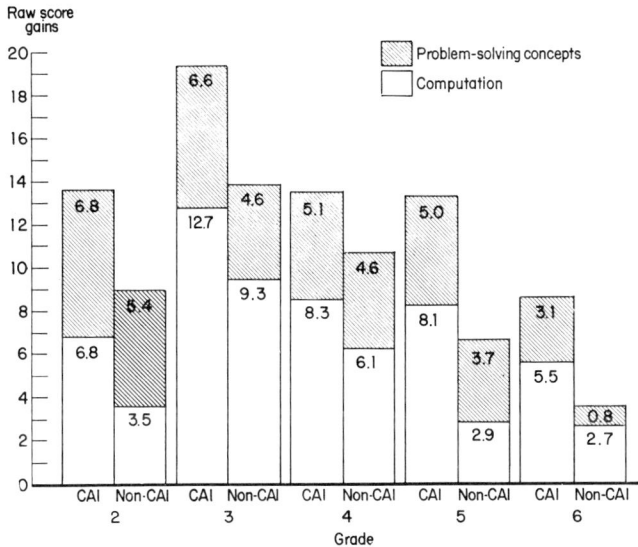

Fig. 11.7. Comparison of MAT Arithmetic Computation raw score gains and Problem-Solving Concept raw score gains earned by students grouped according to grade

Conclusion

As in most studies, prudence must be exercised in drawing conclusions. Two factors are pertinent in the CUNY evaluation study: the time interval for the study was relatively short (five months); and several variables, such as selection of teachers, selection of schools, and number of hours of arithmetic instruction, which were not controlled in the study, could have contributed to the earned gains.

Despite these limitations, the study is meaningful because significant differences were found with large numbers of students across grade level and social class.

The most significant differences in favor of CAI groups occurred—

1. in all students in all schools in grades 2, 3, 4, and 5;
2. in matched pairs of students drawn from the entire school population in grades 2, 3, and 5;
3. in all students in schools located in predominately low socioeconomic areas in grades 2 and 3.

Further information may be obtained by writing to Melvin Mendelsohn, Director of Computer Assisted Instruction, at the Board of Education of the City of New York, 229 East 42d Street, New York, New York 10017.

Mathematics for Spanish-speaking Pupils (MSP)

SIDNEY SHARRON

GLORIA COX

No two school districts are alike; no two schools are alike; and no two classes are alike; yet the similarities often outweigh the differences. The report that follows describes what took place when a committee responded to a need of a specific portion of the student population in the Los Angeles City Unified School District. To repeat, similarities often outweigh differences, and if one looks on this report as a kind of model that may be generally adaptable to other situations, then at least the start may be made to meet a variety of needs in a classroom situation.

Background

In May of 1967 the California state legislature modified the Education Code to permit school districts to offer bilingual instruction when it is advantageous to the pupils. The new legislation reaffirmed the state policy to ensure the mastery of English by all pupils; but it also provided a means by which bilingual instruction could accompany the systematic, sequential, and regular instruction in the English language.

Achievement tests and dropout studies indicate that the average level of educational achievement in East Los Angeles schools is below that of the pupils in the District as a whole. Most of these pupils are of Mexican descent, and the probable reasons for the low achievement could be separated into two main categories: (1) cultural, linguistic, social, and economic factors that appear to be characteristic of the Mexican-American population and (2) the other factors that are common to low-achieving pupils in general. Many differences exist within the Mexican-American school population with respect to the degree of acculturation, dominance of English or Spanish, and school achievement; but in recognizing these differences, one must guard against equating "Mexican-American pupil" with "low achiever."

A large number of Mexican-American pupils do not speak English until they enter school. The beginning school experience is usually one of complete failure because the pupil is not able to communicate with his teacher. To say the least, it is obvious that a pupil will have difficulty in understanding mathematical concepts if he does not understand the language.

Development

In November 1967 a committee of District personnel proposed that a pilot seventh-grade mathematics program be developed for junior high schools having a large number of Spanish-speaking pupils. A competent, bilingual Mexican-American teacher of mathematics in one of the East Los Angeles high schools was chosen to work as a consultant with the mathematics supervisor in developing and implementing the program. It is interesting to note that the consultant's first language was Spanish and that she was unable to speak English when she entered kindergarten.

It was intended that this project would offer a means of finding ways to improve computational skills of bilingual pupils of the Mexican-American community who are achieving below grade level in mathematics. The thinking was that the pupil may respond more favorably to a mathematics class that is presented in an atmosphere in tune with his environment, his social behavior, and his means of communication.

A search for suitable mathematics textbooks, written in Spanish and/or English but depending mostly on the mathematical notation for developing concepts and practice, proved fruitless. Although some texts were found that were written in both English and Spanish versions, the level of both the mathematics and the language used was beyond the comprehension of the students the project was trying to reach. Consequently, the writing team prepared their own text material. With the start of the spring semester (February 1968) there were six junior high schools engaged in the pilot program. During the summer of 1968 the text was expanded to cover the full year of seventh-grade mathematics, and during the 1968/69 school year the same six junior high schools offered this special mathematics program. Students selected for this program were required to have parental consent.

Description of the program

The text is a consumable, write-in collection of sequential mathematics lessons consisting of sixteen parts. Each part has approximately seven or eight lessons using 16 pages, making the total text 256 pages long. There is a pupil's text, English version; a pupil's text, Spanish version; and an annotated teacher's edition in English. The content is built around an elementary introduction to the basic operations, first on whole numbers and then on nonnegative rationals. It is assumed that the pupils who will use this material have not been successful in mathematics and that it may be rewarding to start with a careful elementary presentation, using simple language when the mathematical notation is not adequate, and gradually increase the level of mathematical activity to bring it into the mainstream of the regular seventh-grade course. The general topics include:

Addition, subtraction, multiplication, and division of whole numbers and the same operations for nonnegative rationals, including decimal fractions
Number patterns and relationships
Introduction to set concepts
Introduction to geometry and geometric constructions
Ordered pairs and graphs
Probability and statistics
Addition and subtraction of integers

The program is not dependent on the text alone, but rather on an interaction between pupil and teacher with the text being a catalyst. Three plans were offered to the school:

Plan 1: *For pupils who speak and read Spanish and cannot function effectively in English*
   A bilingual teacher is to teach mathematics in Spanish. Pupils are to use text materials written in Spanish.

Plan 2: *For pupils who speak but do not read Spanish*
   A bilingual teacher is to teach mathematics in English, speaking Spanish as needed. Pupils are to use text materials written in English.

Plan 3: *For pupils who speak Spanish and have some proficiency in reading Spanish*
   A bilingual teacher is to teach mathematics in English and Spanish. Pupils are to use text materials written in English or Spanish or both.

It was understood that a school could elect to offer any one of these plans, any combination of them, or perhaps a plan of its own.

Figures 11.8 and 11.9 show lesson sheets taken from the English and Spanish editions of *Mathematics Lessons (MSP Project)*, book 2 (for junior high school), which was published by the Los Angeles City Schools in 1968.

Results and evaluation

The students responded favorably to the program, and most of the students asked to continue in the class the following fall semester. Questionnaires were sent to the parents, and the general response was favorable. An interesting side effect was that some parents were able, for the first time, to help their children with their school work. For the first time, these parents were able to read the textbook the student brought home.

An evaluation of the program was made, using forms X and W of the California Arithmetic Test as a pretest and a posttest respectively. A statistically significant difference at the .05 confidence level was found in favor of the experimental group when the relative starting points of the experimental group and the control group were considered.

Conclusion

Initially, the design of the project was determined by a committee in response to a need made clear through requests from teachers,

MATHEMATICS LESSONS
(MSP Project)

Name _____

Date _____

Part X   **Lesson 6**

FILL IN THE ☐ WITH $=$, $<$, OR $>$ TO MAKE THE SENTENCE TRUE.

Sample: 1.2 ☐ 2.1   *Sample:*   .3 ☐ .1

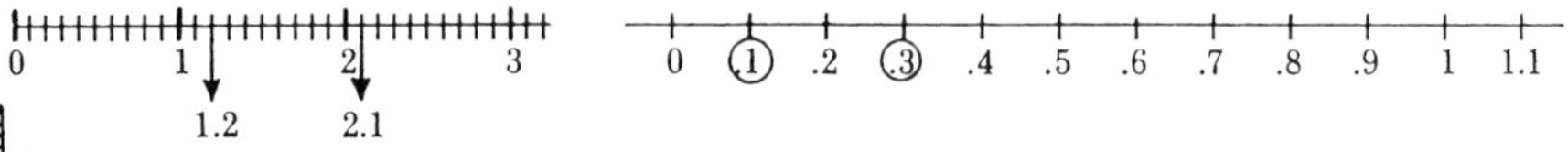

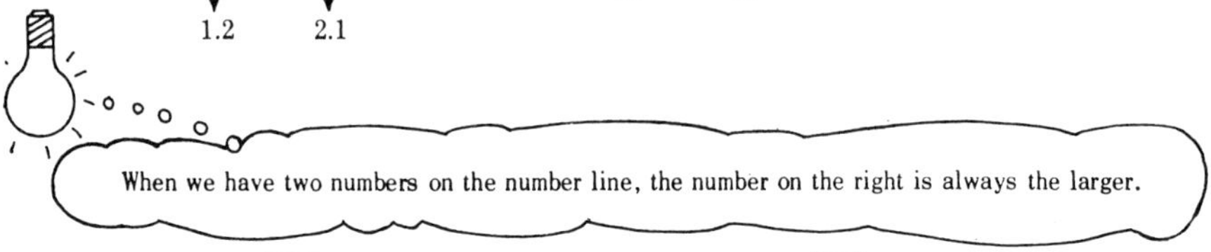

When we have two numbers on the number line, the number on the right is always the larger.

So,   1.2 $<$ 2.1   and   .3 $>$ .1

START FILLING.

         a   b

1.   .5 ☐ .7   .9 ☐ .6

2.   2.4 ☐ 1.9   3.5 ☐ 4

3.   .78 ☐ .89   .99 ☐ .88

4.   .231 ☐ .046   1.46 ☐ 14.60

5.   19.66 ☐ 19.76   17.09 ☐ 17.20

6.   19.68 ☐ $19\frac{68}{100}$ .0025 ☐ .0024

Los Angeles City Schools   •   Division of Instructional Planning and Services   •   Copyright © 1968

Fig. 11.8. English version

LECCIONES DE MATEMÁTICAS
(MSP Project)

Nombre _____
Fecha _____

Parte X   *Lección 6*

ESCRIBAN =, <, o > EN EL ☐ PARA QUE LA FRASE SEA CORRECTA.

Ejemplo: 1.2 ☐ 2.1   *Ejemplo:* .3 ☐ .1

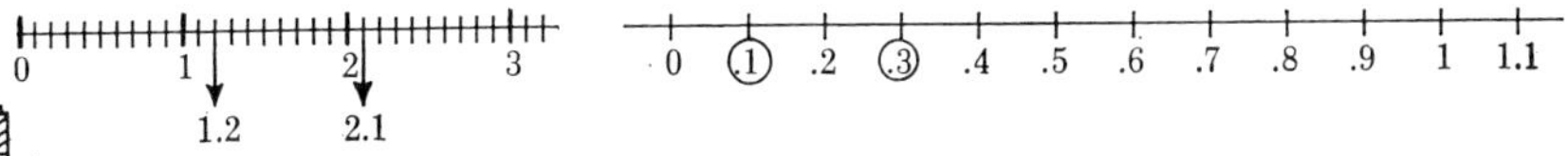

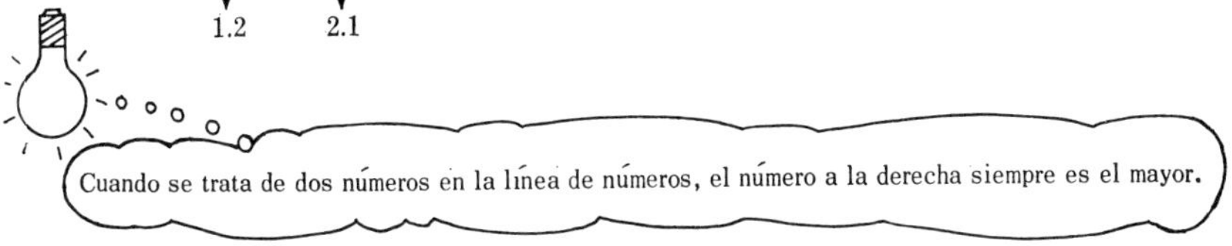

|++++++++|++++++++|++++++++| ─┼──┼──┼──┼──┼──┼──┼──┼──┼──┼──┼─
0   1   2↓   3   0 ① .2 ③ .4 .5 .6 .7 .8 .9 1 1.1
         1.2   2.1

Cuando se trata de dos números en la línea de números, el número a la derecha siempre es el mayor.

Así es que, 1.2 < 2.1   y   .3 > .1

EMPIECEN A ESCRIBIR.
            a   b

1.   .5 ☐ .7   .9 ☐ .6

2.   2.4 ☐ 1.9   3.5 ☐ 4

3.   .78 ☐ .89   .99 ☐ .88

4.   .231 ☐ .046   1.46 ☐ 14.60

5.   19.66 ☐ 19.76   17.09 ☐ 17.20

6.   19.68 ☐ 19 $\frac{68}{100}$ .0025 ☐ .0024

Los Angeles City Schools • Division of Instructional Planning and Services • Copyright © 1968

Fig. 11.9. Spanish version

pupils, and the community. However, when classroom implementation began, the actual experience of all these groups provided feedback that contributed to the revision and expansion of the text. The following are some of the major points that encouraged and influenced the expansion of the program:

1. One teacher stated that without a course of this type, many of his students would remain almost at a standstill in mathematics education.
2. Five additional junior high schools asked to be included in the program the next year.
3. In one school the teacher asked the students for a written appraisal of the MSP class. The replies were definitely in favor of the program and expressed a desire to continue having classes of this type.
4. Most of the parents that were contacted regarding this project were interested in the approach and agreed to have the children participate in the program.

As a result of this experience, a teacher committee recommended the MSP textbooks for adoption in the Los Angeles City Unified School District, and now these materials are available to any of the junior high schools that wish to use them. The original 5,000 copies have been consumed, and the schools are now working with the materials provided by a second printing.

Although bilingual education is not the most pressing matter in many areas throughout the nation, exposure of this project to other school districts has always been met with a great deal of enthusiasm and interest. One teacher from Canada felt that the same type of program could be carried off successfully in her community, using French instead of Spanish. There have been requests for copies of this material from educators representing many areas, among which are California, Arizona, New Mexico, Texas, New York, and Florida. The address of the Los Angeles City Unified School District is **1849 Blake Avenue, Los Angeles, California 90039**.

Mathematics for Basic Education (Grades 7-11)

VINCENT BRANT

In the summer of 1963 the Board of Education of Baltimore County began the first of several summer workshops to construct a program appropriate to the needs of students classified as slow learners (a program not only for mathematics but for other disciplines as well). By 1969 the program in mathematics, titled "Basic Education in Mathematics," was being implemented to a considerable degree in grades 7-10, as shown in the following data:

Grade 7	1,080 students	46 sections
Grade 8	966 students	44 sections
Grade 9	797 students	36 sections
Grade 10	565 students	26 sections

Work on the grade 11 program was begun in the 1970 summer workshop and completed in the 1971 summer workshop.

The principals in the schools have limited the average class size to 23 students for this special program. They have also provided for parallel scheduling of classes, which permits a low achiever who may have overcome some of his difficulties to be transferred easily to a more advanced section. This procedure avoids "locking" a student in a slow-learner section.

The exploratory 1963 and 1964 summer workshops produced guidelines and recommendations. In particular, the characteristics and needs of the slow learner were identified. Criteria were agreed upon as follows:

MEASURABLE CRITERIA

1. IQ range 75-90 from at least two group tests or an individual test
2. Percentiles on group tests of mental ability and achievement ranging from 0 to 19 (approximately two or more years below grade level in reading comprehension and arithmetic)
3. Teacher grades—consistently below average

TRAITS CRITERIA

1. Limited academic interest
2. Difficulties in planning and carrying out work without supervision

3. Limited creativity and intellectual curiosity
4. Short attention span
5. Severe limitation in the ability to communicate orally or in writing

The philosophy agreed on by the workshop committee may be stated briefly as follows:

1. The slow learner should be educated in his own right and to the maximum of his ability.
2. Any adaptation of an academically oriented program must surely fail.
3. A program of mathematics for the slow learner should be based on the latest developments and research in learning theory and on an appropriate selection and reorganization of mathematical concepts and skills.
4. Proper pacing of the concepts and skills must underlie the structure.
5. All the human resources of the educational system—the mathematics teacher, the principal, the mathematics supervisor, the resource teachers, the guidance counselor, and other specialists—must be brought to bear on this problem.

The writing committee agreed initially to construct a program in mathematics for grades 7–10 only, making this limitation because (1) available research indicated difficulty in identifying the slow learner in the primary grades and (2) the problem of the slow learner seemed to be most acute at the junior high school level.

The 1966 summer workshop produced a resource manual of activities—developmental, recreational, and computational—as a first stage in the work. The selection of topics for instructional activities was based on two considerations—mathematical significance and appeal to the interest and curiosity of the students. This resource manual was unstructured with regard to the sequence of topics and the placement of topics according to grade level. The subsequent summer workshop in 1967 provided structure regarding the grade placement of topics and the continuity of desired behavioral outcomes as they relate to mathematical concepts and skills.

The key features of Basic Education in Mathematics are the use of behavioral objectives, the "banded" approach and sample two-week unit, mathematics laboratories, instructional materials (devices and games), and in-service courses to provide orientation for teachers in this program.

Since the concept of behavioral objectives focuses on the performance of the student, and since slow learners are poor performers, it was decided that behavioral objectives should be a foundation stone in this program. Walbesser's nine "action verbs" were used to construct the behavioral objectives. These action verbs are *identify, distinguish, construct, name, order, describe, state* [a rule], *apply* [the rule], and *demonstrate*. In the course guides, these objectives are stated in terms of the desired behavioral outcomes on the part of the student. Then student activities are designed to achieve these outcomes. Finally, the suggested assessment procedures indicate ways in which the student shows whether or not he has acquired the desired behavior. In effect, the elements of three sets—the set of objectives, the set of learning activities, and the set of asssessment items—should correspond on a one-to-one basis. Thus the guide emphasizes three phases: *objectives, instruction,* and *assessment*. An example of these phases is pictured in

Fig. 11.10

figure 11.10. Other examples may be found in chapter 3 of this yearbook. Although the committee firmly believed that the behavioral-objective approach would materially improve instruction, it was cognizant that an over-zealous and inappropriate use of behavioral objectives might weaken the program. There was agreement about two pitfalls to be avoided:

1. The fact that an instructional activity lends itself well to specifying well-defined behavioral objectives is not sufficient justification for including that activity in the curriculum.
2. The fact that an instructional activity does not lend itself well to specific behavioral objectives is not sufficient cause for the exclusion of that activity from the curriculum.

The 1967 summer workshop contributed scope and a topical sequence to Basic Education in Mathematics. The NCTM "Second Report of the Commission on Post-war Plans" (*Mathematics Teacher*, May 1945) was helpful in determining the terminal competencies for these non-college-bound students. The topical divisions of the curriculum guides listed below are based on areas of mathematical competencies for the slow learner:

Numbers, Operations, and
  Algorithms
Geometry
Measurement
Probability and Statistics

Graphing
Algebra
Logic
Recreational
  Activities

Behaviors were assigned to each concept and skill in each area of mathematical competency. This information is shown in the curriculum guides by a series of charts—master charts and grade-level charts. Sample pages of these charts are shown in figures 11.11 and 11.12. The master charts give overviews of the mathematical content and behaviors that the students are to acquire in grades 7–10. Thus the teacher can use the master charts to obtain a picture of the total mathematics program for the slow-learning student. The grade-level charts for each area are identical with the master chart except that they contain only the information for a specific grade. These are used by the teacher to obtain an overview of those behaviors that should be acquired by the student in a specific area of mathematical competency for that particular year.

To assist the teacher in helping students attain the desired behaviors, the writing committee also constructed for each grade a list of behavioral objectives, which enable the teacher to interpret the details omitted in the charts. The teacher uses these objectives when planning lessons, since they state precisely what is expected of the student. By the end of the year, the students should be able to exhibit most of the behaviors mentioned.

The "banded" approach is another key feature of Basic Education in Mathematics. It is based on one of the traits of the slow learner—a limited span of attention. This approach is simply a flexible way of organizing instructional activities in the class period. Normally, the lesson is divided into three time bands, although it may be divided into two or even four time bands, depending on the nature of the activities. For example, a unit in geometry might be taught along with related activities on fundamental operations. Thus, the unit in geometry is split into smaller parcels and presented over a longer period of time rather than being presented as a two-week concentrated unit. The major portion of the lesson might be presented during a 25-minute segment, since this seems to be about the maximum

UNIT _____ GEOMETRY _____   GRADE(S) _____ Six through Ten _____

TOPIC	NAME	IDENTIFY	DEMON-STRATE	CONSTRUCT	DESCRIBE	STATE THE PRINCIPLE	APPLY THE PRINCIPLE	INTERPRET	ORDER	DISTIN-GUISHING
Point	6	6								
Line	6	6		6	6					
Plane	6	6		7	6					
Closed Path	6	6		6	6					6
Segment	6,7	6,7	7	6,7	6					6
Congruent Segments	9	9	9		9					
Ray	6,7	6,7		6	6					6
Angles	6,7	6,7	7	6	6					
Vertex	7	7			7					
Right Angles	6	6	9	6	6					9
Acute Angles	9	9		9	9					9
Obtuse Angles	9	9		9	9					9
Straight Angles	9	9		9	9					9
Vertical Angles	9	9		9	9	9	9			
Supplementary Angles	9	9		9	9					9
Complementary Angles	9	9		9	9					9
Congruent Angles	9	9	9	9	9					
Triangles	6,7	6,7	10	6	6					

Fig. 11.11

UNIT ____GEOMETRY____   GRADE(S) ____Seven____

TOPIC	NAME	IDENTIFY	DEMON-STRATE	CONSTRUCT	DESCRIBE	STATE THE PRINCIPLE	APPLY THE PRINCIPLE	INTERPRET	ORDER	DISTIN-GUISHING
Plane				7						
Segment	7	7	7	7						
Ray	7	7								
Angles	7	7	7							
Vertex	7	7			7					
Triangles	7	7								
Parallel Lines	7	7	7	7	7					7
Midpoint of Segment	7	7			7					
Quadrilaterals	7	7		7	7					
Trapezoid	7	7		7	7					7
Parallelogram	7	7		7	7					7
Rectangles	7	7		7	7					7
Square	7	7		7	7					7
Rhombus	7	7		7	7					
Circle			7							
Radius			7			7				
Diameter			7			7				
Chord	7		7	7	7					

Fig. 11.12

length of time that these students can concentrate on any one activity. A sample unit of banded lessons is given in figure 11.13.

SAMPLE UNIT OF BANDED LESSONS - Grade 7
OUTLINE OF TOPICS

LESSON	BAND I	BAND II	BAND III
1	Drill-geometric figures	Parallel lines	4-digit numbers
2	Drill-patterns	Symbols for segment and ray, assessment of parallel lines	Puzzle-optical illusions
3	Math Builder	Copying segments -straightedge	Tape-addition
4	Puzzle-multiplication and addition	Copying segments -straightedge and compass	Math Builder
5	Math Builder	Assessment-copying segments	Cross Number Puzzle-place value
6	Drill-patterns	Midpoint-paper folding	Construction of ruler
7	Math Builder	Midpoint-compass and ruler	Puzzle-multiplication and addition
8	Puzzle-division	Assessment-midpoints	Cross Number Puzzle-multiplication
9	Math Builder	Symbols for angle, vertex	Puzzle-renaming numbers
10	Tape-verbal problems	Copying angles-compass and straightedge	Tic-Tac-Toe game
11	Diagnostic Test-addition of whole numbers	Copying angles	Continuation of Tic-Tac-Toe game
12	Puzzle-calendars	Assessment-copying angles	Puzzle-hidden words

Fig. 11.13

Band I is usually a short activity of about 5–10 minutes' duration. For example, students may review their number facts (using a controlled reader projector for mathematics), have an oral number puzzle, or complete a number pattern. The activities that might be used for maintaining skills and arousing curiosity are numerous.

Band II usually contains the major topic for the day. It is about 25 minutes in length. For this activity, specific behavioral objectives are stated. Students are exposed to instructional activities that are designed to enable them to acquire the desired behaviors. Assessment procedures might also be employed here to determine whether students have acquired some of the behaviors specified in the objectives. Remaining objectives may be assessed in other bands of subsequent lessons.

Band III is usually a short activity of 5–10 minutes. This band can be managed in two ways. First, all the students might begin work at the same time on a class activity. Second, as each student completes his work in Band II, he begins some planned individual or small-group activity. For example, he may go to a specified place in the room and choose an interesting puzzle or game, work on an SRA computational-skills kit, or listen to a tape at the listening post. This approach keeps the students actively involved in learning activities rather than just waiting for the class to finish the work in Band II. Thus a more efficient use is made of the student's time.

An important reason for using the banded approach is the necessity of providing continuous experiences for the maintenance of computational skills. Research shows that low-ability students provided with continuous experiences in computational skills reach a maximum that serves as a plateau. However, if experiences in maintaining skills are withdrawn, a marked decrease in these skills results. For this reason, each lesson using the banded approach makes provision for some type of maintenance of computational skills.

For each of the curriculum guides, the writing committee constructed a two-week sample unit which could be used at the beginning of the school year as a detailed illustration of the use of the guide. Each two-week sample unit contains (1) a block plan indicating the topics to be presented each day and (2) detailed lesson plans indicating the materials to be used, the behavioral objectives for Band II, suggested methods of presentation, student worksheets, and assessment items.

The student activities section contains units that may be removed from the guide and used to make thermal ditto masters for student worksheets or transparencies for the teacher.

The use of mathematics laboratories, mathematical devices, and games (many of them homemade) is also an integral part of Basic Education in Mathematics. Materials for this program are being added so that the teacher has a considerable variety with which to motivate students.

Curriculum guides and materials, by themselves, are not sufficient to ensure the success of such a program. A continuing activity of the Office of Mathematics has been the orientation of teachers to this program through a series of in-service courses, which have been granted two hours of professional credit by the Maryland State Department of Education.

This program has not been evaluated through a formal research design because of a lack of personnel and funds. However, informal evaluations by teachers, staff, and outside educators indicate that the program is proceeding quite well. To be sure, much work remains to be done. Additional units and activities need to be constructed. More teachers need to be trained to implement this program. New commercially produced materials have to be analyzed with regard to behavioral objectives. But in general, these efforts have shown the feasibility and practicality of using a behavior-objectives approach so that these objectives have an immediate application in the classroom. Furthermore, the construction of a program for slow learners does not have to depend on state or federal funding, although this is helpful. Basic Education in Mathematics is a project locally initiated and locally funded by Baltimore County.

Owing to a lack of production facilities and limited personnel and funds, the Office of Mathematics has been able to produce only enough guides for use in the county schools. Thus it has not been possible to produce enough guides for general distribution or purchase.

For further information, interested educators may contact Vincent Brant, Coordinator, Office of Mathematics, Board of Education of Baltimore County, 6901 North Charles Street, Towson, Maryland 21204.

The Mathematics Laboratory at the Sir R. L. Borden Secondary School

MRS. L. R. STROBEL

The Sir R. L. Borden Secondary School in Scarborough, Ontario, was opened more than five years ago specifically to accommodate the underachiever. A condition of enollment is a record of failure at the elementary level. The total enrollment averages 700, the course is three years long, and the average entrance age is 13.4 years.

The school year is divided into four ten-week terms. There are no formal exams. The student is in shop classes half the day and in academic classes the other half. He may choose a program of three shops, of which one is a major and two are related, from twenty-six different shops. These include culinary arts, painting and decorating, plumbing, hairdressing, textiles, auto service, and so on. Of his four academic subjects, English and mathematics are compulsory.

The principal problem in rekindling the reluctant learner's enthusiasm for school is one of motivation. Mathematics, because it involves mental discipline, is particularly demanding for those who have trouble accepting any discipline, social, physical, or mental. To compound the problem, these youngsters are creatures of their environment, and this environment includes the sophisticated techniques of television, films, and advertising. Teaching techniques must be as persuasive.

Variety of techniques

The math lab facilitates the use of a variety of teaching techniques, particularly those techniques encouraging student involvement. The reluctant learner is most highly motivated when he is directly, personally, and constructively involved. Different mathematical topics lend themselves to different techniques. The development of computational and equation-solving skills involves a great deal of drill. In order to introduce variety into the repetitive nature of drill, the desk calculators, the skill-builder filmstrips, and the computational skill-building kits are valuable aids. The overhead projector has many advantages when teaching geometry, particularly in constructions and graphs. In areas where the steps involved in the solution of a problem are more important than the arithmetic, the desk calculators free the students from the frustrations of involved computations and enable the teaching of topics that would otherwise be too discouraging. Filmstrips are effective in many areas, including taxation and insurance. The lab environment provides an excellent setting for group or individual projects where the information must be researched and organized by the student. Materials are readily available and the equipment familiar to the student. Change of pace, variety of material, and variety of approach are essential to the maintenance of a high level of interest.

The math lab is the integration of filmstrips, teaching aids, tape recordings, records, transparencies, desk calculators, workshop material, and programmed learning material. Each room is equipped with a math-builder projector; a filmstrip projector; an overhead projector, trolley (or cart), and screen; and an SRA computational skill-building kit. Available when needed are a film-loop projector, a class set of twelve desk calculators, a filmstrip reviewer, a tape recorder, a record player, movie projector, and an opaque projector. The equipment is arranged on trolleys for convenience and ease of use.

The course is organized into topics of four or five weeks' duration. The transparencies, filmstrips, teaching aids, and all other appropriate materials are cataloged and contained in a teaching kit for each topic. A teacher may choose from a variety of from ten to twelve topics for each grade, ranging from geometry, algebra of sets, and arithmetic to budgeting, math in the shops and at home, insurance, and taxation. He is free to choose a program suitable to the needs and abilities of his particular classes. Because only one teacher is teaching a given topic at a given time, the teaching kit is available without interruption for the length of the topic. Each topic is concluded with a project week. Working individually or in pairs, the students research practical applications of the preceding topic or "discover" ramifications.

The two basic premises of the math lab are involvement, particularly student involvement, and variety. Although the freer learning atmosphere is not to be confused with poor discipline, the classical silence of the traditional classroom is gone. Students cannot exchange ideas and remain mute! This means more pressure on the teacher to guide and direct, with the resulting expenditure of energy. Energy cannot be wasted in hunting up equipment and teaching material. With the organization of the math lab, the teacher is encouraged to use the wide assortment of materials, equipment, and techniques which inspire learning for learning's sake.

Guidelines

Choosing a suitable program is left to the individual teacher's judgment, but with the following guidelines:

1. The course in each grade will consist of nine or ten topics. Compulsory topics must be covered. Optional topics are left to the teacher's choice, and their selection should be governed by the caliber of the class.

2. Four projects are compulsory in each grade. Each project should take one week of classroom time and be related to the preceding topic.

3. Flow charting should be used to emphasize a logical development in solutions of more-than-one-step problems. Use flow charting in small doses and only for important emphasis.

4. Use desk calculators to *verify* all work. Except for problems where the logical development of a solution is more important than the arithmetic computation, the student must do the arithmetic first. In the former instances arithmetic may be done with calculators.

The program has been extended to include teaching the related shop mathematics in the shop itself. After a few years of experimenting it has been found that the most effective way to implement the plan is to schedule each mathematics teacher with three periods in a six-day cycle for shop mathematics. He is then free to go to the shops on a regular basis.

By assigning each mathematics teacher a certain number of shops and leaving it up to him and the shop teacher to decide on the material to be covered, it is possible to meet each individual shop's needs. Also, the shop teachers do not feel the mathematics department is imposing a program on them.

It turns out to be a very interesting form of team teaching, with the mathematics teacher and the technical teacher each bringing his particular perspective to the same problem. It also provides new insights for both.

Perhaps the reluctant learner's problem is so obvious, so pronounced, that few objections are raised when radical changes in the art of teaching are used in an attempt to find solutions. As positive results develop with increasing regularity, the doors gradually open to an atmosphere where education is not only a means to an end but an end in itself.

For further information about this program, write to Mrs. L. R. Strobel at the Sir R. L. Borden Secondary School, 200 Poplar Road, West Hills, Scarborough, Ontario.

Project SEED

WILLIAM F. JOHNTZ

Project SEED, Special Elementary Education for the Disadvantaged, is a program designed to improve the academic achievement of disadvantaged children by teaching them abstract, conceptually oriented mathematics in the elementary grades. The major focus of Project SEED at the present time is on inner-city ghetto children, predominantly black. Work has also been done, however, with Mexican-American, American-Indian, poor-white Appalachian, and Eskimo children.

Two of the most important reasons for the disadvantaged child's poor academic performance are these:

1. He enters kindergarten *inadequately prepared* to learn reading skills because he lacks the kinds of verbal experiences common to middle-class children (books in the home, frequent conversations with adults, enriched vocabulary, nursery school, trips to the library, etc.). Consequently, he is behind his more advantaged classmates from the start.

2. By the time he enters school, the disadvantaged child, especially if black, has already acquired a *negative self-image* that impedes his cognitive development. Consequently, instead of catching up with more advantaged children, he tends to fall further and further behind as he progresses through school.

Project SEED is based on these major assumptions:

1. Young children in general are capable of understanding and performing abstract, conceptually oriented mathematics. Page and Davis both reported ten years ago that young children not only are able to understand high-level mathematics but also become enthusiastically and creatively involved in learning the subject when it is well taught. Their work suggests that mathematical talent is, contrary to popular belief, universal if cultivated before it is destroyed by teachers who do not understand it and consequently dislike it. (Later work in Project SEED suggests further that there is a universal enthusiasm for mathematics until it, too, is destroyed. Children have chosen Project SEED

by popular vote in preference to extracurricular activities such as music, art, and physical education.)

2. Few children, even those who are advantaged, have had previous experience in abstract, conceptually oriented mathematics when they enter the first grade. The disadvantaged child, therefore, is not behind others in this subject as he is in language skills and, to some extent, the familiar arithmetic skills.

3. Abstract, conceptually oriented mathematics is seldom a familiar part of any child's environment; therefore, it is "culture free"—the disadvantaged child cannot use it to compare himself unfavorably with others.

4. Abstract, conceptually oriented mathematics is a high-status, intellectually demanding subject. Success in this subject helps the disadvantaged child improve his poor self-image, thereby enabling him to perform better in all subjects, including mathematics.

The discovery method is crucial to the success of Project SEED. Course content evolves, not from lectures, not from demonstrations, not from exercises in textbooks, but from questions posed orally by the teacher to the students in a group situation. The teacher never gives answers; he only asks questions. If a student asks a question, the teacher, instead of answering, asks a further question designed to lead the student to the answer. If a student gives an incorrect answer, the teacher does not say, "That is wrong." To tell a child, especially a disadvantaged child, that he is wrong destroys both his spontaneity and his willingness to take risks. Instead, the teacher asks the student, "How did you find that answer?" The young child often gives an incorrect answer to a mathematical question because he has (1) changed the axiom system underlying the question or (2) made up a new question related to, but different from, the original question. It is indeed ironic that industry rewards the research scientist who can change axiom systems or ask new questions while the typical elementary school teacher punishes the child who will do the same!

(It is not intended that these remarks be misconstrued as a sweeping criticism of elementary school teachers, who, for the most part, perform a heroic and largely thankless job. They, too, are victims of hopelessly inadequate mathematics education.)

Because of the demands of the discovery method, the teacher who is well trained in mathematics and enthusiastic about the subject is a necessary condition to the success of Project SEED. Only such persons possess the mathematical fluency needed to ask provocative questions that will guide the student to the self-discovery of the concepts and structure of mathematics. Therefore, a Project SEED teacher must have at least a baccalaureate degree in mathematics, preferably more. Most of those presently teaching in the project have had several years of postgraduate work in mathematics. An ever-increasing number have Ph.D.'s, including several who are university professors or research scientists.

It should be stressed here that Project SEED never *replaces* the regular arithmetic program. It is always, however, offered *on a daily basis during school hours to a regular class*. Students are never specially selected for Project SEED.

Topics introduced to a fifth-grade Project SEED class typically include an examination of the properties of exponentiation treated as a binary operation over the rationals, including zero, negative, and fractional exponents. The log operation, general summation, and limits are then employed as analytical tools in the study of rational and irrational numbers. For instance, the students are led to discover that the $\log_B A$ is irrational whenever A is even and B is odd, or vice versa. Then the topic of limits and infinite series is taken up and developed to the point where the students are led to see that a number D is rational if and only if it can be represented as a repeating N-mal number for some fixed N.

Project SEED offers the universities of this country a unique opportunity to involve some of their top-level personnel—that is, mathematicians and graduate students in mathematics—in community work *on a daily basis in a nonconsultative, nonresearch role*. A version of Project SEED called The Community Teaching Fellowship Program became the number one item in the University of California's 1969 Urban Crisis Program, receiving more funds than any other item in the package.

For the first time in history, industries have also been able to involve top research personnel in community work on a daily basis in a nonconsultative, nonresearch role through Project SEED. Research mathematicians and physicists from IBM have been teaching Project SEED classes for two years. More than forty research personnel from Bell Laboratories have indicated an interest in working in Project SEED.

Project SEED offers school districts a unique kind of in-service training that is actually an integral part of the program itself.

Considerable effort is spent enlisting the support and cooperation of the staff in any school in which Project SEED will be implemented; classroom teachers are asked to participate as colleagues in planning the program. Project SEED stipulates that the classroom teacher must be present, observing and participating when necessary, while the mathematics specialist teaches. The teacher's daily presence helps her in three ways. First, because the mathematical concepts introduced in Project SEED are altogether different from anything the typical elementary teacher has been exposed to, she inevitably learns an enormous amount of mathematics and finds that her appreciation of the subject is greatly enhanced. The cooperative spirit in which Project SEED is introduced to the schools further facilitates her receptiveness.

Second, her daily presence helps her to improve her teaching methods. The discovery method used in Project SEED provides the participating teacher with an excellent model of classroom questioning and related procedures. She can adapt what she observes to her own teaching—in other subjects as well as in mathematics. Finally, and most important, by observing so-called low achievers achieve at very high levels, the teacher is helped to raise her expectations for *all* children.

Mindful of the need for in-service training, most Project SEED mathematics specialists set aside one day out of five to work with classroom teachers as a regular part of the ongoing program.

Statewide evaluations in California and Michigan by the California Institute of Technology and American Institutes for Research, respectively, reveal that children in Project SEED not only are able to perform abstract, conceptually oriented mathematics, but also that their arithmetic computational skills have improved enormously. These findings were confirmed by similar evaluations in Seattle, Washington, and New Haven, Connecticut. Other evaluations in Berkeley and in Del Paso Heights, California, show significant improvement by children in Project SEED classes in IQ scores and attitudes toward self and school. The California and Michigan studies also revealed consistently positive responses to Project SEED from classroom teachers who were involved in the program.

Project SEED, Incorporated, a nonprofit corporation, has the extremely low cost figure of $150 per child per year based on an assumed class size of thirty. This is far lower than other compensatory education programs that even approach Project SEED's level of proven success. There are three reasons why the SEED price is so low: (1) Project SEED specialists work with the whole class. Most successful compensatory education programs involve one adult working with a few pupils. (2) Project SEED has no materials or gadgets to sell, only the skills of a highly trained teacher who can reach children from even the most deprived backgrounds. (3) All the corporate people who work in SEED are volunteers. This helps to bring down the national per child per year cost.

Information about Project SEED may be obtained by writing its director, William F. Johntz, 1011 Keith Avenue, Berkeley, California 94708.

Chicago's Attempts to Meet the Needs of the Inner-City Child via Math Labs

JESSIE L. SCOTT

I hear, and I forget.
I see, and I remember.
I do, and I understand.

The philosophy of this Chinese proverb is the basis for the eight elementary school math labs in Area B, Chicago Public Schools. There is a lab for each district, similar in layout to the one pictured in figure 11.14. The labs are located in the following districts and schools and serve the grades indicated: District 9, Smyth, grades K–8; District 10, Crown, grades K–6; District 11, Doolittle-East, grades 4–8; District 12, Edwards, grades K–8; District 15, Owen, grades K–8; District 19, Cooper Upper Grade Center, grades 7–8; District 23, Woodson-North, grades 4–6; and District 26, Healy, grades K–8.

Each lab has a lab teacher and provides a wide variety of materials and experiences so that a child can discover meanings and relationships himself. Each lab is so organized and conducted as to meet the needs of its school population and community. Two of these labs are for Spanish-speaking children.

This article will attempt to describe one lab in detail. Doolittle-East is located in inner-city Chicago. The enrollment is 1,078. The school is at the 30.6 percent poverty level for purposes of the Elementary and Secondary Education Act. This means that 330 of the chil-

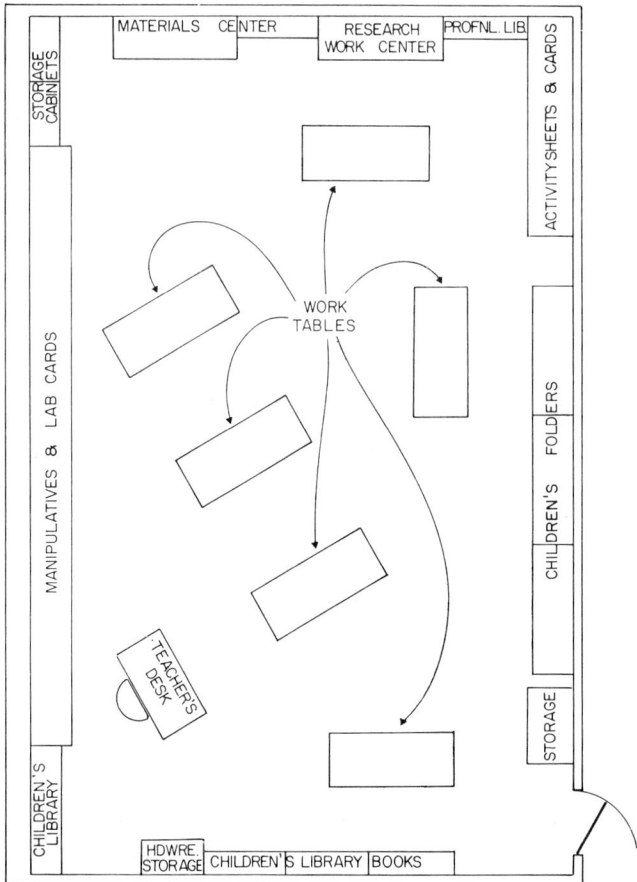

Fig. 11.14. Math lab for Doolittle-East

dren come from families in which the income is less than $2,000 a year or they receive over $2,000 a year from Aid for Dependent Children or some other type of welfare. Over 90 percent are eligible for the free lunch program because of the level of the family income.

Characteristics, Objectives, Teacher's Role

The school had to realize that there are certain similar characteristics found among these children because they live in an inner-city area:

1. The child is more interested in survival in a community of gangs than in anything else.

2. He and his parents do not often think of the school in terms of his learning experiences.
3. He distrusts teachers and principals.
4. It is very hard to motivate him.
5. His attendance is very irregular because he often has to babysit for younger brothers and sisters and feels that no one cares if he is regular in his attendance.
6. He expects failure.
7. He cannot relate to the social situations in most textbooks.
8. He does not see that mathematics has any importance for him.
9. He lacks a quiet place in which to study.
10. He has little respect for property.
11. He has low reading scores because of his environment.
12. He needs to sense immediate success.
13. He seldom has the basic materials (pencils, paper, etc.).
14. He "tunes you out" when you are teaching.

Table 11.5 shows the test results for the city-wide 1968/69 testing program.

After taking a good, hard look at the picture, Doolittle-East planned its math lab with the assistance of a consultant.

These objectives were set up:

1. Free the children to think for themselves.
2. Provide many materials so that the children can use many senses to learn.
3. Provide experiences that will have relevance for them.
4. Establish an atmosphere that will foster a relationship of trust and respect.
5. Provide activities and practice that will be enjoyable.
6. Provide materials and experiences that will lead the children to discover relationships and patterns.
7. Develop a positive attitude toward learning.
8. Provide opportunities for the continuous progress of each child through the mathematical strands.
9. Provide materials and experiences to meet the needs and abilities of average, below-average, and advanced pupils.
10. Train the children in the necessary mathematical skills.
11. Provide experiences with which a child can be successful.

The math-lab teacher was selected. She had a master's degree in teaching mathematics and ten years of experience in teaching inner-

TABLE 11.5

Results of a Testing Program in Chicago, 1968/69

Grade and Quartile	Scores					
	School Learning Ability from Intelligence Tests					
	National		City		School	
	IQ	PR*	IQ	PR*	IQ	PR*
Grade 6:						
Q3	111	75	106	65	103	57
Q2	100	50	95	38	93	33
Q1	89	25	84	16	82	13
Grade 8:						
Q3	111	75	108	69	102	55
Q2	100	50	95	38	94	35
Q1	89	25	85	17	86	19
	Arithmetic Computation					
	National		City		School	
	GE†	PR*	GE†	PR*	GE†	PR*
Grade 6:						
Q3	7.4	75	7.4	75	7.3	73
Q2	6.5	50	6.1	35	6.3	44
Q1	5.8	25	5.4	16	5.6	20
Grade 8:						
Q3	9.5	75	8.6	55	7.5	35
Q2	8.4	50	6.9	28	6.6	24
Q1	6.7	25	5.9	13	5.9	13
	Reading					
	National		City		School	
	GE†	PR*	GE†	PR*	GE†	PR*
Grade 6:						
Q3	9.0	75	7.1	55	6.9	53
Q2	6.7	50	5.3	29	5.4	31
Q1	5.1	25	4.3	13	4.3	13
Grade 8:						
Q3	10.1	75	9.0	59	8.0	49
Q2	8.1	50	6.9	38	6.4	32
Q1	5.8	25	5.0	14	5.3	18

* PR stands for "percentile rank."
† stands for "grade equivalent."

city children. Materials were purchased that would help children discover concepts in all the mathematical strands. (A partial list of these materials may be found at the end of this article.)

The math lab is not a program in itself, but a supplement to the activities carried on by the classroom teacher. The math-lab teacher may initiate a project or provide experiences related to the topics being studied in the classroom. The role of the math-lab teacher is to—

1. create a relaxed atmosphere;
2. lead the children to discover relationships;
3. set up materials in the activity centers prior to the arrival of pupils in the lab;
4. tape directions for lab activities that will present reading problems caused by the technical vocabulary;
5. write activity cards and rewrite commercially written activity directions at appropriate reading levels for the students;
6. determine individual children's weaknesses and assign appropriate laboratory activities;
7. correlate activities with those of the classroom teacher;
8. determine how the children are grouped in the lab;
9. encourage work in research and individual projects.

The children are scheduled for periods in the lab. When a teacher brings her entire class, she works with the lab teacher, so that the pupil-teacher ratio is approximately 15 to 1. Small groups of seventh and eighth graders may report to the lab to work in the research center during their study periods if they have requested permission prior to the time of the study period. The schedule of periods in the lab for any particular child changes periodically, depending on the achievement of the child and the consequent change in need. Table 11.6 shows a typical schedule.

TABLE 11.6

Typical Lab Schedule

Time	Monday	Tuesday	Wednesday	Thursday	Friday
9:15–10:00	Prep.*	7th #118	Prep.	7th #316	Prep.
10:00–10:40	7th #116	Prep.	6th #300	Prep.	6th #306
10:40–11:20	8th #216	8th #216	8th #216	8th #216	8th #261
[Lunch]					
12:20–1:00	8th #212	8th #212	8th #212	8th #212	8th #212
1:00–1:40	8th #210	8th #210	8th #210	7th #210	7th #218
1:40–2:25	4th #106 or 5th #201	4th #307	4th #101	4th #103	Research
2:25–3:10	8th #312	5th #207 6th #302	5th #100 6th #206	5th #105 6th #202	Research Projects

* Prep. indicates preparation period.

A Typical Period in the Lab

Fourth-grade class

All the fourth-grade children were using Alge blocks in their work with equivalent fractions. The activity cards were on transparencies and projected on the screen. The classroom teacher had requested that the children engage in the same activity.

Fifth-grade class

A class of fifth-grade pupils were engaged in activities according to their abilities:

One group was discovering equivalent fractions by using Alge blocks.

Another group was discovering equivalent fractions by using Cuisenaire rods.

Each child in the two groups had a card like the one in figure 11.15 to guide his thinking.

	Halves	Thirds	Fourths	Fifths	Sixths	Sevenths	Eights	Ninths	Tenths
$\frac{1}{2}$	X								
$\frac{1}{3}$									
$\frac{2}{3}$									
$\frac{1}{4}$									
$\frac{2}{4}$									
$\frac{3}{4}$									
$\frac{1}{5}$									

Fig. 11.15

A third group was using Cuisenaire rods to discover prime numbers. See figures 11.16–11.18.

A fourth group, made up of advanced pupils, was working on polyhedra with straws and pipe cleaners.

Other groups

On one occasion a group of nineteen eighth graders from three eighth-grade rooms sought help. They had received low scores on the standardized test. They were given a standardized test; then the pupils

1. Place a red rod in your work space. Can you make a train with two rods the same color that would be as long as the red one?

Red	
?	?

2. Three rods?
3. Four rods?

Fig. 11.16. Card A

1. Place a light green rod in your work space.
2. Can you build a train with two cars the same color that is the same length as the light green rod?
3. Three cars?
4. Four cars?
5. Five cars?

Fig. 11.17. Card B

1. Look at your trains.
2. Are there any others like the train for the red rod?
3. Name them.
4. If the red rod is 2, what are the factors of 2? Of 3? Of 5? Of 7?

Fig. 11.18. Card J

and the lab teacher made an item analysis and a study of errors. Next they conferred with the lab teacher regarding a program for improvement. They selected their activities and determined their curriculum. They were scheduled into the lab each day in small groups. Individual progress conferences were held constantly.

One group of eight students requested a retest after a month. As is characteristic of inner-city children, they must see that they are being successful immediately. Table 11.7 shows the results.

TABLE 11.7

COMPARISON OF TEST RESULTS

Date	Score of Child							
	A	B	C	D	E	F	G	H
21 Jan.	5.4	4.9	5.1	4.8	5.1	5.3	4.2	3.4
26 Feb.	5.9	4.2	6.5	7.1	5.4	5.8	4.2	4.0

The math lab is also used as a resource center by principals and teachers from other schools in the area. Teachers are taught mathematics methods courses in the lab.

There is constant in-service training for the math-lab teacher.

The only evaluation at this time is based on teacher observation of pupil behavior and willingness to participate in lab activities, some transfer from lab actvities to classroom activites, and comments of pupils and teachers.

Reaction of Children

A questionnaire was given to the children. They wrote their comments about the lab and put them in a large envelope. They were asked not to sign the questionnaire. Here are some of the comments of the children:

"I think it helps kids a lot. It makes me feel at ease. I like it a lot."
"It just seems to me as if we can't or don't get as much done as we should."
"I am more interested in math."
"Math used to be a very complicated subject, but now it isn't so hard."
"I felt that math was alright before and very interesting after working in the lab."
"The math lab is lots of fun."
"I think it's the best place to learn."

"You get to do more in the lab."
"I still don't like math."
"The lab has many things to stimulate the brain. It has many challenging things."
"It gives me a more vivid understanding of the word *mathematics*, what it means, and its many uses and—believe me—the math lab can restore your brain with all of these answers and many more."
"I used to think that math was a boring subject."
"I know more now."
"The teacher explains the work instead of just telling you to do this."
"Miss Thompson figured some easy way to do math."
"I was excited in the lab."
"I understand my work more better."
"It is a nice place to make what you feel like doing."
"I feel that we should have it more often."
"I feel like I had the brains to do the things I was asked to do."
"Math is getting harder every day."
"Math was nothing I wanted until I went to the lab."
"It makes you want to do math more."
"Every school should have one."
"I would die if anything happens to the lab."
"I used to think math was a disaster."
"All other mathematics seems simple."
"It has made math become my best subject."
"I felt as if I wasn't learning enough before, and the math lab made me see that I was right."

For further information about the program, please write to Barbara Thompson, Doolittle-East Math Lab, 525 East 35th Street, Chicago, Illinois 60616, or Jessie L. Scott, Math Consultant, Area B Office, Curriculum Services, Edwards School, 4815 South Karlov Avenue, Chicago, Illinois 60632.

Lab Materials

A partial list of lab materials is given below. In addition to the items mentioned, a number of miscellaneous articles are useful—rubber bands, pipe cleaners, rice, beans, straws, rulers, protractors, tape recorders, overhead projector, previewer, and so on.

Dimensions	Battleship
Qwik-Save	Sum Times
Spare Time (bowling)	Dignity
Madagascar Madness	Numerals Jigsaw

Desk Calculator
Color Cubes
Perimeter Area Boards
Computing Abacus
Desk Tape Number Line
Winning Touch
Four by Four
Experiments in Mathematics
Tri-Nim
Configurations
On-Sets
WFF'N PROOF
Chinese Abacus
Timer, Stopwatch
Map Measurer
Cross-Number Puzzles
Geoboard
Thread Sculpture
Pattern Blocks
Attribute Games and Problems
Shape Analysis Matching
Cards, Box 1, Box 2
Psyche-Paths
Tangle
Parquetry Blocks
Qubic
Cuisenaire Rods
Place-Value Board
Mathematics Using Strings
Sage Kit
Developing Number Experiences
Twin Choice, Decks 1 through 8
Come Out Even
Bali Buttons
Clinometer
Hexed
I'm Out
Think
Tri-Grams
Solitaire Puzzle
Tuf

Spirograph
100 Square Graph Stamp Scale
Avoirdupois Precision
Napier's Rods Demonstrators and
    Pupils' Sets
Compasses
Alge Blocks
Soma
Red Cards and Green Cards
Burns Pupil Boards
Quiet Counters
Kahlah
Cubical Counting Blocks
Walker Geo Cards
Tower Puzzle
Discs
Peg Game
Weights and Springs
Centimeter Blocks
Mathematical Balance
Ascobloc
Heads Up
Numble
Who Is Your Favorite?
Measurement Kits
Dial-A-Matic
Prime Ed Trundle Wheel
Transparent Globe Laboratory
Tongue Depressors
Fact Pacer
Flat Shapes
Mathematical Shapes
Shapes with Tubes
Mirrors
Pi-O
Map Making
Yardstick
Meter Stick
Dienes Multibase Arithmetic Blocks
Poly-O

University of Denver Mathematics Laboratory Programs for Teachers

RUTH I. HOFFMAN

A typical classroom in remedial mathematics at the secondary school has the student sitting at a desk in one-to-one correspondence with a piece of paper and his own discouragement. He is engaged in firmly retreading his old failures in exactly the same patterns that have persisted for many years.

In an effort to upset this unfruitful educational pursuit, several programs are in operation at the University of Denver Mathematics Laboratory:

Programs to *train teachers* in the mathematics-laboratory approach to teaching low achievers in mathematics

Programs to *train teachers of teachers* in the same approach

Programs to establish *satellite centers* for this approach throughout Colorado

A *depository for materials* that can be checked out by any teacher in the state for use in his classroom or for his own experimentation and planning

Model—program COLAMDA

The programs for teacher training have used as a model the project COLAMDA (Committee on the Low Achiever in Mathematics, Denver Area), a program funded by Title III, Elementary and Secondary Education Act, that had its origin and early-stage development at the University of Denver. For this project, "low achiever" identifies students in grades 7–12 enrolled in remedial classes with two typical educational records: (1) two or more years below grade level in problem solving and computational skills as measured by a standardized test and (2) a record of unsuccessful experiences in previous mathematics classes.

COLAMDA provides an opportunity for teachers to become a part of a working model through individualized training in instructional techniques and methods, exploration, experimentation, idea exchange, and preparation of materials.

The teacher-training segment of the project places primary emphasis on favorable change in the attitudes of teachers toward the teaching of the low achiever, identification of known successful instructional techniques and methods, development of realistic objectives, and transposition of pure mathematical theory into a usable form for low-achiever instruction. Each new project participant is required to attend a workshop designed with the above objectives in mind.

Learning activities and teacher "idea cards" have been prepared by a project writing team to assist the teacher in personalizing instruction by supplementing the existing district materials. The activities are intended to be student-interest oriented and open-ended in structure to provide for individual differences in mathematics skill development, interest, and age levels.

Philosophy

The philosophy of the program is the simple one that a low achiever is a student who has become so embittered by habitual failure that he hates mathematics. There is little possibility of this student's learning mathematics until an attitude change has been effected. A new, interesting, involvement approach with many and varied pieces of equipment brings about this change. The laboratory setting gives an opportunity to go back to basic concepts for a new approach to understanding—one that avoids the stigma of doing dull drill on very basic and elementary topics. The laboratory approach, when properly carried out, unifies ideas that were previously isolated items of memorization.

Characteristics of the low achiever

The characteristics of the low achiever are dislike of mathematics and school, irregular attendance, poor self-image, poor reading habits, short attention span, and limited success with academic endeavors—all these qualities pointing to the student as a potential dropout.

The mathematics laboratory

The low-achiever program is one of involvement, with students using as many of their five senses as possible in learning; therefore the teachers must experience the same process in teacher-training programs. For this reason the manner of teaching mathematics is a complete departure from former classroom procedures and is, in effect, a mathematics-laboratory procedure.

It is difficult to define a mathematics laboratory, but the following phrases characterize it to some extent:

Active, materials-centered situation

Questioning atmosphere and a continuous involvement with problem-solving situations

Teaching role that of a *catalyst* in the activity between student and knowledge

Physical plant with *equipment*

A place where a student learns by *doing,* with appropriate objects available

Inexpensive and easily assembled apparatus to give students an opportunity to arrive at mathematical ideas through *experiments* —comparing, recording, and analyzing to develop mathematical relations based on physical evidence

The activities and materials in a laboratory are anything that leads to modeling mathematical ideas and concepts physically, or to assembling physical models to represent mathematical principles. The following are samples of the kinds of activities and materials that characterize a mathematics laboratory:

Printed software

Hardware—calculators, adders, tape recorder, overhead projectors, tachistoscope, video tape recorder, and so forth

Manipulative and concrete aids—abaci, geoboards, Cuisenaire rods, grids, chips, and so forth

Activities simulating real-life situations

Physical involvement—experimenting, collecting data, building devices

Field work—measurement and estimation

Multisensory aids—dictating machines, projectuals, video tapes, films, filmstrips, audio tapes, tachistoscope

Games

Programs of teacher training

Several programs for teachers of low achievers have been held at the University of Denver. The first few, where a teacher might pay his own way or be funded by his district, were open to any teacher interested in low achievers. Some were for COLAMDA teachers. One was for a special group, returning Peace Corps teachers; this program was funded by the Office of Education under the Education Professions Development Act program.

All these programs, ranging from two to five weeks, were based on involvement activities. Teachers did laboratory experiments as their students would do them. These were not presented in isolation but related to the mathematical concepts the activity exemplified. The teachers also had time, guidance, and material to make usable equipment for their own classrooms. Since the COLAMDA project was the model used, the teachers were provided with a complete set of COLAMDA activity cards and student sheets. The cards are keyed to the mathematical skill or concept they aid and also to the type of activity—that is, hardware, simulation, experiment, and so forth.

The program for Peace Corpsmen continued into the school year, with thirty two-hour meetings, where the same laboratory experience was used with two extensions: one to computer-extended mathematics and one to cooperative creation of new laboratory tools.

Programs to train teachers of teachers

Two programs have been conducted to train teachers of teachers. The first was funded by the National Science Foundation through the Cooperative College-School Science Program (CCSSP). Twenty-five qualified *secondary* school teachers received training in an involvement program for the *elementary* school. These teachers then trained an additional 750 *elementary* teachers during the spring semester of 1969.

The second program, also funded through the CCSSP, extended the ongoing mathematics projects at the laboratory to a *statewide* basis, using five *regional* centers. Thus 120 secondary teachers received specific training concerning the implementation of the laboratory approach for low achievers.

One outcome of this program is 135 laboratory programs in secondary mathematics in Colorado. Another outcome is the strategic location of trained resource personnel available for extension programs by the local districts throughout the state.

The establishment of satellite centers

The five teams trained as teachers of teachers now have continuing programs in their areas. They are conducting training programs for teachers under the auspices of a college or a school district. These five geographical locations have now become satellite centers for presenting the involvement program to other teachers of low achievers. Evaluation studies show that they are tremendously successful, and their programs are received enthusiastically by the teachers in these areas.

An exciting new program has sprung up in Riverton, Wyoming, called WYOLAMP (Wyoming Low Achiever Mathematics Program). It had its origin in the COLAMDA model and is developing with a similar philosophy and similar goals. It has two excellent innovative aspects: the collection of the low-achiever materials for the *elementary* schools and the incorporation of occupational packets into the secondary low-achiever program.

A depository of material for low achievers

The final phase of the work at the University of Denver provides continuing support for personnel trained in earlier programs. It does this by making materials and equipment available on a check-out basis to any interested teacher in the state. These might be individual items or classroom sets of manipulative materials or resource materials. Included are such items as geoboards, abaci, grids, chips, games (commercial or teacher-made), films, tapes, books, guides, enrichment material, film loops, projectuals, measuring instruments, and many others.

This brief description cannot express the spirit of cooperation that has developed among all participants and the workshop staff, nor does it incorporate many tangential studies that have evolved. For example, some graduate students created special computer-assisted instruction units for junior high school low achievers—units that have been successfully used at schools where teletype terminals are available.

One program leads to many new and innovative programs, and the cooperative effort of a university, the State Department of Education, and local school districts (all of which participated in the above programs) is a powerful combination for helping the low achiever get out of his classroom dilemma and away from his one-to-one correspondence with a piece of paper and his own discouragement .

For further information on this program, write to Dr. Ruth Irene Hoffman, Mathematics Laboratory, University of Denver, Denver, Colorado 80210.

12

The Training of Teachers

DORA HELEN SKYPEK

TIMMY SAID, "Teach them how to keep order—*kindly* order."
A second grader in an inner-city school, Timmy was a guest of the undergraduate honorary sorority in education. The dialogue with his hostess, a student teacher in Timmy's classroom, was not going as planned. She had asked, "How do you like arithmetic?" Somewhat startled when he replied, "I don't," she protested, "But this afternoon you said that you did."

To help in eliciting a positive response from Timmy, the writer interrupted the interview with a question of her own. Explaining that she was a teacher of teachers, she asked, "What do you think is the most important thing I should teach people who will teach in your school?"

Timmy relaxed his defensive stance and said, "Teach them how to keep order." Then he amended the request by adding "—kindly order."

Fantini and Weinstein have investigated the classroom management strategy that Timmy calls "kindly" order. They call it *strength with sensitivity*. They describe a strong and sensitive teacher as a person who "can maintain a consistent orderly structure in which learners can operate and, at the same time, indicate that he is constantly aware of what is going on with the pupils. The pupils are treated as

402

important and respected persons with feelings, attitudes, and experiences that are worthy of attention." (38, p. 324.)

Timmy seems to be asking for just that: an orderly classroom structure in which he can get on with the business of learning arithmetic or reading or whatever and, at the same time, a "kindly" structure in which his worth as an individual is respected. The low achiever—and Timmy is one—has often been characterized as not wanting to learn, but that seems not to be the case with this seven-year-old. Why else would he have asked for order? It is important to note that classroom order is not, however, a sufficient condition for learning in the case of the slow learner. John Holt makes the point in this account:

> During this past vacation I visited a school that was still in session. It has the reputation of being very "good" and "tough." The headmistress, who was very nice, asked me where I had taught. When I told her, she said with false humility, "I'm afraid you'll find us very old-fashioned." But she made me welcome, and particularly urged me to visit the arithmetic class of her fourth-grade teacher, who had been there for many years and was generally felt to be a jewel among teachers and the pride of the school. I went. Soon after I arrived the class began. The children had done some multiplication problems and, in turn, were reading answers from their marked papers. All went smoothly until, right after a child had read his answer, another child raised his hand. "What is it, Jimmy?" the teacher asked, with just the faintest hint in her voice that this interruption could not be really necessary. "Well, I didn't get that answer," said Jimmy, "I got . . ." but before he could say more, the teacher said, "Now, Jimmy, I'm sure we don't want to hear any *wrong* answers." And that was the last word out of Jimmy.
>
> This woman is far ahead of most teachers in intelligence, education, and experience. She is articulate, cultivated, has had a good schooling, and is married to a college professor. And in the twenty years or more that she has been teaching it has apparently never occurred to her that it might be worth taking a moment now and then to hear these unsuccessful Jimmies talk about their wrong answers, on the chance that from their talk she might learn something about their thinking and what was making the answers come out wrong. What makes everyone call her such a good teacher? I suppose it is the ability to manage children effortlessly, which she does. And for all I know, even the Jimmies may think she is a good teacher; it would never occur to them that it was this nice lady's fault that they couldn't understand arithmetic; no, it must be their own fault, for being so stupid. [52, pp. 141-42]

Just as the headmistress in this school does, too many administrators equate the "ability to manage children effortlessly" with good teaching. In fact, an orderly classroom structure and sensitivity to all learners are often thought to be incompatible.

The experience of a first-grade teacher is pertinent as an example. She had been teaching for only two years when she participated in a summer institute for teachers of disadvantaged youth. The assigned reading of Sylvia Ashton-Warner's *Teacher* made a great impact on her. The following September she asked for the first graders who had not passed their "readiness" tests. She let the children select the words they wanted to learn to read and wrote them on large cards, one word to a card. The children studied the words, traced them with their fingers and pencils, and carried them around with them as "their" words. Arithmetic activities with attribute blocks and Cuisenaire rods were supplemented by trips to a sandpile at a nearby construction site. Filling cartons with sand and discussing the number of smaller cartons required to fill larger cartons provided experiences in counting, in studying relationships, and in developing conservation concepts. When maintenance men came during class to replace one of the overhead neon tubes, she joined the children as an interested spectator. In the ensuing discussion she discovered that for these children the word *light* meant an electric light bulb hanging from the middle of a ceiling. Accordingly, with the help of the repairmen, she turned what in many classrooms might have been an unwelcome interruption into an exciting and informative science lesson.

This first-grade teacher was *sensitive* to the learners in her room, seeking cues from them and adapting the instruction to them. Her established limits for a consistent orderly structure in the classroom were, however, broader than those approved by her supervisor. Her newly developed sensitivity to learners, expressed in her evaluation of the summer institute—"I see now that the school must get ready for children instead of expecting them to be ready for school"— was not highly valued. She was transferred to another school; at the end of the school year she resigned from the public school system.

There is a need to rethink what is meant by order in the classroom, by teacher strength. To exercise authority need not mean to ignore the need and the right of children to be respected as worthy individuals. To have his feelings, attitudes, and talents treated as worthy of his teacher's attention is among the more important classroom conditions for every learner, especially the low-achieving youngster, no matter what his age or what the socioeconomic status of his parents may be. Consider the case of Mike, a tenth grader. His junior high school teachers generally agreed that the boy was an underachiever, that he had the intelligence to make better grades than the Cs and Ds on his report cards but he was lazy and lacked motivation. At the beginning of the tenth grade, owing to scheduling difficulties, he was placed in a geometry honors class where the teacher listened when Mike said, "But I think this theorem could be proved another way." Sensitive to Mike's imaginative but nonconformist approach to learning, the teacher encouraged him to write "original" proofs—that is, proofs different from the ones suggested in the textbook.

He became an A student in geometry and, with his self-image as a learner of worth somewhat restored, he began to spend more time on other subjects. However, his "original" papers in English and history were returned to him marked $\cancel{A}$C (that is, a grade of "A" revised to "C"). The explanations for the revised grades usually went something like this: "Your papers are imaginative and exciting to read, but you *must* master the mechanics of spelling and punctuation." That was the only school year of his experience in which Mike *almost* fulfilled his human potential.

The study of classroom management strategies has, in general, been only a peripheral concern of the curriculum reforms and in-service teacher-training programs in mathematics of the past two decades. There have occurred major improvements in the mathematics curriculum, in upgrading teacher knowledge in mathematics, and in innovative classroom methods that engage the learner in active participation in the learning process. However, the benefits of reforms and innovations have accrued largely to the bright, college-bound students. The majority of students have been less affected by the improved curricula. To serve these children—the slow learners, the disadvantaged, the underachievers—is the concern and purpose of the several in-service training programs described below.

Some In-Service Training Programs for Teachers of Slow Learners

A program series of three summer institutes and an academic-year degree program directed by the writer and designed for mathematics teachers (and supervisors) of disadvantaged youth in grades K–8 is discussed in some detail. Two other in-service programs are more briefly described, with attention focused on unique or unusual features.

Programs for teachers of mathematics, grades K–8, Emory University

The first institute, in 1966, included three major components: a teacher-training mathematics laboratory, a teaching practicum in an elementary school serving an urban community, and a seminar with field experiences in the sociology of poverty and minority groups. Succeeding summer institutes added seminars in the problems of teaching mathematics to slow learners, in intergroup relations, and in language development.

The preliminary report of the Conference on the Low Achiever in Mathematics, a conference sponsored by the U.S. Office of Education and the National Council of Teachers of Mathematics in March 1964, included this statement:

> Evidence from research in psycho-pedagogies clearly indicates that active experimentation in which the child handles concrete objects and observes what happens precedes the formal operation stage in learning mathematical ideas. For slum children who come to school with a paucity of experience with manipulation of objects, the elementary teacher must provide the first selected planned environment in which active sensory experiences can take place. Only after the codification of experiences can the real search for structure begin. [108, p. 13]

The ability of elementary school teachers to provide selected sensory experiences conducive to the evolution of mathematical ideas is dependent on a knowledge of mathematics and a knowledge of how children learn mathematics. On the twofold assumption that an adult may also learn from active experimentation in which he handles concrete embodiments of mathematical principles and structures and observes what happens and that a teacher is more likely to teach as he has been taught, each institute was designed around a teacher-training mathematics laboratory. Other planned experiences were incorporated into the program in order to develop—

1. teacher knowledge of the mathematical principles fundamental to arithmetic and understanding of the psychological aspects of mathematics learning;
2. teacher competency in classroom use of concrete materials embodying mathematical principles and structures;
3. teacher awareness of the importance of viewing the child as a person of worth and a responsible learning agent;
4. teacher sensitivity and a flexible willingness to adapt instruction to the experiential needs of disadvantaged youth.

Thirty to forty participants were selected each summer from among experienced teachers and supervisors of mathematics in inner-city elementary schools. Recommendations of school administrators were major factors in the selection procedure. The institute staff included university instructors in the disparate disciplines of mathematics, sociology, educational psychology, and reading and language development. Psychiatrists and experienced elementary school teachers were also on the staff during the last two summers. In an effort to combat the fragmentation of the usual teacher-education programs, the staff met often in formal planning sessions and informally with participants during their free time. Interdisciplinary interest and communication became increasingly greater so that a remarkable synthesis of the various components was achieved during the third summer.

Participants were encouraged, in large measure, to direct their own learning. There were no assigned term papers, research papers, or curriculum units to be written, and no examinations. Grades of B were awarded for satisfactory completion of the program. A variety of materials and books were available in laboratory, reading, and study rooms—rooms set aside for the participants' exclusive use. These rooms were open during the participants' free time, and materials could be checked out.

The teacher-training mathematics laboratory. In the mathematics laboratory each participant was encouraged to work at his own pace, using task cards involving manipulative materials, related texts, and optional sets of supplementary materials. The "math lab" supervisor and assistants gradually assumed the roles of supportive consultants as the participants pursued their individual interests.

A brief description of the materials used somewhat systematically in the teacher-training laboratory and the rationale for their use follow. The order in which the materials were introduced is indicated. Commercial sources, guides, and textbooks are included in the references at the end of this chapter.

1. *Attribute blocks (A-blocks)*

   The universal set consists of forty-eight wooden blocks, each of which is a unique combination of one of four shapes, three colors, two sizes, and two thicknesses. They provide experiences in learning to classify, to discriminate, and to abstract—

   a) concepts of properties of objects;

   b) concepts of properties of sets of objects, e.g., number;

   c) concepts of logical relations between objects and between sets;

d) concepts of operations on sets;
e) related concepts of relations and of operations on numbers.

2. *Dienes Multibase Arithmetic Blocks (MABs)*

These consist of sets of wooden blocks whose volumes increase geometrically according to some specific base number; the blocks are thus a physical embodiment of base systems of numerical representation. For instance, let a 1-by-1-by-1 cm cube represent a *unit*. The next larger piece in a "base *b*" set of blocks would be a *b*-by-1-by-1 cm rectangular prism called a *long;* a *b*-by-*b*-by-1 cm prism is called a *flat;* and the *b*-by-*b*-by-*b* cm prism is called a *block*. The attention of children working with the materials, exchanging *b units* for 1 *long*, or *b longs* for 1 *flat*, or 1 *block* for *b flats*, is directed to the structure of computational techniques of "carrying" and "borrowing," or regrouping.

3. *Cuisenaire rods*

These are pieces of wood having a cross section of 1 cm by 1 cm and varying in length from 1 to 10 centimeters, in increments of 1 centimeter. To each length there corresponds a specific color; the 1-cm rods are painted white, the 2-cm rods are red, the 3-cm rods are light green, and so on. The Cuisenaire rods provide learning experiences for a large number of mathematical notions, including the basic arithmetical operations, rational numbers, bases, and volume.

4. *Geoboards*

Geoboards, typically, are square-shaped pieces of wood, measuring 10 inches on a side, with a 5-by-5 array of nails, 2 inches apart, that is a physical model of a set of points. A rubber band stretched around two points is a model of a straight line segment; a rubber band stretched around three noncollinear points represents a triangle; and so on. The study of polygons and measures of polygons is based on manipulation of the rubber bands around sets of nails and observations of the physical models of segments and interior regions of the polygons.

5. *"Red and green pieces"*

These consist of small pieces of wood, red or green, and triangular, diamond-shaped, or square. Depending on how piles of pieces are "named" or how equivalence relations are defined among "piles," these materials can be used to embody the ideas of the natural numbers, the integers, one- and two-dimensional vectors, and matrices. It was amazing to see how far the participants and their students were able to progress into "abstract mathematics"—from the integers to matrix algebra and group structures—using these very simple materials.

6. *Cardboard or wooden representations of square, rectangular, or triangular regions*

These representations were used in the study of transformational geometry. Translations, reflections, and rotations were employed to examine properties of geometrical figures and group structures generated by certain transformations. Children, in particular, found the "flipper" games among the most exciting activities presented during the summer.

7. *Calculators and hand-operated adding machines*

These pieces of equipment were available in the math lab and in the practicum. Their use (particularly with slow learners) seems to hold much promise for improving computational skills, for individualizing instruction, for motivational purposes, and for the development of marketable skills. A unit on flow charts was introduced in connection with the use of mechanical computing devices.

8. *Other materials available*

Dienes's Algebraical Experience Materials, Stern's Structural Arithmetic Blocks, filmstrips, programmed units, Madison Project Shoebox Labs, Mirror Cards, measuring tapes, stopwatches, abaci, and other mathematical aids were also available to the participants for individual or small-group explorations.

Many of the materials were homemade, either by the participants and staff or by the University shop. Activities paralleled, as nearly as possible, those of an elementary or junior high school math lab.

The major problem in the laboratory occurred during the first summer. There was one supervisor for thirty participants. Directed activities in which all participants were involved worked well. However, as the supervisor diminished his direction of the total group and encouraged participants to assume direction and responsibility for their own learning, activity slowed down and some participants protested. Experienced teachers are, in general, accustomed to being passive learners in a classroom setting. Old habits and attitudes about learning are hard to change. An active, hands-on approach, in which they follow directions on task cards for manipulating concrete materials, then record data and draw generalizations, is not in their repertoire of experiences or expectations in advanced study.

In subsequent programs alumni of former institutes joined the staff as laboratory assistants, one assistant for each group of ten participants. As instruction became more individualized, the teacher-participants did learn to direct much of their own learning. The length of time necessary for immersion in the hands-on approach, before the learner became self-directed, differed for individual teachers. Initially most elementary school teachers needed more support and encouragement than was generally assumed necessary (unlike young children, who are not as inhibited). As they worked together in groups of two, three, or four, they learned firsthand the role that social exchange of ideas, questions, and conjectures can have in learning mathematics. The existence of different learning styles became increasingly evident to them, and the right of the learner to options in the problem-solving process became increasingly important.

The practicum for experienced teachers. The primary purpose of the practicum was that teachers should learn *how children learn* through observing both verbal and nonverbal behaviors that indicate learning and, also, how to modify teaching behaviors in order to modify learning behaviors. The number of students assigned to each participant varied from not more than two to as many as eight. Supervisors observed that, in general, a teacher learned to interact with students on an individual basis when there were only one or two students. When there were three or more, learning ceased to be a joint venture and became teacher-directed. There were no specified topics to teach and no measures taken of children's learning. In general, the teachers chose to use materials with which they were working in the mathematics laboratory.

Each summer, principals of local inner-city schools recruited fifty or so students from grades 2–7 and assigned classroom space for the participants and their students to work together in small groups. School records, including reading and arithmetic achievement scores, were available to the teachers only at the discretion of the supervisory staff. The first day with only one or two children was somewhat traumatic for many experienced teachers. To sit across the table from a child in order to learn from that child something about how learning occurs is quite different from standing in front of a class of thirty children on the first day of school with permanent record folders, lesson plans, and textbooks and with expectations for the year pretty well fixed. For many teachers it was a first experience at being totally dependent on the learner for cues, for direction in the teaching act.

Among the supervisors were instructors in mathematics, instructors in educational psychology, and experienced elementary school teachers. The most effective supervision was provided by the educational psychologist, who, not a mathematics educator, could ask "Why are you doing that?" without threatening the teacher, who was himself trying to learn some mathematics. However, the question forced the teacher to clarify his understanding of the mathematics principle embodied in the materials and to identify and evaluate the verbal and nonverbal learning behaviors of the children with whom he was working. The experienced elementary school teachers, former institute participants, were also more effective supervisors than were the college instructors in mathematics.

In the practicum, teachers learned to talk less, to ask open-ended questions, to wait for children to think through a problem, to let the children verify for themselves the conjectures they made, to listen, and to interpret nonverbal cues with greater understanding. They found out that what appears to be lack of interest may be a protective cover-up for a feeling of shame or stupidity. Prior convictions about the hostility or indifference of disadvantaged children were dispelled as the teachers discovered that children who experience a measure of success can become enthusiastic learners. The teachers discovered that disadvantaged children can learn mathematics and can become absorbed in problem solving.

Teachers evaluated the practicum and the mathematics laboratory as the most significant of the institute's learning experiences. The academic-year program was an expanded form of the institute program, with the mathematics laboratory as an adjunct to each of five formal courses in mathematics. Within the framework of graduate-degree requirements, the practicum replaced the usual research project and was scheduled in cooperation with three local elementary schools. The fifteen teachers (full-time graduate students) worked in teams of five, each team spending one day per week for a period of six months in the assigned schools.

In general, the teachers defined their own roles in the schools—as resource teachers in mathematics, as math-lab directors, as assistant teachers, as remedial teachers, or as instructors of in-service workshops. Each teacher experimentally tried many roles. Instruments for supervision were observations by staff and principals, weekly logs by team leaders, and consultations. As in the short-term institutes, teachers in this program thought the practicum to be the most meaningful experience. Their usual, somewhat prescribed classroom roles were denied them. The result was a freedom to experiment with various teaching behaviors, to develop curriculum, and to assess their behaviors in terms of learners' behaviors.

The practicum must also be assessed in terms of other program components. Lectures, readings, and seminars provided an academic knowledge not only of mathematics and learning theories but of the sociology and language patterns of poverty and minority groups.

The practicum was the laboratory for applying and evaluating academic learning; and whatever else it provided, it gave each teacher an experience in sensitivity to the learner.

TRAINING LAB: STUDY OF TRANSFORMATIONAL GEOMETRY AND GROUP STRUCTURE THROUGH MANIPULATION OF MODELS

TRAINING LAB: STUDY OF LOGICAL OPERATIONS THROUGH MANIPULATION OF SETS OF A-BLOCKS

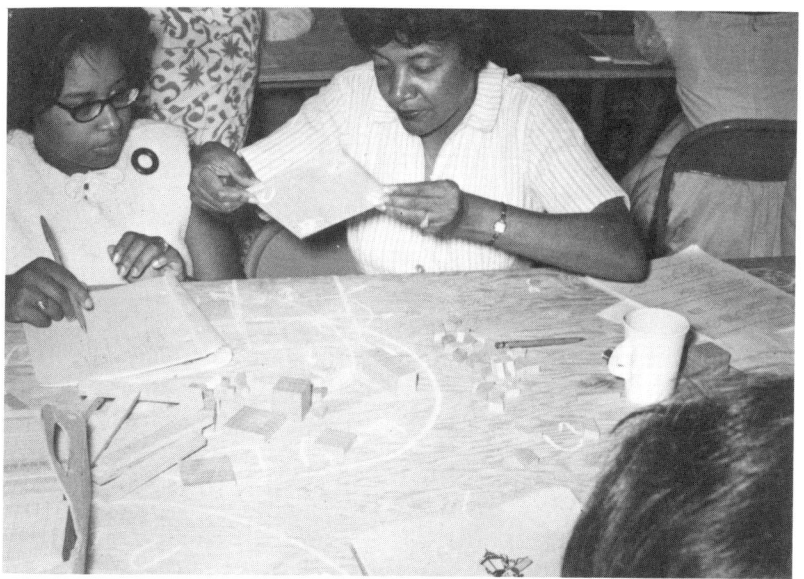

Training Lab: Study of Multiplication through Manipulation of Cuisenaire Rods

Training Lab: Mathematical Games with A-Blocks

Training Lab: The Human Computer

Teaching Practicum: Venn Diagram in Wood and Coat-hanger Wire

TEACHING PRACTICUM: JOINT VENTURE IN MULTIPLICATION WITH CUISENAIRE RODS

TEACHING PRACTICUM: POLYGONS IN NAILS AND RUBBER BANDS (GEOBOARDS)

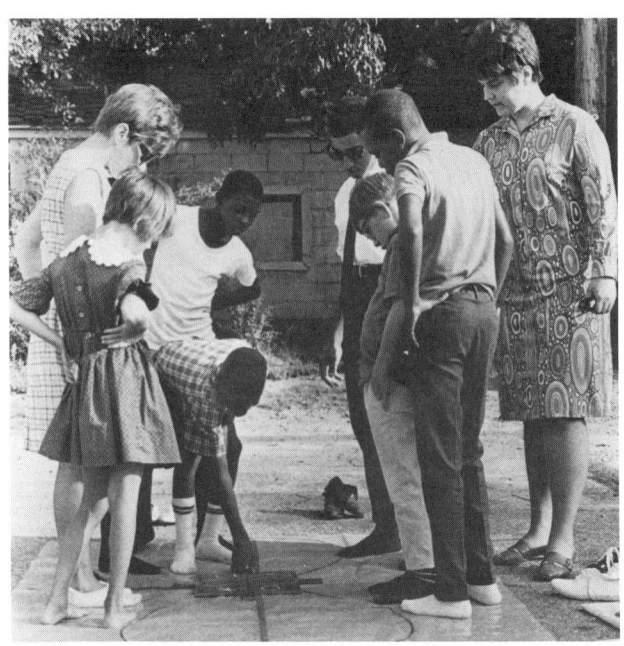

Teaching Practicum: Transformational Geometry—the "Flipper" Game

Teaching Practicum: Second Graders Using Adding Machines

Training in sensitivity. After the first summer, there were structured training experiences in sensitivity. The weekly institute seminars on intergroup relations were restricted to not more than ten teachers in each group and were directed by a psychiatrist. During the third summer institute, participants shared a required dormitory "live-in" experience of two weeks' duration at the beginning of the term. No family members or other observers were allowed. During the academic-year program, a two-day encounter group was scheduled, as was a two-day workshop in behavior modification. The reactions of teachers to these experiences were mixed—from quite positive (the majority) to slightly negative.

According to Fantini and Weinstein, strength and sensitivity, as characteristics of the teaching act, consist of interactions with the learner in a variety of ways and, as such, are behaviors. One learns teaching behaviors, not through reading about the teaching act, but through *behaving*—through experimenting with a range of possible behaviors and assessing the effectiveness of different teaching behaviors, according to certain purposes and certain learners. (38, pp. 330–31.) Structured training experiences in sensitivity to learners also included videotaping and role playing as described below.

Videotaping with experienced teachers. During the third summer institute, a research investigation in the "development and standardization of an instrument for assessing videotaped data of teacher management in the elementary classroom" (96, p. 1) made extensive use of the practicum. Each of the forty participants was videotaped in four ten-minute segments, with the four recorded segments occurring at intervals of approximately one week. After being taped, each teacher met with his supervisor to view his tape and discuss his behavior in terms of a management code. Thus the code served as a basic instrument of supervision throughout the practicum.

> The Process Code is the core of the instrument. It is designed to permit the description of teacher behavior in the service of traditional learning theory elements. Attention getting, setting up for student response, taking feedback from the students, and reinforcement of the students are behaviors coded here. Pilot research indicates that these elements occur throughout the teacher-student interaction and can be coded at regular intervals with a high degree of inter-coder reliability (in excess of .90).
>
> The Event Code is an amplification of the Process Code in an effort to describe the managerial behavior of the teacher in a more episodic

way. The pilot research indicates that every teacher has a highly stable style which can be punctuated by any number of measurable incidents of more or less regularity which contribute to a description of teacher management. The teacher herself may initiate interactions with the students which demonstrate unusual awareness of the student, or lack of it (Teacher With-it-ness). Again, the teacher may permit the flow of classroom activity to modify (Wandering). Finally, there may arise incidents beyond the control of the teacher to which she must respond in order to maintain management of her class (Disruptive Outbursts).

The scope of the code is limited to the description of those interactions with the student, of which the teacher becomes a part, in her role as the adult who is responsible for the creation and maintenance of a teaching-learning situation. [96, p. 1]

In addition to using the code to assist each teacher in assessing his teaching style and the behaviors that characterize him in a uniquely personal way, the participants and supervisory staff used the tapes to explore teaching strategies in terms of specific instructional objectives and learner needs or problems.

It is well to note that the reaction of experienced teachers to viewing themselves for the first time is highly personal—"I didn't know those pants were so baggy." The second time they view themselves, they are professionally hypercritical—relatively minor incidents are singled out for attention. However, in the third viewing they can begin to focus on the teaching-learning environment as a whole and can view themselves somewhat objectively. For many teachers the major observable change attributable to viewing themselves was a reduction in their talking behavior and an increase in their listening and attending behavior.

Role playing for experienced teachers. In the academic-year program, the role-playing device was employed. A start was made with a list entitled "Behavioral Objectives for Elementary Mathematics Education," from *Improving Mathematics Education for Elementary School Teachers,* the report of a 1967 conference sponsored by the National Science Foundation and the Science and Mathematics Teaching Center of Michigan State University (55, pp. 14–16).

From the thirty-seven objectives listed, twenty were selected as teaching behaviors with which to experiment. Five of these were assigned to all the teachers, and the remaining ones were assigned individually. Each person had to play the role of a teacher while other members of the seminar played the roles of students. The one in the teaching role was told what grade he was teaching (or was given a description of a particular classroom situation) and was assigned a concept to teach. He was charged with exhibiting the behavior specified in the objective.

For instance, one of the objectives in the list is "Given an objective, outline an inductive sequence of experiences to carry out the objective." One teacher assigned the role of exhibiting this particular behavior was told that he was teaching an average seventh-grade class and that he was to guide the class in discovering the generalization "If a and b are two natural numbers and $a \geq b$, then $(a - b)(a + b) = a^2 - b^2$."

The assignment proved to be a difficult one; the teacher had majored in mathematics as an undergraduate and found it difficult to start at the low level of skill mastery on which the others, now in the role of average seventh graders, insisted that he must. Of several different sequences of experiences that he might have provided, the following sequence is one:

Teacher: Let's find the products of the following pairs of numbers. As you compute the products, search for patterns relating the sequence of products to the sequence of factor pairs.

$$13 \times 13 =$$
$$12 \times 14 =$$
$$11 \times 15 =$$
$$10 \times 16 =$$
$$9 \times 17 =$$
$$\vdots$$
$$1 \times 25 =$$
$$0 \times 26 =$$

The computation of products results in this sequence:

$$13 \times 13 = 169$$
$$12 \times 14 = 168$$
$$11 \times 15 = 165$$
$$10 \times 16 = 160$$
$$9 \times 17 = 153$$
$$\vdots$$
$$1 \times 25 = 25$$
$$0 \times 26 = 0$$

The search for patterns begins. Learners easily spot the pattern on the left side: The first factor in each sentence is one less and the second factor is one more than are the first and second factors, respectively, in the preceding sentence. They also discover the pattern of decrease in magnitudes of the products. When asked, "What else can you say about this sequence?" some learners may begin to relate 13 × 13 to, say, 9 × 17 and write:

$$9 \times 17 = (13 - 4) \times (13 + 4)$$

Then

$$10 \times 16 = (13 - 3) \times (13 + 3)$$

and

$$1 \times 25 = (13 - 12) \times (13 + 12)$$

The decrease in magnitude from 13 × 13 to 9 × 17 is 16. The decrease in magnitude from 13 × 13 to 10 × 16 is 9. The sequence then looks like this:

$$13 \times 13 = 169$$
$$12 \times 14 = 168$$
$$11 \times 15 = 165$$
$$(13 - 3) \times (13 + 3) = 10 \times 16 = 160 = 169 - 9$$
$$(13 - 4) \times (13 + 4) = 9 \times 17 = 153 = 169 - 16$$
$$\vdots$$
$$(13 - 12) \times (13 + 12) = 1 \times 25 = 25 = 169 - 144$$
$$0 \times 26 = 0$$

Cues from the learners should determine the further search for patterns. The teacher could ask, "What can you say about the numbers 169, 9, 16, 144, . . . ?" It may be necessary to leave this particular sequence and begin a new one. (Children do not recognize this kind of activity as drill!) Try the following:

$$16 \times 16 =$$
$$15 \times 17 =$$
$$14 \times 18 =$$
$$13 \times 19 =$$
$$12 \times 20 =$$
$$\vdots$$
$$1 \times 31 =$$
$$0 \times 32 =$$

Assuming that the students have been writing "frame" sentences, the teacher will leave it to the students to discover

$$(\Box - \triangle) \times (\Box + \triangle) = \Box^2 - \triangle^2.$$

The emphasis is on using cues that the learners provide and adapting the give-and-take of instruction to the learners.

Another behavioral objective in the list is "Given a variety of pupil contributions, react positively to all of them." All the teachers were responsible for exhibiting positive reactions in the following situation:

Assume that you as the teacher have asked five second-grade students to write on the chalkboard "the sum of two fours." Here are the written responses:

$$24$$
$$2 + 4 = 6$$
$$4 + 4$$
$$44$$
$$\text{⧊} + \text{⧊} = 8$$

Admittedly, the set of responses is contrived to elicit judgments of "wrong" from teachers. However, if a positive response to student work is desirable teaching behavior—that is, if teacher responses or judgments are to be "kindly" or show respect for the child as a worthy learning agent—then response behaviors need to be assessed and positive behaviors practiced.

No consensus was reached as to what kinds of teacher responses constituted positive responses to these "answers." For example, the teachers argued about the degree of positivity in the response "Apparently you didn't understand what I said." Some of the teachers rated the statement negative in that the student was being blamed for not understanding the teacher. One teacher protested that it was the only positive response she could make. The seminar members were also divided on the response to the sentence $\text{⧊} + \text{⧊} = 8$. Some teachers responded, "Good. You are right; the sum of two fours is eight." Others insisted that the student was not right.

Curriculum development and adaptation. It was not the purpose of these programs to produce curriculum units, although teachers did plan and write many such units for their own use. Sharing ideas, creating homemade models and games, and writing task cards were optional and free-time activities. "Shoebox math labs" were created by the academic-year students as part of their mathematics-laboratory experiences.

The main thrust of the programs was the modification of teacher attitudes and behaviors for the long-range purpose of modifying the behaviors of children who have generally been unsuccessful in mathematics. A number of commercial and experimental units were available for teachers' use in developing and adapting the curriculum in terms of learners' individual needs. One of the four major aims was to prepare the teacher to become a curriculum developer himself, no longer totally dependent on the adopted textbook series or on curricula created by others.

Robert B. Davis has identified pressures in curriculum development with which all classroom teachers and trainers of teachers of mathematics will become increasingly involved. "They include a technology which is becoming more complicated more rapidly than almost anyone seems to realize. . . . They include also the multiple crises of our largest cities, in which the future of our society and the future of our education are inextricably intertwined." (25, p. 2.)

One bright promise from the modern computer technology is a structure for individualizing learning. The mathematics laboratory also provides for individualization according to learning needs. Both structures, according to Davis, are "concerned with methods for revising the curriculum much more often—at least as often as once a year, say—than was possible during the textbook-using period of American education history" (25, p. 11).

Another pressure for change in the curriculum is the crisis in urban education. Fantini and Weinstein suggest changes toward a "relevant" curriculum. Their test for revelance is "the correspondence of the curriculum to the condition and pattern of experience of the learner." In "Toward a Relevant Curriculum" (38, chap. 10), they identify and discuss dimensions for change under the following subheads:

From a Uniform to a Diversified Curriculum
From a Symbolistic to an Experiential Curriculum
From Horizontal to Vertical Skill Sequences
From a Remote to an Immediate Curriculum
From a What to a Why Curriculum
From an Academic to a Participating Curriculum
From an Antiseptic to a Reality-oriented Curriculum
Toward a More Affective Curriculum

To move toward a relevant curriculum in mathematics along these dimensions suggests anew that each teacher must become a curriculum developer for his own students. He must know not only mathematics but also "the condition and pattern of experience of the learner," as exemplified in an incident related by Fantini and Weinstein:

An eighth-grade teacher overheard his students discussing their desire to quit school in order "to make some good money." From class discussions he found that, to them, "good money" meant "a dollar-twenty an hour" or "forty bucks a week." A four-week unit evolved from the teacher's perception of his students' interests and needs.

After developing a working definition of good money—the amount one needs for the basic necessities of food, shelter, and clothing—the class consulted newspaper ads for the cost of furnished rooms and the cost of food for themselves, visited a department store to find out other costs, and viewed a film on how to get the most for one's money. "They worked out their complete costs on a yearly, monthly, and weekly basis. The results were compared with their original estimates and discrepancies were discussed."

The problem then was to find out where they could make their newly defined "good money." Checking newspaper ads, the students discovered that "almost without exception, the jobs required special training and *at least* a high school diploma—that dropping out of school is *not* the first step toward making good money." (38, pp. 405–7.)

All dimensions of the authors' definition of a relevant curriculum are exemplified in this account of a remarkable teacher. The writer, however, questions the implications of the authors that in the mathematics curriculum for educationally disadvantaged youth one should abandon the academic, symbolistic, and remote dimensions of the curriculum.

Many activities in an "experiential" curriculum for younger children or underachievers like Mike (the tenth grader mentioned earlier in this chapter) might have little relationship with practical reality for the learner. It is also appropriate to have experiences with culture-free models of mathematical ideas in which the cultural "thingness" of a model does not inhibit the study of classes of mathematical relations. Among experiential needs are the primary needs for sensorimotor experiences and concrete-operational experiences which precede formal operational stages of learning. Many learners have been deprived of such experiences, or they have been denied enough time for the internalization and codification of experiences before being asked to learn the formal, symbolic structures of mathematics. However, it does not follow that a "symbolistic" curriculum is not relevant.

Problem-solving activities need to be grounded not only in the reality of the learners' own cultural experiences, as recorded above, but also in the reality of relatively culture-free models, both concrete and symbolic, which the learner manipulates in both free and directed experiments, observing what happens. Learning to record data from experiments with reality moves from simple treatment of the data to increasingly complex treatment in which the learners rely entirely on symbolic representations of experience. Emphasis is on the *process* of learning. One may ask, "How did you arrive at that conclusion?" and expect the learner to demonstrate with model manipulations or pictorial representations or symbolic representations, depending on the level at which he operates most successfully.

Even in the teaching of computation, teachers are expected to diversify the curriculum to allow for different levels of performance in the exercise of skills. For example, a sixth-grade teacher in a middle-class school posed the problem of two slow learners in her class who could not learn the usual computational algorithm for adding "mixed numbers." They could not understand or reproduce the following process, which all other students in the class had mastered:

$$\text{Given:} \quad 34\frac{3}{7} \qquad \text{Think:} \qquad 34\frac{3}{7} = 34\frac{3\cdot 8}{7\cdot 8} = 34\frac{24}{56}$$

$$+\ 27\frac{5}{8} \qquad \text{and} \qquad 27\frac{5}{8} = 27\frac{5\cdot 7}{8\cdot 7} = 27\frac{35}{56}$$

$$\text{The sum is} \quad 61\frac{59}{56} = 62\frac{3}{56}$$

There is a less efficient process that is also less sophisticated or complex, thus permitting a lower-level performance. Given the same problem, generate sets of fractions equivalent to the given fractions and, by inspection, determine a fraction in the first set and a fraction in the second set such that both fractions have the same denominator, then use the algorithm for adding fractions having the same denominator.

Thus,

$$34\frac{3}{7} = 34 + \left\{\frac{3}{7}, \frac{6}{14}, \frac{9}{21}, \frac{12}{28}, \frac{15}{35}, \frac{18}{42}, \frac{21}{49}, \boxed{\frac{24}{56}}, \cdots\right\}$$

$$+ 27\frac{5}{8} = 27 + \left\{\frac{5}{8}, \frac{10}{16}, \frac{15}{24}, \frac{20}{32}, \frac{25}{40}, \frac{30}{48}, \boxed{\frac{35}{56}}, \cdots\right\}$$

$$61\frac{59}{56}, \quad \text{or} \quad 62\frac{3}{56}$$

The process is tedious, of course. The point is that the slow learners were successful at the less sophisticated level and did acquire a skill in computing sums of mixed numbers.

The institute participants were expected to become curriculum developers primarily through adapting instruction and activities in mathematics to the aptitudes and needs of learners. The staff may have questioned the inclusion of some skills and concepts and the exclusion of others from the present-day curriculum, but the institute programs were designed to serve teachers of today's children in today's classrooms within the limitations of financial and professional resources available to them.

A program for teachers of slow learners, grades 7–10, Baltimore County, Maryland

An in-service course for teachers of slow learners in mathematics has been scheduled each year since 1967 by the Baltimore County school system in conjunction with its instructional program for slow learners in grades 7–10 (12). The in-service classes meet after school for fifteen two-hour sessions during the winter season. Enrollment is limited to twenty-five teachers. The content and structure of the in-service course must be considered in the context of the ongoing curriculum project, a locally initiated and locally funded program.

In 1966, following the school system's identification of the characteristics and needs of slow learners, a summer-workshop group of mathematics supervisors and teachers produced a resource manual of developmental, recreational, and computational activities in mathematics. The writing committee in subsequent summer workshops has revised and expanded the program, with current plans calling for construction of slow-learner programs through grade 12. The specification of behavioral objectives as they relate to mathematical concepts and skills is the basis of the curriculum project.

Teachers of slow learners are involved in the planning, production, and evaluation of instructional units. The writing committee for the first junior high school manual, used in 1966/67, included three elementary, six junior high, and three senior high teachers, in addition to members of the Office of Mathematics staff. Teachers participating in the experimental program during the first year developed one of the unique features of the current instructional program, a method of teaching called the "banded" approach. This particular approach recognizes the limited span of attenion of slow learners and provides for a variety of topics and activities in each lesson. The major band is devoted to the developmental activity for which specific behavioral objectives have been written, and it is generally sandwiched between two bands of shorter duration. The shorter bands include skill-maintenance activities, exploratory math-lab activities, pattern searches, or games and puzzles.

The more structured in-service training program, in which teachers may earn two hours of professional credit, is taught by a local mathematics supervisor, assisted by other members of the Office of Mathematics staff and the writing committee. Among the activities and topics included are the following: testing and guidance, the nature of slow learners, behavioral objectives, the mathematical significance of activities and games already written into the student program, the construction of additional games or activities, visits to classrooms using the program, and the exchange of ideas and experiences with other teachers of slow learners. (12.)

Among the unique and positive features of the program is the *context* in which in-service training occurs. The people who have written the instructional program and who have supervised its implementation in classrooms are also instructing the teachers' in-service courses. As part of their training, the teachers are developing and testing instructional units to be incorporated into the curriculum guide. Academic and laboratory components of the classes for teachers are, thus, much more closely correlated with the instructional program and classroom needs than any university-based training could be.

Other special features of the in-service course are the same as those that mark the instructional program for students: the specification of learning behaviors and the banded approach. The instructors of the teachers write behavioral objectives for their classes, just as the teachers will write behavioral objectives for *their* students. These trainers of teachers ask, "What do we expect the teachers to be able to do?" and then attempt to specify the desired outcomes in terms of observable behaviors.

For teachers who attend training programs during after-school hours, the banded approach is a change from the usual sleep-inducing, two-hour-lecture format of many in-service courses. A variety of topics and activities induce, instead, a change of pace which encourages active, creative, even enthusiastic, participation in learning. In the banded approach, flexibility is the key. The bands may vary in number and duration, depending on the topic being presented or the interests and needs of the teachers.

To date, any evaluation of the in-service program is largely subjective. However, the Coordinator of Mathematics reports that there is a discernible preference on the part of mathematics teachers for classes of slow learners rather than classes in general mathematics. The fact that teachers *ask* for slow learners seems to the writer a positive measure of the effectiveness of one school system's efforts in behalf of slow learners.

Cooperative teacher-training projects, grades 7–12, University of Denver and Douglas County Schools, Colorado

The features characterizing a series of cooperative in-service programs for teachers of low achievers in the Denver metropolitan schools are summarized in the description of two concurrently scheduled 1969/70 programs: a University of Denver–sponsored project for training returning members of the Peace Corps to teach the disadvantaged and low achievers in mathematics, grades 7–9; and the teacher-training component of COLAMDA (Committee on Low Achievers in Mathematics—Denver Area). The University-based program, designed to make use of "the special experience and qualities of the returning Peace Corps workers" (51, p. 1), consisted of a summer institute of five weeks' duration, followed by thirty weekly meetings during the academic year. COLAMDA project teachers in the training program were selected by their supervisors on the basis of their "commitment to develop a better learning atmosphere" for slow learners (92, p. 74). The teachers, each of whom taught a class in general, or basic, mathematics, attended a two-week workshop during the summer; training experiences during the school year were individualized through weekly classroom visits by the director of the project or one of his assistants.

Participants in both programs taught in junior or senior high schools in the Denver area. That the two programs were cooperative efforts, complementary in nature, is evidenced by the fact that the planning and instructional staff for both programs included the director of the University-sponsored project, the director of the Douglas

County COLAMDA project, and a state supervisor of mathematics from the Colorado State Department of Education.

In a brief review and evaluation of the University-based institute, the director identified its strengths and its weakness as follows:

The major strengths were (1) the training of teachers in mathematics in a laboratory setting, the format of which was "manipulation, simulation, and measurement"; (2) the tying of laboratory experiences to specific mathematics concepts; and (3) the systematic study of the mathematics content in the junior and senior high school curriculum, with some advanced topics included "to raise the teachers' sights" (50).

The major problem identified by the director is also a national one and a particular educational need to which the institute program was addressed. According to the original proposal (51, p. 2),

> Peace Corps workers who choose to enter teaching in the United States after their return are frequently disappointed that they are absorbed into rigidly controlled organizations where they are unable to use those very qualities which make them valuable to the Peace Corps—empathy for the disadvantaged and the ability and the patience to impart to the disadvantaged a desire to learn as well as learning itself. On the other hand, urban schools in disadvantaged areas . . . find it difficult to staff courses with teachers having those qualities.

Of the ten returning corpsmen in the institute, three of them did experience difficulty in adjusting to the regimentation of the public schools. Other participants in the program were twenty experienced teachers. The Peace Corps workers were "cooperative, excited, and enthusiastic" about their training and, together with the experienced teachers, generated a "good group chemistry" (50).

The summer workshop employed the mathematics laboratory as the central device in training teachers in mathematics and in methodology. Experiences included the use of desk calculators in simulated classroom experiments and assignments in mathematics. Flowcharting was studied as an aid to problem analysis. Teachers had access to a computer terminal and developed units in computer-aided instruction. They learned classroom uses of audiographics. Experiences with manipulative devices such as geoboards, Cuisenaire rods, and abaci were provided. Participants also studied the value of the controlled use of games, puzzles, and other motivational techniques for slow learners.

The laboratory experiences were carefully and explicitly related to skill acquisition and the clarification of concepts. Equipment purchased for the workshop was placed in the schools for student use during the academic year, as were the participant-created kits of manipulative materials and measurement tools. Mathematics content emphasized fundamental concepts in computing with real numbers and was developed concurrently with classroom techniques for working with students who lack foundational concepts and skills. The basic geometric and algebraic content of junior high school mathematics was reviewed, with emphasis on methodologies employing experimentation, discovery, and problem analysis.

The thirty two-hour in-service meetings were given over to participant discussion of classroom successes and problems, mathematics content related to classroom topics, expanded laboratory activities, and (in one out of every six meetings) topics in mathematics of intellectual interest to the participants without regard for classroom applications. The director reports that the interest and involvement were "tremendous, with perfect attendance" throughout the series of thirty lessons.

The COLAMDA project is a joint curriculum-development and teacher-training endeavor for the purposes of developing

> an effective program model for low achievers in mathematics, grades 7–12. . . . The teacher training segment of the project plans primary emphasis on favorable teacher attitude change toward the teaching of the low-achiever, identification of known successful instructional techniques and methods, development of realistic objectives and transposition of pure math theory into a usable form for low-achiever instruction. Each new project participant is required to attend a workshop designed on the above concerns. [92, p. 74]

Twenty-two teachers were enrolled in the 1969/70 training program. The mathematics laboratory was again the central training device in the summer workshop, with individualized instruction during the academic year. Desk calculators, adding machines, flowcharting, instructional aids, games, puzzles, manipulative materials, and overhead projectuals were used in the multisensory approaches to learning mathematics. Instructional techniques and methods were studied in the laboratory and in the classroom, and classroom materials and kits were prepared.

COLAMDA project objectives and evaluation procedures are stated in terms of five major concerns for a program model for low achievers: (1) student performance in mathematics, (2) student attitudes toward mathematics, (3) teacher attitudes toward teaching low-achiever mathematics, (4) the development or selection of field-tested materials and teaching aids, and (5) the collection of data on mathematics skills needed for entry-level jobs in the community, as well as those necessary for everyday living (92, pp. 77–79).

The evaluation procedure with regard to "favorable teacher attitudes toward teaching low-achiever mathematics" includes two criteria.

[The goal] to effect favorable teacher attitude . . . will be attained if there is—

a) An increased commitment by each teacher to working with low-achievers in mathematics. This commitment will be measured by responses of teachers in an interview, with additional information gathered from steering committee observations, building principal observations, and on observations by the project staff.

b) Evidence of flexibility and adaptation in using material and equipment in an effort to adapt to individual differences of students. Data on this will be from interviews, material inventory and observation of laboratory usage. [92, p. 76]

Few measurable results of teacher-training programs in mathematics for slow learners have been reported. Most of the published reports are descriptive in nature, and the evaluations of change in teaching behaviors are largely subjective. The ultimate measure, of course, is student performance in mathematics. Perhaps at some time in the future there will be more specific guidelines for training teachers of slow learners. The fact is that the institutions whose programs are described herein felt they could not wait for answers in the future. To paraphrase Baltimore County's coordinator of mathematics, "The slow learners . . . were with us here and now— and in great abundance. The urgency of the situation prompted the [institutions] to make a start using the best available sources, consultants and the experience of dedicated teachers." (12, p. 47.) Although the answers are still not in, the writer recommends the directions that have been charted.

Recommendations

The nature of workshops for teachers of slow learners in mathematics will depend on many factors, such as administrative leadership and support, teacher commitment and prior training in contemporary mathematics, identification and recruitment of resource people and organizations, time schedules, and financial support. The suggestions that follow are by no means exhaustive of the possible structures or resources for in-service teacher training.

Short-term workshops (25–40 hours)

For teachers of grades 7–12. In the October 1969 issue of the *Mathematics Teacher* Milton W. Beckmann describes a short-term workshop held at the University of Nebraska (8). The schedule of topics is included in his article, consultants are identified, and resource materials and organizations are named. The workshop is recommended to university-based mathematics educators, school district supervisors, and departmental chairmen as a prototype for short-term workshops.

The fifteen sessions of two and one-half hours each could be modified to meet the time limitations of other in-service arrangements—for instance, that of a district faculty's preplanning week and four or five subsequent released-time, after-school, or Saturday morning meetings.

At each session there were from two to five presentations, including reports on books and articles related to low achievers in mathematics, descriptions of low-achiever materials and projects, involvement in the laboratory type of experiences, films, games, and invited lectures by master teachers. A one-day conference was held in conjunction with the workshop, and on this day the presentations were made by nationally known experts in the field of teaching low achievers in mathematics.

Detailed reports of each day's session were reproduced and distributed to all members for their permanent reference file.

It is evident from Beckmann's description that major factors in the success of the workshop were strong and concerned leadership; cooperative preplanning; and the active involvement of participating teachers in the collecting, reviewing, and developing of materials.

For teachers of grades 1–10. The in-service instructor with limited resources might consider a program based on experimentation with selected "models" of teaching behaviors. A collection of professional periodicals is an excellent source of possible models—that is, descriptive reports by individual teachers of classroom materials and strategies which they have tried and found successful with slow learners. (See references at the end of this chapter for suggested readings from the *Arithmetic Teacher* and the *Mathematics Teacher*.)

In the majority of the reports, the preparation of materials and the teaching strategies are sufficiently detailed to allow for emulation by other teachers.

Participation during the period of the workshop might consist of two hours each week in after-school or released-time meetings and one regular classroom period each week in which experimental approaches suggested by the models are tried. In planning for the initial in-service meeting, a large number of recent issues of periodicals should be assembled and one or two model classroom experiences identified for simulation. The games, worksheets, or manipulative aids necessary in the simulation will have to be collected or reproduced, and the workshop member selected for the instructor's role may find it helpful to pilot the described experiences in his own classroom first.

Following the workshop simulations and related discussions, the teachers can be asked to search the periodicals on hand and select one or more models which they will try in their own classrooms before the next meeting. At that time they should be prepared to share or demonstrate the materials they have used and to discuss their students' reactions. Subsequent workshop activities should continue the pattern of experimenting with a range of "model" teaching behaviors and then assessing the effectiveness of different teaching behaviors in terms of instructional objectives and learners' behaviors.

During one in-service simulation, teachers should be assigned individual or group projects in measurement, the physical acts of measuring to be carried out during the meeting just as students in the mathematics classroom should be permitted to make their own measurements. For instance, the teachers could measure the dimensions of the room in meters; determine the speed of automobiles passing in front of the building; measure the height of a flagpole; estimate the number of beans in a large jar and find ways to verify their estimations without counting; estimate and measure the capacity or volume of a variety of containers; make several different paper models of a square foot or a square yard (with at least one foot-square model and one yard-square model); demonstrate with cardboard or paper models that 144 square inches equal 1 square foot and 9 square feet equal 1 square yard. Teachers who have themselves engaged in the physical act of measuring are more likely to provide the same real and practical approaches to measurement in their own classrooms.

A change of pace can be introduced at the in-service meetings with films borrowed from state and local professional libraries; demonstrations by commercial distributors of manipulative materials or activities units; display and demonstration of student-created work; new materials and games which a "search" committee has located, reviewed, or developed; and, if possible, with consultants who are knowledgeable about some of the nationally known programs.

The proposed structure can provide the direction and the mutual support and encouragement that many teachers need in order to initiate changes in established classroom procedures. Experimentation with different teaching behaviors is, of course, not the whole solution to the problem of teaching mathematics to slow learners, but it is a first step. It is hoped that sustained practice in experimentation will unleash the creative powers of teachers to continue seeking solutions to the problem long after the in-service program is completed.

For teachers of grades K–6. An alternate structure for a short-term workshop might be an intensive five- or six-day schedule of seminars and laboratory sessions. The director of the workshop could begin by planning and equipping a teaching demonstration center that could also serve as a prototype for student learning centers. (For suggestions, see chapter 8 on the laboratory approach and, in the present chapter, the descriptions already given of teacher-training mathematics laboratories.) The cost of equipment and materials can vary, depending on whether one purchases commercially prepared manipulative materials and games, or contracts with local industrial arts departments or hobbyists for specified materials, or makes many of the materials himself with the help of teacher-participants.

Money is well spent for selected professional books and periodicals, programmed units in mathematics, collections of experimental student units, teachers' guides, and task cards for use with manipulative materials. (This yearbook will be an invaluable sourcebook.) Pre-workshop arrangements should include the recruitment of experienced and enthusiastic teachers or consultants to direct the simulated classroom activities with laboratory materials.

However one varies or modifies the sequence of major topics suggested in the chart, a "banded" approach is recommended. With the greater time band devoted to the major topic, the time bands of shorter duration should allow for individual or small-group work with materials that have already been introduced and the creation and construction of teacher-developed materials.

Meetings	Major Topics
1, 2	Discussion of preassigned readings, particularly chapters 1 and 2 of this yearbook. Brief review of Piagetian learning theory and related research, with emphasis on number concepts and conservations. Demonstrations. Classroom simulation with attribute blocks. Review and discussion of Hess and Shipman's "Congnititive Elements in Maternal Behavior" (48, pp. 57–85). Relating and discussing the above.
3, 4	Simulated classroom experiences with Cuisenaire rods.
5	Simulated classroom experiences with the Dienes Multibase Arithmetic Blocks.
6, 7, 8, 9	Study of Wirtz, Botel, and Beberman's four-part set of books (106), which is recommended for purchase by each teacher. (Under each of two titles there are two books: a teacher's guide and a book of student work forms that purchasers may duplicate as they wish.) Viewing the set of ten related films showing classroom lessons in which the activities and strategies described in the teacher's guides are used.
10, 11	Using geoboards in simulated classroom activities, as suggested in exercises in chapter 8. Doing projects in measurement.
12	Review by workshop members of Nuffield Foundation booklets (73) and Biggs and Maclean's *Freedom to Learn* (11). Evaluation of workshop: "Where do we go from here?"

Laboratory activities should be related to the development of mathematical concepts and the acquisition of skills. Resources other than those used in connection with major topics should be provided for outside reading and exploration. Active teacher involvement in a variety of flexible and experimental approaches to the teaching-learning act is the immediate goal of the short-term workshop.

Professional credit in-service course (50 hours or more)

A new and promising trend in mathematics curriculum development ignores the traditionally horizontal and fragmented treatment of elementary mathematics and emphasizes instead a collection of "strands." The strands identify the big ideas in mathematics, such as relations and functions, numbers and numeration, operations and properties, geometry, measurement, and probability and statistics. Guidelines for implementing a strands approach ignore the arbitrary structures of grade levels, administrative divisions, and branches in elementary mathematics—that is, eight years of arithmetic, one of algebra, and one of geometry. Instead, the guidelines suggest early, intuitive experiences of the readiness type in each of the strands, with the developmental nature of mathematical and logical ideas adjusted to maturational stages in learning.

The in-service training of teachers of slow learners in mathematics could profit from a strands approach. Instruction and exchange of ideas among teachers along the vertical dimension of grade placements would better serve the needs for individualizing learning. Participants in the course should be recruited from those who teach basic, or general, mathematics in a senior high school and those who teach slow learners in the feeder junior high and elementary schools. Content strands of the course may include, or be selected from, the topics that constitute the chapter divisions of this yearbook.

In the content of strands in mathematics and in teaching mathematics to slow learners there is considerable overlap among grades and administrative divisions. It is apparent from a review of the training programs described in this chapter that many basic assumptions, materials, and strategies in the mathematics laboratories for teachers of grades K–8 and teachers of grades 7–12 are the same. The recommended prototypes for short-term workshops, with few modifications, are appropriate for teachers in any administrative division. The fact is that instruction in mathematics for slow learners must be in terms of individual students' developmental needs and interests, not grade-level placements.

It is especially important to include primary-grade teachers in any such program. Because problems of slow learners are more glaringly evident at the upper-elementary and secondary grade levels than they are in the first and second grades, the greater efforts to solve the problems have been in remedial programs rather than in early public school programs. However, if teachers of primary grades were more acutely aware of the future expectations for their students, some of the problems might be prevented. For instance, in order to ensure an adequate and sound development of the concepts and skills employed in computation, the first-grade teacher, the fourth-grade teacher, the seventh-grade teacher—all teachers who serve the same child over the period of years he must attend school—need to talk to one another in an effort to identify and remedy potential problem areas. The following anecdote makes the point.

The teachers in an inner-city school (grades K–7) were discussing problems in teaching computation. The fourth-grade teacher had complained that his students did not understand the place-value principles involved in computing differences such as 43 − 17. In the ensuing discussion a first-grade teacher remarked that she had just completed a unit on place value and that all her students knew what 17, 43, and all two-digit numbers meant. When asked to demonstrate what these first graders had learned about 43, she wrote, "43 = Ⓧ Ⓧ Ⓧ Ⓧ ///." Further questioning elicited the information that her first graders had spent about four weeks learning to write that all two-digit numbers are equal to Xs with rings drawn around them and tally marks with fingers drawn under them. The skill is of little value in preparation for the fourth grade. How does one "borrow" one of those Ⓧ 's and take it apart to have a lot of /'s?

These first graders were not unintelligent or unteachable. They had learned well what they were told to learn. Children from a poor socioeconomic community, they will be labeled "slow learners" in the fourth grade. Their poor performance in computation will be unjustly attributed to their "poor cultural background." During the four weeks allotted to learning about place value, these children should have been tying string around physical objects in bundles of ten, or putting rubber bands around bundles of ten singles, or putting singles into paper sacks or boxes and then counting the bundles and the singles left over. As they bundled objects and counted, the teacher could have instructed them in the arbitrary convention of recording their counts of bundles and singles. That is, to record the physical reality of 4 bundles and 3 singles, one uses a coding scheme in which the count of bundles is written to the *left* of the count of singles, and one reads the symbol "43" as "4 bundles and 3 singles" or "4 tens and 3 ones" or "forty-three."

All teachers who are responsible for first experiences, reinforcement experiences, or remedial experiences in learning to use the decimal numeration system should recognize that it is an arbitrary and complex coding system and that the development of skills in computation is dependent to a great extent on the development of skills in using the code. Much of the trouble that slow learners have with computation stems from an incomplete understanding of the numeration, or number coding, system.

A joint study by primary and upper-grade teachers of the strand on characteristics and needs of slow learners should point up the physically oriented learning styles of many children and the concomitant need for a great deal more physical input in the primary grades before coding takes place. A joint study of the strand on reaching the slow learner through behavioral objectives should lead to the writing of performance objectives and the identification of enabling skills; these activities could, in turn, provide more specific directions for primary-grade teachers in the curriculum choices they must make and more specific guidelines for middle- and upper-grade teachers in diagnostic and prescriptive measures. A joint study of the strands on multisensory aids and the laboratory approach would suggest the means—materials and strategies—by which school faculties could provide a more consistent and purposeful sequence of activities across the grades to meet the needs for physical input in the achievement of the specified objectives.

Creative and ingenious leadership will be needed in planning and implementing a professional credit course along the vertical dimensions of selected strands for teachers whose training and experiences have equipped them with quite different sets of concerns and expectations. However, the common concern with a particular population of learners in a particular content area should provide a focus the instructor can use in the planning and execution of the course. For instance, if teachers are recruited from schools in a particular geographic area, then the strand on the characteristics and needs of slow learners (see chap. 1) can provide a context in which *their* slow learners' characteristics and needs can be more specifically delineated. In turn, the instructor and teachers can use this set of characteristics and needs as a guide for determining the inclusion of other strands.

To provide for differences in abilities, needs, and interests, learning can be individualized through laboratory experiences; teacher options within a required reading list; individual and small-group assignments in reviewing, collecting and developing materials for presentation to the total group; experimentation with new materials and teaching strategies in a practicum; and individual conferences. It is through the identification and discussion of common problems along the developmental dimensions of a strands approach that each teacher can acquire a greater awareness of his role and his responsibility in the sequenced learning experiences of his students.

Concluding Remarks

Whether or not in-service training programs use a strands approach, the major recommendations are these: The usual lecture format should be avoided and multisensory aids employed in instructing teachers in mathematics. Each teacher should be actively engaged in reviewing, collecting, and developing materials for use in the course and in his classroom. Experimentation with a range of possible teaching behaviors and assessment of different behaviors in terms of instructional objectives and learning behaviors should be supported. Teacher exchange of ideas and experiences should be encouraged.

Although the suggested content for in-service programs appears to be a smorgasbord of topics, activities, and strategies, it is important that the supervisor-instructor provide a structure of rather clear-cut objectives and direction, at least in the major instructional "bands."

The ultimate goal of the recommended programs is the establishment of classroom environments in which purposeful, creative, and self-directed learning in mathematics can take place. The intermediate goal should be to establish a comparable structure for training the classroom teachers of mathematics.

REFERENCES

1. Abbott, Janet S. *Learn to Fold, Fold to Learn.* Teacher's ed. Pasadena, Calif.: Franklin Publications, 1968.
2. ———. *Mirror Magic.* Teacher's ed. Pasadena, Calif.: Franklin Publications, 1968.
3. Almy, Millie, Edward Chittenden, and Paula Miller. *Young Children's Thinking: Studies of Some Aspects of Piaget's Theory.* New York: Teachers College Press, 1966.
4. Ashton-Warner, Sylvia. *Teacher.* New York: Simon & Schuster, 1963.
5. Association of Teachers of Mathematics [Great Britain]. *Notes on Mathematics in the Primary School.* London: Cambridge University Press, 1967. Also available as paperback from the New York branch of Cambridge University Press and the Cuisenaire Company of America, Inc., 12 Church St., New Rochelle, N.Y. 10805.
6. ———. *Some Lessons in Mathematics: A Handbook on the Teaching of "Modern" Mathematics.* Edited by T. J. Fletcher. New York: Cambridge University Press, 1964.
7. Bachrach, Beatrice. "Do Your First Graders Measure Up? (A Report of a Unit with Disadvantaged Learners)." *Arithmetic Teacher* 16 (November 1969): 537–38.
8. Beckmann, Milton W. "Teaching the Low Achiever in Mathematics." *Mathematics Teacher* 62 (October 1969): 443–46.
9. Bereiter, Carl, and Siegfried Engelman. *Teaching Disadvantaged Children in the Preschool.* Englewood Cliffs, N.J.: Prentice-Hall, 1966.
10. Biggs, Edith E. "Trial and Experiment." *Arithmetic Teacher* 17 (January 1970): 26–32.

11. Biggs, Edith E., and James R. MacLean. *Freedom to Learn: An Active Learning Approach to Mathematics.* Don Mills, Ont.: Addison-Wesley (Canada), 1969.
12. Brant, Vincent. "Behavioral Objectives and the Slow Learner—an Action Approach." In *Report of a Conference: Programs in Mathematics for Low Achievers,* pp. 29–70. Charlottesville, Va.: Association of State Supervisors of Mathematics, 1970.
13. Bruner, Jerome. *The Process of Education.* Cambridge, Mass.: Harvard University Press, 1961.
14. ———. *Toward a Theory of Instruction.* Cambridge, Mass.: Harvard University Press, Belknap Press, 1966; New York: W. W. Norton & Co., 1968.
15. Burt, Bruce C. "Drawing Conclusions from Samples (an Activity for the Low Achiever)." *Arithmetic Teacher* 16 (November 1969): 539–41.
16. Bye, Nikoline. "Self-Service In-Service." *Mathematics Teacher* 61 (October 1968): 630–33.
17. Cambridge Conference on Teacher Training. *Goals for Mathematical Education of Elementary School Teachers: A Report of the Conference.* Published for Education Development Center. Boston: Houghton Mifflin Co., 1967.
18. Chandler, Arnold M. "Mathematics and the Low Achiever." *Arithmetic Teacher* 17 (March 1970): 196–98.
19. Clarkson, David M. "Mathematical Activity." *Arithmetic Teacher* 15 (October 1968): 493–98.
20. Cohen, Donald. *Inquiry in Mathematics via the Geo-Board.* New York: Walker Teaching Aids, 1967.
21. Davidson, Jessica. *Using the Cuisenaire Rods: A Photo/Text Guide for Teachers.* New Rochelle, N.Y.: Cuisenaire Co. of America, 1969.
22. Davidson, Patricia S. "An Annotated Bibliography of Suggested Manipulative Devices." *Arithmetic Teacher* 15 (October 1968): 509–24.
23. Davidson, Patricia S., and Arlene W. Fair. "A Mathematics Laboratory—from Dream to Reality." *Arithmetic Teacher* 17 (February 1970): 105–10.
24. Davies, Robert A. "Low Achiever Lesson in Primes." *Arithmetic Teacher* 16 (November 1969): 529–32.
25. Davis, Robert B. *The Changing Curriculum: Mathematics.* Washington, D.C.: Association for Supervision and Curriculum Development, 1967.
26. ———. *Discovery in Mathematics: A Text for Teachers.* The Madison Project. Reading, Mass.: Addison-Wesley Publishing Co., 1964.
27. ———. *Explorations in Mathematics: A Text for Teachers.* Reading, Mass.: Addison-Wesley Publishing Co., 1966.
28. Denholm, Richard A. *Making and Using Graphs and Nomographs.* Teacher's ed. Pasadena, Calif.: Franklin Publications, 1968.
29. Dienes, Zoltan P. "Comments of Some Problems of Teacher Education in Mathematics." *Arithmetic Teacher* 17 (March 1970): 263–69.
30. ———. *Modern Mathematics for Young Children.* New York: Herder & Herder, 1965.
31. Dienes, Zoltan P., and E. W. Golding. *Exploration of Space and Practical Measurement.* Mathematics Experience Programme, edited by Zoltan P. Dienes. New York: Herder & Herder, 1966.
32. ———. *Learning Logic, Logical Games.* Mathematics Experience Pro-

gramme, edited by Zoltan P. Dienes. New York: Herder & Herder, 1966.
33. ———. *Sets, Numbers, and Powers.* Mathematics Experience Programme, edited by Zoltan P. Dienes. New York: Herder & Herder, 1966.
34. Duckworth, Eleanor. "Piaget Rediscovered." *Arithmetic Teacher* 11 (November 1964): 496–99.
35. Dutton, Wilbur H. "Teaching Time Concepts to Culturally Disadvantaged Primary-Age Children." *Arithmetic Teacher* 14 (May 1967): 358–64.
36. Elder, Florence. "Mathematics for the Below-Average Achiever in High School." *Mathematics Teacher* 60 (March 1967): 235–40.
37. Elkins, Deborah, and Hilda Taba. *Teaching Strategies for the Culturally Disadvantaged.* Chicago: Rand McNally & Co., 1966.
38. Fantini, Mario D., and Gerald Weinstein. *The Disadvantaged: Challenge to Education.* New York: Harper & Row, 1968.
39. Fitzgerald, William M. "A Mathematics Laboratory for Prospective Elementary School Teachers." *Arithmetic Teacher* 15 (October 1968): 547–49.
40. Foley, Jack, and Leroy B. Smith. "Summer In-Service Experiences in Teaching Noncollege Preparatory Mathematics." *Mathematics Teacher* 61 (April 1968): 437–40.
41. Fremont, Herbert. "Some Thoughts on Teaching Mathematics to Disadvantaged Groups." *Arithmetic Teacher* 11 (May 1964): 319–22.
42. Fremont, Herbert, and Neal Ehrenberg. "The Hidden Potential of Low Achievers." *Mathematics Teacher* 59 (October 1966): 551–57.
43. Gagné, Robert M. *The Conditions of Learning.* 2d ed. New York: Holt, Rinehart & Winston, 1970.
44. Gibney, Thomas C. "Multiplication for the Slow Learner." *Arithmetic Teacher* 9 (February 1962): 74–76.
45. Groenendyk, E. A., and Terry E. Shoemaker. *Experimental Ninth Grade General Mathematics.* Teacher's ed. Pella, Iowa: Central University of Iowa Press, 1965.
46. Harper, E. Harold, and Leslie P. Steffe. *The Effects of Selected Experiences on the Ability of Kindergarten and First Grade Children to Conserve Numerousness.* U.S. Office of Education Cooperative Research Project 2850, Technical Report no. 38. Madison: University of Wisconsin, Research and Development Center for Learning and Re-Education, 1968.
47. Heard, Ida Mae. "Making and Using Graphs in the Kindergarten Mathematics Program." *Arithmetic Teacher* 15 (October 1968): 504–6.
48. Hess, Robert D., and Virginia C. Shipman. *The Craft of Teaching and the Schooling of Teachers.* Proceedings of the First National Conference of the U.S. Office of Education Tri-University Project in Elementary Education, Denver, 18–20 September 1967. Lincoln, Nebr.: Tri-University Curriculum Center, 1967.
49. Higgins, Jon L. "Sugar-Cube Mathematics." *Arithmetic Teacher* 16 (October 1969): 427–31.
50. Hoffman, Ruth Irene. "The Slow Learner—Changing His View of Math." *Bulletin of the National Association of Secondary School Principals* 52 (April 1968): 86–97.
51. ———. "A Special Training Program for Returning Peace Corps Workers for Teaching the Disadvantaged and Low Achievers in Mathematics, Grades 7–9." Mimeographed. Proposal to U.S. Office of Education for Operating Grant, University of Denver, May 1968.

52. Holt, John. *How Children Fail*. New York: Pitman Publishing Corp., 1964.
53. ———. *How Children Learn*. New York: Pitman Publishing Corp., 1968.
54. Homan, Doris Ruth. "The Child with a Learning Disability in Arithmetic." *Arithmetic Teacher* 17 (March 1970): 199–203.
55. Houston, Robert. *Improving Mathematics Education for Elementary School Teachers*. Lansing, Mich.: Michigan State University, 1967.
56. Hunt, Joseph M. *Intelligence and Experience*. New York: Ronald Press, 1961.
57. Inhelder, Barbel, and Jean Piaget. *The Growth of Logical Thinking from Childhood to Adolescence*. Translated by Anne Parsons and Stanley Milgram. New York: Basic Books, 1958.
58. Keiffer, Mildred C. "The Development of Teaching Materials for Low-Achieving Pupils in Seventh- and Eighth-Grade Mathematics." *Arithmetic Teacher* 15 (November 1968): 599–604.
59. Kennedy, Leonard M., and Robert Alves. "In-Service Education for Elementary School Mathematics Teachers: Responses to Nine Questions." *Arithmetic Teacher* 11 (November 1964): 506–9.
60. Kessler, Bernard M. "A Discovery Approach to the Introduction of Flowcharting in the Elementary Grades." *Arithmetic Teacher* 17 (March 1970): 220–24.
61. Kohl, Herbert R. *Thirty-six Children*. New York: New American Library, 1967.
62. Loftus, Sonja. "Fibonacci Numbers: Fun and Fundamentals for the Slow Learner." *Arithmetic Teacher* 17 (March 1970): 204–8.
63. Mager, Robert F. *Preparing Instructional Objectives*. Palo Alto, Calif.: Fearon Publishers, 1962.
64. May, Lola J. "Learning Laboratories in Elementary Schools in Winnetka." *Arithmetic Teacher* 15 (October 1968): 501–3.
65. Mintz, Natalie, and Herbert Fremont. "Some Practical Ideas for Teaching Mathematics to Disadvantaged Children." *Arithmetic Teacher* 12 (April 1965): 258–60.
66. Morrisett, Lloyd M., and John Vinsonhaler, eds. *Mathematical Learning*. Society for Research and Development Monographs, vol. 30, no. 1, serial no. 99. Chicago: University of Chicago Press, 1965.
67. National Council of Teachers of Mathematics. *The Growth of Mathematical Ideas, Grades K-12*. Twenty-fourth Yearbook. Washington, D.C.: The Council, 1959.
68. ———. *More Topics in Mathematics for Elementary School Teachers*. Thirtieth Yearbook. Washington, D.C.: The Council, 1969.
69. ———. *Topics in Mathematics for Elementary School Teachers*. Twenty-ninth Yearbook. Washington, D.C.: The Council, 1964.
70. National Society for the Study of Education. *Mathematics Education*. Sixty-ninth Yearbook, pt. 1, edited by Edward G. Begle. Chicago: University of Chicago Press.
71. Noar, Gertrude. *The Teacher and Integration*. Washington, D.C.: Student National Education Association, 1966.
72. Noddings, Nellie L. "Providing for Individual Rates of Learning in Mathematics." *Mathematics Teacher* 62 (November 1969): 543–45.

73. Nuffield Foundation. *Nuffield Mathematics Project* series. New York: John Wiley & Sons, 1967–69.
74. Passow, A. Harry, ed. *Education in Depressed Areas.* New York: Bureau of Publication, Teachers College, Columbia University, 1963; Teachers College Press, 1968.
75. Passow, A. Harry, Miriam Goldberg, and Abraham Tannenbaum, eds. *Education of the Disadvantaged.* New York: Holt, Rinehart & Winston, 1967.
76. Pearcy, J. F. F., and K. Lewis. *Experiments in Mathematics, Stage 1, Stage 2,* and *Stage 3.* Boston: Houghton Mifflin Co., 1966, 1967.
77. Pettigrew, Thomas F. *A Profile of the Negro American.* Princeton, N.J.: D. Van Nostrand Co., 1964.
78. Piaget, Jean. *The Child's Conception of Number.* Translated by C. Gattegno and F. M. Hodgson. 1952. Reprint. New York: Humanities Press.
79. ———. *The Language and Thought of the Child.* Translated by Marjorie Gabain. 1926. Reprint. Cleveland: World Publishing Co., Meridian Books, 1955.
80. Piaget, Jean, and Barbel Inhelder. *The Psychology of the Child.* Translated by Helen Weaver. New York: Basic Books, 1969.
81. Piaget, Jean, Barbel Inhelder, and Alina Szeminska. *The Child's Conception of Geometry.* New York: Basic Books, 1960.
82. Potter, Mary, and Virgil Mallory. *Education in Mathematics for the Slow Learner.* Washington, D.C.: National Council of Teachers of Mathematics, 1958.
83. Proctor, Amelia D. "A World of Hope—Helping Slow Learners Enjoy Mathematics." *Mathematics Teacher* 58 (February 1965): 118–22.
84. Rogers, Carl L. *Freedom to Learn.* Columbus, Ohio: Charles E. Merrill Books, 1969.
85. Roper, Susan. *Paper and Pencil Geometry.* Teacher's ed. Pasadena, Calif.: Franklin Publications, 1968.
86. Ross, Ramon. "Diagnosis and Correction of Arithmetic Underachievement." *Arithmetic Teacher* 10 (January 1963): 22–27.
87. Schaefer, Anne W., and Albert H. Mauthe. "Problem Solving with Enthusiasm—the Mathematics Laboratory." *Arithmetic Teacher* 17 (January 1970): 7–14.
88. Schools Council. *Mathematics in the Primary Schools,* Curriculum Bulletin no. 1. 2d ed. London: Her Majesty's Stationery Office, 1966.
89. School Mathematics Study Group. *Developing Mathematics Readiness in Pre-School Programs.* Pasadena, Calif.: A. C. Vroman Co.
90. ———. *Preliminary Report on an Experiment with Junior High Very Low Achievers in Mathematics.* SMSG Reports, no. 6, edited by E. G. Begle. Stanford: Stanford University, 1968.
91. ———. *The Slow Learner Project: The Secondary School "Slow Learner" in Mathematics.* SMSG Reports, no. 5, edited by E. G. Begle. Stanford: Stanford University, 1968.
92. Shoemaker, Terry. "Teaching the Low Achiever—Success or Failure." Mimeographed. Paper read at National Conference of State Supervisors of Mathematics, University of Virginia, 4–9 December 1969.
93. Shulman, Lee S., and Evan R. Keislar, eds. *Learning by Discovery: A Critical Appraisal.* Rand McNally Education Series. Chicago: Rand McNally & Co., 1966.

94. Sigel, Irving E., and Frank H. Hooper. *Logical Thinking in Children: Research Based on Piaget's Theory.* New York: Holt, Rinehart & Winston, 1968.
95. Steffe, Leslie P. *The Performance of First Grade Children in Four Levels of Conservation of Numerousness and Three IQ Groups when Solving Arithmetic Addition Problems.* U.S. Office of Education Cooperative Research Project 2850, Technical Report no. 14. Madison: University of Wisconsin, Research and Development Center for Learning and Re-Education, 1968.
96. Steward, David S., and Margaret S. Steward. "Development and Standardization of an Instrument for Assessing Video-Taped Data of Teacher Management in the Elementary Classroom." Mimeographed. Research report under Program for Increasing Educational Activity at Emory University, contract no. OEC 2-6-062707-2127, 1969.
97. Swan, Malcolm D., and Orville E. Jones. "Preservice Teachers Clarify Mathematical Percepts through Field Experiences." *Arithmetic Teacher* 16 (December 1969): 643-45.
98. Swart, William L. "A Laboratory Plan for Teaching Measurement in Grades 1-8." *Arithmetic Teacher* 14 (December 1967): 652-53.
99. Sweet, Raymond. "Organizing a Mathematics Laboratory." *Mathematics Teacher* 60 (February 1967): 117-20.
100. Tinti, Robert. "Mathematics through Cardboard Carpentry (a Unit for Low Achievers)." *Arithmetic Teacher* 17 (March 1970): 209-10.
101. Travers, Kenneth J. "Computation: Low Achievers' Stumbling Block or Stepping Stone?" *Arithmetic Teacher* 16 (November 1969): 523-28.
102. Trivett, John V. *Mathematical Awareness,* pt. 1 and pt. 2. New Rochelle, N.Y.: Cuisenaire Co. of America, 1963.
103. Unkel, Esther. "Arithmetic Is a Joyous Experience for Elementary School Children in Great Britain." *Arithmetic Teacher* 15 (February 1968): 133-37.
104. Walter, Marion. "A Second Example of Informal Geometry: Milk Cartons." *Arithmetic Teacher* 16 (May 1969): 368-70. Reprinted in *Readings in Geometry from the "Arithmetic Teacher,"* pp. 48-50. Washington, D.C.: National Council of Teachers of Mathematics, 1970.
105. Weiss, Sol. "Innovations and Research in the Teaching of Mathematics to the Terminal Student." *Mathematics Teacher* 60 (October 1967): 611-18.
106. Wirtz, Robert W., Morton Botel, and Max Beberman. *Teacher's Guide* and *Work Forms* for *Developing Insights into Elementary Mathematics: Operations with Whole Numbers* and *Teacher's Guide* and *Work Forms* for *Toward Improving Computation.* 4 pts., not available separately. Washington, D.C.: Curriculum Development Associates, 1968, 1970.
107. Woodby, Lauren G., ed. *The Low Achiever in Mathematics.* Report of a conference sponsored by the U.S. Office of Education and the National Council of Teachers of Mathematics. U.S. Office of Education Bulletin 1965, no. 31. Washington, D.C.: Government Printing Office, 1965.
108. ———. *Preliminary Report of the Conference on the Low Achiever in Mathematics.* Washington, D.C.: National Council of Teachers of Mathematics, 1964.
109. Young, J. W. A. "The Teaching of Mathematics." Excerpts from a text first printed in 1906. *Mathematics Teacher* 61 (March 1968): 287-95.

Appendix A: Activities, Games, and Applications

THOMAS E. ROWAN
WILLIAM G. McKENZIE

This beginning section of Appendix A suggests activities—including applications and games—that are suitable for slow learners of mathematics. Many of the activities are adaptable to various topics. Some are included because they are motivational *and* because they can be used to move the pupil toward some specific and valued mathematical goal. A few are included because of their motivational value alone. It is left to the teacher to match the appropriate activities with specific objectives. Many of the activities are useful, in some form, for both the elementary and secondary levels. Again, the decision in this regard is left to the teacher, since the curriculum at these levels may vary from one part of the country to another. We hope you will find many useful ideas here and that this presentation will serve as a base on which to build an increasing collection of such ideas.

Lightning addition

The pupils select three 3-digit numerals, which are recorded on the chalkboard and on paper by the pupils. The teacher then supplies two 3-digit numerals and asks the students to find the sum of the five addends. The teacher or a pupil who knows the method then writes the sum on the chalkboard without going through the addition. The pupils check this sum on their papers. Students can be challenged to find the secret or can be told the secret after their appetites are sufficiently whetted.

Example: The students supply 453, 721, and 584. The teacher adds 546 and 415 to this and immediately writes the sum 2,719.

$$\left.\begin{array}{r}453\\721\\584\end{array}\right\} \text{students}$$
$$\left.\begin{array}{r}546\\415\end{array}\right\} \text{teacher}$$
$$\overline{2,719}$$

The secret is in the fact that the teacher selected the "nines complements" of two of the student numbers—453 and 584, in this case. Note that $453 + 546 = 584 + 415 = 999$. Thus $999 + 999 = 2,000 - 2$, and the addition is solved by adding this to the remaining addend, 721. Thus $721 + 2,000 - 2 = 2,719$, the sum.

This procedure can be done with other variations. You can use more addends, or more digits per addend. The students always supply one more than half the addends. Consider these examples:

$$\left.\begin{array}{r}35\\28\\74\\23\end{array}\right\} \text{students}$$
$$\left.\begin{array}{r}64\\25\\76\end{array}\right\} \text{teacher}$$
$$\overline{325} = 28 + 300 - 3$$

$$\left.\begin{array}{r}7,683\\2,931\end{array}\right\} \text{students}$$
$$\underline{7,068} - \text{teacher}$$
$$17,682 = 7,683 + 10,000 - 1$$

An interesting variation is for the teacher to supply the answer immediately after the pupils have given the first addend. In this case, the teacher simply uses the first number as the key number and supplies the "nines complement" for each additional addend later given by the pupils.

$$838 - \text{students}$$
$$\left.\begin{array}{r}136\\728\end{array}\right\} \text{students' additional}$$
$$\left.\begin{array}{r}863\\271\end{array}\right\} \text{teacher}$$
$$\overline{2,836} = 838 + 2,000 - 2$$

A version of nim for class competition

Nim is an ancient mathematical game that takes various forms. The following is just one version that has been adapted for group competition.

In this version, the objective is to be the player to add the addend that produces the goal number. Any goal number may be used, but for beginning play it is best to use a fairly easy one. Let's consider an example using 11. The players take turns adding addends until the goal is reached, and the one to reach it wins. The addends that can be used are selected by the teacher or players. In the case with the goal of 11, suppose we use the addends 1 and 2. The game might then progress as follows:

    First player: 1,   5,   8,   11 (the goal)
    Second player: 3,   6,   9,

The game can be adapted for groups as follows: The class is divided into two teams of equal numbers. If there is an odd number of students, one might serve as judge and/or scorekeeper. Each team is then subdivided into pairs. If each team has an odd number, one member can be team captain. A player is permitted to talk to his partner but to no other team member. A pair from the first team plays a pair from the second team; and this is repeated, alternating the first play, until all pairs have played. The team gets one point for each game won by a pair from that team. Players will ordinarily look for the system that will assure victory. After the teams have played, the teacher may invite anyone from either team to challenge him to a game. If the student wins, then his team gets two extra points. If he loses, then the team loses one point. It is also possible to record the results in various ways. Sometimes they are recorded as follows:

$$1, 2, 4, 6, 8, 9, (11)$$

Other times they may be recorded so that the pupils do a little more figuring.

$$1 + 2 + 2 + 1 + 2 + 1 + 2$$

The game can be adapted to the abilities of the students, as well as adjusted according to experience in playing, by changing the goal and/or the addends. Thus a goal of 14, 21, 100, or any other number might be used. The addends 1 and 2 can be used, or the number of addends can be increased. For a goal of 21 the addends could be 1, 2, and 3. With a goal of 100, the addends might be 1, 2, 3, ... , 9.

ACTIVITIES, GAMES, AND APPLICATIONS 447

The game gives practice with basic addition and encourages the pupils to seek a strategy that will ensure victory. Although the underlying strategy is basically the same for all games, it is likely that many pupils will initially find the strategy only for particular games, so that each change of addends or goal produces new competition.

The strategy for a particular version of the game can be built around discovery of a certain set of "key" numbers. For instance, in the game to 11 that was described above, the first player can always win if he knows the key numbers 2, 5, and 8; then he is assured of being the one to get 11. Such a set of key numbers can be found for each version of the game, although it will sometimes be the first player who has the advantage and at other times the second player. The general formula for winning any game is based on recognizing that where n is the largest addend, repeatedly substracting $n + 1$ from the goal until such subtraction is no longer possible yields the key numbers. Thus, in the game of 11, the key numbers are $11 - 3 = 8, 8 - 3 = 5$, and $5 - 3 = 2$. If the goal were 12 and the addends 1 and 2, the key numbers would be $12 - 3 = 9, 9 - 3 = 6, 6 - 3 = 3$, and $3 - 3 = 0$. Since 0 is not allowed as an addend, the *second* player can always win if he knows the strategy.

Many variations of this game can be found in books dealing with mathematical recreations; others might be designed by the creative teacher for his particular class.

Magic squares

This is an interesting way to review addition (and subtraction).

To make a magic square, we must place a different number in each cell in such a way that the sum of every horizontal row of cells, the sum of every vertical column of cells, and the sums of the diagonals will be the same number. Magic squares may be made that have an odd number of cells or an even number of cells. Following are the directions for constructing a 9-celled magic square, using the numbers from 1 to 9, inclusive.

Directions:

1. Draw a square with 9 cells.
2. Place the number 1 in the middle cell of the top row, as seen in figure A.1.
3. By moving diagonally up to the right, we begin to fill in the other spaces, but this puts us out of the top of the square. When this occurs, we simply drop to the last cell in that column.

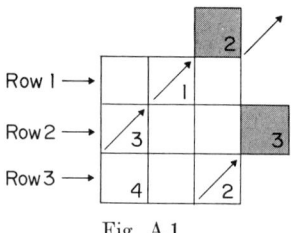

Fig. A.1

4. Moving diagonally from the 2 puts us out of the side of the square. When this happens, we simply go all the way to the left of that row.
5. Moving diagonally from 3 up to the right, we find ourselves in a space that is already occupied. When this occurs, go back to the starting point of 3 and put the number 4 in the cell below the 3. This rule also applies if you move out of the square on the main diagonal.
6. Continue until all cells are filled, as in figure A.2. Ask the class to observe anything unusual resulting from the arrangement of the numbers. It should be apparent to the student that the sum of the numbers of each row, column, and diagonal is 15.

8	1	6
3	5	7
4	9	2

Fig. A.2. Magic square 1

This 9-celled magic square is made with 9 consecutive whole numbers. To change the square, each number in magic square 1 may be increased by the same number. If each number in magic square 1 is increased by 1, the result is the magic square seen in figure A.3.

9	2	7
4	6	8
5	10	3

Fig. A.3. Magic square 2

ACTIVITIES, GAMES, AND APPLICATIONS 449

Using this method, squares can be made for class use by omitting numerals in certain cells, as in figure A.4.

25		23
20	22	24
	26	

Fig. A.4. Magic square 3

This square was constructed by increasing each number in magic square 1 by 17. Each number can also be multiplied (or divided) by the same number to create a new magic square. Division will produce squares with fractions.

One can make more difficult magic squares using 16 cells, 25 cells, and so on.

To construct a magic square containing 16 cells, we do the following:

1. Construct the square and put in all 16 numbers consecutively, beginning in the upper left-hand corner, as seen in figure A.5.

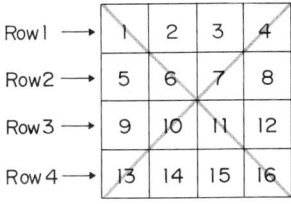

Fig. A.5

2. Reverse the numbers in both diagonals of the square. This will yield the completed square, seen in figure A.6.

16	2	3	13
5	11	10	8
9	7	6	12
4	14	15	1

Fig. A.6. Magic square 4

By omitting several of the numbers in the magic square, the students may be motivated to discover the pattern at the same time that they are reviewing the addition and subtraction facts.

Magic squares of 25 cells, 49 cells, or any odd number of cells may be made by following the directions given for the square of 9 cells. Even-numbered magic squares beyond 16 are possible to make but are not included here.

Discover the rule

Rules or formulas for the students to discover are shown at the right of the tabular information that supplies the necessary clues.

1.

a	4	8	0	10	5	11	16	9
b	8	16	0	20				

$2a = b$

2.

a	2	7	0	9	6	18	16	11
b	10	15	8	17				

$a + 8 = b$

3.

a	3	7	0	10	5	8	6	1
b	18	26	12					

$2a + 12 = b$

4.

	3	14	2			6	12	15	$a - b$
a	6	15		7		11			
b	3	1	3	2	5		4		
	9	16	18		12			25	$a + b$

5.

	3	4		3			29	18	$a - b$
	9	8	8		11	12	31		$a + b$
a	6	6		9					
b	3	2	4	3		5			
	18	12		18					ab
	25	19			25	42		47	$ab + 7$

ACTIVITIES, GAMES, AND APPLICATIONS 451

6.

a	3	7	0	10	5	8	6	1
b	5	9	2					

$a + 2 = b$

Shortcuts in multiplication

Since 25 can be expressed as $\frac{100}{4}$, multiplication by 25 can be done in two simple steps:

1. Divide by 4.
2. Multiply by 100.

Example: 25×48

$$\frac{100}{4} \times 48$$

$$\frac{100}{\cancel{4}} \times \frac{\cancel{48}^{12}}{1} = 1{,}200$$

If the number being multiplied is not a multiple of 4, there are three cases to consider:

a) A remainder of 1

Example: 25×73

$$\frac{100}{4} \times 73$$

$$\frac{100}{\cancel{4}} \times \frac{\cancel{73}^{18\frac{1}{4}}}{1} = 100 \times 18.25 = 1{,}825$$

b) A remainder of 2

Example: 25×86

$$\frac{100}{\cancel{4}} \times \frac{\cancel{86}^{21\frac{2}{4}}}{1} = 100 \times 21.50 = 2{,}150$$

c) A remainder of 3

Example: 25 × 39

$$\frac{100}{\underset{1}{\cancel{4}}} \times \frac{\cancel{39}^{9\frac{3}{4}}}{1} = 100 \times 9.75 = 975$$

Multiplication by 50—since 50 can be expressed as $\frac{100}{2}$—can be used by following a technique similar to that used in multiplication by 25:

1. Divide by 2.
2. Multiply by 100.

Example: 50 × 78

$$\frac{100}{2} \times 78$$

$$\frac{100}{\underset{1}{\cancel{2}}} \times \frac{\cancel{78}^{39}}{1} = 3{,}900$$

If the number being multiplied is not an even number, the only possible remainder is 1.

Example: 50 × 93

$$\frac{100}{\underset{1}{\cancel{2}}} \times \frac{\cancel{93}^{46\frac{1}{2}}}{1} = 100 \times 46.50 = 4{,}650$$

An interesting discussion can follow the presentation of these two shortcuts, based on the following questions: What are the possible endings, tens and units digits, for multiples of 25? Of 50?

A different kind of shortcut becomes apparent when we consider multiplication problems involving 11. In the first example shown below the 5 in the product is the same as the units digit of the multiplicand. The 8 is the sum of the tens and units digits. The 3 is the same as the tens digit.

First example:

$$\begin{array}{r} 35 \\ \times 11 \\ \hline 35 \\ 35 \\ \hline 385 \end{array}$$

Other examples:

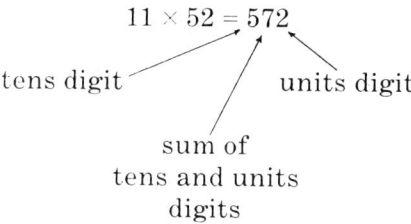

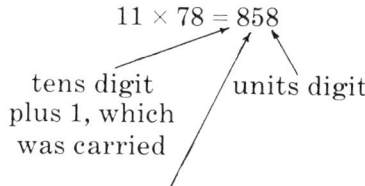

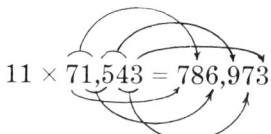

Fibonacci numbers

An interesting sequence of numbers, called Fibonacci numbers, can be generated in the following manner:

Begin with two ones, 1, 1; add these to get the next number, 2, of the sequence 1, 1, 2; then add 1 and 2, and so on, for the sequence seen below.

$$1, 1, 2, 3, 5, 8, 13, 21, 34, 55, 89, 144, 233, \ldots$$

The sequence has many interesting properties. For example: $2 \times 3 = 6$; $1 \times 5 = 5$; $3 \times 5 = 15$; $2 \times 8 = 16$; $5 \times 8 = 40$; $3 \times 13 = 39$.

For any four successive numbers, the product of the two in the middle will be 1 more or less than the product of the outer two.

$3^2 = 9$; $5 \times 2 = 10$ $\qquad$ $8^2 = 64$; $5 \times 13 = 65$

$$13^2 = 169; \quad 8 \times 21 = 168$$

The square of a Fibonacci number will be 1 more or less than the product of the two adjacent to it. Squaring Fibonacci numbers we get a sequence that begins as shown in the upper line of figure A.7. Adding the products as shown in the lower line of the figure, we get alternate Fibonacci numbers.

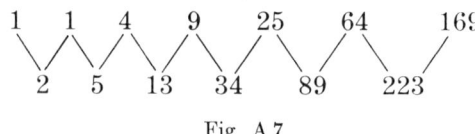

Fig. A.7

Writing the Fibonacci sequence vertically, ask a student to draw a line under one of the numbers. You can immediately give him the sum of all the numbers above the line. The sum always turns out to be 1 less than the second number below the line.

Example:

1
1
2
3
5
8
13
21
—
34
55
89

The sum of the numbers above the line is 1 less than 55, or 54.

Number patterns

Complete this pattern:

$$1 \times 8 + 1 = 9$$
$$12 \times 8 + 2 = 98$$
$$123 \times 8 + 3 = 987$$
$$1{,}234 \times 8 + 4 = 9{,}876$$
$$12{,}345 \times 8 + 5 =$$
$$123{,}456 \times 8 + 6 =$$
$$1{,}234{,}567 \times 8 + 7 =$$
$$12{,}345{,}678 \times 8 + 8 =$$
$$123{,}456{,}789 \times 8 + 9 =$$

Give the first few products in each pattern. Have the pupils complete the patterns and check some of the products by regular multiplication.

76,923 × 1 = 076,923
76,923 × 10 = 769,230
76,923 × 9 = 692,307
76,923 × 12 = 923,076
76,923 × 3 = 230,769
76,923 × 4 = 307,692

76,923 × 2 = 153,846
76,923 × 7 = 538,461
76,923 × 5 = 384,615
76,923 × 11 = 846,153
76,923 × 6 = 461,538
76,932 × 8 = 615,384

Palindromic numbers

A palindromic word is reversible, as are MOM and LEVEL. A palindromic number is also reversible, as are **363**, **13131**, and **66**. An interesting way of forming a palindromic number is to select some number, reverse the digits, add, and then repeat the entire routine until a palindrome is produced. For example:

```
    18          238           20
  + 81        + 832         + 02
   ――          ――――           ――
    99         1070            22
             + 0701
              ――――
               1771
```

The number of additions required varies with the number used to start. For instance, **196** requires **100** additions.

The lattice method of multiplication

The use of the lattice method or form is simple in its operation because it presumes only a knowledge of the primary multiplication facts and the ability to add. There is no renaming during multiplication. This was an early method used for multiplication, and it was also known by the names *gelosia*, *jalousie*, and "grating."

As a first step in the multiplication of **419** by **375**, see figure A.8.

Obtain products of the separate factors and in the corresponding squares write the products, with the numeral representing the ones digit of the product written *below* the diagonal and the numeral representing the tens digit written *above* the diagonal. For examples, see the top row of the completed diagram (fig. A.9): 4 × 3 = 12,

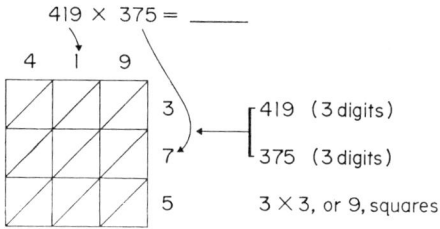

Fig. A.8

so in the appropriate square 2 is written below the diagonal and 1 is written above it; 1 × 3 = 3, so 3 is written below the diagonal and a 0 inserted above it; 9 × 3 = 27, so 7 is written below the diagonal and 2 above it. The final product is obtained by adding the digits in the diagonals, beginning with the diagonal in the lower right-hand corner, and adding the numerals in each diagonal until all the additions have been performed. Numerals are carried into the next diagonal row of numerals where necessary, as in ordinary addition. When the numerals thus obtained are read from left to right around the lattice frame, the product of the two given factors is obtained, as seen in figure A.9.

The method works because of the distributive property.

$$419$$
$$\underline{375}$$

$$2{,}700 = 300 \times 9$$
$$3{,}000 = 300 \times 10$$
$$120{,}000 = 300 \times 400$$

$$630 = 70 \times 9$$
$$700 = 70 \times 10$$
$$28{,}000 = 70 \times 400$$

$$45 = 5 \times 9$$
$$50 = 5 \times 10$$
$$2{,}000 = 5 \times 400$$

$$157{,}125$$

ACTIVITIES, GAMES, AND APPLICATIONS 457

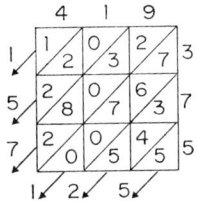

Fig. A.9

Napier's bones

John Napier developed a method of multiplication closely related to lattice multiplication that is considered to be a forerunner of modern computing machines. Prepare a set of strips (bones) with multiples of the digits 0 through 9, together with an index stick bearing each of the digits 1 through 9. Figure A.10 shows the bone for 7.

To find a product, use the bones and the index stick as shown in figure A.11; for 8 × 369, place the index beside the bones for 3, 6, and 9.

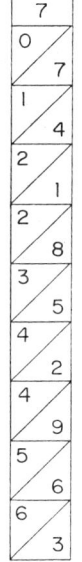

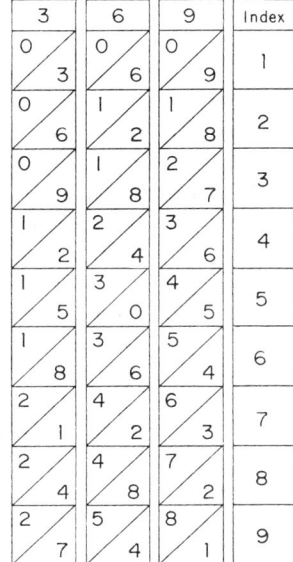

Fig. A.10 Fig. A.11

To find the product, use the row alongside the 8 on the index stick. As with lattice multiplication, add on the diagonals. Thus 8 × 369 = 2,952, as seen in figure A.12.

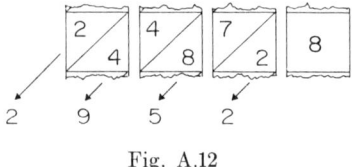

Fig. A.12

To compute in situations such as 427 × 369, we use the row beside the index 4, the row beside the index 2, and the row beside the index 7. We get three partial products and then add them in such a way as to allow for the place value. Thus:

```
    1476
    0738
 +  2583
  ------
  157563 = 427 × 369
```

Baseball game

This game of baseball reinforces the basic number facts for addition, subtraction, multiplication, and division of natural numbers.

The only special equipment needed consists of a color wheel (see fig. A.13) and flash cards, which can be made of poster paper; the chalkboard can be used for a scoreboard (see fig. A.14), tallies of runs, and records of the positions of men on base. The flash-card computations consist of the basic addition and multiplication facts, with the inverse operations included. They are made in four sets, in increasing difficulty according to the value assigned to them, as shown in the examples in figure A.15.

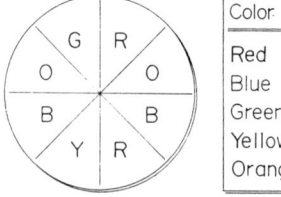

Fig. A.13. Color wheel and values

ACTIVITIES, GAMES, AND APPLICATIONS   459

Inning	1	2	3	4	5	6	7	8	9
Team 1									
Team 2									

Fig. A.14. Scoreboard

After choosing three field officials, separate the rest of the class into two teams.

Duties of the officials:
1. Determine, by spinning the color wheel, the type of hit the batter will attempt to make (an out is automatic when orange is spun).
2. Pick at random, for the batter, a flash card from the appropriate set.
3. Keep tally of runs and position of men on base, and make the proper entries on the scoreboard.

As the year progresses, the flash cards should become more difficult with the inclusion of fractions, properties, percent equivalents, decimal fraction equivalents, and so on.

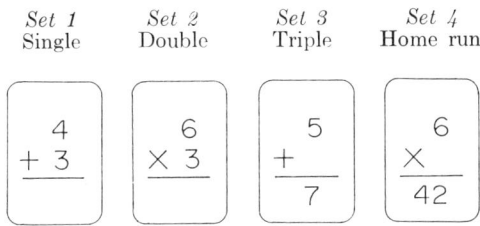

Fig. A.15

Exponents by discovery

This activity can be used to lead to the idea of exponents, providing drill with fundamental operations at the same time. It is really the familiar arithmetic game "What's My Rule?" in a special version.

Duplicate enough cards of the type shown in figure A.16 to permit each pupil to have an ample supply.

The activity can be accompanied by a story of some sort if desired. For instance, the card could be an order card in a shipping department and the pupils are to guess how to interpret it.

The card is marked with **X**'s or by punching holes above the numerals. The pupils' job is to write the appropriate number in the lower left-hand

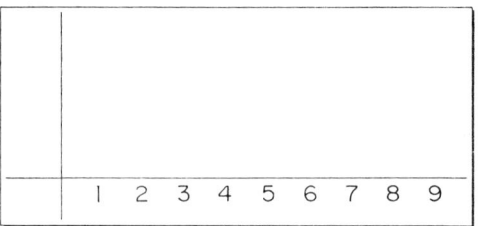

Fig. A.16

box. If there are two **X**'s over the 3, a 9 is written in the box. If there are two **X**'s over 2 *and* two **X**'s over 5, a 29 is written in the lower left-hand box. With enough examples from the teacher, the pupils will soon discover the three **X**'s over the 2 means $2^3 = 8$ should be written in the box. Two **X**'s over 4 and four **X**'s over 3 means $4^2 + 3^4 = 16 + 81 = 97$ should be written in the box. Later, if **X**'s are used, the card can be eliminated and $\genfrac{}{}{0pt}{}{\mathbf{X}}{2}$ written as an abbreviation for the information on the card. This can then be further abbreviated to 2^2 and the raised 2 called an "**X**-ponent."

Arithmetic with exponents

Would you believe that even some of the slowest junior and senior high school students could find the answer to

$$\frac{6{,}561^2 \times 243^3 \times 729}{19{,}683^2 \times 59{,}049}$$

in just a few seconds? To do so, the following concepts must be developed: The symbol 3^4 means that 3 is used as a factor 4 times $(3 \times 3 \times 3 \times 3)$; 3^2 means that 3 is used as a factor 2 times. So $3^4 \times 3^2$ means that 3 is used as a factor $4 + 2$, or 6, times. After a few such examples, the student will see that

$$3^a \times 3^b = 3^{a+b}$$

Similar examples with other base numbers should be used until the general rule $a^x \cdot a^y = a^{x+y}$ is developed.

The quantity $3^4 \div 3^2$ can be written as

$$\frac{3 \times 3 \times 3 \times 3}{3 \times 3}$$

By dividing numerator and denominator by 3 repeatedly until all the 3s in the denominator are used up, we are left with 3×3, or 3^2. So when dividing by 3^2, we "took away" two of the 3s in 3^4. With a few other examples, the student will be led to the generalization that

$$\frac{a^x}{a^y} = a^{x-y}$$

Next, have the class complete a table of powers of 3, through 3^{10}.

$3^1 = 3$ $3^6 = 729$
$3^2 = 9$ $3^7 = 2{,}187$
$3^3 = 27$ $3^8 = 6{,}561$
$3^4 = 81$ $3^9 = 19{,}683$
$3^5 = 243$ $3^{10} = 59{,}049$

Ask the class to find the product 27×81 by inspection. Some will see that this is $3^3 \times 3^4$, or 3^7, which is 2,187. In like manner $59{,}049 \div 729$ becomes $3^{10} \div 3^6$, or 3^4, which is 81. After some practice, the class should be able to tackle the original problem:

$$\frac{(3^8)^2 \times (3^5)^3 \times 3^6}{(3^9)^2 \times 3^{10}} = \frac{3^8 \times 3^8 \times 3^5 \times 3^5 \times 3^5 \times 3^6}{3^9 \times 3^9 \times 3^{10}} = \frac{3^{37}}{3^{28}} = 3^9$$

So the answer is 19,683.

Similar tables using other bases should also be used to apply the same principle.

For example:

$$\frac{512^2 \times 256^3}{1{,}024 \times 128^4}$$

can be expressed as

$$\frac{(2^9)^2 \times (2^8)^3}{2^{10} \times (2^7)^4} = \frac{2^{18} \times 2^{24}}{2^{10} \times 2^{28}} = \frac{2^{42}}{2^{38}} = 2^4 = 16$$

Number shapes

Present to the class the array of dots shown in figure A.17.

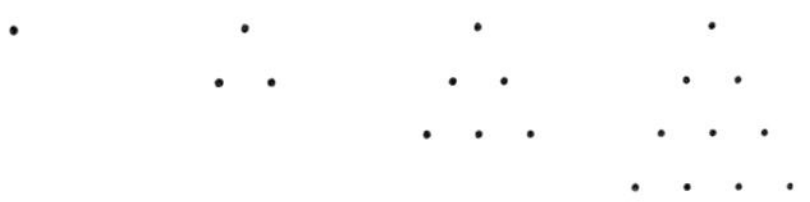

Fig. A.17

Ask the students to continue the pattern through the next two sets of dots. Then ask if anyone can predict how many dots would be in the next set, without actually drawing it.

Hopefully, some of the students will associate the dots with the following sequence of numbers, called the set of triangular numbers:

$$1, 3, 6, 10, 15, 21, 28, \ldots$$

If zero is included, subtracting consecutive pairs of triangular numbers produces the result shown in figure A.18.

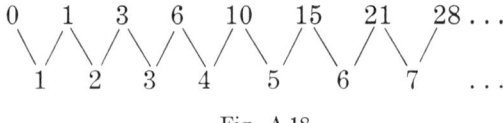

Fig. A.18

Adding consecutive pairs produces the set of square numbers, which can also be represented geometrically, as shown in figure A.19.

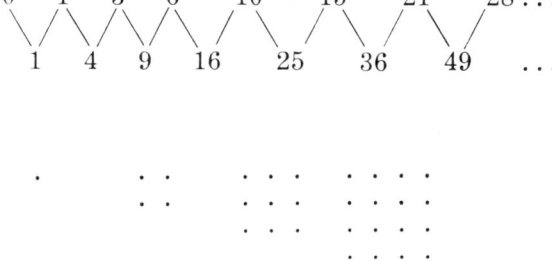

Fig. A.19

Subtracting consecutive square numbers produces the set shown in figure A.20.

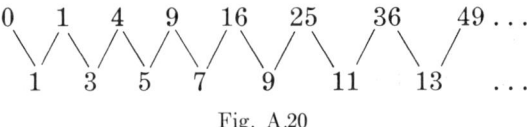

Fig. A.20

Naming numbers

The student can be asked to see if he can construct a name for each whole number from 1 through 10 using exactly four 4s, any of the operations +, −, ×, and ÷, and place value.

ACTIVITIES, GAMES, AND APPLICATIONS 463

Some examples are shown below:

$$1 = \frac{4}{4} + (4 - 4)$$
$$2 = \frac{4}{4} + \frac{4}{4}$$
$$3 = \frac{4 + 4 + 4}{4}$$
$$4 = 4 + 4 \times (4 - 4)$$
$$5 = \frac{(4 \times 4) + 4}{4}$$

$$6 = \frac{4 + 4}{4} + 4$$
$$7 = (4 + 4) - \frac{4}{4}$$
$$8 = (4 + 4) + (4 - 4)$$
$$9 = (4 + 4) + \frac{4}{4}$$
$$10 = \frac{44 - 4}{4}$$

Of course, there are other ways to construct most of these. The level of difficulty can be varied by extending the set to be named (e.g., 1 through 20), using additional operations (e.g., exponents, factorials, etc.), or using other numbers as the base set in place of four 4s.

Here are two examples of numbers greater than 10, using additional operations and four 4s.

$$4 + \frac{4 + 4!}{4} = 11 \quad \text{and} \quad \frac{4^4}{4 \times 4} = 16$$

This activity gives good practice with fundamental operations and replaces much routine drill.

Bingtac

This game appeared in the April 1969 issue of the *Arithmetic Teacher*, in an article written by Russell L. Williams.

Make several sets of wooden cubes with the numerals 4–9 on their faces and duplicate enough copies of the grid shown in figure A.21 to give several to each pupil.

	4	5	6	7	8	9
4						
5						
6						
7						
8						
9						

Fig. A.21

The game can be played with two to four players. They first decide on addition or multiplication as the operation to be indicated in the upper left-hand corner of the grid. Then they roll one cube to see who gets the highest number and plays first. Each player takes a turn rolling two cubes and placing the sum or product of the resulting numbers in its appropriate space on *his* grid. If a double is thrown, the player gets an extra turn. The first player to get six in a row, column, or diagonal correct wins and calls out "Bingtac." If the player gives a wrong sum or product, he loses that turn. It was pointed out that it is wise not to have the pupils play too long on any one day, perhaps half an hour or less.

Multiplication by doubling and halving

Consider the multiplication $2 \times 4 = 8$.

$$2 \times 4 = \tfrac{1}{2}(2) \times (2 \times 4)$$
$$= 1 \times 8$$
$$= 8$$

Consider also the multiplication $8 \times 11 = 88$.

$$8 \times 11 = 4 \times 22$$
$$= 2 \times 44$$
$$= 1 \times 88$$
$$= 88$$

In each case we have taken half of one factor and doubled the other until the product is achieved. This process can be adapted even when one factor is an odd number by using the distributive principle and saving all addends of the form $(1 \times a)$ where a is any whole number.

$$15 \times 23 = (14 + 1) \times 23$$
$$= (14 \times 23) + (1 \times 23)$$
$$14 \times 23 = 7 \times 46$$
$$= (6 + 1) \times 46$$
$$= (6 \times 46) + (1 \times 46)$$
$$6 \times 46 = 3 \times 92$$
$$= (2 + 1) \times 92$$
$$= (2 \times 92) + (1 \times 92)$$
$$2 \times 92 = 1 \times 184$$

Thus,

$15 \times 23 = (1 \times 23) + (1 \times 46) + (1 \times 92) + (1 \times 184)$
$= 23 + 46 + 92 + 184$
$= 345$

Here is another example: $18 \times 19 = ?$

$18 \times 19 = 9 \times 38$
$= (8 + 1) \times 38$
$= (8 \times 38) + (1 \times 38)$
$8 \times 38 = 4 \times 76$
$= 2 \times 152$
$= 1 \times 304$
$18 \times 19 = (1 \times 304) + (1 \times 38) = 304 + 38 = 342$

Multiplication by doubling and summing

Any whole number can be expressed as a sum of powers of two. Listing these powers we get: $2^0 = 1$, $2^1 = 2$, $2^2 = 4$, $2^3 = 8$, $2^4 = 16$, ... Consider $3 = 2 + 1$, $5 = 4 + 1$, $6 = 4 + 2$, $7 = 4 + 2 + 1$, $9 = 8 + 1$, $10 = 8 + 2$, and so on. This is not a proof of the statement, but it does illustrate it. Let's consider a large number, $45 = 32 + 8 + 4 + 1 = 2^5 + 2^3 + 2^2 + 2^0$.

This principle can be used to multiply two whole numbers. Consider $10 \times 13 = 130$. This can be solved in the following way, noting that $10 = 8 + 2$.

$1 \times 13 = 13$
$2 \times 13 = 26$
$4 \times 13 = 52$ Double each time
$8 \times 13 = 104$

But $10 \times 13 = (8 + 2) \times 13 = (8 \times 13) + (2 \times 13) = 104 + 26 = 130$.

Another example: 33×45

$33 = 32 + 1$ $1 \times 45 = 45$
$33 \times 45 = (32 + 1) \times 45$ $2 \times 45 = 90$
$= (32 \times 45) + (1 \times 45)$ $4 \times 45 = 180$
$= 1{,}440 + 45$ $8 \times 45 = 360$
$= 1{,}485$ $16 \times 45 = 720$
                            $32 \times 45 = 1{,}440$

The secret of this process is that the first factor is being written as a base-two numeral and the second factor is being multiplied by powers of two through a simple doubling process. The product is thus found by simply adding those products that occur where there are ones in the base-two numeral of the first factor. Thus,

$$33_{ten} = 100001_{two} = (1 \times 2^5) + (1 \times 2^0) = 32 + 1$$

Binary magic

Reproduce the four charts seen in figure A.22, either on a ditto, giving one set to each student, or on tagboard that is large enough for the entire class to see.

A			B			C			D	
1	9		2	10		4	12		8	12
3	11		3	11		5	13		9	13
5	13		6	14		6	14		10	14
7	15		7	15		7	15		11	15

Fig. A.22

Ask one of the students to select a number from 1 through 15, informing the class of his choice. Then ask the class to tell you on which of the charts, A, B, C, or D, the number appears. You can then tell them the number they are thinking of by simply finding the sum of the numbers in the upper left-hand corner of the charts the students name.

For example, if they choose 13, they will name charts A, C, and D. You will then add 1, 4, and 8, giving you 13.

The charts are set up by representing the numbers from 1 through 15 in the binary system (see fig. A.23).

All the numerals having a one in the ones column appear on chart A, those having a one in the twos column are on chart B, those with a one in the fours column are on chart C, and chart D contains those having a one in the eights column.

The yes and no responses from the students tell you how to represent the numeral in the binary system.

Taking the example we have already used, 13, we see that the results are as shown below.

$$\begin{array}{cccc} D & C & B & A \\ (8) & (4) & (2) & (1) \\ \text{Yes} & \text{Yes} & \text{No} & \text{Yes} \\ 1(8) & + 1(4) & + 0(2) & + 1(1) \end{array}$$

Base-Ten Numeral	Base-Two Numeral			
	8	4	2	1
1				1
2			1	0
3			1	1
4		1	0	0
.				
.				
.				
14	1	1	1	0
15	1	1	1	1
	D	C	B	A

Fig. A.23

An interesting variation of this activity is to prepare a punch card for each of the numbers 1 through 15, representing them in the binary system as is illustrated in figure A.24.

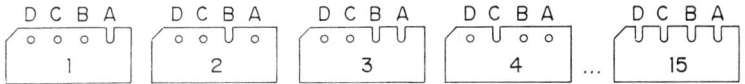

Fig. A.24

Again have the students select a number from 1 through 15, and let you know on which chart it appears.

By using a knitting needle, the cards are then separated in the following manner:

If the numeral appears on chart A, put the needle through slot A and separate the cards into two sets. Discard those that remain on the needle. If the numeral is not on chart B, put the needle through the B slot of the remaining cards, this time keeping the cards that stay on the needle. Continue this through the four charts. When you get to the fourth chart, if the response is yes, the number selected will be represented on the card that falls off the needle; if the response is no, it will be the one remaining on the needle.

If you wish to use more numbers, a fifth chart will extend the set through 31, and a sixth chart will extend it through 63.

Odd vs. even

This is a game between two players or two teams. One player or team uses all the even digits, the other uses all the odd digits. Players take turns placing the numbers on a tic-tac-toe grid. The first player or team to place a third number in a row, column, or diagonal such that the sum is 15 wins. The game can be varied by expanding the board to 4 by 4 or 5 by 5, and using the numbers 1–16 and 1–25, respectively, with sums of 34 and 65. Another possibility would be to use the 9-cell square with multiplication to either of the products 120 or 105 (two goal numbers are desirable in multiplication so that one is odd, the other even). This may be further varied by having each team pick its own goal number before play begins.

Turn, Turn, Turn

A novel addition game that can be played using a single die gives good practice with fundamental addition while encouraging the pupil to develop strategies. This can be played with an ordinary die taken from a game, or a large-size die can be made from a wooden cube cut to about 1½ or 2 inches on an edge. The die will have the numbers from 1 through 6 on it, arranged so that opposite faces always add up to 7.

The game requires two players. One player rolls the die to start the game. The number on the top face becomes the first addend. The second player can turn the die to any of the four faces adjacent to the top face, but cannot use the top face or the face that is opposite the top face. The number turned to becomes the second addend. The players alternate turning the cube to produce new addends until a goal number is reached. The player who turns the cube to show the addend that gets the sum closest to the goal number without exceeding it wins. A good goal number might be 21; another is 50. Players should be encouraged to analyze the game for strategies that increase their chances of winning.

First addend is 1.   Second addend is 2.

Fig. A.25. In this example of Turn, Turn, Turn, the players continue turning until the addends give the sum of 21 or the sum closest to 21 without exceeding that goal.

Mathematical mind reading

To find the number of brothers and sisters a student has (assuming that the student has no more than 9 brothers or 9 sisters), tell him to follow these directions:

1. Write down the number of brothers you have.
2. Double this number.
3. Add 1.
4. Multiply this result by 5.
5. Add the number of sisters you have.
6. Tell your result.

When you hear the result, subtract 5 from it to obtain the number of brothers (shown by the tens digit) and the number of sisters (shown by the units digit). For example, if his result is 17, subtracting 5 gives 12, showing 1 brother and 2 sisters.

An explanation of why this "mathematical mind reading" works becomes apparent when the steps performed by this student are given below in both arithmetical and algebraic terms, with x representing the number of brothers and y representing the number of sisters.

	Arithmetical	Algebraic
1.	1	x
2.	2 × 1, or 2	$2x$
3.	2 + 1, or 3	$2x + 1$
4.	3 × 5, or 15	$5(2x + 1)$, or $10x + 5$
5.	15 + 2, or 17	$10x + 5 + y$
6.	17	$10x + 5 + y$

Solution: $10x + 5 + y - 5 = 10x + y$

Operations with fractions

The distributive property of multiplication over addition can be used to multiply certain whole numbers and mixed numbers mentally.

For example, $5 \times 7\frac{3}{5}$:

$$5 \times (7 + \tfrac{3}{5}) = (5 \times 7) + (5 \times \tfrac{3}{5})$$
$$= 35 + 3$$
$$= 38$$

After working several examples of this type, where the product is a whole number, more difficult examples can be used.

For example, $4 \times 3\frac{2}{5}$:

$$4 \times (3 + \tfrac{2}{5}) = (4 \times 3) + (4 \times \tfrac{2}{5})$$
$$= 12 + \tfrac{8}{5}$$
$$= 12 + 1\tfrac{3}{5}$$
$$= 13\tfrac{3}{5}$$

An approach to dividing fractions is illustrated by the following examples:

Example 1: $\dfrac{3}{4} \div \dfrac{2}{3}$

Express the problem as $\dfrac{\frac{3}{4}}{\frac{2}{3}}$.

Find the least common denominator for the two fractions and multiply this by the numerator and denominator of the complex fraction.

$$\dfrac{\frac{3}{4}}{\frac{2}{3}} \times \dfrac{12}{12} = \dfrac{\frac{3}{4}}{\frac{2}{3}} \times \dfrac{\frac{12}{1}}{\frac{12}{1}} = \dfrac{9}{8}$$

Example 2: $3\tfrac{2}{9} \div 4\tfrac{5}{6}$

$$\dfrac{3\frac{2}{9}}{4\frac{5}{6}} \times \dfrac{18}{18} = \dfrac{3 \times 18 + \frac{2}{9} \times 18}{4 \times 18 + \frac{5}{6} \times 18} = \dfrac{54 + 4}{72 + 15} = \dfrac{58}{87}$$

Copy numbers

This idea was first suggested to the writer by Dr. Lola J. May of Winnetka, Illinois.

An area of frequent difficulty is addition and subtraction of fractions. Copy numbers may be used with students who seem to be unable to make progress with the usual algorithm.

Note that:

$$\dfrac{5}{6} = \dfrac{5+5}{6+6} = \dfrac{5+5+5}{6+6+6} = \dfrac{5+5+5+5}{6+6+6+6}$$

$$\dfrac{3}{4} = \dfrac{3+3}{4+4} = \dfrac{3+3+3}{4+4+4} = \dfrac{3+3+3+3}{4+4+4+4}$$

These are the "copy numbers." Now, suppose we are adding $\frac{5}{6}$ and $\frac{3}{4}$. Set up the problem in the vertical form and develop the copy numbers one at a time, beginning with the smaller denominator and always working with the fraction having the smaller sum in its denominator.

(1) $\quad \begin{aligned} \frac{5}{6} &= \frac{5}{6} \\ +\frac{3}{4} &= \frac{3+3}{4+4} \end{aligned}$ (2) $\quad \begin{aligned} \frac{5}{6} &= \frac{5+5}{6+6} \\ +\frac{3}{4} &= \frac{3+3}{4+4} \end{aligned}$ (3) $\quad \begin{aligned} \frac{5}{6} &= \frac{5+5}{6+6} \\ +\frac{3}{4} &= \frac{3+3+3}{4+4+4} \end{aligned}$

At this point, we note that $6 + 6 = 4 + 4 + 4$; this tells us we have gone far enough. Now we can complete the addition.

$$\begin{aligned} \frac{5}{6} &= \frac{5+5}{6+6} &&= \frac{10}{12} \\ +\frac{3}{4} &= \frac{3+3+3}{4+4+4} &&= \frac{9}{12} \\ & && \;\;\;\frac{19}{12} \end{aligned}$$

Of course, it is not necessary to write everything over three times. That was done only to spell out the separate steps. Here is one more example, without rewriting.

$$\begin{aligned} \frac{5}{7} &= \frac{5+5+5}{7+7+7} &&= \frac{15}{21} \\ -\frac{2}{3} &= \frac{2+2+2+2+2+2+2}{3+3+3+3+3+3+3} &&= \frac{14}{21} \\ & && \;\;\;\frac{1}{21} \end{aligned}$$

Sometimes the process is very quick; at other times it takes time, just as is the case with finding the least common denominator for the standard algorithm. It does enable the student to successfully add fractions with unlike denominators even when he is unable to use the standard algorithm.

Whole Numbers Down

Whole Numbers Down is a card game that can be played by two, three, or four pupils at one time. It gives excellent practice in adding fractions.

The materials needed for the game consist simply of a special deck of cards. These can be made by the teacher or by a capable student. The background for each card is poster paper cut to approximately the size of a regular playing card—or, to eliminate cutting, a three-by-five-inch index card could be substituted. On a lighter-weight paper, cards to be cut to the appropriate size should be made up as shown by the examples in figure A.26.

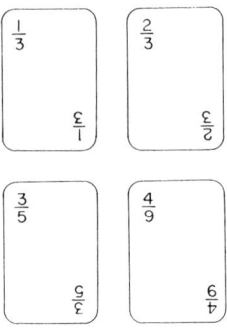

Fig. A.26

The cards showing the fractions should then be cut out and glued to the heavier cards. A complete set should consist of 40 cards with various fractions.

The game is played by shuffling and dealing four cards to each player. The remaining cards are placed face down in the center of the playing area, then the top one is turned face up. The first player either takes the face-up card or draws one from the top of the pile. He then makes up combinations of cards in his hand that add to any whole number; he lays these whole-number sums down face up in front of him. Finally, he discards one card. The first player to get rid of all of his cards ends the hand, and each player gets the total of the points he has put down on the table minus ½ point for each card in his hand. The game is won by the first player to get 25 points. Anyone who lays down a set of cards not having a whole-number sum must return these cards to his hand and take an extra card from the pile without discarding.

Seven

Practice in multiplication and division, as well as the recognition of patterns, can be accomplished in the following ways:

Ask the class to multiply 142,857 by 1, then by 2, 3, 4, 5, 6, and 7.

After they have done two or three, ask if anyone can give the rest of the products by inspection.

ACTIVITIES, GAMES, AND APPLICATIONS 473

$1 \times 142{,}857 = 142{,}857$ $\qquad 5 \times 142{,}857 = 714{,}285$
$2 \times 142{,}857 = 285{,}714$ $\qquad 6 \times 142{,}857 = 857{,}142$
$3 \times 142{,}857 = 428{,}571$ $\qquad 7 \times 142{,}857 = 999{,}999$
$4 \times 142{,}857 = 571{,}428$

Ask the class to change $\frac{1}{7}$, $\frac{2}{7}$, $\frac{3}{7}$, $\frac{4}{7}$, $\frac{5}{7}$, and $\frac{6}{7}$ to decimal fractions, carrying the division out to 12 places.

Again, after two or three are worked, ask if anyone can see a special pattern that would enable him to get the rest of the quotient by inspection.

Sum and product

Find two fractions that will give the same answer whether they are multiplied or added together. Is there a pattern for making such pairs of fractions? ($\frac{7}{4}$ and $\frac{7}{3}$, $\frac{9}{4}$ and $\frac{9}{5}$, etc.)

Regular hexagons

After learning to construct a regular hexagon in a circle it is a simple matter to make a triangle and to make regular polygons with sides of 12, 24, 48, . . . by bisecting a side of the polygon and its corresponding arc.

For the *hexagon* use r as radius for a circle, and, using this same radius, mark off points around the circumference of the circle. By connecting the consecutive points, a regular hexagon is formed. If every second point is connected, an equilateral triangle is formed. By drawing two triangles, ACE and DRF, a six-pointed star is formed, as seen in figure A.29. Many designs can be created by students from the basic regular hexagon.

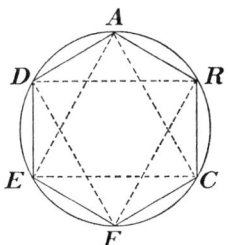

Fig. A.29

Squares

Construct the perpendicular bisector of the diameter of a circle. Connect the four consecutive points on the circumference and have a

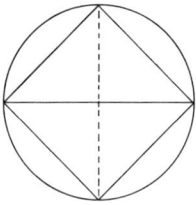

Fig. A.30

perfect square, as seen in figure A.30. By bisecting a side of the square and its corresponding arc, a regular octagon can be constructed. Continuing in this way, regular polygons of 16, 32, 64, . . . sides can be constructed.

Symmetry

The idea of symmetry can be introduced to a class, small group, or individual using a discovery approach. A fairly large set of cutout shapes (either geometric shapes or the capital letters of the alphabet) is required for this activity. About half the shapes should have line symmetry; the other half should be nonsymmetrical.

The activity begins when the teacher writes "Yes" as a heading for one section of a chalkboard or flannel board and "No" as a heading for another section. A letter or geometric shape is then selected and held up for the pupils to see. They are to guess if it is a yes or a no. After all have had the opportunity to express their opinion, the teacher places the shape (using masking tape, magnets, glued-on flannel, or something similar) in the proper section of the board. The shapes are selected one by one for this process. Any pupil who feels he knows the principle determining the yes shapes can either write his theory or state it aloud after all members of the group have had ample opportunity to guess. The principle could also be described nonverbally by having the pupils fold the shapes to show matching halves.

The activity can be made more challenging or can be extended at another time by including figures that have symmetry with respect to a point in addition to those having line symmetry.

An individualized version can be developed by putting the shapes on flash cards with "Yes" or "No" on the back. The pupil would try to classify a card properly without looking at the back, then he could check his response. He would put it into the proper set and continue this process until he felt he could describe the principle either orally or in writing for the teacher to check.

ACTIVITIES, GAMES, AND APPLICATIONS

Spatial relationships

To aid in developing spatial perception in geometry, exercises of the following type may help (build models).

Using six Popsicle sticks of equal length, how can they be arranged so that four triangles are formed whose sides are the length of the Popsicle sticks? The answer is seen in figure A.31.

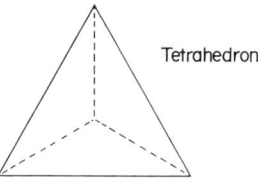

Fig. A.31

Ask the students to visualize a 3-inch cube that is painted red. Assume that this cube is cut into 27 one-inch cubes as in figure A.32.

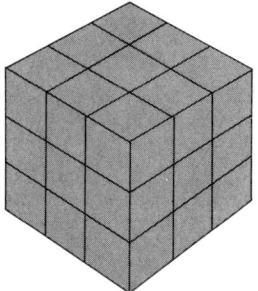

Fig. A.32

How many of these one-inch cubes will have red paint on none of their faces? On one face only? On two faces only? On more than three faces? Alphabet blocks or sugar cubes are two things that can be used to build a model if the students cannot visualize the cube.

Elementary surveying:
Use of clinometer to determine the size of an angle

This activity could follow a review of either the concept of similar triangles or the concept of scale drawings.

Heights of flagpoles and buildings or rockets may be solved by the shadow method and similar triangles. Another interesting method is to use a clinometer to determine the angle of elevation. Once the angle is determined, either scale drawing or trigonometry can be used to determine distances.

This activity gives every student the opportunity to discover surveying techniques for himself, since he will make his own clinometer and use it.

Directions for construction:

1. Use a rectangular piece of heavy cardboard, about 9 by 14 inches in size.

2. Place a protractor close to the edge in the upper right-hand corner, as shown in figure A.33.

3. Attach a string with a weight at point *A*, figure A.33.

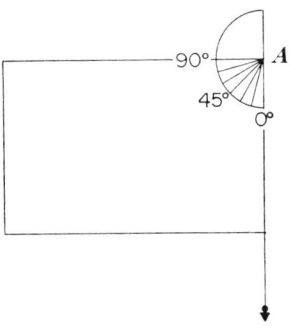

Fig. A.33

Directions for use:

1. The student stands at point *P*, an arbitrary distance (not too close) from a flagpole, as shown in figure A.34. In this figure *P* is at a distance of 50 feet from the flagpole.

2. Standing at point *P*, the student sights along the edge of the instrument to the top of the flagpole.

3. The string will remain in vertical position because of the attached weight and will cross the protractor at a point that repre-

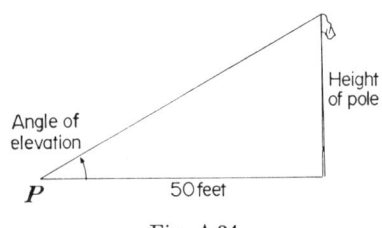

Fig. A.34

ACTIVITIES, GAMES, AND APPLICATIONS 477

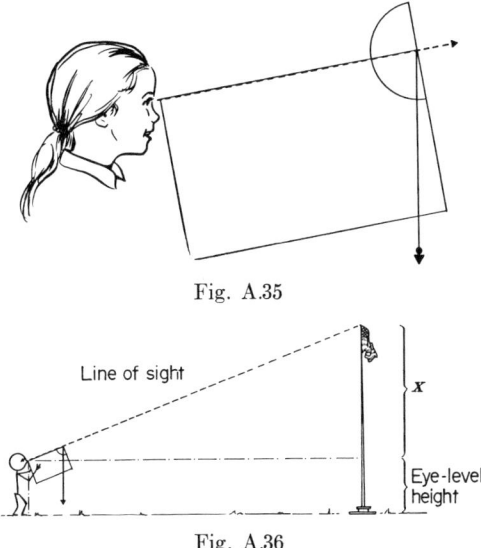

Fig. A.35

Fig. A.36

sents the measure of the angle of elevation. Figure A.35 shows the position for a reading of an angle of elevation of 20°. Figure A.36 is a diagram of the scene.

4. Solve the problem by the use of a scale drawing. Graph paper is ideal for this purpose. Note that construction of a scale drawing will give the height of the flagpole (x in fig. A.36) *above* the student's horizontal line of sight. The student should be sure to remember to add his eye-level height to the value of x to get the final answer.

The Möbius strip

A Möbius strip can be constructed in the following way: Take a strip of paper (adding-machine tape is quite good), give one end half a twist, and tape the two edges together. In figure A.37, A would be joined to A', B to B'.

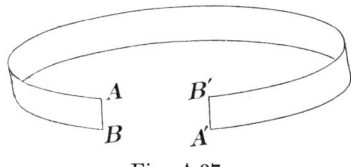

Fig. A.37

The Möbius strip has many interesting characteristics, which the following experiments illustrate.

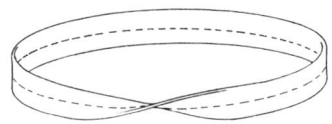

Fig. A.38

Ask the students to color one side red and the other side blue. (They will discover, no doubt greatly to their surprise, that this cannot be done. This will help to prepare them for further surprises in the additional experiments.)

Ask them to cut the Möbius strip in half, along the dotted line, as seen in figure A.38.

Then cut the halves in half.

Instead of cutting it in half, try to cut it into thirds.

Make a double Möbius strip (see fig. A.39). Join A to A', B to B', C to C', and D to D'. Verify that there are really two strips by running some object between the two strips all the way around. Then separate the strips. Then put them back together.

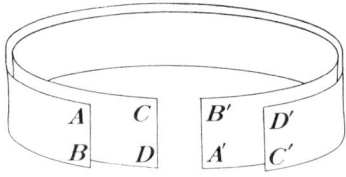

Fig. A.39

Probability

This activity is designed to help the student discover for himself a method for predicting the outcome for certain events.

Have a student flip a single coin several times and record the results in the following way:

Example:

```
    x
    x
    x   x
    x   x      6 heads (H), 4 tails (T)
    x   x
    x   x
    ─────
    H   T
```

Then let the students work in pairs, noting the heads-or-tails outcome of each pair of flips as shown in the example below.

ACTIVITIES, GAMES, AND APPLICATIONS 479

```
              x
              x
              x
              x              2H—3
              x    x         1H, 1T—8
         x    x    x         2T—4
         x    x    x
         x    x    x
        H,H  H,T  T,T
              or
              T,H
```

Next, have three students working together. Here is an example of possible results:

```
                   x
                   x
              x    x
              x    x
              x    x                3H—4
              x    x                2H, 1T—10
              x    x    x           1H, 2T—12
              x    x    x           3T—6
         x    x    x    x
         x    x    x    x
         x    x    x    x
         x    x    x    x
        HHH  HTH  HTT  TTT
             HHT  THT
```

Some observations the students might be expected to make on the second and third examples are: When two coins were flipped at once, there were about twice as many times one head and one tail appeared as there were times either two heads or two tails were gotten. When three coins were flipped, the number of times two heads and one tail appeared was about the same as the number of times two tails and one head appeared. There were about three times as many times for either of these as there were of getting three heads or three tails.

Divide the class into groups of three or four. Each group should have a pair of dice and a sheet of paper to record the results of rolling the dice. The results can be recorded as seen in the tabulation of possible results below.

```
                        x
                        x
                    x   x
                x       x   x   x
                x   x   x   x   x
            x   x   x   x   x   x   x
            x   x   x   x   x   x   x
            x   x   x   x   x   x   x   x   x
        x   x   x   x   x   x   x   x   x   x
        x   x   x   x   x   x   x   x   x   x   x
        x   x   x   x   x   x   x   x   x   x   x
        2   3   4   5   6   7   8   9  10  11  12
```

A similar table should then be made using the ordered pairs that result in the various sums:

```
                            (6,1)
                    (5,1)   (5,2)   (6,2)
            (4,1)   (4,2)   (4,3)   (5,3)   (6,3)
        (3,1)   (3,2)   (3,3)   (3,4)   (4,4)   (5,4)   (6,4)
    (2,1)   (2,2)   (2,3)   (2,4)   (2,5)   (3,5)   (4,5)   (5,5)   (6,5)
(1,1)   (1,2)   (1,3)   (1,4)   (1,5)   (1,6)   (2,6)   (3,6)   (4,6)   (5,6)   (6,6)
  2       3       4       5       6       7       8       9      10      11      12
```

The students should then observe that the table shows 36 different possible combinations: There is 1 way out of 36 of getting 2, there are 2 ways of getting 3, 6 ways of getting 7, and so on.

Games with coordinate axes

There are a variety of games that can be played on coordinate axes. One of these is the game that is sometimes called "Battleship." There are different versions of the game to be found, and the following is just one possibility.

Three pupils cooperate in this activity. It is a very simple way to enable them to name and identify ordered pairs on a set of coordinate axes. One pupil serves as the judge, the others are players. Each player has a sheet of graph paper or a teacher-made version of a coordinate grid, with the axes marked. The judge puts a curve around four adjacent points on his grid. The others are not allowed to see which four points have been identified. The opponents then take turns calling out an ordered pair, which they each mark on their respective grids. If one of them selects a point from the four that were chosen as the battleship, the judge calls out, "Hit." The opponent who hits the fourth point of the battleship wins the game.

ACTIVITIES, GAMES, AND APPLICATIONS   481

Then the winner becomes the judge, and the former judge plays the loser. The first person to win three games is the champion.

Another game involving the coordinate grid is a version of tic-tac-toe. Two players choose a grid of dimension agreeable to both, or the teacher can pick the playing grid. The players take turns naming ordered pairs and marking points on the grid, perhaps with their first initial. Players score a point for three in a row vertically, horizontally, or diagonally. The player with the greatest number of points when the grid is filled wins. The game can be varied by requiring four or more in a row for a point or by extending it outside the first quadrant of the grid. A player who names one ordered pair and marks a different one loses his next turn. This can be used as a group game similar to nim, which was described earlier.

Cross-number puzzle

Fig. A.38

Horizontal
1. The L.C.D. of $7/8$ and $5/6$.
3. Change $5/8$ to number of 24ths.
5. Change $36/3$ to a whole number.
6. $6\frac{2}{3} + 5\frac{1}{4} + 3\frac{5}{6} + 2\frac{1}{4}$
8. $7\frac{1}{2} - 3\frac{1}{2}$
9. $8\frac{2}{3} \times 1\frac{2}{3}$
10. $\frac{1}{4}$ of what number is 28?
12. $46\frac{1}{2} \div 7\frac{3}{4}$
13. Subtract $7\frac{1}{3}$ from $13\frac{1}{4}$ and add $2\frac{1}{12}$.
14. Add $27\frac{5}{8}$, $32\frac{1}{3}$, $16\frac{5}{24}$, and $44\frac{5}{6}$.
16. Multiply $13\frac{5}{7}$ by $2\frac{1}{3}$.
18. Divide $29\frac{1}{2}$ by $7\frac{3}{8}$.
19. $19\frac{1}{2}$ is $\frac{3}{4}$ of what number?
20. $5\frac{3}{5} \times 1\frac{1}{2}$ divided by $\frac{3}{5}$
21. Simplify
$$\frac{12\frac{3}{5} \times 2\frac{1}{2}}{1\frac{1}{2}}$$
23. Divide the product of $17\frac{1}{2}$ and $\frac{2}{5}$ by $\frac{7}{12}$.

Vertical
1. Divide 14 by $\frac{1}{16}$.
2. Change $\frac{1}{4}$ to number of 16ths.
3. $\frac{1}{2} + \frac{1}{6} + \frac{1}{3}$
4. Find $\frac{3}{4}$ of 72.
5. $6\frac{7}{8} \times 1\frac{3}{5}$
6. Divide $3\frac{3}{10}$ by $\frac{3}{10}$.
7. Add $148\frac{3}{4}$, $210\frac{2}{3}$, $56\frac{1}{6}$, and $402\frac{5}{12}$.
11. Change $16/8$ to a whole number.
12. Multiply the difference of $120\frac{1}{5}$ and $27\frac{1}{2}$ by $6\frac{2}{3}$.
14. $\frac{2}{5} \times 1\frac{1}{2} \times 1\frac{2}{3}$
15. 12 is $\frac{3}{4}$ of what number?
16. Take $\frac{1}{5}$ of 390.
17. L.C.D. of $\frac{1}{8}$, $\frac{1}{3}$, $\frac{3}{4}$, and $\frac{5}{12}$
18. $\frac{3}{4}$ of what number is $31\frac{1}{2}$?
22. $1\frac{1}{5} \times 2\frac{1}{2}$ divided by 3
23. Simplify
$$\frac{5\frac{1}{2} - 2\frac{1}{4}}{1\frac{3}{4} + 1\frac{1}{2}}$$

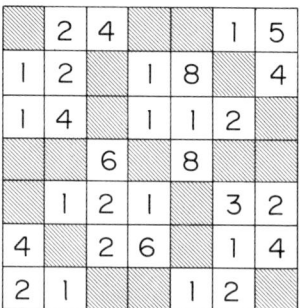

Fig. A.39. Solution

A Selected Bibliography of Games and Enrichment Activities

Abraham, Robert Morrison, comp. *Diversions and Pastimes: A Second Series of Winter Nights Entertainment.* New York: E. P. Dutton & Co., 1935; Gloucester, Mass.: Peter Smith, n.d.

Adler, Irving. *Magic House of Numbers.* Illustrated by Ruth Adler. New York: John Day Co., 1957.

———. *Mathematics: The Story of Numbers, Symbols, and Space.* New York: Simon & Schuster, 1958.

Amir-Moez, Ali R. *Ruler, Compass, and Fun.* New ed. Boston: Ginn & Co., 1966.

Anderson, Raymond W. *Romping through Mathematics.* New York: Alfred A. Knopf, 1947.

Asimov, Isaac. *Realm of Numbers.* Boston: Houghton Mifflin Co., 1959.

Bakst, Aaron. *Mathematical Puzzles and Pastimes.* 2d ed. Princeton, N.J.: D. Van Nostrand Co., 1965.

———. *Mathematics, Its Magic and Mastery.* 3d ed. Princeton, N.J.: D. Van Nostrand Co., 1967.

Ball, W. W. R. *Mathematical Recreations and Essays.* 11th ed., revised by H. S. M. Coxeter, 1939. Reprint. New York: Macmillan Co., 1960.

Barr, Stephen. *A Miscellany of Puzzles: Mathematical and Otherwise.* New York: Thomas Y. Crowell Co., 1965.

———. *Second Miscellany of Puzzles: Mathematical and Otherwise.* New York: Macmillan Co., 1969.

Bezuska, Stanley. *Contemporary Motivated Mathematics.* Chestnut Hill, Mass.: Boston College Press, 1969.

Biggs, Edith E., and James R. MacLean. *Freedom to Learn: An Active Learning Approach to Mathematics.* Don Mills, Ont.: Addison-Wesley (Canada), 1969.

Brades, Louise G. *Cross-Number Puzzles.* Portland, Maine: J. Weston Walch, 1957.

———. *Math Can Be Fun.* Portland, Maine: J. Weston Walch, 1956.

Burnett, Major J. C. *Easy Methods for the Construction of Magic Squares.* London: Rider, 1936.

Court, Nathan A. *Mathematics in Fun and Earnest.* New York: Dial Press, 1958.

Crescimbeni, Joseph. *Arithmetic Enrichment Activities for Elementary School Children.* W. Nyack, N.Y.: Prentice-Hall, Parker Publishing Co., 1965.
Cutler, Ann, and Rudolph McShane. *The Trachtenberg Speed System of Basic Mathematics.* Garden City, N.Y.: Doubleday & Co., 1960.
Degrazia, Joseph. *Math Is Fun.* New York: Emerson Books, 1954.
Experiences in Mathematical Discovery. 8 units. Washington, D.C.: National Council of Teachers of Mathematics, 1966–67, 1970.
Fitzgerald, W. *Laboratory Manual for Elementary Mathematics.* Boston: Prindle, Weber & Schmidt, 1969.
Fowler, H. Walter, Jr. *Kites.* New York: Ronald Press Co., 1953.
Freeman, Mae Blacker, and Ira M. Freeman. *Fun with Figures.* New York: Random House, 1946.
Friend, John Albert Newton. *Numbers: Fun and Facts.* New York: Charles Scribner's Sons, 1954.
Gamow, George, and Marvin Stern. *Puzzle-Math.* New York: Viking Press, 1958.
Gardner, Martin. *Mathematics, Magic, and Mystery.* New York: Dover Publications, 1956.
———. *The Unexpected Hanging and Other Mathematical Diversions.* New York: Simon & Schuster, 1969.
Gardner, Martin, ed. *The Scientific American Book of Mathematical Puzzles and Diversions.* New York: Simon & Schuster, 1964.
———. *The Second Scientific American Book of Mathematical Puzzles and Diversions.* New York: Simon & Schuster, 1965.
Golomb, Solomon. *Polyominoes.* New York: Charles Scribner's Sons, 1965.
Johnson, Donovan A. *Paper Folding for the Mathematics Class.* Washington, D.C.: National Council of Teachers of Mathematics, 1957.
Johnson, Donovan A., and W. H. Glenn. Exploring Mathematics on Your Own series. 9 units. Manchester, Mo.: McGraw-Hill Book Co., Webster Div., 1960–63.
Kaufman, Gerald. *The Book of Modern Puzzles.* New York: Dover Publications, 1954.
Kinnaird, Clark, ed. *Encyclopedia of Puzzles and Pastimes,* New York: Citadel Press, 1946.
Kraitchik, Maurice. *Mathematical Recreations.* New York: Dover Publications, 1953.
Leeming, Joseph. *Fun with Puzzles.* Philadelphia: J. B. Lippincott Co., 1946.
———. *More Fun with Puzzles.* Philadelphia: J. B. Lippincott Co., 1947.
———. *Take a Number: Mathematics for the Two Billion.* New York: Ronald Press Co., 1946.
MacMahon, P. A. *New Mathematical Pastimes.* New York: Cambridge University Press, 1930.
Marsh, Leonard George. *Children Explore Mathematics.* 4 bks. New York: Arco Publishing Co., 1964, 1967–68.
Merrill, Helen A. *Mathematical Excursions.* New York: Dover Publications, 1958.
Meyer, Jerome S. *Fun with Mathematics.* Reprint. New York: Fawcett World Library.
Mott-Smith, Geoffrey. *Mathematical Puzzles for Beginners and Enthusiasts.* 2d rev. ed. New York: Dover Publications, 1954.

Potter, Mary V., and Virgil Mallory. *Education in Mathematics for the Slow Learner.* Washington, D.C.: National Council of Teachers of Mathematics, 1958.

Proskauer, Julien J. *Puzzles for Everyone.* New York: Harper & Brothers, 1944.

Schaaf, William L. *A Bibliography of Recreational Mathematics.* 2 vols. Washington, D.C.: National Council of Teachers of Mathematics, 1970.

———. *Recreational Mathematics: A Guide to the Literature.* 3d ed. Washington, D.C.: National Council of Teachers of Mathematics, 1963.

Simon, William. *Mathematical Magic.* New York: Charles Scribner's Sons, 1964.

Spitzer, Herbert F. *Enrichment of Arithmetic.* New York: McGraw-Hill Book Co., 1964.

Sources of Mathematics Teaching Aids

Addison-Wesley Publishing Co.
Schools Division
Sand Hill Rd.
Menlo Park, Calif. 94025

American Seating Co.
901 Broadway, NW
Grand Rapids, Mich. 49502

Edmund Scientific Co.
300 Edscorp Bldg.
Barrington, N.J. 08007

Educational Development Laboratories
Huntington, N.Y. 11744

Harcourt Brace Jovanovich
757 3d Ave.
New York, N.Y. 10017

Holt, Rinehart & Winston
383 Madison Ave.
New York, N.Y. 10017

Ideal School Supply Co.
1000 S. Lavergne Ave.
Oaklawn, Ill. 60453

Instructo Products Co.
1635 N. 55th St.
Philadelphia, Pa. 19131

Judy Co.
310 N. 2d St.
Minneapolis, Minn. 55401

Math-Master Labs
Box 310
Big Springs, Tex. 79720

Milton Bradley Co.
Springfield, Mass. 01101

Sargent-Welch Scientific Co.
7300 N. Linder Ave.
Skokie, Ill. 60076

Science Materials Center
59 4th Ave.
New York, N.Y. 10003

Science Research Associates
259 E. Erie St.
Chicago, Ill. 60611

A Bibliography of Articles from the "Arithmetic Teacher," 1960–1970

1960 "Bibliography of Books for Enrichment in Arithmetic," by Ruth K. Carlson and Charles H. Tyldsley. April, pp. 189–93.

1962 "Arithmetic Baseball," by Donald Inbidy. November, pp. 390–91.

1963 "Arithmetic Is Fun," by Lois Rapp. May, pp. 256–58.

"Experiment in Enrichment—Fourth Grade," by Francis H. Hildebrand. February, pp. 68–71.

"The Game of Five," by Harold J. Shurlow. May, pp. 290–91.

"The Role of Games, Puzzles, and Riddles in Elementary Mathematics," by Dora Dohler. November, pp. 450–52.

ACTIVITIES, GAMES, AND APPLICATIONS 485

"Seesaw Game," by Helen Parker. November, pp. 449–50.

1964 "Fun, Fact, and Fancy," by Cada R. Parrish. January, pp. 39–41.

"Kalah—an Ancient Game of Mathematical Skill," by John B. Haggerty. May, pp. 326–30.

"Mathematics for Summer Fun," by Morris Rosenthal and Marvin Sitts. May, pp. 323–25.

1965 "Easy Construction of Magic Squares for Classroom Use," by John Cappon, Sr. February, pp. 100–105.

"Game to Review Basic Properties and Vocabulary," by Bernadine F. Condron. March, pp. 227–28.

"The Magic Box," by Thomas J. Jennings. May, pp. 377–78.

"A Mathematical Diversion," by David C. Bishop. October, p. 430.

"Nu—Tic-Tac-Toe," by Harry D. Ruderman. November, pp. 571–72.

"The 'Object-A-Screen': A Machine for Teaching Elementary Mathematics," by Chester L. Uncapher, Jr. October, pp. 462–65.

"Pegboard Geometry," by Lewis B. Smith. April, pp. 271–74.

"Some Practical Ideas for Teaching Mathematics to Disadvantaged Children," by Natalie Mintz and Herbert Fremont. April, pp. 258–60.

1966 "Developing Arithmetical Inquiry with Enrichment Aids," by Joseph Crescimbeni. January, pp. 49–51.

"A Game of Fractions," by Charlotte W. Junge. October, p. 494.

"Games for the Early Grades," by Edwina Deans. February, pp. 140–41.

"More Games for the Early Grades," by Edwina Deans. March, pp. 238–40.

"Rings and Strings," by James E. Major. October, pp. 457–60.

"The Witch's Best Game," by C. Winston Smith, Jr. December, pp. 683–84.

1967 "Tic-Tac-Toe—a Mathematical Game for Grades 4 through 9," by Robert A. Timmons. October, pp. 506–8.

"Tinkertoy Geometry," by Pauline L. Richards. October, pp. 468–69.

1968 "'Arithmecode' Puzzle," by David F. Winick. February, pp. 178–79.

"Arithmetic Card Games," by Martin H. Hunt. December, pp. 736–38.

"Enrichment with Exponents," by Earl L. McCallon and Paul J. Cowan. January, p. 70.

"Finger Multiplication," by Louisa R. Alger. April, pp. 341–43.

"Interest Getters," by Karl G. Zahn. April, pp. 372–74.

"Just for Fun," by J. D. Caldwell. May, pp. 464–65.

"Math for the Low, Slow, and Fidgety," by Jane G. Stenzel. January, pp. 30–34.

"Placo—a Number-Place Game," by Robert C. Calvo. May, pp. 465–66.

1969 "Bingtac," by Russell L. Williams. April, pp. 310–11.

"Fun Can Be Mathematics," by Audrey Kopp and Robert Hamada. November, pp. 575–77.

"A Game with Shapes," by Daisy Gogan. April, pp. 283–84.

"Magic Square Patterns," by Jeannie Gorts. April, pp. 314–16.

"Mathematical Puzzles and Games," by Jay A. Hickerson. February, pp. 85, 114.

"Secret Number Sentence," by William L. Swart. February, pp. 113–14.

1970 "Fibonacci Numbers: Fun and Fundamentals for the Slow Learner," by Sonja Loftus. March, pp. 204–8.
"Fostering Enthusiasm through Child-created Games," by Sarah R. Golden. February, pp. 111–15.
"Polygonal Numbers: A Study of Patterns," by Margaret A. Hervey and Bonnie H. Litwiller. January, pp. 33–38.

A Bibliography of Articles from the "Mathematics Teacher," 1960–1970

1960 "Graphing Pictures," by Frances Gross. April, pp. 295–96.
1961 "Nomography," by C. R. Wylie, Jr. November, pp. 531–37. *See also* January 1962, p. 82, for "Erratum" on this article.
1963 "Pattern Multiplication," by Robert L. Page. May, pp. 316–18.
1964 "An Experiment with Low Achievers in Arithmetic," by Kenneth E. Easterday. November, pp. 462–68.
1965 "A World of Hope—Helping Slow Learners Enjoy Mathematics," by Amelia D. Proctor. February, pp. 118–22.
1967 "A Christmas Puzzle," by Sister Anne Agnes von Steiger, C.S.J. December, pp. 848–49.
"An Application of Triangular Numbers to Counting," by Charles L. Hamberg and Thomas M. Green. April, pp. 339–42.
"Gambling Doesn't Pay!" by Andrew Sterrett. March, pp. 210–15.
1968 "A Christmas Tree for 1968," by Lucille Groenke. December, pp. 764, 787.
"The Effect of Modified Programmed Lectures and Mathematical Games upon Achievement and Attitude of Ninth-Grade Low Achievers in Mathematics," by Thomas Jones. October, pp. 603–7.
"A Magic Square for the New Year," by Martin Gardner. January, p. 18.
1969 "Art," by Carmelita C. Cadle. March, p. 217.
1970 "An Intuitive Approach to Square Numbers," by George F. Edmonds. February, pp. 113–17.
"The Magic of a Square," by Herta T. Freitag and Arthur H. Freitag. January, pp. 5–14.
"Teaching General Mathematics: A Semi-Laboratory Approach," by Jack Wilkinson. November, pp. 571–77.

Appendix B: Sample Lessons

Exploring Large Numbers (for Slow Junior High or Upper Elementary Students)

NEIL WALLEN
Assistant Principal, Coral Way Elementary School
Miami, Florida

Objective

Given a number of common uniform objects (dimes, dollars, paper clips, etc.—in the principal activity here, dimes), the learner should demonstrate an understanding of this number by relating some of these uniform objects to a small unit of measure and then to some single larger object (a specific mountain, tower, building, etc.) whose measure is thereby more easily comprehended.

Materials for each student

Over 20 dimes   Worksheet
Ruler   Conversion table

Teacher-guided activities

1. Give each student a number of dimes and a ruler. Ask him to find approximately the number of dimes in a 1-inch stack (20).

2. Ask questions such as these: How high would a stack of 40 dimes be? How high would a stack of 60 dimes be?

3. Have the student estimate how high a stack containing 1,000,000 would be. (The correct answer is not to be expected at this time.)

4. Have the student complete the worksheet (fig. B.1).

Inches	Dimes	Inches	Dimes	Inches	Dimes	Inches	Dimes	Inches	Dimes
10,000	200,000	1,000	20,000	100	2,000	10	200	1	20
Inches	Dimes	Inches	Dimes	Inches	Dimes	Inches	Dimes	Inches	Dimes
20,000	400,000	2,000	40,000	200	4,000	20	400	2	40
Inches	Dimes	Inches	Dimes	Inches	Dimes	Inches	Dimes	Inches	Dimes
				300	6,000	30	600	3	60
Inches	Dimes	Inches	Dimes	Inches	Dimes	Inches	Dimes	Inches	Dimes
						40	800	4	80
Inches	Dimes	Inches	Dimes	Inches	Dimes	Inches	Dimes	Inches	Dimes
		5,000	100,000					5	100
Inches	Dimes	Inches	Dimes	Inches	Dimes	Inches	Dimes	Inches	Dimes
Inches	Dimes	Inches	Dimes	Inches	Dimes	Inches	Dimes	Inches	Dimes
Inches	Dimes	Inches	Dimes	Inches	Dimes	Inches	Dimes	Inches	Dimes
80,000	1,600,000								
Inches	Dimes	Inches	Dimes	Inches	Dimes	Inches	Dimes	Inches	Dimes

Fig. B.1. Worksheet

5. Discuss the worksheet. Have the student check his estimation made in activity 3 in the following way, using the worksheet.

Dimes	Inches High
200,000	→ 10,000
200,000	→ 10,000
200,000	→ 10,000
200,000	→ 10,000
200,000	→ 10,000
1,000,000	→ 50,000

SAMPLE LESSONS 489

6. Using the conversion table (fig. B.2), change the number of inches (50,000) to the number of feet.

Inches	Feet	Inches	Feet
12	1	840	70
60	5	960	80
120	10	1,080	90
240	20	1,200	100
360	30	12,000	1,000
480	40	24,000	2,000
600	50	36,000	3,000
720	60	48,000	4,000

Fig. B.2 Conversion table

7. Ask, "If 1,000,000 people each place 3 dimes on a stack, how high would the stack be in feet?"

```
    Dimes              Feet
  1,000,000  ———→   4,166 2/3
  1,000,000  ———→   4,166 2/3
  1,000,000  ———→   4,166 2/3
  ─────────
  3,000,000  ———→  12,498 6/3 = 12,500 ft.
```

8. Have the children name objects that measure about 12,500 feet Look in encyclopedias, dictionaries, and other reference materials for information such as height of mountains. For example, Fuji in Japan is **12,388** feet high.

Reinforcement activities

1. Count the sheets of paper in a stack 1 inch high. Using a similar procedure, determine how high a stack of 1,000,000 sheets of paper would be.

2. Count the number of paper clips in a string 1 foot long. Find the length of a string containing 1,000,000 clips.

Triangular and Square Numbers

GAETANA LEVINSON
Montclair State College
Upper Montclair, New Jersey

The following is a lesson plan written specifically for the student. It is a lesson on triangular and square numbers and would be used in a unit on the study of number character and personality. Other topics in this unit could include a study of the properties of even and odd numbers, prime and composite numbers, perfect numbers, the divisibility rules—in fact, a general "Who's Who" among the integers.

Please note that the lesson as given here has been completed. Responses of the students are indicated by being circled.

References used in the construction of this lesson follow the lesson itself.

Hi!
I'm myself. I'm me.
My name is Triangular.
I am a set of numbers.

I have character, like you. Just as some of you are tall and fat and cheerful and honest, numbers have character, too. There are even numbers and odd numbers and prime numbers and square numbers and many other numbers. All with different personalities.

Do you know what I look like?

I'll give you a hint.

You've seen one of me at the bowling alley as an array of 10 bowling pins. You've seen part of me in the sky, in the formation of birds flying south in the winter. Pool players use one of my forms to store the 15 balls of that game when they are not in use.

Now do you know what I look like?

Well, I just happen to have a few pictures of myself. This is the first one.

As you can see, sometimes I am quite small. Here I am called the first triangular number. My nickname is T(1).

This is the second one.

Here I am as the second triangular number, called T(2). Do you see that I get bigger if you put down two circles in the second row?

Unfortunately, I've only one other picture of myself. This is the third one.

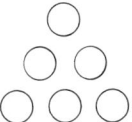

See how the line of three circles in the third row makes me bigger still. This is me as the third triangular number, T(3).

Gee, I'm pretty. But I wish I had more pictures of myself. Could you draw a picture of me? I'll help.

492   THE SLOW LEARNER IN MATHEMATICS

First, see how my pattern forms a triangle. How many circles are there in each side of the triangle? (Equal number.) What kind of triangle does my form take? (Equilateral.)

Now you can draw a picture of me at the bowling alley. (Fig. B.3.)

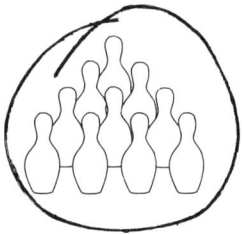

Fig. B.3

How do I look? (Equilateral.)

How many rows did it take to form me? (4.)

What would I be called? (T(4).)

How many circles did you use? (10.)

I just love having my picture drawn. Please draw another. I know, a picture of me on the pool table. (Fig. B.4.)

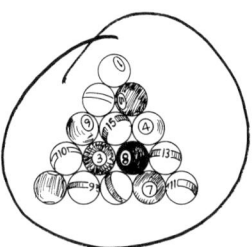

Fig. B.4

How did it turn out?
How many rows did it take to form me this time? (5.)
What would I be called here? (T(5).)
How many circles did you use? (15.)

SAMPLE LESSONS 493

Say, you certainly can draw a nice picture of me. Do you think you could draw me when I am called T(8)? And T(10)? Please try. (Fig. B.5.)

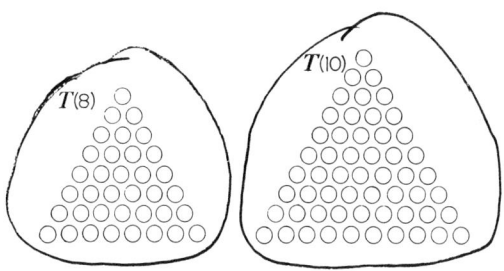

Fig. B.5

How many rows are there in T(8)? (8) T(10)? (10)
How many circles did you use in T(8)? (36) T(10)? (55)
Did you actually count them?
There must be an easier way, and I bet *you* could determine it. You seem so-o-o smart. (Sigh!)

Now you know what I *look like*. But you still don't know me—how I'm made—the real me. Or do you?
Look at me again when I am called T(1). See that I equal 1 circle, or 1. Then look at me at T(2). See that I equal 1 circle plus 2 circles, or 3.
At T(3) I am (1 + 2 + 3) circles; in other words, I equal 6.
Here's my chart! (Fig. B.6.)
Complete it, and you should know me quite well.

Well, you've done it. Here are the first 10 members of me (and me in general). Now that you've seen a part of the real me, how would you define me?
[Seek students' definitions—in their own words.]
My character can be summarized by saying that I am a number equal to the sum of consecutive integers beginning with one (1).
Now we are true friends.

Nick-name	1st Row	2nd Row	3rd Row	4th Row	5th Row	6th Row	7th Row	8th Row	9th Row	10th Row	Sum	Triangular Number
$T(1)$	1	/	/	/	/	/	/	/	/	/		1
$T(2)$	1	2	/	/	/	/	/	/	/	/	1+2	3
$T(3)$	1	2	3	/	/	/	/	/	/	/	1+2+3	6
$T(4)$	①	②	③	④							1+2+3+4	10
$T(5)$	①	②	③	④	⑤							15
$T(6)$	①	②	③	④	⑤	⑥						21
$T(7)$	①	②	③	④	⑤	⑥	⑦					28
$T(8)$	①	②	③	④	⑤	⑥	⑦	⑧				36
$T(9)$	①	②	③	④	⑤	⑥	⑦	⑧	⑨			45
$T(10)$	①	②	③	④	⑤	⑥	⑦	⑧	⑨	⑩		55
$T(r)$	1	2	3	4	5	6	7	8	9	10	to r	$\frac{r(r+1)}{2}$

Fig. B.6

Oh, here comes one of my favorite cousins, Square Number.

You've met him already? Yes, I imagine you would have. He really gets around. That's right. He is the product of another number by itself. ($2 \times 2 = 4$, $3 \times 3 = 3^2 = 9$, etc.) And, of course, you met him when you studied the area of a square ($A = s^2$) and the area of a circle ($A = \pi r^2$). But why not talk to him for a while, anyway? You might discover something new in his character.

Hi!
I'm Square Number.
I noticed you looking at some pictures of my cousin, Tri.
Would you like to see some of me? Good.

This is me, at 1^2. You see I was only a baby of 1. (They called me $S(1)$ here.)

Now here I am at 4^2, when I was 16. Notice my terrific pattern.

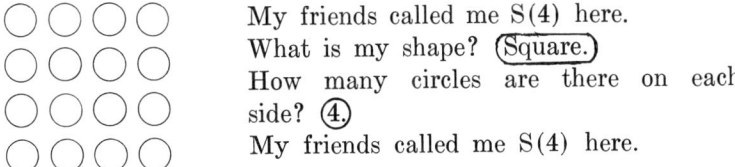

My friends called me $S(4)$ here.
What is my shape? (Square.)
How many circles are there on each side? (4.)
My friends called me $S(4)$ here.

My cousin tells me that you draw pictures of us numbers quite well. Could I interest you in sketching me when I was 2^2, 3^2, and 5^2? Fig. B.7.)

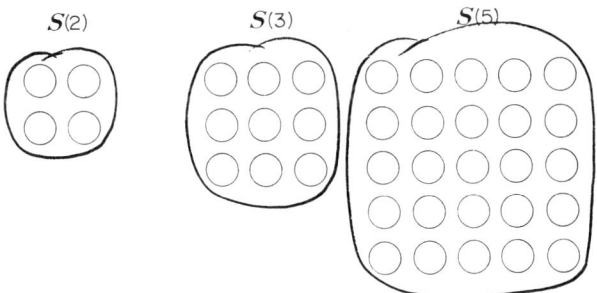

Fig. B.7

Very good likenesses, I must say.

But you haven't captured my resemblance to my cousin, Triangular. What?? You don't see it? Well, please allow me to show you.

First, let us look at your sketches of me at 2^2, 3^2, and 5^2. At 2^2, when I was called S(2), my shape was square. What is the length of each side of this square? ②

How many circles were used to form me? ④
Now, at S(3), what is the length of each side? ③
How many circles were used to form me here? ⑨
Once more at S(5). Is my shape still the same? (Yes.)
How long is each side? ⑤
How many circles were drawn to sketch me? ㉕
(I'm glad to see that you didn't count but simply thought 5^2 means 5 × 5, which equals 25.)

Now, let us try again. What are the first and second triangular numbers? (1 and 3.)

What is their sum? ④

How does this sum compare with the second square number, S(2)? (Same.)

See how you drew me at S(2)?

Now see how I can capture my resemblance to triangular number by arranging the first and second triangular numbers to form S(2).

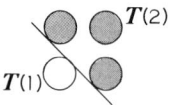

Again, the resemblance can be seen when S(3) is sketched as an arrangement of the second and third triangular numbers.

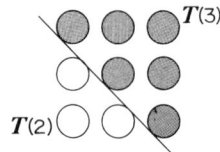

SAMPLE LESSONS

Now do you see my resemblance to Triangular Number? Right! I can be represented as the sum of two consecutive triangular numbers.

Sketch me again at $S(4)$ and $S(5)$ as the sum of two consecutive triangular numbers. (Fig. B.8.)

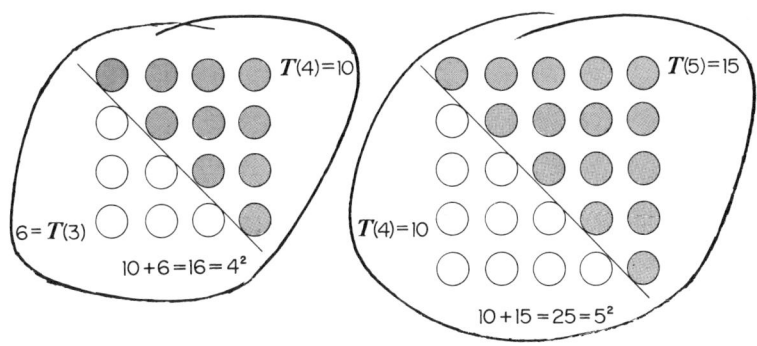

Fig. B.8

Yes indeed! A very good resemblance.

Here is a chart of our relationship. (Fig. B.9.) Complete it, and you will see it quite well.

First triangular number	Second triangular number	Sum of two consecutive triangular numbers	Sum	Square number	
1		1 + 0	1	1^2	1
3	1	3 + 1	4	2^2	4
6	3	6 + 3	9	3^2	9
10	6	10 + 6	16	4^2	16
(15)	10	(15 + 10)	(25)	5^2	(25)
(21)	15	(21 + 15)	(36)	6^2	(36)
(28)	(21)	(28 + 21)	(49)	7^2	(49)
(36)	(28)	(36 + 28)	(64)	8^2	(64)
(45)	(36)	(45 + 36)	(81)	9^2	(81)
55	(45)	(55 + 45)	(100)	10^2	(100)

Fig. B.9

Very good, indeed.

Well, I must dash. It has been a real pleasure having you see the relationship to cousin Triangular. See you again. —Bye, Triangular. Bye, students.

Good-bye, Square Number.

And good-bye to you again. I'm happy we met. It would be fun if we could have another visit. I'm sure my other cousins, Pentagonal and Hexagonal, would be very happy to have you discover their characters, too.

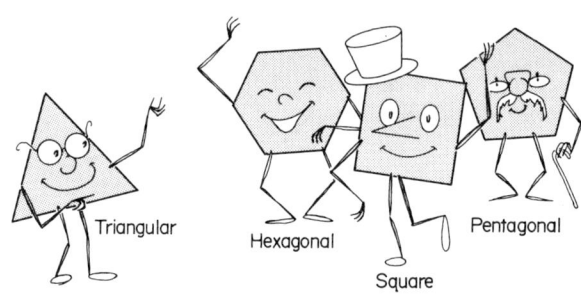

REFERENCES

Adler, Irving. *Magic House of Numbers,* p. 44. New York: John Day Co., 1957.

———. *A New Look at Arithmetic,* p. 57. New York: John Day Co., 1964.

Beiler, Albert. *Recreations in the Theory of Numbers: The Queen of Mathematics Entertains,* p. 185. New York: Dover Publications, 1964.

Davis, Philip. *The Lore of Large Numbers,* p. 85. Toronto, Ont.: Random House of Canada, 1961.

Linear Measurement
(Grades 4–7)

MARY Y. NESBIT
*Former Supervisor of Elementary Mathematics, Dade County Public Schools
Miami, Florida*

Objective

Given an object less than 10 feet in length, the learner should be able to estimate its length using body measurements and report the estimate in feet and inches.

Materials for the teacher

References given at the end of the lesson and any available book on the history of measurement

Materials for each student

Foot ruler
Yardstick
Paper and pencil

Teacher-guided activities

1. Led by the teacher (who has used the reference sources), the students can discuss old ways of measuring and how they led to some of the standard units of our present linear measure.

2. Students make a table of early measures of length: digit, hand or palm, span, cubit, foot, and pace.

Example:
    4 fingers = 1 palm
    3 palms = 1 span
    2 spans = 1 cubit
    2 cubits = 1 yard

3. Students may measure given line segments, a textbook, a desk, or other available objects, using the body measure they feel is most appropriate. Ask them to record these measurements.

4. Let small groups of students work together to compare the measurements they have recorded. To give a variety of measures the teacher, an aide, and any available adult may be included in the groups.

Example:

Measure your desk by palms.
How many palms long is it?
How many palms wide is it?
Compare the width of your palm to the palms of several friends and to your teacher's and aide's palms.

5. Suggest that each group make a table containing body measurements and comparisons of these measurements to the standard unit to which they are related.

Example (see fig. B.10):

Description of Measurement	First Person	Second Person	Third Person	Fourth Person
Standard unit—*Inch*				
Width of thumb...............				
Width of two fingers...........				
Distance from knuckle to joint of thumb..............				
Distance from joint to end of thumb...................				
Standard unit—*Foot*				
Length of foot................				
Standard unit—*Yard*				
Distance from nose to thumb of outstretched arm............				

Fig. B.10

6. Pick the student whose thumb measures nearest an *inch*. Pick the student whose foot measures nearest a *foot*. How many thumb-inches are in the foot-foot?

7. Ask each student to find his *own* body measures that are nearest to an inch and to a foot. Provide objects for each to measure, using his own body measures.

Follow-up activities

1. Estimate measurements of the following:

a) Length of room in inches, feet, and yards
b) Distance in inches a bicycle wheel travels in one revolution
c) Dimensions of the chalkboard in inches and feet

2. Measure the length of a block by using the body-foot. Remeasure, using a yardstick or tape measure.

3. Check the estimates made in follow-up activity 1 by using the appropriate unit of measure.

4. Make a record similar to the one shown in figure B.11.

Object	Estimate	Accurate measure	Amount over or under estimate
Speller (height)	9 inches	11 inches	− 2 inches
Chalkboard (length)	10 feet	9 feet	+ 1 foot

Fig. B.11

REFERENCES

Horne, Sylvia. *Learning about Measurement*. Franklin Mathematics Series. Chicago: Lyons & Carnahan, Educational Div., Meredith Corp., 1970.

Johnson, Donovan A., and William H. Glenn. *The World of Measurement*. Exploring Mathematics on Your Own series. St. Louis: Webster Publishing Co., 1961.

A "Sticky" Experiment—a Lab Approach and Behavioral Objectives

VINCENT BRANT
Coordinator, Office of Mathematics, Board of Education of Baltimore County
Towson, Maryland

The following lesson is an illustration of the kind of activity appropriate for slow learners. This may be used as an activity in the elementary grades to introduce the basic facts in multiplication. Observe that the model is based on the Cartesian product of two sets. This model may also be used for children who forget their basic facts in multiplication. In other words, it represents an algorithm of a lower order of abstraction and enables the child to perform successfully, although at a slower rate, until he convinces himself that it would be much easier to commit these basic facts to memory.

Objectives

The student should be able to do the following:
1. Identify the horizontal and vertical positions of lines
2. Name the horizontal and vertical positions of lines
3. Draw (place) lines in horizontal and vertical positions
4. Name and identify intersections of horizontal and vertical lines
5. State the rule that the number of intersections of horizontal and vertical lines is equal to the product of the number of horizontal lines and the number of vertical lines
6. Apply the above rule

Materials for each student

18 sticks
Preliminary worksheet
Summary worksheet

Plan

1. Distribute the sticks and worksheets.
2. Emphasize the necessity of careful reading and recording.
3. Have an additional activity ready for those children who finish before others.

Preliminary Worksheet

1. The sticks in these experiments will represent lines.
2. When a stick is placed on your desk as in the diagram below, we say that the stick represents a *horizontal* line.

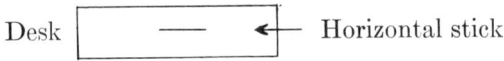

3. When a line is placed on your desk as in the diagram below, we say that it represents a *vertical* line.

Desk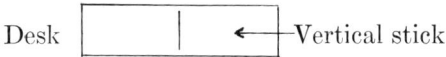

Experiment 1
1. Place one stick in a horizontal position on your desk.
2. Place another stick in a vertical position on top of the first stick as shown below.

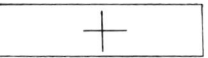

3. Do they cross each other?_____
4. How many times do they intersect (cross each other)?_____
5. Record your findings in the chart below.

	Number of horizontal lines	Number of vertical lines	Number of intersections
Experiment 1			

Experiment 2
1. Place 2 sticks in a horizontal position on your desk.
2. Place 1 stick in a vertical position on top of the horizontal sticks.
3. Count the number of intersections of the horizontal and vertical sticks; that is, the number of places where they cross.
4. Record this information in the chart on the summary worksheet.

Experiment 3
1. Place 3 sticks in a horizontal position on your desk.
2. Place 2 sticks in a vertical position on top of the horizontal sticks.
3. Count the number of intersections of the horizontal and vertical sticks.
4. Record this information in the chart on the summary worksheet.

Experiment 4
1. Place 3 sticks in a horizontal position on your desk.
2. Place 5 sticks in a vertical position on top of the horizontal sticks.
3. Count the number of intersections of the horizontal and vertical sticks.

4. Record this information in the chart on the summary worksheet.

Experiment 5
1. Place 6 sticks in a horizontal position on your desk.
2. Place 4 sticks in a vertical position on top of the horizontal sticks.
3. Count the number of intersections of the horizontal and vertical sticks.
4. Record this information in the chart on the summary worksheet.

You will probably notice that there is a rule that will tell you how to find the number of intersections *without counting*. If you know this rule, write it in the spaces provided in the middle of the summary worksheet.

If you have not discovered this rule, do experiment 6.

Experiment 6
1. Place 4 sticks in a horizontal position on your desk.
2. Place 8 sticks in a vertical position on top of the horizontal sticks.
3. Count the number of intersections of the horizontal and vertical sticks.
4. Record this information in the chart on the summary worksheet.

Now, to discover the rule, compare the numbers in the different rows. There is a relationship or rule connecting the three numbers in each row. When you have discovered the rule, write it in the space provided in the middle of the summary worksheet. Test the rule, as directed there, and check your answers by comparing them with the correct answers at the bottom of the worksheet.

	Number of horizontal lines	Number of vertical lines	Number of intersections
Experiment 1	1	1	1
Experiment 2			
Experiment 3			
Experiment 4			
Experiment 5			
Experiment 6			

Rule

The rule for finding the number of intersections of horizontal and vertical lines is_____

Testing your rule

By this time, you have probably discovered the rule. It should provide a shortcut for finding the number of intersections *without counting*. Test your rule by finding the number of intersections for the following exercises. You can check your answers by comparing them with the correct answers at the bottom of this worksheet.

1. 6 horizontal sticks and 5 vertical sticks
2. 7 horizontal sticks and 9 vertical sticks
3. 9 horizontal sticks and 8 vertical sticks

If you should ever forget your basic facts of multiplication, you can always use the idea in this experiment. For example, if you forget the answer to 5 × 4, you can draw 5 horizontal and 4 vertical lines on your paper, and then count the number of intersections.

Correct answers
   1. 30   2. 63   3. 72

Area of a Rectangle (Fourth Grade)

MARILYN POTTORFF
*Fourth-Grade Teacher, F. C. Martin Elementary School
Richmond Heights, Florida*

Objective

Given a number of horizontal units less than 11 and a number of vertical units less than 11, the student should learn to compute the area of a rectangle.

Materials for the teacher

  Dotted grid on chalkboard
  Large demonstration geoboard, if available

Materials for each student

  1 dotted sheet of rectangles and two other shapes, as in figure B.12
  1 data sheet, figure B.13
  Individual geoboard, if available

Teacher-guided activities

When children look over the dotted sheets, tell them, "We're going to find the number of square units in each of the rectangles shown."

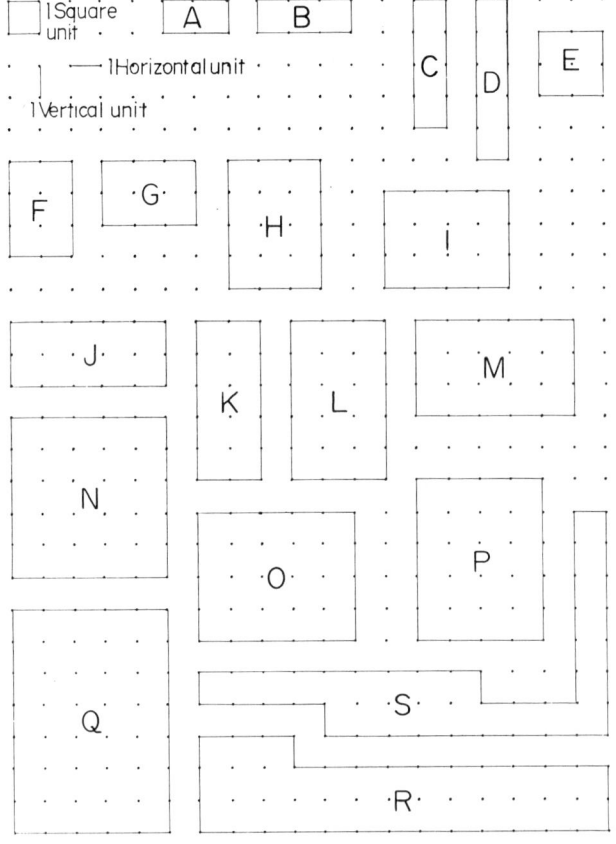

Fig. B.12. Dotted sheet

SAMPLE LESSONS 507

Show on the chalkboard grid one vertical unit, one horizontal unit, and one square unit.

Relate "vertical" to vertical take-off aircraft.

Relate "horizontal" to horizon.

Discuss the data sheet (fig. B.13) and procedure for each set of answers. Make clear that the children count the line segment from one dot to the next—not the dots.

	A	B	C	D	E	F
Vertical units						
Horizontal units						
Square units						
	G	H	I	J	K	L
Vertical units						
Horizontal units						
Square units						
	M	N	O	P	Q	
Vertical units						
Horizonal units						
Square units						

For those who think they're smart:

R = _____ square units   S = _____ square units

Fig. B.13. Data sheet

Do rectangle A of figure B.12 on the chalkboard or geoboard. Work A, E, and H together. The teacher or a child should write the following answers on the board, filling in a simulated portion of the data sheet.

	A	B	C	D	E	F
Vertical units	1	1	4	5	2	3
Horizontal units	2	3	1	1	2	2
Square units	2	3	4	5	4	6

More figures may be worked out together (as needed).

The teacher should duplicate the outline of the figure and the dots, since children often have difficulty seeing the square units. As in a portion of the illustration below, count the number of square units by drawing in connecting lines between dots.

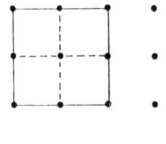

Review results, using the data sheet, after the first few examples. Allow the children to complete independently the second row of the dotted sheet (G, H, and I).

Continuation of teacher-guided activities

Ask the children if they see any relationship between the horizontal and vertical units and the square units of each rectangle.

Allow them to do independently the third row of the dotted sheet (J–M).

Ask: "Do you see a shortcut [multiplication] yet?"

Allow the children to complete rectangles through Q. (Do not do R and S at the present time, since they are not rectangles.)

"OK. Suppose you knew this chalkboard was 7 vertical units and 10 horizontal units." [Write this on the board in data-sheet form.]

Vertical units	7
Horizontal units	10
Square units	70

"Can you tell me how many square units it would contain?"

As the children figure out the shortcut, don't ask for the rule; rather, give them a simple rectangle to figure out by saying, for example, "Three vertical and 7 horizontal units—how many square units?"

For children who seem to have the concept, ask: "How many square units in a 3-by-7 rectangle? How many square units in a 7-by-3 rectangle?"

Extensions

1. For those who have caught on, prepare worksheets without dots, like the one shown below. Later, graduate to larger numbers as their skills warrant. For groups who have skill using a tape measure, suggest they measure the room, recording length and width to the nearest foot, and find the area.

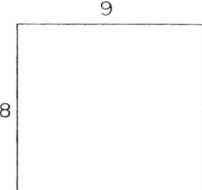

2. Prepare sheets with dots only and allow the children to make up their own figures, such as the R and S of figure B.12.

Long Division
(Upper Grades)

JAMES R. PEARSON
Coordinator of Media Valuation, Dade County Public Schools
Miami, Florida

Objective

To enable the student to realize the objective of this lesson, prelesson work should have been done with an array approach to multiplication, of course; this work should also include 1 digit times multiples of 10, since this is merely basic multiplication-facts drill hidden behind "big numbers" (i.e., 8×60 is *really* 8×6 multiplied by 10). The objective of the lesson is that the student, given a division problem having a 3-digit dividend and a 1-digit divisor, with a remainder of 0, should learn to compute the quotient.

Materials for the teacher

Chalkboard
Large "array" card

Materials for each student

Scrap paper and pencils
Multiplication tables (if necessary)
Worksheets

Teacher-guided activities

Hold up the array card shown below and review the fact that the

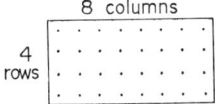

32 objects in the array may be represented by the multiplication of the number of rows, 4, by the number of columns, 8: $4 \times 8 = 32$.

The division sentence might be $32 \div 4 =$ what? (8.)

Suppose the array looked like this:

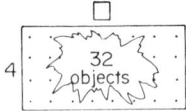

Now we can write $4 \times \square = 32$. Is there a division sentence we can write? ($32 \div 4 = \square$.)

Review 1 digit times a multiple of 10.
Now, on the board, show:

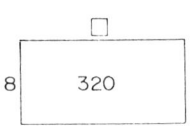

How can this be written? ($8 \times \square = 320$.) Are we sure a whole number can be put in the box? (We can't always be sure.) At any rate, let's use less than or equal to ($\leq$). We can call it "equal or not quite equal to."

Is *this* true, whether or not the $\square$ represents a whole number: $320 \div 8 = \square$? (Yes.) How many tens in 320? (32.)

Write $8 \times \square \leq 32$ tens. Now it's easy: 8 times *what* is "equal or not quite equal to" 32? (4.) Yes, but 4 what? [Point to the space after the box, wait to hear "tens," and write $8 \times [4]$ tens ≤ 32 tens. Also ask the students to fill in $8 \times \square \leq 320$.]

SAMPLE LESSONS   511

Continue with other examples, such as 240 ÷ 6 = ☐, 639 ÷ 9 = ☐, and 490 ÷ 7 = ☐.

Look at this example: 504 ÷ 7 = ☐

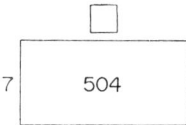

How can we write this as multiplication? (7 × ☐ ≤ 504.) How many tens in 504? (50.) Will someone write a sentence using tens? (7 × ☐ tens ≤ 50 tens.) How many tens? (7.) Write 7 × [7] tens ≤ 50 tens. What is [write] 7 × 70 = ☐? (490.) That's not exactly 504. What can we do to find out how much more than 490 we have? (Subtract: 504 − 490.) Now we have a 7 × 70 array (490) plus a 7 × ☐ array with 14 in it.

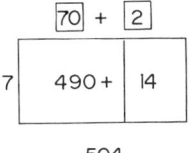

Now what goes in the box? (2.) So 7 × [2] = 14.

   504
  −490
    14

Then 504 ÷ 7 = ☐. (72.)

Continue with other examples, such as 384 ÷ 8 = ☐, 301 ÷ 4 = ☐, and 125 ÷ 5 = ☐.

Finally:

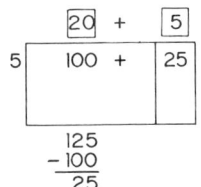

125 ÷ 5 = [25]

5 × [20] ≤ 12 tens

  125
 −100
   25

(Leave the above on the board.)
Or we could write it like this:

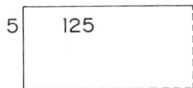

Now erase the dotted lines:

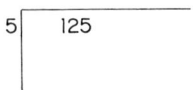

A.

$$\begin{array}{r}20\\5\overline{\smash{)}125}\\-100\\\hline 25\end{array}$$

A. We already found that $5 \times 20 = 100$, and we subtracted the 100 to see how many we had left. Let's subtract *here* this time. We find there is a $5 \times \square$ array left with 25 in it.

B.

$$\begin{array}{r}25\\5\\20\\5\overline{\smash{)}125}\\-100\\\hline 25\\25\end{array}$$

B. Now $5 \times \boxed{5} = 25$, so we'll write that above the 20 and add *up*. Now, fill in: $125 \div 5 = \square$. (25.)

Now, we'll do the next one like this: $444 \div 6 = \square$.

A.

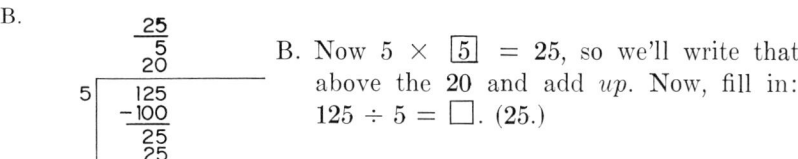

A. Can someone write the "equal or not quite equal" sentence? ($6 \times \square \leq 444$.)

How many tens in 444? (44.) Now, write the "tens" sentence, $6 \times \boxed{7}$ tens ≤ 44 tens, and $6 \times 70 = 420$. How much more than 420 is this? (Someone subtract $444 - 420$.)

B.

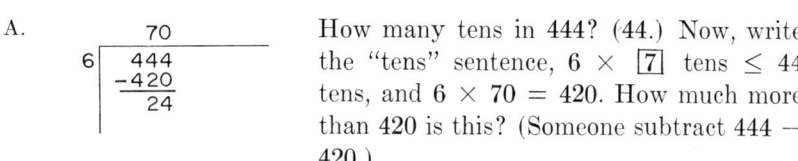

B. There's 24 left, and that's an easy fact. ($6 \times 4 = 24$.) When we add *up* we get 74.

Extensions

Worksheets with the following types of work will provide practice:

$372 \div 4 = \Box$; $\_ \times \Box \leq \_$; $\_ \times \Box$ tens $\leq \_$ tens

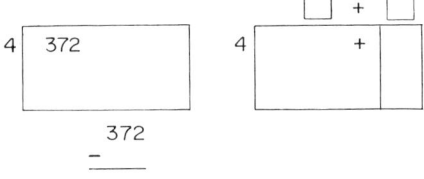

$9\overline{)468}$

$468 \div 9 = \Box$

$\_ \times \Box$ tens $\leq \_$ tens

REFERENCES

Biggs, Edith E., and James R. MacLean. *Freedom to Learn: An Active Learning Approach to Mathematics,* pp. 119–20. Don Mills, Ont.: Addison-Wesley (Canada), 1969.

Dienes, Z. P. *Mathematics in the Primary School,* pp. 96–98, 107–10. London: Macmillan & Co., 1964.

Diagnostic Analysis of Mathematics Skills

JAMES F. SKARBEK
Principal, Lansdowne Elementary School
Baltimore County, Maryland

Oral analysis is a diagnostic technique in which the teacher not only observes the child's work but also has him talk aloud as he solves the problem. The technique enables the teacher to discover how the child is thinking about number and number operations. By asking probing questions, the teacher gains insight into what skills have been mastered and further insight into what generalizations have been only partially understood. The technique can readily be implemented using informal exercises or test items at any level of learning. Although oral analysis is valuable for use with all pupils, it is especially appropriate for use with slow learners.

In order to illustrate oral analysis, the following examples were selected from a fourth-grade diagnostic exercise administered at the beginning of the school year. The children had been introduced to the subtraction skill of renaming as a part of their third-grade program; the skill had not been reviewed in the fourth grade prior to the diagnostic exercise. A tape recorder was employed to record the explanations offered by the children. Each computation is reproduced as it appeared on the child's paper.

Illustration A

Before reading the explanation offered by pupil A, analyze his algorithm. How would one explain the changing of 6 hundreds to 4 hundreds in the sum?

Computation

$$\begin{array}{r} 4\ 1\ 1 \\ \cancel{6}\ 0\ 4 \\ -5\ 4\ 5 \\ \hline 6\ 9\ \end{array}$$

Student Explanation (on tape)

Four minus five, you can't take that, so you'll have to take [pause] you can't take one from zero, so you take one from the number six and that will give you the number fourteen and fourteen minus five is nine and then you come to the number zero and zero minus four [pause]. You can't take four from zero, so you come from the number six again and take one from there, and that will give you the number ten, and ten minus four is six, and since you took two from the number six, that would make the number four and four minus five is [pause]. You can't take that so you just leave it blank, and the number is number sixty-nine.

Through your analysis of the algorithm were you able to assess pupil A's understanding? The explanation revealed that pupil A partially understood the concept that in subtraction of whole numbers every column must have a sum that is greater than or the same as the known addend. Specifically, the child recognized that the sums named

SAMPLE LESSONS 515

in the ones column and in the tens column were not larger than the known addends and therefore realized that the sum had to be renamed. However, the child did not understand the concept of renaming. Further questioning would be necessary to reveal the child's understanding of place value.

Illustration B

As you read the explanation of pupil B, assess his understanding of the operation.

Computation	Student Explanation (on tape)
5 9 10 6 0 4 −5 4 5 5 5	You can't take four [pause] five from four, so you take a hundred out of the hundreds place and put nine in the tens column and then ten in the ones column, and then you subtract ten from [pause] five from ten and put down five, and then you subtract nine from four, and then you get your answer is five, and five take away five equals zero.

The explanation indicated pupil B's understanding that the operation required renaming. The child skillfully handled the zero difficulty when renaming 6 hundreds to 5 hundreds 9 tens and 10 ones. The difficulty occurred in providing for the 4 ones represented in the original sum. Confusion was evidenced, however, in the application of the concept that subtraction is the inverse operation of addition. In two instances, pupil B began to subtract the sum rather than the known addend; in the third instance, he reversed the numbers but computed the missing addend.

Illustration C

Review pupil C's algorithm and analyze the explanation. Based on your assessment of his understanding, what teaching suggestions could be offered to help pupil C?

Computation	Student Explanation (on tape)
5 4 9̸ 1̸ 0 −2 4 0 3 0 0	Zero minus zero equals zero [pause]. I crossed out the one 'cause you can't take four from one, and I took a four from the nine, and the one became the four, and four minus four is zero, and of course the [pause] nine is now five, so I get five minus two equals three.

Obviously, pupil C is attempting to function at a level beyond his understanding. Further diagnosis is required to ascertain pupil C's ability to subtract 2- and 3-digit numerals when renaming is not required. An instructional program should provide for a review of expanded notation using number frames and place-value pockets to develop the idea that a number can be named in many ways. The concept of expanded notation should then be used to develop an understanding of renaming. Expanded notation and renaming should then be applied to 2-digit numerals and 3-digit numerals before the short subtraction algorithm is developed.

Illustration D

In contrast to the preceding answers, the answer of pupil D is correct. As you read the explanation, attempt to identify the method employed. What recommendations should be offered concerning an instructional program for pupil D?

Computation	Student Explanation (on tape)
$\begin{array}{r} 6\ 0\ 4 \\ -5\ 4\ 5 \\ \hline 5\ 9 \end{array}$	Well, you can't take five from four, so you have to make a four a fourteen, and five from fourteen would be nine, and then you have to make the four a five, from ten would be five, and you have to make the other five a six, and six from six would be zero.

It should be noted that an inspection of the written computation does not reveal the take-away equal-additions method; only through oral analysis is the method evident to the teacher. Further discussion with the child revealed that the procedure was taught to the child by a parent. The instructional program should provide for pupil D's understanding of the method being used by the class. The instructional program should also emphasize that there are different methods to perform number operations and that each method has certain advantages. The ultimate choice of method belongs to the child.

Conclusion

Oral analysis is unique in revealing the mental reactions of a child. It enables the teacher to assess the manner of individual learning and to program instruction based on that assessment.

Fractions
(Grades 4–6)

MARGARET H. BERGE
District Mathematics Teacher, Southwest District, Dade County Public Schools
Miami, Florida

Objective

Given fractional numbers, the student should learn to identify equivalent and nonequivalent fractions orally or by writing the symbols $=$, $<$, $>$, and $\neq$.

Materials for the teacher

6 egg cartons, painted in different colors: 1 whole carton, the others cut into halves, thirds, fourths, sixths, and twelfths
These egg cartons nest together neatly and compactly.

Materials for each student

6 egg cartons, as listed for the teacher (children enjoy gathering and preparing this material)
1 large, unruled, laminated card
1 crayon
1 tissue or paper towel for cleaning the laminated card after each response

Teacher-guided activities

During this lesson, have students show answers on the laminated cards as often as possible so that you can evaluate the response of each student. Discussion of answers and proofs, using nests, should follow to allow students to verbalize their responses and to clarify misconceptions.

Display 1 whole egg carton and ask students to write a number or a word on their card, with the crayon, that tells *how many* the carton will hold. Ask them to show their answers when you say, "Show me."

Discuss the correctness of "12" or "dozen." Suggest that for the activities today "1 dozen" be used to name the container.

Look through your nest of containers and find one that will hold ½ dozen. The lesson might then proceed as follows. The responses of the students, when given, are shown in parentheses.

How many of these do you have? (2.)

If we fit these 2 into our 1-dozen container, how do they compare in size? Do the 2 parts fill the dozen container? (Yes.)

How many parts do you have that show ½ dozen? (2.)

Are the 2 parts the same size? (Yes.)

Show me 1 of these 2 parts.

You have shown me 1 part of 2 parts. [Show this on the chalkboard as indicated below.]

```
   1     part
out of..........
   2     parts
```

We can also write this as ½.

Tell me two ways to read this symbol. (½ or 1 part out of 2 parts.)

Look through your nest and find 3 parts of a dozen that are the same size.

Fit the 3 parts into the dozen container and tell how they compare in size, or how they fit.

Write the color of your 3 parts on your card and *show me*.

Show me 1 part out of 3 parts. [Place the following on the chalkboard.]

```
   1     part
out of..........
   3     parts
```

If we called 1 part out of 2 parts ½, what symbol can we use to show 1 part out of 3 parts? (⅓.)

How do we read this symbol? (⅓ or 1 part out of 3 parts.)

Show me

```
   2     parts
out of..........
   3     parts
```

or ⅔ of 1 dozen.

SAMPLE LESSONS

[Continue the same procedure with fourths, sixths, and twelfths until the children demonstrate the fraction by identifying the part named by the denominator and the number of parts specified by the numerator.]
Show me $\frac{1}{2}$ dozen.
Show me $\frac{1}{12}$ dozen.
How many $\frac{1}{12}$s will it take to fill $\frac{1}{2}$?
Use your nests to find out and write your answer on your card, and *show me.* (6.)
Next, think about this:

| 6 parts |
| out of |
| ? parts |

or $\frac{6}{?}$, is another name for $\frac{1}{2}$.
Write True or False on your card for this equation: $\frac{6}{12} = \frac{1}{2}$. (True.)
How do you know?
Show me $\frac{1}{4}$ dozen.
Show me $\frac{1}{12}$ dozen.
How many $\frac{1}{12}$s will it take to fill $\frac{1}{4}$?
Write True or False on your card for this equation: $\frac{1}{4} = \frac{3}{12}$. (True.)
How do you know?
Write True or False for this equation: $\frac{1}{4} = \frac{4}{12}$. (False.)
How do you know?
Write the answer on your card: How many $\frac{1}{12}$s equal 1 dozen? (12.)
Write True or False: $\frac{12}{12} = 1$. (True.) $\frac{6}{6} = 1$. (True.) $\frac{2}{3} = 1$. (False.)
Show me $\frac{1}{3}$ dozen.
Show me $\frac{1}{6}$ dozen.
How many $\frac{1}{6}$s of a dozen will it take to fill $\frac{1}{3}$ dozen?
Next, think about this:

| ? parts |
| out of |
| 6 parts |

or $\frac{?}{6}$, is another name for $\frac{1}{3}$.
Write True or False on your card for this equation: $\frac{2}{6} = \frac{1}{3}$. (True.)
[Continue with other equivalent fractions.]
Use your nests to find which is larger, $\frac{1}{2}$ or $\frac{3}{4}$. Use them again to find which is larger, $\frac{2}{3}$ or $\frac{5}{6}$.
[Continue with other comparisons, allowing the children to manipu-

late their nests to discover relationships. A sample worksheet is shown here.]

Use your nest of cartons to compare the fractions.
Put <, >, or = in the frames.

$\frac{1}{2} \square \frac{1}{4}$ $\qquad$ $\frac{5}{6} \square \frac{2}{3}$

$\frac{1}{4} \square \frac{1}{3}$ $\qquad$ $\frac{4}{6} \square \frac{3}{4}$

$\frac{2}{2} \square 1$ $\qquad$ $\frac{2}{12} \square \frac{1}{6}$

$1 \square \frac{4}{4}$ $\qquad$ $\frac{4}{12} \square \frac{5}{6}$

$\frac{3}{3} \square 1$ $\qquad$ $\frac{6}{12} \square \frac{1}{2}$

$\frac{2}{3} \square \frac{3}{4}$ $\qquad$ $\frac{7}{12} \square \frac{2}{3}$

Follow-up

This lesson should be followed by naming and comparing fractional parts of number lines and regions using fifths, sevenths, eighths, and others.

Index

Achievement, 1–13 passim, 29–36 passim, 129–30, 133, 163, 330, 351, 365
Action verbs, 81, 83–90, 372–73, 376. *See also* Performance, verbs
Administration, classroom and school, 319–44
Aides, teacher, 160, 270, 323, 324, 336, 339, 340–41
Allport, Gordon, 306
Aptitude, 27, 29, 30, 42, 330
Arithmetic Teacher (NCTM), 153, 157, 158, 264, 431, 463
Asbell, Bernard, 8, 15
Assessment, 59, 133, 373, 377. *See also* Evaluation
  tasks, 57, 72–74, 82–90, 93–101
Attitudes, 1, 33–34, 41, 104, 137, 292, 333, 350–54 passim, 386, 389, 398, 403, 429–30
  of teachers, 327, 398, 409, 422, 429–30
Audiovisual materials, 39, 324, 341. *See also* Bulletin boards; Chalkboards; Models; Projectors; Recording equipment; Visual aids and materials
Ausubel, David P., 4
Axline, Virginia
  Dibs: In Search of Self, 289

Baltimore County program, 59, 96, 178–79, 345, 425–27
  "banded" approach in the, 178–79, 372, 374–78, 426–27
  behaviorial objectives in the, 96–101, 372–79, 425–26

Mathematics for Basic Education, 97–101, 345–46, 371–79
Beberman, Max, 434
Beckmann, Milton W., 431
Begle, Edward G., 35
Behavior problems, student, 117–21. *See also* Control of class
Behavioral indicators, 298–305. *See also* Behavioral objectives
Behavioral objectives, 36–37, 52–102, 175, 330, 437, 501–2. *See also* Behavioral indicators
  in the Baltimore County program, 96–101, 372–79, 425–26
  characteristics of, 69–72
  in teacher training, 52–55, 418–21
  and teaching, 91–93
Behavioral scientist, 52, 58, 59, 73
Bentzen, Frances, 12
Berger, Emil J., 36
Biggs, Edith E., 115, 434
  Freedom to Learn (with MacLean), 115, 124, 271, 434
Bilingual instruction. *See* "Mathematics for Spanish-speaking Pupils (MSP)"
Blackboards. *See* Chalkboards
Bloom, Benjamin S., 38–40, 59, 293, 299–304, 306, 309, 313
  Taxonomy of Educational Objectives: The Classification of Educational Goals. Handbook 1, *Cognitive Domain*, 40, 59, 293, 298–304, 309, 313
Botel, Morton, 434

Brant, Vincent, 346, 371, 379
Brownell, William Arthur, 298, 301, 307, 308, 311
Brueckner, Leo J., 129
Bruner, Jerome S., 8, 11, 284, 286
Bugelski, Bergen Richard, 110
Bulletin boards, 107, 110, 150, 167, 190, 204, 212, 218, 321–30 passim

California Achievement Tests, 129, 349, 351, 367
California Test of Mental Maturity, 32
Callahan, John J., 36
Cambridge Conference on School Mathematics, 249
Carroll, John B., 36, 288
Castaneda, Albert M., 35
Cawley, John F., 33
Chalkboards, 107, 139, 144, 150, 152, 164, 167, 188, 190, 191, 196, 197, 208, 210–18 passim, 321–26 passim, 474, 507
Characteristics of slow learners, 2–12, 104, 283, 371–72, 398, 437. *See also* Disadvantaged children, characteristics of; Inner-city children, characteristics of
  affective functioning, deficient in, 1, 6, 13, 22
  attention span, short, 8–9, 104, 169, 180–81, 183, 187, 218, 350–51, 372, 374
  cognitive functioning, deficient in, 1, 2, 4, 22
  goals, short-range, 18
  learning style, physical and slow, 5–6, 22, 436
  self-image, negative, 1–13, 22, 104, 182, 223, 383, 384, 398
  sex differences and, 11–12, 22
  skills
    school, deficient in, 8–9
    social, deficient in, 9–10, 22
Chips, 249–57, 264, 265, 268
  chip trading, 221, 249–56, 337
  games with, 250–53
Classroom, 105–21, 323–24
  atmosphere, 105, 112–21, 391
  contingency-managed, 324–27
  management, 319, 320–31, 402–5
  organizing for learning in the, 135–37
  physical environment of the, 14, 105–7, 172
  the self-contained, 326–27

Classroom Questions: What Kinds? (Sanders), 309
Cobb, Margaret V., 35
Cognitive domain
  development in the, 383
  functioning in, slow learners, 1, 2, 4, 22
  levels of behavior in the, 40–41, 298–99
  taxonomy of behaviors in the, 298–305
  variables in the, 4–6
"Committee on the Low Achiever in Mathematics—Denver Area" (COLAMDA), 397–401, 427–30
Computation, 12, 32, 41, 131–58 passim, 165, 352, 362–63, 378
Computer-assisted instruction (CAI), 136, 337, 401
  in McComb, Mississippi, Schools, 36
  in New York City Schools, 337, 345, 355–64
Conditions of Learning, The (Gagné), 301
Conference on the Low Achiever in Mathematics (USOE and NCTM), 406
Control of class, 327–30. *See also* Behavior problems, student
Cook, J. Marvin, 59, 92
Copeland, Richard W., 340
Cox, Gloria, 345, 364
Cronbach, Lee J., 33–36, 286
Crowley, Regis F., 333
Cruickshank, W. M., 131
Cuisenaire rods, 36, 115, 149, 249, 262, 264, 266, 392–93, 396, 399, 404, 408, 413, 415, 428, 434
Cultural differences, 2, 3, 6–7, 22
Curriculum
  adjustments for slow learners, 136–37
  development and adaptation, 371–79, 421–27, 429
  logical subtheory of, 284, 286–87
  "mastery," 38–40
  psychological subtheory of, 284–85, 286–87
  sociological subtheory of, 285, 286–87

Davis, Robert B., 15, 116, 422
Deans, Edwina
  "*Space Oriented Mathematics for Early Grades*" (USOE), 157

DeVenny, William S., 345, 349
Diagnosing pupil performance, 23, 130–35, 136, 310–12. *See also* Diagnostic-prescriptive teaching
  analyzing written work as a means of, 132–33
  audio tape and video tape in, 132, 311, 514–16
  observing and interviewing the pupil as a means of, 131–32, 308–9, 513–16
  using tests as a means of, 133–35, 172, 179, 307, 320, 330, 331, 333
Diagnostic-prescriptive teaching, 39, 282–318. *See also* Diagnosing pupil performance
  curriculum variable and, 284–87
  ideographic procedures in, 282, 305, 307–12
  method variable and, 287–90
  nomothetic procedures in, 282, 305–7, 308
  symptomatic approach to diagnosis, 282, 293, 302, 304
Dibs: In Search of Self (Axline), 289
Disadvantaged children, culturally, 1, 6, 7, 15, 17, 32, 36, 104, 137, 149, 151, 160, 337, 355, 383, 384, 405, 406, 411, 423, 427
  characteristics of, 6, 10–11, 109
  socioeconomic status of, 361, 405
Discipline. *See* Control of class
Discovering Meanings in Elementary School Mathematics (Brueckner, Grossnickle, and Reckzeh), 129
Discovery, 157, 159, 183, 287–90, 384–87
Dodson, Joseph Wesley, 33
Drill, 136, 146–47, 174, 179, 270, 325, 349, 355–59, 377, 380, 398, 463. *See also* Practice; Skills, maintaining
Duncan, Frances M., 149
Dunkley, M. E., 32

Easterday, Kenneth E., 36, 346
Eisenberg, Leon, 3
Elementary Arithmetic and Learning Aids (USOE, Spross), 157
Elementary and Secondary Education Act (ESEA), 356, 387, 397
Elkins, Deborah, 23
Engel, Roberta S., 92
Erikson, Erik H., 13–14
Evaluation, 167, 306–8, 330–33. *See also* Assessment
  daily work, 330–31
  formative, 39
  homework, 325, 330
  reporting to parents, 332–33
  summative, 306–7
  testing, 331–32
Experiences in Mathematical Discovery (NCTM), 36

Fantini, Mario D., 7, 402, 417, 422–23
Films. *See* Projectors
First International Congress of Mathematical Education, 35
Flanagan Tests of General Ability, 37
Flow charts, 174–75, 190–92, 207–9, 359, 382, 409, 429
Fort, Jane G., 291
Fowler, William, 3, 7, 17
Freedom to Learn (Biggs and MacLean), 115, 124, 271, 434

Gagné, Robert M., 36, 59, 293, 301–4
  The Conditions of Learning, 301
Games, 5, 16, 39, 105, 112, 114, 115, 149, 151–53, 175, 179, 187–88, 248–53, 266–67, 337, 338, 341, 377, 379, 399, 401, 426, 428, 429, 432, 433, 446–81 passim
Gattegno, C., 225
Geoboards, 5, 221, 224–49, 264–65, 337, 396, 399, 401, 408, 415, 428, 434, 507
  circular spaced, 225–26
  games on, 248–49
  isometric, 225–26
  uses of, 226, 245–49
Glaser, Robert, 30, 31
Gleason, A., 249
Glennon, Vincent J., 286, 287
Glick, Oren, 33–34
Goodman, John O., 33
Grades, 1, 22, 371
Gray, William L., 92
Grossnickle, Foster E., 131
  Discovering Meanings in Elementary School Mathematics (with Brueckner and Reckzeh), 129
Grouping for instruction, 2, 13, 39, 146, 158–60, 333–36
  homogeneous, 20, 135, 319, 338–40
  within class, 130, 158–60, 319, 333–35

Hastings, J. Thomas, 38–39
Hendrickson, Gordon, 298, 301
Herriot, Sarah T., 30, 35

Hierarchies
  of cognitive levels, 40
  of content, 297–98
  of learning outcomes, 39
  of learning types, 36, 301–2
Highet, Gilbert, 290
Hoffman, Ruth Irene, 35, 346, 397, 401
Holt, John, 403
Howitz, Thomas A., 36
Husén, Torsten, 40

Identification of slow learners, 1, 26, 28–30
Improving Mathematics for Elementary School Teachers (Michigan State University), 418
Individual differences, 13, 19, 34–36, 42, 102, 169, 338, 430
  research on, 30–32, 338
Individualized instruction, 36–37, 130, 135, 136, 164, 169–70, 174, 324, 335–38, 355, 397, 409, 422, 429, 435
Individually Prescribed Instruction (IPI), 36–37, 336–37
Inner-city children, 112, 119, 346, 383, 387–95
  characteristics of, 388–89
Institute for Mathematical Studies in the Social Sciences (Stanford University), 356
Instructional activities, 183–218, 444–80, 487–520. *See also* Chips; Cuisenaire rods; Games; Geoboards; Manipulative materials; Models; Projectors; Recording equipment; Written materials
  constructing (*see* Models, constructing)
  cutting paper and string, 183–85, 194–96, 198, 211
  drawing, 196–201, 214–16, 491–98
  graphing, 107, 108, 209–10, 224, 374
  lessons, sample, 487–520
  magic squares, 153, 188–89, 447–50
  mapping, 247, 259
  measuring, 101, 106, 147, 165, 202, 211, 228–45, 337, 432, 475–77, 487–89, 499–501, 505–9
  paper folding, 185–86, 195–96, 198–202, 206–7, 211–14, 218, 337, 338, 477–78
  puzzles, 5, 113, 127, 151, 153, 175, 179, 337, 377, 378, 396, 426–29 passim, 481–82
Intelligence, factors of, 28–31

Intelligence quotient (IQ), 1, 2, 29–30, 32, 42, 129, 371
International Study of Achievement in Mathematics (Husén, ed.), 34–35

Jacobson, Lenore F., 37–38
Jacobson, Ruth S., 36
James, William 306
Jerome, Sister Agnes, 32
Johnson, Donovan A., 338
Johnson, George Orville, 332
Johntz, William F., 346, 383, 387
Judd, Charles H., 308

Kagan, Jerome, 10, 11, 17
Karnes, Merle B., 36
Keislar, Evan R., 289
Kelly, Francis J., 36, 136
Kilpatrick, Jeremy, 40
Klineberg, Otto, 6
Korb, Sister Mary, 336
Krech, David, 292

Laboratory, mathematics, 5, 135–36, 221–81, 311, 323, 346, 372, 379, 422, 433, 435, 501–4
  as an approach to learning, 222–81, 283, 433, 437
  characteristics of a, 222, 399
  in the Chicago City Schools, 387–96
  in the Emory University program for teachers, 407–11
  in the Sir R. L. Borden Secondary School, 346, 380–82
  in the University of Denver programs for teachers, 397–401, 427–30
  materials for a, 262–64, 278–81, 395–96, 399
  purposes of a, 222–24
  starting a, 267–70
  ways of using a, 270–71
Learning
  climate, 170
  environment, 104–28
  independently, 173–75, 180
  rates of, 102
  tasks, sequencing and pacing of, 17–18
Learning Activity Package (Dade County, Florida, Schools), 175–77
Learning by Discovery, A Critical Appraisal (Shulman and Keislar), 289
Leidermann, Gloria F., 33
Lerch, Harold H., 36, 136

INDEX 525

Lesser, Gerald S., 291
Lippitt, Peggy, 20
Lohman, J. E., 20
Low Achiever in Mathematics, The (USOE, Woodby, ed.), 157
Lyda, W. J., 149

MacLean, James R., 115, 434
Madison Project, The, 116, 255, 409
Madaus, George F., 38–39
Mager, Robert F., 3, 59
Manipulative materials, 132, 135–37, 157–58, 221, 224, 267, 269, 428–29, 432, 433. *See also* Chips; Cuisenaire rods; Geoboards; Models
  abacus, 142, 264, 396, 401, 409, 428
  abacus board, 249–53
  attribute materials, 149, 224, 264, 396, 404, 407–8, 412, 413
  balances, 221, 223, 264, 269, 396
  building blocks, 224, 264, 265
  calculators, 5, 174, 264, 380–82, 396, 409, 428
  clinometer, 396, 475–77
  cubes, 224, 257–66, 268, 396
  Dienes Multibase Arithmetic Blocks, 5, 115, 142, 249, 262, 396, 408, 434
  mirror cards, 224, 264, 265, 409
  pattern blocks, 224, 259, 264, 265, 396
  Stern Structural Arithmetic Apparatus, 249, 409
  tangrams, 224, 264, 265
  toys, children's, 157–58
Maryland Elementary Mathematics Inservice Project (MEMIP), 59
Mathematics. *See also* Computation; Patterns in mathematics; Relationships in mathematics
  algebra, 204–10, 374
  categories of content, 40–41
  education, 26, 27, 286
  geometry, 140–42, 149, 150, 194–204, 210–17, 226–48, 366, 374–76
  language (symbolism, vocabulary) of, 133, 137, 148, 149, 248
  taxonomy of content for arithmetic, 282, 293–305, 313
Mathematics for Basic Education. See Baltimore County program
"Mathematics for Spanish-speaking Pupils (MSP)" (Los Angeles), 345, 364–70
Mathematics in Primary Schools, Curriculum Bulletin No. 1, 264

Mathematics Teacher (NCTM), 265, 373, 431
Mathematics Teaching, 265
May, Lola J., 470
Maynard, Freddy Joseph, 36
Meade, Edward J., Jr., 289
Mendelsohn, Melvin, 337, 345, 355, 364
Methods of teaching
  discovery, 384–86
  discovery subtheory of, 287, 289–90
  expository subtheory of, 287–90
  psychotherapy subtheory of, 287, 289–90
Metropolitan Achievement Test (MAT), 360–63
Models, 98, 99, 182, 183, 202–4, 209–10, 216–17, 221
  constructing, 211–12, 473–74
  making use of, 210–11
  patterns for, 212–14
  stacking, 212
Motivation, 15, 19, 139, 288, 291, 380, 444. *See also* Rewards
  extrinsic, 107–8, 111–12
  intrinsic, 108–11
Multisensory aids, 182–220, 437. *See also* Audiovisual materials; Manipulative materials; Visual aids and materials; Projectors

Napier, John, 457
National Council of Teachers of Mathematics (NCTM), 340, 373, 406
  Works: *Arithmetic Teacher,* 153, 157, 158, 264, 431, 463; *Experiences in Mathematical Discovery,* 36; *Mathematics Teacher,* 265, 373, 431; *Second Report of the Commission on Post War Plans,* 373
National Science Foundation (NSF), 400, 418
Needs of slow learners, 2, 8, 12–22, 124–27, 425, 437
  for immediate gratification, 8, 21–22, 110
  for novelty and variety, 15–16, 23, 113–16, 187
  for physicalization, 5, 14–15, 122, 182
  for positive feedback, 21–22, 111, 127
  for predictability in classroom routine, 15, 113, 320
  for proper sequencing and pacing in learning, 17–18
  for relevance in learning, 18–19

for sense of trust, 13–14, 23
for success, 20, 110, 126–27
Neill, A. S., 284–86
Notes on Mathematics in Primary Schools, 264
Nuffield Project, The, 130, 263–64, 434
Nutting, Sue Ellis, 36

Objectives, 52–57, 175. *See also* Behavioral indicators; Behavioral objectives
  instructional, 40, 432
  student understanding of, 171–72
  in textbooks, 91

Paschal, Billy J., 137, 149, 151
Patterns in mathematics, 142–48, 155, 160, 183–86, 211, 224, 247, 249, 257, 366, 378, 389, 420, 426, 450–80 passim, 490–98
Peer group, 9–11
Peer helpers, 19–20, 23
Performance. *See also* Behavioral indicators; Behavioral objectives
  classes, 77–81, 87
  statements, 58–59, 70, 81, 82
  verbs, 74–81 (*see also* Action verbs)
Piaget, Jean, 308
Pikaart, Leonard, 36
Potter, Mary, 329
Practice, 146–48, 157, 158, 159, 174, 389, 447, 463, 468, 471, 472. *See also* Drill; Skills, maintaining
Primary Mathematics, 265
Primary Mental Abilities Tests, 29, 33
Problem solving, 32, 131, 133, 137, 150, 157, 301, 304, 337, 363, 424, 429
Program for Underdeveloped Mathematics Pupils (Palm Beach County, Florida), 180
Programs for slow learners, 345–401
Project SEED, 346, 383–87
Projectors
  film and, 175, 265, 271, 278, 338, 399, 401
  film loops, 381, 401
  filmstrips and, 97, 98, 105, 175, 338, 380, 381, 399, 409
  Math Builder, 179, 377
  opaque, 381
  overhead, 189, 191, 196, 197, 204, 208, 215, 217, 218, 380, 381, 399
  slide, 105
Punishment, 20, 22

Readiness for new learning, 132, 138
Reading
  instruction in reading mathematics, 148–51
  levels, 1, 30, 173, 351, 398
  mathematics, 131, 133, 391
  scores low in, 32, 371, 389
Reckzeh, John, 129
Recording equipment
  audio, 105, 117, 160, 175–77, 311
  recorders, 105, 160, 167, 399, 514
  recordings, 132, 514–16
  tapes, 97, 105, 167, 179, 401
  video, 132, 311, 399, 417–18
Relationships in mathematics, 142–58 passim, 183, 224, 338, 366, 387, 389, 391, 404, 504
Relevance, 7–8, 18–19, 23, 168–69, 286–87, 389, 423
Remediation
  classes for, 135, 319, 397
  instruction for, 35–36, 135, 136, 159, 160, 250, 267, 339
  procedures for, 302
  programs for, 36, 435
  teachers for, 411
Research and the slow learner, 26–51, 283
  on individual differences, 30–32
  on instructional programs, 34–37
  on variables associated with slow learning, 32–33
  predictive of future trends, 37–41
Retention of learning, 283, 298
Rewards, 20–22, 107, 164–65, 168–69, 326, 330, 331. *See also* Motivation
Riessman, Frank, 3, 5, 16
Rising, Gerald R., 338
Romberg, Thomas A., 40
Rosenthal, Robert, 37–38
Ross, Ramon, 32
Rowan, Thomas E., 92

Sanders, Norris M.
  Classroom Questions: What Kinds?, 309
Schacht, Elmer James, 133
School Mathematics Study Group (SMSG), 345, 349–55
  Attitude scales, 354
  Reports, 351
  Secondary Mathematics—Special Edition, 353–55
Science—A Process Approach, 59

INDEX

Scott, Jessie L., 346, 387, 395
Sealey, L., 249
Sears, Robert, 13
Secondary Mathematics—Special Edition (SMSG), 353–55
Second Report of the Commission on Post War Plans (NCTM), 373
Sharpe, H. C., 35
Sharron, Sidney, 345, 364
Shulman, Lee S.
  Learning by Discovery, A Critical Appraisal (with Keislar), 289
Silberman, Charles E., 11, 324
Skills, maintaining, 186–94. *See also* Drill; Practice
Skinner, B. F., 20
Smith, John M., 92
Smith, Robert M., 131
Solnit, A., 2
"Space Oriented Mathematics for the Early Grades" (USOE, Deans), 157
Spearman, Charles Edward, 28
Spross, Patricia
  Elementary Arithmetic and Learning Aids (USOE), 157
Stanford Achievement Test, 351–52
Stanford-Binet Test, 29, 32
Stark, M., 2
Strickland, James Fisher, Jr., 36
Strobel, Mrs. L. R., 346, 380, 382
Suppes, Patrick, 136, 337, 356

Taba, Hilda, 23
Task control, 14–19
Task fitting. *See* Assessment, tasks
Taxonomies
  behavioral, 298–305 (*see also* Bloom, Benjamin S.)
  content, 282, 293–301, 303–5, 313
  of types of learning, 301–5
Taxonomy of Educational Objectives: The Classification of Educational Goals. Handbook 1, *Cognitive Domain* (Bloom, ed.), 40, 59, 293, 298–305, 309, 313
Teachers. *See also* Aides, teacher
  as managers of instruction, 14–18, 23, 170, 417–18
  as strategic change agents, 12–13, 23
  training of (*see* Teacher education)
  use of, 340–41
Teacher education, 397–401, 402–43
  at Emory University, 406–25
  at the University of Denver, 397–401, 427–30

in-service, 372, 379, 385, 394, 405–38
laboratories for, 397–401, 407–14
practicum in, 410–16
role playing in, 418–21
sensitivity training in, 406, 417
strands approach to, 435–37
video tapes and, 417–18
Teaching. *See also* Diagnostic-prescriptive teaching
  sensitivity to slow learners, 124–27, 402–5, 406, 417
  strategies of, 137, 170
  styles of, 163–81, 418
  team, 136, 335–36, 339, 382
  use of reinforcement control in, 20–23
Terman, Lewis Madison, 29
Testing. *See* Assessment; Evaluation
Thorndike, E. L., 28, 30
Thorndike, R. L., 37–38
Thurstone, Louis Leon, 27–29
Transfer of learning, 170, 283, 298
Tutorial help, 39

Underachievers, 1, 29, 38, 159
United States Office of Education (USOE), 157, 175, 180, 356, 400, 406

Visual aids and materials, 136, 137, 142, 146, 157, 176, 183, 322. *See also* Audiovisual materials; Bulletin boards; Chalkboards; Models; Multisensory aids; Projectors; Written materials
  charts, 107, 144, 150, 151, 192–94
  dot paper, 225, 267, 506
  graph paper, 144, 146, 196–201, 211, 215–16, 218, 262, 265, 266, 269, 477, 480
  graphs, 107, 137, 151, 165, 366
  grids, 193, 196–201, 211, 215–16, 225, 229, 399, 401, 480, 506, 507
  nomographs, 204–6
  scales, 151, 192–94

Waetjen, Walter B., 15
Walbesser, Henry H., 59, 94, 372
Watts, Jean C., 291
Weaver, J. Fred, 308
Weinstein, Gerald, 7, 402, 417, 422–23
Williams, Russell L., 463
Wilson, Guy M., 285, 286
Wilson, James W., 39, 40–41
Wilson, John W., 293
Windelband, Wilhelm, 305
Wirtz, Robert W., 434

Wolfson, Bernice J., 335
Wood, R., 40
Woodby, Lauren
  The Low Achiever in Mathematics (USOE, ed.), 157
Woodrow, Herbert A., 31–32
Written materials, 156–57, 221
  flow charts (*see* Flow charts)
  lessons, sample, 487–520
  programmed materials, 39, 117, 157, 176
  supplementary assignment sheets, 153–56
  textbooks, 39, 91, 114, 137, 150–53, 156–57, 175, 221, 222, 269, 271, 384
  workbooks, 16, 39, 114, 157